VISIT US AT

www.syngress.c

Syngress is committed to publishing high-quality books for IT Professionals and delivering those books in media and formats that fit the demands of our customers. We are also committed to extending the utility of the book you purchase via additional materials available from our Web site.

SOLUTIONS WEB SITE

To register your book, visit www.syngress.com/solutions. Once registered, you can access our solutions@syngress.com Web pages. There you will find an assortment of value-added features such as free e-booklets related to the topic of this book, URLs of related Web sites, FAQs from the book, corrections, and any updates from the author(s).

ULTIMATE CDs

Our Ultimate CD product line offers our readers budget-conscious compilations of some of our best-selling backlist titles in Adobe PDF form. These CDs are the perfect way to extend your reference library on key topics pertaining to your area of expertise, including Cisco Engineering, Microsoft Windows System Administration, CyberCrime Investigation, Open Source Security, and Firewall Configuration, to name a few.

DOWNLOADABLE E-BOOKS

For readers who can't wait for hard copy, we offer most of our titles in downloadable Adobe PDF form. These e-books are often available weeks before hard copies and are priced affordably.

SYNGRESS OUTLET

Our outlet store at syngress.com features overstocked, out-of-print, or slightly hurt books at significant savings.

SITE LICENSING

Syngress has a well-established program for site licensing our e-books onto servers in corporations, educational institutions, and large organizations. Contact us at sales@syngress.com for more information.

CUSTOM PUBLISHING

Many organizations welcome the ability to combine parts of multiple Syngress books, as well as their own content, into a single volume for their own internal use. Contact us at sales@syngress.com for more information.

SYNGRESS®

DESIGNING AND BUILDING

Enterprise DMZs

Ido Dubrawsky Technical Editor

C. Tate Baumrucker

James Caesar

Mohan Krishnamurthy

Dr. Thomas W. Shinder

Becky Pinkard

Eric Seagren

Laura Hunter

KEY	SERIAL NUMBER
001	HJIRTCV764
002	PO9873D5FG
003	829KM8NJH2
004	LKLKPOP34N
005	CVPLQ6WQ23
006	VBP965T5T5
007	HJJJ863WD3E
008	2987GVTWMK
009	629MP5SDJT
010	IMWQ295T6T

PUBLISHED BY
Syngress Publishing, Inc.
800 Hingham Street
Rockland, MA 02370

Designing and Building Enterprise DMZs

Printed in Canada
1 2 3 4 5 6 7 8 9 0
ISBN: 1-59749-100-4

Publisher: Andrew Williams
Acquisitions Editor: Erin Heffernan
Technical Editor: Ido Dubrawsky
Cover Designer: Michael Kavish

Page Layout and Art: Patricia Lupien
Copy Editor: Darlene Bordwell, Audrey Doyle
Indexer: Nara Wood

Distributed by O'Reilly Media, Inc. in the United States and Canada.
For information on rights, translations, and bulk sales, contact Matt Pedersen, Director of Sales and Rights, at Syngress Publishing; email matt@syngress.com or fax to 781-681-3585.

Technical Editor

Ido Dubrawsky (CISSP, CCNA, CCDA) is the Chief Security Advisor for Microsoft's Communication Sector North America, a division of the Mobile and Embedded Devices Group. Prior to working at Microsoft, Ido was the acting Security Consulting Practice Lead at AT&T's Callisma subsidiary and a Senior Security Consultant. Before joining AT&T, Ido was a Network Security Architect for Cisco Systems, Inc., SAFE Architecture Team. He has worked in the systems and network administration field for almost 20 years in a variety of environments from government to academia to private enterprise. He has a wide range of experience in various networks, from small to large and relatively simple to complex. Ido is the primary author of three major SAFE white papers and has written, and spoken, extensively on security topics. He is a regular contributor to the SecurityFocus website on a variety of topics covering security issues. Previously, he worked in Cisco Systems, Inc. Secure Consulting Group, providing network security posture assessments and consulting services for a wide range of clients. In addition to providing penetration-testing consultation, he also conducted security architecture reviews and policy and process reviews. He holds a B.Sc. and a M.Sc. in Aerospace Engineering from the University of Texas at Austin.

Contributing Authors

Cherie Amon (CCSA/CCSE) has been installing, configuring and supporting Check Point products since 1997. Cherie is also the Technical Editor and co-author of *Check Point Next Generation Security Administration* (Syngress Publishing, ISBN: 1-928994-74-1) and contributing author of *Nokia Network Security Solutions Handbook* (Syngress Publishing, ISBN: 1-931836-70-1). She is also a contributing author of *Check Point NG VPN-1/FireWall-1: Advanced Configurations and Troubleshooting* (Syngress Publishing, ISBN: 1-931836-97-3).

C. Tate Baumrucker (CISSP, Sun Enterprise Engineer, MCSE) is a Principal Architect with Callisma, a completely owned subsidiary of AT&T. Tate is responsible for leading engineering teams in the design and implementation of secure and highly available systems infrastructures and networks. He is industry-recognized as a subject-matter expert in security, network performance, and LAN support systems, such as HTTP, SMTP, DNS, and DHCP. For 11 years, Tate has provided business and technical consulting services in enterprise and service-provider industries and to the Department of Defense, and currently works as the Principal Architect of Network Performance for the Pentagon's enterprise-wide networks. Tate has contributed to other Syngress books, including *Managing Cisco Network Security* (ISBN: 1-928994-17-2), *Cisco Security Specialist's Guide to PIX Firewall* (ISBN: 1-931836-63-9), and *Cisco Security Professional's Guide to Secure Intrusion Detection Systems* (ISBN: 1-932266-69-0).

Tate resides in Washington, DC with his wife, Evelyne and two daughters, Elise and Margot.

James Caesar (CCIE #14995, CCSE Plus) is currently a Network Analyst for Ceridian Corporation, where he is responsible for design and implementation of the company's global network infrastructure, including the DMZ environment which supports Ceridian's many Web-based products. James was a co-author for other Syngress titles, including *Managing Cisco Network Security, 2nd Edition* (ISBN: 1931836566) and *Check Point NG VPN-1/Firewall-1*(ISBN: 1931836973). James holds his bachelor's degree in Electrical Engineering from the Georgia Institute of Technology and lives outside of Atlanta, GA with his wife, Julie.

Eli Faskha (CCSI, CCSA, CCSE, CCSE+, CCAE, MCP). Based in Panama City, Panama, Eli is Founder and President of Soluciones Seguras, a company that specializes in network security and is the only Check Point Gold Partner in Central America and the only

Nokia Internet Security partner in Panama. He was Assistant Technical Editor for *Configuring Check Point NGX VPN-1/FireWall-1* (ISBN: 1597490318), a Syngress Publishing book. Eli is the most experienced Check Point Certified Security Instructor and Nokia Instructor in the region, and has taught participants from almost twenty different countries. A 1993 graduate of the University of Pennsylvania's Wharton School and Moore School of Engineering, he also received an MBA from Georgetown University in 1995. Eli has more than 8 years of Internet development and networking experience, starting with Web development of the largest Internet portal in Panama in 1999 and 2000, managing a Verisign affiliate in 2001, and running his own company since then. Eli has written several articles for the local media and has been recognized for his contributions to Internet development in Panama.

Laura E. Hunter (CISSP, MCSE: Security, MCDBA, Microsoft MVP) is an IT Project Leader and Systems Manager at the University of Pennsylvania, where she provides network planning, implementation, and troubleshooting services for various business units and schools within the university. Her specialties include Windows 2000 and 2003 Active Directory design and implementation, troubleshooting, and security topics. Laura has more than a decade of experience with Windows computers; her previous experience includes a position as the Director of Computer Services for the Salvation Army and as the LAN administrator for a medical supply firm. She is a contributor to the TechTarget family of Web sites, and to *Redmond Magazine* (formerly *Microsoft Certified Professional Magazine*).

Laura has previously contributed to the *Syngress Windows Server 2003 MCSE/MCSA DVD Guide & Training System* series as a DVD presenter, author, and technical reviewer, and is the author of the *Active Directory Consultant's Field Guide* (ISBN: 1-59059-492-4) from APress. Laura is a three-time recipient of the prestigious Microsoft MVP award in the area of Windows Server—Networking. Laura graduated with honors from the University of Pennsylvania and also works as a freelance writer, trainer, speaker, and consultant.

Mohan Krishnamurthy Madwachar (JNCIW-FW, CWNA, and CCSA) is an AVP of Infrastructure Services for ADG Infotek, Inc. ADG Infotek is an IT Services Company headquartered in Gurgaon, India. Mohan operates from ADG's East Brunswick office in New Jersey. ADG Infotek is part of a leading systems integration group that has branches in 7 countries and executes projects in nearly 15 countries. Mohan is a key contributor to their infrastructure services division and plays a significant role in the organization's Network Security and Training initiatives. Mohan's tenure with companies such as Schlumberger Omnes and Secure Network Solutions India adds to his experience and expertise in implementing large and complex network and security projects.

Mohan holds leading IT industry certifications, and is a member of the IEEE and PMI.

Mohan dedicates his contributions to this book to his father Krishnamurthy Madwachar and mother Radha Madwachar who have been his inspiration and support for his career achievements. Mohan also writes in newspaper columns on various subjects and has contributed to leading content companies as a technical writer and a subject-matter expert.

Wesley J Noonan (Houston, Texas) has worked in the computer industry for more than 12 years, specializing in Windows-based networks and network infrastructure security design and implementation. He is a Staff Quality Engineer for NetIQ, working on their security solutions product line. Wes is the author of *Hardening Network Infrastructure* (ISBN: 0072255021), and is a contributing/ co-author for *The CISSP Training Guide, Hardening Network Security* (ISBN: 0072257032) and *Firewall Fundamentals* (ISBN: 1587052210). Wes is the technical editor for *Hacking Exposed: Cisco Networks* (ISBN: 0072259175). Wes also contributes to "Redmond" magazine, writing on the subjects of network infrastructure and security, and he maintains a Windows Network Security section called "Ask the Experts" for Techtarget.com (http://searchwindowssecurity. techtarget.com/ateAnswers/0,289620,sid45_tax298206,00.html). Wes has also presented at TechMentor 2004.

Wes lives in Houston, Texas.

Becky Pinkard (CCSA, CCNA, GCIA) has worked in the information technology industry for over 10 years. She is currently a senior security architect with a Fortune 50 company where she is fortunate enough to work with security technology on a daily basis. Becky's main areas of interest are intrusion detection, pen testing, vulnerability assessments, risk management, and forensics. She is a SANS Certified Instructor and has taught for the SANS Institute since 2001. She participated on the Strategic Advisory Council for the Center for Internet Security where she edited the first draft of the CIS Windows NT benchmark. Becky holds a bachelor's degree from Texas A&M University and is a member of the North Texas chapter of InfraGard. She'd like to send out hacker-like greetz to her wonderful partner, awesome family and incredible friends - *you are all loved beyond compare.*

Eric S. Seagren (CISA, CISSP-ISSAP, SCNP, CCNA, CNE-4, MCP+I, MCSE-NT) has ten years of experience in the computer industry, with the last eight years spent in the financial services industry working for a fortune 100 company. Eric started his computer career working on Novell servers and performing general network troubleshooting for a small Houston-based company. While working in the financial services industry, his duties have included server administration, disaster recovery, business continuity coordination, Y2K remediation, network vulnerability assessment, and risk managements. Eric has spent the last few years as an IT architect and risk analyst, designing and evaluating secure, scalable, and redundant networks.

Eric has contributed to several books as a contributing author or technical editor. These include; *Hardening Network Security* (McGraw-Hill), *Hardening Network Infrastructure* (McGraw-Hill), *Hacking Exposed: Cisco Networks* (McGraw-Hill), *Configuring Checkpoint NGX VPN-1/FireWall-1* (ISBN: 1-597490-31-8), a Syngress Publishing book and *Firewall Fundamentals* (Cisco Press). He has also received a CTM from Toastmasters of America.

Thomas W. Shinder, M.D. is the primary content creator and driving force for www.isaserver.org. He is co-owner of TACTEAM and he has provided Microsoft Internet Security and Acceleration Server firewall consultation and strategic guidance to major enterprises including Microsoft, HP, Exxon and the United States Federal Government. Tom is also the coauthor of *Dr. Tom Shinder's Configuring ISA Server 2004* (ISBN: 1931836191), published by Syngress.

Darren Windham (CISSP, Security+) works for McAfee, Inc., supporting enterprise-level clients with the implementation, operation, and integration of the McAfee product line. Darren is currently becoming familiar with current technologies supporting Network Access Control (NAC).

Darren's previous experience in technology includes network design, system configuration, security audits, internal investigations, ensuring compliance with GLB, FFIEC, OTS, FDIC, and SOX regulations, and managing technology risks within an organization. He has also worked as a security consultant for local companies including other financial institutions along with networking and server support. Darren was a reviewer for the book *Hacking Exposed: Computer Forensics* (McGraw-Hill Osborne Media, ISBN: 0072256753). Darren was also a contributing author for the book *Winternals Defragmentation, Recovery, and Administration Field Guide* (Syngress Publishing, ISBN: 1-59749-079-2)

Darren is a member of Information Systems Audit and Control Association® (ISACA), North Texas Electronic Crimes Task Force (N-TEC), and the North Texas Snort User Group.

Darren thanks his wife, Jaime, and his three sons, Daniel, Andrew, and Jacob for being his support and inspiration to succeed. Darren would also like to thank his friends and coworkers along the way that have shared their knowledge and experience: Chris Bolton, Dave Cowen, Keith Loyd, Chris Davis, Gabby Cox, and Matt Gair.

Contents

**Appendices A, B, C, and D can be downloaded from
www.syngress.com/solutions.**

## Chapter 1

DMZ Concepts, Layout, and Conceptual Design

Solutions in this chapter:

- **Planning Network Security**
- **DMZ Definitions and History**
- **DMZ Design Fundamentals**
- **Advanced Risks**
- **Advanced Design Strategies**

☑ **Summary**

☑ **Solutions Fast Track**

☑ **Frequently Asked Questions**

Introduction

Since the dawn of the Internet Age, we have witnessed the constant advance of innovative technologies and enjoyed a continuous expansion of access, convenience, and power that networked computer systems provide. From unparalleled communications around the globe to the simple act of paying bills from a cellular phone, it seems that nothing is impossible. Yet, with this progress comes a similarly constant and increasing threat against our privacy, our financial security, and the very lifestyle we treasure.

Each year brings news of larger and more devastating technological security incidents in both commercial and federal sectors. Last year, we saw the compromise of several massive credit card databases, including Card Systems and Lowe's. Just recently, confidential data, including the Social Security numbers and medical histories of thousands of U.S. veterans was stolen, only to be recovered later. Was the data that held the identity of those veterans copied and sold? Will that singular incident cost the U.S. government millions of dollars and wreak havoc on thousands of citizens?

The statistical trends of security incidents have not and will not decline; our increased access to more valuable and critical data provides too great an incentive to amateur hackers and professional criminals. The Mazu Networks *2006 Internal Threat Report* finds that, "although enterprises are clearly more educated and aware of the risks posed by internal network vulnerabilities than ever before, they continue to fall victim to a growing number of attacks that circumvent perimeter and endpoint security solutions. In 2005, malicious attacks became increasingly ominous, with a large number of incidents focused on criminal activities such as identity theft and extortion versus traditional hacker exploits such as Web site defacement or vandalism. Additionally, network services such as instant messaging, IP telephony and SOAP/XML joined existing attack vectors like e-mail, Web traffic and browser-based exploits. This growth in attack type, frequency and vector has exceeded the capabilities of traditional security technologies and has rendered status quo defense strategies ineffective."

So, what then are our options as security professionals? What actions can we take to protect against these threats? One step is the secure design of computer services networks or demilitarized zones (DMZs). A DMZ is a network construct that provides secure segregation of networks that host services for users, visitors, or partners. This separation is accomplished using firewalls and multiple layers of filtering to control access and protect critical systems. This book is designed to be a definitive work for your use in understanding the concepts of protection, the terminology and components of DMZ structure, and DMZ design in enterprise networks.

Along the way, the authors of this book will provide you with the information you need to appropriately design, implement, monitor, and maintain a secure and functional DMZ structure. The book contains not only the theory, but the "how to" information that you require to successfully protect your networks from attack. Information is available about various DMZ-related hardware and software implementations (including Cisco PIX and ASA, Nokia, Check Point, Microsoft ISA Server, and others) that will be useful in planning and implementing your own DMZ.

Chapter 1 provides a great deal of background information to refresh your knowledge of security concepts and defines DMZ terminology to improve your understanding and create a common ground for subsequent chapters in the book. This chapter also explores DMZ design basics before expanding into advanced risks and the advanced designs that might be used to better protect your networks. After reviewing these basic concepts, Chapter 2 discusses the procedures and placement for Windows-based services within the DMZ and internal networks, and Chapter 3 covers UNIX-based services within the DMZ and internal networks. It is imperative that you read this first section of the book because it will give you the underlying fundamentals and concepts you need to accurately design a DMZ.

Planning Network Security

Successfully implementing security for your network and computer systems begins with a written plan that is evaluated and accepted by all critical stakeholders in your organization. This initial plan will be used to define the starting parameters for security policies and the overall direction and goals for your protection plan. The plan will contain the decision-making information leading to the design of a functional DMZ that meets the needs and level of protection for your organization.

Planning for network security requires an evaluation of the risks involved with loss of data, unauthorized access to data, and information compromise, among other things. The plan must consider cost factors, staff knowledge and training, and the hardware and platforms currently in use in the current and future organization. As we will see, the DMZ plan and concept provides a multilayered security capability, but as with anything that involves multiple components, administration costs and equipment costs increase with the complexity of the design.

Fortunately, there are many templates and published standards to assist you in the creation of functional security plans. These blueprints must be customized to match your needs and environment, but they provide excellent and holistic examples of things to consider in your own plan. We'll discuss some of these products later in the chapter.

Finally, it should be understood that no security plan is ever a final plan. Instead, we work continuously to revise and update the plan in an ongoing effort to provide the best possible coverage that minimizes the risk of intrusion and damage in an evolving environment. Of course, before we can provide a meaningful and effective evaluation of the areas we need to protect, we must understand the components that have to be protected. In the next few sections of this chapter, we look more closely at the fundamentals of security and define more precisely what exactly we are trying to protect.

Security Fundamentals

When discussing the fundamentals of security in our networks, we use the *confidentiality, integrity, and availability (CIA)* triad model as a starting point. This CIA triad provides security professionals with the paths they needed to assess their security stance and a set of rules that make it somewhat easier to group tools and procedures for evaluation. Using CIA as an evaluation method is still a good practice and sound methodology today, but we must consider a number of other factors that weren't covered at the time that the CIA concept was developed.

Until a few years ago, for instance, providing CIA for our infrastructure included the use of simple proxy-based firewalls combined with Network Address Translation (NAT) between outside (untrusted) networks and our internal (trusted) network. At that time, that system served the purpose for which it was designed; it provided a perimeter defense between the untrusted and trusted security zones and limited access to internal networks and services. Figure 1.1 illustrates the original configuration we might have used.

Figure 1.1 Original Basic Firewall Configuration

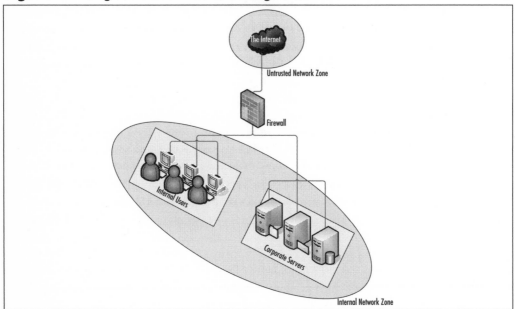

Since those days, however, we've greatly expanded the role of our network infrastructure and system resources to provide information to employee, partner, and public requests for information. We provide varied data to different types of consumers, so it makes sense to segment these service networks in different ways. Additionally, the freely available tools and the relative ease with which various probing and spoofing attacks can be mounted force us to isolate our networks and protect the information that is contained in them. That same growth in the availability of tools and attack methodologies has necessitated the expansion of the CIA concepts that were originally handled through a single-firewall design. A new, greatly expanded multilayer approach must be employed to ensure proper protection of our assets. This is where we begin to consider the use of the DMZ concept, allowing us to better segregate and divide our networks. Figure 1.2 demonstrates a generic DMZ configuration.

Figure 1.2 Generic DMZ Configuration

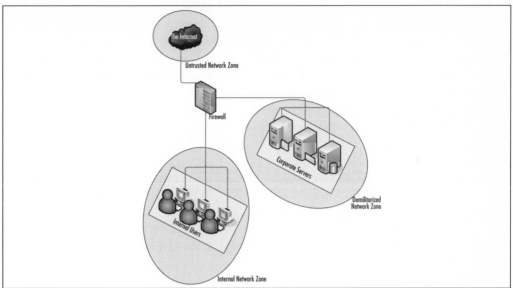

One reason for this new design is our need to provide services to some employees and others outside of the Internal Network Zone environment when we might not want to allow those services to be available to everyone. The addition of the extra layer of filtering provided by the second firewall (or more) in the control environment allows us to more finely control access to the data and servers hosting that data. This in turn allows us to more fully implement the second part of the triad, *integrity*. If we can control these access points more closely through access control lists and user accounts, for instance, it is much more likely that we will succeed in maintaining the integrity of the data and keeping it in a protected and undamaged state.

Perhaps more important, including additional security zones in the form of DMZs limits the scope of systems vulnerabilities; compromised systems on untrusted or DMZ networks may present less of a potential threat to critical, internal-only systems. As we'll see through our study in this book, the DMZ design and flexibility contribute greatly to the administrator's ability to ensure CIA and still provide services to those who need them.

NOTE

The firewall configurations we will use act primarily to route and restrict traffic flow to and from particular network segments. As we will see in later sections of the chapter, those configurations are varied and depend on required protections and functionality.

Identifying Risks to Data

As we continue to review the basics of security, it is necessary to understand some of the risks that occur in relation to our data. One of the important things we have learned as systems operators and administrators is that it is paramount to protect the data that we are charged with controlling, maintaining, and providing. We understand that there is a necessity to perform backup operations, provide disaster recovery services, and generally keep the information highly available and intact. While you prepare to develop your plan for protection, consider that there are now many more potential causes of data loss and corruption than at any time previously in the history of computing. Here are a few of the ways data can be lost:

- Hardware failure
    - Power disruption
- External attacks:
    - Enumeration of your network
    - Access to confidential data
    - Modification of critical data
    - Destruction of data
- Internal attacks:
    - Unauthorized access
    - Theft of information
    - Disclosure of information to others
    - Destruction of data
- Natural and other disasters:
    - Water, flooding
    - Fire
    - Ground movement
    - Weather disasters (hurricanes, tornados, ice storms, others)
    - War

Human and software failures:
    - Inadvertent deletion of data
    - Corruption of data

- Disregard for physical security of equipment/network

- Configuration errors

Are all these risks to data relevant to the DMZ? Although it's possible that not all will relate directly to the consideration of your DMZ and its implementation, we'll see that the overall planning required for the DMZ and its design must incorporate overall, systematic security planning. Thus, we must consider all these potential problem areas as risks when we plan to provide protection for the data sources in our systems.

Identifying Risks to Services

Maintaining the security of services being provided to partners, employees, and customers can be a difficult task. The continued growth of shared information and the availability of technologies providing network-based information and services to an ever-growing user base outside our internal networks generate a number of risks to the information we provide. Additional sources of risk are created through the multitude of services we provide to the end user. With each passing day, customer demand for functionality grows. What was once simply e-mail, Web, and secure online purchasing now involves mobile technologies such as personal digital assistants (PDAs), mobile phones, and wireless services. New protocols and languages are developed to accommodate new functions but are delivered with evolving vulnerabilities that create risk to the services we offer individuals and companies outside our internal networks. Some of the things that can be classified as risks to services are:

Denial-of-service (DoS) attacks:

- Unauthorized use of services such as mail relaying

- Compromise of poorly configured system and services, such as:

    - DNS server zone transfers

    - Active and unprotected Telnet service

    - File Transfer Protocol (FTP) server file root unsecured or not otherwise protected

- Interception or diversion of services or service information

    Unauthorized remote control of systems

As you can see, the risks of service disruption are not limited to failure of our systems; they also incorporate the risks of attack and lack of availability of services provided to us by others that could impact our operation. It must be understood that every service has inherent vulnerabilities. Our job as security professionals is to fully identify, understand, and overcome these vulnerabilities through secure configuration and proper network design. To assist in this effort, the SANS Institute publishes the most common services vulnerabilities on its Web site, at www.sans.org/top20. We must anticipate those risks as we design our security plans.

Identifying Potential Threats

As you prepare your overall security plan and DMZ, it is important that you identify and evaluate the potential risks and threats to your network, systems, and data. You must evaluate your risks thoroughly during the identification process and assign priority to the risks. This will help determine the order in which you gain funding and apply protection, thereby reducing the likelihood of loss resulting from those risks and threats if they materialize. This methodology should be applied to anything that could potentially disrupt, slow, or damage your systems, data, or credibility. Some potential threats to consider include:

- Outside hacker attacks:
    - Trojans, worms, and virus attacks
    - DoS or distributed denial-of-service (DDoS) attacks
    - Compromise or loss of internal confidential information
    - Network monitoring and data interception
    - Internal attacks by employees
    - Hardware failures
- Loss of critical systems

This identification process creates the basis for your security plan, policies, and implementation of your security environment. You should realize that this is an ongoing evaluation and is subject to change as conditions evolve within your company and its associated assets. We have learned that security is a process and is never truly "finished." However, a good basic evaluation goes a long way toward creating the most secure system that we can achieve.

Introducing Common Security Standards

Security and network professionals use a number of currently accepted procedures and standards to conduct our business and ensure that we are following industry best practices. Although we, as network and systems administrators, have a responsibility to try to attain perfection in the availability and integrity of our data, we also have constraints placed on us in accomplishing those conditions. Those constraints include budgets, physical plant capability, and training of users and technicians to maintain the security and integrity of the data. These constraints do not relieve us of our responsibility for maintaining the data safely and securely. To that end, we currently employ some accepted security standards that help us perform our tasks to the best possible level. In this section, we review some of the common security standards and briefly discuss them:

- **Confidentiality, integrity, and availability (CIA)** CIA is a commonly accepted benchmark for evaluating information systems security. Over the past few years, the CIA processes have expanded to include more comprehensive guidelines that incorporate the process of defining risk and use of risk management tools to provide a more complete method of protection. The components of CIA are:

- *Confidentiality* infers that individuals have access to only that which they are expressly permitted. It involves privacy of communications, secure storage of sensitive data, and granular control for the authentication, authorization, and auditing of system use.

- *Integrity* relates to the validity of data, which means our information is protected from corruption, modification, or deletion while it is stored, used, or transmitted.

- *Availability* means continual accessibility to our networks, systems and data. It includes the aspects of resistance to attack, proper scalability, redundancy, contingency systems, and ease of use.

- **Least privilege** This concept is used by the security team to define levels of access to resources. Individuals should have access to only what is necessary to do their jobs. Denying access by default and providing access by exception is also part of least privilege. As security professionals, we know this can be a challenging task, but it is potentially the largest cause of internal security breaches.

- **Defense in depth** The idea that no single system, methodology, or human being can individually secure an environment leads us to the concept of defense in depth. In principle, the concept implies a multitiered approach to provide security. Some simple examples of defense in depth include the use of vendor firewalls, the application of several types of intrusion prevention systems (IPS) or intrusion detection systems (IDS), and, of course, the use of DMZs to protect our network. Holistically, defense in depth involves the use of multiple *types* of defense strategies that, in aggregate, provide a comprehensive security stance.

Remember, too, that security involves multiple dimensions that should be applied when creating our security plans. These include:

- **Physical** The hardware that stores data and provides services must remain physically inaccessible to unauthorized users. A secure physical environment prevents access to systems using cipher locks, biometrics, smart cards, and other technologies.

- **Personnel** The individuals responsible for system administration, security, and maintenance in your company must be trusted and reliable. Proper human resources practices such as background verification and routine law enforcement checkups can help ensure a trusted workforce.

- **Procedural** Perhaps the most critical dimension to security is procedural awareness. Human mistakes due to improper training, missing written procedures, or sheer incompetence presents an enormous risk to your company. To offset this risk, training must be an essential part of your security plan.

- **Technical** For each new threat we face, a solution will eventually be developed. These are the technical responses to these threats that you will deploy as part of your overall security plan and may include firewalls, IPS, IDS, aggregation and correlation facilities, to name a few.

These are the fundamental and standard aspects of security. Now let's revisit some of the means by which we construct our security policies, plans, and procedures.

Policies, Plans, and Procedures

Earlier in this chapter, we mentioned that it is important to provide and conduct an initial baseline security audit and institute a security plan for the organization. Along with this practice, it is equally important to provide adequate information not only to the individuals in charge of security, but to everyone in the organization. Everyone must cooperate in this plan to achieve the desired goal of information and services security and integrity in your environment. To that end, we must provide additional service beyond the security evaluation and plan. This means working with a planning team that includes legal, human resources, and management input to prepare the documentation.

At a minimum, your security plan should provide documentation and supporting work that includes:

Acceptable-use policies:

- Permitted activities

- Disciplines for infractions

- Auditing policies

- Disaster recovery plans

- Reporting hierarchy and escalation paths

- Overall security policy:

  - What needs protection and from what type of attack?

  - What methodologies will be utilized for protection?

  - Who is responsible for implementation, monitoring, and maintenance?

  - Risk analysis—what is vulnerable and what is the impact if lost/damaged/compromised?

- Growth and service needs projections

User training and education plans

As previously mentioned, there are several bodies of work that we can leverage to complete a comprehensive security policy and plan. One such document is ISO/IEC 17799:2005, which establishes guidelines and general principles for initiating, implementing, maintaining, and improving information security management in an organization. Although everything within the ISO/IEC 17799 standard might not apply to your specific objectives, it is an invaluable source of elements included in a holistic plan and makes an excellent reference.

The objectives set forth in the standard include general guidance on typical goals of information security and provides best practices in information security management, including:

- Security policy

- Organization of information security

- Asset management

- Human resources security

- Physical and environmental security

- Communications and operations management

- Access control

- Information systems acquisition, development, and maintenance

- Information security incident management

- Business continuity management

- Compliance

This standard is provided as a practical guideline in developing security standards and effective security management practices.

Many documents and processes are necessary for the proper implementation and enforcement of a security stance after delivery of your overall security plan. Figure 1.3 provides a brief pictorial view of what is involved in the security policy planning stage. This process is necessary and must be completed and maintained throughout your company's life span before proceeding to the tasks of designing the DMZ. Without the security policy in place, DMZ design may be ineffective and not cost-effective, because it may have to be reconfigured to fit with the organization's overall security needs.

DMZ Definitions and History

In the security fundamentals section of this chapter, we began to discuss some of the terminology and definitions relating to our work with DMZ structure and its components. Before we proceed to a more in-depth discussion of the DMZ, we need to review the definitions its components. Furthermore, we'll briefly discuss the history of the DMZ and the philosophy that has led to its implementation for protection. To begin, we define some common terms that we will use throughout the book as we discuss DMZs. Table 1.1 details and defines these terms.

Figure 1.3 The Path to Completion of a Security Policy Document

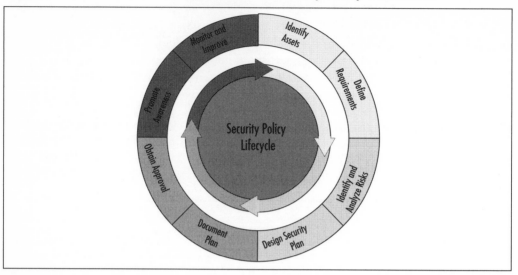

Table 1.1 DMZ Definitions

Term	Definition or Description
DMZ	In computer networks, a demilitarized zone, or DMZ, is a computer host or small network inserted as a "neutral zone" between a company's private network and the outside public network. The DMZ prevents outside users from getting direct access to a server that has company data. (The term comes from the geographic buffer zone that was set up between North Korea and South Korea following the United Nations' "police action" there in the early 1950s.)
Bastion host (untrusted host)	A machine (usually a server) located in the DMZ with strong host-level protection and minimal services. It is used as a gateway between the inside and the outside of networks. The bastion host is normally not the firewall but a separate machine that will probably be sacrificial in the design. The notation "untrusted host" may be used because the bastion host is always considered to be potentially compromised and therefore should not be fully trusted by internal network clients.
Firewall	A hardware device or software package that provides filtering and/or provision of rules to allow or deny specific types of network traffic to flow between internal and external networks.
Proxy server	An application-based translation of network access requests. Provisions for local user authentication for access to untrusted networks. Logging and control of port/protocol access may be possible. Normally used to connect two networks.

Continued

Table 1.1 continued DMZ Definitions

Term	Definition or Description
Network Address Translation (NAT)	Application-based translation of IP headers to masquerade internal IP networks. Can be deployed in a one-to-one or one-to-many relationship, Port Address Translation (PAT). Originally conceived to provide additional IP space in the form of RFC 1918 addresses.
Packet filtering	The use of a set of rules to open or close ports to specific protocols (such as allowing Transmission Control Protocol [TCP] or User Datagram Protocol [UDP] packets) or protocol ID(s), such as allowing or blocking Internet Control Message Protocol (ICMP).
Stateful packet filtering	A hardware- or software-based process in firewalls that inspect transient flows to ensure proper standards-based protocol activity.
Screened subnet	An isolated network containing hosts that need to be accessible from both the untrusted external network and the internal network. An example is the placement of a bastion host in a dual-firewall network, with the bastion host in the network between the firewalls. A screened subnet is often a part of a DMZ implementation.
Screening router	An often used initial screening method to limit traffic to and from a protected network. It may employ various methods of packet filtering and protocol limitation and act as a limited initial firewall device.
Intrusion detection system (IDS)	A hardware or software system that "listens" to transient network flows and sends alerts based on signature matching or anomalous traffic.
Intrusion prevention system (IPS)	An inline hardware or software system that "listens" to transient network flows, sends alerts based on signature matching or anomalous traffic, and terminates malicious traffic on detection.
Honeypot or honeynet	Devices or a network of devices that appear to have vulnerable services but are actually used to collect information about potential threats, hackers, and malicious code access.

DMZ use has become a necessary method of providing a multilayered, defense–in–depth approach to security. The use of DMZ structures developed as a response to evolving business requirements in which increased numbers of services were deployed for multiple, yet functionally disparate, consumers of data. These new technologies and designs have provided a higher level of protection for the data and services we are charged with protecting.

DMZ Concepts

The use of a DMZ and its overall design and implementation can be relatively simple or extremely complex, depending on the needs of the particular business or network system. The DMZ concept was born as the need for separation of networks became more acute; we began to provide more access to services for individuals or partners outside our trusted, internal network infrastructure. A primary reason that the DMZ is a critical component of security design is the realization that a single type of protection is subject to failure. This failure can arise from configuration errors, planning errors, equipment failure, or deliberate action on the part of an internal employee or external attack force. The DMZ has proven to be more secure and to offer multiple layers of protection for the security of the protected networks and machines. Over time, it has proven to be very flexible, scalable, redundant, and robust in its ability to provide the ongoing protection companies need. DMZ design now includes the ability to use multiple products (both hardware- and software-based) on multiple platforms to achieve the necessary level of protection.

To provide a common understanding of DMZ design, let's examine a number of conceptual paths for traffic flow into service networks and DMZs. Before we look at the conceptual paths, let's make sure that we understand the basic configurations and layouts that can be used for firewall and DMZ network. In the following figures, we'll see and discuss these configurations. Please note that each of these configurations is useful to protect assets on both internal and external networks such as the Internet. Our first configuration is shown in Figure 1.4.

Figure 1.4 A Basic Network With a Single Firewall

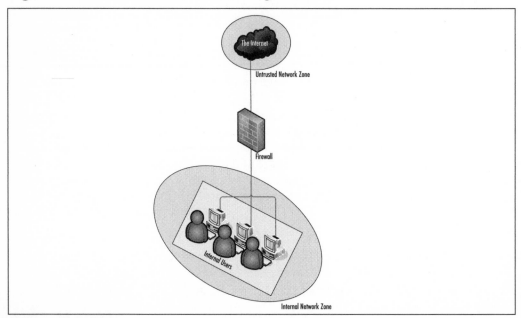

In Figure 1.4, we can see the basic configuration that would be used in a simple network situation where there was no need to provide external services. This configuration would typically be used to begin to protect a small business or home network. It could also be used within an internal network to protect an inner network that needed to be divided and isolated from the main network. This situation could include payroll, finance, or development divisions that must protect their information and keep it away from general network use and view.

Figure 1.5 details a protection design that would allow for the implementation and provision of services outside the protected network. In this design, it would be absolutely imperative that rules be enacted to not allow the untrusted host to access the internal network. Security of the bastion host machine would be accomplished on the machine itself, and only minimal and absolutely necessary services would be enabled or installed on that machine. In this design, we might be providing a Web presence that did not involve e-commerce or the necessity to dynamically update content. This design would not be used for provision of virtual private network (VPN) connections, File Transfer Protocol (FTP) services, or other services that required other content updates to be performed regularly.

Figure 1.5 Basic Network, Single Firewall and Bastion Host (Untrusted Host)

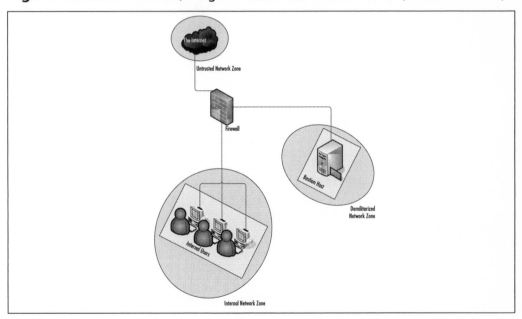

Figure 1.6 shows a basic DMZ structure. In this design, the bastion host is partially protected by the firewall. Rather than the full exposure that would result to the bastion host shown in Figure 1.5, this setup would allow us to specify that the bastion host in Figure 1.6 could be allowed full outbound connection, but the firewall could be configured to allow only port 80 traffic inbound to the bastion host (assuming it was a Web server) or others as

necessary for connection from outside. This design would allow connection from the internal network to the bastion host if it was necessary. This design would potentially allow updating of Web server content from the internal network if allowed by a firewall rule, which could allow traffic to and from the bastion host on specific ports, as designated. (There is more on that topic later in the chapter.)

Figure 1.6 A Basic Firewall With a DMZ

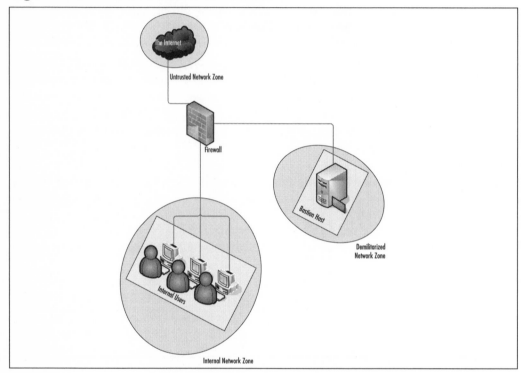

Figure 1.7 shows a generic multitiered DMZ configuration. Because firewalls are now capable of virtualization through inspection of 802.1q Virtual LAN (VLAN) tags, we no longer require physically separate firewalls or firewall interfaces. In this arrangement, a single trunked interface is connected to the DMZ, and the firewall enforces separate security policies based on the inspected VLAN tags. This configuration is recommended when your DMZ networks exist within the same security zone. Should you have separate security zones for your DMZ, you may wish to provide physical separation on multiple switches to mitigate VLAN hopping risks. The bastion host can be protected from the outside and allowed to connect to or from the internal network, or even another separate DMZ network. In this arrangement, like the conditions in Figure 1.6, flow can be controlled to and from both of the networks, away from the DMZ. This configuration and method are more likely to be used if more than one bastion host is needed or if a traditional multitiered application environment is present in the DMZ.

Figure 1.7 A Multitiered Firewall With a DMZ

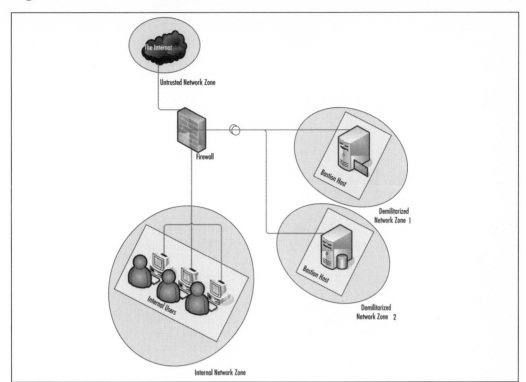

Traffic Flow Concepts

Now that we've had a quick tour of some generic designs, let's take a look at the way network traffic typically flows through these designs. Be sure to note the differences between the levels and the flow of traffic and protections offered in each design.

Figure 1.8 illustrates the flow pattern for information through a basic single-firewall setup. This type of traffic control can be achieved through hardware or software and is the basis for familiar products such as Internet Connection Sharing (ICS) and the NAT functionality provided by digital subscriber line (DSL) and cable modems used for connection to the Internet. Note that flow is unrestricted outbound, but the basic configuration will drop all inbound connections that did not originate from the internal network.

Figure 1.9 reviews the traffic flow in a network containing a bastion host and a single firewall. This network configuration does not produce a DMZ; the protection of the bastion host is configured individually on the host and requires extreme care in setup. Inbound traffic from the untrusted network or the bastion host is dropped at the firewall, providing protection to the internal network. Outbound traffic from the internal network is allowed.

Figure 1.8 Basic Single-Firewall Flow

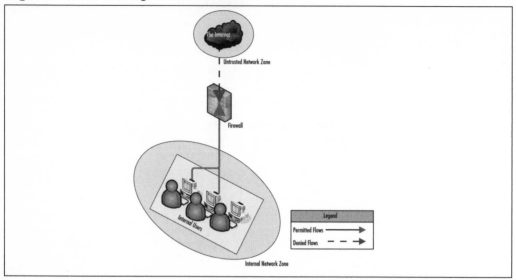

Figure 1.9 A Basic Firewall With Bastion Host Flow

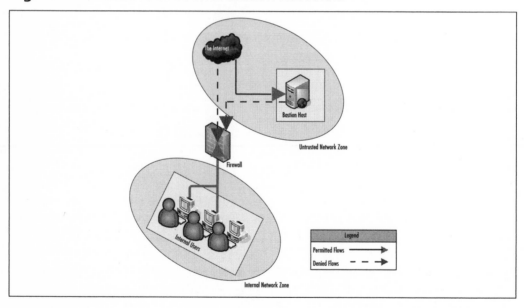

Figure 1.10 shows the patterns of traffic as we implement a DMZ design. In this form, inbound traffic flows through to the bastion host if allowed through the firewall and is dropped if destined for the internal network. Two-way traffic is permitted as specified between the internal network and the bastion host, and outbound traffic from the internal network flows through the firewall and out, generally without restriction.

Figure 1.10 A Basic Single Firewall With DMZ Flow

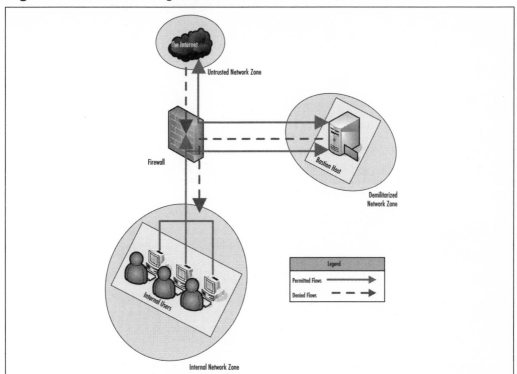

Figure 1.11 contains a more complex flow path for information but provides the most capability in these basic designs to allow for configuration and provision of services to the outside. In this case, we have truly established a DMZ, separated and protected from both the internal and external networks. This type of configuration is used quite often when there is a need to provide more than one type of service to the public or outside world, such as e-mail, Web servers, DNS, and so forth. Traffic to the bastion host can be allowed or denied as necessary from both the external and internal networks, and incoming traffic to the internal network can be dropped at the external firewall. Outbound traffic from the internal network can be allowed or restricted either to the bastion host (DMZ network) or the external network.

As you can see, there is a great amount of flexibility in the design and function of your protection mechanisms. In the sections that follow, we expand further on conditions for the use of various configurations and on the planning that must be done to implement them.

Figure 1.11 A Multitiered Firewall With a DMZ Flow

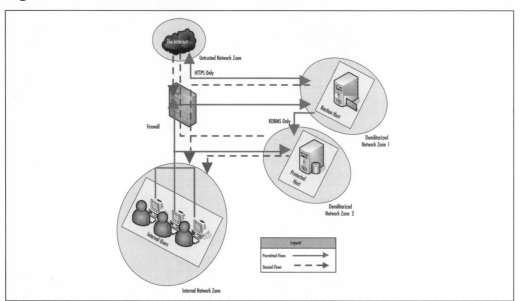

Networks With and Without DMZs

As we pursue our discussions about the creation of DMZ structures, it is appropriate to also take a look at the reasoning behind the structures of the DMZ and when and where we'd want to implement a DMZ or perhaps use some other alternative.

During our preview of the concepts of DMZs, we saw in Figures 1.4–1.7 some examples of potential designs for network protection and access. Your design may incorporate any or all of these types of configurations, depending on your organization's needs. For instance, Figure 1.4 shows a configuration that may occur in a home network installation or perhaps with a small business environment that outsources its services or information for customers at a collocation facility. This design would be suitable under these conditions, provided that configurations are correct and monitored for change.

Figure 1.5 illustrates a network design with a bastion host located outside the firewall. In this design, the bastion host must be stripped of all unnecessary functionality and services and protected locally with appropriate file permissions and access control mechanisms. This design is suitable for an organization that provides minimal services to an external network, such as a simple Web server. Access to the internal network from the bastion host is generally not allowed, because the bastion host is subject to compromise and therefore untrusted.

Figure 1.6 details the first of the actual DMZ designs and incorporates a screened subnet. In this type of design, the firewall controls the flow of information from network to network and provides more protection to the bastion host from external flows. This design might be used when it is necessary to regularly update the content of a Web server or provide a front end for mail or other services that need contact with both the internal and external networks. Although better for security purposes than Figure 1.5, this design still infers an untrusted relationship between the bastion host and the internal network.

Finally, Figure 1.7 provides a design that allows for the placement of many types of service in the DMZ. Traffic can be very finely controlled between the various networks through access at the firewall, and services can be provided at multiple levels to both internal and external networks.

In the next section, we profile some of the advantages and disadvantages of the common approaches to DMZ architecture and provide a checklist to help you decide what is appropriate for your DMZ design.

Pros and Cons of DMZ Basic Designs

Table 1.2 details the advantages and disadvantages of the various types of basic design discussed in the preceding section.

Table 1.2 Pros and Cons of Basic DMZ Designs   193.192

Basic Design	Advantages	Disadvantages	Recommended Use
Single firewall	Inexpensive, fairly easy configuration, low maintenance	Much lower security capabilities, no growth or expansion potential	Home, small office/home office (SOHO), small business with outsourced services
Single firewall with bastion host	Lower cost than more robust alternatives, simple design	Bastion host vulnerable to compromise, inconvenient to update content, loss of functionality other than for absolutely required services; not scalable	Small business with minimal services and/or static content that doesn't require frequent updates
Single firewall with screened subnet and bastion host	Firewall provides protection to both internal network and bastion host, limiting compromise risk while providing some flexibility	Increased complexity, requires split DNS	Larger businesses with multiple networks requiring access to the bastion host for dynamic information

Continued

Table 1.2 continued Pros and Cons of Basic DMZ Designs

Basic Design	Advantages	Disadvantages	Recommended Use
Multitiered firewall with DMZ	Allows for multiple service-providing hosts in the DMZ; protects bastion hosts in the DMZ from other DMZ host networks, allows fine granularity of control; limits fault domain after compromise	Requires more hardware and software for implementation of this design; increased complexity, requires more configuration work and monitoring, requires split DNS	Larger operations that require the capability to offer multiple types of Web access and services to both the internal and external networks involved

Configuring & Implementing…

Bastion Hosts

Bastion hosts must be individually secured and hardened because they are always in a position that could be attacked or probed. This means that before placement, a bastion host must be stripped of unnecessary services, fully updated with the latest patches and software updates, and isolated from other trusted machines and networks. This reduces the possibility that its compromise would allow for connection to (and potential compromise of) the protected networks and resources. This also means that a machine being used for this purpose should have no user accounts relative to the protected network or directory services structure, which could lead to enumeration of your internal network.

DMZ Design Fundamentals

DMZ design, like security design, is always a work in progress. As in security planning and analysis, we find DMZ design carries great flexibility and change potential to keep the protection levels we put in place in an effective state. Ongoing work is required so that the system's security is always as high as possible within time and budget constraints while still allowing appropriate users and visitors access to information and services. You will find that the time and funds spent in design and preparation for the implementation are very good investments if the process is focused and effective; this effort will lead to a high level of success and an optimal level of protection for the network you are protecting.

In this section of the chapter, we explore the fundamentals of the design process. To make decisions about our initial design, we incorporate the information we discussed in relation to security and traffic flow. Additionally, we'll build on that information and review some other areas of concern that could affect the way we design our DMZ structure.

> **NOTE**
>
> In this section we look at design of a DMZ from a logical point of view. Physical design and configuration are covered in following chapters, based on the vendor-based solution you choose to deploy.

Why Design Is So Important

Design of the DMZ is critically important to the overall protection of your internal network—and the success of your firewall and DMZ deployment. The DMZ design can incorporate sections that isolate incoming VPN traffic, Web traffic, partner connections, employee connections, and public access to information provided by your organization. Design of the DMZ structure throughout the organization can protect internal resources from internal attack. As we discussed in the security section, it has been well documented that much of the risk of data loss, corruption, and breach actually exists *inside* the network perimeter. Our tendency is to protect assets from external harm but to disregard the dangers that come from our own internal equipment, policies, and employees.

These attacks or disruptions do not arise solely from disgruntled employees. In fact, many of the most damaging conditions that occur are due to inadvertent mistakes made by well-intentioned employees. Each and all of these entry points is a potential source of loss for your organization and ultimately can provide an attack point to defeat your other defenses. Additionally, the design of your DMZ will allow you to implement a multilayered approach to securing your resources without single points of failure in your plan. This minimizes the problems and loss of protection that can occur because of poorly configured rule sets or access control lists (ACLs), as well as reducing the problems that occur due to hardware configuration errors. In the last chapters of this book, we investigate how to mitigate risk by testing your network infrastructure to ensure that firewalls, routers, switches, and hosts are thoroughly hardened.

Designing End-to-End Security for Data Transmission Between Hosts on the Network

Proper DMZ design, in conjunction with the security policy and plan developed previously, allows for end-to-end protection of your network and services. The importance of this capability is explored more fully later in the chapter when we review some of the security problems inherent in the current implementation of TCP/IPv4 and the transmission of data. The use of one or more of the many currently available firewall products or appliances will most often afford the opportunity not only to block or filter specific protocols but also to protect the data as it is being transmitted. This protection may take the form of encryption using available cryptographic transports to protect data. Additionally, proper use of the technologies available within this design provides the necessary functions in the concepts of CIA and defense in depth that we have discussed in earlier sections.

This need to provide end-to-end security requires that we are conversant with and remember basic network traffic patterns and protocols. The next few sections help remind us about these requirements and further illustrate the need to design the DMZ with this capability in mind.

Traffic Flow and Protocol Fundamentals

The ability to granularly and holistically control traffic flow through the DMZ is a major benefit of DMZ designs that include multi-tiered firewalls. In modern hardware and software-based firewalls, we can control traffic flowing in and out of the network or DMZ through packet filtering based on port numbers or by allowing or denying the use of entire protocols suites. For instance, a firewall rule set might include a statement that blocks communication via ICMP, which would block protocol 1. A statement that allows IPSec traffic using ESP or AH would be written allowing protocol 50 for ESP or 51 for AH. (For a listing of the protocol IDs, visit www.iana.org/assignments/protocol-numbers.) Remember that the optimal rule of security follows the principle of least privilege; we must include in our design the capability to allow only the absolutely necessary traffic into and out of the various portions of the DMZ structure and deny all other traffic.

DMZ Protocols

Protocol use within a DMZ environment is highly variable based on the specific needs of an organization. Often some of these protocols are problematic to our security stance. We should be well aware of the potential risks associated with the protocol used in various software implementations and those that are frequently and actively attacked due to known vulnerabilities and weak code. Table 1.3 provides a brief overview of some known issues with various protocols. This table is not intended to be all-inclusive; rather, it is demonstrative that when designing a plan for DMZ structure, the DMZ designer must be aware of many protocols' limitations.

Table 1.3 Protocols With Known Weaknesses

Protocol	Basic Weakness
File Transfer Protocol (FTP)	No encryption, exposing usernames, passwords, and payload in clear text
Telnet	Vulnerable to buffer overflow attacks, replay, and spoofing to gain privilege and discover passwords, allowing potential for breach of service
Hypertext Transfer Protocol (HTTP)	Many security vulnerabilities within various vendor software implementations; poor HTTP server configuration allows privilege escalation and compromise
Lightweight Directory Access Protocol (LDAP) and Microsoft Directory Services	Some implementations are subject to buffer overflow and DoS attacks, with possibility of privilege elevation
Simple Network Management Protocol (SNMP)	DoS and buffer overflow attacks are possible as are security risks posed by administrators who leave the community names and other information in default configurations; some conditions can result in privilege escalation and compromise
Secure Shell (SSH)	Privilege escalation, system compromise when code run under root credentials, DoS attacks
Domain Name Services (DNS)	Many security vulnerabilities within various vendor software implementations allow privilege escalation and compromise; widespread deployment needed for Internet use

Designing for Protection in Relation to the Inherent Flaws of TCP/IPv4

The current implementation of TCP/IPv4 contains a number of well-documented flaws that should be considered in the design of both your security plan and your DMZ. Some of these problems are corrected in IPv6, but since implementation of this technology isn't completely standardized or on the immediate horizon, we must accommodate the weaknesses of the existing protocols in implementing our DMZ design. We must plan for certain known problems, such as:

- SYN attacks, a DoS condition resulting from overflow of the wait buffer

- IP spoofing, allowing the attacker to pretend it is another host

- Sequence guessing, allowing reassembly or delivery of forged packets

- Connection hijacking, allowing man-in-the-middle attacks

You can find a good discussion of the problems with TCP/IPv4 in Stephen Bellovin's *Security Problems in the TCP/IP Protocol Suite*, available at www.cs.columbia.edu/~smb/papers/ipext.pdf. A more complete discussion of the flaws and improvements made in TCP/IPv6 is available at www.linuxsecurity.com/resource_files/documentation/tcpip-security.html. The design that we create for our DMZ structure will accommodate the weaknesses of the TCP/IP protocol and provide the protection necessary to stymie these attacks and their resulting potential for security breaches. To accomplish that goal, we need to consider these various problems and design functional protections in the design and firewall and ACL rules while considering the use of other protocols such as IPSec and L2TP to protect the data on the wire.

Public and Private IP Addressing

One of the primary reasons that the DMZ concepts have been so useful is that network administrators have a greatly expanded capability to use private addressing schemes. As you will recall, the initial TCP/IPv4 implementations were based on classful subnet masks, which inherently limited flexibility in network designs. With the advent of classless addressing and improvements provided with the acceptance of that concept, much greater utilization has been made of functions such as NAT to provide addressing for the internal network, without exposing that network to the dangers of the public network. The DMZ design must incorporate the methods and equipment being used for address translation and routing as it provides a method of hiding internal addresses from unwanted contact.

Therefore, we should plan to use RFC 1918-based private IP addressing ranges, which are shown in Table 1.4.

Table 1.4 Private IP Address Ranges

Private IP Range	CIDR Mask	Decimal Mask
10.0.0.0–10.255.255.255	/8	255.0.0.0
172.16.0.0–172.31.255.255	/16	255.255.0.0
192.168.0.0–192.168.255.255	/24	255.255.255.0

Use of private address space allows us much greater flexibility in the segregation of the DMZ and assures that the contacts between the protected network, the DMZ, and the outside world are more difficult for would-be attackers to penetrate.

Ports

Knowledge of various ports used in network communication is an extremely important tool toward our ability to filter access levels and establish ACL functions on devices and in software implementations used to protect our assets. Recall that ports 0–1023 are reserved for specific uses and that all other ports are functionally available for use by applications.

Registered ports include those from 1024 through 49151, and dynamic and/or private ports (used by applications for communication and session maintenance) are those from 49152 through 65535. The entire port list can be found at www.iana.org/port-numbers.

That means, of course, that the DMZ design must incorporate rules that block all traffic that is not necessary for the function of the DMZ or communications that must be carried through that area. Generally, this involves creating a rule set for the ACL that restricts or blocks all unused ports on a per-protocol basis to assure that the traffic is actually stopped. These rules that are created become an integral part of the DMZ defense. Security adminis-trators often start from one of two "all or nothing" configurations: either all ports are open and administrators close ports as problems occur (bad), or all ports are initially closed and administrators open ports as required (good, but requiring a great deal of administration and monitoring in a new network that has not been fully documented). Either method can be considered in your design, but the latter incorporates the concept of least privilege and pro-vides much more security as you begin your quest to prevent system compromise.

The SANS Institute (www.sans.org) recommends the port actions shown in Table 1.5 at a minimum as you design your DMZ and firewall blocking rules from external networks.

Table 1.5 Common Ports to Block

Protocol	Port	Service Name
TCP	21	FTP
TCP	25	SMTP
TCP/UDP	53	DNS
TCP/UDP	67, 68	DHCP
TCP/UDP	69	TFTP
TCP	80	WWW, HTTP
TCP/UDP	88	Kerberos
TCP	135	RPC/DCE Endpoint Mapper
UDP	137	NetBIOS Name Service
UDP	138	NetBIOS Datagram Service
TCP	139	NetBIOS Session Service
TCP	143	IMAP
TCP/UDP	389	LDAP
TCP	443	HTTP over SSL/TLS
TCP/UDP	445	Microsoft SMB/CIFS
TCP/UDP	464	Kerberos lpasswd
UDP	500	Internet Key Exchange, IKE (IPSec)
TCP	593	HTTP RPC Endpoint Mapper

Continued

Table 1.5 Common Ports to Block

Protocol	Port	Service Name
TCP	636	LDAP over SSL/TLS
TCP/UDP	1433, 1434	MS SQL Server
TCP	3268	AD Global Catalog
TCP	3269	AD Global Catalog over SSL
TCP	3389	Windows Terminal Server
ICMP	N/A	Internet Control Messaging Protocol (ICMP)

The OSI Model

While we are reviewing the basics prior to designing our DMZ structure, we should also look briefly at the basis for traffic flow in our networks and how the data is transported and delivered from host to host. This review is not intended to be all inclusive but rather to demonstrate that these traffic flow designs strongly influence technology considerations in properly defending our machines and data from attack or misuse. Recall that there exist two different but complementary designs of data traffic flow and processing for network communication. The first is the *Open Systems Interconnection (OSI) model*, which formed the basis for all network communication as originally conceived. The OSI was followed, during the development of the TCP/IP protocol suite, by the *TCP/IP model*, which combines the functions of the OSI model layers. Figure 1.12 details the components of the two models.

Figure 1.12 The OSI and TCP/IP Models

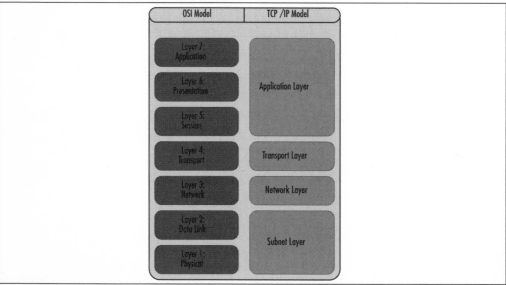

Recall that in both models, packets are assembled and headers from each layer are added as a packet is encapsulated and prepared for transport on the physical media. The header contains information about the processing that occurred, to guide reassembly by the receiving machine. Through either process, when the packet is being sent from the sender to the receiver, a negotiated port is used to deliver the information to the receiving machine. While you're making design decisions for the DMZ access restrictions, it is important to keep in mind your communication needs for your existing or proposed services and applications. The launch point of the communication becomes important as we consider the design, because we must provide for communication that starts at the Application Layer differently than the communication that is occurring at lower layers such as the Transport Layer or below. The various layers of the models provide the DMZ designer with a number of different places to institute the desired controls that are used to restrict or allow traffic into and out of the DMZ.

Identifying Potential Risks from the Internet

Part of the identification process for identifying Internet-based risks is a thorough review of the original baseline analysis performed during security planning. Risks identified from that analysis should be a part of your comprehensive DMZ design plan and should consider a number of potential problems, including, but certainly not limited to:

Virus and Trojan introduction to the network:

- Possibility of enumeration of the network
- Various entry points to the network
- Unauthorized disclosure of information
- Remote control usage:
    - VNC
    - Microsoft's Terminal Services
    - PCAnywhere and similar products

Possible weak configurations allowing elevated access privileges

Evaluation and inclusion of these potential areas of entry and attack, along with others that may be defined in your plan, should be constantly reviewed during the design process and again at regular intervals to verify that the discovered risks are mitigated through proper security design and enforcement.

Using Firewalls to Protect Network Resources

Firewalls have long been and continue to be an integral part in the planning process for DMZ deployments. The design can include any or all of the basic designs we discussed earlier in the chapter and may very well incorporate multiple types of configurations, depending on your organization's needs to protect data and resources from various threat areas. Firewalls are not the only component of the design that is important, but they do play a major part in allowing the administrator control of traffic, and thus they provide a higher level of protection.

Part of the design process includes evaluating and checking the performance of different hardware- and software-based firewall products. Later chapters of this book discuss some of the most used technologies, such as Check Point and Check Point NG, PIX, Nokia, and Microsoft's ISA Server. Additionally, firewall considerations are explored during discussions of wireless network protection and the methods of protecting networks using Sun and Microsoft network operating system (NOS) software.

Using Screened Subnets to Protect Network Resources

As you proceed to a more advance design for your DMZ, conditions may drive the decision to employ screened subnets for protection or provision of services. The screened subnet, in some designs, actually becomes synonymous with DMZ in usage. However, the screened subnet is actually a security enhanced version of the multihomed screened host configurations that were used in the past. It involves the use of more hardware but provides a more secure basis for configuration and blocking unauthorized access.

The screened subnet that we looked at earlier in the chapter can be configured in a number of configurations, dependent on your needs. The most simple of construction involves a multiple-interface firewall with the capability to filter traffic to more than one network. Although simple than others, this design might not be appropriate to use in your environment if you plan to offer services such as Web, e-mail, FTP, or VPN connections from the public network to your private network. In these situations, a good case could be made for the multitiered firewall approach, perhaps with multiple screened subnets that provide different services or access based on criteria that you have identified during your planning process. Certainly, if offering services that involve e-commerce or access to confidential records (such as HIPAA-compliant patient records), your plan will most likely need to include multiple screened subnets, following the earlier suggestions that a multilayer approach be used to restrict access and prevent attacks from outside.

Securing Public Access to a Screened Subnet

Public access to screened subnets is secured and restricted through a multilayer process, using a screening router to begin providing protection and a firewall in the next layer to protect the access point coming into the screened subnet. Figure 1.13 shows a possible configuration to begin this protection process.

Figure 1.13 A Basic Screened Subnet

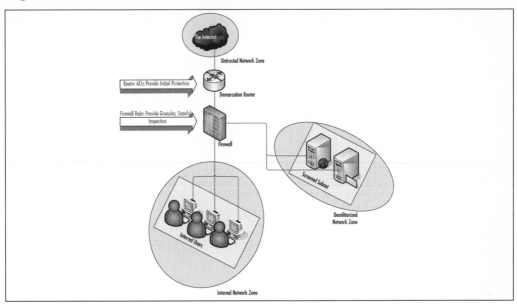

In this configuration, it is possible to limit the inbound traffic initially by configuring a rule set on the router; this piece might be provided by an Internet service provider (ISP), for example. Further levels of security can be developed in your plan as needed to protect assets on the screened subnet by firewall rule sets and hardening of the server providing services. Additionally, this design could be expanded or used for services or administration of screened subnets, providing greater security to the internal network as well.

Designing & Planning…

Know What You Want to Secure First

As you begin your DMZ design process, you must first be clear about the elements for which your design is intended. A design that is only intended to superficially limit internal users' access to the Internet, for instance, requires much less planning and design work than a system protecting resources from multiple access points or providing multiple services to the public network or users from remote locations. An appropriate path to follow for your initial design might look like this:

Continued

1. Perform baseline security analysis of existing infrastructure, including OS and application analysis:

- Perform baseline network mapping and performance monitoring
- Identify risk to resources and appropriate mitigation processes
- Identify potential security threats, both external and internal
- Identify needed access points from external sources:
  - Public networks
  - VPN access
  - Extranets
  - Remote access services
- Identify critical services

2. Plan your DMZ

Traffic and Security Risks

After beginning to research the necessary components for designing your protection plan, you will reach a point at which you will assess the actual risks to the security of your enterprise network. One of the first tools you might consider in this part of your evaluation is the SANS Top 20 list of the current most critical vulnerabilities, to review the most commonly vulnerable services. You can view this list at www.sans.org/top20; it is updated frequently. This information can help you to at least begin to identify some of the risks involved and then to design a more effective plan to secure what you need to secure.

More appropriately, you should list all services in the DMZ that are required for business operations. This list should detail the vendor and version of software on each system. This continually evolving list can be used to investigate specific vulnerabilities within your environment. Armed with this information, you can proceed to mitigate the known risks and weak points within your DMZ.

As we continue with our overview of DMZ design principles, we also need to discuss the management of resources and the challenges that occur in designing for administration and control of the DMZ. The following sections detail a number of the areas that we must be aware of during our consideration of design and DMZ implementation.

Application Servers in the DMZ

Application server placement in the DMZ must be designed with tight controls in mind. As in other screened subnet configurations, the basic security of the operating system must first be assured on the local machine, with all applicable patches and software updates applied. All unused services should be disabled or removed if possible.

We spend a great deal of time in this book covering the hardening of your systems (Windows 2000, Sun Solaris, and the like) within the DMZ. Additionally, functionality of the application servers located in the DMZ should be limited to specific tasks that do not involve critical corporate data or information. Therefore, although it is acceptable to place a Web server in the DMZ with a supporting database server, neither of those servers should contain confidential or critical corporate information, because they are still located in an area in which they are considered untrusted. Critical or confidential information should not be accessible from or stored in the DMZ. For instance, as discussed in the following section, it is not acceptable to store any type of internal network authentication information on machines in the DMZ. Likewise, front-end servers or application proxy servers can be placed in the DMZ for other needs, such as an SMTP gateway or a DNS forwarder. In these instances, neither the mail nor the DNS server should store any information about the internal network or allow general communication to pass unchecked to or from the internal network. Traffic to these servers from the internal network should pass through a firewall, restricting traffic to individual machines in both directions, using specific port and address information.

Domain Controllers in the DMZ

Domain controllers for Windows networks or other directory services authentication servers should never have those services located within the DMZ. It is feasible in some configurations to provide a front end to these critical servers from within the DMZ, but it is not recommended, because compromise of a bastion host allowed to communicate with the internal network through the firewall could lead to compromise of the entire internal system. Access to your internal network that requires authentication should instead be handled in your design by the use of VPN solutions, including RADIUS and TACACS+, discussed in the next section. It is possible, however, that domain controllers need to be placed within the DMZ, depending on the services you plan to provide in the DMZ. For instance, if you were running a cluster that is highly available from the Internet on Windows 2000 servers, the cluster will not operate correctly without a domain controller present. For that reason, you have to accurately assess what you will need and analyze how to implement and secure it.

RADIUS-Based Authentication Servers in the DMZ

Remote Authentication Dial-In User Service (RADIUS) servers, by definition and usage, are required to have full access to the authentication information provided by the Directory Services system in the enterprise. For this reason, the RADIUS server must be fully protected from attack and patched completely to avoid DoS conditions. The preferred option would have the RADIUS server located in the internal network, with proxied requests coming from a Routing and Remote Access Services (RRAS) server allowed through the firewall to the RADIUS server only from the specified RRAS servers. Additionally, it would make sense to plan for the use of IPSec to further protect that traffic. Regardless, understand that you must analyze the need and deploy the choices based on a proper design that provides the required service but still remains secure.

VPN DMZ Design Concepts

VPN usage has grown during the past few years. Many organizations embraced the possibility of VPN use as a method to communicate securely from remote offices. This led to a surge of connectivity that was requested in order to allow home "teleworkers" to perform their job functions without entering the secured environs of the actual workplace and its network.

A number of changes have been implemented in VPN technology in the recent past, and these have modified the thought process that we must undertake as we design our DMZ infrastructure. To begin, VPN solutions should be created in a separate DMZ space, away from the other parts of the Internet-facing infrastructure and apart from your internal network space. VPN technologies now incorporate the capability to enter your company network space through public switched telephone network (PSTN) connections, Frame Relay connections, and the public Internet. Each of these connection types must be included in the plan, and entry points must be carefully controlled to allow the required access and protection of information while not allowing a back-door entry to the internal networks.

A number of these plans are discussed in subsequent chapters of this book as different firewall configurations and designs are considered and discussed. When we're looking at the possibilities for VPN implementation and protection, it is extremely important to utilize all potential security tools available, including IPSec and its authentication and encryption possibilities as well as IDS and IPS. It is also important to evaluate the actual network design, in order to use RFC 1918 (private) addressing in the internal network and properly secure the addressing within the VPN, which should be registered addresses. Chapter 10 covers this topic more fully.

Advanced Risks

After you've considered the basic issues for connectivity to your infrastructure in your design, it is appropriate to begin to explore and plan for other areas that might need protection through your DMZ design. There are nearly infinite overall design possibilities, including the ability to protect not only the internal network but e-commerce, business partner, and extranet connections. Additionally, your enterprise may be involved in the creation of hosted services, in which you are providing protection to Web, FTP, or other servers that require unique protections as well as the ability to provide management capabilities. This section visits a number of those potential areas that may be appropriate for coverage in your overall DMZ design.

Business Partner Connections

Business partner connections can provide a unique challenge to the DMZ designer. Often there is a requirement to provide access to and from enterprise resource planning (ERP) packages such as those from Oracle, SAP, Microsoft Dynamics, and others that are currently in use, to provide project management, packaging, and collaboration tools to members of multiple organizations.

One of the challenges that arises quickly is the question of how to appropriately allow connectivity between organizations with proper authentication and protection of information for all parties. Many of the basic designs that we've discussed, including the use of specifically screened subnets for VPN access, provide partial solutions to these issues, but each case also requires an in-depth evaluation and most certainly collaboration between the DMZ designers to appropriately channel the access entry points, remote access if needed, and authentication of the users from various entities to maintain the requirements of CIA. Chapter 10 covers this configuration more fully.

Extranets

Of the possibilities that can be explored in relation to business partner connections for an enterprise, extranets provide a great deal of flexibility in their implementation and use. Extranets can be XML-powered Web browser-based information stores, can allow contact by customers seeking catalog information, and can allow real-time or close to real-time tracking capabilities of shipments and the supply chain. Additionally, the extranet can be configured for collaborative efforts and used between business partners for the ultimate capability to share information and processes while working on joint projects. Extranets, much like the earlier discussion of VPN access, are usually placed on isolated DMZ segments to segregate them from the hosting network's operations. These DMZ segments will house and host machines that allow the use of ERP software and the warehousing of common information. The use of extranet applications is most often Web browser based for the client that is seeking the information and not normally for storing highly sensitive data, although the data should still be protected.

Web and FTP Sites

Customer-based Web and FTP sites that are provided or hosted by your organization can also cause the DMZ design to change in various ways. Hosting the information on customer-based sites requires the same processes that we've looked at in relation to hosting our own Web and FTP servers in the DMZ, with an additional requirement that some sort of remote management capability be provided for the customer to administer and monitor the sites. This hosting can lead to a plan that permits administrative access from Internet-based, untrusted sources and must be carefully explored. Ensure that your DMZ design will not be compromised by the methods used to allow remote access to these servers and their administration by the client customer. It may be appropriate to host customer-based operations in a separate DMZ segment, away from your operation altogether.

E-Commerce Services

Among the possibilities that we may include in our overall DMZ design scheme is the possibility of hosting or supporting e-commerce services. As with other DMZ design considerations, the DMZ segment hosting e-commerce services must provide a level of isolation that protects such things as credit card information and transactions. It can include restrictions that block access from noncustomer address ranges, and it can also include restrictions on traffic to limit it to ports for Web services and Secure Sockets Layer (SSL), to protect the internal records generated by the services' action. E-commerce activities should also include restrictions that disable IP forwarding between servers and segregation of services such as noncritical database information among different servers for load balancing and to distribute security to a higher degree. No contact should be allowed between the e-commerce DMZ servers inbound to the internal network. E-commerce applications benefit greatly from multitiered DMZ structures where the traditional application tiers (Web front end, database, and so on) are segmented and protected from each other with tightly restricted, minimal connectivity.

E-Mail Services

E-mail services are among the most used (and abused) network services that are provided through a combination of access points, both external and internal. SMTP gateways should be located in segregated DMZ subnets with firewalls allowing access into and out of the mail subnet for SMTP (TCP port 25) and DNS (UDP/TCP port 53). This setup should also include mail relay settings on the DMZ mail gateway that prevent relaying mail from networks other than the internal network or other trusted networks. The external firewall that allows access to the SMTP gateway should be configured to block outbound SMTP traffic that did not originate at the gateway. Finally, the server should be configured to only send mail to accepted internal addresses while rejecting all other communications. Great care must be used in the proper configuration of mail servers from all vendors when access is granted in any fashion from the external networks.

Advanced Design Strategies

Up to this point, we've directed our discussion to access path design and the methods of securing access to the internal network from the external network. In most cases, the DMZ is used to block incoming traffic and control it more completely through the multiple layers that are placed in the design, because this approach offers tighter control to stop access to the internal network. In the past, standard DMZ designs almost always defaulted to a condition in which the internal network's access to the external public network was unrestricted. As threats have grown in complexity, it has become clear that outbound access restrictions are often needed to prevent perpetuation of malicious traffic such as worms and viruses.

Before we complete our discussion of basic designs, it is appropriate to explore briefly some of the ways we might consider blocking access from the internal network to the external network, either wholly or in part, if the security design we created earlier indicates a need to do so. In the next section, we visit some of the common conditions that your organization might want to block or limit in your efforts to protect your assets and information.

Advanced DMZ Design Concepts

Intranet users have regularly been allowed full and unrestricted access to public network resources via the DMZ structure. Often the protection for the internal network involves using NAT or proxy-based connectivity to allow outward flow while restricting inbound requests to the internal network. You should think about some special considerations while you are working in this area. Let's list some of them and consider them in thought patterns as an addition to the overall design:

- Traditional local area network (LAN)-based protocols such as Microsoft CIFS should generally not be used outbound to transmit and received data from wide area network (WAN) destinations.

- Known worm propagation protocols and ports should be denied outbound access to prevent the spread of malicious traffic, should a system be compromised on an internal network.

- DMZ design lends itself to allowing control of unnecessary services that may be present on the external network. For instance, the DMZ design may incorporate outbound blocking of ports to services providing instant messaging, non-business-related networks, and other restrictions as appropriate to your system.

- Known management ports for externally located devices and services should be blocked from the internal network.

Additionally, we must look at the applications that are in use from the internal network to determine the appropriate level of outbound access to accommodate those applications.

As we continue through the book, we'll find that a number of other considerations must be taken into account as we create the design plan. For instance, although many DMZ configurations allow access to a Web server that we are operating, there must be a method in place to advise us of the presence of potential hackers working within our borders. To this end, the DMZ design must also include provisions for IDS and IPS placement in the various levels of the DMZ structure for evaluation of and alarm during intrusion attempts. This is most notably required when encrypted flows are permitted into your DMZ. As with all services that we provide, the Web services servers must be continually evaluated and kept up to date in their levels of security and service packs.

Another conceptual area that must be mentioned is the difference between a DMZ that is established for the purpose of isolating or segregating the public network from your private network and a DMZ that is used for the purpose of isolating or segregating a portion of your internal network. The design you create should include the capability to establish internal DMZ structures to protect confidential information from the general LAN operation. This could include segregation of financial data or provisions for VPN access to the internal network that does not originate from the public network (such as Frame Relay PVC channels or PSTN modem access). Again, when dealing with these special cases, the designer must be absolutely sure that the design does not introduce a back-door situation that allows public network bypass of the DMZ structure through compromise of a host machine.

Remote Administration Concepts

Remote management and administration of the various pieces of hardware within the DMZ design you implement provide another challenge for the designer. Although it is extremely tempting to use the built-in capabilities of the various operating systems and the management software provided for many of our hardware devices, it is very important to thoroughly review alternatives. Use of these tools for normal management from within the internal network could be a quick recipe for security breach and disaster.

It is certainly technologically possible to access the equipment in the DMZ through use of SSH, Telnet, or Microsoft's Terminal Services and to create firewall rules allowing traffic on the necessary ports to accomplish this task. So, what's the problem with using the built-in tools? These management tools, including SNMP-based traps and management agents, rely on the integrity of the network and the systems on which they are loaded to provide reports and management capabilities used to control the configuration of hardware and servers. What happens when the underlying network capability is degraded, reduced, or overloaded through an equipment failure or a DoS attack? What happens when the server itself is compromised? No management is possible, because we now can't reach the equipment. Overcoming this problem necessitates the concept of *in-band* versus *out-of-band* management of your systems.

The alternative of providing out-of-band management capabilities can be accomplished in a number of ways, including serial connections to secured management ports on the devices to be managed or a separate management screened subnet, such as illustrated in Figure 1.14.

In this simplified design, the servers located in the DMZ are each configured as a multi-homed machine, with the additional adapters configured to accept communications only from the designated management workstation(s), if your security policy allows multiple administrative units. Optimally, this second interface is a dedicated management port commonly found on today's server platforms. The outside firewall is configured to allow specific port-based traffic to flow from the management workstation to the servers, and the management workstation is not accessible from either the untrusted network or the protected LAN. This approach eliminates much of the security vulnerability that is presented when management options include only in-band tools.

Figure 1.14 A Method to Provide Out-of-Band Management in the DMZ

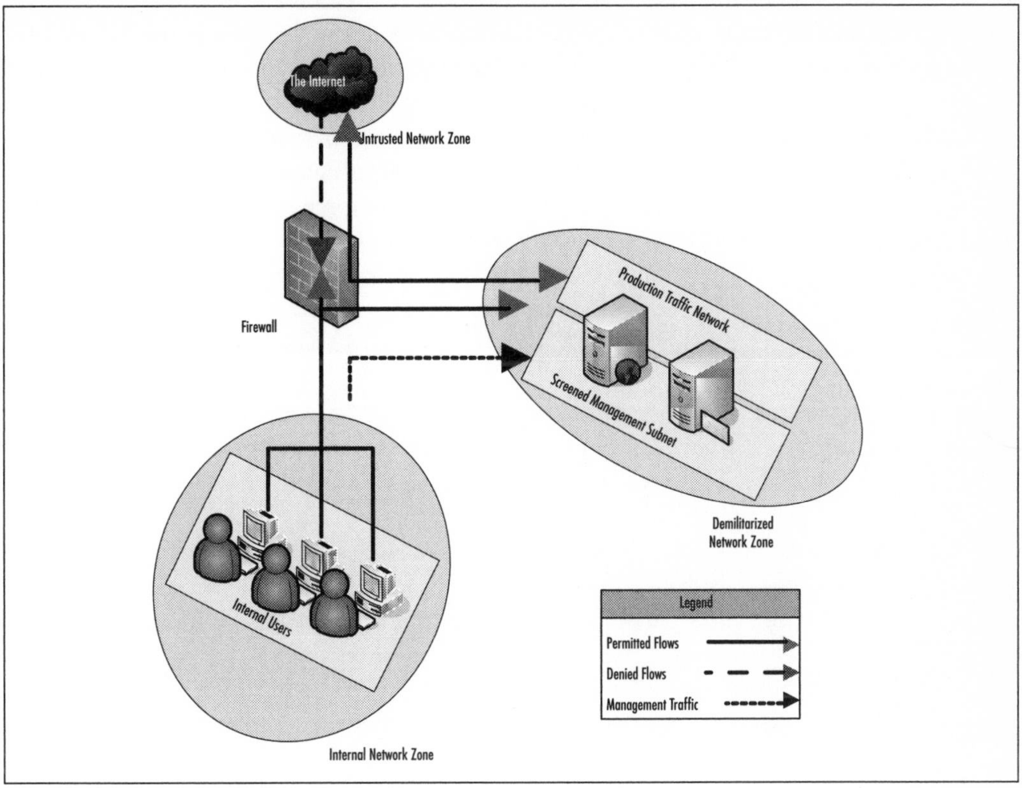

Authentication Design

Earlier in the chapter, we mentioned that it is generally inappropriate to locate a RADIUS or TACACS+ server in a DMZ segment, because it creates a condition in which the authentication information is potentially accessible to the public network. In some environments, it might be necessary to implement a plan to accommodate the authentication of users entering the DMZ from a public network. In this case, the DMZ design should include a separate authentication DMZ segment and the equipment in that segment should be hardened, as previously detailed in our discussion of placement. At this point, it is possible to provide an RRAS server in the DMZ with no internal account information and utilize ACLs and packet filtering at the firewall to restrict and encrypt the traffic between the two machines to the authentication traffic. It is recommended that this process utilize IPSec, and it would require that Protocol ID 51 for IPSec and IKE traffic on port 500 (UDP) be allowed for the communication to occur. It is also possible that other third-party authentication products such as Cisco's CiscoSecure ACS could provide a gateway and controls to allow this functionality.

Summary

Chapter 1 provided the opportunity to explore and review a number of important concepts in our preparation for designing an effective and secure DMZ structure. DMZ design includes a number of important steps that make the overall design process smoother and less subject to compromise. These steps include performing a complete physical and logical security analysis of the systems to be protected, followed by the adoption of an enterprise security policy to detail the path of management, monitoring, enforcement, and responsibility for various areas of the enterprise's security. Once we have completed a security analysis and have a security policy that has management support, we have the opportunity to think about the design of the DMZ structure. With a plan it is possible to incorporate the principles of security, such as defense in depth and CIA, into the design, to assure a higher level of security in the DMZ.

Generically, we create the basic DMZ structure after we have identified the assets and resources that need protection. This simple plan is followed by an evaluation of how the information currently flows in the organization and how it should be handled to securely isolate and protect the systems from compromise.

When the generic tasks have been completed, the design begins to take shape as we configure and define the various levels of the DMZ structure to provide necessary services to customers, employees, and partners. We're aware at this point that there are nearly infinite possibilities in the use of various equipment and configurations, and we're charged with creating a design that is functional and economically feasible in the reduction of risk. Here we begin to consider not only the best logical design but also the design that might be the most feasible to protect our data.

We find as we proceed that the level of service that we are providing and the connectivity needs of the various partners and operations greatly affect the level of configuration within the DMZ structure. We also find that it is possible to allow connectivity in multiple levels for various services while always striving to protect the internal network from harm.

Solutions Fast Track

Planning Network Security

- ☑ DMZ design requires that we first evaluate the physical and logical security and needs of the organization.

- ☑ The overall security plan and evaluation require input from all concerned parties in the organization, at levels ranging from human resources to the legal department to the chief security officer, to provide a valid analysis.

☑ Following the completion of the security plan, it is imperative that an overall enterprise security policy be written, approved, and implemented to assist in the evaluation of the need for DMZ protection. Without this document and definition of responsibility, DMZ design is fruitless.

DMZ Definitions and History

☑ DMZ use has been increasingly important as the de facto enterprise architecture design for security while at the same time offering an ever-increasing array of services and connections to services in the network.

☑ The multilayer approach of using bastion hosts, screened subnets, IDS/IPS, and firewalls to provide finer and finer control of access when approaching the interior network has proven to be an effective means to securing the DMZ structure.

☑ DMZ design is never static. Like security plans and policies, DMZ designs are a work in progress at all times, and it should be understood that the design is an evolving effort, subject to constant upgrade and tweaking.

DMZ Design Fundamentals

☑ Multiple design possibilities exist, depending on the level of protection that is required in the particular enterprise configuration.

☑ DMZ designs generally consist of firewalls and segments that are protected from each other by firewall rules and routing as well as the use of RFC 1918 addressing on the internal network.

☑ DMZ design depends on the architect's ability to accurately assess the actual risks so that he or she can design adequate protection.

Advanced Risks

☑ Outside the normal DMZ structure, many other conditions could arise that require evaluation. These conditions include restriction of access to the public networks from the private networks, not only the protection of the public network access to the internal network.

☑ Business-to-business (B2B) and e-commerce activities require special consideration to provide protection of partner and customer data and information. They also demand a level of design separate from basic needs.

☑ Provision of e-mail services and VPN connectivity to the private network via connection through the DMZ with a connection to the public network requires special considerations prior to design.

Advanced Design Strategies

■ Consider the methods that might be used to provide VPN services to special connections, such as Frame Relay and PVC circuits or Internet-based home users.

■ Limit or restrict outbound traffic from the internal network to inappropriate services, such as FTP or messaging services.

■ Provide for out-of-band management capabilities on all DMZ design segments as well as intrusion detection services where they are appropriate.

Frequently Asked Questions

The following Frequently Asked Questions, answered by the authors of this book, are designed to both measure your understanding of the concepts presented in this chapter and to assist you with real-life implementation of these concepts. To have your questions about this chapter answered by the author, browse to **www.syngress.com/solutions** and click on the **"Ask the Author"** form.

Q: What is the difference between a DMZ and a screened subnet?

A: Although the terms are sometimes used interchangeably, the screened subnet is a variation of the screened host configurations that required dual or multihomed hosts to provide protection. In the case of the DMZ, the protection is most often provided through the use of screening routers and firewall appliances or software to more securely limit traffic and eliminate single points of failure.

Q: You mention that a security policy must be in place before designing a DMZ. Why should I go to all that trouble?

A: It is important that administrators have a clear goal and vision about the levels of protection that you are responsible for and that you are expected to maintain. It is impossible to navigate the complexities of the DMZ design stage without first having a path to follow.

Q: Could you explain the difference between out-of-band and in-band management?

A: In-band management tools require that the network being managed and the devices connected to it utilize the same network. In the case of network problems or DoS attacks, the administrator would be unable to manage the equipment or rectify the problem. With out-of-band tools in place, management occurs on a different level, which may be a separate segment or serial port-based interaction with a console port on equipment. This capability is very important in the maintenance of your DMZ structure.

Q: A client has an outside office that needs to be able to authenticate to the internal network. The client would like to accomplish this task as inexpensively as possible while still maintaining security. What would you recommend?

A: In this case, the normal recommendation would be to use a modem-based RAS to allow access to the internal network, unless there is already a substantial DMZ structure in place to accommodate the traffic from the remote office.

Q: To provide the levels of security that are required in the large enterprise environment, what path would you recommend toward achieving the most complete design?

A: As we've discussed throughout the chapter, the most complete design requires security analysis, policy creation, and discussion with all stakeholders to appropriately implement the DMZ plan and structure.

Q: I thought that RADIUS was only for billing purposes?

A: Actually, RADIUS does have the capability to log access times and traffic, thus making auditing a simpler process. Its main use, however, is to screen the authentication process from outside networks and limit communication via the authentication mechanisms of our internal networks.

## Chapter 2

Windows DMZ Design

Solutions in this chapter:

- **Introducing Windows DMZ Security**
- **What's New in Windows Server 2003 and R2**
- **Building a Windows DMZ**
- **Looking Ahead to Windows Longhorn**
- **Windows DMZ Design Planning List**

☑ Summary

☑ Solutions Fast Track

☑ Frequently Asked Questions

Introduction

Microsoft has taken great strides in the past few years to enhance its security posture. Windows 2000 and Windows Server 2003 are as secure as Microsoft can make them, so it's very important that you follow this chapter closely; everything you learn here will be used in your network's demilitarized zone (DMZ).

In Chapter 1 we learned what a DMZ is, its fundamental security concepts, and how to design a basic DMZ with traffic flows. In this chapter we start to populate the DMZ with systems and the specifics of designing those systems to work within the DMZ. From Chapter 1, you'll recall what you learned about the basic DMZ and its overall reason for existence as well as its basic design. Building on the content of Chapter 1, this chapter shows you how to use your Windows systems within the DMZ design. We cover how to design a Windows-based network solution that will work within and around the DMZ segment. It's important to know this information as a security administrator or engineer because the DMZ (as you are now starting to see) can be very complex to work with. It will grow even more complex as we move through this book. (Chapter 13 and Appendix A focus entirely on how to lock down and harden Windows services such as IIS, so if you are only looking to harden systems, you might want to jump directly to those sections of the book.)

In this chapter you learn about Windows security but only as it relates to the DMZ. In other words, this chapter is not a general Windows security chapter but rather is customized to fit the needs of designing security within the DMZ. Of course, the chapter covers many security topics revolving around Windows security, but all the content is tailored, for the most part, to security administrators working within a DMZ environment.

The last section of this chapter discusses basic traffic flows and the services and protocols Microsoft products use. With this information, you can design your systems so that all needed traffic will go through the firewalls, as well as preventing traffic that you do not want to go through the firewall. In later chapters, we show you how to configure those firewalls to allow the traffic to pass; you can come back to this chapter to get the data you need (such as port numbers for access control lists) to engineer your solution. As mentioned before, you need to read this book in its entirety to be able to complete your solution if you are not sure what to do at all, but if you have a Cisco PIX firewall that you need to implement with a Windows IIS Server, you can probably just read this chapter, the PIX chapter (Chapter 6), and the chapter on how to secure Windows 2000 and Windows 2003 bastion hosts on the DMZ segment (Chapter 13).

This chapter can serve as a rough design document to help you place your Windows systems and the services they run within the DMZ. Many administrators wonder how to place their systems within the DMZ, especially when those systems are Web or FTP servers that face the Internet and are publicly accessible. This job can be nerve-wracking, especially with all the past publicity about Microsoft being an insecure system with many bugs, unchecked buffers, and a plethora of other problems, resulting in its products becoming the biggest target on the Internet today. This chapter (and following chapters) will remedy those fears by providing you with the answers and solutions you need, not only to place the systems in and around the DMZ but also to protect them.

> **NOTE**
>
> If you are looking for a book on how to harden and implement security with Windows 2000 or Windows Server 2003 in more granular detail without a focus on the DMZ segment, you can check out this Syngress title:
>
> - *MCSA/MCSE Exam 70-291 Study Guide & DVD Training System Implementing, Managing, and Maintaining a Windows Server 2003 Network Infrastructure* (ISBN: 1931836922)

Introducing Windows DMZ Security

In this section we take a broad look at security concepts for Windows systems, tailoring all the content to DMZ-based hosts. This section of the chapter covers the following details:

- Fundamental Windows DMZ design

- Windows DMZ bastion hosts design

- Engineering Windows traffic in the DMZ

An introduction to Windows DMZ security must start with a general discussion of the concepts of applying a secure foundation to the core services running within the DMZ, all based on the Microsoft product line. In discussing Windows-based security in the DMZ, we need to look at a few general concepts. What will be publicly accessible? Why do you need these services available? How will you control access to and from such resources? How will you maintain these services? Everything else is all about hardening the systems. Let's look at the general design. Remember, DMZs are the best place for you to place and secure your publicly used information and services such as an e-commerce site, a Web site, an FTP site, VPN-based services, and so on. In this chapter we look at proper placement of these needed services.

In this section of the chapter we also look at basic Windows DMZ bastion host design. This is really about placement of servers and reasons you would place them in specific locations on your network.

Remember, you need to understand three very important concepts: why you are building a DMZ, where to place specific services, and how to engineer the traffic to and from those services. After that, you can worry about locking down those individual systems.

Fundamental Windows DMZ Design

Before we look at the fundamentals of securing the DMZ segment and its hosts, we need a general idea of what it's going to look like on a map. All good network designers plan the topology (hopefully with a topology map) and figure out in advance traffic flows, logical addressing, and any other factors that would affect the system's planned operation. If you choose not to follow this recommendation, you could find yourself very discouraged when the network does not function properly and systems cannot be accessed due to a simple (or complex) mistake you made in the design. A DMZ segment can be one of the most complicated network segments to design and implement. When you add Windows to the mix, you not only have to be an expert in security—you also must be an expert in network engineering, Windows 2000 and Windows 2003 system design, and the services to be made available. Look at it from this perspective: You want to set up a DMZ segment with a PIX firewall and a Windows-based Web server. This should not be a complicated task, but think of all the areas you need to focus on:

- Network engineering
- Systems engineering
- Security analysis

Now take a look at Figure 2.1, which points out all three of these areas.

Figure 2.1 Fundamental DMZ Design

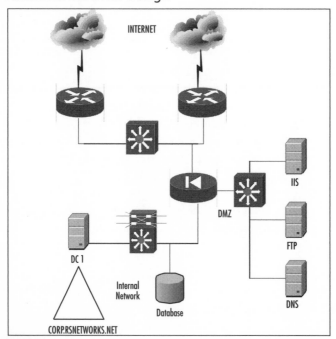

The reason we have segmented this figure into three sections is that it represents how you should design each section. Let's take a look at each section in more detail.

> **NOTE**
>
> In Figure 2.1, note also the use of high availability in your design. If your resources need to be in high demand, it is critical that you design high-availability features so that you can keep your services available in time of disaster. Here you can see the need for firewalls, redundant routers, and Internet connections to different points of presence (POPs), highly available Web services, and database services. Never rule out high availability for your solution if you can afford to implement it.

Network Engineering the DMZ

Your first step in designing a Windows-based DMZ is to select all the networking hardware you will need. You must do an assessment of your needs to figure out what the hardware infrastructure will cost your company. When you are looking at the networking end of it, you should ask yourself, "What devices will I need, and how should I scale them?" Exploring these questions will bring answers based on networking gear and costs. Since we've already mentioned Cisco, let's stick with that company's products for this example. In Figure 2.1 we looked at a very basic network infrastructure, but the future needs are quite high, so let's say that we decide to scale up the network hardware. We interviewed all departments that are part of the project to design and implement a DMZ infrastructure with an IIS Web server. After talking to everyone involved, we came up with a few important items:

1. We need to scale up the number of connections to the Internet, since the VPN services, external DNS, and other services will be added sooner rather than later. For this reason, we might need to have more port availability on our switch that is publicly accessible via the Internet.

2. We need to add more bandwidth and site-to-site VPN services off the external Internet routers. This need will become critical next year. This tells us that we had better not skimp on the Internet-facing routers, and we must make sure that we purchase models that either have crypto cards (to use IPSec for VPNs) installed or that are upgradeable to them.

3. We need to eventually set up a load-balanced solution with multiple IIS servers and a possible backend database cluster. This tells us that we will need to scale the firewall, switches, and all other infrastructure to meet the needs for a possible e-commerce site, a load-balanced cluster, and so on.

Can you see why you must really plan this project very well? There is nothing more frustrating than having to constantly replace equipment because you have not anticipated future needs and requirements. It always winds up costing more in the long run, so make sure that you perform a detailed needs assessment up front, and scale your design to what you might need in the future.

> ### NOTE
>
> Even if your management team or project stakeholders decide it's not in the best interest of the project, organization, or IT group to scale resources up or out (which adds immensely to the cost of the project), at least they'll remember you brought it up—and when the need comes up in the future (as it usually will), it will be on record that you at least tried!

Now you have performed a needs analysis and have designed the infrastructure. (The initial design is shown in Figure 2.1.) You have noted that a redundant firewall should be used to ease the pain of failure as well as your scaling requirements. The management team responsible for purchasing and approving this design has stated that all is approved except the redundant firewall, which will be considered and purchased at a later date.

After you run a test (maybe even a pilot or prototype) of your network design, you are ready to implement it. Again, this chapter focuses on overall design. Since this book was written with all types of systems in mind, you can replace that firewall (currently PIX) with a Nokia firewall, a Check Point firewall, or Microsoft ISA Server. This book allows for that flexibility in design so that you can pretty much replace that firewall with whatever you are currently using or plan to use. We look at the specifics of adding rules and so on in later chapters.

Now that you have an idea of network design, let's continue with our plan to design it. Take a look at Figure 2.2.

Since you have already selected your vendor's product line (Cisco) and have your needs analysis done, you can lay out your infrastructure. In Figure 2.2 you see that we have used Cisco routers, switches, and a firewall to build our DMZ segment. The Layer 3 switches in the internal network position were already in place. This is the LAN's default gateway and the switch responsible for segmenting the LAN into virtual LANs (VLANs). Chapter 9 of this book is all about building those VLANs; for now, we'll focus on design.

Figure 2.2 Network Design of the DMZ

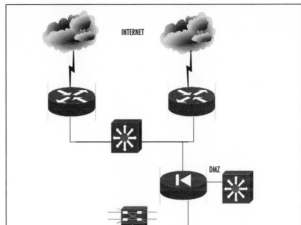

We've decided to use the following components for our DMZ:

- Two Cisco 3725 routers with T1 WAN interface cards (WICs) with which to connect to the Internet and Fast Ethernet ports to the external switch. We decided on two routers because we want to have a highly available solution to the Internet. If one link goes down, we have another to use, and we can offset the load in times of high demand. We chose this router model because we foresaw a future need to implement site-to-site VPNs, add more redundancy to the network, and leave room for a possible later upgrade in not only bandwidth but also in the number of connections for backup lines.

- We selected two Cisco switches for our external public network segment and for the DMZ. Now you have to do some research (or refer to Chapter 9 for more information), but your switch choice will be based on how many ports you need, the amount of traffic you will have going through it, the quality-of-service enhancements you would like, and other features such as dual power supply. Your switch should be scaled to what you need and scaled up (or out) based on future needs. The best piece of advice we can offer you in terms of a decision on a switch is to research very heavily on the vendor's Web site to find what each model offers and how it can fit into your design, based on current and future needs as well as cost.

- We selected a Cisco PIX firewall to be the "traffic cop" among the Internet, the DMZ, and the private LAN. Again, Chapter 6 focuses on this design (you will be shown the exact configuration to implement this solution), and that is where you can find all the details on a specific model. One design flaw we pointed out (but had to live with) was the single-firewall design. We originally asked for a redundant solution (two firewalls with failover, as you will see in Chapter 9), but the cost was too high for now and the need was not as great. Again, this solution was implemented to make the DMZ and to control traffic to and from it, so the needed design was met with this requirement, but a second redundant firewall would be ideal.

NOTE

When planning your infrastructure, you always need to ensure that you plan the proper equipment list, no matter what vendor you pick. If you are purchasing this much equipment, presales support could be in order. Ask your vendor to show you user limits per device (the number of users who can simultaneously use this device without affecting its performance) as well as what type of traffic you will be pumping through it. Many times, the vendor can help you design your network so that you don't fall short on what you need or you don't go into overkill where you might not need the extra power.

You can see that implementing a DMZ is not a cakewalk; it's all based on needs and analysis. It is something that you have to really plan out and design so that it comes out the way you want it and need it instead of becoming a costly disaster. In addition, note that we have only designed the actual infrastructure—we have not even plugged any intelligence into it. Future chapters point out how to add intelligence so that you can configure rules and other settings to make all the components work together. In the next section, we look at adding the systems into the segment.

Designing & Planning…

What Is a Site-to-Site VPN?

We have alluded to the need for a site-to-site VPN as a future requirement in our design. The purpose of this VPN is twofold. First, we want you to "think outside the box" and consider that there are such things as future requirements when designing a DMZ. Second, we want to ensure that this book is relevant to today's and tomorrow's future technology trends. Let's look at the Cisco router that we selected for this DMZ design as an example.

Continued

Key features for the Cisco 3725 and 3745 are:

- Two integrated 10/100 LAN ports
- Two integrated Advanced Integration Module (AIM) slots
- Three integrated WIC slots
- Two (Cisco 3725) or four (Cisco 3745) Network Module (NM) slots
- One (Cisco 3725) or two (Cisco 3745) High-Density Service Module (HDSM)-capable slots
- ??32MB Compact Flash (default); 128MB maximum
- ??128MB DRAM (default, single 128MB DIMM); 256MB DRAM maximum
- Optional in-line power for 16-port EtherSwitch NM and 36-port EtherSwitch HDSM
- Support for all major WAN protocols and media: FR, ISDN, X.25, ATM, fractional T1/E1, T1/E1, xDSL, T3/E3, HSSI
- Support for selected NMs, WICs, and AIMs from the Cisco 1700, 2600 and 3600 Series 2 RU (Cisco 3725) or 3 RU (Cisco 3745) rack-mountable chassis

The VPN and encryption AIM are:

- AIM-VPN/HP DES/3DES VPN Advanced Integration Module for 3660 and 3745—High Performance
- AIM-VPN/EP DES/3DES VPN Advanced Integration Module for 2600 and 3725—Enhanced Performance

You are using this router because of the addition of the VPN and encryption AIM that are available with it. You need this added crypto card to be able to tunnel from one site to another over the Internet. You understand why we selected the router we did (for its scaling and functionality), so you need to know what a site-to-site VPN is, now that you have the router hardware lined up. A site-to-site VPN (as shown in Figure 2.3) is a network solution that utilizes both public and private IP Internet connections to establish the WAN between all sites that you want to connect to, such as remote branch offices, business-to-business partner connections, and so on.

The benefits of using this solution are many. For one, VPN technology can run over public or private Internet-based solutions. In other words, you can utilize this design in just about any country in the world. Frame Relay (especially in international deployments) can be quite costly, so you might want to utilize a VPN connection to connect a remote branch more cheaply than with a costly Frame Relay connection. You can also augment your WAN with a backup solution based on VPN. VPN services are better in some ways because all VPN traffic takes place at Layer 3, without delving down to Layer 2 of the OSI model. Since there

Continued

is no breakdown of data and rebuilding of data, it can be argued that a VPN solution is better when you're trying to utilize voice over IP (VOIP), and the like. (Keep in mind that both VPN and VoIP technologies would benefit from QoS or policy-based routing to avoid performance degradation.) The difference we mentioned before (public vs. private VPN technologies) is that a public VPN network setup will utilize any ISP's Internet service, whereas a private VPN network would be, for example, AT&T's private IP VPN network built only for use with private business and not publicly accessible via the Internet, if you do not want it to be, using a Layer 3 private network. Both can be used at the same time with this solution, adding another degree of flexibility to your design.

Figure 2.3 A VPN-Based Network

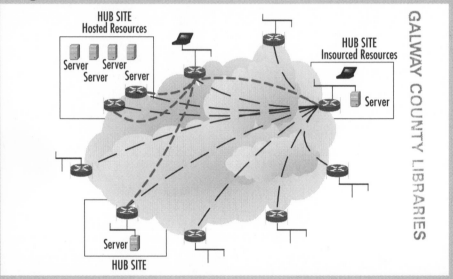

The reason this information is so important is that in the future, you might only have an Internet connection to worry about for all your remote e-mail, Internet access, and WAN access. Therefore, the DMZ becomes even more critical at this point in the design phase. Each router you see in Figure 2.3 should be fire-walled (with a DMZ, if the services are needed) especially if you are not using an ISP's private VPN solution. One last note: The design used in Figure 2.3 is called a *partial mesh*. This keeps the tunnel endpoint to a minimum, with no more than one to three hops to get to any site from any site. A full mesh keeps hop counts down, but tunnel maintenance is harder to maintain because you will have many more tunnels to maintain with a full mesh. Conversely, a partial mesh keeps the hop count down but requires more complex routing solutions for full site-to-site connectivity.

Now that you have designed your network, it is time to populate the segment with systems. In the next section we look at systems engineering your DMZ.

Systems Engineering the DMZ

You can now start to populate the DMZ and its surrounding areas. First, you need to think about access to and from the DMZ and the services that are needed. The reason behind this initial thought is that your end users, customers, potential customers, and outsiders will be able to utilize needed resources and only those needed resources—nothing more, nothing less. To start the engineering process, you must first make certain that you have these answers! What do you need? You should make sure that users can obtain the information that they need about your company without accessing the internal network and accessing only the DMZ or safely accessing the internal network, if you chose not to implement a DMZ. Working with DMZs can be tricky (hence the need for this book), so if you can, it's always better to segment Internet-based resources via the DMZ for an added level of safety.

Now that you know your network layout, you have to think about other access to and from the DMZ. Your secret, protected, confidential, and proprietary information should be stored behind your firewall and DMZ on your internal network. Servers on the DMZ shouldn't contain sensitive trade secrets, source code, proprietary information, or anything that can be used against you or your company—or that can be used to exploit or hack into your systems. (There's more on DMZ hacking techniques in Chapter 14.) A breach of your DMZ servers should at worst create an annoyance in the form of downtime while you recover from the security breach.

Here are examples of systems that could wind up on your DMZ:

- **A Web server that holds public information** This can be IIS (since we are discussing Microsoft technologies in this chapter) or any other publicly accessible Web server. You can also think of FTP services, NNTP services, and other Web-based services to be accessed and utilized.

- **Electronic commerce-based solutions always wind up on the DMZ** The front end of an e-commerce transaction server is the one through which orders are placed. Keep the back end, where you store client information, behind the firewall. You want to design this system properly because if you don't, you could compromise your entire client database (or personal and private data) if your system is exploited.

- **A mail server that relays outside mail to the inside** This will be a highly utilized solution, especially since spam and other e-mail exploits are common DMZ host-based targets of attack.

- **VPN solutions are prevalent in the DMZ** Other than the site-to-site VPN we already learned about, you also have VPN solutions in which you have a remote access solution so that clients can attach over the Internet to get to their files and other data they need on the corporate network. This data also has to be publicly accessible via the DMZ.

■ **Security devices** These include intrusion detection solutions, honeypots, and other items you will learn about in Chapter 15.

These areas all need to be addressed when it comes to providing a solution for your systems and where to place them within the DMZ or around it.

Take a look at Figure 2.4, which shows the placement of the systems within the DMZ. We have placed all the publicly accessible systems (such as Web, FTP, and DNS) on the DMZ so that Internet users can access them and not come into and through our internal network, which is to remain private. You can also see that we have placed our domain controller and all-important data (such as a SQL Server database) on the internal network. This approach keeps these resources secure and accessed only via proper channels, not exposed to the Internet for malicious exploits to take place.

Figure 2.4 Systems on the DMZ

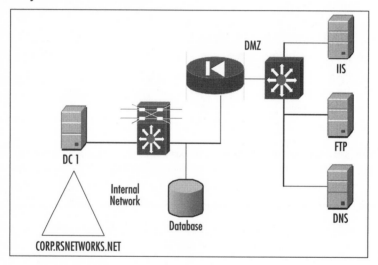

Security Analysis for the DMZ

Once you have finalized the DMZ network segment design and placed your systems where they need to be (and you understand why they need to be there), you have to consider the security of such systems. To learn how to harden the systems themselves, read through the chapters in this book that concern security measures you need to take in the DMZ. If you want to implement an IDS for intrusion detection, for example, you can read Chapter 15 to learn how to do that, but to understand placement for your DMZ, take a look at Figure 2.5.

Figure 2.5 Implementing Security in the DMZ

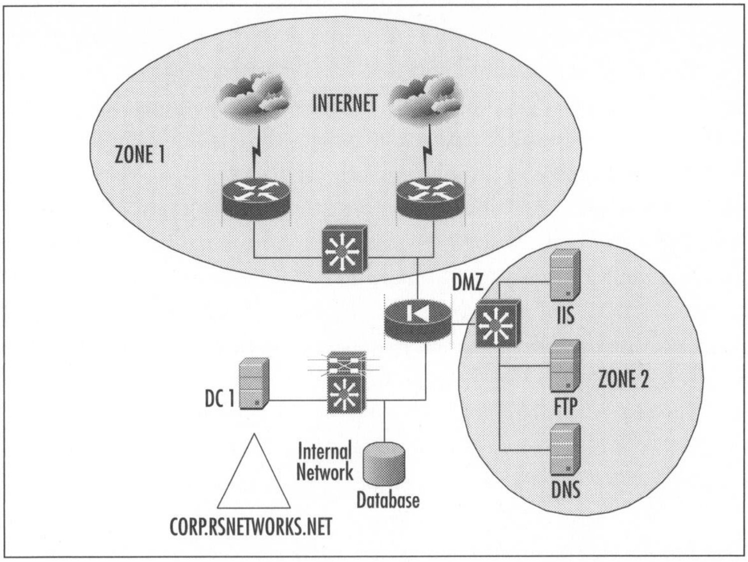

To keep the security analysis potion of your DMZ design to a minimum (the rest of the book is based on configuring security), you need to know the two biggest targets of attack and what you should be concerned about when considering your design.

Zone 1

Zone 1 of Figure 2.5 is the location of your public Internet connection and where you are traditionally most vulnerable to exploitation. Zone 1 is where you need to consider your external router and switch security as well as the outside port of your firewall. You can read Chapter 13 to learn how to lock down this zone. Furthermore, Zone 1 is where you would consider placing your network-based IDS (although you can place it just about anywhere, depending on what you are trying to capture) as well as your honeypot. You can read Chapter 15 to learn about IDSs and their implementation around the DMZ.

Zone 2

Zone 2 is the actual DMZ. The DMZ is where we have placed our Windows 2000 servers and the services they offer, such as external DNS and Web services. To learn how to harden the systems on the DMZ (also called *bastion hosts*), read Chapter 13.

New Features in Windows Server 2003 R2

For a number of reasons, the notion of the network perimeter has evolved over time. Part of this is due to the increased prevalence of high-speed residential Internet connectivity as well as an overall increase in connected e-commerce ventures for both new and existing companies. Because companies rely more and more on the Internet to do business, many are searching for better ways to improve their ability to interact with vendors, suppliers, and customers, without "giving away the store"—in other words, without providing more access to the internal network than an external user in one of these roles requires. For example, Windows Server 2003 allows you to create trust relationships between two separate Active Directory forests, but in many instances, granting this level of access to a customer or business partner would be undesirable or simply impractical.

To help address this challenge, Windows Server 2003 R2 includes a new feature called the *Active Directory Federation Service*, or ADFS. This service provides an alternative to the traditional DMZ environment and creates an environment where two separate organizations or distinct subsidiaries of a larger parent company can create a *federation agreement* to allow one party to provide access to its resources across the Internet. For example, Airplanes.com, an airplane manufacturer, can configure a federation agreement with its business partner Airplaneparts.com, in which Airplanes.com employees can access resources on the Airplaneparts.com internal network using their company's existing Internet connection. The federation agreement configures the business rules that dictate which resources can be accessed by whom, as well s the technical controls that will be used to authenticate users: smart cards, Active Directory logons, the Microsoft Passport service, and the like.

> **NOTE**
>
> As of this writing, ADFS can be used only to secure Web-based applications; traditional client/server applications cannot leverage ADFS for authentication or authorization.

Building a Windows DMZ

Building a Windows DMZ is not very difficult; however, there are many moving parts that you need to be concerned with in the initial design and for consistent maintenance.

Consider this situation: You are the systems engineer responsible for designing, implementing, and maintaining a Windows DMZ segment that consists of an IIS Web server, an FTP site, an external DNS server, and an e-mail relay. That doesn't sound like a lot, but this is one tall order. Consider the following: You will have to know (or find the people who know) how to configure hardware such as routers, switches, and the firewall. You must have security applied to these items and others, such as an IDS if you need it or if the design requires it. You have to place bastion hosts on the DMZ and configure security on them, including hardening the base OS (Windows 2000 as well as Windows 2003) and then applying the needed services and hardening them, too. Lastly, you need to know how to engineer the traffic to and from those services to other front-end or back-end systems, depending on what the design calls for. In this last example, consider having an internal DNS namespace and an external DNS namespace. How do you configure them to work together through the firewall? This is the point behind this chapter (and much of this book), which is to get you to think about these details so that your DMZ is a success, works properly, can be maintained, and is secure.

Now that we have taken a look at the fundamentals of laying out the hardware to create the DMZ, let's examine the details of populating it with a Windows solution.

Designing the DMZ Windows Style

Now that you have the fundamental placement, design, and understanding, let's get into more detail concerning the Windows platform, since there is much to think about and much to plan. In this section we cover domain models (how to configure your domain), devices that sit on your DMZ segment, the names and definitions of systems revolving around the DMZ, and much more. In this section we look specifically at the domain model, which can confuse many architects who might not know the exact placement of the domain controllers (DCs) and where the logical boundaries of the domain sit with the DMZ segment.

Domain Considerations

Building a domain with a DMZ segment can be confusing. For one, you have probably heard many times that you should never expose an Active Directory DC to a public network such as the Internet. If this advice is sound, how in the world do you set up domain-based logins if you need a domain-based account for a particular service to work? Consider the following: You need to implement a load-balanced cluster in your DMZ, and for the service to work, the cluster account must log into a domain. If this were the case, where would you place the DC? Figure 2.6 offers a possible solution.

Figure 2.6 A Cluster in a DMZ

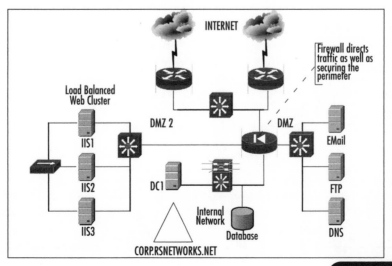

This solution is not impossible, but it can be tricky. Think of the traffic flow and other issues you need to consider with your design:

1. As you can see, your IIS load-balanced cluster will need to be accessible to the Internet users who will want to see your Web site.

2. If e-commerce solutions are available, the IIS servers need to know how to get to the back-end database, if that is what you need for your solution. You must have a way to get your IIS servers to communicate through the firewall to get to the SQL server. Alternately, you can segment the back-end database into a DMZ of its own rather than placing it on the internal LAN. Your design can be augmented by doing so and then placing restrictions on the traffic flow between the Web cluster DMZ and the database DMZ.

3. You have two DMZ segments from your PIX firewall. You need to know how to set security levels on each and how to deny traffic coming from one segment to the other. If someone exploits your DNS server and if you have not applies security so that it does not allow this type of activity, it might only be a matter of time before they get to your second DMZ.

4. Your cluster needs to access a DC if it is using the Cluster Service, though the DC in question does not necessarily need to be a DC on the internal LAN. Since this is a load-balanced solution, you can forego that need, but if you place a cluster on the DMZ, you need a nearby DC to service your requests. Alternately, you can deploy a hardware-based load-balancer instead.

5. Your firewall should be configured to allow for external public Internet traffic to come to your Web sites, but your Web servers can only make requests to the database of the DC behind the firewall or a database server in a separate DMZ. The Web servers need to deliver what was requested of them to the Internet users.

6. Your firewall should also be configured so that your internal DNS server (not shown) can communicate with its forwarder on the DMZ. The internal e-mail server (also not shown) should be able to send e-mail back and forth to the relay on the DMZ. Users should be able to get to the FTP site.

As you can see, now that you have planned it, you only need to pay for it, implement it, and maintain it. That's easier said than done, which is why you have this book. Remember, this chapter is conceptual in nature; it's not until you get to some of the later chapters that you actually learn how to configure all these elements on the firewall.

NOTE

Depending on the model and type of firewall you use, you can in fact have different DMZ segments with different services on each, to add even more security to your DMZ segments and hosts.

The Internet Connection

Your Windows DMZ solution needs to allow for Internet access. What must be known about the Internet connection is that it should be able to handle the site's required bandwidth needs. If you are using this Internet connection as your LAN's Internet access for surfing and e-mail, and you decide to use it for a VPN as well, you need to analyze your requirements first. You can do a traffic flow analysis to ascertain the requirements quite quickly, but you need to know how to do the analysis and have the tools with which to do the analysis. If you do not, it is in your best interests to work with an outside vendor that does have the required tools and experience. Failing to do so will almost always result in bad performance and increased cost later, when you need to reprovision the lines to a higher bandwidth. Everything you need to consider is shown in Figure 2.7.

Figure 2.7 Internet Connection Considerations

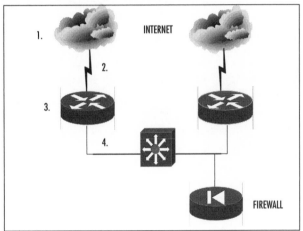

Figure 2.7 shows four sections:

1. The first section you need to consider is the actual ISP you are connecting to. You see here that we have two clouds; the reasoning is that our Internet connection should be highly available. We suggest having at least two connections if your company's livelihood depends on use of the Internet. You can also diversify the connections between providers and points of presence (POPs). If you have both POPs in, let's say, New York, and if New York develops a major problem (or a single ISP goes down completely), you will still be available on the Internet. If you have serious concerns about high availability, you should also consider geographically dispersed servers and/or deploying a disaster recovery site.

2. Make sure you size your connections properly for high availability. Most vendors and ISPs have sizing tools that help you determine how much bandwidth you

need to the Internet. If we had two T1s here, we would have almost 3MB of traffic to and from the Internet, which is not too bad at all.

3. Make sure that you have a properly sized router. Make sure that the router can handle all the Internet-based traffic, both coming and going. Processing power, available memory, and other factors can hinder your response time, so do not make the router the bottleneck on the Internet.

4. Do not let the last leg of the segment (for the Internet connection), which is the connection into the firewall, be the bottleneck. Make certain that you have 100MB/full duplex or better here if possible. Most firewalls allow for Fast Ethernet connectivity.

Remember, anyone can connect to and use the Internet, so the number (and frequency) of your vulnerabilities will become much higher. Always make certain that all these areas are secured properly; you can learn how to lock all this down in later chapters in this book.

Wide Area Network Link

A WAN link is really not much different from the Internet connection (they both use some form of leased lines), but in a traditional sense, a WAN link describes the connections from your company to others through the use of private lines. When we say *private*, we mean in the sense that it is not accessible via the Internet, which is a publicly accessible arena. The WAN link (T1, Frame Relay, ISDN) connects your remote sites up to the backbone located within the core site. Most traditional designs show a hub-and-spoke formation. Here, in Figure 2.8, a hub and spoke are shown connected to an Internet-based segment with a DMZ.

Figure 2.8 A WAN Connected to a Backbone with an Internet Connection

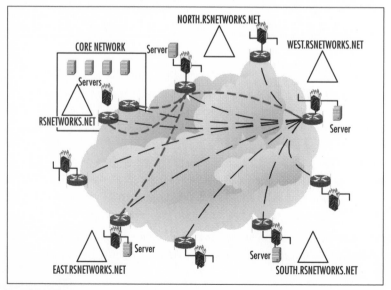

The reason that this concept is so important is that you will have to know how to get traffic from the LAN to either the WAN links or perhaps out to the Internet. How do you do this? Let's go through the process step by step while looking at Figure 2.8:

1. You need to consider the design. In Figure 2.8, we have a core network (where the major resources are located) connected to the Internet and also to a Frame Relay network with two remote sites. How do you direct the traffic? How do the remote sites access the Internet?

2. Look at Area 1; you can see that the Internet connection has been established correctly, as shown in the last section. Now you need to visualize how users will gain access the Internet; to the user, this process should be transparent: Click the Web browser and out you go! This is set via the proxy settings in the Web browser (as shown in Figure 2.9) or via the default gateway of the client (as shown in Figure 2.10). The proxy setting will be valuable to you if you use a proxy server to get to the Internet. (A proxy server DMZ-based system is described in Chapter 8, when we take a granular look at ISA Server.) If you need to see what your default gateway is set to, you can do an *IPCONFIG /all* to get all the IP settings for your Windows NT or 2000/2003 system. If you are using older *9x* versions, *WINIPCFG* will do the same. You need to know your default gateway because this is how you will direct traffic in an enterprise DMZ. Remember, if you have only an Internet connection, the Internet connection-based router (or the firewall in front of it) can be your default gateway.

Figure 2.9 Proxy Settings for a Web Browser

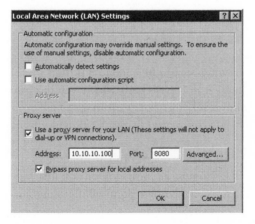

Figure 2.10 Default Gateway Settings for a LAN Client

```
Microsoft Windows 2000 [Version 5.00.2195]
(C) Copyright 1985-2000 Microsoft Corp.
```

```
C:\>ipconfig /all

Windows 2000 IP Configuration

Host Name . . . . . . . . . . . : SHIMONSKI-LAPTOP
Primary DNS Suffix  . . . . . . . :
Node Type . . . . . . . . . . . : Hybrid
IP Routing Enabled. . . . . . . : No
WINS Proxy Enabled. . . . . . . : No
DNS Suffix Search List. . . . . : rsnetworks.net

Ethernet adapter Local Area Connection 3:

Connection-specific DNS Suffix  . : rsnetworks.net
Description . . . . . . . . . . : Wireless Network PC Card
Physical Address. . . . . . . . : 00-23-15-26-1E-3D
DHCP Enabled. . . . . . . . . . : Yes
Autoconfiguration Enabled . . . . : Yes
IP Address. . . . . . . . . . . : 192.168.2.100
Subnet Mask . . . . . . . . . . : 255.255.255.0
Default Gateway . . . . . . . . : 192.168.2.1
DHCP Server . . . . . . . . . . : 192.168.2.101
DNS Servers . . . . . . . . . . : 192.168.2.102
                                  192.168.2.103
Lease Obtained. . . . . . . . . : Sunday, May 25, 2003 8:04:49 AM
Lease Expires . . . . . . . . . : Monday, May 26, 2003 8:04:49 AM
C:\>
```

3. Now that you understand that portion, you need to understand Area 2, which is the default gateway for the LAN, as shown in Figure 2.8. Now you need to engineer the WAN link behind your default gateway, or it must be the default gateway if you have an Internet connection to get to. To get to the Internet or the Internet-based proxy/firewall, you need to know how to view the routes in your router. In Figure 2.11, we did a *show IP route* command on the Cisco router. This gave us a routing table, of which we show only the beginning. You can see here that the last line shows what's called the *gateway of last resort*. Your Windows systems will need to know what this is to get out to the Internet if they are connected anywhere on your internal LAN or if they are one of your remote sites. Figure 2.12 shows you the command to add this route.

Figure 2.11 The Routing Table on the WAN Router

```
WANROUTER#sh ip route
Codes: C - connected, S - static, I - IGRP, R - RIP, M - mobile, B - BGP
       D - EIGRP, EX - EIGRP external, O - OSPF, IA - OSPF inter area
       N1 - OSPF NSSA external type 1, N2 - OSPF NSSA external type 2
       E1 - OSPF external type 1, E2 - OSPF external type 2, E - EGP
       i - IS-IS, L1 - IS-IS level-1, L2 - IS-IS level-2, ia - IS-IS
       * - candidate default, U - per-user static route, o - ODR
       P - periodic downloaded static route

Gateway of last resort is 10.10.10.100 to network 0.0.0.0
```

Figure 2.12 Adding a Route to the Router

```
ip route 0.0.0.0 0.0.0.0 10.10.10.100
```

4. Area 3 is the frame cloud. The frame cloud needs to be engineered and provisioned properly, with the proper access port size and Committed Information Rate (CIR) based on your needs. Make sure you size the frame cloud properly and ask for a bandwidth and utilization report a few months after you use it, to make sure you are not overpaying for what you don't need or undercutting your remote sites by not giving them the bandwidth they need to do their jobs. Remember, you need to allow your remote sites to access the Internet through your core, so you need to properly size the frame links (or any other WAN connection technology).

5. Last but not least, take a look at the remote sites. Note that these sites need to travel up to the core router, and then the core router needs to send the Internet requests up the firewall, which directs the requests out to the Internet. Look at Figure 2.13. It clearly shows the traffic flow needs. And remember the gateway of last resort we saw in Figure 2.11? This same gateway will be used in the remote-side router, with one exception—the IP address of the gateway will be the core router, as shown in Figure 2.14.

Figure 2.13 Internet Traffic Out from a Remote Site

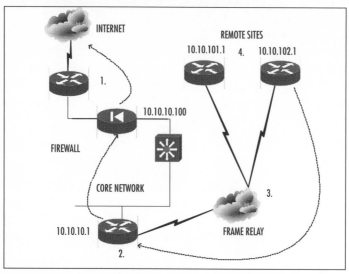

Figure 2.14 The Routing Table on the WAN Router

```
WANROUTER#sh ip route
Codes: C - connected, S - static, I - IGRP, R - RIP, M - mobile, B - BGP
       D - EIGRP, EX - EIGRP external, O - OSPF, IA - OSPF inter area
       N1 - OSPF NSSA external type 1, N2 - OSPF NSSA external type 2
       E1 - OSPF external type 1, E2 - OSPF external type 2, E - EGP
       i - IS-IS, L1 - IS-IS level-1, L2 - IS-IS level-2, ia - IS-IS
       * - candidate default, U - per-user static route, o - ODR
       P - periodic downloaded static route

Gateway of last resort is 10.10.10.1 to network 0.0.0.0
```

Take another look at Figure 2.13. It is imperative that you understand the flow here. A user at a remote site needs to access the Internet via the WAN link. The user is on the remote site LAN with an IP address of 10.10.102.5/24, given via a DHCP server. The default gateway for the LAN is the 10.10.102.1 router. The user makes a request of the Internet, and because the IP address is not local to the LAN (10.10.10.100), the request must be forwarded to the default gateway on the LAN. Because of the route added (as shown in Figure 2.14), the router knows to forward the request up through the Frame Relay WAN to 10.10.10.1, which is the main core router through which the Internet is connected. You should start to see the picture here now. The core router sends the request to the firewall (or proxy, or whatever you have configured), and it forwards the request once again to the Internet router on the perimeter of your network.

NOTE

Never forget: You will need to configure the route back to the remote site as well. You can add a routing protocol or static routes in reverse, depending on what you need to do. For help, you can use *ping* and tracing tools (*tracert* for Windows and *Traceroute* for UNIX) to figure out how to get to and from each site.

As you can see, it's very important that you know how to design and engineer the WAN link (in conjunction with the Internet connection) or you will be running around in circles trying to figure out why your Windows workstations cannot communicate over the Internet.

Server and Domain Isolation Using IPSec

As an alternative to a physical DMZ, you can use IPSec to create logical groupings of trusted hosts on your network and to prevent untrusted computers from being able to communicate with your domain computers. In other words, you can *isolate* the computers within an Active Directory domain so that they cannot exchange any network traffic with computers that are not domain members. This approach is useful for environments that have numerous "visiting users" who need basic Internet access (such as salespeople or conference attendees visiting a corporate campus) but who should not have access to sensitive resources stored on corporate file and application servers. Microsoft has published a great deal of information about server and domain isolation; it can be found at www.microsoft.com/sdisolation.

DMZ Perimeter Security

The DMZ is an isolated segment through which you simply allow services to Internet users while still maintaining some form of security on your network. To allow users to come into your corporate network unknown, unwatched, and consistently will surely lead to an attack somewhere down the line, if not instantly. In this section we look at all the areas you need to consider while building your Windows DMZ. In the last section we took a look at where your internal resources need to be, how they need to be laid out, and some special considerations to take into account. Here we look at the reverse of your protected network (where your LAN meets your internal firewall port), which is the unprotected network. This is your DMZ and Internet connection, which make up your network perimeter. Although the claim is that they are "unprotected," we will make them "highly protected"—or as much as we can! Let's take a look.

The External Router

The external router is the router that connects you to the Internet. Again, there can be more than one, and it's recommended (depending on your needs) that you have at least two connections the Internet. The external router connects the protected network and DMZ to the WAN Link. The router provides the first opportunity to actively permit or deny access for clients and servers and for network services. This means that you can apply ACLs, AAA, logging, and much more to the first line of defense of your network. You will want to read Chapter 13 in its entirety to learn how to lock down the Internet router, but for now, simply understand its importance in the design.

The Firewall

As you already know, a firewall is the "traffic cop" in the middle of your DMZ, public Internet, and private LAN that handles incoming and outgoing traffic and places that traffic where it needs to be against the rules that you create for it—simple as that. Your firewall, if configured properly, will aid you in building and maintaining security on your perimeter network. A firewall is simply an enforcer of a security policy. (Security policy is explained in detail in the sidebar, "Guidelines for Creating a Good Security Policy-Based DMZ.") A firewall should reside at the perimeter of your network and protect your data from malicious attackers and wrongdoers. As shown in Figure 2.15, your firewall can have many interfaces.

Figure 2.15 Firewall Interfaces

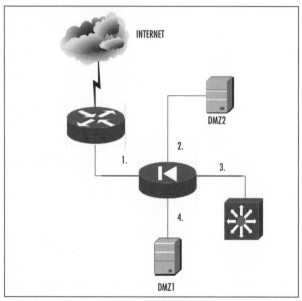

Let's look at each section to see what these interfaces can connect to. Section 1 is the external WAN port on the firewall. This is the Ethernet connection that connects your system to the external router. Section 2 is the first DMZ leg and has IIS Web services on it. Section 3 is the connection into the corporate network—the private network. Section 4 is the second DMZ leg with a DNS server on it. The point here is to show you that you could have multiple DMZs set by one single firewall! As you will see in Chapter 5, there are many ways you can deliver secure services though multiple DMZs with only one firewall. Three interfaces are recommended: one for incoming traffic, one for access to the demilitarized zone, and one that connects to the protected network. But remember, if you need more than one DMZ, you can create multiple ones.

NOTE

In Chapter 8, you will learn all about Microsoft's Windows-based proxy and firewall product, ISA Server. ISA (which stands for *Internet Acceleration and Security*) allows you to build a DMZ firewall and create a protected solution with a Microsoft product.

Designing & Planning…

Guidelines for Creating a Good Security Policy-Based DMZ

We mentioned the importance of a firewall and alluded to the fact that a firewall is essentially the enforcer of a security policy. This means that your firewall will be configured to mirror the needs and requests of the corporation. For instance, if you want to create a security policy that states, "No remote user can pass the DMZ. Only users needing to access our IIS Web server from the Internet can access that single server, and nowhere else can they go though or pass the DMZ," all you need to do is configure the rules on the firewall (PIX, Check Point, Nokia, ISA) to reflect that need, as shown in Figure 2.16.

Let's examine that need against what we actually configured: We need to have only Internet users access the IIS server at 12.10.11.2. This is done through the firewall and its ruleset; you add a rule to the firewall stating that any user needing to get to an IIS server should be sourced from the Internet. The firewall also knows that if the IIS server is compromised, no request from the 12.10.11 network needs to go to the 10.10.10.0 subnet in the private network. As you see from Request 2 in the figure, you can't allow users to go through the firewall to attach to the Web server, because this capability is not in the security policy.

Continued

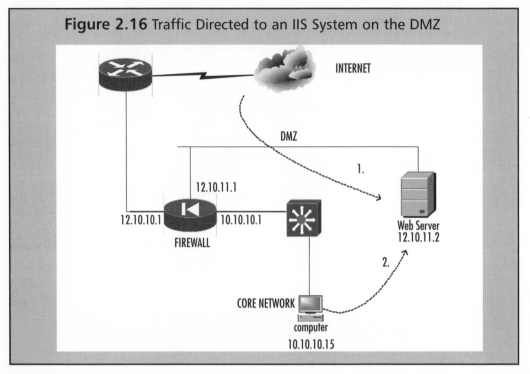

Figure 2.16 Traffic Directed to an IIS System on the DMZ

Extra DMZ Routers

Sometimes (if the size and complexity of the network dictate) you'll need a router on each leg of the firewall. This concept is illustrated in Figure 2.17. At times, you will get requests to either add security to the segment you are working on or add more and more devices to it, where you might need to either route or direct traffic. Some firewalls will not route like a router; in other words, a firewall might route the RIPv1 protocol, whereas a router will route IS-IS, OSPF, EIGRP, RIP, and so on. A router does just that—it routes. A firewall can in fact route if it is configured to do so, but often, depending on how paranoid you are, you could decide to keep these services dependent on the device in which they sit. You might even want to separate these roles, even if you are using a true enterprise-class firewall that is capable of handling multiple routing protocols.

The added routers can increase security and flexibility, but they can also add complexity. The only real time you need to use this is when the firewall is not part of the protected net-work. The DMZ router filters on the services the DMZ provides and denies all other traffic. A good way to envision this concept is if you have a firewall that will do NAT. If the firewall provides NAT, the DMZ router will verify that all connections originate from the firewall, which will add to your safety. With the internal network router (shown in Figure 2.19), you can see another level of security against attack. The threat that lingers most on the internal network is the end user. If configured properly, the internal router can be used to protect your firewall and DMZ from internal attack. The rules you set up on the router should mimic those configured on the firewall. Router hardening and lockdown are covered in Chapter 13 of this book.

Figure 2.17 Extra Routers Added to the DMZ Segment

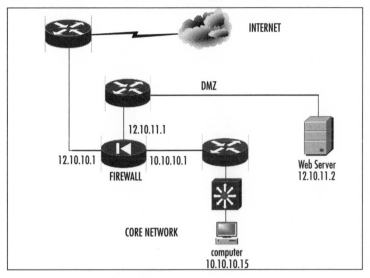

Name Resolution for the DMZ

Too often, DNS and WINS servers are misplaced when people work with the DMZ. Is there a specific design you need to follow? In essence, yes, there is. The importance of name resolution in the DMZ matters only if you in fact need it. Let's look at a quick design map so you can follow along. Figure 2.18 shows you that it is very important to use static addressing on your DMZ and on your public Internet segments so that a publicly accessible resource like a Web server will not continually receive a new IP address from DHCP; this would make it difficult for outside users to access this resource consistently, since its IP address would not be a "known quantity." If a hacker is able to tap into and exploit your DNS server, for example, she would gain access to all IP and name information for your network. If your DMZ is not very large (which it normally is not), you should use static addressing. DNS, WINS, and even DHCP are more suitable for the internal network, where you are more likely to have more hosts, so it is safer to put it there and only have to look for internal attacks.

Figure 2.18 Name Resolution in the DMZ

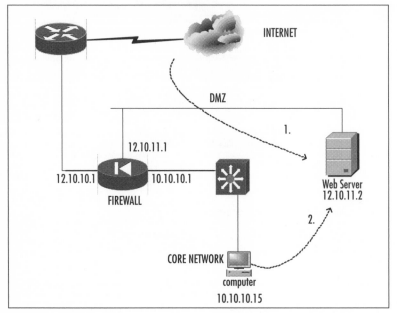

DMZ Mail Services

Too often, mistakes are made with e-mail service placement due to the administrator's lack of knowledge of how and where to place such services! There are really only two ways to place an e-mail server easily within a DMZ. For one, you can place the e-mail server (only one for this example) in the private network. The firewall in front of the e-mail server would be responsible for taking all requests in and out of the network and for securing the traffic to the e-mail server. Due to the server's design, it made the relaying of outbound Internet-based e-mail the responsibility of the e-mail server—only one single server. The question then, however, is, "Why would we want to expose our e-mail server to the public Internet? What if somehow there was a way to attack the e-mail server directly through the firewall?" (Not to mention the deluge of spam and virus-infected e-mail messages that would be clogging up your internal mail server as a result.) Figure 2.19 shows you the design we are talking about. You can see the e-mail server behind the firewall, allowing public Internet access directly to your private corporate network.

Figure 2.19 E-Mail Server Behind the Firewall

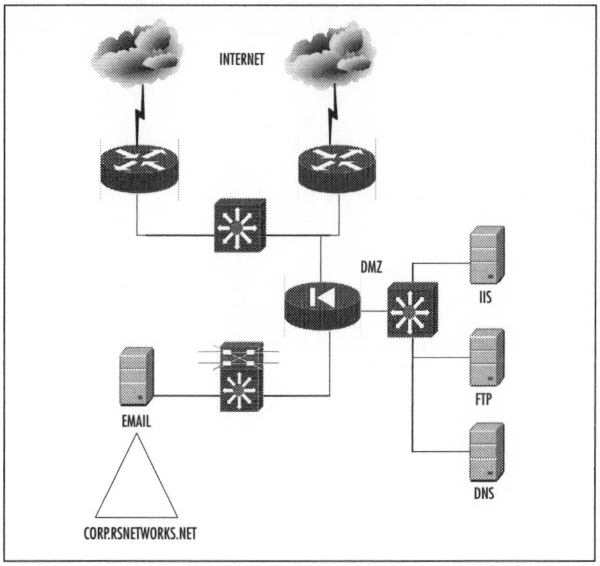

Mail Relay

Several risks are associated with the receipt of e-mail from potentially untrusted entities outside the site. Now that you can visualize this situation, let's consider an alternative. Would you want your Microsoft Exchange server exposed in this manner? Would you want your Sendmail server attacked and penetrated so that the attacker has direct access into your network? Of course you wouldn't. Because of this vulnerability, it is common to simply add another e-mail server to the DMZ segment and use this server as a relay to and from the protected e-mail server in the private network. The server now becomes what's called an *e-mail relay,* and it will relay the mail to and from the Internet and to and from the mail server. If mail relays (IIS has an SMTP service that can be used as a relay) are compromised, you can simply reinstall the server from scratch and not lose a thing, because all the server did was relay traffic.

Web Servers

Web servers are the most common form of DMZ-based hosts today. Other services are needed, such as DNS and e-mail, but if you really think about it, the main reason DMZs even exist is due to the public Internet Web surfer feeding frenzy. Almost every company in business in the world now has a publicly accessible Web site, which means that just about every company worldwide either has an Internet presence or is looking to have one. Thanks to all these personal invitations to companies' corporate networks, it is imperative that you also plan your security completely or your network could be exploited.

External Web Server

Organizations frequently have data they want to publish to the external network via a Web server. Again, to allow direct access to the Web server via the Internet while the server is sitting in your private and protected LAN would create a significant security vulnerability. For that reason, allow an external Web server to be placed on the DMZ. This way you can allow all your visitors to come directly to your IIS server and not have them exploit that server only to find ways to get to other systems. If the IIS server is external on the DMZ, you can at least have some defense against it if it is compromised in any way.

Internal Web Server

Your internal Web server is nothing more than an intranet you set up for HTTP and other Web-based access for use within the LAN and not for public access. Your internal Web server will be secure from the Internet only if you never directly connect it to the Internet. Once you do, you move the server out to the DMZ and it becomes an external Web server.

Designing Windows DNS in the DMZ

The last (and most common) services to see on the DMZ, both internally and externally, are the DNS servers for your organization. If you are using DNS to resolve your company's IP address to easy-to-remember names, this section is for you. DNS services are now the single most common service used for name resolution; WINS and NetBIOS-based name resolution is still around for some Microsoft application support, but even this will be phased out over time. Because of DNS's growing use, it is important that when you plan your Windows network, you are able to design the Internet namespace and the external namespace for the organization. You can also set up your own primary servers in the DMZ, or you can forward requests to others.

Figure 2.20 shows both solutions at work. For one, you can set up an internal namespace called PRIVATEDNS.NET. This is the company's Windows DNS solution that the entire Active Directory depends on. We do not want to expose that to the Internet if we don't have to. Now we can put a forwarder on the DNS server that resides in the DMZ. This is called the *external DNS server*, which will be explained shortly. The last scenario is to host your own public DNS servers. That means that even more traffic will come to your site, since others can use your DNS servers as well. If you opt to do this, make certain that you secure your DNS servers as well as possible, since they will be exposed to external attackers.

Figure 2.20 Examining DNS in the DMZ

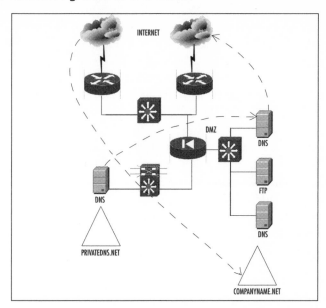

External DNS Server

The external DNS server resides in the DMZ and is for public use. The only information that should be on the external DNS server is the information that needs to be advertised to Internet clients—nothing more. You can use a Windows 2000 or Windows 2003 server, but it is not uncommon to see Linux on the DMZ doing DNS forwarding. Not one piece of internal DNS information should be kept on this system. The internal DNS server is unable to communicate directly with the external network, because it will be configured to send queries and receive the responses via the external DNS server. You have to ensure that DNS UDP and TCP connections are allowed through the firewall to the external DNS server or your solution might not work.

Engineering Windows Traffic in the DMZ

Once you have finalized the DMZ network segment design and placed your systems where they need to be (and understand why they need to be there), you have to consider traffic and applications flows, ACLs, and filtering. In this section we review the concepts you need to allow for the proper traffic to flow where it is needed to and from the DMZ segment.

Traffic engineering can be tough. Think of it like this: You build your DMZ (using whatever firewall product you like—PIX, Nokia, Check Point, ISA), and now you have to let services in and out. Other chapters in this book show you exactly how to do that (with these exact vendor products), but it is important that you at least understand the concept of it here as well as the fundamentals of design. Each chapter of the book grows more detailed in discussing to how to configure each device, but the concepts of design and the initial layout are the most important by far.

First, you need to know what a port is. A *port number* is a number assigned to a service. You can think of an IP address and a port number as analogous to a street address and an apartment number. If you have ever lived in an apartment, you know that everyone in the apartment complex has the same street address. So what tells the mail carrier where to put everyone's mail? The apartment number does. If it weren't for the apartment number, all organization would end once the mail got to your street address. You would have to search through everyone's mail to find yours. This is the same concept behind IP addresses and port numbers. The port number is used by a particular service. When a request is made, the port number tells the computer which service it wants to talk to. You could say that the port number defines the endpoints of a connection. The format for using port numbers is the IP address followed by a colon and the port number. For example, let's say that we want to connect to the IP address 10.10.10.10 and we want to use the port for HTTP (port 80). The syntax would be 10.10.10.10:80.

There are three port categories:

- Well-known ports
- Registered ports
- Dynamic/private ports

The Internet Corporation for Assigned Names and Numbers (ICANN) is responsible for managing port numbers. The well-known port numbers range from 0 to 1023. The registered port numbers range from 1024 to 49151. The dynamic and private ports range from 49152 to 65535. Most systems use the well-known port numbers to run system processes or privileged programs. ICANN doesn't control the registered port numbers. Most of the time these numbers are used with nonsystem processes or nonprivileged programs, such as an ordinary user running a program. Table 2.1 lists the well-known port numbers.

Table 2.1 Well-Known Port Numbers

Port Number	Transport Layer Protocol	Description
7	TCP, UDP	Echo
13	TCP, UDP	Daytime
19	TCP, UDP	Character generator
20	TCP, UDP	File Transfer Protocol (default data)
21	TCP, UDP	File Transfer Protocol (control)
22	TCP, UDP	SSH Remote Login Protocol
23	TCP, UDP	Telnet
25	TCP, UDP	Simple Mail Transfer Protocol (SMTP)

Continued

Table 2.1 continued Well-Known Port Numbers

Port Number	Transport Layer Protocol	Description
53	TCP, UDP	Domain Name Server (DNS)
67	TCP, UDP	Bootstrap Protocol Server
68	TCP, UDP	Bootstrap Protocol Client
69	TCP, UDP	Trivial File Transfer Protocol (TFTP)
79	TCP, UDP	Finger
80	TCP, UDP	World Wide Web HTTP
88	TCP, UDP	Kerberos
110	TCP, UDP	Post Office Protocol Version 3 (POP 3)
118	TCP, UDP	SQL Services
119	TCP, UDP	Network News Transfer Protocol (NNTP)
123	TCP, UDP	Network Time Protocol
137	TCP, UDP	NETBIOS Name Service
138	TCP, UDP	NETBIOS Datagram Service
139	TCP, UDP	NETBIOS Session Service
143	TCP, UDP	Internet Message Access Protocol (IMAP4)
156	TCP, UDP	SQL Service
161	TCP, UDP	SNMP
162	TCP, UDP	SNMPTRAP
179	TCP, UDP	Border Gateway Protocol
194	TCP, UDP	Internet Relay Chat Protocol
213	TCP, UDP	IPX
369	TCP, UDP	Rpc2portmap
389	TCP, UDP	Lightweight Directory Access Protocol (LDAP)
401	TCP, UDP	Uninterruptible Power Supply (UPS)
443	TCP, UDP	HTTP over TLS/SSL (HTTPS)
445	TCP, UDP	Microsoft-DS
464	TCP, UDP	Kpasswd
500	TCP, UDP	Isakmp
513	TCP	Remote login via Telnet (login)
514	UDP	Syslog
530	TCP, UDP	Rpc

Continued

www.syngress.com

Table 2.1 continued Well-Known Port Numbers

Port Number	Transport Layer Protocol	Description
563	TCP, UDP	NNTP over TLS/SSL (NNTPS)
568	TCP, UDP	Microsoft shuttle
569	TCP, UDP	Microsoft rome
593	TCP, UDP	HTTP RPC Ep map
631	TCP, UDP	Internet Printing Protocol (IPP)
636	TCP, UDP	LDAP over TLS/SSL (LDAPS)
637	TCP, UDP	Lanserver
689	TCP, UDP	NMAP
691	TCP, UDP	MS Exchange Routing
749	TCP, UDP	Kerberos administration
750	TCP, UDP	Kerberos version iv

What is so important about these ports is that when you get to later chapters of this book, you will have to come back here to get the numbers to plug into the ACLs and filters you create with your firewall of choice. Make sure that you understand the placement of DMZ hosts and what traffic to let through before you attempt to configure your firewall, because the firewall configuration will solely depend on that information (port, service, placement) first! You can't direct traffic if you don't know where to send it and what numbers you need to plug in to get that movement in the first place. If you have the network design shown in Figure 2.21, what traffic map would you design?

Figure 2.21 Windows Traffic in the DMZ

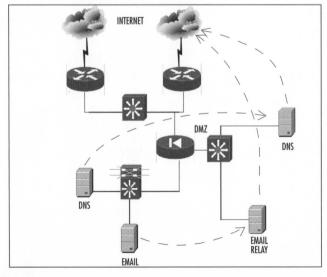

Let's look at this subject in more detail:

- You have an internal DNS server that needs to communicate with an external DNS server to forward queries.

- You have an external DNS server that needs to communicate with the Internet DNS.

- You have an e-mail server and its e-mail relay to the Internet to consider.

- You have an e-mail relay that needs to send mail to the Internet.

Now that you have looked at the traffic map, you need to configure the rules in the firewall. You will have to use DNS and e-mail ports from Table 2.1. For DNS, you can use port 53, and for e-mail services, you'll use SMTP to send mail on ports 25. Again, there are many more services and many more ports, but if you lay out the map and think about the communication paths, you can easily plug in the numbers and then go to the appropriate chapter in the book to find out how to configure the necessary rules, filters, and ACLs.

Assessing Network Data Visibility Risks

Now that you have engineered the traffic to flow into and out of your network, what is really the risk of others seeing this traffic? Tools to eavesdrop on traffic are freely available on the Internet and can cause you much pain when you try to build a Windows DMZ. Depending on the structure of your network, an attacker can use a network sniffer to explore and map the hosts it contains. We won't spend too much time on this topic, because it's really the concept you have to get down here. You need to think about the problems you could encounter while building your DMZ, if you do let certain traffic traverse your network and over the Internet, and decide which ports and services to allow or disable.

Configuring & Implementing...

Disable NetBIOS and SMB!

Disabling NetBIOS on servers in untrusted networks (or anywhere in general) is always a good idea. Just remember to test before you do, in case an application you are using is dependent on that service. Other than that, disable away. NetBIOS is by far the poorest form of secure name resolution you can find. Always use DNS if you can, but in case your Windows networks contain any legacy systems (anything predating Windows 2000), you are sure to need NetBIOS. Always disable NetBIOS if it's not needed on your DMZ hosts or they will be exploited, without question. Servers in the perimeter network should have all

Continued

unnecessary protocols disabled, including NetBIOS and server message block (SMB). These protocols should both be disabled to counter the threat of user enumeration. You can think of user enumeration as a form of information gathering so that the attacker can find other ways to attack from the information he or she has gathered. This information includes domain and trust details, shares, user information, groups and user rights, and even Registry information. You will want to disable NetBIOS whenever possible. To do this from a firewall, you can block all communication using the following ports:

- UDP/137 (NetBIOS name service)
- UDP/138 (NetBIOS datagram service)
- TCP/139 (NetBIOS session service)

SMB uses the following ports:

- TCP/139
- TCP/445

To disable these on a host, you can remove File and Printer Sharing for Microsoft Networks and Client for Microsoft Networks using the **Transmission Control Protocol/Internet Protocol (TCP/IP) Properties** dialog box in your **Local Area Connection** properties. Once you have done that, there is one more option. This is the easy way to disable SMB:

- Open the **Device Manager**. (You can get to it from the **Control Panel** of the Computer Management Console.)
- Once you open Device Manager (in **Computer Management** view, as shown in Figure 2.22), you can then show the hidden devices (where the driver is) by right-clicking the **Device Manager** icon and selecting **View** and then **Show Hidden Devices**.
- Expand the **Non-Plug and Play Drivers**.
- Right-click **NetBIOS over Tcpip**, and then click **Disable**. Once this is done, you will disable the SMB direct host listener on TCP/445 and UDP 445.
- Close the **Computer Management** console to finish.

You can also use the Windows Firewall or IPSec policies to control file and print sharing traffic on an individual computer or on multiple computers in an Active Directory domain using Group Policy Objects.

In sum, these steps show you how to engineer traffic on a Windows 2000 and a Windows 2003 network. You need to know how to direct traffic as well as how to enable and disable it. An attacker can research just as easily as you can, and this is what they are looking for—the exploits you have forgotten about and left wide open.

Continued

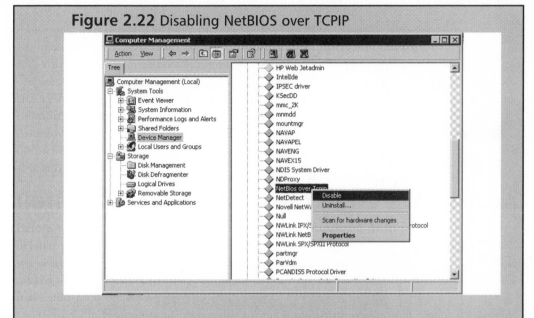

Figure 2.22 Disabling NetBIOS over TCPIP

Not all traffic engineering is completely without repercussion to a production environment, so you need to test your efforts before going live into production. You could disable a service or driver only to find out an application that depended on it no longer functions properly. When you disable the NetBIOS over TCP/IP driver, for instance, you have effectively disabled the nbt.sys driver. This driver could be used by another application. Just be careful and test your applications in a test environment before making "live" changes.

Windows DMZ Design Planning List

Until now we have looked at ways to build a Windows DMZ. We have covered the network hardware needs and basic layout, the devices that will populate the DMZ, the types of systems you need to place on your DMZ, and the engineering of traffic through the DMZ. The last thing you need to know is the population of systems in the DMZ, such as Windows hosts, DNS servers, and others. Again, this information is covered in detail in Chapter 13.

For you to properly plan your Windows 2000/2003 DMZ, follow these checklists to get yourself from start to finish. These are by no means all-inclusive lists, but they should serve you well in getting started, getting the foundation of what is needed up and running. Then, if necessary, you can populate the list with more items you need or want.

To successfully start your Windows 2000/2003 DMZ implementation, begin with our initial discussion on planning: network engineering, systems engineering, and security analysis.

- Network engineering

- First, start with your vision. You must have current network topology maps handy and a map of what it is you plan to do. There are many examples through this chapter and this book on how to make a proper topology map for your organization.

- After the planning stage, you can either start to work on a prototype, or pilot, or go live. No matter what you decide, you should do some testing or visit a location (or another business) to analyze their Windows 2000 DMZ solution to see if your scaling requirements are right.

- Don't undercut yourself. If you need to scale up or out, plan that in now, so you can get a jump on future requirements.

- Get the devices you need, lay them out, test them, and then implement them into the design.

- Make certain that you harden your network engineering devices. They will be exposed to the Internet and are just as vulnerable to attack as your Web or DNS servers.

- Systems engineering

  - Plan the placement (logically and physically) of your DMZ hosts. Since you are using Windows 2000 or Windows 2003, you can look at IIS for a Web and FTP server as well as an SMTP relay, Windows 2000/2003 DNS services, Exchange 2000/2003, ISA Server 2004, and so on.

  - Once you plan your systems, you need to engineer the communications between devices in the DMZ and behind it.

  - Once you have the planned communications, you can start implementation.

- Bastion hosts installation and lockdown

  - As you populate the DMZ with hosts to provide services, you need to harden them.

  - Harden the base Windows 2000/2003 operating system first. (You'll find details in Chapter 13.)

  - Harden each individual service you implement. (You'll find details in Chapter 13 and Appendix A.)

- Security analysis

  - Run tests on your Windows DMZ to ensure that all devices are locked down, hardened, secure, and ready to provide services to the public Internet.

  - Test all connections and all devices, and use a plethora of tools to test different types of attack.

- Run service packs, hotfixes, and anything else to test, harden, secure, and tighten up the perimeter or your network could be exploited. You can refer to Chapter 14 to learn how to hack the DMZ and test it.

A Look Forward to Longhorn

The next release of the Windows Server operating system, currently codenamed Longhorn, will have a number of new features that provide additional capabilities for securing DMZ and other perimeter and remote networks. The three major features that administrators will find useful in this arena are the Read-Only Domain Controller (RODC), Server Core, and Network Access Protection (NAP).

Introducing the Read-Only Domain Controller

The RODC is being designed for environments such as a branch office, where you need to deploy a domain controller but you cannot guarantee its physical security. Unlike the Backup Domain Controller (BDC) from NT 4.0, RODC will store only a configurable subset of your Active Directory database in its local copy of the AD database. For example, if you have a branch office with only 20 users, you can configure an RODC in that location so that it stores only those 20 user accounts in its local database. If any users other than those 20 need to authenticate at the local branch, they'll need to contact a DC in the main office to authenticate; if the WAN link between the branch office and the main office is unavailable, any user whose credentials haven't been stored on the local RODC (including domain administrators) will be unable to log in. (You can still log on using a local administrative account for troubleshooting.) In addition, accounts belonging to certain "special" groups such as domain admins and enterprise admins will not be cached on an RODC by default. This increases the security of your domain controllers by minimizing the number of account passwords that will be compromised if an RODC is hacked or physically stolen.

Slimming Down with Server Core

In addition to the full-blown version of Longhorn Server, you will also be able to install Longhorn in a *Server Core* configuration, which allows you to deploy a small-fingerprint version of Longhorn Server, with an installation size that's as little as 500MB. Server Core cannot run anything requiring a graphical user interface (GUI), the .NET Framework, or any component that relies on managed code. This simplified configuration allows you to deploy modular servers that are dedicated to only one or two components, such as domain controller or file/print services.

Using Network Access Protection

In an era of laptop computers, pervasive wireless access, and high-speed Internet access in a majority of homes, virtual private networks (VPNs) have blurred the notion of the network perimeter much more than it has been in the past. This creates new risks for an enterprise network, since administrators often can't maintain a strict level of control over these laptops and other remote computers; VPNs can often become a threat vector through which viruses and malware can infect an internal network. To help combat this problem, Longhorn will offer Network Access Protection (NAP), which will bring a "quarantine" feature for any wired or wireless clients connecting to a corporate network. Using NAP, you can prevent a remote client from accessing your network resources until it has passed one or more "health checks" that can ensure that a remote client has the appropriate antivirus software installed with up-to-date definitions and that a client is running a particular operating system and patch level; it can even scan incoming clients for particular malware infections or other vulnerabilities. Using NAP, you can extend the logical perimeter of your network to include remote clients in a much safer and more controlled manner.

Summary

Although this is only the second chapter in the book, you should start to see many concepts coming together. The demilitarized zone, or DMZ, is probably the most difficult segment to design and engineer on your network. In this chapter in particular, you should have acquired the foundation to lay out and build a Windows-based DMZ. Again, it's not merely knowing Windows, Cisco, or any other vendor's products that will get you through the design and implementation of a Windows DMZ, but all this knowledge put together underlies a simple set of concepts: Design the network, design the systems, and then test them all for security. We looked at that process in great detail in this chapter. You learned how to lay out all the hardware you need, set up a plan and a design with a topology map, plan where the systems will be placed—in front of, behind, and within the DMZ segment formed by the firewall you use. Other chapters focus on more granular aspects such as bastion hosts, hardening, testing, and so on, but this chapter should have laid the groundwork for your design.

When considering Microsoft Windows (or any other vendor OS), you need to consider system placement and traffic engineering. You need to know exactly what ports and services that OS needs to rely on to communicate and function properly. Although Windows Server 2003 is a much more secure operating system than its predecessors, it is only as secure as you can make it. Therefore, it's very important that you followed the content of this chapter closely, since everything you learned here will be used in the DMZ of your network. The DMZ is the segment exposed to the Internet, so it is critical that you understand the concepts not only in this chapter but in this entire book. We can't stress it enough: If you place Windows servers on your DMZ, pay close attention to hardening techniques and proper traffic flows, or you could be exploited.

In this chapter we covered how you can design a Windows-based network solution that will work within and around the DMZ segment. It's important to know how to perform this task as a security administrator or engineer because the DMZ can be very complex to work with and around. In this chapter you learned how to use your Windows systems within the DMZ design.

Lastly, this chapter focused not on learning Windows security concepts but on how to design the proper DMZ layout. In other chapters you will learn the granular details needed to implement security, harden systems, and test those systems to ensure that they are secured properly.

This chapter should have served as a rough design document to help you place your Windows systems and the services they run within the DMZ. It is common for many administrators to wonder how to place their systems within the DMZ, especially when they are Web or FTP servers facing the Internet and publicly accessible. As we mentioned in the chapter, this job can be nerve shattering, especially with all the publicity Microsoft has gotten in the past as being an insecure system with many bugs, unchecked buffers, and a plethora of other problems resulting in becoming the biggest target on the Internet today. This chapter should help you remedy those fears by providing you with the answers and solutions you need to not only place the systems in and around the DMZ but also to protect them.

Solutions Fast Track

Introducing Windows DMZ Security

■   To begin, we need a general idea of what it's going to look like on a map. All good network designers plan the topology (hopefully with a topology map) and figure out traffic flows, logical addressing, and any other factors that would affect the systems operating as advertised. If you choose not to follow this recommendation, you could find yourself very discouraged when the network does not function properly and systems cannot be accessed because of a simple (or complex) mistake you made in the design.

■   The DMZ segment can be one of the most complicated segments to design and implement on the network. When you add Windows to the mix, you not only have to be an expert in security but also network engineering as well as Windows system design and the services to be made available. In sum, make sure you plan your implementation very closely.

■   The three main sections you need to consider when you're building your Windows DMZ are network engineering, systems engineering, and security analysis.

■   Your first step in designing a Windows-based DMZ is to select all the networking hardware you will need. You must assess your needs, trying to figure out what the hardware infrastructure will cost your company. You need to look at needs first. When you are looking at the networking end of it, you should ask yourself, "What devices will I need, and how should I scale them?" Exploring these questions will bring about answers based on networking gear and costs.

■   When planning your infrastructure, you always need to ensure that you plan the proper equipment list, no matter what vendor you pick. If you are purchasing this much equipment, presales support might be in order. Ask you vendor to show you user limits per device (how many users can simultaneously use this device without affecting its performance) as well as the type of traffic you will be pumping through it. Often, the vendor can help you design your network so that you don't fall short on what you need or do not go into overkill where you might not need the extra power.

■   When you want to populate the DMZ with Windows hosts, you need to think about access to and from the DMZ and the services that are needed. The reason behind this initial thought is that your end users, customers, potential customers, and outsiders will be able to utilize needed resources and only those needed resources—nothing more, nothing less. To start the engineering process, you have to first make certain that you have these answers! You should make sure that users can obtain the information that they need about your company without accessing the internal network and only by accessing the DMZ or accessing the Internal network safely, if you chose not to implement a DMZ. If you can, it's always better to segment Internet-based resources via the DMZ for an added level of safety. Now that you know your network layout, you have to think about other access to and from the DMZ.

- Your secret, protected, confidential, and proprietary information should be stored behind your firewall and DMZ on your internal network. Servers on the DMZ shouldn't contain sensitive trade secrets, source code, proprietary information, or anything that can be used against you or your company—or be used to exploit or hack your systems. (There's more on DMZ hacking techniques in Chapter 14.) A breach of your DMZ servers should at worst create an annoyance in the form of downtime while you recover from the security breach.

- A Web server that holds public information is a common example of a DMZ host. This can be IIS (since we are discussing Microsoft technologies in this chapter) or any other publicly accessible Web server. You can also think of FTP services, NNTP services, and other Web-based services to be accessed and utilized.

- Electronic commerce-based solutions always wind up on the DMZ. This is the front end of an e-commerce transaction server through which orders are placed. Keep the back end, where you store client information, behind the firewall. You want to design this properly; if you don't, you could potentially compromise your entire client database (or personal and private data) if it's exploited.

- A mail server that relays outside mail to the inside will be a highly utilized solution in the DMZ, especially since spam and other e-mail exploits are common DMZ host-based targets for attacks.

- VPN solutions are prevalent in the DMZ. Other than the site-to-site VPNs we already learned about, you also have VPN solutions in which you will have a remote access solution so that clients can attach over the Internet to get to their files and other data needed on the corporate network. This also has to be publicly accessible via the DMZ.

Building a Windows DMZ

- Depending on the model and type of firewall you use, you can in fact have different DMZ segments with different services on each to add even more security to your DMZ segments and hosts. This might be necessary if you plan to segment your DMZ hosts even further. This would mean that you could place an IIS load-balanced cluster on one DMZ and an e-mail relay on another.

- Your Windows solution revolving around the DMZ needs to allow for Internet access. The Internet connection should be able to handle the bandwidth needs of the site. If you are using this Internet connection as your LAN's Internet access for surfing and e-mail and you decide to use it for a VPN as well, you need to analyze your requirements first.

- A traffic flow analysis can be done to ascertain the needed requirements (for WAN links, Internet connections, and so on) quite quickly, but you need to know how to do the analysis and have the tools to do so. If you do not, it is in your best interests to work with an outside vendor that does have the tools and experience to do so. Not doing so will almost always result in bad performance and increased cost later when you need to reprovision the lines to a higher bandwidth.

- Sometimes (if the size and complexity of the network dictate) you'll need a router on each leg of the firewall. At times, you will get requests to either add security to the segment you are working on or add more and more devices to it, where you might need to either route or direct traffic. You might decide to keep these services dependent on the device in which they sit. Keep your devices dedicated to what they do best when you can afford to do so and can use the added security.

- Too often, administrators mistake where to put DNS and WINS servers when working with the DMZ. Be sure to control where your public and private resources are published so that you are not exposing details of private hosts to the public over the Internet.

- Know how to place an e-mail server on the DMZ. You could place it in the private network. The firewall in front of the e-mail server would be responsible for taking all requests in and out of the network and responsible for securing the traffic to the e-mail server. Due to the design of the server, it made the relaying of outbound Internet-based e-mail the responsibility of the e-mail server—only one single server. The question is then, however, "Why would we want to expose our e-mail server to the public Internet? What if there was a way to attack the e-mail server directly through the firewall?"

- It is common to simply add another e-mail server to the DMZ segment and use this as a relay to and from the protected e-mail server in the private network. The server now becomes an e-mail relay, and it will relay the mail to and from the Internet and to and from the mail server. If mail relays (IIS has an SMTP service that can be used as a relay) are compromised, you can reinstall the server from scratch and not lose a thing because all the server did was relay traffic. (Keep in mind that this approach could still incur downtime for your organization, so it is still advisable to create a high-availability scheme that will minimize this risk.)

- Web servers are the most common form of DMZ-based hosts today. Other services, such as DNS and e-mail, are needed, but if you really think about it, the main reason DMZs even exist is because of the public Internet Web surfer feeding frenzy. Almost every company in the world now has a publicly accessible Web site, which means that just about every company worldwide either has an Internet presence or is looking to have one. Because of all these personal invitations to their corporate networks, it is imperative that you also think out your security completely or your network could be exploited.

- Organizations frequently have data they want to publish to the external network via a Web server. To allow direct access to the Web server via the Internet while the server is sitting in your private and protected LAN would be suicide. For that reason, we allow an external Web server to be placed on the DMZ. This way, you can allow all your visitors to come directly to your IIS server and not have them exploit that server only to find ways to get to other systems. If the IIS server is external on the DMZ, you can at least have some defense against it if it is compromised in any way.

- The last (and very common) services to see on the DMZ both internally and externally are the DNS servers for your organization. DNS services are now more than ever the most common service used for name resolution. Because of DNS's growing use, it is important that when you lay out your Windows 2000/Windows 2003 network, you are able to design the Internet namespace and the external namespace for the organization.

- Once you have finalized the DMZ network segment design and placed your systems where they need to be (and understand why they need to be there), you have to consider traffic and applications flows, ACLs, and filtering.

Windows DMZ Design Planning List

- To successfully start your Windows DMZ implementation, you need to start with our initial discussion on planning: network engineering, systems engineering, and security analysis.

- To properly plan your Windows DMZ, follow the steps in our checklist to get yourself from start to finish. You can use the list incorporated in the end of this chapter to do the planning you need.

Frequently Asked Questions

The following Frequently Asked Questions, answered by the authors of this book, are designed to both measure your understanding of the concepts presented in this chapter and to assist you with real-life implementation of these concepts. To have your questions about this chapter answered by the author, browse to **www.syngress.com/solutions** and click on the **"Ask the Author"** form.

Q: I would like to protect my Windows DMZ. What do hackers use to test, check, and penetrate my DMZ?

A: Tools that allow people to eavesdrop on traffic are freely available on the Internet and can cause you much pain when you're trying to build a Windows DMZ. Regardless of the types of traffic traversing your network, a network sniffer is all someone needs to learn, map, and disable your network. You need to think about the problems you could encounter while building your DMZ when you do let various types of traffic traverse your network and over the Internet.

Q: I need to look at allowing specific traffic through my firewall, and I am unsure who handles such assignments. Where should I look for this information?

A: The Internet Assigned Numbers Authority (IANA) is responsible for managing port numbers. The well-known port numbers range from 0 to 1023. The registered port numbers range from 1024 to 49151. The dynamic and private ports range from 49152 to 65535. Most systems use the well-known port numbers to run system processes or privileged programs. Most of the time they are used with nonsystem processes or nonprivileged programs, such as an ordinary user running a program. Visit www.iana.org for more information.

Q: What is the most common form of DMZ-based system in use today, and what is commonly seen on DMZs big or small?

A: Web servers are the most common form of DMZ-based hosts today. Other services are needed, such as DNS and e-mail, but if you really think about it, the main reason DMZs even exist is because of the public Internet Web surfer feeding frenzy. Because of all these personal invitations to companies' corporate networks, it is imperative that you also think out security completely or your network could be exploited.

Q: I am planning out a new DMZ infrastructure. I am unsure about the hardware I need or what vendor to select. What should I do to start my plan?

A: When planning your infrastructure, you always need to ensure that you plan for the proper equipment, no matter what vendor you pick. If you are purchasing that much equipment, presales support could be in order. Ask your vendor to show you user limits per device (how many users can simultaneously use this device without affecting its performance) as well as the type of traffic you will be pumping through it. Many times, the vendor can help you to design your network so that you don't fall short on what you need or do not go into overkill where you may not need the extra power.

Q: I want to implement a DMZ, but I am hearing from management that there might be a future need for an e-commerce site. How does this affect my design now? Should I plan for this functionality, even though I do not know exactly when it might happen?

A: If there is a need to eventually set up a load-balanced solution with multiple IIS servers and a possible back-end database cluster, you should plan for it in the design stages of the initial DMZ setup so that you don't have to repurchase new gear for it later. You should also see if this can be amended into the project plan by the stakeholders and the project manager so that, if possible, the need can be finalized and you can scale your equipment for it before, not after, the fact. Always get a needs analysis and a future needs analysis done early in the design phase of the project so that you know what you might want to incorporate in the design (such as load balancing). If e-commerce is the need, you need to scale the firewall, switches, and all other infrastructure to meet the needs for a possible e-commerce site, a load-balanced cluster, and so on.

Q: Why would I need a site-to-site VPN, and how does it affect my Windows DMZ design?

A: If there is a need to add more bandwidth and site-to-site VPN services off the external Internet routers, you should at least be familiar with the design and why you are implementing it. For one, the VPN used in this manner replaces your current Frame Relay or other WAN technologies, or if this is a new installation, you can forego using these technologies in the first place. All the VPN does is encrypt your data over a public or private medium so that you can have the private-line feeling without the private-line price premium. These are popping up left and right as companies try to save money, so it is important that you know how to design them into your DMZ. You should also ensure that you purchase models either with crypto cards (to use IPSec for VPNs) installed or upgradeable to them.

Q: When I plan my Internet connection, I am unsure as to what type of switch I need behind the external router, or if I even need a switch at all. Can't I just use a crossover cable to go from the router port to the firewall port?

A: If you need to scale up the number of connections to the Internet, such as the need for VPN services, intrusion detection systems, honey pots, other routers and so on, or you have other services that will be added sooner rather than later, you might need to put a switch in between the firewall and the external router. You might need more port availability on the switch so if you can get a switch, you have set yourself up to scale out in the future if needed. If this need is not there, you can skip this implementation and simply use a patch or crossover cable to connect your systems instead.

## Chapter 3

Sun Solaris DMZ Design

Solutions in this chapter:

- New Features of Sun Solaris 10
- Placement of Servers
- The Firewall Ruleset
- System Design
- High Availability
- Implementation: The Quick and Dirty Details
- Hardening Checklist for DMZ Servers and Solaris

- ☑ Summary
- ☑ Solutions Fast Track
- ☑ Frequently Asked Questions

Introduction

Solaris is a commercial UNIX operating system distributed by Sun Microsystems. The combination of Sun hardware and software makes systems that use Solaris some of the best-performing servers in the world. However, Solaris can be used as more than just an ancillary of services, such as database, Web, and mail. With roots in the Berkeley Software Distribution (BSD) UNIX world, Solaris is well equipped to perform as a DMZ server.

In this chapter, we discuss the use of Sun hardware and Solaris as a DMZ system. We begin with the new features of Sun Solaris 10, followed by a discussion of the placement of servers in configurations to make the most of resources. We also discuss the use of firewall rules and how they can be implemented to provide security to the private and public network segments of a DMZ implementation.

After discussing the use of Solaris as a DMZ system, we focus on the Solaris system itself. The object of this discussion is examining the factors in creating a secure system to act as the DMZ server. Of the design, implementation, and maintenance phases common to every server, we focus on the design and implementation phases. In the discussion of these phases, we outline specific methods that can be applied to systems to create a secure design as well as to maintain the system's integrity during the implementation. Let's begin with a discussion of the new features of Sun Solaris 10 followed by the placement of Solaris DMZ servers.

New Features of Sun Solaris 10

Sun hardware platform supports Windows, Linux, Trusted Solaris, and the standard Solaris. Sun has introduced new features to increase security, scalability, stability, and performance in Solaris 10. Features such as predictive self-healing, ZFS file system, cluster volume manager, Grand Unified Boot Loader (GRUB) on the $x86$ platform, OSPFv2 and BGP-4 routing protocol support, IP Filter IPv6 support, SSL acceleration, IP Filter Firewall, Web console, and zones deserve mention here.

Let's look at some of the features that are helpful in deploying Sun Solaris as a DMZ platform in your organization.

- **Zones** Later in this book you will read about Juniper Networks' virtualization concepts. Zones are nothing but virtualized OS services, or simply put, multiple instances of Solaris OS running on a single hardware platform. Sun calls them as *containers.* This approach helps administrators decide on the amount of resources to be allocated to applications and services without interfering with each other. For security or manageability purposes, if you had considered running services such as Web and mail in different server hardware, now you don't need to do that. Run multiple services on a single hardware platform, isolating them with zones. Failure or nonperformance of one of the virtual operating systems doesn't impact the performance of another application running in a completely different OS instance. Resources such as memory and CPU are shared among the virtual operating system instances, however, appearing to the individual virtual OS as though the resources are dedicated to itself.

- **ZFS** Zettabyte File System, or ZFS, introduced in Sun Solaris 10, uses a concept of *pooled storage,* bringing performance enhancement and integration of file systems with volume management.

- **Reduced Networking Software Group** Solaris 10 allows you to build a secure server with only those services that are absolutely necessary for you to run a designated application. You get the control of what is installed and what is not from the installation stage itself, facilitated by a text-based console and various administration utilities. You may add and remove software packages and enable or disable services and network interfaces as needed. This ensures that you don't enable some services inadvertently, which could cause a security loophole later in the network.

For a complete list of new features, refer to www.sun.com/software/solaris/whats_new.jsp.

Placement of Servers

We can draw a parallel between the placement of a Solaris system that will provide DMZ services and the purchase of real estate with the mantra "location, location, location." Just as you do not want to purchase real estate that was previously a dump site, you don't want to put the DMZ server in a location on the network that is a metaphoric trash heap, cluttered with the equivalent of network garbage. Placing the system that will function as the DMZ server at a position in the network that is both efficient and secure is of the utmost importance.

Placing the system on the DMZ usually depends on network requirements. Some network configurations, such as smaller networks, may place the DMZ server directly behind the router, as demonstrated in Figure 3.1.

Figure 3.1 Basic Implementation of a Solaris DMZ Server in a Small Network

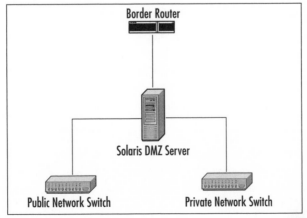

Although this is not the most ideal configuration because it does not permit easy scaling of network resources or easy integration of high availability, this design should be sufficient for smaller networks. We can see from the diagram that network traffic first enters via the network router and next goes directly to the DMZ server.

From there, the traffic proceeds to its next hop in the network infrastructure, which in this case is a switch on the public or on the private network. The router has a valid routable address on both interfaces. The DMZ server has a valid address on two interfaces, and on one interface it has a private network address. Traffic coming from and going to the private interface is translated using Network Address Translation (NAT).

In this type of configuration, the DMZ server is capable of handling a couple of networks. However, when traffic grows to the point that the DMZ server can no longer handle the load, the network needs to be redesigned to scale outward, to handle the additional traffic.

In addition, this configuration makes it difficult to monitor the network outside the DMZ server with network intrusion detection (IDS) tools. However, for small offices or businesses, this configuration is a workable solution.

In Figure 3.2, we see a configuration that is a little more advanced and scalable. When traffic enters the network, it crosses the border router. It then immediately goes to a switch, where it is passed to the DMZ server. From the DMZ server, it proceeds to the switch on the public network or the switch on the private network.

Figure 3.2 Advanced Implementation of a Solaris DMZ Server With External Switches and NIDS

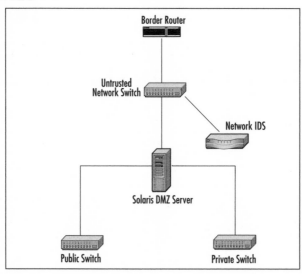

We should discuss a few noteworthy things in this configuration. First, we have a switch immediately behind the router. This is an important feature in the design because as the network grows, we may potentially add address space. In doing so, we could decide to add this network space to a different DMZ altogether due to business requirements. Placing a switch immediately behind the router gives us the ability to expand or contract the network as necessary. If a switch is not used, we could connect, via a patch or crossover cable, the border router directly to the Solaris system.

Also worth noting in this configuration is the IDS monitoring the network outside the DMZ. Note that it is connected only to the network outside the DMZ and has no other access. The host is connected to the outside network to provide monitoring of attempted attacks. Information gathered from this sensor could be crucial in identifying attacked and/or compromised hosts or, in most cases, a passive scan on the DMZ. Furthermore, this system has no other network access because it is in an unprotected location and could potentially be the victim of an attack itself. This situation can be mitigated through access controls on the border router and DMZ systems, though the possibility will always exist due to the location of the system.

However, IDS is outdated because it does not prevent an intrusion from happening. Therefore, security administrators consider deploying an intrusion prevention system (IPS) to detect and block intrusions. Sophisticated appliances are available in IPS to perform an application layer level of scanning and detecting intrusions. Often these systems are used to block denial of service (DoS) or distributed denial of service (DDoS), worms, Trojans, and backdoor attacks. IPS is also used to block application layer traffic, such as chat programs and peer-to-peer (P2P) applications, to enhance security in a corporate network. If you are planning to deploy IPS, you should consider modifying the network design because IPS is normally placed behind the firewall. This enables IPS to focus only on the traffic that is already permitted by the firewall and therefore concentrate only on the contents of a packet, to detect malicious traffic. Organizations that want to know where the attack is happening (much before the firewall drops the traffic) can still place the IPS between the router and the firewall. However, you need to consider the performance impact before doing so.

We must also consider the need for high availability. The configuration shown in Figure 3.3 differs slightly from the one shown in Figure 3.2 and illustrates a highly available configuration.

This figure contains many features similar to those in Figure 3.2. However, what is different is that rather than one DMZ system connected to the external network switch, three DMZs are connected to the external network switch. Additionally, there are several connections from these DMZ systems to the same public and private networks. We also see a connection between the DMZ systems. You may also consider implementing firewall and server load-balancing appliances such as BIG IP from F5, Cisco Content Service Switches (CSS), or Nortel Networks Alteon load balancers. These dedicated load-balancing appliances can offload the load balancing and high-availability loads from the servers.

Figure 3.3 Solaris DMZ Servers in a Conceptual Highly Available Configuration

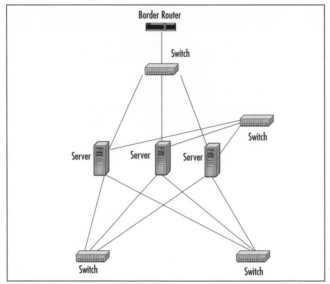

This configuration shows a DMZ server cluster. All systems in the cluster maintain an active connection to other systems in the cluster via the switch. The only system in the cluster that maintains active connections outside the failover information switch is the active DMZ system. When the primary DMZ system fails, it deactivates (or is deactivated) via information over the failover communication network, and the next system in the cluster brings up its network interfaces to perform the job of the primary DMZ server.

These general network component configurations enhance network security. However, this is only part of the design. Equally important is the firewall ruleset, which we discuss in the next section.

The Firewall Ruleset

The firewall ruleset dictates the exact types of network activity permitted by the DMZ server. As the implementers of a DMZ system, we are responsible for the first line of security of both the public and private networks. This important task cannot be taken lightly.

In this section, we focus more on the firewall rulesets as they relate to the various requirements of the DMZ host. In each segment of the network handled by the DMZ server, we have a different set of requirements and expectations. We start with the private network rules, discussing the ideal private network firewall policy.

Following our discussion of the private network segment, we focus on the public network requirements and firewall ruleset. Some of the inherent risks of public network access are also outlined. We end our discussion of firewall rulesets with a brief examination of requirements for local host security.

The Private Network Rules

Because the security of both the public and private networks depends on a secure DMZ server, the firewall ruleset must be well conceived and sufficiently secure. Although the firewall ruleset must be secure enough to prevent attack and compromise, it is equally important that the network at least be usable. Our quest to create a secure network should not necessitate jackboots as work footwear and an iron fist as a policy enforcement tool.

Therefore, we must evaluate the services a user needs to meet business requirements, and we must balance our firewall policy against restricting the services a user does not need. It is often easier to inventory the services users need than the services they don't need. Although business networks are typically infinitely complex, let's keep it simple and say that our users need only Web, mail, and domain name service (DNS) access. Such a planning of permissible traffic is commonly referred to as *whitelisting*. It is always easy to downsize what you want rather than list everything you do not want (*blacklisting*). Commonly used firewall rules include a *stealth rule* that prevents any direct connection to the firewall (*any to fw, drop,* meaning traffic from any source with firewall as destination will be dropped). This rule is placed on the top of the ruleset. The *cleanup rule* drops all the traffic that any other rule does not permit. This rule is normally placed last in the sequence of rules. Most of the firewalls implement this rule as an *implicit rule*, which means that the rule exists, regardless of whether you create it or not.

Configuring & Implementing...

DMZs and Internet Chat Clients

Internet chat clients have become a popular means of communication, and business is no exception to the trend. Often it is more productive and easier for coworkers to open an instant message (IM) to communicate rather than to perform a context switch by turning away from the computer and picking up the phone or physically leaving the workspace to consult with a colleague.

However, Internet chat clients are the bane of DMZ security. Many such clients piggyback communication on top of other protocols to circumvent filtering or even to scan the firewall to determine how to reach the outside. Due to problems inherent with these clients, it is possible for a remote user to exploit an issue that would result in a client-side attack. The attacker could gain access to

Continued

> the user's system with the privileges of the user and thus initiate a connection to the outside world that allows the attacker access.
>
> It is difficult to prevent the use of these clients at the DMZ level, and it might be better to approach this issue with a security policy.

In Figure 3.4, we show a network design with a router at the top of the network. From the router, we go to a switch, then to the DMZ server. The DMZ server connects to switches on both the public and private networks. On the private network, we see a mail server. On the public network, we see a mail server, a DNS server, and a Web proxy server.

Figure 3.4 A Solaris DMZ Server With Hosts on the Public and Private Networks

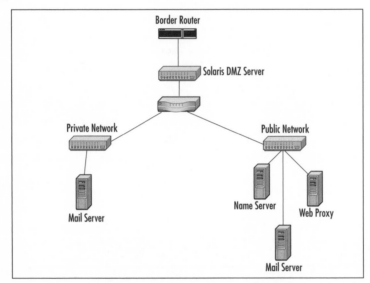

Even though users do not need access to the mail server outside the private network, the mail server on the private network needs the ability to access mail outside the network. The most secure way to do this is to allow the internal mail server to contact the mail server in the DMZ for mail rather than allowing the mail server in the DMZ to indiscriminately send traffic through the firewall on port 25 to the internal mail server. This can be done using a tool such as *rsync* over SSH. Alternately, you may use the Fetchmail service over SSL to deliver mails to the Sendmail mail service in the internal network. We want the internal mail server to perform this task as a stateful action to prevent the piggybacking of traffic on the connection.

In terms of Web access, giving users unfettered access to the Web is, at the least, risky. Wise network design involves using a proxy server to filter potentially malicious Web content. However, we do not want to keep this proxy server at a location where it could pose a risk to the security of the private network. Therefore, we assume that the proxy server is in the DMZ.

To maintain the security of the private network, we want to place a firewall rule entry for the proxy server. This rule maintains the state of outgoing user connections to the proxy server, like that of the mail server, except this rule goes to the proxy server. Once these two rules are configured, we fall to our last rule in the ruleset, which expressly denies any other incoming or outgoing traffic.

Finally, we must take into consideration the domain name service. We use the domain name server on the public network to provide this service to users. The firewall ruleset for the private network permits querying of the name server from the private network. We see an example of this configuration in Figure 3.5.

Figure 3.5 An Example of Rules Implemented on the Solaris DMZ Server for Private Network Traffic

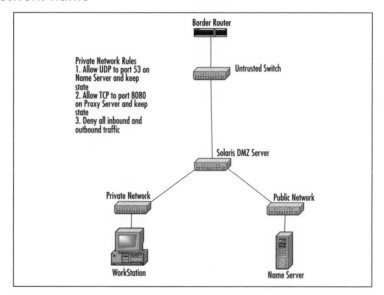

Now that we have a secure configuration for our private network, let's examine our public network configuration.

The Public Network Rules

The requirements for the public network often differ significantly from those for the private network. The public network usually provides a number of services available to the public Internet and some for private network users as well. The biggest consideration here is that the public network also requires accessibility by external users, which increases the exposure to potential attacks.

Public networks are conceptually much like private networks. They require giving users the ability to access services and should limit users' ability to deviate outside of accessing the allowed service set. In the previous section, the services we discussed were mail, Web, and name service. Let's assume that these services are also required on the public network.

In terms of Web service, we have already established that users of the private network will use a proxy server to access outside content. The proxy server needs access outside the public network, so we create a rule that maintains state, allowing access from the proxy server to networks outside the public network. The rule enforces the policy that the proxy server process may connect to any system on any port and must maintain state. No outside server is permitted to connect directly to the proxy server or the proxy server process.

The mail server on the public network requires different configuration. SMTP is a two-way protocol that requires the ability of the mail server to connect to outside mail servers as well as receive connections from outside mail servers. In the previously described private network configuration, the mail server on the private network will likely forward the mail to the public mail server. From the public mail server, the mail will then be sent to the appropriate receiving server. The public ruleset should be configured to allow both incoming and outgoing connections that maintain state to the mail server process on the public mail server.

Finally, we must configure the public firewall ruleset for the domain name server. In the previous section, we stated that the name server would accept resolution requests from hosts on the private network. For the public network, we must alter this capability a bit. On the public network, the name server should only accept replies from other name servers. This name server should not be authoritative for the domain and should not otherwise accept resolution requests from users outside the public or private networks. Domain name service is inherently insecure. Although the only means to fix domain name service is a complete revision of the protocol itself, this configuration will at least insulate the service against many attacks. The public firewall rule should permit outbound requests from the domain name service process to any host on port 53 and should permit only responses to requests, if possible. In Figure 3.6, we see a manifest of firewall rules applied to the public network.

NOTE

The site www.cve.mitre.org/cve/ maintains the list of common vulnerabilities and exposures (CVE). Do a search on DNS to learn about the security threats and exploits available on DNS.

You can secure DNS by implementing DNS Security Extensions (DNSSEC). This adds security to the domain name system. DNS security threats such as *cache poisoning* can be avoided by using DNSSEC. For more information, visit www.dnssec.net.

Hardening tips, tricks, and techniques for bastion hosts located on the public network-based DMZ can be found throughout this book.

Figure 3.6 An Example of Rules Implemented on the DMZ Server for the Public Network

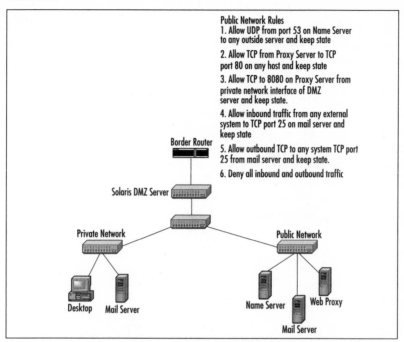

Public Network Rules
1. Allow UDP from port 53 on Name Server to any outside server and keep state

2. Allow TCP from Proxy Server to TCP port 80 on any host and keep state

3. Allow TCP to 8080 on Proxy Server from private network interface of DMZ server and keep state.

4. Allow inbound traffic from any external system to TCP port 25 on mail server and keep state

5. Allow outbound TCP to any system TCP port 25 from mail server and keep state.

6. Deny all inbound and outbound traffic

Border Router

Solaris DMZ Server

Private Network

Public Network

Desktop   Mail Server

Name Server   Web Proxy

Mail Server

Now that we have discussed the use of the Solaris DMZ server, let's focus on the server's design and implementation details.

Server Rules

We have addressed the rules for both the public and private networks, but we have not discussed the rules for the host itself. Essentially, the DMZ host is the linchpin of the network, and accordingly, it must be resilient to remote attacks. The ideal implementation keeps the host unreachable, if not basically invisible, from all systems except the system from which remote administration may be performed.

As such, the firewall ruleset implementation is pretty easy to conceptualize. Generally, the best policy is to deny all traffic to the host from all systems. Rules to permit traffic to the host for administration should be carefully implemented; we want to permit the administration host access to the administrative service on the DMZ server, but we do not want to give the host total access, in the event that it is compromised.

In that same vein, it might be helpful to give hosts from which administrative access will be performed a static IP address on the private network. It is generally not the best idea to use DHCP to assign addresses to these hosts, since this could potentially allow another host to acquire the address through either legitimate or illegitimate means. Furthermore, it makes it possible in the firewall ruleset to specifically allocate access to the administrative interface of the DMZ server from the private IP address of the administration station. This concept is shown in Figure 3.7.

Figure 3.7 An Example of Rules Implemented on the Solaris DMZ Server to Protect the DMZ Server

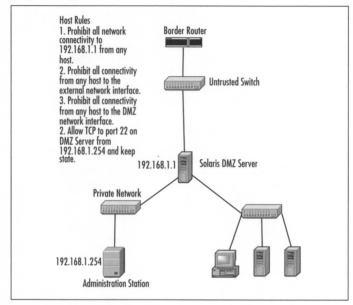

System Design

In the previous sections, we focused on the role of the DMZ server within the network. We discussed DMZ design, firewall rulesets for private networks, and firewall rulesets for public networks. These topics apply to the use of the DMZ server in the network environment; let's now focus our attention more closely on the design details of the server.

The process of deploying any type of server can be broken into three distinct phases:

1. The planning phase
2. The implementation phase
3. The maintenance phase

Let's look at a brief description of each of these phases. The *planning phase* typically involves designing the system. Details such as operating system selection, hardware selection, third-party software selection, operating system software installation details, and the like are decided during this phase. The planning phase is followed by the *implementation phase,* which entails assembling the hardware, securely installing the software according to specifications decided in the planning phase, configuring the host to meet design requirements, and testing the host to ensure stability and reliability. After the implementation phase has been completed, the system is placed into production, thus beginning the *maintenance phase*. During the maintenance phase, the system is continually monitored for signs of intrusion and performance issues. Additionally, the system is regularly patched with all critical and security-specific patches made available by the vendors of the software installed on the DMZ system over the course of its production life.

Our focus in this section is on the planning phase. We discuss two of the more popular firewall software packages available for Solaris. Selection of a firewall software package is important during the planning phase. However, we also want to fill in many of the other blanks, such as the hardware on which the DMZ server will operate, the operating system revision that will be used for the implementation, and similar details.

When a building is constructed, blueprints specify the minute details, from measurements and plumbing to storage closets. The foundation must first be designed before the structural design can begin. Once the foundation is designed, floor upon floor of the building climbs into the sky until the structure design is completed. Then the details such as plumbing, drywall, and paint are applied to the building. Designing a DMZ server, or any server for that matter, is not much different in concept. We start by designing the foundation—selecting hardware. We then select software, which can be likened to designing the structure. Then we complete the details such as service offerings, security features, and configuration details—the proverbial plumbing, drywall, and paint.

NOTE

Sun BluePrints offer industry-standard security and best practices. Topics covered include file system integrity, authentication, encryption, architecture of various security modules of Solaris and security tools such as auditing, fingerprint database, and Solaris Security Toolkit (SST). Sun BluePrints can be found at www.sun.com/software/security/blueprints/.

Hardware Selection: The Foundation

It goes without saying that the hardware is the base of the entire system. The proper selection of hardware, to use another analogy, can be likened to buying a car. Sure, one can buy a Ferrari if it is affordable. But the problem is, if we bought a Ferrari, once we marry and have kids, we would be stuck with a two-seat car and have to buy another car to fit our family and lifestyle. Arguably, if you can afford a Ferrari, you are likely to be able to afford a decent family car as well. However, if you are like everybody else working in technology these days, thoughts are not of a nice, new, shiny Volvo but instead a 1974 Pinto station wagon with minimal rust—paint optional.

Hardware selection is a process of picking a system with enough room to handle the current load yet scalable enough to add capacity for growth. This is a particularly important factor to consider in selecting hardware for a DMZ server. The two reasons are growth of network traffic and expansion of administered networks.

Growth of network traffic happens, plain and simple. A company could have an increase in network traffic thanks to increased popularity in the company Web site due to expanded offerings or other reasons, constituting an increased load through the public network segment. In addition, more staff could be hired, all requiring access to the Internet, which could constitute an increase in private network traffic and thus more load on the DMZ server.

A system that handles network traffic needs an abundance of two specific resources: processing power and memory (RAM). It is in RAM that the traffic is momentarily stored, evaluated against the configured firewall ruleset, processed, and either rejected or sent on its merry way to the destination.

Because of the resource needs as well as the likely possibility of growth, you should consider hardware that is capable of being expanded. Minimally, select hardware that is capable of adding RAM as well as faster processors.

An older example of such as system is the Sun E420R. This rack-mountable system is designed to handle two disks internally, which is sufficient for our purposes. On the main board, the system is capable of handling 4GB of RAM and four Ultra-Sparc II processors. A newer example of a system capable of handling our needs is the rack-mountable Sun V480 Server. This system, like the E420R, has the ability to handle two disks internally. It is capable of handling up to four Ultra-Sparc III processors and up to 32GB of RAM. Sun's newer server range, based on AMD Opteron with four AMD processors and high-performance $x64$ computing, also offers the ability to handle large amounts of memory. The Sun x4600 series with four or eight single- or dual-core AMD processors offers to support 128GB of RAM when the 4GB memory chips are released. For more options before you decide on your Sun hardware platform, visit www.sun.com/servers/ and view by processor family.

Another factor to consider is the ability to add network interfaces. Select a system with space on the bus that's sufficient to add network interfaces. With Sun systems, two types of interface are available. We discuss these interfaces in more detail in the network hardware considerations section that follows.

From this discussion, we can draw a few conclusions about hardware selection. The first and more obvious is that we should select hardware capable of handling the load. Second, we should select hardware that is capable of being scaled to fit our current needs as well as our future needs. The difference between selecting hardware that cannot be expanded and hardware that can be expanded equates to purchasing and building a new DMZ server once a year.

Let's focus in a little more detail on the common DMZ hardware requirements as well as network hardware considerations.

Common DMZ Hardware Requirements

Solaris is predominantly used on Sun or Sun-clone hardware. In some instances, it is also possible to use Intel-based Solaris to create a DMZ server and provide service to a network. However, due to variances in Intel-based hardware and the idiosyncrasies involved in making a working configuration on this platform, we omit Intel Solaris from our discussion. Instead, we focus this discussion entirely on Sun and Sun-clone hardware.

For the purpose of this discussion, Sun hardware is essentially the same across the board, whether you're using a 10BaseT (le) interface on a SparcStation20, a fast-Ethernet Interface on an Ultra80, or Gigabit interface on an Enterprise system.

To create the standard three-legged DMZ system configuration, we require at least three network interfaces. These interfaces can be provided in one of two ways. We can use three separate interfaces, such as single Ethernet cards, each using a separate opening on the bus. This would provide us three separate cards, leaving the single point of failure on the system bus rather than in one network component.

Another configuration could be the use of a tool specifically designed for the job. This tool comes in the form of a Sun quad interface card. These are single cards containing, as their name implies, four network interfaces in one card. This gives us the benefit of consolidating all our network components into one slot on the system bus, leaving room for other components such as fiber channel cards or the like.

Of the card types available, the Ethernet cards, used in a set of three, would comprise the *le0, le1,* and *le2* interfaces on the system. The corresponding quad Ethernet card would give us interfaces *qe0* through *qe3.* The Fast Ethernet cards would give us *hme0* through *hme2,* with the quad Fast Ethernet card giving us interfaces *qfe0* through *qfe3.*

Network Hardware Considerations

We must take a couple issues into consideration when we're planning to use a Solaris system as the DMZ server. The first of these issues is the speed of the cards the system will use to service the network. The second issue is the hardware on the network to which the DMZ server will provide service.

We must pay particularly close attention to the first issue when we're using separate Ethernet interfaces. In this type of configuration, the primary interface on the host will most likely be used as one leg in the DMZ configuration. Therefore, the additional two cards you purchase should have similar characteristics.

For example, most Sun SparcStation20 systems were distributed with a stock 10BaseT Ethernet interface. Therefore, wisdom would lead us to purchase additional 10BaseT Ethernet interfaces. This train of thought applies to other systems, such as the Ultra80, which, by default, includes a 10/100 fast Ethernet interface, and so forth.

In light of the first issue, we must also consider the second issue, which are the requirements of our network neighbors. Where possible, we want to use hardware that is at least of the same speed of the systems with which the DMZ server will be communicating. Typically, we want to place a DMZ server in a location between switches or between a router and a switch. In standard configurations, switches and routers have, at a minimum, Fast Ethernet interfaces.

Although it is possible to get by using interfaces of slower speeds than our neighbors, doing so creates a senseless bottleneck in the network. Minimal requirements should be using interfaces of the same speed as our network neighbors. A rule of thumb is to use interfaces that are at least as fast and capable of higher speeds than our network neighbors for future growth in network traffic and changes in network configuration.

Drawing on the previous section about DMZ hardware requirements, we must again consider the type of cards we will use to get the job done. Current ability to perform and future scalability are as important in this scenario as our budget. Getting the job done with separate Ethernet cards could be the cheaper solution, but when the network grows in the future, we will be forced to either replace the system with one that will provide additional slots on the bus for single Ethernet cards or, more realistically, convert the single Ethernet cards to quad Ethernet cards. Consider making this type of hardware a standard selection, because it provides multiple interfaces of the same speed and offers immediate scalability in a standard three-leg DMZ configuration, since one interface on the quad card is free, as well as the primary interface on the host.

Software Selection: The Structure

In the planning phase, the next most critical decisions concerning a DMZ server are the selections of various software packages. These software packages include the operating system that will run on the host as well as the firewall software package and any other third-party software packages that might be required. In using Sun hardware, it is a given that Solaris is the operating system of choice; it provides the best performance on the hardware, has the best symmetric multiprocessing code of operating systems, and provides the best support for Sun hardware.

Solaris is versatile enough to function well as a networking operating system, having its roots in the Berkeley implementations of Unix. Like the Berkeley Operating Systems, Solaris, with the appropriate hardware, is capable of acting as a router in its default implementation. Unlike the BSD Operating Systems, Solaris requires additional software to provide advanced features such as packet filtering and stateful inspection.

One common theme across all networks is that no a single common software package is used to implement DMZ and firewall services. The fact of the matter is that although most available software packages offer a plethora of common features, the decision to use one particular type or brand of software often boils down to two factors: in-house expertise and money. The questions, "Do we have the expertise to use this software?" and "Can we afford this software?" are the two influences on which selection is ultimately made.

This is not to say that there are not a number of other factors that come into play. One such factor is support. For example, some software might not offer the most cutting-edge features. However, when the price and accessibility of support are factored in, the return on investment significantly increases. Along that same vein, having an in-house expert who is capable of modifying the source code of a free software package to fulfill business requirements and resolve issues with the minimum amount of downtime can far outweigh the initial investment in software and support as well as the turnaround time typically required with external support.

Popular Firewall Software Packages

There are many players in the firewall software market. Naming and describing them all could easily turn into a chapter in and of itself. Instead, here we discuss Check Point FireWall-1, which is the most commonly used firewall software package available for Solaris.

Check Point FireWall-1

Though the statistics are a couple years old, at one point it was estimated that FireWall-1 was deployed on one of every four firewall implementations. FireWall-1's feature set as well as its complexity have made it quite popular with enterprises. The complexity of the software has also led to the creation of several levels of certification for use of the product itself. This says little about the product but more about its widespread use.

Check Point has roughly everything one would expect from a standard firewall package. It uses stateful packet filtering, works with multiple interfaces, and can perform NAT services. Some deployments can be configured to provide failover services in the event of loss of one firewall.

Prior to using FireWall-1 for a DMZ implementation, it is recommended that people using the software familiarize themselves with the package. Although the slick GUI for configuration could put some users at ease, inexperience with the software can minimally lead to a very frustrating experience. Table 3.1 shows the Check Point NGX modules available on Solaris platform.

Table 3.1 Check Point NGX Products on the Solaris Platform

Products	Available on Solaris UltraSPARC 8, 9, and 10
SmartConsole GUI	X*
SmartPortal	X
VPN-1 Power (VPN-1 Pro) including QoS, Policy Server	X
VPN-1 UTM (VPN-1 Express/ Express CI)	
VPN-1 VSX	
SmartCenter Server	X
SmartPortal	X
ClusterXL (VPN-1 Power Module)	X

Continued

Table 3.1 continued Check Point NGX Products on the Solaris Platform

Products	Available on Solaris UltraSPARC 8, 9, and 10
UserAuthority	X
Eventia Reporter—Server	X
SmartView Monitor	X
VPN-1 Accelerator Driver II	X
VPN-1 Accelerator Driver III	X
Performance Pack	X
SmartLSM—Enabled Management	X
SmartLSM—Enabled ROBO Gateways	
SmartLSM—Enabled CO Gateways	X
Advanced routing	
SecureXL TurboCard	
SSL Network Extender—Server	X
Provider-1/ SiteManager-1 Server	X
Provider-1/ SiteManager-1 GUI	X

* SmartConsole clients SmartView Monitor, SmartLSM, Eventia Reporter Client, and the SecureClient Packaging Tool are not supported on Solaris UltraSPARC platforms.

Table 3.2 shows the minimum hardware requirements of Check Point NGX R61 (Sun).

Table 3.2 Minimum Hardware Requirements of Check Point NGX R61

Hardware	Minimum Requirement
VPN-1 Power SmartCenter Server or Enforcement Module	
Processor	UltraSparc II
Memory	128Mbytes RAM (256Mbytes recommended)
Disk space	100MB for installation
Network interface	1 or more network interfaces
Media drive	CD-ROM drive

Continued

Table 3.2 continued Minimum Hardware Requirements of Check Point NGX R61

Hardware	Minimum Requirement
SmartConsole	
Processor	UltraSparc III
Memory	128Mbytes RAM
Disk space	100MB for installation
Network interface	1 network interface
Media drive	CD-ROM drive
Graphics	800x600 video adapter
Eventia Reporter*	
Processor	UltraSparc III 900Mhz
Memory	1GB RAM
Disk space	80MB for installation 60GB for database
Network interface	1 network interface
Media drive	CD-ROM drive
Graphics	1024x768 video adapter

* SmartConsole clients SmartView Monitor, SmartLSM, Eventia Reporter Client, and the SecureClient Packaging Tool are not supported on Solaris UltraSPARC platforms.

TIP

For more information on Check Point hardware and software requirements, visit www.checkpoint.com/ngx/upgrade/requirements.html.

You can install Check Point SmartCenter server and SmartConsole GUI on the same server. However, in normal practice SmartConsole GUI is installed on the security administrator's desktop. Figure 3.8 shows the SmartConsole GUI.

High Availability of the DMZ Server

Another design issue that should be addressed in the planning phase is high availability. Designing, building, and deploying a DMZ server are crucial steps in securing a network. However, if the DMZ server fails, an outage of all network resources occurs until the system is either fixed or replaced. This includes a public network outage, which means public-facing systems in the DMZ cannot be reached by systems on outside networks. This also means network connectivity from the private network to external networks is affected.

Figure 3.8 The SmartConsole GUI

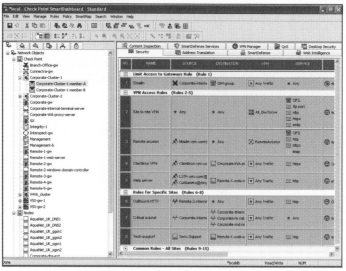

Failure may occur for one of any number of reasons. Often, catastrophic failure such as the failure of a component in the system can result in the system becoming completely unavailable and requiring that the component is either repaired or replaced before normal network operations can resume. The goal of high availability is to minimize the amount of time lost when the DMZ server fails.

High availability is created by deploying two or more systems to perform the same job in what is called a *cluster*. One system in the cluster sits by idly while the other system serves client requests. The serving system continually monitors itself and sends information to its peers about its current state of operation. Should the system performing the job fail, the next system in the cluster identifies the failure and takes over the job performed by the failed system.

Let's discuss some high-availability packages in a little more detail.

Check Point Cluster

Check Point FireWall-1 has a diverse set of features. One of these features is high availability, made possible through the ClusterXL module.

The ClusterXL module is diverse in its function. It can enable a cluster of FireWall-1 servers to act as failover systems. It can also be configured as a load-balancing system, which can aid in handling networks prone to large spikes of network activity. If an HA module is implemented, the firewall system acts as Active/Passive, in which one firewall acts as the primary firewall and the second remains a standby. When you deploy ClusterXL (additional licensing required), the firewall system acts as Active/Active, in which both the firewalls handle traffic and perform load balancing. Figure 3.9 shows the Check Point cluster.

Figure 3.9 Check Point Firewall ClusterXL

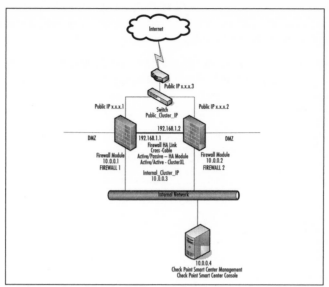

After you install Check Point firewall modules on two separate servers for clustering, SmartCenter management on another server, and the Smart Center GUI on a desktop or administrator's computer, you need to create a cluster object and add the two firewall modules as members in the cluster. Figure 3.10 shows cluster object members.

Figure 3.10 Cluster Object Members

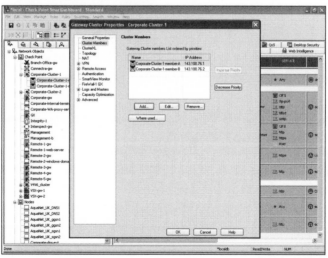

ClusterXL may be configured in unicast or multicast mode. Both these modes require specific configurations. Figure 3.11 shows ClusterXL properties. For more details, refer to the

Check Point documentation at www.checkpoint.com/support/technical/documents/docs_r61.html.

Figure 3.11 Cluster Object Members

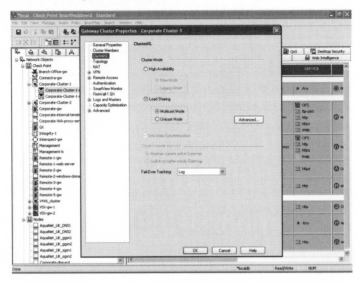

Implementing a firewall cluster in a multicast mode means that both firewall modules need to be reachable from the router all the time and therefore responding to multicast queries. This could require that an ARP entry be added to the router. Multicast MAC addresses can be found in the cluster advance properties screen. Use the following command to add the entry:

```
router(config)# arp public_ip_of_the_cluster 0100.5e3c.6e42 arpa
```

IP Filter Firewall

Solaris provides configuration files such as ipf.conf, ipnat.conf, and ippoo.conf. These files are found in the /etc/ipf directory. By rightly editing these files you can utilize your Sun Solaris server as a firewall or a NAT device.

You can configure packet filtering and NAT rules using an IP filter firewall. The syntax for a packet filtering rule is:

```
action [in | out] option keyword, ...
```

For example:

```
block in quick from 192.168.10.0/24 to any
```

This rule will *block* all *incoming traffic* from the *network* 192.168.10.0/24

You may also implement NAT rules using an IP filter firewall. The syntax to implement a NAT rule is:

```
command interface-name parameters
```

If you want to translate the outgoing traffic from the *le0* interface that has a source network address 192.168.10.0/24 to 10.1.1.0/24, you need to create this rule:

```
map le0 192.168.10.0/24 -> 10.1.1.0/24
```

Before you configure packet-filtering rules or NAT rules, ensure that you know the source and destination network or network objects, the type of protocol or service, and whether you want to permit or reject the traffic and/or translate.

Security Features of Sun Solaris 10

The Solaris 10 operating system comes bundled with an integrated packet-filtering firewall and IP filter. It is an open-source, cross-platform packet filter. The IP filter is used to manage the type of traffic and the traffic flow to and from a system.

Solaris also provides the Automated Security Enhancement Tool (ASET) that helps you monitor and control system security. This eliminates any manual work of hardening. You need to choose one of the security levels such as low, medium, or high. Once ASET is executed, it increases your system security by tightening the file access. The Low level sets the file system attributes at a standard level. At this level only a security check is performed. The Medium level sets the file system to a security level that is adequate for most environments. At this level system files and parameters are modified. The High level ensures that the system's security is set to the highest levels. This means that minimum access is available to system files, and most of the file system parameters are modified.

ASET performs several tasks, including tuning system file permissions, system file checks, user and group checks, system configuration file checks, environment variable checks, and EEPROM checks. More information is available on the security services volume of Sun Solaris 10 system administration guide (http://docs.sun.com).

Veritas Cluster Server

Cluster Server by Veritas is another high-availability software package. Cluster Server is independent of other applications on the system and is not dependent on any one application. This independence offers the advantage of allowing a group of DMZ servers using firewall software packages that are not highly available to be configured into a cluster of failover hosts.

Cluster Server requires cluster configurations that have a means of communication between all nodes in the cluster via a network interface. This is a circumstance in which our previous discussion about the user of quad Ethernet cards applies. With an extra interface on the DMZ server, we can group together the DMZ server and backups into a cluster, making the network highly available.

Sun Cluster

Sun Cluster is another high-availability package. As the name implies, it is distributed and maintained by Sun. Sun Cluster is written specifically for Solaris and Sun hardware.

Like Veritas Cluster Server, Sun Cluster is independent of any particular application. Also like Veritas Cluster Server, the Sun Cluster software package can be used to make roughly any firewall software system highly available.

Host Security Software

Ensuring the reliability and integrity of the DMZ system means using host integrity-monitoring software to report activity that could indicate intrusion. Like many other security measures, integrity monitoring is a reactive measure that involves notifying staff responsible for the system in the event of noisy and messy compromise. However, knowing of a compromise after the fact is far better than never knowing about it at all.

For the most part, host integrity-monitoring software works in one of two ways. One method that host integrity software uses to monitor the system is monitoring activity on the local system's ports to identify activity that could indicate a compromise. Any activity that is known by the software to represent a likely intrusion is reported.

The other method is the creation of a database of cryptographic hashes of binaries installed on the system. When the host integrity software is installed and configured, the software crawls the directories it is configured to monitor and creates the hash database. The host's integrity is maintained by checking the hashes of the monitored binaries and directories against the hashes contained in the database.

Although it might seem intuitive to use software that monitors both the ports on the DMZ server and the hashes of local binaries, it is best to use software that monitors only the local hashes. The reason for this is a matter of exposure. The addition of any network-aware services additionally exposes the system to attack.

Of the software available for host integrity monitoring, two packages are most commonly used. The first is the commercially available Tripwire package. The other widely used software package for this purpose is the Aide software package.

Cisco Security Agent, Cisco's solution for end-point security is available for Sun Solaris 8 and 9 server platforms.

Other Software Considerations

To properly place a DMZ server in the network infrastructure, we typically put it in a location that is ideal for a number of other services. Often, it seems like a good idea to place services on the DMZ system that are used for the infrastructure of the network. These services can include things such as Web servers, domain name servers, mail servers, or other such services.

You must resist this temptation. As we discuss in the configuration section, the host that will be providing DMZ and firewall infrastructure to the network should run with the minimal number of services possible. There are many reasons for this approach; here we focus on two.

First, the DMZ server is dedicated to handling network traffic. As previously stated, this is extremely RAM- and processor-intensive activity. Running additional services consumes additional resources that could otherwise be dedicated to handling network traffic. Although the impact might not be readily apparent on a lightly loaded network, as the network traffic load handled by the DMZ server increases, the impact becomes much more apparent. Often, such a situation results in failure of systems to connect to hosts, because the system drops packets due to limited resources.

Second and more important: Running network services on the system increases the system's exposure to potential vulnerabilities and thus potential attacks. The cornucopia of past vulnerabilities in the Berkeley Internet Name Daemon (BIND), in addition to the likely future continuation of the BIND vulnerability saga, is a prime example of the dangers of deploying services on the host. Sendmail and the numerous and frequent vulnerabilities in the software are other examples. Even intrusion detection software packages such as Snort are not immune to remote vulnerabilities, as displayed recently in the Snort TCP Stream Reassembly Buffer Overflow Vulnerability by the research team of Core Security Technologies.

Increasing the exposure to remote vulnerabilities with the DMZ server is, to put it bluntly, stupid. Should the system be compromised, an attacker is granted not only access to all hosts on the DMZ but full access to all hosts on the private network segment as well. Once the DMZ system is compromised, the network's integrity can no longer be trusted, and the attacker can direct traffic to wherever whim may lead.

The selection of hardware and software is important in the reliability, stability, and performance of the DMZ server. However, the next step in the planning phase has a far greater impact on the security and integrity of the system. Let's discuss the design of a secure system configuration.

Configuration: The Plumbing and Other Details

The configuration portion of system design is the stage in which we lay out the way the host will be implemented. We previously discussed the selection of hardware and software and the surrounding impact on performance; in this section we discuss the configuration details of hardware and software as they relate to security. Configuration can make the difference between a stable, reliable DMZ server that is resistant to remote attacks and one that is exposed and thus prone to attack and compromise when the next remote vulnerability is discovered.

Creating a secure DMZ server configuration requires the use of two distinct concepts: creating a secure configuration and using layers of security in our configuration. Because most security measures are reactive in nature, making security the basis of configuration at this stage is a fundamental change to the way security is typically handled, making it a proactive measure.

Our network will be only as secure as the design of the DMZ server itself. We must therefore create a configuration that exposes our DMZ server to no more risks than necessary. Let's look in depth at creating a secure configuration.

Disk Layout and Considerations

Before you can decide on a disk design, you must first gather some information. First, it is necessary to determine the size of the disks. This information can be gathered from the documentation or marketing literature for the selected system hardware. Or, if the disks will be hosted on a storage system such as a RAID cabinet, get the size information for the allocated disks in the cabinet.

Now that you have the information about the disks, the next step is to decide on the type of file system the host will use. In some configurations, such as a cluster, the stock UFS file system might be sufficient. However, in other configurations, it might be wise to use a different file system, such as a journaling file system. One example of such a system is the Veritas File System.

Another consideration is disk failover. Using a RAID cabinet simplifies this issue, since many RAID cabinets handle the disk issues on the storage server side, allowing us to merely identify the device on which the data is located in the system PROM and configuring the disk cluster in the cabinet to worry about the failover for us. However, in configurations such as our previously mentioned hardware, we could be using local disks. In this case, we might have to use additional software to provide redundancy in the event of disk failure.

This task can be accomplished through other software packages, one of which is the Solstice DiskSuite. DiskSuite is a soft solution to creating RAID configurations. Using disks on the local system, DiskSuite can be used to create RAID 0, RAID 1, RAID 0+1 (also called *ten*), and RAID 5 configurations. Depending on business needs and availability of storage, the best solution is typically a RAID 0+1 configuration.

Once we've attended to these details, we can decide the layout of the disk. For our purposes, we assume the use of a 36GB disk. Although recommendations on disk layout vary, we can safely allocate space of the following minimums to the various file systems:

- For the root partition (/), a minimum for 500MB

- For the swap partition, at least twice the amount of physical memory (RAM)

- For the /usr partition, at least 1.5GB

- For the /opt partition, at least 500MB

- For the user home partition (typically /export/home), at least 1GB

- For the /var partition, as much of the remaining space as possible

Allocating as much space as possible to the /var partition gives us the benefits of plentiful log space. Even with this minimum recommended configuration, a system with 1GB of physical memory and a 36GB disk will have 31.5GB of space for log information. Although this might seem like a massive amount of space, a busy DMZ server with increased auditing and logging enabled will easily gobble up this space (as we see in the next section). Logging on a separate server from the DMZ will not only provide additional security—it also improves the performance of the DMZ server itself.

Sun Solaris 10 introduces ZFS, which offers data integrity and scalability. With a *pooled storage* model, it eliminates issues with respect to creating partitions and unutilized storage space. File systems can draw storage for their requirements from a common pool of storage, therefore utilizing only as much space as required. This model ensures that the combined I/O bandwidth is available to all the file systems.

Backup and restore features of ZFS use snapshots to create full or incremental backups. ZFS provides built-in compression facilities. ZFS offers significant performance improvements over UFS.

Increasing the Verbosity of Local Auditing

Local auditing is an important factor in preserving the integrity of a host. Audit data is the first line of information in which intrusion might be apparent. Audit trails also have a legal significance; whenever there is an intrusion, log data becomes evidence that may be admissible in court. For these reasons, audit configurations must be increased in verbosity.

Solaris includes a number of auditing choices with a stock installation of software. As with every UNIX implementation, Solaris provides the standard system-logging facility, Syslog. Syslog is a good source of basic system information, but in addition to the standard audit trail provided by Syslog, Solaris additionally implements other utilities, such as the Basic Security Module, or BSM, as it is commonly known.

BSM is a highly configurable, robust, low-level auditing tool. It is disabled in default implementations of Solaris but can easily be enabled. BSM logs data when system calls of an interest in regard to security are invoked. Data written to the BSM files is in binary format. The BSM configuration file is located at /etc/security/audit_control. More information about BSM is available through http://docs.sun.com.

You can enable BSM as a root user by issuing:

```
#/etc/telinit 1 (To bring the system to single-user mode)
# cd /etc/security
# ./bsmconv (To enable BSM)
```

Disable BSM by issuing:

```
# /etc/telinit 6 (To bring the system to single-user mode)
# cd /etc/security
# ./bsmconv
```

A typical audit_control file will look like this:

```
flags:lo,ad,-all,^-fc
minfree:25
dir:/etc/security/audit/server1/files
#
#This is to audit when the file system of server1 is filled by at least 75%
#
```

The preceding script monitors *server1,* and as soon as the file system of *server1* gets filled up by at least 75 percent (minimum free is 25 percent, as per this example), it runs the warning script. The flags define that all logins and administrative operations should be audited. ^-*fc* means that file system creation failures are to be ignored. All other failures must be audited.

Increased auditing directly translates to log files of increased size. Often, data generated by auditing falls into one of two categories: It is either too much and thus too cumbersome to review, or it is not understood and thus auditing is turned off. These problems are often a matter of proper BSM configuration. However, it goes without saying that large amounts of data can still be generated, even with proper configuration. This data is important and should be reviewed regularly. It should also be preserved for future reference, which we discuss in the next section.

Backup Considerations

DMZ servers, like all systems, have data that is irreplaceable. On other systems, this data could be customer information, credit card numbers, or other business information. On DMZ servers, business information equates to system logs, audit data, and firewall logs.

As mentioned in the previous section, this data is crucial, especially from a legal aspect. Therefore, this data must be backed up and saved for future reference and analysis. For this reason, we must take into consideration the backup of DMZ servers.

Since a Solaris DMZ server is, at its root, a Solaris server, its backup differs little from other systems. Designing a backup solution is the same process as for any other host. However, we must consider the system's sensitivity.

Because a DMZ server is often the linchpin of networks, and because compromise of the system constitutes compromise of the network, we must make every effort to isolate the DMZ server from attack, and backup is no exception. Although it is sufficient for other systems to initiate backups via storage networks and backup servers, it is important for the DMZ server to keep its data backed up in a location that is isolated from other systems. Additionally, media should be, if possible, in an append-only configuration.

Two other issues to consider are storage constraints and backup software. Will storage constraints permit nightly backup of the entire system? Or is a better solution to back up only the important files? These questions cannot be answered without evaluating the resources at your site.

Backup software, on the other hand, is a much easier issue to tackle. If you're using a configuration such as a master backup repository and NetBackup, the solution is pretty clear. On the other hand, if nothing as formal is in place, *ufsdump,* included with Solaris and a DLT drive, could be the best solution.

Remote Administration

Most servers are administered remotely through either a graphical tool or a tool that uses the command-line interface. Often, the servers are stored in a location that either is uncomfortable to work in, such as a cooled server room, or requires travel to the site to administer, which in most operations departments, whether a remote colocation facility or the next room, is out of the question. DMZ servers are no different than any other server in this regard.

You must plan for remote administration and the impact on DMZ servers. It is not recommended that you provide any remote services that could increase potential exposure to attack, but sometimes this simply is not an option. If you're using services for remote administration, you must provide access control for these services, such as firewall rules. Additionally, the use of cryptographically secure services such as Secure Shell (SSH) is recommended because these services are less prone to peers and intermediaries on the network eavesdropping on potentially sensitive information such as passwords.

Putting the Puzzle Together

Before we can create a secure configuration, we must first know what to expect from a default configuration. After we have selected our operating system and third-party software, we need an idea of what to expect in terms of services, requirements, and default insecurities caused by the interactivity of all components. Having this information will better equip us to make informed decisions.

This is the phase in which we gather as much information as possible about the system in question. In many cases we can go online to get most of the pertinent details about default services started by the operating system and third-party software. Vendor sites as well as other third-party sites contain a wealth of information that can help us determine hurdles we might face in creating a secure configuration.

Should this approach not yield sufficient information or should we decide to take a more hands-on approach for our specific configuration, we can always create a test implementation. This implementation is really no more than an experiment. The installation procedure is not meant to be secure, and the software installation is not meant to be kept for future production use. The idea is to put together all the components, hardware and software, to see how they all interact with one another.

Once we have created a test implementation, we must gather information from it. To gather local information about the default configuration, we can usually use local system tools. These tools include *ps(1)* and *netstat(1M)*. We use *ps* to gather information about the processes started by default on the system, as shown in Figure 3.12.

Once we have gathered process table information, we gather network socket table information with *netstat*, as shown in Figure 3.13.

Once we have gathered this information, we can create a model of our design.

Figure 3.12 Getting a List of Executing Processes With the *ps* Command

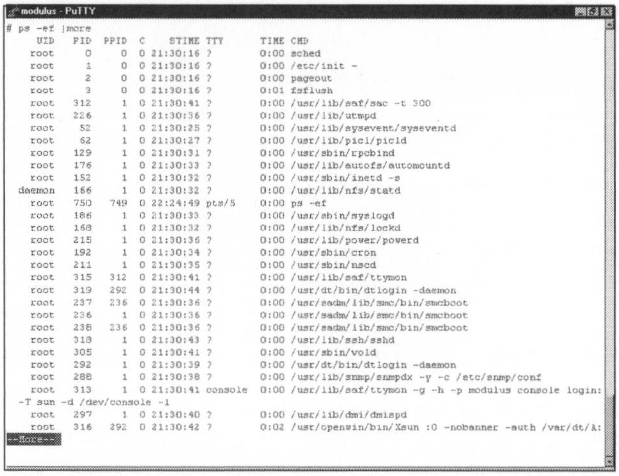

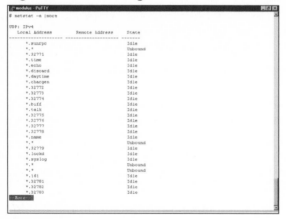

Figure 3.13 Getting a List of Listening Services With the *netstat* Command

Layering Local Security

The problem with most systems implemented on the Internet is that they are designed like candy: Many have a hard exterior that is crunchy and difficult to bite through, but once the hard shell has been breached, the center is soft and chewy.

This problem is not the fault of any one person in particular. Vendors design and create software this way. Administrators implement software this way. Security personnel run vulnerability scanners against the network and make the assumption that because there are no scanner events detailing remotely exploitable bugs, the systems are secure.

To Sun's credit, the company is making strides to combat this complacency. In Solaris versions through 7, we have file access control lists, an extension of the UNIX permission model designed to provide more granular access control. With Solaris 8, Sun implemented role-based access control (RBAC), which can be used to add power to or remove power from certain users. Security in 9 and 10 have been enhanced to meet the changing demands

Other third-party security software packages exist as well. Two additional features are restricted shells and restrictive environments. Let's briefly focus on each of these topics.

File Access Control Lists

As previously mentioned, file access control lists are an extension of the UNIX permission set. They are implemented at the file system level and designed to enforce security policy on a much more granular level. The tools *setfacl(1)* and *getfacl(1)* are used to manipulate these permissions.

The difference between standard permissions and file access control lists can be likened to allowing an entire group access to a specific file versus being able to select exactly which members of the group can access the file. Access control lists can also be used to limit which users in the world can read or execute a world-readable and/or world-executable file. A brief example of these programs appears in Figure 3.14.

Figure 3.14 Using *setfacl* and *getfacl* to Add and Restrict Access Permissions for Individual Users

In implementations in which there is a small user base, file access control lists might be handy. By adding granular access control lists to programs that might be sensitive, such as *setuid* and *setgid* executables, you can effectively put these programs out of reach of the unprivileged attacker. Although this solution cannot mitigate every single potential risk and attack, it definitely raises the bar.

DMZ servers are not and should not be designed to handle local users outside of administrative staff, due to the sensitivity of the system. However, this solution provides an additional layer of security against unprivileged local users. It is not a useful countermeasure in attacks that result in remote administrative compromise.

Role-Based Access Control

Role-based access control, also known as RBAC, is another useful enhancement to the UNIX permission model. RBAC is designed to allow administrators to delegate certain permissions within the system to roles, giving power to role users. RBAC can also be used to remove power from users.

The removal of power from users consists of creating traditional UNIX user accounts as roles. This way, you are given the ability to granularly specify exactly what the user can and cannot do. Creating a role for these users can limit the impact of system compromise through a specific user account.

Restricted Shells

Restricted shells are an older solution to untrusted user access. Their name implies exactly what they are: shells that are restricted. The restriction comes in the form of not permitting a user the ability to change certain profile information or escape his or her home directory.

Restricted shells can be useful in the event of a compromise of a user account on the DMZ system. If a user account is compromised through either a stolen password or a brute-force attack, the attacker gains access to an account in which the user can only execute programs contained in the home directory. Used in combination with RBAC, this can be a powerful configuration, because the user has the ability to only change to a role. However, if a program is made available within the directory that allows the user to execute shell commands, as is the case with most text editors, it is possible for the user to escape the restricted home directory by executing a standard shell.

Restrictive Environments

Restrictive environments are another useful means of mitigating risk locally. Like most other security measures, restrictive environments are, at best, a flaky solution if used as a sole means of maintaining host security. However, when coupled with other security measures, restrictive environments can significantly mitigate risk and increase the delta between a user gaining unauthorized access to a system and discovery of that breach.

Restrictive environments are often implemented in the form of a root directory change, also known as *chroot*. The principle is to create a pseudo-root directory from which a process executes. If the process is ever compromised due to vulnerability in execution, the attacker gaining access to the system with the privileges of the process is restricted to the pseudo-root directory. Known problems with *chroot* in some implementations can allow a user to escape the pseudo-root directory. However, as an additional layer of security, *chroot* is an excellent obstacle that can increase the precious amount of time leading to discovery from when a restricted account is compromised to when administrative privilege is compromised.

Auditing Local File Permissions

Local file permissions can be the boon or bane of a DMZ system security model, and they have resulted in many heated arguments. In many modern UNIX systems, files installed on a system during a default implementation could put the system at unnecessary risk. This is not necessarily the fault of the vendor; the program is written based on a user request and often given privileged execution status due to the need to access information or perform operations that require privilege. However, unintentional programming errors within the program make it a risk to the integrity of the entire system.

It is possible to mitigate this risk through local file permission auditing. This is a process that requires research and attention to detail. It is possible to reduce the execution permissions of many programs. However, reckless removal of permissions can minimally result in breaking applications on the system but can have more severe consequences, such as making the system unusable.

Two methods can be used to enhance local file permissions and reduce privileges where possible: manual auditing and automated security tools. The selection of methods is a matter of both size of the job and personal preference. We discuss each method here.

Manual File Permission Auditing

Auditing file permissions manually can be tedious work, especially if the person doing the auditing is not intimately familiar with the operating system's idiosyncrasies. Not knowing how to use tools supplied on the local system nor where to locate documentation and information about various programs can cause the job to escalate from the level of an exercise in frustration to the level of an exercise in restraining oneself from beating the system with a sledgehammer, especially when the usual unrealistic deadlines loom.

For people who are more comfortable with the system or who at least have the luxury of time, manual file system auditing can be beneficial in that it both allows you to get even more familiar with the operating system and allows you total control in local file permission security. This discussion assumes that the previous idea of building a test system that is used merely for information gathering in design is possible.

The two most useful system utilities for auditing local file permissions are *find(1)* and *man(1)*. Using *find* to locate files on the system installed with elevated privilege, as shown in Figure 3.15, makes the task significantly easier.

Upon compiling a list of executables installed with elevated privileges, you must understand the purpose of the executable to determine whether or not permissions may be lowered. For example, the *su(1M)* program is installed with *setuid* root privileges. Removing the *setuid* bit, however, usually has negative consequences because users can no longer use the *su* program to log into a different account from the shell, including that of root. This is where the man program becomes handy. Understanding the purpose of the program, how it integrates into the environment, and whether or not it really needs elevated execution privileges in the configuration is essential and can only be obtained through research and wisdom.

Figure 3.15 Using *find* to Get a List of Files With *setuid* Privileges on a Solaris System

```
# find / -perm -4000 -print |more
/usr/openwin/bin/xlock
/usr/openwin/bin/sys-suspend
/usr/openwin/bin/kcms_configure
/usr/openwin/bin/sparcv9/kcms_configure
/usr/openwin/bin/kcms_calibrate
/usr/openwin/lib/mkcookie
/usr/bin/sparcv7/newtask
/usr/bin/sparcv7/uptime
/usr/bin/sparcv7/w
/usr/bin/at
/usr/bin/atq
/usr/bin/atrm
/usr/bin/crontab
/usr/bin/eject
/usr/bin/fdformat
/usr/bin/login
/usr/bin/newgrp
/usr/bin/passwd
/usr/bin/pfexec
/usr/bin/su
/usr/bin/tip
/usr/bin/sparcv9/newtask
/usr/bin/sparcv9/uptime
/usr/bin/sparcv9/w
/usr/bin/chkey
/usr/bin/cancel
/usr/bin/lp
/usr/bin/lpset
/usr/bin/lpstat
/usr/bin/admintool
/usr/bin/rcp
/usr/bin/rdist
--More--
```

For programs not documented in manual pages, other resources exist. A good starting point is the Sun documentation site, at http://docs.sun.com. If documentation of the program does not exist there, resorting to a search engine might be in order. If you can't locate any documentation on the program, the rule of thumb, "If it ain't broke, don't fix it," applies.

Automated File Permission Auditing

For readers with less time to perform file permission auditing or who are uncomfortable with it, it is likely a relief to know that others have already done much of the work of figuring out which programs really need elevated privileges. If digging into the system is not on your agenda for the day and you're apt to trust free tools, one of two widely used programs can perform much of this work for you.

The first of these programs is the Computer Oracle and Password System, or COPS. Originally written by legendary security professionals Dan Farmer and Gene Spafford, COPS audits the local system for insecure file permissions, executables with elevated privileges, and weak passwords. Although it is somewhat dated, the program is well written and still extremely useful. It can be downloaded from the U.S. Department of Energy Computer Incident Advisory Capability at ciac.llnl.gov/ciac/ToolsUnixSysMon.html.

Another available tool is the Yet Another Solaris Security Package, or YASSP, as it is commonly called. YASSP is written specifically for Solaris and performs many of the same functions as COPS. This program is also a bit dated but is an excellent utility for enhancing local file permission security.

One final tool we will mention is the FixModes script. Written by Casper Dik of Sun fame, FixModes is another utility designed specifically for Solaris. It audits the file system of the host for programs with insecure permissions and makes changes necessary to enhance local security.

Building the Model for Future Use

As a kid, I was astonished by models. My friends used to build incredibly detailed, scaled versions of things like planes, aircraft carriers, battleships, and helicopters. Because I lacked the manual dexterity and artistic gifts of many of my peers, my finished models often left much to be desired. An attempt at a model of the *U. S. S. Enterprise* once resulted in something that resembled a model train wreck.

So, if the thought of creating a model of a system brings out *your* anxiety of past childhood shortcomings, worry not; for this model, we need little more than a text editor or a pencil and paper if we want to use a low-tech solution. The process of creating a model can be approached by two methods: either listing what we need or listing what we don't need. In most configurations, it is easier to take the former route to creating a model than it is to take the latter.

In Table 3.3, we have created a model of a system using the method of listing what we need. As you can see, we have specifically listed our requirements on the left, and on the right we've made an inventory of items to fulfill our needs. We can be as minimal or as fancy as we want with our model; what counts is that we list everything we need and everything we are going to do to fulfill the requirements.

Table 3.3 A Model of a System Design Listing Only the Requirements of the Host

Network Service Requirements Description	Inventory
Access to services required from the private network	HTTP; SMTP; DNS
Access to services required from the public network for the private network	HTTP; SMTP
Access to services required from the public network for untrusted sources	HTTP; SMTP; DNS; FTP
Access required to DMZ host	SSH from private network

Host Requirements Description	Inventory
Speed of network connections	100BaseT
Number of network interfaces (minimum of three)	Five
Number of disks	Two
Disk size	36GB
Auditing utility	Basic Security Module
Backup method	Local DLT drive

Continued

Table 3.3 continued A Model of a System Design Listing Only the
Requirements of the Host

Host Requirements Description	Inventory
Remote administration	SSH
High-availability software	Veritas Cluster Server
Local intrusion detection software	Tripwire
Firewall software	IPFilter
Software to harden system	Solaris Security Toolkit

Here are some things to keep in mind when you're building a model:

1. Ensure that hardware includes all the components necessary to create a DMZ server. This includes a minimum of three network interfaces.

2. Ensure that sufficient space is available for the configuration on the available drives, and allocate enough space for the file systems. Allocate as much space as possible to the file system that will be maintaining logs.

3. Plan to increase system audit verbosity.

4. Ensure that the backup solution is sufficiently secure, and take into account any limitations in storage that might exist.

5. Do not install any more software than absolutely required to perform the job. Third-party applications, such as firewall software, could have minimum software requirements. Consult vendor documentation for specific details.

6. Plan for high availability of the server.

7. Plan on implementing host integrity-checking software.

8. Plan to implement multiple layers of security.

9. Plan to audit local file permissions.

10. Disable all unnecessary processes. This is especially important of processes that are network-aware and could expose the system to potential attack.

11. Do not plan on providing network services from the DMZ server.

Once you've filled in as many of the blanks on these details as possible, you should proceed with design review. A peer review might also be helpful in this phase; a second set of eyes of a person with different ideas on design could be helpful in identifying any missed details or potential shortcomings in design. Upon successful review, implementation, which we discuss next, can proceed.

Implementation: The Quick and Dirty Details

The implementation phase of a DMZ server is pretty straightforward. As with all systems, the process consists of assembling the hardware, installing the software, installing the patches, then configuring the system. Whereas the process is the same across roughly all systems, we want to take particular precautions to ensure the integrity of the system through the entire evolution.

In this section, we look at the details necessary to ensure host integrity through this phase. Rather than giving a specific step-by-step outline of how you should install software on a server, we instead create a list of general guidelines that can be used to provide the maximum host security during the implementation process.

Media Integrity

A secure implementation cannot begin without first obtaining valid media. Acquiring valid media usually is done in one of two ways: It is purchased from the vendor and delivered by a sales representative or mail, or it is downloaded via the Internet. Verifying the integrity of media delivered in hard form, such as a CD, is relatively easy; simply look at the shrink-wrap to see if it has been tampered with.

Verifying the integrity of media downloaded via the Internet, however, is a bit more difficult. To verify the integrity of such media, the vendor must give us some secure means of checking its validity. This is typically done through cryptography.

Often, the vendor makes available a file containing a one-way cryptographic hash value, usually on the same page as the media or within a link of the media. The file is then signed with a cryptographic key that can be verified as valid. This task is typically performed with a utility such as Pretty Good Privacy (PGP) or GNU Privacy Guard (GPG). Once the integrity of the media is verified, it is safe to proceed.

Physical Host Security

During the installation process, physical security of the host should be maintained. One way to ensure physical security is to not leave the host unattended during the installation process. However, if there is not adequate time to sit around and watch the installation bar slowly progress from the left to the right side of the screen, another method is to ensure that the system is stored in a secure location while unattended.

A secure location can be one of two things. One secure location is a locked office. The system can be placed in the office with the door locked while unattended. Another secure location is a rack. Both of these locations make the common assumption about locks, which are designed to keep the honest man out.

Host Network Security

As we've continuously emphasized in previous sections, the host should not be exposed to any unnecessary risk. With that in mind, the system should not be connected to any network resources at any point during the implementation phase. Keeping the system disconnected eliminates the possibility of any incoming remote attacks by entirely eliminating the vector.

Even though it is considered generally safe to implement systems with a connection to the network plugged into the host, this is making an assumption that could create a window of exposure. Although none is currently known in Solaris, past vulnerabilities that could permit a remote attacker to gain unauthorized access to the system have been discovered in operating systems. This would be an ideal time for the attacker to compromise the host, since it has little in terms of defense in place.

Additionally, just because no vulnerabilities are currently known in the installation process does not mean they do not exist. Furthermore, even after installation, a window exists in which vulnerable services executing on the host could be compromised. As we're seen recently, the time worms require to propagate across the Internet has significantly decreased, making any window of exposure unacceptable. In short, do not permit network connectivity to the host at any point during the implementation phase.

Patch Application

Prior to attempting to apply to the implementation the secure configuration details we have developed, we should apply the recommended patch cluster to the host. This cluster, usually downloaded from SunSolve, comes in the form of a large, tarred, and compressed archive of updates to the system.

Configuring & Implementing...

Solaris Patch Management

Like every other operating system, Solaris patches are periodically released. The reasons for these patches vary, but they are often released for one of two reasons: system stability or system security.

The main clearinghouse for Solaris patches is the SunSolve site, located at http://sunsolve.sun.com. From this site, you can gain access to the latest patch cluster via either HTTP or FTP download. In addition, automated tools are available to manage patches on Solaris systems, such as the Sun PatchManager utility for Solaris 8 and 9. Sun Solaris 10 offers Sun Update Connection service that delivers latest patches and updates to your Solaris 10 server.

Although it requires network access to attain, the archive should be transferred to the system in the most secure means possible. Often, this is by way of "sneakernet," which is to say archiving the patch cluster onto media and physically carrying it to the system.

Patches should be applied to the system before you attempt to implement configuration and hardening procedures. The reason for this is that when patches are applied to a system, the details of a configuration are often overwritten. Therefore, configuring and hardening the system, then applying the patches could result in the unexpected exposure of the system to potential attack due to configuration changes by the patches.

To summarize the creation of secure implementation leading up to hardening, we should minimally fulfill the following requirements:

1. Verify media integrity prior to system installation. This applies mainly to media obtained from the Internet.

2. Provide physical security to the host during the implementation phase. The system should never be left unattended during the implementation phase without being locked in a secure location, such as an office or a rack.

3. Protect the system from attacks via the network during the implementation phase. This means not connecting the host to any network until the implementation phase has been completed.

4. Apply all patches to the system as a last step before conducting hardening and secure configuration procedures on the host. Patches will often change configurations, which could leave the host exposed to remote attack.

Solaris System Hardening

In some groups, system hardening is thought of as a separate phase in the system life cycle. However, system hardening is really just a subsection of system implementation. Hardening occurs before the system is connected to any network and should be periodically reevaluated and performed again. This is because configuration is always apt to change, whether the changes come from administrative staff or other sources such as system patches.

The hardening of the system amounts to no more than the application of the design principles we developed during the planning phase. During the planning phase, we made several decisions about disabling this and that, changing the permission on files, and so forth. This phase of the implementation is where the rubber meets the road in terms of our original design.

Two methods can be used to harden a Solaris system, each with its benefits and drawbacks. One method, manual hardening, consists of making by hand the changes that we detailed in our system model during the planning phase. This method has the benefit of giving us complete control over the hardening process. The drawbacks of this method are the amount of time involved manually hardening the host, the esoteric knowledge required to create a hardened configuration, and human error. Manual hardening and configuration of

Solaris DMZ servers is not for administrators who lack an intimate knowledge of UNIX systems and Solaris.

The other method of hardening hosts is the use of automated hardening tools. We have mentioned these tools before. Automated tools have the benefit of giving us a speedy, hardened configuration. Automated tools are also not prone to missed details due to human error. However, automated security tools have the distinct drawback of applying chainsaw methodology to system security. Additionally, you must trust another person's idea of a hardened system, thus relinquishing control of the configuration.

The decision of manual or automated hardening ultimately rests with the person implementing the system. The two important factors that influence the decision are time and expertise. In the next two sections, we discuss manual and automated hardening. In the manual hardening section, we discuss the steps that are generally considered the hardening best practices. In the automated hardening section, rather than discussing the functions of the tools themselves (they essentially all work the same way), we discuss a few different available tools and highlight some of their features.

Manual System Hardening

We should preface this discussion with a short definition of system hardening. In the previous sections, we have emphasized the importance of limiting exposure so many times, it is almost painful to mention it again. However, be ready to feel the pain, because we are about to discuss it again.

System hardening is, for the most part, the limiting of exposure. The way hardening differs from other security precautions is that although many other security precautions require the addition of software to enhance security, hardening typically involves the *removal* of software. In addition to the removal of software, it is also a procedural activity that typically involves the changing of permissions on files and directories as well as the removal or disabling of other components and features prone to abuse on the system.

Based on our initial design, we know which software and services we intend to keep. Our first step in hardening is to remove the software that we do not intend to keep. Afterward, we remove the services we do not intend to keep. We follow this step with some additional configuration variables that may enhance security.

NOTE

You need to understand the architecture of Solaris, the purpose of individual services and directories, and dependency of one service on another to function smoothly before you start tweaking the system. Always ensure that you do one change at a time, and check the system for stability before you proceed further. Document every change you make, including the files removed, services stopped, and configuration file edits.

Software Removal

No matter how much attention to detail we pay to the host during installation and how careful we are about the software we install, we inevitably end up with unintended software installed on the system. This is a fact that we must resign ourselves to and make plans to spend time combing through the installed software, removing that which we do not need.

Post-installation, we can get a list of installed software using tools distributed with the operating system. The two most important tools available for this job are the *pkginfo(1)* and *pkgrm(1M)* tools, installed with all Solaris installations by default. The *pkginfo* tool allows users to query the package database for installed packages in Sun package format, whereas *pkgrm* allows users to remove packages installed in Sun package format.

To get a listing of installed packages, one must first execute the *pkginfo* program. As shown in Figure 3.16, *pkginfo* displays the contents of the entire package database with the following information:

- The category into which the package falls
- The package instance
- A brief description of the package

Figure 3.16 Getting a List of Installed Packages With the *pkginfo* Command

```
# pkginfo |more
system      FJSVcpc      Fujitsu CPU Performance Counter package
system      FJSVcpcx     Fujitsu CPU Performance Counter package (64-bit)
system      FJSVhea      Fujitsu SunOS Header Files
system      FJSVmdb      Fujitsu Platform Modular Debugger
system      FJSVmdbx     Fujitsu Platform Modular Debugger (64-bit)
system      FJSVvplr     Fujitsu platform links
system      FJSVvplu     Fujitsu usr/platform links
system      IPLTadcon    Administration Server Console
system      IPLTadman    Administration Server Documentation
system      IPLTadmin    Administration Server
system      IPLTcons     Console Client Base
system      IPLTdscon    Directory Server Console
system      IPLTdsman    Directory Server Documentation
system      IPLTdsr      Directory Server (root)
system      IPLTdsu      Directory Server (usr)
system      IPLTjss      Network Security Services for Java
system      IPLTnls      Nationalization Languages and Localization Support
system      IPLTnspr     Portable Runtime Interface
system      IPLTnss      Network Security Services
system      IPLTpldap    PerLDAP
system      NATEvplr     Nature Tech platform links
system      NATEvplu     Nature Tech usr/platform links
application NSCPcom      Netscape Communicator
system      SMEvplr      SME platform links
system      SMEvplu      SME usr/platform links
system      SUNW1251f    Russian 1251 fonts
system      SUNW1394h    Sun IEEE1394 Framework Header Files
system      SUNW1394x    Sun IEEE1394 Framework (64-bit)
ALE         SUNW5xmft    Traditional Chinese (BIG5) X Windows Platform minimum required Fonts Pa
ckage
system      SUNWGlib     GLIB - Library of useful routines for C programming
system      SUNWGtkr     GTK - The GIMP Toolkit (Root)
--More--
```

We can redirect this information to a list for review, because often the output is quite long. Redirecting the output can be extremely helpful, since it can help us create a list of installed packages to evaluate for removal, away from the console. We may also create a copy of this list and edit it to contain only the packages that we want to remove from the system. This type of list is useful if we want to write a script that invokes *pkgrm* to remove the packages.

Though the base of an end-user installation is relatively small, there is room for improvement. Obviously, a DMZ server is not going to require a plethora of language-compatibility packages to provide functionality. We can evaluate eliminating these to support only the language or languages used within our region. In addition, other compatibility packages, such as the packages for NFS, and the audio packages can also likely be removed.

Another suite of software packages to consider removing is the graphical desktop software itself. This comes in the form of Common Desktop Environment (CDE) and OpenWindows software on the Solaris platform. These software suites often contain numerous programs that execute with elevated privileges and have been notoriously "buggy" in the past. Unless required by other third-party applications that will be used on the system, such as firewall software, these suites should also be removed.

Upon removing all packages not required for the stable operation of the system, we should reboot the host and move on to disabling the unnecessary services and processes.

Disabling Services and Processes

The next most important part of hardening a system is the disabling of unnecessary services and processes. The majority of unneeded services and processes should have been eliminated in the software removal phase. We discussed this during the design phase—creating a model of the system and knowing what to expect in terms of default services and processes. However, in spite of our best efforts to eliminate the majority of unneeded software, some issues could still linger.

As we demonstrated in the section "Putting the Puzzle Together," we need to audit the system process table and network sockets table to identify any remaining pieces that might be disabled. The previously mentioned reference documentation, "Back to the Basics: Solaris and inetd.conf" and "Back to the Basics: Solaris and init.d," might also be of benefit during this stage as aids in locating the origins of these services and processes.

Once the service or process is disabled, it might also be beneficial to modify the permissions of the program. Though this step might seem paranoid, we must consider that if a configuration error is ever made, whether out of innocence or malice, preventing the program itself from executing might be a failsafe that prevents a possible attack. It could seem rational to remove the program entirely, although this practice is not recommended due to the possibility of needing the program in some odd future circumstance. With the program in place, to enable it again we merely change the permissions. If it is removed, we must reinstall the program, which could create additional work, requiring reinstall of the program, the application of any required patches, and the modification of the host intrusion detection system.

Once we've completed this step in the hardening process, we might consider implementing the host intrusion detection software, testing the host, and putting it in production, or we could consider additional configuration variables to further protect the host. This is as much a matter of preference as it is time constraints. Let's look in the next section at some miscellaneous configuration variables that could further enhance host security.

Miscellaneous Configuration Variables

A few additional configuration variables could also help enhance host security. Although not critical in nature to protecting the integrity of our DMZ server, they might be helpful in making the system more resistant to attack. These configuration variables might or might not be helpful in each particular configuration, depending on the system requirements. In some cases, these configuration variables might be possible, though in some configurations they could have a negative impact on performance or might not be possible due to software requirements.

The nonexecutable stack setting could be helpful in some configurations. The variable is designed to prevent the execution of code placed in stack memory on a system. In the stack-overflow problem that is commonly reported in various programs, this can prevent an attacker from exploiting the problem to execute arbitrary code, potentially resulting in privilege elevation. On the plus side, this is useful to some extent because it eliminates the ability to take advantage of a subsection of a class of vulnerabilities. On the negative side, it could break software depending on executable stacks, and it does not insulate the system against other types of overflows such as those occurring on the heap or other vulnerabilities such as format string and input validation bugs. A nonexecutable stack can be enabled by placing the following entry in the /etc/system file:

```
set noexec_user_stack=1
```

Systems that have enabled this configuration send a segmentation violation signal (*SIGSEGV*) to programs that attempt to execute code on the stack. This activity is logged by the system log daemon, the log entry containing the name of the program the *SIGSEGV* occurred in, the process ID of the program this occurred in, and the user ID of the system user executing the program. This information could be useful debugging information if the variable is set on a system with software requiring an executable stack. The logging of attempts to execute code on the stack can also be disabled, if desired. It should also be noted that, in some circumstances, it might be possible to bypass this protection.

Another configuration variable that can make a host more resistant to attack is TCP connection request queue size. Solaris implements two queues for handling TCP traffic: the connection request queue and the established connection queue. The separation of the two queues is designed to make a system continuously available to systems that are already connected when a SYN flood occurs while independently handling the deluge of TCP SYN requests in another. In the event that the DMZ server is ever attacked via a SYN flood, the second queue may help the system continue to function, keeping established connections separated and functioning until they are terminated.

The default size of the TCP connection request queue is 1024 connections, although this can be modified from a minimum of one connection to a maximum of 4,294,967,296 connections. To modify the parameter, use the following configuration of the *ndd(1M)* command:

```
ndd -set /dev/tcp tcp_conn_req_max_q0 <number>
```

Here, *<number>* represents the maximum number of requests to keep in the connection request queue table. It is possible to insert this command into an initialization file to automatically set this variable in the later stages of system bootstrap.

Another configuration variable worthy of investigation is the *KEYBOARD_ABORT* parameter. This variable allows you to disable the keyboard abort key sequence (also known as *Stop-A*) from the operating system level. Setting this variable will not prevent a user from pressing **Stop + A** during a certain window of the system boot process. However, when the system has fully booted, this variable will prevent a user from pressing **Stop + A** to enter the EEPROM.

To set this variable, follow this procedure: In the /etc/default/kbd file, use a text editor to monitor the following parameter:

```
#KEYBOARD_ABORT=enable
```

This will reflect the following configuration:

```
KEYBOARD_ABORT=disable
```

One final area of configuration we discuss is that of the OpenBoot parameters. OpenBoot is the firmware used in EEPROM of Sun systems. For the most part, OpenBoot is used only to boot the operating system and to ensure the correct handling of some hardware during boot, but it also has features that can make the system more resistant to attack. These features are the security mode and the security password.

The *security-mode* parameter can be set to disable the modifying of OpenBoot parameters without a password. Additionally, *security-mode* can be set to prevent the system from being booted without knowledge of the OpenBoot password. The most ideal configuration is to use the latter type of configuration, although one must evaluate business requirements before instituting this change.

To configure the OpenBoot software to require a password to boot the system, make the following configuration changes. From the OpenBoot command line, execute the following command to enable password protection:

```
setenv security-mode full
```

This command should be followed with the setting of the OpenBoot password. This can be done with the following command, issued on the OpenBoot command line:

```
setenv security-password <newpassword>
```

Here *<newpassword>* is representative of the desired password for OpenBoot.

To enable only password protection on EEPROM configuration changes, use the word *command* in place of the word *full*. These parameters can also be manipulated from the command line using the *eeprom* command on a running Solaris system. Be careful in applying this security mode. If you forget the password, you will not be able to modify the OpenBoot environment, should the system require maintenance.

Now that we have discussed manual hardening techniques, let's discuss a few of the tools available to do the job for us.

Automated System Hardening

Essentially, automated system hardening involves using a prewritten tool to perform many if not most of the activities we have just discussed. In the section on auditing file permissions, we discussed a few of the more basic tools, including COPS, YASSP, and FixModes. In this section, we mention a couple more and discuss the use of such tools.

All system hardening tools essentially work the same way. They are downloaded and placed on the system that is being hardened, they're unpacked, and if necessary, the source code is written in whatever language is compiled into an executable. Most require some configuration information prior to execution, which can come in the form of a flat text file; others might prompt the user for this information when the program is executed.

Most of these tools are scripts and are interpreted by some shell such as Bourne Shell, Korn Shell, or Perl. Tools that require compilation are typically written in C; therefore, a C compiler such as the GNU C Compiler might be needed. It should be noted that a C compiler it not installed with Solaris, and any C compiler installed on Solaris systems should minimally be installed with restrictive permissions, such as root read/write/execute only.

Let's look at one such hardening toolkit from Sun.

Solaris Security Toolkit

The SST is the Solaris Security Toolkit, also known as the Jumpstart Architecture Security Scripts (JASS). It is available from the Sun Blueprints portion of Sun Microsystems and owes much of its heritage to Alex Noordergraaf, Glenn Burnette, and Keith Watson. You can download it directly from the Sun Blueprints program.

SST is a highly configurable, extensive, flexible tool. It can be run as part of a Jumpstart configuration, where a Solaris system is installed via the network from another Solaris system, or it can be used in a standalone configuration. It adds other security software to the system, such as OpenSSH, when used in the recommended configuration.

After you download and install the SST version 4.2 (available at www.sun.com/download/products.xml?id=42e6becd), you need to execute the following command:

```
# ./jass-execute -h
```

The command executes the *jass* script in standalone mode. You may also execute the following command to harden the Solaris server with the specific driver:

```
# ./jass-execute -h -d secure.driver
```

TIP

You can find the SST documentation at www.sun.com/products-n-solutions/hardware/docs/Software/enterprise_computing/systems_management/sst/index.html.

When you execute this script, it performs specific hardening procedures, including removing or disabling packages and process. If you face any problems after the hardening process, you can reverse the same. To reverse the system changes, execute the following command:

```
# ./jass-execute -u
```

> ## !WARNING
>
> Needless to say, you should understand these processes thoroughly before you perform hardening. Ensure that appropriate backups are available for a quick system restore. Never try these procedures on live production servers. You could get unexpected results, including an unbootable Solaris server, when the some critical packages that are required by other applications are removed by either manual or automatic hardening. It is not recommended to run any other application or services on a DMZ or a firewall server. However, in certain cases (for example, integrating RSA token-based authentication, which requires some agent files be placed directly on the firewall server), you might have to run other applications from the firewall server. Use of appropriate version of Sun Solaris, Check Point firewall modules, patches recommended by Check Point, and patches and fixes released by Sun is recommended. Always do one change at a time and follow change management procedures.

When we have completed the hardening process, we still have two issues that should be addressed. After modifications to the system are complete, we must install, configure, and put into production the host-based intrusion detection system (HIDS). This step should be performed at the very end of the hardening process, since any changes to the system will cause the system to generate an alert. Once we've finished this step, we should conduct performance and stability testing. This can be done with the Sun Validation Test Suite (SunVTS), of which more information is available at http://docs.sun.com.

For more hardening tips specific to Check Point installation, refer to www.checkpoint.com/techsupport/documentation/FW-1_VPN-1_performance.html#solaris.

Designing & Planning…

Host-Based Intrusion Detection System Maintenance

HIDS require periodic maintenance. This is one of the burdens of monitoring the base of installed software on a system.

Continued

You might need to periodically regenerate the checksum database from which the IDS conducts its checks. This might be required when patches have been applied to the system, because the checksums of some monitored programs will likely change. This could also occur in the instance of software installation, removal, or configuration changes in some files.

Hardening Checklists for DMZ Servers and Solaris

Use this checklist as a starting point when hardening your Solaris DMZ servers:

- Has a model or diagram of the host been made?
- Is the host physically secured?
- Has the host been kept segregated from all networks?
- Have all the recommended patches been applied?
- Has increased logging of system activity been implemented?
- Are data backups secure from physical access?
- Are data backups secure from being overwritten?
- Have all remote administration utilities been sufficiently secured?
- Has all unnecessary software been removed?
- Has the system been hardened manually or by using an automated tool?
- Have all unnecessary services been disabled?
- Have all unnecessary processes been disabled?
- Has host security been layered using:
    - Role-based access control?
    - Granular file access control lists?
    - Restrictive environments?
- Have any additional security-enhancing system variables been set?
- Has the firewall rule policy been implemented for the host?
- Has the HIDS been installed?

Summary

In this chapter, we discussed the use of DMZ servers and Solaris. We began our discussion with the new features of Sun Solaris 10 followed by details of the placement of DMZ servers. We examined a Solaris DMZ server implemented as a host directly behind the router, a host attached to a switch behind the router, and a cluster configuration attached to a switch behind the router. We came to the conclusion that configuration is only part of the equation.

In our discussion of firewall rules, we examined rulesets for both the public and private networks. We asserted that our private network should deny all traffic except for access to services required for business needs. Our public network configuration gave us enhanced security by allowing only traffic to the specified services required by both internal and external users.

We shifted our discussion from network use of Solaris as a DMZ system to building a Solaris DMZ system. We began with a discussion of selecting the right hardware to do the job and acquiring a minimum of three network interfaces to perform the job. We also discussed the benefits of using quad Ethernet cards.

Our hardware discussion was followed by an examination of software selection. We stated the fact that additional software would be required to provide DMZ services with a Solaris system, and we briefly mentioned two software packages, Check Point FireWall-1 and IP Filter firewall. This discussion was followed with another about selecting high-availability software to keep a DMZ system available at all times. We examined the options of FireWall-1, Veritas Cluster Server, and Sun Cluster. We advised against the dangerous tendency to place additional network services on the DMZ server and thus put the integrity of the server at risk.

Configuration design was the subject of our next discussion, in which we examined several of the software configuration factors to consider in building a secure design. We examined disk layout, with an emphasis placed on creating a maximum amount of space for log files. We also looked at increasing log verbosity and the reasons to do so, such as acquiring legally admissible evidence. Considerations for backup and using media that is append-only were also noted as desirable.

Regarding configuration design, we also discussed putting the puzzle together by creating a test implementation of the software. This was done to give us an idea of what to expect in a default configuration, from which additional design decisions could be made. We also discussed the importance of using multiple layers of security, including file access control lists, RBAC, restricted shells, and restrictive environments. The necessity of auditing and checking the permissions of programs that execute with privileges and automated programs such as COPS, YASSP, and FixModes that do this job for us also was outlined.

The discussion of system design ended with building a system model. From our model, we were able to make decisions about what services we would require, what services and processes should be disabled, and what security precautions should be taken to protect the host. Our design created a culmination of all the secure system details we had previously discussed.

Implementation was the next topic we examined. Our implementation phase detailed general guidelines to use to preserve the integrity of a host. This included verifying the integrity of media using cryptography, ensuring physical security of the host so as not to allow unauthorized individuals access to the system, and securing the network side of the host by not connecting it to network resources until the implementation is complete. In addition, we noted that patch applications should be the final part of implementation that occurs prior to the hardening process.

We ended the chapter with an examination of the hardening process from both the manual and automated points of view. Of the manual hardening process, we discussed steps such as the removal of unnecessary software, disabling of unnecessary services and processes, and manipulation of miscellaneous configuration variables to enhance host security. We addressed the automated hardening process from the perspective of available tools to perform the job for us, including ASET and SST. We completed our implementation by installing host-based intrusion detection software and a performance-testing software package available for the host.

Solutions Fast Track

Placement of Servers

- ☑ DMZ servers should be placed behind network routers.

- ☑ An ideal DMZ server configuration is placing a switch between the network router and the DMZ server.

- ☑ High-availability configurations require the ability to connect multiple systems to the same network segments.

- ☑ High availability (simple Active/Passive configuration) or clustering (Active/Active) configurations require proper physical cabling and connectivity.

Firewall Ruleset

- ☑ The firewall ruleset is as important as the proper design and configuration of the networks serviced by the DMZ.

- ☑ Private networks should prohibit all network traffic by default and permit outbound access to systems that service business needs, such as Web proxy servers, mail servers, and domain name servers.

- ☑ Public networks should provide access to the required services while not allowing users to deviate connections to reaching unauthorized ports on systems in the DMZ.

System Design

- ☑ Hardware for the job should be evaluated for its expandability, and the proper hardware for the job such as quad Ethernet cards should be used.

- ☑ The proper software for the job, including firewall and high-availability packages, should be selected to provide stable, reliable performance with minimal impact in the case of a server failure.

- ☑ It is wise to create a test installation of a system to evaluate its default state prior to implementing the design.

- ☑ A model should be created of the system design that will serve as a reference during implementation.

Implementation: The Quick and Dirty Details

- ☑ The system should be implemented with the express concern of preserving host integrity. This involves checking media integrity, ensuring physical security of the host, ensuring network security of the host, and applying the recommended patch cluster.

- ☑ The system should be hardened to make it resistant to attacks. This involves either manually manipulating the operating system to create an attack-resistant configuration or using an automated tool to do the job.

- ☑ Host-based intrusion detection software should be installed on the system after hardening.

Hardening Checklist for DMZ Servers and Solaris

- ☑ All services not specifically required for operation of the DMZ server should be disabled. This involves auditing the inetd.conf file as well as the initialization script.

- ☑ All processes not specifically required for system operation should be disabled. This limits exposure to potential attack and lightens the load on system resources.

- ☑ Additional configuration variables that are not mandatory but might be helpful in providing a more secure configuration should be evaluated. These include nonexecutable stacks and EEPROM passwords.

- ☑ Ensure any script that claims to perform automatic hardening has a clear documentation and reversing procedures.

Frequently Asked Questions

The following Frequently Asked Questions, answered by the authors of this book, are designed to both measure your understanding of the concepts presented in this chapter and to assist you with real-life implementation of these concepts. To have your questions about this chapter answered by the author, browse to **www.syngress.com/solutions** and click on the **"Ask the Author"** form.

Q: Can multiple DMZ servers exist behind one router?

A: Absolutely. One of the best reasons for putting a switch behind a router is to allow for growth and distributing of DMZ services to other networks that might be implemented to distribute the load.

Q: Why should all incoming and outgoing network traffic be prohibited by default on the private network?

A: The private network typically contains desktop systems, which often have sensitive information stored on them. Prohibiting traffic into and out of the network prevents the propagation of some types of worms, such as those that use their own SMTP engines, and prevents remote access in the event that a desktop system is compromised via a back door.

Q: Should I implement an IDS or an IPS?

A: Use of IDS in an enterprise network is getting outdated. Consider intrusion prevention system (IPS) that can offer more security compared to IDS, including application layer protection and proactive defense in the absence of timely updates and fixes for unknown attacks.

Q: Why is host security focused on at the design stage rather than at the implementation stage?

A: Making security the basis of design makes the system implementer less apt to miss details such as increasing auditing, host-based intrusion detection, and fixing file permissions. Acknowledging these requirements early in design and reviewing them before implementing also gives the implementer a chance to plug any holes in design that he or she notices.

Q: Why is the name server for the private network on the public segment?

A: Some domain name service packages are a double-barrel shotgun of vulnerability. In one barrel, there is the ammunition of protocol problems in DNS that could lead to it being exploited to deny service or incorrectly resolve domains for users. In the other barrel, there are the consistent problems of remotely exploitable vulnerabilities that gain the attacker access to the host as the name service daemon user; typically root. It is better to place the server in a location in which, if it is compromised, it can only reach certain public systems, rather than it having free reign of the private network.

Q: I have securely implemented a test server during the design phase and would like to implement it into production. Should I do this?

A: If the integrity of the host can be trusted beyond the shadow of a doubt, why not?

Q: I was told never to install a C compiler on a sensitive system, especially one that services the network. Why is it mentioned in this chapter?

A: The belief that a system is more prone to compromise because a C compiler is installed on the host is a myth. First, an abundance of cheap SPARC hardware is floating around that an attacker could acquire to precompile exploit tools. Second, sufficient access controls on the system will prevent an attacker with regular user privileges from executing the C compiler. Third and finally, it is possible to do many if not most of the same things done with a compiler with interpreters such as Perl.

Q: How important is hardening on a firewall or a DMZ server?

A: It is essential to optimize the system by running only those services that are required, therefore increasing the performance and reducing the security risks arising out of commonly deployed (but unused) services. Start from minimal packages and add packages to the server as and when required.

## Chapter 4

Wireless DMZs

Solutions in this chapter:

- **The Need for Wireless DMZs**
- **Designing the Wireless DMZ**
- **Wireless DMZ Examples**
- **Wireless LAN Security Best-Practices Checklist**

☑ **Summary**

☑ **Solutions Fast Track**

☑ **Frequently Asked Questions**

Introduction

The Internet is in the air. Some cities, such as Philadelphia, have municipal WiFi; many coffeehouses such as Starbucks and bookstores such as Barnes and Noble have wireless Internet services for their clientele. McDonald's restaurants provide WiFi hotspots with the Wayport service, and Boingo is another popular WiFi service provider. Wireless networks are everywhere, and their numbers continue to increase every day. If you are curious about the number of wireless LANs (WLANs) in your neighborhood or around your town, it is a simple matter to download some wardriving software and drive around with your laptop and a WiFi network card. If you have never done this, you might be surprised at the number of wireless access points (APs) that you find. You might also be surprised to find how many are wide open, with no encryption and perhaps even the default configuration just as the AP came out of the box. Of course, this book is geared toward the enterprise, but it is important to acknowledge the world of WLANs and their various roles in the different areas.

Many people feel as though a WLAN is, by its very nature, insecure. This is not necessarily the case, since many tools are available to help administrators secure their wireless networks. Of course, administrators need to understand the risks inherent with running a network over airwaves, and therefore they must be familiar with the options available for security. The same tools are available for wired LANs, such as switches, routers, and firewalls, and then there are the tools designed to protect the transmissions themselves, such as WPA/WPA2 encryption and EAP/802.1x authentication. With proper care, administrators can securely deploy WLANs inside their private networks and safely allow employees to utilize this business critical resource while they are mobile around the office. WLANs make it possible for employees to take their laptops into the break room, conference room, or down the hall to work with a colleague as well as allowing organizations such as hospitals to have mobile Internet equipment for doctors and nurses.

Regardless of how you want to implement your WLAN, you need to be familiar with the tools at your disposal for securing, monitoring, and managing your network. We discuss a number of these tools throughout this chapter and provide you with some food for thought on how you can deploy your network.

The Need for Wireless DMZs

Since WLANs can be made secure for the internal, private network, why then should we be concerned with separating the WLAN into its own DMZ? Well, typically a DMZ is a network designed to give the public access to specific internal resources, and you might want to do the same thing for guests visiting your organization without compromising the integrity of your internal resources. In other words, you might want to have your WLAN open to the public so that they too can use the Internet while sitting in your lobby, sleeping in your hotel, or dining in your restaurant. The Internet is so woven into everyday life that patrons to your organization will look favorably on you if they can come to your location and access the Internet with ease.

NOTE

You will learn how to configure and implement a wireless DMZ in Chapter 5.

It is necessary to understand why it's important to secure your WLAN. The WLAN is subject to the same network attacks to which any wired network could be vulnerable. However, there are some attacks that are specific to a wireless network that would not be possible if it weren't broadcast through the air. These will help clarify why you don't want to leave an open access point (a.k.a. a rogue access point) lying around your internal private network.

In general, attacks on wireless networks fall into four basic categories:

- Passive attacks

- Active attacks

- Man-in-the-middle attacks

- Jamming attacks

In the next sections, we examine these four categories in some detail to help you get an idea of what can go wrong with a WLAN.

Passive Attacks on Wireless Networks

A *passive attack* occurs when someone listens to or eavesdrops on network traffic. Armed with a wireless network adapter that supports promiscuous mode and the right software, an eavesdropper can capture network traffic for analysis. When the network interface card (NIC) is in promiscuous mode, every packet that goes past the interface is captured and displayed within the application window. Many tools are available that can sniff the wireless network, completely unbeknown to the administrator. One of the more common wireless sniffers is AiroPeek, from WildPackets (www.wildpackets.com).

A passive attack on a wireless network might not be malicious in nature. In fact, many in the wardriving community claim that their wardriving activities are benign or "educational" in nature. To function, wireless network cards need to scan and detect wireless networks, so it's even possible for someone to be driving around using their laptop and not even be aware of the fact that their network card is scanning and possibly even connecting to open access points as they go. Wireless communication takes place on unlicensed public frequencies that anyone can use. This makes protecting a wireless network from passive attacks more difficult. However, by its very definition, a passive attack might not be an attack at all but merely a reconnaissance mission—information gathering for a future attack.

Of course, the information gathered could be severely limited if you configure encryption on your access point. There is certain network information that an attacker could still obtain, such as a Service Set Identifier (SSID), the channel you're using, MAC and IP addresses, and the type of encryption and cipher being used, but as long as you are using WPA/WPA2, the attacker isn't likely to gain any more information than that without attempting to crack your encryption key, which is no longer a passive activity. The supposed "passive attacker" is merely a bystander. The relative "passivity" of the interaction completely changes when there is criminal intent to either capture or change data on a network the user is not explicitly authorized to access.

Passive attacks are, by their very nature, difficult to detect. If an administrator is using Dynamic Host Configuration Protocol (DHCP) on the wireless network, he or she might notice that an unauthorized Media Access Control (MAC) address has acquired an IP address in the DHCP server logs. Then again, he or she might not. Perhaps the administrator notices a suspicious-looking car sporting an antenna out one of its windows.

NOTE

DHCP is not usually recommended on a WLAN because it makes it just that much easier for an attacker to gain access to your network. The idea is that if the attacker can get past the rest of your configured security mechanisms, having a DHCP lease offered to him or her is just the icing on the cake. It really makes no difference, however, because they can also determine the network address space in use by monitoring the management frames and the initial communications between the client and the AP. Then they can simply choose a static IP address to use instead.

If the car is parked on private property, the driver could be asked to move or possibly be charged with trespassing. However, the legal response may be severely limited, depending on the laws in your jurisdiction. In comparison, circumstances under which the wardriver is susceptible to being charged with a data-related crime depend entirely on the country or state in which the activity takes place.

Passive attacks on wireless networks are extremely common, almost to the point of being ubiquitous. Detecting and reporting on wireless networks has become a popular hobby for many wireless wardriving enthusiasts. In fact, this activity is so popular that a new term, *war plugging*, has emerged to describe the behavior of people who actually want to advertise both the availability of their access point (AP) and the services they offer by configuring their SSIDs with text such as "Get_food_here!"

Wardriving

There are many software packages publicly available for wardriving enthusiasts to choose from. One popular Windows-based program is NetStumbler. Some other popular programs that run on multiple operating systems are Kismet and Airsnort. For a list, visit www.wardrive.net/wardriving/tools. Most wardrivers are young and interested in finding free/open WiFi hotspots. Some may be looking for a challenge and want to try to crack WEP keys or WPA keys. You can easily thwart the casual wardriver simply by following the best security practices outlined in this chapter.

NOTE

Wardrivers often make their own Yagi-type (tubular or cylindrical) antenna. Instructions for doing so are easy to find on the Internet, and effective antennas have been made from such items as Pringles potato chip cans. Another type of antenna that can be easily homemade is the *dipole*, which is basically a piece of wire of a length that's a multiple of the wavelength, cut in the center and attached to a piece of cable that is connected to the wireless NIC.

Notes from the Underground...

Tools for Cracking WEP

Several software programs are readily available for cracking WEP by passively monitoring network transmissions. With one of these tools, it could take just 10 minutes of eavesdropping on a busy network to capture enough data to compute and recover WEP keys.

> Aircrack/Aircrack-ng
>
> AirSnort
>
> WEPCrack
>
> WEPlab
>
> KisMAC

WPA may be cracked as well if you have it configured with a passphrase only and that passphrase is susceptible to a brute-force attack. Therefore, it is recommended that you use the WPA-Enterprise with server certificates and authentication.

Sniffing

Originally conceived as a legitimate network and traffic analysis tool, sniffing remains one of the most effective techniques in attacking a wireless network, whether it's to map the network as part of a target reconnaissance, to grab passwords, or to capture unencrypted data.

Sniffing is the electronic form of eavesdropping on the communications that computers transmit across networks. In early networks, the equipment that connected machines allowed every machine on the network to see the traffic of all others. These devices, repeaters and hubs, were very successful at getting machines connected, but they allowed an attacker easy access to all traffic on the network because the attacker only needed to connect to one point to see the entire network's traffic.

Wireless networks function very similarly to the original repeaters and hubs. Every communication across the wireless network is viewable to anyone who happens to be listening to the network. In fact, the person who is listening does not even need to be associated with the network in order to sniff!

The hacker has many tools available to attack and monitor a wireless network. A few of these tools are AiroPeek for Windows, Ethereal (www.ethereal.com) for Windows, UNIX or Linux and TCPDump or ngrep (http://ngrep.sourceforg.net) in a UNIX or Linux environment. These tools work well for sniffing both wired and wireless networks.

Active Attacks on Wireless Networks

Once an attacker has gained sufficient information from the passive attack, he or she can then launch an active attack against the network. There are potentially a large number of active attacks that a hacker can launch against an open wireless network. For the most part, these attacks are identical to the kinds of active attacks that are encountered on wired networks. These include, but are not limited to, unauthorized access, spoofing, DoS, and flooding attacks as well as the introduction of *malware* (malicious software) and the theft of devices.

With the rise in popularity of wireless networks, new variations of traditional attacks specific to wireless networks have emerged, along with specific terms to describe them, such as *drive-by spamming,* in which a spammer sends out tens or hundreds of thousands of spam messages using a compromised wireless network.

Due to the nature of wireless networks and the weaknesses of WEP, unauthorized access and spoofing are the most common threats to wireless networks that use this insecure encryption method. Spoofing occurs when an attacker is able to use an unauthorized station to impersonate an authorized station on a wireless network. MAC addresses are sent in the clear on wireless networks, so it is also a relatively easy matter to discover authorized addresses if someone has implemented MAC filtering. It is also very simple to change the MAC address associated with your network card via the Windows registry or a Unix command.

Once the attacker has authenticated and associated with the wireless network, he or she can then run port scans, use special tools to dump user lists and passwords, impersonate users, connect to shares, and, in general, create havoc on the network through DoS and flooding attacks. These DoS attacks can be traditional in nature, such as a *ping flood, SYN, fragment,* or *DDoS* attacks, or they can be specific to wireless networks through the placement and use of *rogue access points* to prevent wireless traffic from being forwarded properly (similar to the practice of router spoofing on wired networks).

Spoofing (Interception) and Unauthorized Access

One definition of spoofing is an attacker's ability to trick the network equipment into thinking that the address from which a connection is coming is one of the valid and allowed machines from its network. There are several reasons that an attacker would spoof. If the network allows only valid interfaces through MAC or IP address filtering, an attacker would need to determine a valid MAC or IP address to be able to communicate on the network. Once that is accomplished, the attacker could then reprogram his interface with that information, allowing him to connect to the network by impersonating a valid machine.

IEEE 802.11 networks introduce a new form of spoofing: *authentication spoofing*. As described in their paper, *Intercepting Mobile Communications: The Insecurities of 802.11*, authors Borisov, Goldberg, and Wagner identified a way to utilize weaknesses within WEP and the authentication process to spoof authentication into a closed network. The process of authentication, as defined by IEEE 802.11, is very simple. In a shared-key configuration, the AP sends out a 128-byte random string in a cleartext message to the workstation that is attempting to authenticate. The workstation then encrypts the message with the shared key and returns the encrypted message to the AP. If the message matches what the AP is expecting, the workstation is authenticated onto the network and access is allowed.

As described in the paper, if an attacker has knowledge of both the original plaintext and ciphertext messages, it is possible to create a forged encrypted message. By sniffing the wireless network, an attacker is able to accumulate many authentication requests, each of which includes the original plaintext message and the returned ciphertext-encrypted reply. From this, the attacker can easily identify the keystream used to encrypt the response message. The attacker could then use it to forge an authentication message that the AP will accept as a proper authentication.

The ability to forge authentication onto a wireless network is a complex process. No off-the-shelf packages that provide these services are available. Attackers need to either create their own tools or take the time to use AirSnort or WEPCrack to decrypt the secret key.

Denial of Service and Flooding Attacks

The nature of wireless transmission, especially the use of spread-spectrum technology, makes a wireless network especially vulnerable to DoS attacks. The equipment needed to launch such an attack is freely available and very affordable. In fact, many homes and offices contain the equipment that is necessary to deny service to their wireless networks.

A DoS occurs when an attacker has engaged most of the resources a host or network has available, rendering that host or network unavailable to legitimate users. One of the original DoS attacks is known as a *ping flood*. A ping flood utilizes misconfigured equipment along with bad "features" within IP to cause a large number of hosts or devices to send an ICMP echo (ping) to a specified target. When the attack occurs, it tends to use a large portion of the resources of both the network connection and the host being attacked. This makes it very difficult for valid end users to access the host for normal business purposes.

In a wireless network, several events can cause a similar disruption of service. Probably the easiest way to trigger such an event is through a conflict within the wireless spectrum, caused by different devices attempting to use the same frequency. Many new wireless telephones use the same frequency as 802.11 networks. Through either intentional or unintentional uses of another device that uses the 2.4GHz frequency, a simple telephone call could prevent all wireless users from accessing the network.

Another possible attack would be through a massive number of invalid (or valid) authentication requests. If the AP is tied up with thousands of spoofed authentication attempts, authorized users attempting to authenticate themselves would have major difficulties in acquiring a valid session.

As demonstrated earlier, the attacker has many tools for hijacking network connections. If a hacker is able to spoof the machines of a wireless network into thinking that the attacker's machine is their default gateway, not only will the attacker be able to intercept all traffic destined for the wired network—he would also be able to prevent any of the wireless network machines from accessing the wired network. To do this, the hacker needs only to spoof the AP and not forward connections to the end destination, preventing all wireless users from performing valid wireless activities.

Not much effort is needed to create a wireless DoS. In fact, many users create these situations with the equipment found within their homes or offices. In a small apartment building, you could find several APs as well as many wireless telephones, all of which transmit on the same frequency. It would be easy for these users to inadvertently create DoS attacks on their own networks as well as on those of their neighbors.

A hacker who wants to launch a DoS attack against a network with a flood of authentication strings will in most cases not even need to be a highly skilled programmer. Many tools are available to create this type of attack, so even the most unskilled of black hats, the script kiddie, can launch one with little or no knowledge of how it works or why.

Many apartments and older office buildings do not come prewired for the high-tech networks in use today. To add to the problem, if many individuals are setting up their own wireless networks without coordinating the installations, many problems can occur that will be difficult to detect. For instance, only a limited number of frequencies are available to 802.11 networks. Considering these problems, it is not hard to imagine the following situation occurring.

Let's say that a person purchases a wireless AP and several network cards for his home network. When he gets home to his apartment and configures his network, he is extremely happy with how well wireless networking actually works. Then, suddenly, none of the machines on the wireless network are able to communicate. He phones the tech support line of the vendor that made the device. After waiting on hold for 45 minutes, he finds that his network has magically started working again, so he hangs up.

Later that week, the same problem occurs, except that this time he decides to wait on hold when he phones the vendor. While waiting, he goes onto his porch and begins discussing his frustration with his neighbor. During the conversation, his neighbor's kids come out and say that their wireless network is not working.

So they begin to do a few tests (while still waiting on hold, of course). First, the man's neighbor turns off his AP (which is usually off unless the kids are online, to "protect" their network). When this is done, the original person's wireless network starts working again. Then they turn on the neighbor's AP again and the first man's network stops working again.

At this point, a tech support rep finally answers, and the caller describes what has happened. The tech support representative has seen this situation several times and informs the user that he will need to change the frequency used in the device to another channel. He explains that the neighbor's network is utilizing the same channel, causing the two networks to conflict. Once the caller changes the frequency, everything starts working properly.

Man-in-the-Middle Attacks on Wireless Networks

Placing a rogue AP within range of wireless stations is a wireless-specific variation of a man-in-the-middle (MITM) attack. If the attacker knows the SSID the network is using (which, as we have seen, is easily discoverable) and the rogue AP has enough strength, wireless users might have no way of knowing that they are attempting to connect to an unauthorized AP.

Using a rogue AP, an attacker can gain valuable information about the wireless network, such as authentication requests, the secret key that is in use, and so on. Often, the attacker will set up a laptop with two wireless adapters, in which one card is used by the rogue AP and the other is used to forward requests through a wireless bridge to the legitimate AP. With a sufficiently strong antenna, the rogue AP does not have to be located in close proximity to the legitimate AP.

For example, the attacker can run the rogue AP from a car or van parked some distance away from the building. However, it is also common to set up hidden rogue APs (under desks, in closets, or the like) close to and within the same physical area as the legitimate AP. Because of their virtually undetectable nature, the only defense against rogue APs is vigilance through frequent site surveys (using tools such as AirDefense, AirWave, WaveLink and Cisco's SWAN), visual site inspections, and physical security.

Frequent site surveys also have the advantage of uncovering the unauthorized APs that company staff members might have set up in their own work areas, thereby compromising the entire network and completely undoing the hard work that went into securing the network in the first place. This is usually done with no malicious intent but for the convenience of the user, who might want to be able to connect to the network via his or her laptop in meeting rooms, break rooms, or other areas that don't have wired outlets. Even if your company does not use or plan to use a wireless network, you should consider doing regular wireless site surveys to see if someone has violated your company security policy by placing an unauthorized AP on the network, regardless of their intent.

Network Hijacking and Modification

Numerous techniques are available for an attacker to "hijack" a wireless network or session once they are associated with an AP. However, unlike some attacks, network and security administrators might be unable to tell the difference between the hijacker and a legitimate "passenger."

Many tools are available to the network hijacker. These tools are based on basic implementation issues within almost every network device available today. As TCP/IP traffic goes through switches, routers, and APs, each device looks at the destination IP address and compares it with the IP addresses it knows to be local. If the address is not in the table, the device hands the packet off to its default gateway.

This table is used to coordinate the IP address with the MAC addresses that are known to be local to the device. In many situations, this list is a dynamic one that is built up from traffic that is passing through the device and through Address Resolution Protocol (ARP) notifications from new devices joining the network. There is no authentication or verification that the request received by the device is valid. Thus a malicious user is able to send messages to routing devices and APs stating that his MAC address is associated with a known IP address. From then on, all traffic that goes through that router destined for the hijacked IP address will be handed off to the hacker's machine.

If the attacker spoofs as the default gateway or a specific host on the network, all machines trying to get to the network or the spoofed machine will connect to the attacker's machine instead of the gateway or host to which they intended to connect. If the attacker is clever, he will only use this machine to identify passwords and other necessary information, and he'll route the rest of the traffic to the intended recipients. If he does this, the end users will have no idea that this "man in the middle" has intercepted their communications and compromised their passwords and information.

Another clever attack can be accomplished through the use of rogue APs. If the attacker is able to put together an AP with enough strength, the end users might not be able to tell which AP is the authorized one that they should be using. In fact, most will not even know that another is available. Using this technique, the attacker is able to receive authentication requests and information from the end workstation regarding the secret key and where they are attempting to connect.

These rogue APs can also be used to attempt to break into a WEP-configured wireless AP. Utilizing tools such as AirSnort and WEPCrack requires a large amount of data to decrypt the secret key. A hacker sitting in a car in front of your house or office is noticeable and thus will generally not have enough time to finish acquiring sufficient information to break the key. However, if the attacker installs a tiny, easily hidden machine in an inconspicuous location, this machine could sit there long enough to break the key and possibly act as an external AP into the wireless network it has hacked.

Attackers who want to spoof more than their MAC addresses have several tools available. Most of these tools are for use in a UNIX environment and can be found through a simple search for *ARP spoof* at http://packetstormsecurity.org. With these tools, the hacker can easily trick all machines on the wireless network into thinking that the hacker's machine is another machine on the network. Through simple sniffing on the network, an attacker can determine which machines are in high use by the workstations on the network. If the attacker then spoofs the address of one of these machines, the attacker might be able to intercept much of the legitimate traffic on the network.

AirSnort and WEPCrack are freely available. It would take additional resources to build a rogue AP, but these tools will run from any Linux machine. Once an attacker has identified a network for attack and has become a valid member of the network, he or she can gain further information that is not available through simple sniffing.

By simply ARP spoofing the connection with the AP to be that of the host from which he or she wants to steal the passwords, the attacker can cause all wireless users who are attempting to SSH into the host to connect to the rogue machine instead. When these users attempt to sign on with their passwords, the attacker is then able to, first, receive their passwords, and second, pass on the connection to the real end destination. If the attacker does not perform the second step, it will increase the likelihood that the attack will be noticed, because users will begin to complain that they are unable to connect to the host.

Jamming Attacks

The last type of attack is the *jamming attack*. This is a fairly simple attack to pull off and can be done using readily available, off-the-shelf radio frequency (RF) testing tools (although they were not necessarily designed to perform this function). Whereas hackers who want to get information from your network would use other passive and active types of attacks to accomplish their goals, attackers who just want to disrupt your network communications or even shut down a wireless network can jam you without ever being seen. The process of jamming a wireless LAN is similar in many ways to the way a DoS attack would target a network; the difference is that in the case of the wireless network, the attack can be carried out by one person with an overpowering RF signal. This attack can be carried out using any number of products, but the easiest way is with a high-powered RF signal generator, readily available from various vendors.

A jamming attack is sometimes the most difficult type of attack to prevent, because the attacker does not need to gain access to your network. He or she can sit in your parking lot or even further away, depending on the power output of their jamming device. You might be able to readily determine the fact that you are being jammed, but you could find yourself hard-pressed to solve the problem. Indications of a jamming attack include clients' sudden inability to connect to APs where there was previously no problem.

The problem will be evident across all or most of your clients (the ones within the range of the RF jamming device), even though your APs are operating properly. Jamming attacks are sometimes used as the prelude to further attacks. One possible example includes jamming the wireless network, thereby forcing clients to lose their connections with authorized APs. In this time, one or more rogue APs can be made available operating at a higher power than the authorized APs. In some cases RF jamming is not always intentional and could be the result of other, nonhostile sources, such as a nearby communications tower or another WLAN that is operating in the same frequency range. Baby monitors, cordless telephones, microwave ovens, and many other consumer products can also be sources of interference.

You can take some comfort in knowing that although a jamming attack is easy and inexpensive to pull off, it is not the preferred means of attack. For most hackers, the only real victory with a jamming attack is temporarily taking your wireless network offline.

Designing the Wireless DMZ

You've decided that you want to provide a public WiFi network. What do you need to accomplish this goal? If you want to provide Internet access to guests, you might need just an access point (AP) and an Internet router. If you want the wireless DMZ to share the same Internet connection with the rest of your organization, however, you might want to install a firewall or tie them into a new network interface of an existing firewall. An IDP device and a bandwidth management solution is also a good idea, to ensure that the wireless network is not capable of bringing down your Internet connection. If you need to secure the wireless DMZ, you will also need an authentication server.

Placement of Wireless Equipment

Whether you are putting in one wireless access point (WAP) or covering a large campus, you need to be aware of the limitations of the 2.4GHz frequencies. A wall can block your signal or interference from other 2.4GHz devices, such as cordless phones and microwaves, or other access points might cause too much noise and effectively cancel out your signal. If you are more concerned about ensuring that others cannot attempt to snoop or hijack your WLAN, you might want to consider attempting to block the frequency with electromagnetic shielding. Therefore, where you place wireless equipment will depend on your requirements and the area you want to be available for your WLAN. You might want to conduct a site survey to determine the proper number of access points you need based on the expected number of users and your specific environment.

Access to DMZ Services

The process of configuring access to DMZ services is the same whether you are using a WLAN or a wired network. You should have a firewall in place, or at least a router with access control lists (ACLs), to monitor and control connections in the DMZ.

Authentication Considerations

When choosing authentication methods for your WLAN, you must first evaluate the security level you want to achieve and the hardware that you have at your disposal. Some older network cards and access points might not support the new WPA2 standard. If you want to deploy a wireless network as an open access point, you would not consider authentication. If, however, you need to provide a high level of security on your wireless LAN, you will want to ensure that you can support the latest authentication and encryption standard WPA2-Enterprise and utilize client-side certificates with smartcards, to have maximum security. If you fall somewhere in the middle, you have a number of options that are definitely secure enough for the typical network.

WEP

WEP is the basic security encryption mechanism that was provided in the original 802.11b specification from the Institute of Electrical and Electronics Engineers (IEEE). It is based on the RC4 stream cipher and is available in 64-bit and 128-bit implementations. WEP is weakened by the use of a 24-bit initialization vector (IV) that is reused in a short period of time, thus rendering WEP vulnerable to attack by several readily available cracking tools. In late 2002 the Wi-Fi alliance changed the requirements for becoming Wi-Fi certified to include Wi-Fi Protected Access (WPA).

EAP and 802.1x

Extensible Authentication Protocol (EAP) is defined in RFC 3748 (www.ietf.org/rfc/rfc3748.txt) as an authentication framework that supports multiple authentication methods. EAP is most commonly used with either Point-to-Point (PPP) or IEEE 802, where IP layer connectivity might not be available. WPA and WPA2 use EAP as the basis for their authentication mechanism. EAP can be used in either an enterprise mode, which utilizes a central authentication server (such as RADIUS), or a simplified mode using a preshared key.

802.1x is a subset of EAP that is defined as port-based authentication; it plays a major role in the IEEE 802.11i standard. Prior to authentication, only uncontrolled "ports" are open on the AP, in which only EAP traffic is allowed. Once a network client is authenticated, a controlled "port" is open and the client can access additional network resources.

EAP Authentication Methods

There are over 40 EAP methods to choose from, but here we will only talk about four of the best methods available to securely authenticate your users.

EAP-TLS

Transport Layer Security (TLS) is the most widely supported EAP method and was the first to be certified by the Wi-Fi alliance. EAP-TLS requires the use of a client-side certificate, which also makes it the most secure method available.

EAP-FAST

Flexible Authentication via Secure Tunneling (FAST) was developed by Cisco Systems to fix the weaknesses of Lightweight Extensible Authentication Protocol (LEAP). EAP-FAST uses something called a Protected Access Credential (PAC), which can be entered manually or dynamically in the first of three phases. A server certificate is optional but is recommended to increase security.

EAP-TTLS

EAP-Tunneled TLS (TTLS) offers good security through the use of Public Key Infrastructure (PKI) certificates on the server. This method of EAP is widely supported across platforms.

PEAPv0/PEAPv1

PEAPv0/EAP-MSCHAPv2 combines Protected EAP and Microsoft Challenge Handshake Authentication Protocol. It is the most common method of PEAP in use and is supported by Microsoft, Cisco, and other vendors and open source channels. PEAPv1/EAP-GTC, supported by Cisco, was designed to be an alternative to PEAPv0 and allowed the use of an inner authentication protocol other than Microsoft's MSCHAPv2.

WPA/WPA2

Wi-Fi Protected Access (WPA) came about in 2002 and was designed to be an intermediary, forward-compatible subset of standards based on 802.11i, which was in development by the IEEE. WPA uses a 48-bit IV and takes 802.1x authentication and EAP from the 802.11i standard and combines them with TKIP (pronounced "tee-kip"). TKIP resolves security issues found in WEP by providing per-packet key mixing, a message integrity check (MIC) called Michael, and a rekeying mechanism such that existing hardware could be utilized. In short, TKIP replaces WEP without requiring hardware replacement. WPA2 implements the full IEEE 802.11i standard (ratified in June 2004), but it might not work with some older network cards. The main difference between WPA and WPA2 is that the Michael algorithm was replaced by a message authentication code, Counter Mode with Cipher Block Chaining Message Authentication Code Protocol (CCMP), that is considered fully secure, and RC4 was replaced by AES. Microsoft Windows XP fully supported WPA2 as of May 2005. Driver upgrades for network cards may be required as well.

Companies deploying wireless networks with WPA/WPA2 should use the enterprise model with an 802.1x authentication server; however, there is a less secure Pre-Shared Key (PSK) method, which is much like WEP in that each user is given the same passphrase. Although WPA-PSK is less secure than WPA-Enterprise, it is still more secure than WEP alone. If a passphrase is used, the more characters (up to 63) used and the more random, the better the security protecting against brute-force attacks.

Wireless DMZ Components

Now it's time to discuss the physical components of your wireless DMZ, such as access points, network adapters, authentication servers, and wireless gateways. Figure 4.1 depicts a standard DMZ arrangement in which the firewall provides three interfaces: public, private, and DMZ.

Figure 4.1 One Example of a Typical DMZ Arrangement

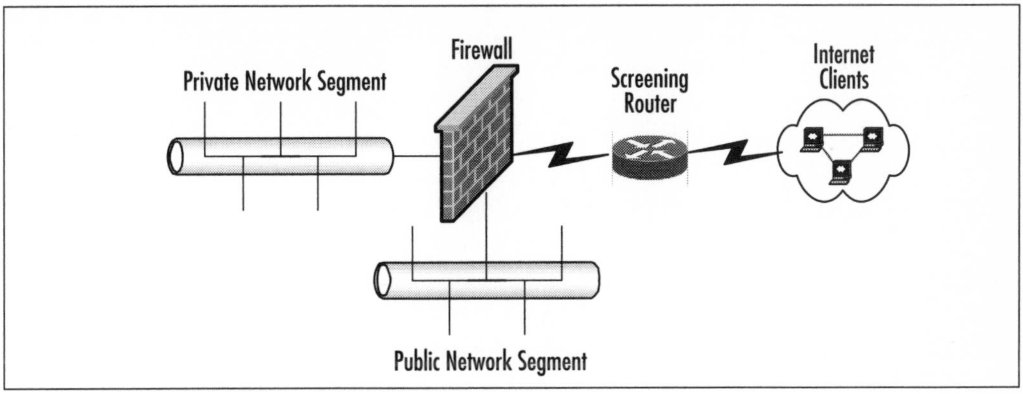

Access Points

In simple terms, an AP is a Layer 2 device that serves as an interface between the wireless network and the wired network. APs are the wireless networking equivalent of a standard Ethernet hub in that they allow multiple clients using the same network technology to access the core network, with a shared amount of bandwidth available to all clients. What sets the AP apart from its less advanced hub brethren is its ability to carry out many other additional functions—functions that will become important to creating your complete solution. Of course, it's no surprise that an AP is one of two items that forms the backbone of the WLAN. When it comes to choosing an AP, however, you have a multitude of choices, each presenting different benefits and costs. The AP you choose should be complementary to the wireless network adapter you choose—meaning that if you opt for a more powerful and advanced AP, you should consider acquiring and using network adapters that can take advantage of the often vendor-specific features provided in the AP.

Network Adapters

The second piece of the puzzle is the network adapter. This, again, should be no big surprise, since you require the proper wireless network adapter to make the connection to begin with. As with the AP, the type of network adapter you choose will determine the types of security solution you can implement.

For example, let's suppose that you decided to use a Cisco Aironet AP with Cisco's Aironet 802.11a/b/g Wireless CardBus network adapters and the Cisco Aironet Desktop Utility software on the client computers. Using this arrangement, you could increase your security by taking advantage of EAP-Flexible Authentication via Secure Tunneling (EAP-FAST), Cisco LEAP, EAP-Transport Layer Security (EAP-TLS), Protected Extensible Authentication Protocol-Generic Token Card (PEAP-GTC), or PEAP-Microsoft Challenge Handshake Authentication Protocol version 2 (PEAP-MSCHAPv2). In Chapter 5, we examine how this combination of hardware and solutions can be used to provide increased security.

Authentication Servers

Authentication servers tie in with the wireless DMZ solution by enabling the AP to authenticate clients that want to legitimately access the network. A Remote Authentication Dial-in User Service (RADIUS) server could be used to verify the identity of the wireless client that's attempting to connect. When a user first attempts to connect to an AP configured to use EAP, the AP hands the authorization over to the authentication server. After successful authentication, the AP opens the port and grants access to the client.

An authentication server can also participate in the 802.11i key management functions. After authenticating a client, the server then provides a unique master key to the client. From this key, a new key is generated and provided to the access point. From there, four more keys are generated, including the Temporal Key 1 and 2 (TK1/TK2), which will be the keys used to encrypt the communications.

Windows Authentication

Microsoft provides an Internet Authentication Service (IAS) server with RADIUS and proxy capabilities to centralize AAA for many types of network access, including wireless connections in Windows Server 2003. The authentication protocols IAS supports for use with wireless networks are:

- Extensible Authentication Protocol-Message Digest 5 CHAP (EAP-MD5 CHAP)
- EAP-Transport Layer Security (EAP-TLS)
- Protected EAP-MS-CHAP v2 (PEAPv0/EAP-MSCHAPv2)

RADIUS

Remote Authentication Dial-in User Service (RADIUS) servers provide network users what's known as AAA: authentication, authorization, and accounting. In short, RADIUS servers are used on the back end of the network to provide a flexible and scalable system to authenticate users attempting to access network services. Originally developed for dial-in access using modems, RADIUS has proven flexible and powerful enough to handle authentication of users through various other connection means, including those attempting to make wireless connections to your network.

When RADIUS servers are combined with 802.1x port-based access control on APs, users are effectively prevented from accessing the network past the AP until they have been authorized against the RADIUS database. EAP-FAST, for example, takes advantage of 802.1x port-based access controls to further increase the security of the wireless and wired network. The RADIUS server performs the critical task of verifying that the user is authorized to gain access to the network through either an internal (native) database or by using the domain database (Active Directory).

NOTE

RADIUS is defined in RFC 2865. The behavior of RADIUS with EAP authentication is defined in RFC 2869. RFC can be searched and viewed online at www.rfc-editor.org. 802.1x is defined by the IEEE in the document located at http://standards.ieee.org/getieee802/download/802.1X-2001.pdf.

Enterprise Wireless Gateways and Wireless Gateways

Driven by the uniquely special needs presented by WLANs and their security, the enterprise wireless gateway (EWG) was created to provide enhanced security and management. An EWG is a specially designed and built hardware device that performs several key functions in one unit:

- **Router** EWGs have at least two Ethernet interfaces, one for the wireless segment and at least one for the wired segment. Many also offer additional failover interfaces for the wired segment. An EWG can also make certain that packets traversing the network destined for other subnets get to their intended source.

- **Firewall** Many of the EWGs currently on the market offer firewall-like services by providing stateful inspection of all traffic passing through them.

- **VPN server** Most EWGs typically provide VPN support, allowing clients to create VPN connections to the EWG (and thus the wired segment). They support IPSec, L2TP, and PPTP as well as authentication for larger implementation.

The EWG is placed between the AP segment and the wired segment to control network access from the WLAN, as discussed in the next section. One example of an EWG is Bluesocket's WG-2000 Wireless Gateway, which is available with both copper or fiber gigabit interface cards and encrypted throughput between 150Mbps and 200Mbps.

Firewalls and Screening Routers

Firewalls and screening routers can still play a role in creating and implementing the WLAN DMZ. They provide the same protection and support that they would in a strictly wired network but are not enough by themselves to account for the various security concerns associated with the WLAN. This is due to the fact that firewalls and screening routers are devices primarily used for traffic filtering via user authentication. When used together with a well-crafted WLAN DMZ security solution, they still have a useful purpose. Cisco, Check Point, Netscreen, and ISA Server are all covered in later chapters of this book.

Other Segmentation Devices

Although not discussed here, there are several other segmentation devices that you should be aware of for use in controlling both traffic and access to your network. This list is presented here in the interests of making our discussion more complete. All these devices (and many more) can be used to segment portions of your network:

- SSH2 servers
- VPN servers
- Virtual LANs (VLANs)
- Layer 3 switches

Wireless DMZ Examples

Armed with a brief introduction to the pieces that make up the wireless DMZ, let's examine a few different scenarios that you could implement for your network.

Figure 4.2 shows an example arrangement that you could use to provide RADIUS authentication for wireless clients attempting to gain access to your network. In this example, both the wireless network adapter and the AP are Cisco products that support the use of WPA2. The process by which the client gains access to the network is outlined briefly here and explained in significantly more detail in Chapter 5:

1. The client computer requests to associate with the AP.

2. The AP, using 802.1x port access controls, blocks all access to the wired network segment.

3. The user performs EAP-FAST authentication to the RADIUS server using the required credentials. This process involves the RADIUS server and the client performing mutual authentication. After this is done, the RADIUS server dynamically generates a master key that will be used by the AP to generate the keys that will secure the connection.

4. The RADIUS server then delivers this dynamic key to the AP, which then generates four new keys with the client.

5. The client and the AP use the WPA2 keys to securely communicate, and the client is now associated with the AP. If required, a DHCP lease will be granted to the wireless client.

6. The client now securely accesses resources on the wired segment of the network.

Figure 4.2 Using RADIUS to Authenticate Users

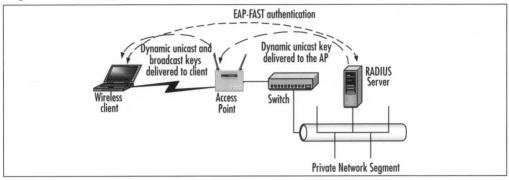

Figure 4.3 shows an example of how you might use a simple wireless gateway such as Bluesocket's WG-2000 to provide authentication and security through an IPSec VPN tunnel, if required. In this scenario, the wireless clients authenticate against the internal database of the WG-200 server, creating a VPN tunnel, if desired.

1. The client computer associates with the AP.

2. The wireless gateway (WG-2000) blocks access to the wired network pending successful user authentication against its internal database.

3. The user authenticates to the WG-2000 server.

4. If required, a DHCP lease will be granted to the wireless client.

5. If desired, a VPN tunnel is constructed to secure traffic.

6. The client now accesses resources on the wired segment of the network.

Figure 4.3 Using a Simple Wireless Gateway to Authenticate Users

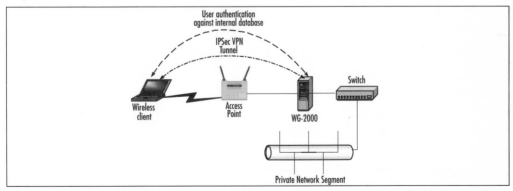

Figure 4.4 shows an overview of the way you might implement an EWG on your network, to provide security for the wireless segment. In this scenario, the wireless clients

authenticate against a RADIUS server with the added benefit of a VPN tunnel being constructed by the EWG to further secure the traffic.

1. The client computer associates with the AP.

2. The client computer creates a VPN tunnel with the EWG.

3. The user performs authentication to the RADIUS server using the required credentials. The EWG acts as an authenticator (a go-between for the client and the RADIUS server).

4. The RADIUS server and the client authenticate per the VPN protocol being used.

5. If required, a DHCP lease will be granted to the wireless client.

6. A VPN tunnel is constructed between the client and the EWG in which to securely pass traffic.

7. The client now securely accesses resources on the wired segment of the network.

Figure 4.4 Using an Enterprise Wireless Gateway to Control Access

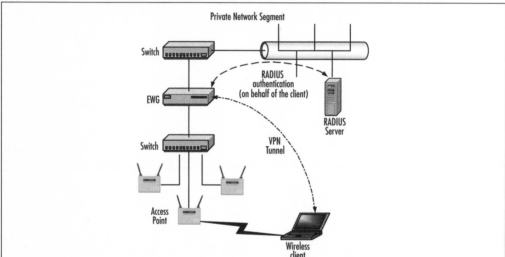

By now, you might be thinking that none of these solutions looks anything like a DMZ. That might be true, but appearances can be deceiving. Remember that the purpose of the DMZ is to keep unwanted (and potentially unsafe) traffic out of the protected internal network. All these solutions offer this capability by controlling access to your wireless network.

Wireless LAN Security Best-Practices Checklist

Although the primary focus here is the implementation of DMZ configurations, you can implement several other "best practices" to further increase the security of your WLAN design. In recent months, the practice of implementing wireless networks has become somewhat routine to many administrators. Unfortunately, there is nothing routine about any network design and implementation. Administrators who want to implement wireless networks should exercise due care and diligence by becoming as familiar as possible with operation and vulnerabilities of wireless networks and *all* the available counter-measures for defending them.

Even though many currently implemented wireless networks support a wide range of features that can potentially be enabled, the sad fact is that most administrators do not use them. The media is full of reports of the informal results of site surveys conducted by wardrivers. These reports provide worrisome information—for example, that most wireless networks are not using encryption and that many wireless networks are using default SSIDs, not to mention the advanced DMZ and VPN solutions we have briefly outlined here. Many of these networks are located in technology-rich areas, such as Silicon Valley, where you would think people would know better, making the information a source of serious concern.

There is really no excuse for failing to implement security features that are available on most wireless networks to minimize security threats. The following checklist is a summary of common best practices that could be employed on many current or future wireless networks:

- Perform a risk analysis of your network.

- Develop relevant and comprehensive security policies and implement them throughout your network.

- Carefully review the available security features of wireless devices to see if they fulfill your security requirements. The 802.11 and Wi-Fi standards specify only a subset of features that are available on a wide range of devices. Over and above these standards, supported features vary widely; this is where the DMZ or the VPN comes into play.

- Wireless vendors are continually addressing the security weaknesses of wireless networks. Check the wireless vendors' Web sites frequently for firmware updates and apply them to all wireless devices. You could leave your network exposed if you fail to update even one device with the most recent firmware.

- Always use WPA or WPA2 encryption.

- Always change the default administrative password used to manage the AP. The default passwords for wireless APs are well known. If possible, use a password generator to create a difficult and sufficiently complex password. Never use a word found in the dictionary.

www.syngress.com

- Change the default SSID of the AP. The default SSIDs for APs from various vendors are well known, such as *tsunami* and *Linksys* for Cisco and Linksys APs, respectively. A fairly inclusive listing of default SSIDs can be found at www.remote-exploit.org/index.php/Wlan_defaults.

- Do not put any kind of identifying information in the SSID, such as the company name, address, products, divisions, and so on. By doing so, you are either simply providing too much information and/or are advertising information that could make your network appear to be of sufficient interest to warrant further attacker effort.

- If possible, disable SSID broadcasts.

- Do not use shared-key authentication. Although it can protect your network against specific types of DoS attack, other kinds of DoS attacks are still possible. Shared-key authentication exposes your encryption keys to compromise.

- Learn how to use site survey tools and conduct frequent site surveys to detect the presence of rogue APs and to detect vulnerabilities in your own network.

- Don't place the AP near windows. Try to place it in the center of the building so that interference will hamper the efforts of wardrivers and others trying to detect your traffic. Ideally, your wireless signal would radiate only to the outside walls of the building and not beyond. Try to come as close to that ideal as possible. You might want to look at some references focusing on wireless network signal radiation patterns. For a start, see http://safari.awprofessional.com/1587051648/app02 and http://www.neugc.org/COMMON%20Corner%20Jan06.pdf.

- If possible, purchase an AP that allows you to reduce the size of the wireless zone (cell sizing) by changing the power output.

- Educate yourself in the operation and security of wireless networks.

- Educate your users about safe computing practices, in the context of using both wired and wireless networks.

Summary

Wireless LANs are attractive to many companies and home users because of the increased productivity that results from the convenience and flexibility of being able to connect to the network without the use of wires. WLANs are especially attractive when they can reduce costs by circumventing the need to install cabling to support users on the network. For these and other reasons, WLANs have become very popular. However, WLAN technology has often been implemented poorly and without due consideration given to network security. For the most part, these poor implementations result from a lack of understanding of the nature of wireless networks and the measures that can be taken to secure them.

WLANs that are not configured properly are inherently insecure due to the fact that they radiate radio signals containing network traffic that can be viewed and potentially compromised by anyone within range of the signal. With the proper antennas, the range of WLANs is much greater than is commonly assumed. Many administrators wrongly believe that their networks are secure; they think that the interference created by walls and other physical obstructions, combined with the relative low power of wireless devices, will contain the wireless signal sufficiently. Often, this is not the case.

The goal of the DMZ is to control traffic crossing the network segment and to prevent unauthorized traffic from entering the protected private network; this result is offered by implementing the solutions that were outlined in this chapter. The most important thing that you, as the network administrator, can do is to fully understand your organization's security requirements and implement those requirements by making numerous solutions available. We examine the actual configuration and implementation of some of these solutions in Chapter 5.

Solutions Fast Track

The Need for Wireless DMZs

☑ Attacks on wireless networks fall into four basic categories: passive attacks, active attacks, man-in-the-middle attacks, and jamming attacks.

☑ Examining the common threats to both wired and wireless networks provides a solid understanding in the basics of security principles and allows the network administrator to fully assess the risks associated with using wireless and other technologies.

☑ Threats can come from simple design issues, where multiple devices utilize the same setup, or intentional DoS attacks, which can result in the corruption or loss of data.

☑ Electronic eavesdropping, or sniffing, is passive and undetectable to intrusion detection devices.

☑ Tools that can be used to sniff networks are available for Windows (such as Ethereal and AiroPeek) and UNIX (such as TCPDump and ngrep).

☑ Sniffing traffic allows attackers to identify additional resources that can be compromised.

☑ Even encrypted networks have been shown to disclose vital information, such as the Service Set Identifier (SSID), the channel you're using, MAC addresses and IP addresses, and the type of encryption and cipher being used.

Designing the Wireless DMZ

☑ The ability to freely gain access to a wireless segment of a network and then subsequently gain access to the wired segment is what makes implementing the wireless DMZ different from implementing the typical wired network DMZ. Therefore, the issue of creating a form of DMZ for the WLAN actually begins with controlling access to that WLAN.

☑ Whereas wired DMZs typically use firewalls and routers, WDMZs require other network hardware components, such as APs, RADIUS servers, network adapters, and EWGs.

Wireless DMZ Examples

☑ WDMZ designs can come in many forms. They all must, however, provide the same basic function: authenticating users and controlling access to the WLAN.

☑ You can opt to use a RADIUS-based solution to perform network authentication and authorization.

☑ You can use proprietary solutions such as EAP-FAST to provide additional protection. VPNs can be used to further secure communications on wireless clients.

Wireless LAN Security Best-Practices Checklist

☑ Perform a risk analysis and implement standardized security policies for your wireless and wired networks.

☑ In addition to deploying a WLAN DMZ, there are several other things that you can do to add protection and increase security of your WLAN, such as placing your AP in a secure location, disabling SSID broadcasts, and using WPA2 encryption along with 802.1x port-based authentication.

☑ Security begins with education. You should gain a full understanding of the security threats your WLAN is subject to. You should then gain a full understanding of how your wireless network hardware components can be used to put together a robust security solution.

Frequently Asked Questions

The following Frequently Asked Questions, answered by the authors of this book, are designed to both measure your understanding of the concepts presented in this chapter and to assist you with real-life implementation of these concepts. To have your questions about this chapter answered by the author, browse to **www.syngress.com/solutions** and click on the **"Ask the Author"** form.

Q: Do I really need to understand the fundamentals of security in order to protect my network?

A: Yes. You might be able to utilize the configuration options available to you from your equipment provider without a full understanding of security fundamentals. However, without a solid background in how security is accomplished, you will never be able to protect your assets from the unknown threats to your network through misconfiguration, back doors provided by the vendor, or new exploits that have not been patched by your vendor.

Q: Given all the problems with wireless network security, wouldn't it be better to avoid using a wireless network in the first place?

A: Yes and no. How does the implementation of a properly secured wireless network impact your business model? Does this wireless network provide a useful function to your organization by allowing users to become more productive as they perform their assigned tasks? The decision to implement a wireless network is one that should not be taken lightly. Planning, just as with any network deployment, is the key to success. Don't simply put up a wireless network because it seems like a good idea; make sure that you have a clear-cut reason and plan of action before you get started. It's better to figure out how to secure your wireless network before you actually start installing it, thus preventing attackers from taking advantage of the easy pickings you have offered them.

Q: How can I protect my wireless network from eavesdropping by unauthorized individuals?

A: Certain eavesdropping is unavoidable unless you can contain your wireless network in a Faraday cage. The best method to secure your communications is by encrypting the traffic with WPA or WPA2. No encryption will expose all your data to cleartext inspection and WEP can be cracked too easily.

Q: I've heard time and again that WEP is insecure. What makes WEP so insecure?

A: WEP is insecure mainly because the 24-bit initialization vector (IV) is too short and because the same IV is reused.

Q: How can I prevent unauthorized users from authenticating and associating with my AP?

A: There are a number of ways to accomplish this goal. The best choice for enterprise networks is to enable WPA2 and 802.1x port access control such as that offered by EAP-FAST with a back-end authentication server.

Chapter 5

Implementing Wireless DMZs

Solutions in this chapter:

- **Implementing RADIUS With Cisco LEAP**

- **Installing and Configuring Juniper Steel-Belted RADIUS**

- **Implementing Windows Active Directory Domain Authentication With Cisco EAP and RADIUS**

- **Implementing PEAP**

☑ **Summary**

☑ **Solutions Fast Track**

☑ **Frequently Asked Questions**

Introduction

In Chapter 4, we examined the various reasons that your wireless network segment is not to be trusted in the same way that you would normally trust a wired network segment. In addition, we discussed the reasons that a wireless DMZ (WDMZ) is needed. We also looked at some basic WDMZ designs; we implement those designs in this chapter. (For a refresher on WDMZ fundamentals, please review Chapter 4.) With a wired DMZ, you are attempting to (for the most part) control the type of traffic going into and out of your network. This is not completely the case with WDMZ implementations. The number-one concern with WLANs is controlling access—who can get on the wireless network and how we can control that access.

The ways you can implement security on a wireless network are varied and limited only by imagination. As outlined in Chapter 4, measures taken to increase security are not limited to implementing DMZs or VPNs but also include many actions that could be characterized as good administrative practices. In the following sections, we examine some potential solutions that you might implement to provide the net effect of a DMZ for your WLAN.

These solutions are certainly not all inclusive—you can add to them as you see fit or even create your own solutions. To increase your network's security, you need to control access to wireless networks. You'll find a wide range of products in the market to achieve this goal.

This chapter looks at a couple of products in depth so that you can utilize them immediately within your WLAN infrastructure.

Implementing RADIUS With Cisco EAP

The use of Remote Authentication Dial In User Service (RADIUS) servers to authenticate network users is a longstanding practice. Using a RADIUS server dynamic per-user, per-session Wired Equivalency Privacy (WEP) keys, combined with initialization vector (IV) randomization, is widely in practice. Enter Cisco's proprietary offering, Lightweight Extensible Authentication Protocol (LEAP). Though proprietary, LEAP is offered by Funk (now Juniper Networks) as well.

LEAP is one of approximately 30 variations of the Extensible Authentication Protocol (EAP). Other variants include EAP-MD5, EAP-TLS, EAP-TTLS, and Protected Extensible Authentication Protocol (PEAP). EAP allows other security products (such as LEAP) to be used to provide additional security to Point-to-Point Protocol (PPP) links through the use of special Application Programming Interfaces (APIs) that are built into operating systems and, in the case of the Cisco Aironet hardware, hardware device firmware.

LEAP (also known as EAP-Cisco Wireless) uses dynamically generated WEP keys, 802.1x port access controls, and mutual authentication to overcome the problems inherent in WEP. The 802.1x protocol is an access control protocol that operates at the port level and sites between any authentication method (LEAP, in this case) and the rest of the network. The 802.1x protocol does not provide authentication to users; rather, it translates messages from the selected authentication method into the correct frame format being used on the network. In the case of our example, the correct frame format is 802.11, but 802.1x can also be used on 802.3 (Ethernet) and 802.5 (Token Ring) networks, to name a few. When you use 802.1x, the choice of the authentication method and key management method is controlled by the specific EAP authentication used (LEAP, in this case). The basic process by which a user gains access to the network when LEAP and 802.1x are in use is explained in Chapter 4.

NOTE

RADIUS is defined by Request for Comment (RFC) 2865. The behavior of RADIUS with EAP authentication is defined in RFC 2869. RFCs can be searched and viewed online at www.rfc-editor.org. The 802.1x protocol is defined by the Institute of Electrical and Electronics Engineers (IEEE) in the document located at http://standards.ieee.org/getieee802/download/802.1X-2001.pdf.

LEAP creates a per-user, per-session dynamic WEP key that is tied to the network logon, thereby addressing the limitations of static WEP keys. Since authentication is performed against a back-end RADIUS database, administrative overhead is minimal after initial installation and configuration.

EAP-FAST (Flexible Authentication via Secure Tunneling), dubbed LEAPv2, implements client/server security to encrypt transactions within a Transport Level Security (TLS) tunnel. Strong shared keys are used to establish tunnels. These keys are unique to users. These shared secrets are also known as Protected Access Credentials, or PACs. PACs can be distributed manually or automatically to client devices. Number of messages exchanged are fewer than a PKI-based deployment and thus faster. EAP-FAST is faster than other protocols.

LEAP Features

Through the use of dynamically generated WEP keys, LEAP enhances the basic security WEP provides by significantly decreasing the predictability to the user hoping to determine the WEP key through the use of a WEP key-cracking utility. In addition, the WEP keys that are generated can be tied to the specific user session and, if desired, to the network login as well. Through the use of Cisco (or other third-party components that support LEAP) hardware from end to end, you can provide a robust and scalable security solution that silently increases network security, not only by authenticating users but also by encrypting wireless network traffic without the use of a VPN tunnel. (You can, however, opt for the additional network overhead and implement a VPN tunnel as well to further secure the communications.)

Cisco LEAP provides the following security enhancements:

- **Mutual authentication** Mutual authentication is performed between the client and the RADIUS server. In addition, the AP and the RADIUS server perform mutual authentication. Using mutual authentication between the involved components prevents the introduction of both rogue APs and RADIUS servers. Furthermore, you provide a solid authentication method to control access to the wireless network segment (and thus the wired network behind it). All communications between the AP and the RADIUS servers is carried out using a secure channel, further reducing any possibility of eavesdropping or spoofing. LEAP does this by supporting dynamic derivation of session keys. It relies on a shared secret, logon password, and challenge response between the user and the RADIUS server.

- **Secure-key derivation** A preconfigured, shared-secret secure key is used to construct responses to mutual authentication challenges. It is put through an irreversible one-way hash that makes recovery or replay impossible and is useful for one time only at the start of the authentication process.

- **Dynamic WEP keys** Dynamic per-user, per-session WEP keys are created to easily allow administrators to quickly move away from statically configured WEP keys, thus significantly increasing security. The single largest security vulnerability of a properly secured wireless network (using standard 802.11b security measures) is the use of static WEP keys that are subject to discovery through special software such as WEPcrack and AirCrack. In addition, maintaining static WEP keys in an enterprise environment is administratively prohibitive. Using LEAP, the session-specific WEP keys that are created are unique to that specific user and are not used by any other user. In addition, the broadcast WEP key (which is statically configured in the AP) is encrypted using the session key before being delivered to the client. In 802.1x authentication, two WEP keys are used. To encrypt Unicast traffic, a per-user key is used. A broadcast key is used to encrypt broadcast and multicast traffic. This key is shared by all the clients associated with a specific AP. Since each session key is unique to the user and can be tied to a network login, LEAP also completely eliminates common vulnerabilities due to lost or stolen network adapters and devices. In a static WEP key scenario, imagine that an employee of your company lost his wireless adapter; anybody can pick up the hardware and get access to your wireless LAN because the key is stored in the firmware.

- **Reauthentication policies** You can set policies that force users to periodically reauthenticate to the RADIUS server and thus receive fresh session keys. This policy can further reduce the window for network attacks because the WEP keys are rotated even more frequently.

- **Initialization vector changes** The IV is incremented on a per-packet basis, so hackers cannot find a predetermined, predictable sequence to exploit. The capability to change the IV with every packet, combined with dynamic keying and reauthentication, greatly increases security and makes it that much more difficult for an attacker to gain access to the wireless network.

TIP

Do a Web search and you might find many products for WEP cracking. Some of the most commonly used utilities are WEPCrack, AirCrack, AirSnort, Kismet, Airodump, and Aireplay.

NOTE

WEP is a shared-key authentication process that uses a pseudo-random number generator and the RC4 stream cipher. The RC4 stream cipher is adequate; however, the weakness in WEP lies in the IV. In most implementations, the IV starts at 0 and is incremented by 1 for each packet transmitted on the network. Given the relatively small number of IVs available (2^{24}), the IV will roll over, given enough time—as little as one to five hours in a busy network. The IV is transmitted in clear text with each encrypted packet, thus allowing an attacker to easily create a table of packets and compare known packet information to determine the WEP key. Several freeware utilities are available for just this task.

Building a Cisco LEAP Solution

To put together a Cisco EAP (LEAP) with RADIUS solution, you need the following components:

- A Cisco Aironet AP that supports LEAP. Currently, this includes the 350, 1100, and 1200 models. The 350 is the oldest of the bunch and offers the least amount of configurability. The 1100 is the newest and offers both CLI- and GUI-based management and configuration.

- A compatible network adapter that supports LEAP (for example, Cisco Aironet 21).

- The most up-to-date network adapter driver, firmware, and Aironet Client Utility (ACU). You can download this driver using the Aironet Wireless Software Selector on the Cisco Web site at www.cisco.com/pcgi-bin/Software/WLAN/wlplanner.cgi.

- A RADIUS server application that supports LEAP. For our purposes, we use Juniper's Steel-Belted RADIUS/Enterprise Edition.

NOTE

Cisco response to dictionary attacks on Cisco LEAP is an interesting read to learn how to handle dictionary attacks. Read the Cisco technology document (which requires CCO logon) at www.cisco.com/en/US/partner/products/hw/wireless/ps430/prod_bulletin09186a00801cc901.html.

Installing and Configuring Juniper Steel-Belted RADIUS

Steel-Belted RADIUS (SBR) is an implementation of the RADIUS protocol. Apart from remote users, SBR supports wireless LANs and works with a wide range of network authentication products and technologies. It helps you implement authentication and access control policy for your organization.

NOTE

SBR is the authentication software from Funk Software, which is now a part of Juniper Networks. When you visit www.funk.com. the Web site redirects you to www.juniper.net/welcome_funk.html.

The features of SBR are:

- Support for wide range of network access components
- Graphical administration
- Centralized management and access control
- Support for wide range of authentication protocols
- Support for 802.1x-based APs
- Wide range of authentication, including token-based and third-party authentication devices

SBR implements authentication (verifying the user), authorization (the level of access on the protected network), and accounting (record of actual network activities, often used for billing and diagnosis), on the basis of the RADIUS protocol.

The components of SBR solution include:

- Access Client, such as wireless clients, dial-in users, wired 802.1x users, and remote office users

- Access Server/RADIUS client, including APs, Remote Access Servers (RAS), 802.1x compatible switches, and VPNs

- RADIUS Server, which implements authentication, authorization, and accounting

- Back-end resources, such as authentication server, SecurID, TACACS+, Remote RADIUS servers, and external database (SQL, Windows Active Directory, or LDAP)

RADIUS Authentication Process

The following are the steps involved in the process (see Figure 5.1) of RADIUS authentication:

1 The supplicant initiates a connection request to a RADIUS client (in this scenario, a wireless AP).

2 The RADIUS client passes the authentication request to the SBR server.

3 The SBR server refers to the local database (native) or external database (such as SQL, LDAP, or Active Directory) to verify the user logon parameters provided by the access client.

4 The SBR server authenticates the user and provides authorization attributes or rejects the user if the parameters are incorrect.

5 If the user is authenticated successfully, the connection is accepted; otherwise, it's rejected.

Figure 5.1 RADIUS Authentication Process

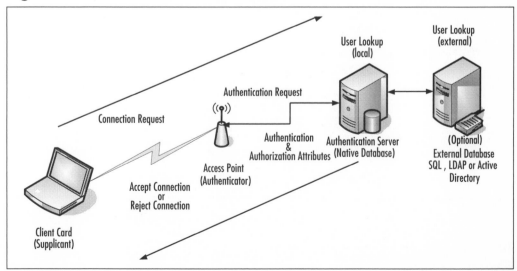

Installing Steel-Belted RADIUS

SBR is available on a wide range of platforms, including Windows, Linux, and Solaris. SBR software components include:

- SBR server

- SBR administration software

- Odyssey client (optional)

SBR can be implemented with Microsoft Windows XP native wireless client or third-party clients such as Cisco Access Client Utility (ACU). SBR in a Cisco implementation supports Cisco LEAP, EAP-FAST, and Microsoft PEAP-MS CHAPv2 protocols.

In this section, we look at the implementation of Juniper SBR with the Cisco LEAP authentication protocol. To get started with your LEAP/RADIUS solution, you first need to install and configure the RADIUS server of your choice. Perform the following steps to get SBR installed and configured for LEAP:

1. Download the SBR installation package from the Juniper Networks Web site (www.juniper.net/customers/support/products/sbr_series.jsp). You can download a 30-day trial if you are not ready to purchase. The current version is SBR 5.4. In addition, download the Windows binaries SBRNT_Admin_54.exe, SBRNT_ALL_54, and optionally, the Odyssey client (odyc45.exe). Execute **SBRNT_ALL_54** to install the SBR server. On a test environment, both the administration software and the server software can reside on the same physical server.

2. Provide your name and your organization's name as well your product key. Note that you can opt to exercise the 30-day trial if you desire. Click **Next** to continue.

3. On the next page, select the **Enterprise Edition** option and click **Next** to continue. Figure 5.2 shows Steel-Belted RADIUS server editions from which to choose.

Figure 5.2 The Steel-Belted RADIUS Server Editions

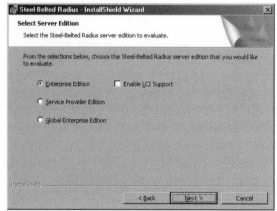

4. Click **Yes** to accept the end–user license agreement (EULA).

5. Click **Next** to start the setup routine.

6. Select your installation location.

7. Select the **SBR standalone server** option and continue the installation.

8. When the installation has completed, the Steel-Belted RADIUS server is installed as a service. You may verify the installation from **Start | Control Panel | Administrative Tools | Services**.

9. Launch **RADIUS Administrator**. The admin application opens. Select the **Local** option and click the **Connect** button, as shown in Figure 5.3.

Figure 5.3 The Steel-Belted RADIUS Administrator Window

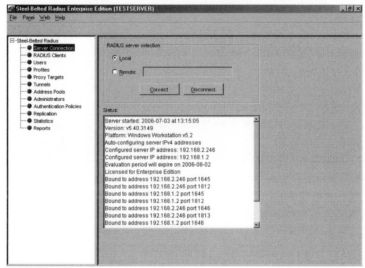

10. Close the SBR admin application to begin the configuration of SBR for LEAP.

11. Navigate to the **SBR installation directory** (c:\radius\service) and open the **Service** folder. Locate and open the eap.ini file for editing. For this example, we use native RADIUS authentication, meaning that users will be authenticating directly against the SBR RADIUS database. (You can, optionally, configure SBR for Windows domain authentication, as discussed later in this chapter.) Under the **[Native–User]** heading, remove the semicolon from the first three items to enable LEAP. Save and close the **eap.ini** file (see Figure 5.4).

Figure 5.4 Configuring SBR for LEAP

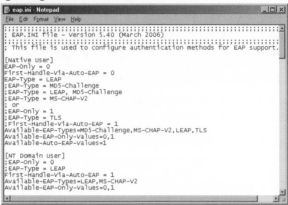

12. From the **Services** console, located in the **Administrative Tools** folder, restart the **Steel-Belted RADIUS service** to force it to reload the eap.ini file. Launch the **SBR Admin** application and connect to the local server as shown in Figure 5.5.

Figure 5.5 Restarting the Steel-Belted RADIUS Service

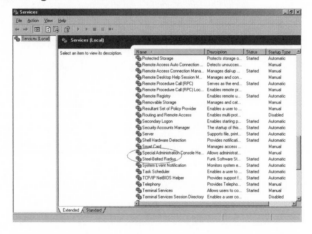

13. Click the **RADIUS Clients** option to configure SBR for the Cisco AP, as shown in Figure 5.6. Note that the AP is the RADIUS client since it is performing authentication on behalf of the wireless network client. Click the **Add** button to create a new client, and click **OK** to confirm it. Next, specify the **client IP address** (the IP address assigned to the AP) and the **type of client** (Cisco Aironet AP).

14. Type a password in the **Shared secret** box to enter the shared secret to be used for the AP and SBR servers to authenticate each other, as shown in Figure 5.6. (Remember your shared secret; you will need it again when you configure the AP later.) Click the **OK** button to confirm the client details.

Figure 5.6 Configuring the RADIUS Client Properties

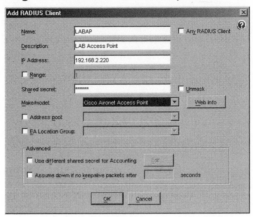

15. Click the **Users** option to create native users (users internal to the SBR server), as shown in Figure 5.7. Click the **Add** button to add a new username. After entering the username and password, click **OK** to confirm it.

Figure 5.7 Creating Native Users

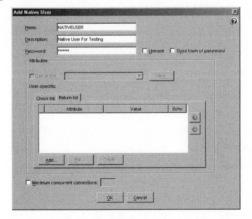

16. Click **Windows Domain User** and **Windows Domain Group** to configure authentication methods while implementing authentication for Windows users.

17. Click the **Authentication Policies** option to set the authentication methods (and their order) to be used, as shown in Figure 5.8. Since we are using native users, ensure that the **Native User** option is placed first in the list. Choose **LEAP** and **MS-CHAP-V2**. Click **Save** to confirm the changes.

Figure 5.8 Selecting the Authentication Methods

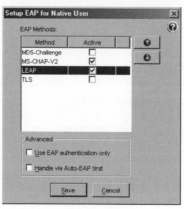

Configuring Cisco LEAP

Once the RADIUS server is installed and configured, the hard work is behind you. All that is left is to configure LEAP on the AP and the client network adapter. To configure LEAP on the AP, perform the following steps. (Note that the exact screen will vary among various APs models—the end configuration is the same, however. For this discussion, a Cisco Aironet 1200 AP is used, with all configurations performed via the Web interface instead of the CLI.)

1. Log in to your AP via the Web interface.

2. Configure your network SSID and enable EAP authentication, as shown in Figure 5.9. Save your settings to the AP after configuring them.

Figure 5.9 Enabling EAP Authentication

3. Enter a 128-bit broadcast WEP key, as shown in Figure 5.10. Save your settings to the AP after configuring them.

Figure 5.10 Entering the Broadcast WEP Key

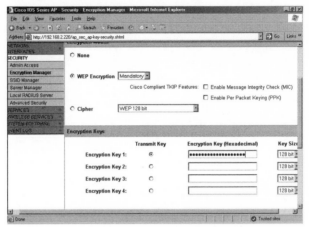

4. Configure your RADIUS server IP address and shared-secret key information, as shown in Figure 5.11.

Figure 5.11 Configuring the RADIUS Server Information

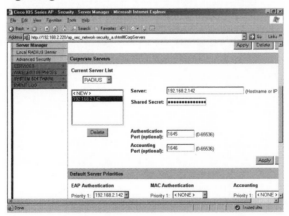

To enable the wireless client for LEAP, first ensure that it is using the most recent firmware and drivers, as discussed previously. Once you've got the most up-to-date files, proceed as follows to get the client configured and authenticated using LEAP:

1. Launch the Cisco ACU, shown in Figure 5.12. Notice that the ACU reports that the network adapter is not associated with the AP. This is normal at this point because the AP is configured to require LEAP authentication.

Figure 5.12 Using the Cisco ACU

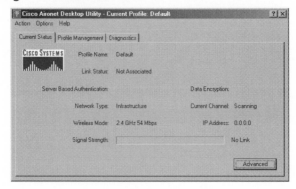

2. Switch to the **Profile Management** tab to create a new profile, as shown in Figure 5.13. Assign a name to the new profile and enter **testssid** (or the name of the SSID).

Figure 5.13 Creating a New Profile

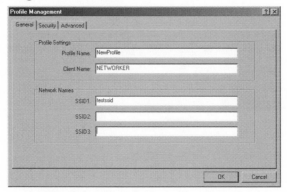

3. Switch to the **Security** tab. Under **Set Security Options**, select the **802.1x** option and select **LEAP** from the drop-down list, as shown in Figure 5.14. After selecting LEAP, click the **Configure** button.

4. On the **LEAP Settings** page, ensure that the **Use Temporary User Name and Password** option is selected with the **Manually Prompt for LEAP User Name and Password** suboption. Remove the check mark from the **Include Windows Logon Domain with User Name** option because we are using Native mode authentication in this example (see Figure 5.15). Click **OK** after making your configuration.

Figure 5.14 Configuring the Authentication Method

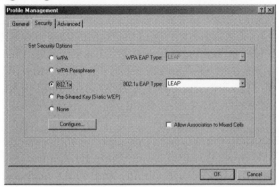

Figure 5.15 Configuring LEAP Options

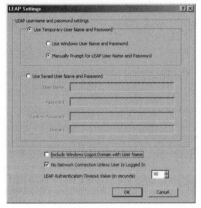

5.   Click **OK** to view the new profile in the Profile Management tab (see Figure 5.16). Click the **Activate** button to activate the new profile.

Figure 5.16 Activating the New Profile

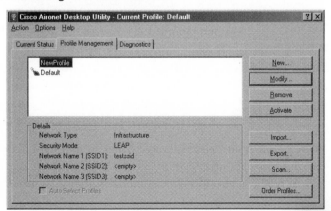

6. Double-click on the new profile to log in.

7. Provide the username and the password of the native user you created in the SBR section.

8. If you look at the SBR Administrator application on the Statistics page, you can see the number of successful and failed authentications (see Figure 5.17).

Figure 5.17 Monitoring the RADIUS Server Statistics

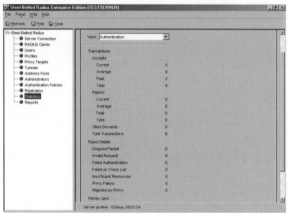

Windows Active Directory Domain Authentication With LEAP and RADIUS

In the preceding sections, we only looked at creating native user accounts in Steel-Belted RADIUS. It is also possible to create AD domain user accounts and have the RADIUS server authenticate directly against Active Directory. This approach offers many advantages, such as preventing dictionary attacks by enforcing account lockout policies. To use domain user accounts for LEAP authentication, you need only perform the following additions and modifications to the procedures outlined earlier in this chapter:

1. Make modifications to the eap.ini file; to enable LEAP, under the **[Windows Domain]** heading, remove the semicolon from the first three items to enable LEAP.

2. From the **Services** console located in the **Administrative Tools** folder, restart the **SBR service** to force it to reload the eap.ini file. Launch the **SBR Admin** application and connect to the local server. On the **Authentication Policies** page, shown in Figure 5.18, ensure that the **Windows Domain User** and **Windows Domain Group** options are enabled and are at or near the top of the list.

Figure 5.18 Checking Authentication Methods

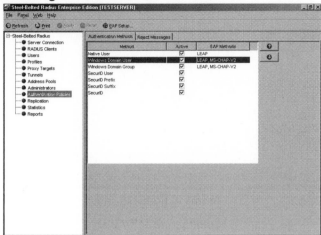

3. Go to the **Users** page and add a new user, as described previously. This time, however, you will have the option to select a domain user, as shown in Figure 5.19. Select your domain user, and click **OK**.

Figure 5.19 Adding a Domain User

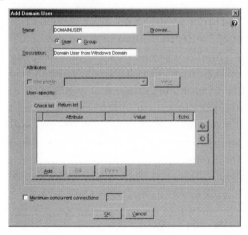

4. Open the **ACU** and edit the profile in use (the one you created previously). Switch to the **Security** tab and click the **Configure** button next to the network security type drop-down box (where **LEAP** is selected). In the LEAP settings dialog box, ensure that the **Use Windows User Name and Password** option is selected (instead of the options you selected for LEAP), as shown in Figure 5.20. In addition, ensure that a check mark is placed next to the **Include Windows Login Domain with User Name** option.

Figure 5.20 Configuring LEAP Options for Domain Authentication

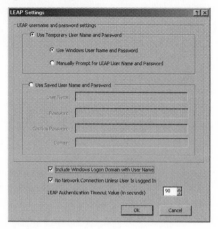

5. Click **OK** to save the settings and exit the profile configuration.

6. Log into the network using LEAP and your domain user credentials.

LEAP Review

Now that you've had a chance to examine the workings of Cisco's LEAP, you should see quite a few benefits to be gained through its use. LEAP, implemented with Juniper (Funk) Software's Steel-Belted RADIUS, is an ideal and very robust security solution for wireless networks of any size. By forcing users to authenticate to a back-end RADIUS server and creating per-user, per-session dynamic WEP keys, LEAP provides greatly enhanced authentication and security for your wireless network.

Cisco has licensed the LEAP technology to several third-party vendors, so you can expect to see many more LEAP-compatible devices in the near future. For example, Apple's AirPort network adapter already supports LEAP with version 2 or better firmware.

Implementing PEAP

Protected Extensible Authentication Protocol (PEAP) is a member of the family of Extensible Authentication Protocols (EAP). PEAP uses Transport Level Security (TLS) to create an encrypted channel between the client supplicant and the RADIUS server. PEAP provides additional security for client-side EAP authentication protocols, such as EAP-MS-CHAP-V2, that can operate through the TLS encrypted channel. PEAP is used as an authentication method for 802.11 wireless and wired client computers but is not supported for VPN or other remote access clients.

Security and ease of deployment make PEAP a popular choice for authentication. The advantages of PEAP are:

- Windows Server 2003, Windows 2000, Windows XP, and Pocket PC 2002 offer support for PEAP (either natively or with a system update), so there is no need for you to install third-party client software.

- Internet Authentication Service (IAS) is the Microsoft implementation of the RADIUS protocol. Windows 2000 Server and Windows Server 2003 support PEAP, so there is no need to install third-party RADIUS software.

NOTE

PEAP addresses many of the EAP security issues highlighted in the recently published Internet Engineering Task Force (IETF) draft, available at www.ietf.org/internet-drafts/draft-ietf-eap-rfc2284bis-0x.txt.

- PEAP uses a TLS channel to protect the user credentials. Other password-based methods (such as LEAP and EAP-MD5) do not create a TLS channel and are exposed to offline dictionary attacks on the user credentials.

- Using the TLS channel from the client to the authentication server, PEAP offers end-to-end protection, not just over the wireless data link. This is particularly important when a mobile user is using a public network to access a private network. For non-TLS schemes (LEAP and EAP-MD5), the password is exposed to attack on the wireless link and across the public network.

- PEAP supports any EAP-compatible methods. PEAP is also defined as an extensible authentication method that can embrace new EAP authentication schemes as they become ratified. Microsoft Windows PEAP supports passwords and certificate authentication and allows any EAP-based method provided by partners to be used within PEAP.

- Within the TLS channel, PEAP hides the EAP type that is negotiated for mutual client/server authentication. This helps prevent an attacker from injecting packets between the client and the network AP. Also, because each packet sent in the TLS channel is encrypted, the PEAP client and server can trust the integrity of the authentication data.

- PEAP offers strong protection against the deployment of unauthorized wireless APs, because the client verifies the RADIUS server's identity before proceeding with further authentication or connectivity. The wireless AP is unable to decrypt the authentication messages protected by PEAP.

- PEAP offers highly secure keys that are used to encrypt the data communications between the clients and wireless APs. New encryption keys are derived for each connection and are shared with authorized wireless APs accepting the connection. Unauthorized wireless APs are not provided with the encryption keys.

- PEAP does not require the deployment of certificates to wireless clients. Only the PEAP server (authentication server) needs to be assigned a certificate. The PEAP server certificate can be managed using an internal certification authority (CA) product or acquired from a certificate management company, such as VeriSign or Thawte.

- Password-based schemes rely on strong passwords to help defend against brute-force hacking. With PEAP, although you should still follow best practices for strong passwords and management, users' credentials are not exposed to the same attack, because their credentials are protected by TLS.

- Microsoft offers native support for PEAP so that a user can use the same logon credentials for all network connections and applications. PEAP integrates seamlessly with Microsoft Windows domain policy, Group Policy, and logon scripts. This means that PEAP by default transparently uses the same logon credentials you type when you first log into your network. Alternatively, you can specify that PEAP authentication should use different logon credentials, if you are not concerned about preserving the "single logon" experience for your users. Non-TLS schemes (LEAP and EAP-MD5) do not support single logon, logon scripts, or Group Policy.

- Authentication schemes for which there are no standards or publicly available specifications will not receive rigorous peer security review. PEAP is an open standard supported under the security framework of the IEEE 802.1X specification and has been submitted to the IETF.

- Windows Server 2003 Group Policy features can be used to centrally configure the properties of PEAP on all Windows XP (Service Pack 1 or later) or Windows Server 2003 wireless clients.

- PEAP offers security and efficiency when used with roaming wireless devices. Authentication latency is frequently a concern with wireless networks because users may need to reconnect to a network through a number of AP devices as they roam. As a result, it is valuable to be able to quickly perform reauthentication. PEAP supports this capability through the TLS session resumption facility, and any EAP method running under PEAP can take advantage of it.

- PEAP provides support for EAP authentication methods such as EAP-TLS and EAP-MS-CHAPV2 that can perform computer authentication. LEAP does not support computer authentication.

- The PEAP protocol specifies an option of hiding a user's name—that is, identity privacy. The Microsoft implementation of PEAP does not support identity privacy at this time.

Windows 2003 Environment PEAP Solution

The components required to implement PEAP in Windows 2003 are:

- Windows 2003 domain controllers
- Microsoft IAS server (RADIUS server)
- APs that allow EAP and PEAP (should be Advanced Encryption Standard, or AES, compatible)
- Client computers with Windows XP SP1, SP2, or better

The additional requirements for implementing PEAP are:

- Server certificates
- Group policy (to automatically configure the client computers)

The optional requirements for implementing PEAP are:

- A management solution for the APs
- Wireless LAN Solution Engine (WLSE)
- Cisco Wireless Domain Service (WDS)

After these requirements are met, you need to do the following to set up PEAP on Windows 2003:

- Set up a Microsoft Certificate Services
- Create Wireless Group, Users, and Computers in Active Directory
- Set up an Internet Authentication Service (IAS) Server
- Configure Load Balancing and Redundancy for RADIUS server

Microsoft Certificate Services

The advantages of using Microsoft Certificate Services are:

- Microsoft Certificate Services come with the Windows server operating system.
- The service is convenient to use if the installation is integrated with Active Directory.

■ The certificate request and installation is straightforward and seamlessly integrated.

■ The authority is automatically installed on all domain computers.

■ After you generate the certificates for the RADIUS server(s), clients install the certificate in their trusted store. You can shut down the certificate server or install a host firewall and block issuing of certificates for other purposes (such as EFS). This ensures that the server runs only when there is a need to issue certificates.

■ If licenses and systems are an issue, the certificate server can be installed in the same computer as the RADIUS server.

Notes from the Underground…

Pros and Cons of Getting a RADIUS Server Certificate from Various Vendors

You might get a certificate from one of these sources:

■ From an online certification authority
   The benefit is that the client computers trust the certificates issued by trusted third parties, such as VeriSign and others. The drawback is that some additional cost is required for each certificate (one certificate for each radius server).

■ From an implementation of Microsoft Certificate Services (this solution uses Microsoft Certificate Services)
   The benefits are that you can use the certificate for other purposes (such as Web servers or EFS) and the propagation of the certification authority can be automated to all client computers. The drawbacks include that there is one more service to maintain, and you must understand the public key infrastructure.

■ From an implementation of a certificate using free software (OPEN SSL)
   The benefits are that it comes free of cost and can be used for other purposes. A disadvantage is that once you generate the certificate for the root certification authority, you need to manually distribute the certificate to all the clients that will use it and put it under the Trusted Authorities.

Configuring a Microsoft Certificate Server

Follow these steps to install and configure the Microsoft Certificate server:

1. Install one or more servers with Windows 2003 domain controller.

2. Install the **Certificate Services** integrated with Active Directory.

3. Using the **Certificate Request Wizard**, request a certificate from the RADIUS server (from the local certificates snap-in).

4. Approve the certificate from the certification authority (certification authority console).

5. Install the certificate in the RADIUS server.

6. Firewall the certificate server so no more certificates can be issued (which provides better security for the computer system itself as well).

TIP

Refer to the Microsoft Technet article at www.microsoft.com/technet/ security/prodtech/windowsserver2003/build_ent_root_ca.mspx to set up and configure a CA in a Windows 2003 domain.

Creating Wireless Group, Users, and Computers in Active Directory

To create a Wireless User Group:

1. Go to **Start | Programs | Administrative Tools | Active Directory Users and Computers**.

2. Right-click on **Users** and select **New | Group**. Provide the Group name and leave the default group **Properties**.

3. Click **OK**.

To create a Wireless Computer object:

1. Go to **Start | Programs | Administrative Tools | Active Directory Users and Computers** to open the Active Directory Users and Computers window, as shown in Figure 5.21.

Figure 5.21 The Active Directory Users and Computers Window

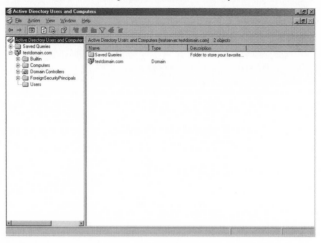

2. Right-click **Computers** and select **New | Computer**. Provide the computer name. Refer to Figure 5.22.

Figure 5.22 Creating a New Computer Object

3. Click **Next**.

4. If it's a managed computer, provide the GUID; otherwise, click **Next** without checking the **This is a managed computer** option (see Figure 5.23).

5. Click **Finish**.

Figure 5.23 Creating a New Computer Object

To create a Wireless User object:

1   Go to **Start | Programs | Administrative Tools | Active Directory Users and Computers**.

2   Right-click **Users** and select **New | User**. Provide the User logon name and other information and click **Next**.

3   Type the User password and other password options.

4   Click **Finish**.

5   Right-click the **New Wireless User** object and select **Properties**.

6   Switch to the **Dial-in** tab, and select the **Allow access** option.

7   Switch to the **Member Of** tab and click **Add**.

8   Choose the **Wireless access group** created earlier.

Setting Up an IAS Server

Follow these steps to install and configure IAS:

1.   Under the RADIUS Clients, add the IP address of each AP. Use a different password for every AP (recommended; see Figure 5.24). If your LAN environment is 100 percent switched and sniffing on the wired LAN is not possible, you might want to opt to use same password for all the APs. To add the IP address of each AP, go to **Start | Programs | Administrative Tools | Internet Authentication Service | RADIUS Clients**, right-click, and select **New RADIUS Client**.

Figure 5.24 Adding RADIUS Clients

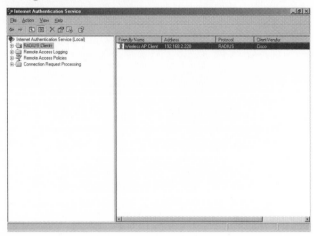

2. Provide a name and the IP address of the AP.

3. Choose the AP vendor from the client vendor list.

4. Provide the shared secret. (The same shared secret needs to be supplied in the AP while configuring the RADIUS server.)

Figure 5.25 illustrates the IAS authentication process to help you understand the steps involved in the RADIUS authentication on Windows 2003.

Figure 5.25 The IAS Authentication Process

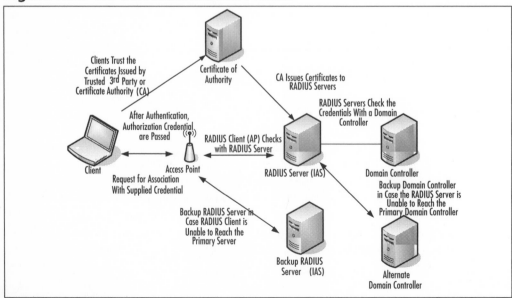

Configuring IAS Server Logging

IAS server logs can provide insight on successful and rejected authentication requests. Figure 5.26 shows IAS log properties.

Figure 5.26 IAS Log Properties

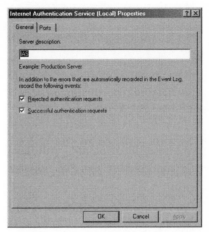

IAS can store its logs in a flat file or in a database on a Microsoft SQL Server (an ideal solution if you do not have a management device). You can use Windows Event Viewer to view the logs. This is a good starting point for troubleshooting. To view the logs in the Event Viewer, select **Remote Access Logging** in the left pane to display Local File and SQL Server options in the right pane. Right-click **Local File** and select **Properties**. You can customize the log properties to include accounting and authentication requests, as shown in Figure 5.27.

Figure 5.27 IAS Log Configuration

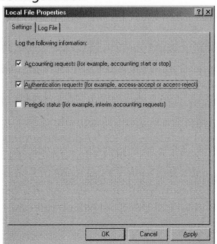

Configuring Remote Access Polices

IAS allows you to have more than one policy on the RADIUS server. Place frequently used policies at the top of the list. Figure 5.28 shows Remote Access Policies.

Figure 5.28 Remote Access Policies of IAS

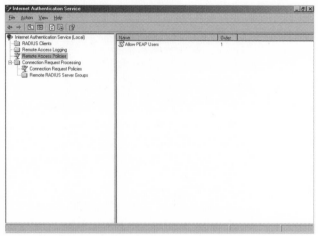

To configure a remote access policy:

1. Right-click **Remote Access Policies** in the left pane and select **New Remote Access Policy**. The New Remote Access Policy Wizard will appear.

2. Provide the policy name.

3. Select the **Wireless (Use for wireless LAN connections Only)** option.

4. Add the **Wireless Group** object.

5. Select the authentication method (Protected EAP, PEAP).

6. Choose the server certificate.

7. Click **Next** and **Finish** to save the policy.

Repeat these steps to create additional policies.

The Wireless Policy

To configure the wireless policy, you need to meet two conditions. First, ensure that the request comes from an AP and that not everyone has wireless access. Second, create a group (as was discussed earlier) and place the computers or users who need wireless access in this group. To configure the wireless policy:

1. Go to **Start** | **Programs** | **Administrative Tools** | **Internet Authentication Service** | **Select Remote Access Policies**. On the right pane, right-click the policy and select **Properties**.

2. In the Wireless AP Policy Properties dialog box, as shown in Figure 5.29, click **Edit Profile**.

Figure 5.29 Wireless Policy Conditions

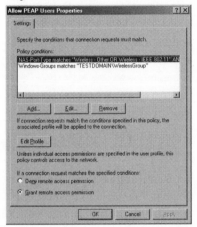

3. Switch to the **Authentication** tab.

4. Click **EAP Methods**.

5. Click **Edit**. You can verify the server certificate in the EAP Protected Properties.

6. Change the default configuration of EAP Methods and Client Timeout Settings in the policy. Figure 5.30 shows EAP methods configuration.

Figure 5.30 EAP Methods

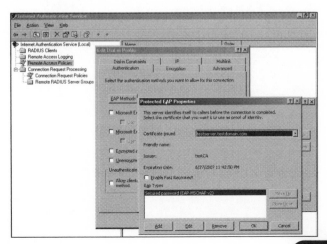

7. With dynamic WEP, the RADIUS server can force the clients to reauthenticate. A new WEP key will be generated for the session. Generation of WEP keys adds to the load of an IAS server. For higher security needs, the timeout can be further reduced from 15 minutes to 3 minutes. Instead, use WPA, which uses a built-in mechanism to rekey the session. You may modify the default timeout settings, as shown in Figure 5.31.

Figure 5.31 Dial-in Constraints and Session Timeout

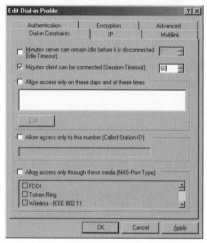

8. Modify the EAP properties of the PEAP policy to choose the server certificate and Fast Reconnect options. Fast Reconnect will allow a user to roam and eliminates the need to reauthenticate. Choose a certificate that was issued for the RADIUS server. Add EAP type MSCHAPv2 to allow usernames and passwords to be used for authentication. Figure 5.32 shows the protected EAP properties.

Figure 5.32 Protected EAP Properties

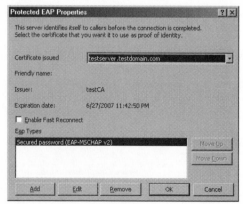

Securing IAS Server

It is quite safe to have a host firewall installed and enabled on the IAS server. The built-in Windows 2003 firewall is adequate for this purpose. You may have to allow access to UDP 1645, 1646 or UDP 1812, 1813 (depending on the RADIUS server configuration and the ports configured on APs). Additional ports may be required for remote administration. You can place IAS in a secured zone with only two open UDP ports.

Configuring the Access Points

The APs are generally not aware of the EAP methods that the client uses to authenticate to the server. There is one specific configuration for individual EAP methods such as EAP, LEAP, TTLS, and EAP-TLS. Before you configure EAP, change the default password, default SNMP communities, and SNMP location.

To configure the AP:

1. Define the SSID.

2. Enable EAP authentication for the SSID.

3. Enable WEP encryption (mandatory requirement).

4. Define the RADIUS server(s) required for the EAP authentication (same password used in the RADIUS server).

You may also use the wizard that will configure these steps.

Group Policy

Use the new Group Policy extensions to configure the wireless LAN adapters of the client computers. You may also write a small application or script that will modify wireless access properties. Then you may send the instructions to apply this policy to the users through e-mail.

NOTE

When a group policy is applied:

- It adds a SSID under the preferred networks of each client computer.
- It applies to the entire organization (domain) or specific containers or organization units.
- The preferred network cannot be removed by the user under normal circumstances.
- You may add other SSIDs (such as home networks).
- The changes on Group Policy Objects are applied to client computers.

If you are using Windows Login Scripts in your environment, remember that Windows XP brings up the login dialog box very quickly. The user might be able to log in with the cached credentials before the wireless authentication process is finished—resulting in an inability to process any login scripts. You may suggest the users to wait for 15 seconds before logging in.

Configure a Windows policy to bring up the login script after the network connections are up and running. This policy poses no issues when the wireless signal reception is good or when there is no signal at all. It becomes a problem when the signal is very weak; the user might be stuck in retransmissions trying to authenticate and so never get to the desktop.

Configuring Load Balancing and Redundancy for RADIUS Server

Failure of the RADIUS server will bring the wireless network down (single point of failure). Therefore, it is recommended to configure a set of APs (about 50 percent) to access the primary RADIUS server (server1) and a second set to access a secondary RADIUS server (server2). Now configure the second set of APs with server2 as the primary server and server1 as the secondary server, as shown in Figure 5.33. You may have to ensure that all the APs are listed on both the RADIUS servers.

Figure 5.33 Configuring Redundancy for RADIUS Servers

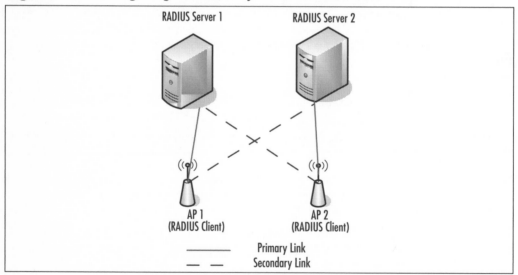

RADIUS Review

The following Phase 1 and Phase 2 steps summarize the RADIUS authentication process. Figure 5.34 provides a pictorial representation of the radius process.

Phase 1

1. AP -> client (EAP-Request Identity)

2. Client -> AP (EAP-Response Identity with Username)

3. AP -> RADIUS (EAP-Response Identity with Username)

4. RADIUS -> Client (EAP-Request/Start PEAP)

5. RADIUS <-> Client (a series of messages that create the TLS channel)

Phase 2:

1. RADIUS -> Client (EAP-Request Identity)

2. Client -> Radius (EAP-Response Identity with Username)

3. RADIUS -> Client (EAP-Request/EAP-MS-CHAP-V2 Challenge with the challenge string)

4. Client -> RADIUS (Response to the challenge and a challenge to the server to authenticate itself)

5. RADIUS -> Client (Success, after checking with the Domain Controller, and response to the challenge)

6. Client -> RADIUS (Success)

7. RADIUS -> AP (EAP Success)

8. Client <-> AP (WEP Encrypted Traffic)

Figure 5.34 RADIUS Process

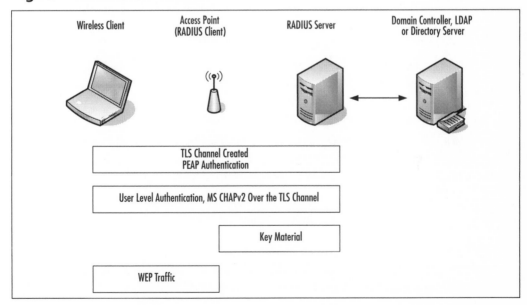

Summary

In this chapter we examined Juniper Steel-Belted RADIUS with Cisco LEAP and Microsoft Windows 2003 PEAP solutions that can be implemented fairly quickly and easily in your network to create the effect of a DMZ. Recall that in most cases the standard DMZ mentality does not apply to wireless networks. You can, however, still create the net effect of limiting traffic and controlling access using these (and many other) types of solutions. The solution you choose will be decided in part by your needs and in part by what you can acquire in your price range.

Cisco's LEAP is a variation of the standard EAP protocol that provided superior 802.1x port-based access control between LEAP-compliant network adapters and APs. Using a back-end RADIUS server designed to work specifically with LEAP, you can achieve a superb level of security through the use of mutual authentication. PEAP can be deployed easily in Windows 2003 environments. Use Windows 2003 group policies to gain granular control.

Solutions Fast Track

Implementing RADIUS with Cisco LEAP

- LEAP addresses all the problems inherent in the use of WEP in a wireless network. The largest vulnerabilities come from static WEP keys and the predictability of IVs. LEAPv2 is further strengthened and should be considered for all newer deployments.

- LEAP creates a per-user, per-session dynamic WEP key that is tied to the network logon, thereby addressing the limitations of static WEP keys. Since authentication is performed against a back-end RADIUS database, administrative overhead is minimal after initial installation and configuration.

- Policies can be set to force users to reauthenticate to the RADIUS server more often and thus receive fresh session keys. This approach can further reduce the window for network attacks because the WEP keys are rotated even more frequently.

- Protected Extensible Authentication Protocol (PEAP) is a member of the family of Extensible Authentication Protocol (EAP) protocols. PEAP uses Transport Level Security (TLS) to create an encrypted channel between the client supplicant and the RADIUS server. PEAP provides additional security for the client-side EAP authentication protocols, such as EAP-MSCHAPv2.

Frequently Asked Questions

The following Frequently Asked Questions, answered by the authors of this book, are designed to both measure your understanding of the concepts presented in this chapter and to assist you with real-life implementation of these concepts. To have your questions about this chapter answered by the author, browse to **www.syngress.com/solutions** and click on the **"Ask the Author"** form.

Q: Isn't just using WEP enough protection from both an authentication and an encryption standpoint?

A: No. Certain tools can break all WEP keys by simply monitoring the network traffic (generally requiring less than 24 hours to do so).

Q: Why is WEP (by the IEEE 802.11b standard) insecure?

A: WEP is insecure for a number of reasons. The first is that the 24-bit IV is too short. Because a new IV is generated for each frame and not for each session, the entire IV key space can be exhausted on a busy network in a matter of hours, resulting in the reuse of IVs. Second, the RC4 algorithm WEP uses has been shown to use a number of weak keys that can be exploited to crack the encryption. Third, because WEP is implemented at Layer 2, it encrypts TCP/IP traffic, which contains a high percentage of well-known and predictable information, making it vulnerable to plain-text attacks.

Q: Where can I find more information on WEP vulnerabilities?

A: Besides being one of the sources that brought WEP vulnerabilities to light, www.isaac.cs.berkeley.edu has links to other Web sites that cover WEP insecurities.

Q: How can I protect my wireless network from eavesdropping by unauthorized individuals?

A: Because wireless devices are half-duplex devices, you cannot wholly prevent your wireless traffic from being listened to by unauthorized individuals. The only defense against eavesdropping is to encrypt Layer 2 and higher traffic whenever possible.

Q: Is LEAP the end-all security solution for wireless networks?

A: No. As we've seen, as good a solution as LEAP is, it still has its weaknesses and vulnerabilities—however small and controllable they might be. The wireless security field is one of the most rapidly changing ones in the area of IT and information security. Newer alternatives, such as EAP-TTLS, are available, and many more will be available in the next few years. The bottom line is that you must find the security solution that offers you the ideal balance—one that gives you the required level of security while still maintaining the desired level of usability.

## Chapter 6

Firewall Design: Cisco PIX and ASA

Solutions in this chapter:

- PIX and ASA Basics

- Securing Your Network Perimeters

- Cisco PIX and ASA Versions and Features

- Making a DMZ and Controlling Traffic

- PIX and ASA Firewall Design and Configuration Checklist

☑ Summary

☑ Solutions Fast Track

☑ Frequently Asked Questions

Introduction

There are many ways to design and build your DMZ, and with so many products on the market, it might be difficult to decide which product is right for you. In the next few chapters we discuss several enterprise-level firewall solutions, including Cisco's PIX and ASA, Check Point's FireWall-1, and Microsoft's ISA 2004. We provide the information you need so that you can decide which firewall meets your DMZ needs in terms of security, performance, functionality, manageability, stability, and reliability. Although all these products provide viable security solutions, they all have different requirements, features, and configuration methods that could lead you to choose one over the other. It is important to understand these products' capabilities and choose the one that meets your DMZ infrastructure performance needs and maintains a high level of security, one that you are comfortable supporting.

Reading this chapter, you will learn how to design and build a DMZ using Cisco's PIX and ASA firewalls. We will advise you on the features of the PIX and the ASA, guide you in the selection of the appropriate PIX and ASA hardware, and discuss different firewall arrangements, as well as direct you on how to configure your firewall to securely pass traffic. By the end of this chapter you should be able to decide whether the PIX or ASA is the right firewall for your DMZ infrastructure and, if you choose it, be able configure, manage, and support the PIX and ASA.

PIX and ASA Basics

Cisco's PIX firewall is one of the industry's best-selling firewalls, providing customers with high levels of security, performance, and reliability. PIX, which stands for *Packet Internet Exchange,* was developed by Network Translation, Inc., in 1994 and purchased by Cisco in October 1995. The PIX firewall is a network appliance that does not use a general operating system like UNIX or Windows; therefore, inherent weaknesses in these operating systems will not degrade the firewall's overall security. The PIX utilizes the Adaptive Security Algorithm (ASA) to analyze every inbound packet, ensures that the network you are protecting is secure, and allows only legitimate traffic to pass through it. Some other features include Network or Port Address Translation (NAT or PAT), URL filtering, content filtering, IPSec VPN tunneling, and intrusion detection.

In 2005 Cisco released a new product to its firewall security product portfolio known as the Cisco Adaptive Security Appliance (ASA, not to be confused with the Adaptive Security Algorithm). The ASA is built on the same basic foundation as the Cisco PIX firewall, including running the same basic software (known as the PIXOS). However, unlike the PIX, which is designed as a purpose-driven firewall, the ASA is designed as a multifunction security device by incorporating not only the same basic PIX firewall functionality but advanced application inspection capabilities through integrated intrusion prevention system functionality as well as integrated flexible VPN connectivity. In a manner of speaking, the Cisco ASA combines the functionality of the PIX firewall, the IPS 4200 Intrusion Prevention System

(IPS), and the VPN 3000 VPN Concentrator into a single device, allowing the ASA to filter traffic through the use of traditional access control lists as well as through the use of the advanced application filtering capabilities of an IPS. In many ways it appears that Cisco is ultimately positioning the ASA as the logical replacement of the PIX firewall.

Cisco provides a complete line of PIX and ASA firewalls to meet your DMZ requirements, ranging from small office/home office (SOHO) to carrier-class firewalls. The entire PIX and ASA line uses the same security algorithm but varies in performance, number of interfaces supported, and interface types. Additionally, the ASA can utilize the IPS functionality to filter based on signatures and traffic-matching patterns defined in the IPS engine. Depending on the chassis and license agreement, the PIX can support up to 10 interfaces; the ASA can support up to 12 interfaces (eight of which can be active at any given time). Additionally, the PIX can support up to 150 virtual interfaces (VLANs), whereas the ASA supports up to 200 virtual interfaces, allowing the DMZ architect to design a large DMZ infrastructure. Cisco's PIX and ASA firewall line gives you the flexibility to support your DMZ infrastructure's needs, no matter its size, complexity, or budget.

As with all Cisco products, hardware and software failures within the PIX and ASA are rare, but they can happen. The PIX and ASA both offer high availability via either Active/Active or Active/Standby failover features. This means that a second PIX or ASA can provide stateful hot standby redundancy, which can maintain current open sessions so that users won't notice that the primary unit has failed. In an Active/Standby scenario, the second firewall is not used at all, remaining in a standby state in the event of a failure. In an Active/Active scenario, the two firewalls can be used for different functionality (for example, housing different DMZ segments), with the functionality contained in one firewall failing over to the other firewall only in the event of a failure. This setup has the benefit of not having a firewall sitting around unused except in the event of a failure. The PIX and ASA security features, purpose-built operating system, long mean time between failures (MTBF), resiliency, and low cost make them some of the most popular firewalls.

NOTE

To avoid confusion as you read this chapter, we use the terms *PIX/ASA* or *firewall* when we refer to functionality or information that is the same for both devices. Where device-specific information needs to be called out, the device in question (PIX or ASA) is specifically mentioned.

Securing Your Network Perimeters

The PIX/ASA is a powerful and versatile tool for securing your network. It can be used to secure your internal network from external parties—for example, with Internet connections to third parties and business partners. The PIX/ASA can also be used on the internal network to protect sensitive data, not only from outside parties but also from unauthorized employees or from employees who might have malicious intent. This book focuses on the network perimeter and the DMZ, but some of the same designs and security features can also be used internally.

The Cisco Perimeter Security Solution

The PIX/ASA provides the DMZ architect with a variety of design possibilities. In the next section, we go through several design possibilities, including a traditional "three-legged" firewall, a multi-DMZ infrastructure using physical interfaces, a multi-DMZ infrastructure using virtual interfaces, and a dual-firewall DMZ infrastructure using an external and an internal firewall. We also discuss adding firewall redundancy so that a single firewall failure would not bring down the entire infrastructure.

Three-Legged Firewall

The most commonly implemented DMZ design in many small and medium-sized corporations is the traditional "three-legged" firewall. This design meets the needs of a site or sites in which internal users require the ability to access the Internet securely as well as send e-mails, access a locally hosted company Web site, or transfer files. Figure 6.1 shows how the traditional "three-legged" firewall fits into the network. The internal interface of the PIX firewall allows internal users to access both the DMZ and the Internet. The external interface connects the PIX/ASA to your local ISP router. The DMZ interface is where Web, FTP, e-mail relay servers, and any other services that the Internet community needs to access are located. This design is very effective for low- to medium-traffic volume DMZ infrastructures that do not require high availability and can afford to have extended downtime in the event of a firewall failure. Remember, if the firewall is down, internal users will not be able to access the Internet, and DMZ services will not be accessible to the Internet community until the firewall is serviced.

If high availability is required, the DMZ architect can consider adding a second PIX/ASA in conjunction with the PIX/ASA's failover feature, which allows the secondary PIX/ASA firewall to back up the primary PIX/ASA in the event of a failure. Figure 6.2 shows how redundancy can be added to the traditional "three-legged" firewall design. This design is ideal for corporations of all sizes, where the Internet/DMZ infrastructure is essential to the business and therefore the organization cannot afford downtime and requires a resilient, highly available solution. Both the primary and secondary PIX/ASA firewalls need to be identical models and have the same interface options. Each PIX/ASA will have an interface on the internal, external, and DMZ LANs. When set up as a redundant pair, the PIX/ASA has the ability to detect problems within the units or on any one of the interfaces and automatically fail over to the backup unit. The PIX/ASA offers the option of *stateful failover*, which means that any open sessions on the primary unit will be automatically transferred to the secondary unit without client sessions disconnecting, so the failure is transparent to end users. For the PIX/ASA to support failover, some additional hardware is required, such as an additional interface to support the optional stateful failover feature and a Cisco proprietary cable for heartbeats between the primary and secondary units. We discuss the PIX/ASA failover feature and its requirements in detail later in this chapter.

Figure 6.1 A Traditional "Three-Legged" Firewall

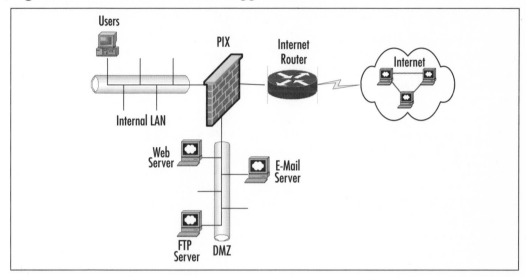

Figure 6.2 A Traditional "Three-Legged" Firewall with Redundancy

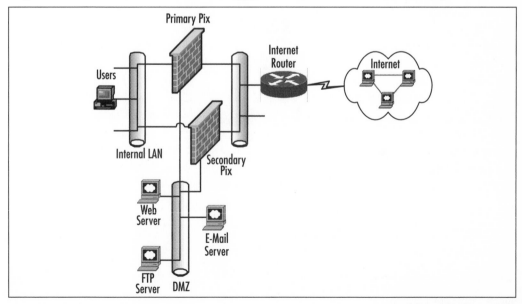

Multi–DMZ Infrastructure Using Physical Interfaces

When you're given the task of building a DMZ in a large DMZ environment or when you need to support multiple service types, it might be desirable to separate them by adding additional "legs" to the DMZ. There are two reasons you might want to use a DMZ leg:

- An additional leg might be necessary if the number of servers has exceeded the number of available IP addresses for hosts on the DMZ subnet. By adding a DMZ interface, you can assign another IP range and add more servers.

- It's a good idea to separate service types onto different DMZ segments. Service types are Web, FTP, e-mail, DNS, VPN, and remote access.

For example, Figure 6.3 shows a multiple-DMZ environment with Web servers, e-mail relays, and FTP servers on the first DMZ leg (DMZ 1) and services such as VPN and dial-in user access on a second DMZ leg (DMZ 2). This setup separates the functions of the DMZs. DMZ 1 supports services that are publicly available over the Internet, such as the company's Web site. DMZ 2 supports remote users accessing resources on the internal LAN via a dial-in or VPN. By making remote users traverse the PIX/ASA, we make the internal LAN environment secure because rules can be set up to restrict remote user access. Adding DMZ legs helps keep the firewall rulesets manageable, especially when each DMZ has different access requirements. It also isolates any errors in configuration, because a change on an access control list (ACL) for one DMZ will not affect the ACL of another DMZ interface.

Figure 6.3 A Multi-DMZ Infrastructure

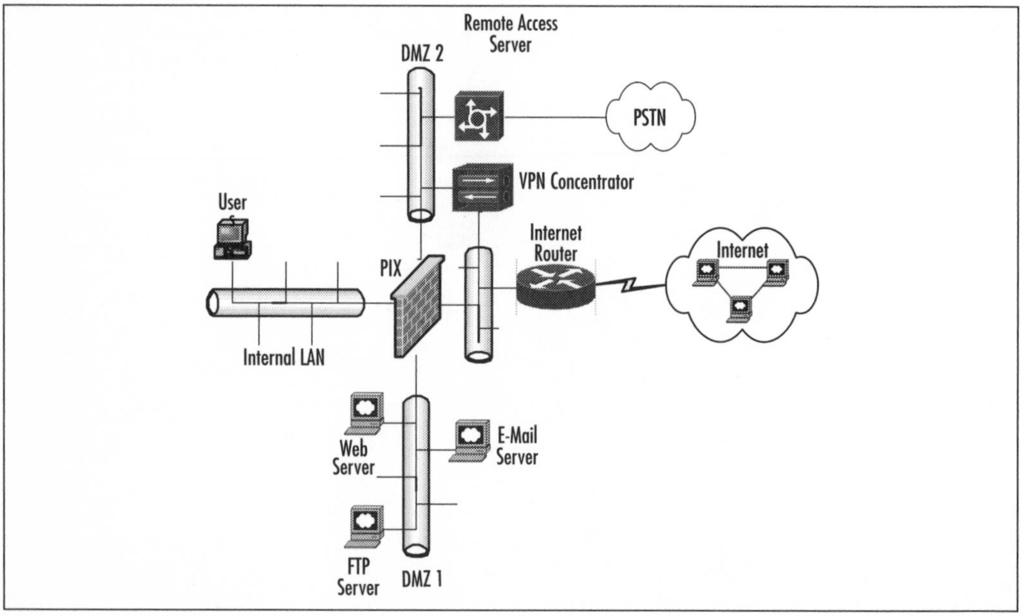

You can add redundancy by adding a secondary PIX/ASA, similar to the redundant traditional "three-legged" firewall design. One of the additional benefits you can take advantage of in a redundant firewall design with multiple-DMZ segments is an Active/Active failover. In an Active/Active scenario, each firewall is actively used for functionality. This traditionally occurs by assigning each DMZ segment to a different firewall as the primary firewall to use. So for example, DMZ1 would be assigned to Firewall1, and DMZ2 would be assigned to Firewall2. In this example, DMZ1 would only fail over to Firewall2 in the event that there was a failure with Firewall1. This approach provides the advantage of being able to run services across both firewalls, effectively load balancing services while at the same time providing full redundancy and failover for all network segments. We discuss the PIX/ASA failover feature and its requirements in detail later in this chapter.

A Multi-DMZ Infrastructure Using Virtual Interfaces

A multi-DMZ infrastructure using virtual interfaces is functionally the same as any other multi-DMZ infrastructure. However, in a physical infrastructure you are limited in the number of DMZ segments that can be created by the number of physical interfaces the firewall supports. If you need more DMZ segments, you need to purchase additional firewalls (and absorb all the related costs, such as maintenance and upkeep). With the latest versions of the PIX/ASA software, you can create virtual interfaces that each belong to a different VLAN. This potentially allows for the creation of hundreds of DMZ segments (with each DMZ segment belonging to a unique VLAN). Building on the example in Figure 6.3, then, you could further segment either physical segment into multiple logical segments. So, for example, DMZ1 could be further segmented into a DMZ for Web services, a DMZ for FTP services, and a DMZ for e-mail services. DMZ2 could then be separated into a DMZ for remote access and a DMZ for VPN access. Each logical interface has its own unique ACLs and rulesets, allowing each ruleset to be managed independently. This approach allows for a much more granular degree of control over the types of traffic that need to be allowed into any given DMZ segment.

Keep one cautionary statement in mind regarding virtual interfaces: For virtual interfaces to be used effectively, the switch that the firewall is connected to must support the use of VLANs, to isolate traffic. This setup is less secure than using separate physical switches, because it is possible for traffic to cross VLANs without going through the firewall. With separate physical switches, that scenario is not possible, because the switches have no connection other than going through the firewall. This type of vulnerability is typically known as a *VLAN-hopping attack*. Although it is not a trivial task to perform and it is extremely rare for such an attack to be successful, it is within the realm of possibility, so it is something to consider. A highly secure environment should probably not use any virtual interfaces, whereas most other environments could potentially take advantage of this functionality. Because of the potential security implications of using VLANs in a DMZ environment, it is recommended that you only use VLANs for DMZs of similar security levels. So, for example, it might be appropriate to separate your Web, FTP, and e-mail traffic into distinct VLANs because they are all at a similar security level. You would not want to separate your internal network and any of your DMZ networks using virtual interfaces and VLANs, however, because they have dramatically different security levels, and if an attack was successful, the attacker could potentially gain access to more valuable internal resources.

A Dual-Firewall DMZ Infrastructure Using External and Internal Firewalls

The designs we've discussed previously are ideal for standard, multipurpose DMZ environments, but the internal/external firewall design (see Figure 6.4) is intended for the specific purpose of supporting an e-commerce site for which various levels of security are required. Large e-commerce sites separate the servers' functions into three components, consisting of a Web server cluster, an application server cluster, and a database cluster, most commonly known as a *three-tier design*. In this design, Internet users accessing an e-commerce site interact with only the Web servers on DMZ1. The job of the Web server is to be the front-end GUI for the e-commerce site. The Web servers in turn call on the application servers on DMZ2 to provide content. The application servers' job is to collect the information the user is requesting and provide content back to the Web server for the user to view.

The application server requests information by making SQL calls to the database servers on DMZ3, which houses the site's data. Each component has a different security requirement, which allows only necessary communication among DMZ1, 2, and 3. The external PIX/ASA only allows users to access the Web site on DMZ1 via HTTP or HTTPS (SSL-enabled HTTP). The user community will not need to access any other part of the site, because the Web server will serve all the necessary content to the users; therefore, access is restricted to DMZ1. The external PIX/ASA will allow the Web servers to make requests to only the application servers on DMZ2 for content. DMZ2 is located between the internal and external firewall sets, with a Layer 3 switch acting as the default gateway for DMZ2 as well as routing traffic though this environment. The internal firewall only allows the application servers to send SQL requests to the database servers located on DMZ3. The internal firewall also allows administrators on the internal LAN to manage the e-commerce environment. For simplicity, Figure 6.4 does not show redundancy, but the internal and external PIX/ASA firewalls can be set up with failover. With the layered security approach, this solution provides a highly scalable and secure design that makes it difficult for hackers to compromise.

Since this is a Cisco-centric chapter, the figure depicts PIX/ASA firewalls being used for both the internal and external firewalls. From a security perspective it is generally recommended that you use two different manufacturers and models of firewall for the internal and the external firewalls, to help reduce the likelihood of a successful attack against both types of firewall. It is common to implement the PIX/ASA for the external firewall while using a more advanced application proxy firewall such as Microsoft ISA Server 2004, Secure Computing Cyberguard TSP, or Secure Computing Sidewinder G2 for the internal firewall.

NOTE

To understand the traffic flows of the DMZ design just described, you should look closely at Figure 6.4 and follow the traffic patterns from host to host. It is imperative that when you design a DMZ, you follow the notes listed here; always draw your scenario and plan it logically before you implement it physically. Because deploying a DMZ scenario is no easy task, your deployment will go more smoothly if you follow this advice.

Figure 6.4 An Internal/External Firewall Sandwich

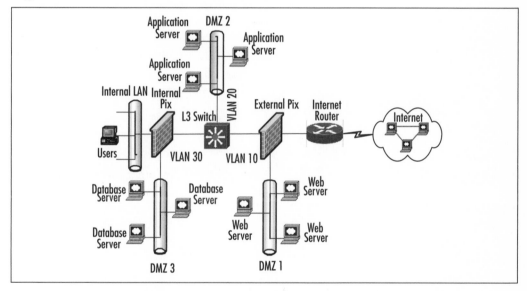

Cisco PIX/ASA Versions and Features

Cisco's PIX/ASA firewall solution provides several different chassis, software features, and licensing and interface options. In this section, we cover in detail the PIX and ASA hardware, features, and options that will help you decide whether the PIX or ASA will provide functionality and performance to meet your DMZ requirements.

Cisco PIX Firewalls

The PIX firewall line consists of five models, ranging from the SOHO model, PIX 501, to the high-performance service provider model, PIX 535. To determine the PIX to choose for your needs, you must first identify the requirements of your enterprise's Internet and DMZ infrastructure. To choose the proper firewall, you need to know some basic information: the number of DMZs (legs or interfaces) the firewall needs, approximate throughput required, number of users accessing resources through the firewall, and whether redundancy is required.

Once you have collected the requirements and have decided on a design, it's time to select the proper hardware that will protect your DMZ infrastructure. With the release of the PIX 7.0 software, the PIX firewall operating system is slightly different for the various PIX models. The PIX 501 and PIX 506E firewalls do not support the PIX 7.0 software release. That means that although all the PIX software versions have the same interface and share probably 90 percent of the same commands and functionality (so features such as NAT, URL filtering, content filtering, and VPN tunneling can be found across the entire line, depending on the software license purchased), some specific pieces of functionality are unique to the PIX 7.0 software. We will talk about those software differences later in this chapter. Notice that the basic differences between the models mostly deal with the chassis interface options, performance, and cost.

The next section details the five PIX model types and presents the information you need to choose the right chassis for your DMZ infrastructure.

The Cisco PIX 501 Firewall

The Cisco PIX 501 is an entry-level firewall designed to meet the needs of small or home offices. The PIX 501 provides SOHO users with the same security level and features as its bigger brothers, but performance is limited. The PIX 501 can support an unlimited number of users concurrently and incorporates a four-port 10/100Mb switch, so home users with broadband service can easily set up a network without purchasing an additional switch. The PIX 501 has a fixed chassis and cannot be upgraded to support additional interfaces, so it does not have the capability to add a third leg (or DMZ leg).

The PIX 501 is strictly designed to be a plug-and-play firewall for very small networks that have broadband access and want to securely access the Internet as well as connect to a central or regional office via a VPN tunnel. It is not designed to support a DMZ infrastructure.

Key items of the PIX 501 firewall include the following:

- A 10-user license allows 10 internal IP addresses to access the Internet simultaneously, and the DHCP server feature supports up to 32 DHCP address assignments

- A 50-user license allows 50 internal IP addresses to access the Internet simultaneously, and the DHCP server feature supports up to 128 DHCP address assignments

- An unlimited user license allows an unlimited number of users to access the Internet simultaneously

- Fixed chassis, integrated four-port switch 10/100Mbps plus one Internet-facing 10/100Mbps port

- A 133MHz processor, 16MB RAM, and 8MB Flash

- Does not support the PIX 7.0 software; at the time of writing, the most recent software version available is the PIX OS 6.3(5)

- 60Mbps clear-text throughput

- Optional encryption licenses are necessary if 168-bit 3DES or 56-bit DES VPN tunnels are needed

- 6Mbps DES VPN throughput

- 3Mbps 3DES VPN throughput

- 4.5Mbps 128-bit AES VPN throughput

- 3.4Mbps 256-bit AES VPN throughput

- Ten VPN peers

- Small chassis (not rack mountable)

The Cisco PIX 506E Firewall

The Cisco PIX 506E, the next level up from the 501, is designed to meet the needs of a remote or branch office. Unlike the 501, it is sold only with an unlimited license restriction that does not limit the number of users concurrently traversing the PIX. The 506E has a clear-text throughput of 100Mbps, which means you will probably max out the Internet connection at the remote site before the PIX becomes oversubscribed. This model supports no specific number of users because turning on features such as VPN tunneling or intrusion detection can reduce overall throughput.

As a guideline, you should not have more than 250 light to moderate Internet users, and if you need VPN tunneling, this number should be reduced further. The PIX 506E is also a fixed chassis and cannot be upgraded to support additional interfaces, so it does not have the capability to add a third leg (or DMZ leg). It does, however, support two virtual interfaces, allowing for the creation of up to two DMZs through the use of virtual interfaces and VLANs. This model has two embedded 100BaseT Ethernet ports, which allow for an internal (protected) interface and an external (Internet-facing) interface.

The PIX 506E is ideal for a small to medium-sized remote or branch office that requires secure Internet connectivity. It also has greater VPN performance that allows for 25 VPN peers. Not only can a VPN tunnel connect the remote/branch site to a central site, but it can also accept remote users to VPN directly to office.

Key characteristics of the PIX 506E firewall include the following:

- No user restriction license

- Fixed chassis, two embedded 10/100Mbps interfaces (internal/Internet facing)

- Two virtual interfaces

- A 300MHz processor, 32MB SDRAM, and 8MB Flash

- Does not support the PIX 7.0 software; at the time of writing, the most recent software version available is the PIX OS 6.3(5)

- 100 Mbps clear-text throughput

- An optional encryption license is necessary if 168-bit 3DES or 56-bit DES VPN tunnels are needed

- 20Mbps DES VPN throughput

- 16Mbps 3DES VPN throughput

- 30Mbps 128-bit AES VPN throughput

- 25Mbps 256-bit AES VPN throughput

- Twenty-five VPN peers

- Small chassis (not rack mountable)

> **NOTE**
>
> It is important that you know the differences between the PIX firewall versions. This knowledge is imperative to solid DMZ design, because some models simply can't be used to create a DMZ, and you don't want to waste your money or your time researching what you do not need. It is clear, however, that if you want to deploy a DMZ segment, your efforts must start with the PIX 515E.

The Cisco PIX 515E Firewall

Previously, we talked about the lower-end Cisco PIX firewalls, which are fixed models, support a small to intermediate number of users, and are *not capable* of supporting a traditional DMZ. Now let's discuss Cisco's enterprise-level firewall, which is modular, more powerful, and supports additional/multiple interfaces where a traditional DMZ can reside.

The Cisco PIX 515E, the first model in the modular line of PIX firewalls, is designed for small to medium-sized businesses but if scaled properly can also be used in larger organizations. The PIX 515E has two embedded 10/100 Ethernet interfaces and can accommodate a variety of interface types, including one- or four-port Fast Ethernet interface cards (used to create the DMZ ports) and/or a VPN accelerator card+ (VAC+) via two internal PCI slots. As we mentioned, optional modules inserted into the PIX 515E can be configured to support a DMZ by adding one- or four-port Fast Ethernet interface cards used to create DMZ legs. The VAC can allow moderate-volume mobile users to remotely access corporate resources or connect remote sites to headquarters via site-to-site IPSec VPN tunnels. The

PIX 515E provides the security, performance, versatility, and cost that make it very popular among network security and DMZ architects.

The PIX 515E is versatile enough to support a significant number of users as well as a DMZ environment that contains Web, e-mail, and FTP servers with volume that will not exceed its 190Mbps throughput. This is adequate for sites that have dual T3s (45Mbps each) or less to the Internet. You might ask, "Two T3s account for 90Mbps total, and it's only half the PIX's 190Mbps limitation?" It must be understood that dual T3s will push 90Mbps in each direction, accounting for 180Mbps of total throughput. However, if you are averaging 70 percent or more utilization or looking for scalability (if plans call for adding a T3 in the future), you should consider upgrading or choosing another chassis such as the PIX 525.

Key characteristics of the PIX 515E firewall include the following:

- License choices are Restricted with a Single DMZ and Unrestricted with Failover (Active/Active or Active/Standby)

- Modular chassis consists of two embedded 10/100 Ethernet ports and two PCI slots (32-bit/33MHz) for optional Fast Ethernet ports or VAC

- Maximum of six Fast Ethernet ports (including the two embedded 10/100 Ethernet ports); this is limited to three (including the two embedded 10/100 Ethernet ports) with the Restricted/DMZ license

- Ten (restricted) or 25 (unrestricted) virtual interfaces

- A 433MHz processor, 64MB (Restricted) or 128MB (Unrestricted) of SDRAM, and 16MB Flash

- 190Mbps clear-text throughput

- 130, 000simultaneous sessions

- Five security contexts

- Optional encryption license is necessary if 168-bit 3DES or 56-bit DES VPN tunnels are needed

- 20Mbps (Restricted) or 63Mbps (Unrestricted w/VAC) or 135Mbps (Unrestricted with VAC+) 3DES VPN throughput

- 130Mbps with VAC+ 128-bit AES VPN throughput

- 130Mbps with VAC+ 256-bit AES VPN throughput

- 2,000 VPN tunnels

- Active/Active and Active/Standby Failover (Unrestricted and Failover)

- Rack-mountable chassis (one rack unit)

> **NOTE**
>
> As with all networking hardware, you need to have a good idea of the type and amount of traffic traversing your network as well as future growth before you can decide to purchase a particular type of hardware. This practice is known as doing a *traffic-flow analysis* on your network segments. Remember, PIX throughput can be adversely affected by turning on features such as NAT, PAT, VPN, intrusion detection, and so on. Keep this in mind when you're sizing your firewall.

The Cisco PIX 525 Firewall

The Cisco PIX 525 firewall is designed to secure large enterprise locations and DMZs with high-volume Web traffic. In addition to the increased throughput, the PIX 525 also can accommodate a wider variety of interface types, including Fast Ethernet, Gigabit Ethernet, and/or a VAC+. The PIX 525 has two embedded 10/100 Ethernet interfaces and is the first model in the PIX line that supports the optional Gigabit Ethernet interface. The PIX 525's capability of supporting up to eight Fast Ethernet interfaces also gives the DMZ architect the freedom to cost-effectively scale the DMZ.

The PIX 525 is ideal for enterprises with large user populations and moderate to heavy Internet access requirements and/or that have DMZ environments requiring significant throughput (not exceeding 370Mbps). With the optional VAC installed, it can also serve as the head end for a remote user VPN and/or a site-to-site VPN WAN, where some or all of your remote sites can be connected to the central enterprise location via IPSec VPN tunnels.

Key characteristics of the PIX 525 firewall include the following:

- License choices are Restricted and Unrestricted with Failover (Active/Active or Active/Standby)

- The modular chassis consists of two embedded 10/100 Ethernet ports and three PCI slots (32-bit/33MHz) for optional Fast Ethernet ports, Gigabit Ethernet, or VAC

- A maximum of ten 10/100 interfaces (including the two embedded 10/100 Ethernet ports) or 3 Gigabit Interfaces in addition to the two embedded 10/100 Ethernet Ports

- 25 (restricted) or 100 (unrestricted) virtual interfaces

- A 600MHz Processor, 128MB (Restricted) or 256MB (Unrestricted) of SDRAM, and 16MB Flash

- 330Mbps clear-text throughput

- 500, 000 simultaneous sessions

- Up to 50 security contexts (unrestricted license only)

- Optional encryption license is necessary if 168-bit 3DES or 56-bit DES VPN tunnels are needed

- 30Mbps (Restricted) or 70Mbps (Unrestricted with VAC) or 145Mbps (Unrestricted with VAC+) 3DES VPN throughput

- 135Mbps with VAC+ 128-bit AES VPN throughput

- 135Mbps with VAC+ 256-bit AES VPN throughput

- 2,000 VPN tunnels (Unrestricted with VAC+)

- Active/Active and Active/Standby Failover (Unrestricted and Failover)

- Rack-mountable chassis (two rack units)

The Cisco PIX 535 Firewall

The PIX 535 is Cisco's top-of-the-line firewall, providing the greatest performance and interface versatility designed for the service provider market. The PIX 535 has over two and a half times more throughput than its predecessor, with clear-text throughput reaching 1.7Gbps. The PIX 535 has nine PCI slots, which can support up to 10 Fast Ethernet interfaces, nine Gigabit Ethernet interfaces, a VAC, or a combination of the three. The PIX 535, with an unrestricted license, can support up to 14 interfaces, but you must consult the documentation before combining interfaces, to determine the number of interface types that can work together. This process can be quite tricky and could cause the firewall not to boot properly. You can find more information about installing a PCI card into the PIX 535 at www.cisco.com/univercd/cc/td/doc/product/iaabu/pix/pix_v53/inst-535/board.htm.

The PIX 535 is ideal for Internet service providers or enterprise locations that offer services to a very large user community, including support for a huge DMZ traffic load. As with the PIX 525, you can install an optional VAC in the PIX 535, and it can also serve as the head end for a remote user VPN and/or a site-to-site VPN WAN, where some or all your remote sites can be connected to the central enterprise location via IPSec VPN tunnels.

Key characteristics of the PIX 535 firewall include the following:

- License choices are Restricted and Unrestricted with Failover (Active/Active or Active/Standby)

- The modular chassis consists of nine PCI slots (four 64-bit/66MHz and five 32-bit/33MHz) for optional Fast Ethernet ports, Gigabit Ethernet, or VAC

- Offers a maximum of 14 interfaces

- 50 (restricted) or 150 (unrestricted) virtual interfaces

- A 1000MHz processor, 512MB (Restricted) or 1024MB (Unrestricted) of SDRAM, and 16MB Flash

- 1.7Gbps clear-text throughput

- 500,000 simultaneous sessions

- Up to 50 security contexts (unrestricted license only)

- An optional encryption license is necessary if 168-bit 3DES or 56-bit DES VPN tunnels are needed

- 45Mbps (Restricted) or 100Mbps (Unrestricted with VAC) or 425Mbps (Unrestricted with VAC+) 3DES VPN

- 495Mbps with VAC+ 128-bit AES VPN throughput

- 425Mbps with VAC+ 256-bit AES VPN throughput

- 2,000 VPN tunnels (Unrestricted with VAC)

- Active/Active or Active/Passive Failover (Unrestricted and Failover)

- Redundant power supplies

- Rack-mountable chassis (three rack units)

Cisco ASA Firewalls

This Cisco ASA firewall line consists of five hardware models that range from a SOHO model, the ASA 5505, to the high-performance service provider model, ASA 5550. The Cisco ASA firewall line also differs from the PIX firewall line in that in addition to the actual hardware models, each model can be further fine tuned into one of five different tailored packages (known as *editions*) that are designed to meet location-specific needs. The two broad categories of edition are the Enterprise Edition and the Business Edition. The Enterprise Edition is further broken down into four location-specific editions: the Firewall Edition, the IPS Edition, the Anti-X Edition, and the VPN Edition. These editions are offered as either bundles of each specific ASA model or through the use of a la carte pricing and the implementation of specific hardware modules in conjunction with software licensing and configuration. An ASA can functionally provide the services of any edition in and of itself, or it can be configured as a combination of the four Enterprise Editions (excluding combining the IPS and Anti-X editions, since only one Security Services Module (SSM) can be installed at a time). Here are some details:

- **Firewall Edition** The Firewall Edition is the base edition for all Cisco ASA firewalls. The Firewall Edition essentially provides the same base firewall functionality that would be provided by a Cisco PIX firewall running the 7.0 PIX software. For all intents and purposes, an ASA running the Firewall Edition is functionality interchangeable with a PIX firewall.

- **IPS Edition** The IPS Edition is designed to provide advanced inspection capabilities to a base ASA through a combination of software licensing and the Advanced Inspection and Prevention Security Services Module (AIP-SSM). There are two models of AIP-SSM: the SSM-AIP-10, which is designed for the ASA 5510 and the ASA 5520, and the SSM-AIP-20, which is designed for the ASA 5520 and the ASA 5540. The IPS Edition cannot be combined with the Anti-X Edition.

- **Anti-X Edition** The Anti-X Edition is designed to provide advanced filtering of network threats including viruses, worms, spyware, spam, and phishing while controlling unwanted e-mail and Web content. Like the IPS Edition, the Anti-X Edition functionality is provided through a combination of software licensing and the Content Security and Control Security Services Module (CSC-SSM). The CSC-SSM utilizes integrated Trend Micro software functionality to provide the appropriate content-filtering functionality. There are two models of the CSC-SSM: the CSC-SSM-10, which is designed for the ASA 5510 and the ASA 5520, and the CSC-SSM-20, which is designed for the ASA 5510, ASA 5520, and ASA 5540. The Anti-X Edition cannot be combined with the IPS Edition.

- **VPN Edition** The VPN edition is designed to provide highly dense VPN connectivity to the ASA firewall through the use of software licensing. This allows an ASA to support up to 5000 VPN peers. The VPN Edition is designed, by and large, to replace the functionality provided by the Cisco VPN 3000 series concentrators.

- **Business Edition** The Business Edition is targeted at the small to medium-sized business (SMB) segment and combines firewall, VPN, and anti-X capabilities into the ASA 5510. Essentially, the Business Edition is an ASA 5510 with the CSC-SSM module installed.

To determine the ASA to choose for your needs, you must first identify the requirements of your enterprise's Internet and DMZ infrastructure as well as whether you have any location-specific needs such as anti-X or IPS functionality. To choose the proper firewall, you need to know some basic information: the number of DMZs (legs or interfaces) the firewall needs, approximate throughput required, number of users accessing resources through the firewall, and whether redundancy is required.

Once you have collected the requirements and have decided on a design, it's time to select the proper hardware that will serve to protect your DMZ infrastructure. The ASA firewalls use the same operating system and, if configured with a specific edition, run the same edition-specific software. This means that all the ASA software versions have the same interface and share the same commands and functionality (so features such as NAT, URL filtering, content filtering, and VPN tunneling can be found across the entire line, depending on the software license purchased). Additionally, the edition-specific software is the same for all models, so configuring the IPS Edition software on an ASA 5510 is the exact same process as configuring an ASA 5540. Notice that the basic differences between the models mostly deal with the chassis interface options, performance, and cost. The next section details the four ASA model types and presents the information you need to choose the right chassis for your DMZ infrastructure.

The Cisco ASA 5505 Firewall

The Cisco ASA5505 is the first model in the line of ASA firewalls; however, it differs from the rest of the ASA firewall product lines because it is not as modular as the rest of the ASA firewalls tend to be. The ASA 5505 is a small form factor device, similar in size to the PIX 501 firewall. The ASA 5505 is designed for the SOHO environment and is perfect for users such as telecommuters and very small remote offices. The ASA 5505 contains an eight-port integrated switch with 2 power over Ethernet ports. Unlike the rest of the ASA firewall, the ASA 5505 does not support the use of the SSM. Instead, it uses what is known as the Security Services Card (SSC). As of this writing, there are no SSCs produced by Cisco, but it is expected that the company will offer similar functionality to what is offered through the larger SSMs.

The ASA 5505 is designed predominantly to support a small environment; however, it does support up to three VLANs, one of which can be used as a restricted or fully functional DMZ, depending on licensing. It is designed to support traffic volumes not exceeding 150Mbps and supports 10 or 25 VPN peers, again depending on licensing. The ASA 5505 is being positioned as the logical replacement for the Cisco PIX 501 firewall and is designed to operate effectively in the same environments (while typically delivering better performance than the PIX).

Key points of interest related to the ASA 5505 include the following:

- License choices are the Base 5505 or the 5505 Security Plus, which provides for stateless Active/Standby Failover

- Quasi-modular chassis consists of an integrated eight-port 10/100 Ethernet switch and one SSC expansion slot

- Supports up to three virtual interfaces

- 256MB of SDRAM, and 64MB Flash

- 150Mbps clear-text throughput

- 10,000 or 25,000 simultaneous sessions (based on licenses)

- 10 to 25 IPSec VPN peers (based on licenses)

- 10 to 25 SSL VPN peers (based on licenses)

- Up to 100Mbps 3DES/AES VPN throughput

- Nonrack-mountable chassis

The Cisco ASA 5510 Firewall

The Cisco ASA 5510, the first model in the modular line of ASA firewalls, is designed for small to medium-sized businesses but if scaled properly can also be used in larger organizations. The ASA 5510 has five embedded 10/100 Ethernet interfaces. Depending on the license, the ASA 5510 supports three interfaces and one out-of-band (OOB) management interface (ASA 5510) or five interfaces (ASA 5510 Security Plus). The ASA 5510 also has a Software Services Module (SSM) port allowing a CSC-SSM, AIP-SSM or a 4GE-SSM to be installed.

The ASA 5510 is versatile enough to support a significant number of users as well as a DMZ environment that contains Web, e-mail, and FTP servers with volume that will not exceed its 300Mbps throughput (150Mbps with the AIP-SSM-10). The ASA 5510 is logically positioned as a replacement for the PIX 515E firewall and is designed to operate effectively in the same environments (while typically delivering better performance than the PIX).

Key characteristics of the ASA 5510 firewall include the following:

- License choices are the Base 5510 or the 5510 Security Plus, which provides for Active/Standby Failover
- Modular chassis consists of five embedded 10/100 Ethernet ports and one SSM expansion slot
- Maximum of five Fast Ethernet ports for the ASA 5510 Security Plus; this is limited to three with the ASA 5510
- 10 (5510) or 25 (5510 Security Plus) Virtual Interfaces
- 256MB of SDRAM, and 64MB Flash
- 300Mbps clear-text throughput
- 150Mbps of threat mitigation throughput with the AIP-SSM-10
- 130,000 simultaneous sessions (50,000 for the ASA 5510)
- 250 IPSec VPN peers
- 10 to 250 SSL VPN peers (based on licenses)
- Up to 170Mbps 3DES/AES VPN throughput
- Active/Standby Failover (ASA 5510 Software Plus)
- Rack-mountable chassis (one rack unit)

The Cisco ASA 5520 Firewall

The Cisco ASA 5520 firewall is designed to secure large enterprise locations and DMZs with high-volume Web traffic. The ASA 5520 provides an increased throughput over the 5510 and generally supports a greater number of VPN clients. The ASA 5520 is also the first

ASA that supports native gigabit network connectivity, Active/Active failover, and multiple security contexts.

The ASA 5520 is ideal for enterprises with moderate to large user populations and moderate to heavy Internet access requirements and/or that have DMZ environments requiring significant throughput (not exceeding 450Mbps). The ASA 5520 is designed as a logical replacement for the PIX 515 or PIX 525 firewalls and is designed to operate effectively in the same environments (while typically delivering better performance than the PIX).

Key characteristics of the ASA 5520 firewall include the following:

- Modular chassis consists of four embedded 10/100/1000 Ethernet ports, one embedded 10/100 Ethernet port, and one SSM expansion slot
- 100 virtual interfaces
- Up to 10 security contexts
- 1024MB of SDRAM, and 64MB Flash
- 450Mbps clear-text throughput
- 375Mbps of threat mitigation throughput with the AIP-SSM-20 (225Mbps throughput with the AIP-SSM-10)
- 4000,000 simultaneous sessions (50,000 for the ASA 5510)
- 750 IPSec VPN peers
- Ten to 750 SSL VPN peers (based on licenses)
- Up to 225Mbps 3DES/AES VPN throughput
- Active/Standby or Active/Active Failover
- VPN clustering and load balancing
- Rack-mountable chassis (one rack unit)

The Cisco ASA 5540 Firewall

The Cisco ASA 5540 firewall is designed to secure large enterprise locations and DMZs with high-volume Web traffic. The ASA 5540 provides an increased throughput over the 5520 and generally supports a greater number of VPN clients, security contexts, and virtual interfaces.

The ASA 5540 is ideal for large enterprises with large user populations and heavy Internet access requirements and/or that have DMZ environments requiring significant throughput (not exceeding 650Mbps). The ASA 5540 is designed as a logical replacement for the PIX 525 firewall and is designed to operate effectively in the same environments (while typically delivering better performance than the PIX as well as the ASA 5520).

Key characteristics of the ASA 5540 firewall include the following:

- Modular chassis consists of four embedded 10/100/1000 Ethernet ports, one embedded 10/100 Ethernet port and one SSM expansion slot

- 200 Virtual Interfaces

- Up to 50 Security Contexts

- 1024MB of SDRAM, and 64MB Flash

- 650Mbps clear-text throughput

- 450Mbps of threat mitigation throughput with the AIP-SSM-20

- 650,000 simultaneous sessions

- 5,000 IPSec VPN peers

- 10 to 2500 SSL VPN peers (based on licenses)

- Up to 325Mbps 3DES/AES VPN throughput

- Active/Standby or Active/Active Failover

- VPN clustering and load balancing

- Rack-mountable chassis (one rack unit)

The Cisco ASA 5550 Firewall

The Cisco ASA 5550 firewall is designed to secure large enterprise and service provider locations and DMZs with high-volume Web traffic. The ASA 5550 provides the largest amount of throughput of any ASA and supports a greater number of VPN clients. The ASA 5550 also supports the largest number of interfaces of any ASA. The ASA supports a total of 12 interfaces, eight 10/100/1000 Ethernet interfaces and four Small Form-Factor Pluggable (SFP) fiber interfaces (in addition to the 10/100 management interface). Of these 12 interfaces, only eight may be active at any given time. The ASA 5550 is designed to function as either a firewall or a VPN concentrator and does not support running the AIP-SSM or the CSC-SSM. (The SSM slot is actually filled with a combination four-port Gigabit Ethernet, four-port SFP SSM expansion card.)

The ASA 5550 is ideal for extremely large enterprises or service providers with large user populations and extremely heavy Internet access requirements and/or that have DMZ environments requiring significant throughput (not exceeding 1.2Gbps).

Key points of interest related to the ASA 5550 firewall include the following:

- Modular chassis consists of eight embedded 10/100/1000 Ethernet ports, four Small Form-Factor Pluggable (SFP) fiber interfaces, and one embedded 10/100 Ethernet port; only eight of the 10/100/1000 Ethernet or SFP interfaces can be active at a time

- 200 virtual interfaces

- Up to 50 security contexts

- 4096MB of SDRAM, and 64MB Flash

- 1.2Gbps clear-text throughput

- Does not support the CSC-SSM or the AIP-SSM (the SSM slot contains a four-port Gigabit Ethernet SSM)

- 650,000 simultaneous sessions

- 5,000 IPSec VPN peers

- 10 to 5000 SSL VPN peers (based on licenses)

- Up to 425Mbps 3DES/AES VPN throughput

- Active/Standby or Active/Active Failover

- VPN clustering and load balancing

- Rack-mountable chassis (one rack unit)

Cisco Firewall Software

With the advent of the Cisco ASA firewalls as well as the two distinct version paths (the 6.x version and the 7.x version) of the PIX Operating System (OS), it can be confusing to understand which operating system will do what is required for an environment. The easiest way to sort it all out is to look at the software features that are shared by all versions of the firewall software (both PIX OS versions as well as the ASA OS) and then look at the features supported by the ASA OS and the 7.x version of the PIX OS.

Common Firewall Software Features

All versions of the PIX and ASA operating system share the same core functionality because they all come from the same base operating system (the PIX 6.x version OS). The PIX/ASA OS is a feature-filled OS that provides a high level of security and performance. Because it is designed solely for the purpose of securing your network infrastructure and has an OS specifically built for it, it doesn't have the weaknesses inherent to general OSs such as Windows or UNIX. However, the PIX/ASA OS's lack of a general OS does not mean that the PIX/ASA has fewer features than its competitors. The PIX/ASA has a full set of security features and, with its streamlined OS and specially designed hardware, it has the ability to outperform many of its competitors.

Features include:

- **Purpose-built operating system** Eliminates the weaknesses found in most general OSs.

- **Adaptive security algorithm (ASA)** Method the PIX/ASA uses to provide stateful packet filtering, which analyzes each packet to ensure only legitimate traffic traverses the PIX/ASA.

- **URL filtering** Can limit URLs accessed by the user's base on a policy defined by the network administrator or a security policy. Requires an external Netpartner's WebSense server or N2H2 server. This URL filtering should not be confused with the filtering provided on the Cisco ASA firewall through the CSC-SSM expansion module.

- **Content filtering** Can block ActiveX or Java applets. This content filtering should not be confused with the filtering provided on the Cisco ASA firewall through the CSC-SSM expansion module.

- **NAT and PAT** Hides internal addressing from the Internet and makes more efficient use of private address space.

- **Cut-through proxy** Authenticates users accessing resources through the PIX/ASA.

- **VPN** Capable of handling mobile user access and site-to-site VPNs utilizing DES, 3DES, and AES encryption methods.

- **Intrusion detection** Enables the PIX to protect against various forms of malicious attack with features such as DNSGuard, FloodGuard, MailGuard, and IPVerify as well as the ability to identify attacks via attack "signatures." This intrusion detection should not be confused with the intrusion prevention provided on the Cisco ASA firewall through the AIP-SSM expansion module.

- **DHCP** Can act as a DHCP client and/or server.

- **Routing functionality** Can support static routes, RIP, and OSPF.

- **Support for RADIUS or TACACS+** Authenticating, authorizing, and accounting for users passing through the PIX or to enabled authentication for those connecting to the PIX's management interfaces.

- **Failover** Provides a resilient, high-availability solution in case of failure.

- **PPP over Ethernet (PPPoE) support** Compatible with xDSL and cable modems.

- **Common Criteria EAL4 Certification** Certain PIX OS versions have achieved the highest level of certification handed out by Common Criteria, an independent international security organization. You can find more information about Common Criteria at www.commoncriteria.org.

NOTE

In this chapter we have discussed how the PIX/ASA would provide stateful inspection. Let's take a closer look at this topic; it is very important to security because stateful inspection provides a deeper level of filtering than ACLs found in routers, which may only filter based on header information. Firewalls that perform stateful inspection analyze individual data packets as they traverse the firewall. In addition to the packet header, stateful inspection also assesses the packet's payload and looks at the application protocol. It can filter based on the source, destination, and service requested by the packet. The term *stateful* inspection refers to the firewall's ability to remember the status of a connection and thereby build a context for each data stream in its memory. With this information available to it, the firewall is able to make more informed policy decisions as well as being able to dynamically permit the return traffic of all requests, without the need for an administrator manually defining the ACL.

ASA and PIX 7.x Firewall Software Features

With the introduction of the PIX 7.x software line, Cisco took the PIX firewall in two distinct directions. The SOHO firewalls (PIX 501 and PIX 506E) remained on the 6.x software base, while the enterprise class firewalls began supporting a more advanced base OS. Additionally, the ASA firewalls were released with the ASA OS 7.x, which is virtually identical to the PIX OS 7.x software. Building on the features contained in the 6.x PIX software, the ASA and PIX 7.x software included a number of additional features:

- **Layer 2 Transparent Firewall** Enables the firewall to operate in line with existing network connections, without requiring any addressing or routing changes.

- **Advanced Web Security Services** Enables deep inspection of Web traffic, giving administrators control over what HTTP commands and methods will be allowed by the firewall.

- **Tunneling Application Control** Allows applications such as instant messenger (such as AOL Instant Messenger, Microsoft Messenger and Yahoo Messenger) or peer-to-peer file sharing applications (such as KaZaA and Gnutella) that tunnel traffic over HTTP to be blocked.

- **3G Mobile Wireless Security Services** Supports 3G Mobile Wireless services using the General Packet Radio Service (GPRS) Tunneling Protocol standard (GTP) while providing advanced GTP inspection to filter traffic accordingly.

- **Enhanced Failover** In addition to the basic Active/Standby failover, supports Active/Active standby failover, allowing both systems to simultaneously pass data.

- **VPN Stateful Failover** Provides Active/Standby stateful failover of VPN connections to ensure that VPN connections are not terminated in the event of a failover.

- **Security Contexts** Allows a single physical firewall to be treated as multiple logical firewalls (security contexts). This allows each security context to have a unique set of security policies, logical interfaces, and administrative domains. Also allows multiple physical firewalls to be consolidated into a single physical appliance while maintaining the separation of management and functionality between each security context.

- **Virtual Interfaces** Supports the creation of VLAN-based virtual interfaces, allowing a single physical interface to have multiple logical addresses, with each virtual interface having a unique security policy.

ASA Firewall Software Features

Although the PIX and ASA OS share many features and functionalities, the ASA firewall software supports some additional features and functionality through either the ASA OS itself or additional software to support the AIP-SSM or CSC-SSM software. The AIP-SSM actually runs the Cisco Intrusion Prevention 5.x software to provide the IPS functionality, while the CSC-SSM utilizes software from Trend Micro, known as Trend Micro InterScan, to provide the advanced content filtering and anti-X functionality.

ASA-specific firewall software features include:

- **Advanced Intrusion Prevention** In conjunction with the AIP-SSM and the Cisco Intrusion Prevention software, the ASA provides signature-based intrusion prevention functionality, allowing the ASA to filter and block traffic not only by the security policy ruleset but based on the configuration of the IPS.

- **Advanced Content Filtering and Anti-X Services** In conjunction with the CSC-SSM and the Trend Micro InterScan software, the ASA provides the ability to perform advanced content filtering of known and unknown attacks and threats, including malware, worms, viruses, Trojans, spyware, adware, phishing, spam, and email and Web content filtering.

- **Remote Access VPN Clustering and Load Balancing** The ASA supports improved VPN scalability and reliability by allowing the ASA to be configured as a member of Cisco VPN 3000 Series Concentrators or ASA 5500 Series VPN clusters of up to 10 devices. This allows for the ASA 5500 to potentially support 50,000 concurrent VPN connections.

The Cisco PIX Device Manager

Cisco provides a few different options to configure and manage PIX firewalls running the 6.x software or earlier, including command-line (CLI) based serial console connection, Telnet, Secure Shell (SSH), and an application with a GUI called the PIX Device Manager (PDM). The PDM provides administrators with a browser-based GUI and gives people who might not be well versed in the PIX CLI the ability to easily configure and monitor the PIX via a Web browser. It is also very secure because the transmissions between the browser and the PIX are made secure by SSL. The PDM provides administrators with configuration wizards, performance graphs, and historical data to help with configuration and troubleshooting tasks. Even though the PDM covers most of the commands needed to configure, manage, and support the PIX, it does not support some commands that can be configured only via the CLI.

The 501 and 506E are initially set up to work out of the box with PDM, but with the higher-end models, it is necessary to initially turn on PDM via the CLI prior to managing it via the PDM. The PDM works on a single device at a time and must be installed on the firewall separately from the PIX OS. To run the PDM, you need an activation key that enables Data Encryption Standard (DES) or Triple DES (3DES). You can find more information about installing the PDM at www.cisco.com/en/US/customer/products/sw/net-mgtsw/ps2032/products_installation_guides_books_list.html.

> **NOTE**
>
> The PDM software is separate from the PIX OS and is located in a separate file on the PIX Flash. Therefore, when you're upgrading software on the PIX, you might also need to upgrade the PDM software. The PDM is available for PIX OS version 6.0 mainline on all chassis types. The PDM does not require a license, but since it supports only encrypted communication to the browser (SSL), an encryption license is required to run the PDM. Cisco provides a no-cost DES license or a 3DES license for a fee.

> **NOTE**
>
> The PDM is limited in that it can manage only one PIX at a time. If you have a large environment and manage a large number of PIX firewalls, you might consider using CiscoWorks VPN and Security Management (VMS) Suite, which provides a Web-based GUI by which an administrator can manage many firewalls from one console. This tool makes managing firewalls easier by defining policies, standardizing configurations, and reducing human configuration errors.

The Cisco Adaptive Security Device Manager

With the release of the PIX OS 7.x and the ASA firewall, Cisco elected to provide a new and more robust management GUI known as the Cisco Adaptive Security Device Manager (ASDM). The ASDM is effectively the upgrade to the PDM for all PIX and ASA firewalls that are running the 7.x version of software. Like the PDM, the ASDM is a separate software file on the firewall. In addition to a browser-based GUI, the ASDM supports a client application that can be installed on the administrator workstation and then connected over the network to multiple firewalls (though each firewall must be managed independently).

Because the ASDM is supported only when running the PIX or ASA 7.x software, it is not supported on the PIX 501 or PIX 506E (you must use the PDM). The ASDM provides administrators with an application or browser-based GUI and gives people who might not be well versed in the PIX/ASA CLI the ability to easily configure and monitor the PIX/ASA via a Web browser or the ASDM client application. It is also very secure because the transmissions between the browser/application and the PIX/ASA are made secure by SSL. The ASDM provides administrators with configuration wizards, performance graphs, and historical data to help with configuration and troubleshooting tasks. Even though the ASDM covers most of the commands needed to configure, manage, and support the PIX, it does not support some commands that can only be configured via the CLI. Otherwise the ASDM and PDM have a very similar GUI and essentially serve the same purpose: to provide a remote management GUI to simplify and augment the traditional console, Telnet, or SSH based CLI.

Cisco PIX Firewall Licensing

Cisco's PIX firewall licensing requires some clarification. There are four categories of license type for all PIX firewalls:

- User licenses
- Platform licenses
- Feature licenses
- Encryption licenses

User Licenses

As the name implies, user licenses are used to define how many internal users can concurrently access the Internet or other external resources. There are three user license levels. The 10-user license and 50-user license are used for the PIX 501 firewall. All other firewalls include an unlimited user license.

Platform Licenses

For the higher-end models (515E and greater), four main license options are available: Restricted (R), Unrestricted (UR), Failover (FO), and Failover-Active/Active (FO-AA). The Restricted license is just that—restricted. It limits the firewall's capabilities; for instance, it does not allow for failover, it limits interface density, and it is shipped with reduced RAM, compared with the Unrestricted license. The Unrestricted license provides all the capabilities of the Restricted license but adds increased LAN interface density, more RAM, VPN acceleration, and failover. The Failover license is used in conjunction with the Unrestricted license to provide Active/Standby failover for the firewall. The backup or redundant PIX can be purchased with the Failover license at reduced cost, which makes the PIX one of the more cost-effective firewalls when it's configured as a redundant pair. In a scenario in which the primary firewall fails the secondary unit with the Failover license, the device will continue to perform all the capabilities the primary device supported. (The secondary unit must have the same optional PCI cards as the primary.) The Failover-Active/Active license is functionally similar to the Failover license, but it supports running the firewalls in an Active/Active failover mode.

NOTE

PIX licenses can be upgraded. When you purchase an upgrade package, you will receive a new activation key that unlocks the software enhancements of the new license as well as any additional hardware to bring the PIX to the correct hardware level to support the license's features. For example, if you upgrade a PIX 515E Restricted license to an Unrestricted license, you will receive an activation key and be able to benefit from another 32MB of RAM and a VAC.

NOTE

For the secondary or backup PIX with a Failover license to support a VPN client or the PCM as the primary, it is necessary to obtain a separate 56-bit DES IPSec license or the 168-bit 3DES IPSec licenses for both the primary and the backup units.

Feature Licenses

Feature licenses are used on the PIX 515E, 525, and 535 firewalls to provide advanced features such as security contexts or GTP/GPRS inspection for the firewall. Security context licensing supports 5, 10, 20, and 50 contexts, with the maximum number of supported security contexts depending on the model of PIX.

Encryption Licenses

When encryption is required to support IPSec VPNs or to enable the ASDM/PDM, it is necessary to obtain either the 56-bit DES encryption license or the 3DES (168-bit)/AES (128, 192 or 256-bit) encryption license. The encryption licenses are available for all models.

Cisco ASA Firewall Licensing

The Cisco ASA licensing is very similar to the PIX licensing. ASA licensing does not include user licensing (all ASA firewalls have an unlimited user license), but it utilizes platform, feature, CSC-SSM, and encryption licenses.

Platform Licenses

The ASA 5510 contains a platform license option that is unique to the 5510. This is known as the 5510 Security Plus. The 5510 Security Plus enables an increased number of concurrent connections and an increased number of virtual interfaces, and most important, it allows for high-availability support. All other ASA devices have a single platform license for all features.

CSC-SSM Licenses

The CSC-SSM is licensed in two ways. The first license is a platform license to support a number of users. By default the CSC-SSM-10 supports 50 users, whereas the CSC-SSM-20 supports 500 users. These licenses can be upgraded to support up to 500 users (CSC-SSM-10) or 1,000 users (CSC-SSM-20).

The CSC-SSM also supports two feature licenses. The base license is included in all CSC-SSMs and provides for antivirus, antispyware, and file-blocking capabilities. This functionality can be enhanced with the Plus License, which adds antispam, antiphishing, content-filter, URL blocking, and URL filtering functionality.

Feature Licenses

Feature licenses are used on the ASA firewalls to provide advanced features such as security contexts or GTP/GPRS inspection for the firewall. Security context licensing supports 5, 10, 20, and 50 contexts, with the maximum number of supported security contexts depending on the model of PIX.

Encryption Licenses

When encryption is required to support IPSec VPNs or to enable the ASDM, it is necessary to obtain either the 56-bit DES encryption license or the 3DES (168-bit)/AES (128, 192 or 256-bit) encryption license. The encryption licenses are available for all models.

Cisco PIX Firewall Version 6.3

PIX Firewall version 6.3 is the latest mainline release of the PIX operating system for the PIX 501 and PIX 506 firewalls. PIX version 6.3 offers many new features as well as performance enhancements. Although many of the new features in this release of code pertain to VPN and support for Voice over IP (VoIP), this release does provide several enhancements that could be useful in a DMZ environment, such as VLAN and OSPF support. PIX OS version 6.3 also fixes several bugs and vulnerabilities found in the previous release. This code does not yet meet the Common Criteria EAL4 certification, but its additional functionality might compel you to upgrade.

New features implemented in PIX version 6.3 include:

- **VLAN support** Enables the PIX to support multiple virtual interfaces via VLAN trunking.

- **OSPF** Supports the Open Shortest Path First (OSPF) dynamic routing protocol.

- **Advanced Encryption Standard (AES)** Support for a new international encryption standard.

- **VPN Acceleration Card+ (VAC+)** The first release to offer support for the new VAC+ PCI Card option.

- **VPN NAT transparency** Circumvents issues arising from using a VPN when NAT/PAT is implemented by dynamically wrapping IPSec VPN packets in a UDP packet Cisco Secure PIX.

- **Access banner** The PIX will display a message to anyone who tries to connect to the PIX's CLI. It is important to configure a banner for legal purposes.

- **Management enhancements** Several enhancements have been made to the CLI, including ACL editing, syslog formats, access banners, and console inactivity timeouts.

For more information on PIX OS 6.3, visit www.cisco.com/warp/customer/cc/pd/fw/sqfw500/prodlit/pix63_ds.htm.

Cisco PIX and ASA Firewall Version 7.2

PIX OS and ASA OS 7.2 is the latest mainline release of the PIX and ASA operating system for all models of PIX or ASA except the PIX 501 and PIX 506E. PIX/ASA OS 7.2 is built on the 6.x software but provides many advanced features and performance enhancements. In addition, the PIX/ASA OS 7.2 makes some fundamental changes to the method and manner in which firewalls, and in particular interfaces and security policies, are configured. Many of these changes will be familiar to users of the Cisco Internetwork Operating System (IOS). For a full breakdown of the changes between the 6.x and 7.x releases, visit www.cisco.com/en/US/products/sw/secursw/ps2120/products_upgrade_guides09186a0080369ee2.html.

New features implemented in PIX/ASA version 7.2 include:

- **Application Inspection and Control** Provides enhanced application inspection and control of a number of new protocols. This functionality is not to be confused with the functionality provided by the AIP-SSM or CSC-SSM.

- **Remote Access and Site-to-Site VPN** Provides improved VPN functionality, including support for Network Admission Control (NAC) and L2TP over IPSec.

- **Network Integration** Provides enhanced network integration capabilities through the support of Point-to-Point Protocol over Ethernet (PPPoE) client functionality, Dynamic DNS, multicast routing enhancements, and private and automatic MAC address assignment for multiple contexts and expands DNS domain name usage when configuring AAA or the *ping, traceroute,* and *copy* commands.

- **Resiliency and Scalability** Supports subsecond (under a second) failover and standby ISP links to define and activate a secondary route in the event that the primary ISP fails.

- **Management and Serviceability** A number of management and serviceability enhancements have been made, including the addition of the *traceroute* command, packet tracer functionality that allows the life span of a packet to be traced through the firewall to determine whether the firewall is behaving as expected. It also includes support for Web Cache Communication Protocol (WCCP) as well as IPv6 security enforcement of IPv6 addresses. Finally, support for inspection, IPS, CSC, and Web filtering has been added to WebVPN clients.

PIX Firewall PCI Card Options

In the previous section, we referred to several of the optional PCI cards that make the higher-end PIX chassis very versatile. These cards give the PIX the ability to handle multiple DMZ legs and increase VPN performance. In this section, we clarify the capabilities of these cards and their uses.

For 10/100Mbps Ethernet requirements, the PIX offers two types of PCI card: a single-port Fast Ethernet card and a four-port Fast Ethernet card. Even though the Fast Ethernet cards are 32-bit/33MHz PCI cards, they can fit in either the 32-bit/33MHz or the 64-bit/66MHz PCI slots on the PIX and can be configured for 10/100Mbps at either half or full duplex. The PIX 525 and 535 both support the Gigabit Ethernet 64-bit/66MHz PCI card. The Gigabit Ethernet multimode fiber PCI interface card can be inserted into either the 32-bit/33MHz or the 64-bit/66MHz PCI slots on the PIX. If you recall, the PIX 535 has both 32-bit/33MHz and 64-bit/66MHz PCI slots, but when inserted into 32-bit/33MHz, the cards will severely degrade device performance, so fill the 64-bit/66MHz PCI slots before inserting a card into the 32-bit/33MHz. The PIX 525 only has 32-

bit/33MHz PCI slots, so you have no choice but to install the card there and not receive the card's full throughput.

The PIX offers VACs, which offload all CPU-intensive encryption calculations, DES, 3DES, or AES, from the main processor and onto the VAC hardware. This improves not only VPN throughput but also overall firewall performance. Without the VAC installed, the encryption algorithm and its computations are performed by the PIX OS and the main CPU, which causes the PIX's overall performance to be severely impacted as the number of IPSec VPN tunnels and load are increased. If you need extensive use of IPSec VPN tunnels, consider installing the optional VAC, because it provides notable improvement in performance and security. At the time of this writing, there were two VAC options: the original VAC and the newer, improved VAC+. Besides increased performance, the VAC+ adds AES hardware acceleration, whereas the original VAC supports only DES and 3DES. It must be noted that VAC+ is only supported by PIX OS version 6.3(1) and later. At some point Cisco will "end of life" the original VAC and sell only the VAC+ as a separate option and include it in the Unrestricted license bundle.

Installing a New PCI Card

You have many things to think about when you're upgrading hardware on the PIX. You must take into account license restrictions, types of interfaces supported by each PIX model, available PCI slots, and cost.

For example, let's say that you are the administrator of an enterprise network and your boss tells you there is a project in the works whereby the company's new Web site will be hosted at your location. You need to build a DMZ environment to accommodate the Web servers. You take a look at your Internet infrastructure; it currently utilizes a PIX 515E, which supports only user access to the Internet. The PIX was originally shipped with the Restricted software license and the two embedded Fast Ethernet interfaces, which are both used by the inside and outside interfaces, and it has no optional PCI cards installed. To support a DMZ where the Web servers will reside, you need to add a third Fast Ethernet interface to the PIX.

You look at Cisco's product catalog for the PIX and notice two options: a one-port Fast Ethernet PCI card and a four-port Fast Ethernet PCI card. Your first inclination might be to order the four-port Fast Ethernet PCI card for scalability reasons, but as we discussed earlier in the chapter, it is important to understand the limitations of the Restricted license. On the PIX 515E, the Restricted license allows for only a total of three Fast Ethernet interfaces, so if you purchase the four-port Fast Ethernet PCI card, you would also have to purchase the Unrestricted license upgrade to take advantage all the installed interfaces. This can be an expensive solution, since most of the PIX's cost is not in the hardware but in the licensing. Another solution is to order the one-port Fast Ethernet PCI card, which will meet your current DMZ requirements, does not require a license upgrade, and costs a fraction of the price of the previous option but does not provide for scalability.

Adding a PCI card to the PIX 515E is a fairly simple process, similar to adding a PCI card to a regular PC. First, shut down and unplug the unit. Remove the top cover from the firewall, exposing the internal components. Next remove the PCI slot faceplate located at the rear of the PIX (fastened by two screws). This action exposes the PCI slots. You can now add the optional PCI card into an open slot (start at the top) and press the PCI card firmly into place. On the faceplate, remove one of the blank PCI slot covers to expose the newly inserted card, then reattach the faceplate and screws. Next, power on the firewall. To verify that installation of the PCI card was successful, you can use the *show version* command, which will display the number of interfaces installed. Refer to the Cisco Web site for further installation procedures, or once you order the extra PCI card, examine its accompanying manual.

ASA Firewall SSM Options

The biggest thing that differentiates an ASA from a PIX firewall is the SSM and the corresponding functionality that it provides. The ASA supports three types of SSM: the AIP-SSM, the CSC-SSM, and the 4GE-SSM.

- **AIP-SSM** This card provides the Intrusion Prevention System functionality that the ASA can utilize for advanced filtering and blocking of traffic. The AIP-SSM runs its own intrusion prevention software in conjunction with the ASA 7.*x* software and can be managed and configured independently of the ASA software. In a manner of speaking, the AIP-SSM combines the features of the Cisco IPS 4200 series sensor and the ASA firewall into a single device.

- **CSC-SSM** This card provides the enhanced content filtering and anti-X functionality that the ASA can utilize for advanced content filtering and blocking of malware. The CSC-SSM runs its own software, provided by Trend Micro, in conjunction with the ASA 7.*x* software that can be managed independently of the ASA software. In a manner of speaking, the CSC-SSM combines the features of the Trend Micro InterScan and the ASA firewall into a single device.

- **4GE-SSM** This card provides four ports of 10/100/1000 Ethernet as well as four SFP fiber ports, allowing the ASA to be expanded to include any combination of the eight ports on the module. Keep in mind that the ASA supports only eight active interfaces at any given time, so, for example, if the four embedded interfaces are in use, only four ports (either Ethernet or SFP) from the 4GE-SSM may be active.

Installing a New SSM

Installing a new SSM is similar to installing a PCI card in a PIX in terms of simplicity. The ASA supports only one SSM at a time, so the only question regarding the SSM and the ASA is which SSM you want to install.

The actual installation is very straightforward: Simply power off the ASA and remove the two screws from the rear left of the chassis that holds the SSM slot cover in place. Insert the SSM into the slot using the provided channels and screw the SSM into the chassis. At that point you merely need to power the SSM back on and connect the SSM to the network, and you are ready to configure the SSM accordingly.

Designing & Planning…

Putting It All Together

If a DMZ is correctly planned and designed, it will make simple the tasks of implementing, maintaining, and supporting the DMZ infrastructure. It is important to note that a DMZ cannot be properly designed without a clear vision of what the DMZ will support. Will the DMZ environment contain a handful of servers that provide the enterprise with basic services and therefore does not require much performance or resiliency? Or will the DMZ environment contain major services that the enterprise needs to be productive and profitable and therefore will need to be in operation at all times? Alternatively, will it be somewhere between these two scenarios? Do you need to perform advanced content filtering or intrusion prevention? There is only one way to determine the category your DMZ infrastructure will fit into: You need to understand the business, the role the DMZ will play, the type of traffic the DMZ will support, the performance you require, and plans for future growth.

Now let's say that you are the network architect for a company called Automania that sells wholesale auto parts. Automania is a standard "bricks and mortar" company that normally does business by in-store sales, phone, fax, and catalog orders, but the company is looking to add the ability to sell auto parts on the Internet. The company sees Internet sales as a way to attract new customers and offer new and existing customers the ability to make purchases 24 hours a day, seven days a week, 365 days a year, which cannot be done without significant expense using conventional methods. The company has hired a consulting firm to design and build the Automania.com Web site, where customers can shop over the Internet. The site's developers have designed an e-commerce site with a shopping cart feature so Internet users can browse for items, check prices, and finally, purchase auto parts. The company projects that the Internet business will show moderate sales at first as regular customers move from the conventional ordering system to the Web-based system, but the business could grow as the site attracts new customers.

Due to budgetary constraints, the developers have designed a small site that requires only two servers—a server that will contain the Web and application functions and a separate server for the database. The developers also had

Continued

the forethought to design a scalable server environment in which the number of servers supporting the site can expand as demand increases. The business expects about 10,000 hits and 1,000 transactions a day at first, then steady growth.

As the network architect for the company, you are given the task of supplying the infrastructure to support the new Automania Web site. The company already has Internet connectivity via a broadband connection, and you are protecting your network using a low-end firewall that was easy to install and worked well but does not have the ability to support a DMZ. Now you realize that you must upgrade for entire Internet infrastructure to host the new Web site. It is now time to gather the information and requirements so you can design and build a DMZ infrastructure that will be able to support the new Web site for its launch and into the future.

You need to begin gathering information, starting with the facts and requirements:

- The facts are that the company is making a strategic move to offer its customers a new method to purchase auto parts as well as to attract new customers.
- The site is important to the growth of the business.
- The Web site will start out small but could grow as sales over the Internet increase.
- The site will be a scalable server environment with a single Web/application server and a database server.
- A DMZ will need to be built on site to support the new Automania.com Web site.
- The infrastructure currently in place is not capable of supporting the new Web site.
- The site is estimated to reach 10,000 hits and 1000 transactions a day at first, then grow steadily.

You next ask questions so you can be informed of data that was missing so that you can move on to designing a solution:

- How much Internet bandwidth is required to support the site?
- What kind of security is needed? Will there be a need for both Web traffic and SSL traffic?
- Does the site require high availability?
- What are the connectivity requirements among the internal network, the Web/application server, and the database server?
- What is the budget for the DMZ infrastructure?

After you asked the questions, the developers and business managers come back to you with their answers. They tell you that since the site will receive only

Continued

10,000 hits and 1,000 transactions a day, they initially need two T1s; as the site grows, they will add bandwidth. Since the site will be processing credit card transactions, both Web traffic (TCP port 80) and SSL (TCP port 443) need to be allowed to access the Web/application server from the Internet. The database should be accessed by only the internal LAN and should respond to Web/application server requests for information.

All Web servers and switches are 100Mbps full-duplex capable devices. Even though the servers can be a single point of failure, the DMZ infrastructure should be built with redundancy. The DMZ infrastructure should be built with scalability in mind, with close attention to the budget—in other words, do not over-engineer the infrastructure.

From this information, you can now start to develop your solution. Analyzing the requirements, you decide that the multileg DMZ with redundant firewalls offers you the most secure and scalable solution that fits your budget. The multileg DMZ allows you to separate the Web/application server into separate DMZs to allow for greater security. DMZ1 will contain the Web/application server, and DMZ2 will contain the database servers. Because users will access only the Web/application server, the firewall rules will be configured so it accesses only the server on DMZ1 via the Web port (TCP port 80) and SSL port (TCP port 443). DMZ2 will allow no connectivity from the Internet; it will only respond to requests made for data by the Web/application server or by the internal LAN for management. Separating the Web/application server and the database servers into different DMZs allows for greater security in the event the Web/application server is compromised by an intruder. Since the Web/application server is directly accessible by the Internet, it is always the most vulnerable. Furthermore, the design allows for the addition of a redundant firewall that will take over for the primary, should the primary go offline.

The next step is to decide on a make and model of the firewall to use for this solution. You choose the Cisco PIX or ASA firewall line because it is a purpose-built firewall appliance and it has a Web-based and a CLI-based management interface, a modular design, strong security features, and performance. As you research the PIX model options, you immediately can cross off the 501 and 506E models because they do not support a third leg (interface) or failover. So you move onto higher-end models. The 515E, 525, and 535 can all meet the needs of your solution in terms of interfaces, failover, and performance, but since the requirements of our DMZ infrastructure are in the low to moderate level and, due to our restrictions on cost, we can choose the PIX 515E. The PIX 515E comes with two embedded 10/100Mbps interfaces (one for the internal interface, one for the outside interface), but since the requirement is for two DMZs, you will need to order the four-port Fast Ethernet PCI card (two for interfaces DMZ1 and DMZ2, one interface for stateful failover, and one interface free). Since high availability is needed in this solution, you need to purchase two PIX 515E firewalls—one with the Unrestricted license and the second with the Failover license.

If your requirements define that you need content filtering or intrusion prevention, you could easily replace the PIX firewall with an ASA firewall to provide

Continued

the required functionality. For example, let's say that in addition to the already defined requirements in this example, you also need to provide intrusion prevention functionality. You could replace the PIX 515E with an ASA 5510 Security Plus or PIX 5520 and meet the organizational needs.

For this example, let's skip the Internet connectivity planning and design; they are discussed in detail in Chapter 9. Once you have gathered all the requirements, designed a solution, and purchased the equipment, you will be ready to configure, test, and launch the site.

Making a DMZ and Controlling Traffic

This section covers how to configure the PIX and ASA's basic and advanced security features to meet your solution's needs. We discuss in detail how to securely access the PIX/ASA and define security levels, NAT, access rules, routing, failover, and other security features.

NOTE

As a general rule, all command examples provided here are the same for both the PIX and the ASA. In most cases, the commands are based on the PIX/ASA 7.x OS. In cases where there are different commands for the PIX 6.x OS, we provide examples of both commands.

Securely Managing the PIX

There are several ways to access the PIX/ASA to configure, troubleshoot, or monitor its status, including console access, Telnet, SSH, PDM (PIX 6.x), and ASDM (PIX 7.x and ASA). In this section, we discuss the advantages and disadvantages of each access method as well as how to configure some of the more secure methods. We also discuss how to authenticate users and manage them via an external RADIUS or TACACS+ server.

The Console

Out of the box, the higher-end PIX chassis, including the PIX 515E and all ASA firewalls, must be initially set up via the console port. Whereas the lower end PIX (PIX 501 and PIX 506E) can also be initially set up via the console port, they are both designed to function as a DHCP server, allowing you to connect over the network using the PDM for the initial setup and configuration. The initial setup can be accomplished using the same method as you use to connect to a Cisco router or switch. You need a terminal program, such as HyperTerminal, configured with the following parameters on the appropriate COM port:

- Bits per second to **9600**
- Data bits to **8**
- Parity to **None**
- Stop bits to **1**
- Flow control to **Hardware**

Connect your PC's COM port to the PIX or ASA's Console port using the adapter and the rolled ribbon cable that came with the PIX/ASA. You now have direct serial access to the PIX or ASA CLI. Access to the console port can be protected by a password or authenticated via a TACACS or RADIUS server. This type of access can be used for general maintenance and monitoring or when access via other methods such as Telnet or SSH is useless due to configuration errors or malfunctions. Accessing the PIX/ASA via the console might be your last option to correct the problem before you have to call Cisco's Technical Assistance Center (TAC) for assistance.

NOTE

Cisco's TAC is responsible for providing Cisco customers with assistance for technical and configuration issues for all Cisco's hardware and software products, including the PIX firewall. Cisco's TAC can be contacted by phone or via the following URL: www.cisco.com/en/US/support/index.html.

Telnet

The PIX/ASA provides the ability to Telnet to the command-line interface. The PIX/ASA allows for five simultaneous Telnet sessions from hosts or networks you specify via the *Telnet address* [*netmask*] [*interface_name*] command. This command allows you to identify the host(s) that can initiate a Telnet session as well as the interface in which to accept the connection.

Telnet access to the PIX/ASA firewall is allowed on all interfaces. However, for increased security on the most vulnerable interface, the outside of the interface with security level 0 (usually the interface facing the Internet), the PIX will accept Telnet sessions to the interface only if it is IPSec protected. Therefore, Telnet access to the outside interface requires extra configuration to support IPSec. Some administrators implement this for remote administration of PIX/ASA firewalls, but use this feature with great caution and only if absolutely necessary. As was the case with the console port, Telnet access can be protected by a password or authenticated via a TACACS or RADIUS server. Remember that Telnet traffic, when not used in conjunction with IPSec, is sent in clear text. If someone is sniffing your network, they can easily capture the PIX or ASA Telnet password or enable password, or if you are using AAA, they will be able to obtain a user ID and password and use them later to open holes in the firewall or perform other malicious activity.

In sum, using Telnet is not recommended, because you could lose your credentials to a malicious attacker who is eavesdropping on your network. A more appropriate solution is to console in, as mentioned previously. An even better in-band alternative is SSH.

SSH

One of the major weaknesses inherent to a Telnet session is that all data is sent in clear text. This can be a serious security vulnerability if someone is able to sniff your Telnet session to the firewall. The PIX/ASA can also support SSH version 1.*x* (version 2.*x* is supported in the 7.*x* software), which gives the administrator secure access to the PIX or ASA CLI. All traffic between the administrator's workstation and the PIX/ASA is encrypted, which makes it difficult for a hacker to capture IDs and passwords or credentials in general. Unlike Telnet, which is available by default on almost every operating system, an SSH version 1.*x* or 2.*x* client is required and usually needs to be installed on the workstation(s) that need to manage the PIX/ASA via SSH. As with Telnet, the PIX/ASA will allow five simultaneous SSH sessions from hosts or networks you specify via the *ssh* command. As with the other access methods, the PIX/ASA can be protected by a password or authenticated via a TACACS or RADIUS server. Unlike Telnet, the PIX/ASA allows SSH connectivity on all interfaces, including the outside interface. To configure SSH, the PIX/ASA firewall needs a DES or 3DES activation key to generate an RSA key pair and support encrypted communication between the client and the PIX/ASA.

The first task in setting up SSH is to create an RSA key pair and save it to the PIX's Flash. The configuration shown in Figure 6.5 identifies the code necessary to generate an RSA key pair, which consists of the PIX or ASA hostname and domain name. Two different commands will need to be run, depending on whether the firewall is running a 6.*x* OS (Figure 6.6) or 7.*x*. For the 7.*x* OS, the *crypto key generate rsa* command generates an RSA key pair with a key modulus of 1024 (which is the default). For the 6.*x* OS, the command *ca generate rsa key 1024* generates an RSA key pair with a key modulus of 1024 bits (the default is 768 bits). This code will not show in the PIX/ASA configuration, but the RSA key-pair configuration can be viewed by executing the *sh crypto key mypubkey rsa* (7.*x*) or *show ca mypubkey rsa* (6.*x*) command. If you are using the 6.*x* OS to save the generated RSA key pair so it will be available after a reboot, you need to save it into Flash by entering the *ca save all* command. With the 7.*x* OS, the RSA key pair is saved when the configuration is saved by running the *copy running-config startup-config* command.

After the RSA key pair is generated, it is time to configure SSH. The example shows a workstation with the IP address 192.168.0.2 that is authorized to initiate an SSH session to the PIX's or ASA's inside interface. Use the *ssh address* [*netmask*] [*interface_name*] command to define the IP host or IP address range that can access the PIX as well as on which interface to accept this connection. The *ssh timeout* command sets the amount of idle time, in minutes, before the session is disconnected.

Figure 6.5 *7.x* OS SSH Configuration Example

```
pixfirewall(config)# hostname ASA5520
ASA5520(config)# domain-name syngress.com
ASA5520(config)# crypto key generate rsa
ASA5520(config)# copy running-config startup-config
ASA5520(config)# ssh 192.168.0.2 255.255.255.255 inside
ASA5520(config)# ssh timeout 60
```

Figure 6.6 *6.x* OS SSH Configuration Example

```
pixfirewall(config)# hostname Pix515
Pix515(config)# domain-name syngress.com
Pix515(config)# ca generate rsa key 1024
Pix515(config)# ca save all
Pix515(config)# ssh 192.168.0.2 255.255.255.255 inside
Pix515(config)# ssh timeout 60
```

An authorized workstation—in this case, 192.168.0.2—with an SSH client can complete a session with the PIX. The SSH client will require a username and password, but if you are using only local passwords, you might ask, "What is my username?" In this case, the username is *pix,* but if AAA is configured, the username is your TACACS+ or RADIUS username and password.

The PIX Device Manager

The PDM provides administrators with a browser-based GUI that can be used to configure the PIX (running the 6.*x* OS) without having to know how to administer the CLI. The PDM provides administrators who are not well versed in the PIX CLI the ability to easily configure and monitor the PIX via a Java applet. All transmission between the browser and the PIX is secure via SSL. The PDM will provide you with configuration wizards, performance graphs, and historical data. To run the PDM, you need an activation key that enables DES or Triple DES 3DES on the PIX. It is important to remember that the PDM software is separate for the PIX OS (although the PDM is dependent on the firewall running the 6.*x* OS) and needs to be loaded into Flash separately (assuming it was not shipped with the PIX already loaded) before it can be used to manage the PIX. The PDM feature is not enabled on the higher-end PIX models (PIX 515E and greater) by default. For the PIX to accept and respond to HTTP requests, you need to enable the HTTP server within the PIX OS with the *http server enable* command. As with the other methods, you need to specify the interface and the IP address or IP range that can access PDM.

> **NOTE**
>
> Unlike the Web-based management interface on Cisco routers, PDM is a very useful tool for novice and even advanced firewall administrators. Besides the PDM providing a powerful GUI, all the traffic between the PIX and the browser is encrypted, which is lacking from the router's HTTP server implementation. As with all unused services, if you are not planning to use PDM, make sure the HTTP server is disabled.

Figure 6.7 shows how to enable the HTTP server and specify that the host with the IP address 192.168.0.2 is the only device able to access the PDM. Once the PDM is enabled (and assuming you've already configured the interfaces on the PIX), you will be able to access the PIX via your Web browser using this URL: https://192.168.0.1. (In this example, the IP address of the PIX's inside interface is 192.168.0.1.)

You will be prompted to accept certificates and then prompted for a username and password. If you are using RADIUS or TACACS+ to authenticate access to the PIX, use the username and passwords assigned to you. If you are not using RADIUS or TACACS+, leave the username prompt empty and enter the enable password at the password prompt. In this chapter, we concentrate on the PIX CLI as the preferred method of configuring and managing the PIX, and as we mentioned earlier, there some advanced commands that the PDM does not support. If you do not need the PDM, make sure you disable the HTTP server on the PIX using the *no http server enable* command. Although the PDM can be very useful for managing and supporting the PIX, we recommend using SSH as the only form of device-centric remote administration of the PIX. For monitoring multiple firewalls, CiscoWorks VMS should be considered. Even though the PDM provides secure communication, it might be wise to disable it to reduce the entry points in the PIX's management interface, therefore limiting the PIX's exposure to attacks. SSH provides secure communication as well as access to all the PIX's CLI commands.

Figure 6.7 PDM Configuration Example

```
Pix515(config)# http server enable
Pix515(config)# http 192.168.0.2 255.255.255.255 inside
```

The Adaptive Security Device Manager

As previously mentioned, the ASDM is the logical replacement of the PDM for all PIX and ASA running the 7.x software. Like the PDM, the ASDM is a separate software image and must be installed independently of the OS, even though it depends on the OS to function.

ASDM is a Java-based GUI used to manage the Cisco PIX firewall. It consists of a software image that runs from Flash memory on the PIX firewall, enabling administrative access via a Secure Sockets Layer (SSL) encrypted HTTPS session. ASDM completely replaces PDM, which was available for versions before 7.0. ASDM allows firewall administrators to work from a variety of authorized workstations configured with a compatible browser and includes nearly all PIX CLI functionality. For example, using ASDM, administrators can add, modify, and delete firewall rulesets, configure NAT, or set up a VPN.

In addition to altering PIX configurations, ASDM facilitates administrative monitoring of the PIX firewall through powerful graph and table displays for near-real-time insight into PIX performance. This chapter introduces ASDM and provides detailed information for using it to configure and monitor the PIX firewall.

There are two methods of accessing the ASDM from a client computer. The first method is by using a Web browser in the same fashion as with the PDM. The second method is by using a client application known as the Cisco ASDM Launcher. The ASDM Launcher provides a browser-independent method of connecting to the ASDM. In both cases the traffic between the client is securely transmitted via SSL.

Figure 6.8 shows how to enable the HTTP server on the firewall, specify the ASDM image to load on the firewall (an optional command that is required ibkt if you have multiple ASDM images installed on the firewall), and specify that the host with the IP address 192.168.0.2 is the only device able to access the ASDM. Once the ASDM is enabled (and assuming you've already configured the interfaces on the PIX/ASA), you will be able to access the PIX/ASA via your Web browser using the URL https://192.168.0.1 or via the ADSM Launcher using the IP address 192.168.0.1. (In this example, the IP address of the PIX/ASA's inside interface is 192.168.0.1.)

Figure 6.8 ASDM Configuration Example

```
ASA5520(config)# http server enable
ASA5520(config)# asdm image flash:/asdm-521.bin
ASA5520(config)# http 192.168.0.2 255.255.255.255 inside
```

NOTE

Some corporate security managers only access the PIX or ASA console port via a secure, nonnetworked terminal in the data center or another form of secure out-of-band management. To reduce the risk of a hacker breaking into the PIX or ASA using admin accounts and making unauthorized changes for other possible attacks, they will not permit access methods such as Telnet, SSH, the PDM, ASDM, or CSPM. Although this access method is very secure, it makes PIX/ASA management and support very difficult.

Authenticating Management Access to the PIX

Suppose you have a large organization in which many administrators have access to the PIX/ASA for management and the security policy calls for each admin to have a unique ID and password so that changes to the PIX/ASA can be tracked and administrators can be held accountable.

To accomplish this task, the PIX/ASA has a feature called *authentication, authorization, and accounting* (also known as *AAA*). AAA can authenticate users managing the PIX/ASA via CLI, ASDM, or the PDM tool. AAA can be applied to admins accessing the PIX/ASA via the following methods: console, Telnet, SSH, and HTTP. With AAA configured, the PIX/ASA will authenticate the username and password information with a local ID or an external RADIUS or TACACS+ server. If the PIX/ASA receives an "Accept" response from the RADIUS or TACACS+ server, the user will be allowed to gain access to the PIX/ASA. If a "Reject" message is received, the user will be denied access. The AAA feature can also limit the commands by authorizing each command an admin enters. This tool is useful if you have many administrators who have access to the PIX/ASA. You might want an administrator to have the ability to troubleshoot the PIX/ASA, which requires the use of *show* and *clear* commands, and provide other senior or advanced administrators the ability to make configuration changes to interfaces, access rules, routing, and so on. Unlike Cisco routers and switches, the PIX/ASA currently does not support accounting, which logs changes administrators make. However, the PIX/ASA can provide AAA services for traffic passing through the PIX/ASA, as we discuss in detail later in this chapter.

Figure 6.9 details the configuration needed to implement authentication of administrative access to the PIX/ASA. The *aaa-server* command sets the server that will authenticate the admin IDs to either RADIUS or TACACS+. This command is also used to identify the interface on the PIX/ASA in which the RADIUS or TACACS+ resides, its IP address, and the encryption key used for encrypted communication between the PIX/ASA and the server and assigns it a group tag. In this example, we authenticate to a TACACS+ server. The IP address of the server is *192.168.1.50*, the shared encrypted key is *mykey,* and we assigned it the group tag of *AuthAdmin.* The *aaa authentication* command specifies the access method and matches it to a group tag. This example shows how to configure authentication for each of the methods discussed in this section. The last line in this example enables command authorization using the *aaa authorization* command. Before you enable command authorization, make sure that you are logged into the firewall with a user account that is authorized to run commands or you may find yourself locked out of the firewall. You can do this by running the command *show curpriv* and verifying that the user you are logged in as is defined on the AAA server and has the appropriate command authorization level.

NOTE

The Cisco Secure Access Control Server (ACS), which can act as either a
TACACS+ or RADIUS server, also needs to be configured to complete the AAA
implementation. You can find more information on ACS on Cisco's Web site at
www.cisco.com/univercd/cc/td/doc/product/access/acs_soft/csacs4nt/acs31/acsuse
r/index.htm.

Figure 6.9 Configuring AAA for the 6.x OS

```
Pix515(config)# aaa-server AuthAdmin protocol tacacs+
Pix515(config)# aaa-server AuthAdmin (inside) host 192.168.1.50 mykey
    timeout 5
Pix515(config)# aaa authentication serial console AuthAdmin
Pix515(config)# aaa authentication Telnet console AuthAdmin
Pix515(config)# aaa authentication ssh console AuthAdmin
Pix515(config)# aaa authentication http console AuthAdmin
Pix515(config)# aaa authentication enable console AuthAdmin
Pix515(config)# aaa authorization command AuthAdmin
```

The same basic commands are used to configure AAA for either the 6.x or 7.x PIX/ASA
software. The only minor difference is that on the PIX 7.x software the *aaa-server* commands
bring you into an AAA server configuration mode, from which you must exit before running the rest of the commands. Figure 6.10 illustrates the 7.x configuration commands.

Figure 6.10 Configuring AAA for the 7.x OS

```
ASA5520(config)# aaa-server AuthAdmin protocol tacacs+
ASA5520(config-aaa-server-group)# exit
ASA5520(config)# aaa-server AuthAdmin (inside) host 10.21.120.46 mypubkey timeout
5
ASA5520(config-aaa-server-host)# exit
ASA5520(config)# aaa authentication ssh console AuthAdmin
ASA5520(config)# aaa authentication serial console AuthAdmin
ASA5520(config)# aaa authentication Telnet console AuthAdmin
ASA5520(config)# aaa authentication http console AuthAdmin
ASA5520(config)# aaa authentication enable console AuthAdmin
ASA5520(config)# aaa authorization command AuthAdmin
```

PIX/ASA Configuration Basics

In this section, we cover the basic configuration steps needed to set up the PIX/ASA to provide internal user access to the Internet, support for a DMZ, and connectivity to the Internet. Here we discuss how to define interfaces, configure NAT, set access rules, and enable routing. By the end of this section, you will be familiar with the basic configuration steps for the PIX/ASA and be able to apply these steps to the configuration of your PIX/ASA firewall.

Defining Interfaces

Before configuring the interfaces on the PIX/ASA, you must have your design laid out and know the function of each PIX/ASA interface. This process includes:

- Naming the interface

- Assigning a security level

- Configuring an IP address

- Setting the speed and duplex of the interface

The commands required to perform these tasks differ based on whether the firewall is running the 6.x or 7.x version of the OS. We will first look at the 6.x OS commands, then the 7.x OS commands. Figure 6.11 shows a design for a traditional "three-legged" firewall, detailing the number of interfaces and their IP addresses required to implement this environment. The switches connecting the PIX/ASA to the inside, outside, and DMZ LANs are all capable of running at 100Mbps full duplex. Once the basic information has been compiled, we can begin to add the configuration needed to set up the interfaces on the PIX/ASA.

Figure 6.11 PIX/ASA Interface Configuration

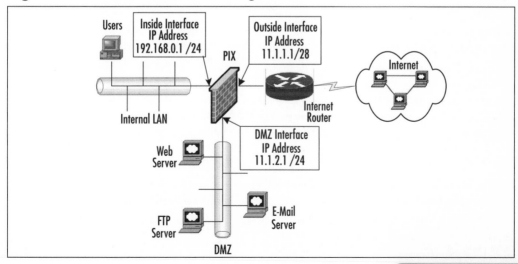

In configuring the interface, the first step is to name and define a security level for each active interface. When the PIX/ASA boots up, it assigns a hardware ID to each interface it detects and is licensed for. In this example, we have a PIX 515E with an optional one-port Fast Ethernet card inserted into one of the chassis' open PCI slots. The two embedded PIX 515E Fast Ethernet interfaces are assigned the hardware IDs *ethernet0* and *ethernet1*. The optional one-port Fast Ethernet card is assigned *ethernet2*. The PIX will allow you to logically name the PIX's interfaces, so you can rename them something more relevant. The only exception to this is the 6.*x* OS, which requires the interface with security level 100 (we discuss security levels in the next paragraph) to be named *inside*. For example, the default interface name for the optional one-port Fast Ethernet is *intf2*, but we will rename it to better describe its usage and call it *DMZ*, since it will house the DMZ LAN.

Once we choose the function and naming convention for the PIX's or ASA's interfaces, we must now decide on a security level for each interface. You can assign a security level between 0 and 100, where 0 is the least secure interface and 100 is the most secure interface. The most secure interface on the PIX/ASA is always the inside interface, which has a security level of 100, and the least secure is usually your Internet-facing interface, or the outside interface, which has a security level of 0. The security levels are designed to let the PIX/ASA know how to treat packets entering its interfaces. Sessions originating and entering the PIX/ASA on an interface with a high security level will be permitted by default to travel through PIX/ASA on any interface with a lower security level and allow packets associated with this session to return.

However, a session originating from a lower security interface will not be forwarded to an interface with a higher security level unless explicitly permitted by an ACL. Other interfaces, such as the DMZ interface in Figure 6.11, need to be assigned a value between 1 and 99, which signifies semitrusted networks and treats them as such, allowing them only default access to the lower security interfaces, such as the outside interface or another DMZ interface with a lower security level.

For example, a user on the internal LAN can access a Web site on the Internet because the user's HTTP request will originate from the PIX/ASA's inside interface and be permitted to exit the outside interface and return due to the fact the inside interface has a greater security level than the outside interface. The same is true if the user wants to access a Web site located on the DMZ interface of the PIX/ASA, because the inside interface has a greater security level than the DMZ interface. If the user moved his or her workstation to the DMZ LAN, he or she would still be able to access a Web site on the Internet because the DMZ interface has a greater security level than the outside interface. However, if the user tried to access any resources on the PIX/ASA's inside interface, access would be denied because the DMZ interface has a lower security level than the inside interface unless access was explicitly allowed. Packets originating from the Internet and entering the PIX/ASA from the outside interface will not be forwarded on any of the PIX/ASA's other interfaces unless explicitly allowed via an ACL. Later in this chapter, we will discuss how to configure the PIX/ASA to allow access from an interface with a lower security level to an interface with a higher security level using ACLs.

NOTE

Prior to PIX OS version 5.3, it was necessary to define the outside interface as Ethernet0 and the inside interface as Ethernet1. Although this is not a requirement for PIX OS version 5.3 and greater, it is recommended that you continue to use this convention.

PIX OS 6.x Interface Configuration

The naming and assignment of the security level of an interface is implemented differently for the PIX 6.x OS and the PIX/ASA 7.x OS. For the PIX 6.x OS, it is implemented using the *nameif* command. Figure 6.12 shows how to configure the DMZ infrastructure pictured in Figure 6.11. Within the *nameif* command, you need to associate the hardware ID to a logical name and a security level. In this case, Ethernet0 and Ethernet1 are left at their defaults, which are *outside* with a security level of 100 and *inside* with a security level of 0, respectively. The default configuration on Ethernet2 is overwritten and changed to *DMZ* with a security level of 50.

Figure 6.12 Configuring Interface Names and Security Levels

```
Pix515(config)# nameif ethernet0 outside security0
Pix515(config)# nameif ethernet1 inside security100
Pix515(config)# nameif ethernet2 DMZ security50
```

NOTE

For the 6.x OS, the interface assigned security level 100 can only be named *inside*. This is no longer the case with the PIX/ASA 7.x OS. When assigning security levels, keep expansion in mind and allow some space between security levels in case you have to add another interface with a security level that sits between two previously configured interfaces.

The next step is to configure the IP addresses for each of the active interfaces on the PIX. IP addresses should always be statically assigned to each active interface, except in the case where you are connecting to a broadband service provider that is assigning IP addresses dynamically to the PIX's outside IP address via DHCP. The *ip address if_name ip_address [netmask]* command is used to assign static IP addresses to each of the PIX's interfaces, as shown in Figure 6.13.

Figure 6.13 Configuring IP Addresses

```
Pix515(config)# ip address inside 192.168.0.1 255.255.255.0
Pix515(config)# ip address outside 11.1.1.1 255.255.255.240
Pix515(config)# ip address DMZ 11.1.2.1 255.255.255.0
```

The last step in the configuration of the PIX's interfaces is to set the speed and duplex and turn up the interface. By default, all the PIX's interfaces are disabled and set to autodetect speed and duplex settings. In the prior DMZ example, we said that all the segments were capable of running at 100Mb full duplex.

Figure 6.14 shows the use of the *interface hardware_id [hardware_speed] [shutdown]* command to configure each interface as 100Mbps full duplex as well as activating each interface by simply not adding the *shutdown* keyword to the *interface* command.

Figure 6.14 Setting Interface Speed and Duplex

```
Pix515(config)# interface ethernet0 100full
Pix515(config)# interface ethernet1 100full
Pix515(config)# interface ethernet2 100full
```

NOTE

It is always a good idea to hard-code the speed and duplex settings into both the PIX and the switch. It is common for the autodetect feature not to detect the correct settings, and you could end up with a speed or duplex mismatch, which will cause errors on the interfaces. In addition, if you have already configured your PIX but you do not think it is performing optimally, check these settings on the PIX and the switch to make sure they match. This is one of the major culprits in performance-related issues, especially in new installations.

PIX OS 7.*x* Interface Configuration

For the PIX/ASA 7.*x* OS, the same fundamental tasks need to be performed: naming and assigning a security level to an interface, assigning an IP address, and setting the interface speed and duplex. However, the commands to perform these tasks are different. With the PIX/ASA 7.*x* OS, Cisco made the interface configuration functions work more like they do in the Cisco IOS. This means that instead of using multiple commands to perform each task, you enter an interface configuration mode and perform the configuration of the naming, security-level assignment, IP address assignment, and speed and duplex settings from there, as shown in Figure 6.15. The configuration uses the interface configuration subcommand *nameif* to assign the appropriate name to the interface. The command *security-level* is used to assign the appropriate security level. The *ip address ip_address [netmask]* command is used to assign an IP address to the interface. The command *speed* is used to assign the interface speed (default is *auto*), whereas the command *duplex* is used to assign the interface duplex mode (default is *auto*).

Figure 6.15 PIX/ASA 7.*x* Interface Configuration

```
ASA5520(config)# interface ethernet0
ASA5520(config-if)# nameif outside
ASA5520(config-if)# security-level 0
ASA5520(config-if)# ip address 11.1.1.1 255.255.255.240
ASA5520(config-if)# speed 100
ASA5520(config-if)# duplex full
# The next 6 lines configure the inside interface
ASA5520(config-if)# interface ethernet1
ASA5520(config-if)# nameif inside
ASA5520(config-if)# security-level 100
ASA5520(config-if)# ip address 192.168.0.1 255.255.255.0
ASA5520(config-if)# speed 100
ASA5520(config-if)# duplex full
# The next 6 lines configure the DMZ interface
ASA5520(config-if)# interface ethernet2
ASA5520(config-if)# nameif DMZ
ASA5520(config-if)# security-level 50
ASA5520(config-if)# ip address 11.1.2.1 255.255.255.0
ASA5520(config-if)# speed 100
ASA5520(config-if)# duplex full
```

Verifying the Interface Configuration

Use the *show interface* command to display all interfaces on the PIX/ASA as well as its name, status, IP address, statistics, and settings. The display in Figure 6.16 shows a PIX with three interfaces (the output is from the 7.*x* OS; the 6.*x* OS is the same command with slightly different output). This command displays a good deal of useful information, but for the purpose of setting up the firewall's interface, let's focus on the first line of each interface, which displays the status of that particular interface, IP address, and the speed and duplex settings (highlighted in bold in the figures). The first line for each interface shows you the name of the interface as the availability of the interface would, shown as either "up" or "down." This line also shows the status of the line protocol. If line protocol is "up," the interface is operational and able to send and receive traffic; or it will show "down" when the cable is not plugged in or there is a problem with the cable. You can also use this command to view the automatically or statically discovered speed and duplex settings as well as the IP address assigned to each interface.

Figure 6.16 Show Interface Display

```
Pix515# show interface
Interface Ethernet0 "outside", is up, line protocol is up
  Hardware is i82559, BW 100 Mbps
        Full-Duplex(Full-duplex), 100 Mbps(100 Mbps)
        MAC address 0004.9ad0.b5a0, MTU 1500
        IP address 11.1.1.1, subnet mask 255.255.255.240
        0 packets input, 0 bytes, 0 no buffer
        Received 0 broadcasts, 0 runts, 0 giants
        0 input errors, 0 CRC, 0 frame, 0 overrun, 0 ignored, 0 abort
        0 L2 decode drops
        196 packets output, 12544 bytes, 0 underruns
        0 output errors, 0 collisions, 0 interface resets
        0 babbles, 0 late collisions, 0 deferred
        0 lost carrier, 0 no carrier
        input queue (curr/max blocks): hardware (128/128) software (0/0)
        output queue (curr/max blocks): hardware (0/14) software (0/1)
  Traffic Statistics for "outside":
        0 packets input, 0 bytes
        196 packets output, 5488 bytes
        0 packets dropped
      1 minute input rate 0 pkts/sec,  0 bytes/sec
      1 minute output rate 0 pkts/sec,  0 bytes/sec
      1 minute drop rate, 0 pkts/sec
      5 minute input rate 0 pkts/sec,  0 bytes/sec
      5 minute output rate 0 pkts/sec,  0 bytes/sec
      5 minute drop rate, 0 pkts/sec
Interface Ethernet1 "inside", is up, line protocol is up
  Hardware is i82559, BW 100 Mbps
        Full-Duplex(Full-duplex), 100 Mbps(100 Mbps)
        MAC address 0004.9ad0.b5a1, MTU 1500
        IP address 192.168.0.1, subnet mask 255.255.255.0
        47552 packets input, 4385636 bytes, 0 no buffer
        Received 37037 broadcasts, 0 runts, 0 giants
        0 input errors, 0 CRC, 0 frame, 0 overrun, 0 ignored, 0 abort
        0 L2 decode drops
```

```
        13512 packets output, 5890064 bytes, 0 underruns
        0 output errors, 0 collisions, 0 interface resets
        0 babbles, 0 late collisions, 0 deferred
        0 lost carrier, 0 no carrier
        input queue (curr/max blocks): hardware (128/128) software (0/26)
        output queue (curr/max blocks): hardware (0/40) software (0/1)
    Traffic Statistics for "inside":
        47531 packets input, 3693104 bytes
        13517 packets output, 5674180 bytes
        25966 packets dropped
      1 minute input rate 5 pkts/sec,  412 bytes/sec
      1 minute output rate 2 pkts/sec,  257 bytes/sec
      1 minute drop rate, 2 pkts/sec
      5 minute input rate 3 pkts/sec,  342 bytes/sec
      5 minute output rate 0 pkts/sec,  0 bytes/sec
      5 minute drop rate, 2 pkts/sec
Interface Ethernet2 "DMZ", is up, line protocol is up
  Hardware is i82559, BW 100 Mbps
        Full-Duplex(Full-duplex), 100 Mbps(100 Mbps)
        MAC address 0003.47dd.ec4d, MTU 1500
        IP address 11.1.2.1, subnet mask 255.255.255.0
        0 packets input, 0 bytes, 0 no buffer
        Received 0 broadcasts, 0 runts, 0 giants
        0 input errors, 0 CRC, 0 frame, 0 overrun, 0 ignored, 0 abort
        0 L2 decode drops
        2 packets output, 128 bytes, 0 underruns
        0 output errors, 0 collisions, 0 interface resets
        0 babbles, 0 late collisions, 0 deferred
        0 lost carrier, 0 no carrier
        input queue (curr/max blocks): hardware (128/128) software (0/0)
        output queue (curr/max blocks): hardware (0/1) software (0/1)
    Traffic Statistics for "DMZ":
        0 packets input, 0 bytes
        2 packets output, 56 bytes
        0 packets dropped
      1 minute input rate 0 pkts/sec,  0 bytes/sec
      1 minute output rate 0 pkts/sec,  0 bytes/sec
      1 minute drop rate, 0 pkts/sec
      5 minute input rate 0 pkts/sec,  0 bytes/sec
      5 minute output rate 0 pkts/sec,  0 bytes/sec
      5 minute drop rate, 0 pkts/sec
```

Configuring NAT

Network Address Translation (NAT) is one of the basic features of the PIX/ASA firewall. NAT converts private, internal IP addresses into publicly routable addresses. You might want to translate, or *to NAT* (using the term as a verb to describe this process), your internal addresses because they are nonroutable private addresses or to discourage attacks from the Internet. Request for Comment (RFC) 1918 lists the addresses that are available for private use on the internal network. The Internet Assigned Numbers Authority (IANA) has reserved the following three blocks of the IP address space for private networks:

- 10.0.0.0 through 10.255.255.255 (10 /8 prefix)

- 172.16.0.0 through 172.31.255.255 (172.16 /12 prefix)

- 192.168.0.0 through 192.168.255.255 (192.168 /16 prefix)

NOTE

You can learn more about RFC 1918 by visiting the RFC document online: www.cis.ohio-state.edu/cgi-bin/rfc/rfc1918.html.

If you are using these addresses on your internal LAN and clients on the internal LAN need to communicate with Internet resources, you need to NAT these addresses to public addresses to be routed throughout the Internet. Public addresses are typically IP addresses assigned to your organization by the Network Information Center (NIC) or by your ISP. The problem facing IPv4 is that the public address pool is being slowly depleted, so network administrators may no longer be able to assign public addresses to all clients on their internal LANs and have them access Internet resources without the use of NAT. For this reason, administrators are forced to assign private addresses to internal clients and use their allocated public addresses for NAT address pools and for DMZ-provided services directly accessible by the Internet, such as Web and e-mail relays.

NAT makes it possible for a small number of public IP addresses to provide Internet connectivity for a large range of hosts. PAT is sometimes used synonymously with NAT. However, NAT and PAT function slightly differently. NAT can provide a static one-to-one IP mapping between private and public addresses or dynamically map a large number of internal private addresses to a pool of public addresses. The problem with Dynamic NAT is that once the pool of public addresses has been exhausted, the PIX/ASA will not be able to NAT additional internal address until an address in the public pool is free, whereas PAT can map very large numbers of private addresses to a single public IP address. PAT dynamically maps a connection requested from the private address range and assigns it a unique port number on a single public address as a connection is requested. As a result, a single public IP address can support up to 65,535 connections.

Table 6.1 shows four addresses PAT'd to a single IP address. Notice that the only difference is the translated port. The PIX will hold a similar table in memory so that it knows to which real address to send the reply traffic.

Table 6.1 Port Address Translation

Real Address	Real Port	Translated Address	Translated Port
192.168.1.2	1234	11.1.1.1	1024
192.168.1.3	1444	11.1.1.1	1025
192.168.1.4	1500	11.1.1.1	1026
192.168.1.5	1234	11.1.1.1	1027

For the PIX 6.*x* OS, NAT configuration statements are required for all connectivity through the PIX/ASA, even if NAT is not required. You need to configure the PIX not to NAT and let the real address flow through without being translated. With the 7.*x* OS, this is no longer the case. Cisco introduced the *nat-control* command, which eliminates the requirement for address translation policies to be in place. We will talk more about *nat-control* later in this chapter.

In this section, we break down the NAT configuration into two parts—outbound NAT and inbound NAT—because they require different commands to implement. Outbound NAT occurs when a device on a secure interface needs to communicate through a less secure interface to reach its destination. Inbound NAT occurs when a device on a less secure interface needs to communicate through a more secure interface to reach its destination. We will also break down the examples into both 6.*x* and 7.*x* OS sections because Cisco fundamentally changed some of the NAT configurations and functionality in the 7.*x* OS for both the PIX and the ASA.

NOTE

This book details how to set up a DMZ environment, but the PIX/ASA and all its features, including NAT, can be configured to accommodate many different requirements or designs. In this NAT section, we focus on how to set up NAT for some conventional DMZ designs. Keep in mind that the PIX's and ASA's NAT and PAT features can be configured for a variety of scenarios, including connecting networks with conflicting IP addressing. You might have conflicting network addresses when your company acquires a company (or your company becomes acquired) with the same internal network numbering scheme. In today's world of mergers and acquisitions, this configuration will become a definite reality for most firewall administrators.

Outbound NAT

With the PIX/ASA 7.*x* OS, Cisco introduced a new command that fundamentally changed how the firewall handled NAT. Historically, whether you actually intended to perform NAT or not, you always needed to configure NAT on the firewall, even if the configuration was nothing more than configuring the firewall to not NAT any traffic. If you did not do this, the firewall would simply not permit any outbound traffic. In the 7.*x* OS, this behavior was changed to allow the firewall, by default, to permit all outbound traffic, even if NAT is not configured. The command that controls this functionality is the *nat-control* command.

By default, the *nat-control* command is disabled (*no nat-control*), which configures the firewall to allow traffic from a higher security-level interface (for example, *inside*) to pass to a lower security level interface (for example, *outside*) without NAT. If you want the firewall to perform outbound NAT, you must run the *nat-control* command, as shown in Figure 6.17. The rest of this section assumes that *nat-control* has been configured on the firewall, thus requiring NAT or PAT configuration commands to allow the firewall to pass outbound traffic.

Figure 6.17 Configuring *nat-control* on a Firewall

```
houqepixfw01(config)# nat-control
```

For the 6.*x* OS, when a connection from a more secure interface to a less secure interface is necessary, a NAT or PAT statement needs to be configured, regardless of whether you need to NAT or PAT the address on the interface with the higher security interface. For the 7.*x* OS, if the *nat-control* command has been enabled, a NAT or PAT statement also needs to be configured. This tells the PIX/ASA whether or not to NAT or PAT the packets as they pass through the PIX. For example, if users on the inside interface, which are on private address space, need to access the Internet, they must be translated to a public address space that is routable on the Internet. The three options to configure outbound address translation are Static NAT, Dynamic NAT, and Dynamic PAT.

Outbound connections usually call for Dynamic NAT or Dynamic PAT. Configuring outbound NAT usually requires two steps. The first step is to identify whether NAT is required for a specified range of IP addresses and, if it is, assign it a NAT ID. The second step is to assign the NAT ID to a public address pool for Dynamic NAT or a single public address to be used by PAT.

The *nat* [(*real_ifc*)] *nat_id real_ip* [*mask* [*dns*] [**outside** | *norandomseq*] [*max_conns* [*emb_limit*]]]] (6.*x* OS) or **nat** (*real_ifc*) *nat_id real_ip* [*mask* [*dns*] [**outside**] [[***tcp***] *tcp_max_conns* [*emb_limit*]][*udp udp_max_conns*] [*norandomseq*]] (7.*x* OS) command is used to complete Step 1. As you can see, the commands are very similar, with the 7.*x* command having a few new options. The *nat* command requires you to configure the interface to which the NAT should be applied, the NAT ID, the range of IP addresses to be translated, and connection limits. The *real_ifc* parameter tells the PIX to NAT connections initiated from the specified PIX interface that match the IP address range specified by the *real_ip mask* parameters. The *nat_id* parameter is used to group the hosts to be translated and will be used later, in Step 2. If the *nat_id* parameter is set to 0, the PIX will not NAT the specified range.

The *max_conns, tcp_max_conns, udp_max_conns,* and *emb_limit* parameters specify the connection limits and the embryonic limit, respectively. The connection limit is the number of simultaneous connections allowed by the PIX initiated by the specified IP range. In the 6.*x* OS, the maximum number of connections is defined as a single value (*max_conns*) for both TCP and UDP connections. In the 7.*x* OS, you can define separate maximum connection values for TCP (*tcp_max_conns*) or UDP (*udp_max_conns*) accordingly. The embryonic limit is the number of connections that have started but have not completed, meaning that they have not completed the three-way handshake. By default, both these parameters are set to 0, which means that the PIX will allow an unlimited number of active connections and an unlimited number of embryonic connections or incomplete connections. Setting these parameters to numbers other than 0 allows the PIX to limit the number of connections made by the specified IP range and protect your network from propagating (but not being targeted by) SYN or flood attacks.

These parameters are relevant in both internally and externally initiated connections settings. They will also protect your network from SYN or flood attacks initiated from the Internet. Since this type of protection is more relevant on connections initiated outside your network, we discuss the importance of setting these parameters later in the "Inbound NAT" section. Keep in mind that if you know the number of connections your internal users need and want that will prevent internal clients from acting as a propagation point for flood attacks, it's a good idea to set the connection and embryonic limits to a value other than 0. Be careful not to set them too low, which would prevent valid connections passing through the PIX. Once they're set, you need to monitor the number of connections from time to time to verify that increased usage from normal growth is not about to eclipse your limits, in which case you need to adjust your settings.

The *dns, outside,* and *norandomseq* parameters are generally not used in most environments. The *dns* parameter causes the firewall to rewrite the DNS A record from the mapped value to the real value. The *outside* parameter is required if the interface you are configuring NAT on is on a lower security level than the interface than the interface that will be identified by the corresponding *global* statement (the second step in configuring outbound NAT). This is known as *outside* or *bidirectional NAT*. The *norandomseq* parameter disables TCP ISN randomization protection. TCP sequence randomization is a security enhancement that limits an attacker's ability to successfully achieve a TCP hijack attack. It should be disabled only if there is another inline firewall that is also randomizing sequence numbers, because both firewalls randomizing the sequence numbers can scramble the data.

The *nat [(real_ifc)] 0 access-list acl_name* command tells the PIX not to NAT packets that match the criteria set by an access list. The use of an access list gives the PIX flexibility not only based on source IP addresses, as the standard *nat* command does, but also on destination IP address. For this command to function, it requires the creation of an ACL and the *nat* command with the *0 access-list* option. The ACL used with the *nat* command only matches on Layer 3 and must not contain any port specification. (We explore ACLs in depth later in this chapter.) Although this functionality might sound similar to the *no nat-control* functionality in the 7.x OS, there is a subtle difference. With the *no nat-control* command, you are not using NAT on the firewall at all. With the *NAT 0* command, you are using NAT on the firewall but are configuring a mechanism to bypass NAT for a specific scenario. Although functionally the traffic is not being NAT'd in either case, it's important to understand that subtle difference.

The second step assigns the NAT ID to a global address pool for Dynamic NAT or a single public address to be used by PAT. The *global [(mapped_ifc)] nat_id {mapped_ip[-mapped_ip] [netmask mask] | interface}* command is used to tie the IP address range specified with the *nat* command to an IP address or a range of global IP addresses. In an outbound connection scenario where internal users need to access resources on the Internet, the global addresses need to be in the public address range so they can be routed throughout the Internet. The *mapped_ifc* parameter is the outbound interface where the translated IP address will exit. The *nat_id* parameter ties the *global* command to the *nat* command, which identifies the IP addresses that need to be translated. The next parameter specifies whether the firewall should perform Dynamic NAT or Dynamic PAT. If only one global IP address is specified in the *mapped_ip* parameter, the firewall will perform Dynamic PAT, but if a range of global IP addresses is specified (*mapped_ip-mapped_ip*], the firewall will perform Dynamic NAT. The *mask* parameter specifies the mask for the global IP addresses. If the *nat* command has a 0 specified as its *nat_id*, no *global* command is needed, since the 0 NAT ID means "do not NAT."

We use the diagram in Figure 6.18 as an example of how the *nat* and *global* commands work together to provide Dynamic NAT and PAT. We have a network with two internal LAN subnets, a PIX to provide secure access to the Internet for internal users and to support a DMZ with Web, e-mail, and FTP servers. Since the two-user subnet is on private address space, the IP addresses of internal PCs need to be translated to a public IP address to access Internet resource. The servers on the DMZ already have public addresses, so they can initiate connections to resources on the Internet without the aid of NAT. The setup has several requirements, which are listed in Table 6.2. We need to configure PAT so that all user PCs on internal LAN A can access the Internet via a single public address. Users on internal LAN B also need to access the Internet, but they have a special requirement that will enable the first seven addresses to be dynamically NAT'd and the rest can be translated via PAT. All access from the internal LAN to the DMZ should not be translated, nor should any access from the DMZ to the Internet.

Figure 6.18 NAT Example

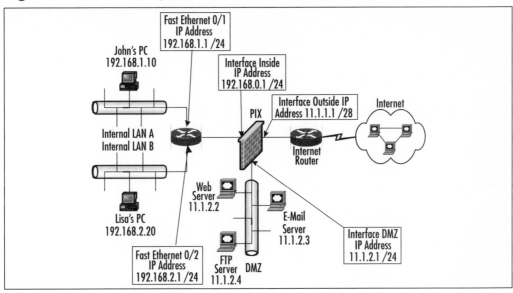

Table 6.2 Outbound NAT

Network/Device	Actual Address	Translated Address	Method
Internal LAN A	192.168.1.0 /24	11.1.1.2 /28	All PAT
Internal LAN B	192.168.2.0 /24	11.1.1.3–11.1.1.9 /28	Dynamic NAT (first seven addresses)
Internal LAN B	192.168.2.0 /24	11.1.1.10 /28	PAT (remaining addresses)
Web server	11.1.2.2 /24	11.1.2.2 /24	No NAT
E-mail server	11.1.2.3 /24	11.1.2.3 /24	No NAT
FTP server	11.1.2.4 /24	11.1.2.4 /24	No NAT

Figure 6.19 exhibits the configuration necessary to fulfill the PAT requirements of internal LAN A and the special NAT and PAT requirements of internal LAN B. The first step is to assign each internal LAN a separate NAT ID via the *nat* command. NAT ID 1 is assigned to internal LAN A, and NAT ID 2 is assigned to internal LAB B. Using the *global* command with a single global IP address and specifying NAT ID 1 will enable Dynamic PAT for all IP address on internal LAN A. All communication initiated from internal LAN A will exit the PIX with an IP address of 11.1.1.2. To meet the special needs of internal LAN B, we first have to use the *global* command with a NAT ID of 2 and a global IP address range between 11.1.1.3 and 11.1.1.9, which allows for seven dynamic one-to-one NAT translations. Once the Dynamic NAT pool has been depleted, the remaining connections

will be dynamically PAT'd to 11.1.1.10. If an IP address in the Dynamic NAT pool is freed up, the next connection request will be dynamically NAT'd before returning to PAT.

Figure 6.19 Outbound NAT Configuration, Part 1

```
Pix515(config)# nat-control     #This command is only required for the 7.x OS
Pix515(config)# nat (inside) 1 192.168.1.0 255.255.255.0 0 0
Pix515(config)# nat (inside) 2 192.168.2.0 255.255.255.0 0 0
Pix515(config)# global (outside) 1 11.1.1.2 netmask 255.255.255.240
Pix515(config)# global (outside) 2 11.1.1.3-11.1.1.9 netmask 255.255.
   255.240
Pix515(config)# global (outside) 2 11.1.1.10 netmask 255.255.255.240
```

Figure 6.20 exhibits the configuration necessary to fulfill requirements where internal users can access the DMZ and servers on the DMZ can access the Internet without NAT. To allow all internal users access to the DMZ without NAT requires the *nat* command with *0 access-list* option. This form of the *nat* command is necessary because, as you might recall, we already assigned the internal LAN A and LAN B NAT IDs that call for NAT. To override this behavior when internal users access the DMZ, we must specifically tell the PIX not to NAT internal LAN IP addresses when they access the DMZ.

The first step is to specify an ACL called *Inside2DMZ,* which specifies the source address as the internal address ranges (192.168.1.0 /24 and 192.168.2.0 /24) and the destination address of the DMZ address range (11.1.2.0 /24) to be excluded from the NAT translation. The next step is to apply the access list to the *nat* command, which lets the PIX know not to NAT internal IP addresses accessing the DMZ. To satisfy the last requirement, which lets the servers on the DMZ access the Internet with the aid of NAT, we specify the DMZ interface and the DMZ IP address range with the NAT ID of 0, which means to not NAT this range on this interface.

Figure 6.20 Outbound NAT Configuration, Part 2

```
Pix515(config)# access-list Inside2DMZ permit ip 192.168.1.0 255.255.255.
   0 11.1.2.0 255.255.255.0
Pix515(config)# access-list Inside2DMZ permit ip 192.168.2.0 255.255.255.
   0 11.1.2.0 255.255.255.0
Pix515(config)# nat (inside) 0 access-list Inside2DMZ
Pix515(config)# nat (DMZ) 0 11.1.2.0 255.255.255.0 0 0
```

Inbound NAT

By default, the PIX/ASA will not allow access from an interface with a lower security level to access an interface with a higher security level. This type of inbound access has to been explicitly defined. The first step to allow this type of access is to define a NAT statement; the second step is to apply access rules. In this section, we discuss how to set up NAT to allow users on the Internet to access the PIX/ASA semisecure interfaces or DMZ interfaces. Access initiated directly from the Internet to the inside interface, or internal LAN, should be prohibited. Normal security policies prevent such access and only allow clients on the Internet to interact with devices on the DMZ.

As with outbound NAT, for the PIX 6.*x* OS it is necessary to configure a NAT statement, regardless of whether network address translation needs to take place. With the PIX/ASA 7.*x* OS, this is not the case. Inbound NAT also has two options to configure address translation: Static NAT and Static PAT. In setting up a DMZ, the most common option is the Static NAT option, where there is a one-to-one IP address mapping. Because there is a one-to-one mapping, this does not save public address space.

Another common configuration is Static PAT. Unlike Static NAT, Static PAT does save address space because it uses one public IP address and, depending on the port on which a request comes in, it translates to any number of private addresses. For example, you can have one IP address exposed to the Internet and have clients on the Internet make requests to this IP address for services such as Web content (TCP port 80) or SMTP (TCP port 25). Depending on the port the request is received on, the PIX will map and forward the request to the real IP of the Web or mail servers, respectively. This section focuses on the Static NAT and PAT commands needed to set up access to the DMZ. To configure Static NAT, the *static* command is used. As with the *nat* command, the static command is slightly different, depending on whether you are using the 6.*x* or 7.*x* OS. For the 6.*x* OS, the command is *static (real_ifc, mapped_ifc) {mapped_ip | interface} {real_ip [netmask mask] | access-list acl_name} [dns][norandomseq] [max_conns [emb_limit]]*. For the 7.*x* OS, the command is *static (real_ifc,mapped_ifc) mapped_ip {real_ip [netmask mask] | access-list access_list_name | interface} [dns] [[tcp] max_conns [emb_limit]] [udp udp_max_conns] [norandomseq [nailed]]*. As with the *nat* command, the *static* commands are fundamentally the same, although the 7.*x* OS supports more parameters. Many of the parameters for the *static* command have the same meaning and function as with the *nat* command, so we won't review them again. What is important are the functions and meanings of the parameters that are unique to the *static* command.

The syntax of this command can be confusing, so special attention is required because the command asks for the interface names in the reverse order than it asks for the IP addresses. In this form, the *static* command maps a virtual IP address on the less secure interface to the actual IP address on the more secure interface, creating a one-to-one IP mapping. The *real_ifc*, the interface with the higher security level, and *mapped_ifc*, the interface with lower security level, parameters specify the PIX's interfaces on which the address translation needs to occur. The *mapped_ip* parameter is the virtual IP on the PIX's less secure interface that will be mapped to the real IP address specified by the *real_ip* parameter on the PIX's more secure interface. The *mask* parameter in one-to-one static mapping is set to 255.255.255.255 or host mask but can also be used for a net static. A net static is useful in a situation in which you need to translate an entire network but want to keep the host portion of the IP address the same. Figure 6.21 is an example of how to change the netmask so that all hosts on network 11.1.1.0 /24 (outside) translate to a host on 10.1.2.0 /24 (DMZ). In other words, 11.1.1.1 will be translated into 10.1.2.1, 11.1.1.2 to 10.1.2.2, 11.1.1.3 to 10.1.2.3, and 11.1.1.254 to 10.1.2.254.

Figure 6.21 Inbound Net Static NAT Example

```
Pix515(config)# static (DMZ,outside) 11.1.1.0 10.1.2.0 netmask 255.255.
    255.0 0 0
```

Figure 6.22 is an example of a one-to-one NAT configuration. In this example, there is a DMZ interface on the PIX with servers on the 10.1.2.0 /24 subnet. Since the 10.1.2.0 /24 subnet is in the private range of addresses, it cannot be routed on the Internet. The PIX's outside interface is on the 11.1.1.0 /28 subnet, which is in the public address range. We have a Web server on the DMZ with an IP address of 10.1.2.2 that needs to accessed by the Internet, but since it's on a private address, it cannot be accessed by the Internet, so we need to configure NAT using the *static* command. In this example, we create a one-to-one IP mapping between 10.1.2.2 and 11.1.1.11. Users on the Internet will now be able to access the Web server via the 11.1.1.11 address, and the PIX will then translate the destination address to the real address, 10.1.2.2, and forward the packet to the Web server. The Web server will then reply to the HTML request with the source address 10.1.2.2 and the destination address of the user. The PIX will receive the return packet and this time change the source address from 10.1.2.2 to 11.1.1.11 and forward the packet. The user on the Internet will receive the Web page and will never know that NAT has taken place.

Figure 6.22 Inbound NAT Configuration with NAT

```
Pix515(config)# static (DMZ,outside) 11.1.1.11 10.1.2.2 netmask 255.255.
    255.255 0 0
```

As we mentioned earlier, a NAT statement is required for the inbound connectivity, even if address translation is not required (this is true for all versions of OS software). In this case the *static* command has a slightly different syntax, *static (real_ifc, mapped_ifc) real_ip real_ip [netmask][conn_limit [em_limit]]*. You can see that the *mapped_ip* parameter has been replaced by a duplicate *real_ip* parameter. This simply tells the PIX not to NAT the specified the IP address or range and make the IP address visible to the less secure interface "as is." This is known as identity NAT. Figure 6.23 is an example of an inbound identity NAT configuration. The network 11.1.2.0 /24, located on the PIX's DMZ interface (refer back to Figure 6.18), is made visible to the outside interface, so clients on the Internet can directly communicate with the servers on the DMZ without the use of NAT.

Figure 6.23 Inbound NAT Configuration Without NAT

```
Pix515(config)# static (DMZ,outside) 11.1.2.0 11.1.2.0 netmask 255.255.
   255.0 0 0
```

Configuring Static PAT, also known as *port redirection*, is slightly different from config-uring Static NAT in that you do not specify a mapping based only on an IP address but also on the port. The *static (real_ifc, mapped_ifc) (tcp, udp) mapped_ip_mapped_port real_ip real_port [netmask][max_conns [emb_limit]]* command is used to define Static PAT; as you might notice, it is very similar to Static NAT except that you are also defining ports. Static PAT works with only TCP and UDP packets. Figure 6.24 shows how to configure Static PAT for Web and SMTP traffic. In this example, if a request came to the IP address of the PIX's outside interface on TCP port 80 (WWW) or TCP port 25 (SMTP), it would be translated and for-warded to the real IP addresses of the Web server (10.1.2.2) and mail server (10.1.2.3), respectively. Notice that we supplemented the parameter *mapped_ip* with the keyword *inter-face,* which means to use the IP address of the outside interface as the *mapped_ip*.

Figure 6.24 Inbound Static PAT Configuration

```
Pix515(config)# static (DMZ,outside) tcp interface www 10.1.2.2 www
Pix515(config)# static (DMZ,outside) tcp interface smtp 10.1.2.3 smtp
```

In the previous section, we mentioned how setting the connection and embryonic limits could protect your internal network from propagating SYN attacks; in this section, we dis-cuss how to protect the servers on your DMZ from SYN and flood attacks initiated from the Internet. If you recall, the connection limit is the number of simultaneous connections allowed by the PIX/ASA initiated by the specified IP range, and the embryonic limit is the number of connections that have started but have not completed, meaning that the three-way handshake has not been completed. Setting the embryonic limit (*emb_limit*) parameter in the *static* command to a value other than 0 (0 means unlimited) enables SYN attack pre-vention via the PIX/ASA's TCP Intercept feature. Once the embryonic threshold is exceeded, the PIX will enter TCP Intercept mode, where the PIX/ASA will complete the three-way handshake on behalf of the server by intercepting all SYN packets and reply on behalf of the server with an empty SYN/ACK. The PIX/ASA will keep the state informa-tion, drop the packet, and wait for a reply from the client.

If the client replies with an ACK, the PIX/ASA will then complete the three-way hand-shake with the server, and the server will be able to communicate with the client. If the client fails to respond, the PIX/ASA sends exponential backoffs to the client. The PIX/ASA will operate in TCP Intercept mode until the number of embryonic connections falls below the threshold.

It is also a good idea to set the connection limit (*max_conns*) to a value other than the default unlimited connection setting. Setting the connection limit can help mitigate the risk of flood attacks to servers that might be incapable of protecting themselves from this form of attack. For example, if you have an e-mail server that never exceeds a specific number of open sessions with other e-mail servers or clients and you would like to protect it from flood attacks, which can render the server useless, consider setting the connection and embryonic limit on the PIX/ASA's *static* command. Figure 6.25 shows a Static NAT configuration for an e-mail server located on the PIX's DMZ interface. The e-mail server's real IP address is 10.1.2.3 and is mapped to a publicly accessible address of 11.1.1.12. The connection and embryonic connection limits are set to 100 and 25, respectively, meaning that the PIX will allow a no more than 100 simultaneous connections. If there are more than 25 embryonic connections, the PIX goes into TCP Intercept mode to protect the e-mail server from SYN or flood attacks. Be careful not set the limit too low, because that will prevent valid connections to pass through the PIX/ASA. Once the limit is set, you need to monitor the number of connections from time to time to verify that increased usage from normal growth is not about to eclipse your limits, in which case you will need to adjust your settings.

Figure 6.25 Preventing SYN and Flood Attacks

```
Pix515(config)# static (DMZ,outside) 11.1.1.12 10.1.2.3 netmask 255.255.
    255.255 100 25
```

> **NOTE**
>
> In PIX OS version 5.2 and later, the PIX/ASA will operate in TCP Intercept mode (also known as *Flood Defender*) once the embryonic limit has been reached. In TCP Intercept mode, the PIX/ASA will complete the three-way handshake on behalf of the server by intercepting all SYN packets and reply on behalf of the server with an empty SYN/ACK. The PIX/ASA will keep the state information, drop the packet, and wait for a reply from the client. If the client replies with an ACK, the PIX/ASA will then complete the three-way handshake with the server, and the server will be able to communicate with the client. If the client fails to respond, the PIX/ASA sends exponential backoffs to the clients. The PIX/ASA will operate in TCP Intercept mode until the number of embryonic connections falls below the threshold. Prior to PIX OS version 5.2, if the PIX's embryonic limit was reached, it would allow no new connections to the server until the number embryonic connections fell below the threshold—in essence, accomplishing what a hacker wanted to do, which was to disrupt services provided by the server.

Verifying and Monitoring NAT

The PIX/ASA provides several commands in order to properly maintain, support, and troubleshoot the NAT feature. The *show xlate* and *clear xlate* commands provide the ability to show and clear NAT translations (also known as translation slots), respectively. The *show xlate* command shows active NAT and PAT translations. The *clear xlate* command clears active NAT or PAT translations and should be used when certain configuration changes are made to the PIX/ASA, including any changes related to the *aaa-server, access-list, alias, conduit, global, nat, route,* or *static* commands. It can also be useful for troubleshooting NAT or PAT problems. The *show conn* command is useful to identify all active connections and can be used to decide on values for the connection limit parameter in the *nat* and *static* commands. The *show static* command can be used to view all the static NAT translations.

Configuring Access Rules

One of the PIX/ASA's most important features is the ACL feature, which is used to create access rules that determine what connections can flow outbound from the PIX/ASA (egress filtering) or inbound to protected resources (ingress filtering). The ACLs allow the PIX/ASA to permit or deny access based on source IP address and/or port and destination IP address and/or port. Creating an ACL requires the use of the *access-list* command, where the firewall administrator can permit or deny access based on set criteria. It is important to remember that ACLs operate on a first-match basis, meaning that the PIX/ASA will work its way down the list and, when it finds a match, it will perform the specified action, whether a permit or deny. It will stop without proceeding to the next line. As you create an ACL, remember that order is important, especially with complex ACLs. Be careful to not permit access to an item higher in the list and then have an explicit deny for it later in the ACL, or vice versa. If ACLs are not carefully thought out, they might not have the desired effect of tight security, leaving security holes in your network. Furthermore, at the end of all ACLs is in implicit deny, meaning that if the PIX/ASA finished processing the access list lines and did not find a match, the traffic will be denied.

The creation of an ACL requires the *access-list* command. This command is very similar to the *access-list* command found in Cisco's router IOS. With the PIX/ASA 7.*x* OS, Cisco made some changes to how the *access-list* command functions. In the 6.*x* OS, an access list was simply an access list. With the 7.*x* OS, however, the *access-list* command was made to function even more like the Cisco IOS by supporting multiple types of access lists. For example, the *access-list standard* is used to identify the destination IP addresses of OSPF routes, whereas the *access-list webtype* command is used to for WebVPN traffic. The *access-list extended* command, however, is the access–list mechanism that provides the same functionality as the PIX 6.*x access-list* command. The examples in this section will use the 7.*x access-list extended* syntax, but you should realize that the commands can be used with minor syntax modifications for any PIX running the 6.*x* OS.

For the PIX 6.x OS, the syntax of the *access-list* command is *access-list id* [line *line-num*] {deny | permit}{*protocol* | object-group *protocol_obj_grp_id*{*source_addr source_mask*} | object-group *network_obj_grp_id* [*operator port* [*port*] | interface *if_name* | object-group *service_obj_grp_id*] {*destination_addr* | *remote_addr*} {*destination_mask* | *remote_mask*} | object-group *network_obj_grp_id* [*operator port* [*port*] | object-group *service_obj_grp_id*]} [log [[disable | default] | [*level*]]] [interval *secs*]]. For the PIX/ASA 7.x OS, the syntax of the *access-list* command is *access-list id* [line *line-number*] [extended] {deny | permit}{*protocol* | object-group *protocol_obj_grp_id*}{*src_ip mask* | interface *ifc_name* | object-group *network_obj_grp_id*} [*operator port* | object-group *service_obj_grp_id*] {*dest_ip mask* | interface *ifc_name* | object-group *network_obj_grp_id*} [*operator port* | object-group *service_obj_grp_id* | object-group *icmp_type_obj_grp_id*][log [[*level*] [interval *secs*] | disable | default]] [inactive | time–range *time_range_name*].

At this point the odds are probably in favor of looking at those two complex syntaxes and thinking, "There is no way I am going to be able to sort this command out." The good news is that for most ACLs and for the purposes of the examples in this chapter, the *access-list* command syntax can be broken down into a number of commonly implemented parameters. For the 6.x OS, the basic syntax is *access-list id action protocol source_address operator src_port destination_address operator dest_port*. For the 7.x OS, the basic syntax is *access-list id extended action protocol source_address operator src_port destination_address operator dest_port*. These commands allow the firewall administrator to specify the actions, permit or deny, to packets that match a certain criteria and logically group them so they can be applied as a set of rules to a specific interface. The *id* parameter is used to logically group and name a list of access rules that will later be used by the *access-group* command to assign the rules list to an interface. The *id* can be a number or a name. The *action* parameter tells the PIX what to do with the packet if there is a match. The valid values are *permit*, which allows the packet to be forwarded, or *deny*, which drops the packet and does not allow connectivity. The *protocol* parameter is the name or number of the IP protocol, which includes but is not limited to IP, TCP, UDP, and ICMP. The *source_address*, *src_port*, *destination_address,* and *dest_port* parameters specify the elements on which the PIX/ASA will determine a match. To be considered a match, the packet in question must identically match all the configured parameters, which can include the IP address and/or port of the source and/or destination. If no source or destination port is specified, the PIX/ASA assumes you will permit or deny access regardless of the port, but if port specification is required, an operator is necessary. Valid operators include *lt* for less than, *gt* for greater than, *eq* for equal, *neq* for not equal, and *range* for an inclusive range.

NOTE

Although the PIX/ASA 7.x OS, uses a slightly different syntax for the *access-list* command (notably the use of the *extended* parameter), you can actually enter an access list on the 7.x OS using the PIX 6.x *access-list* syntax. In that instance, the PIX/ASA will automatically assume that the access list is an extended access list.

To apply an ACL to an interface, use the *access-group* command. For the PIX 6.*x* OS PIX, ACLs can only be applied inbound to an interface. With the PIX/ASA 7.*x* OS, this has been changed to work in a similar fashion to the Cisco IOS by allowing the ACL to be applied to either inbound or outbound traffic on the interface. The *access-group id [in | out] interface if_name* command is straightforward. There are only three parameters that you will typically need to deal with. The *id* is the name or number of the ACL created with associated *access-list* command. The *if_name* parameter sets the ACL to the specified interface. For the 6.*x* OS, the *in* parameter is used to specify that the ACL is applied to inbound traffic. For the 7.*x* OS, you can use either the *in* or the *out* parameter, with the *out* parameter applying the ACL to outbound traffic in the interface. Only one ACL can be applied per interface in the 6.*x* OS, whereas you can have one inbound and one outbound ACL applied per interface in the 7.*x* OS.

> ## NOTE
>
> Like the Cisco router IOS ACLs, the PIX processes its ACLs on a first-match basis and has an implicit *deny all* at the end of the ACL. However, unlike Cisco router IOS, PIX ACLs do not use a wildcard; instead, they use a regular subnet mask in the ACL definition.

Creating an Outbound Access Control List (Egress Filtering)

The PIX/ASA, by default, allows all connections initiated from a higher security-level interface to a lower-level interface. If you want to control access from the more secure interface, you can do so by creating an ACL and applying it to the interface with the higher security level. For example, if your security policy states that users from the internal network cannot initiate FTP sessions with servers on the Internet, you could prevent FTPs by implementing an outbound ACL. An outbound ACL allows the PIX/ASA to permit or deny access based on source IP address and/or port. Destination IP address and/or port or can be used with user authentication to assign an ACL to a specific user. In this section, we discuss filtering only up to Layer 4 (the transport layer), but we do discuss user authentication and content filtering, such as URL, ActiveX, and Java filtering, later in this chapter. To create and apply an outbound ACL is a two-step process. The first step is to create the ACL with the *access-list* command, and the second step is to apply the ACL to an interface with the *access-group* command.

If you recall the diagram in Figure 6.18, we had a PIX connecting two internal LANs, a DMZ, and the Internet. Figure 6.26 shows how to configure the PIX to allow only internal LAN A to connect to Internet sites via the standard Web port (WWW port 80), secure Web sites (SSL port 443), FTP sites (FTP port 21) on the Internet, and the local DMZ. Internal LAN B can access only the local DMZ. The first three lines of this ACL permit internal LAN A to access any resource on the Internet via TCP ports 80, 443, and 21. The next two lines allow both internal LAN A and LAN B to access the DMZ. Because access to the Internet was not explicitly permitted from internal LAN B, it will be denied. The last line in Figure 6.26 applies the ACL named *OutboundACL* inbound to the inside interface of the PIX. The syntax used in this example is the PIX 6.x syntax since it is valid for both the 6.*x* and 7.*x* OS.

Figure 6.26 Configuring and Applying Outbound ACLs

```
Pix515(config)# access-list OutboundACL permit tcp 192.168.1.0 255.255.
    255.0  any eq www
Pix515(config)# access-list OutboundACL permit tcp 192.168.1.0 255.255.
    255.0  any eq 443
Pix515(config)# access-list OutboundACL permit tcp 192.168.1.0 255.255.
    255.0  any eq ftp
Pix515(config)# access-list OutboundACL permit ip 192.168.1.0 255.255.
    255.0 11.1.2.0 255.255.255.0
Pix515(config)# access-list OutboundACL permit ip 192.168.2.0 255.255.
    255.0 11.1.2.0 255.255.255.0
Pix515(config)# access-group OutboundACL in interface inside
```

NOTE

Conduits, *outbound*, and *apply* commands have all been replaced by the *access-list* and the *access-group* commands. If you are still using these commands, consider converting them to the new commands. As of PIX/ASA OS 7.*x*, these commands are no longer supported and can no longer be entered into the firewall configuration.

Creating an Inbound Access Control List (Ingress Filtering)

Unlike outbound connections, the PIX/ASA, by default, will not permit traffic initiated from a less secure interface to a more secure interface. For example, for a client on the Internet to be permitted to access the Web server on the local DMZ, an explicit ACL that permits port 80 traffic must be created; otherwise, access will be denied. Inbound access lists are created and applied to interfaces using the same steps as outbound connections. Because the inbound ACL gives users on the Internet connectivity to your protected resources, it is very important to understand the importance of the inbound ACL. Any mistakes on this ACL can open security holes that hackers can exploit and use to enter your network for malicious purposes.

When creating inbound ACLs, be sure to be specific as possible. Figure 6.27 shows how to configure access from the Internet to specific TCP ports on the servers on the DMZ. The ACL allows any host of the Internet to access Web content (TCP port 80 or WWW) on the Web server, send mail to the mail relay server (TCP port 25 or SMTP), and send FTPs (TCP port 21 or FTP) to the FTP server. As with all ACLs, any access not explicitly permitted will be denied via an implicit *deny* statement at the end of the ACL. The ACL is applied to the outside interface using the *access-group* command. The syntax used in this example is the PIX 6.*x* syntax since it is valid for both the 6.*x* and 7.*x* OS.

Figure 6.27 Inbound Access List Configuration

```
Pix515(config)# access-list InboundACL permit tcp any host 11.1.2.2 eq www
Pix515(config)# access-list InboundACL permit tcp any host 11.1.2.3 eq smtp
Pix515(config)# access-list InboundACL permit tcp any host 11.1.2.4 eq ftp
Pix515(config)# access-group InboundACL in interface outside
```

NOTE

It's important to remember that the concept of an inbound or outbound ACL is typically not a technical term; rather, it's just a term of convenience used to logically describe the ACL and the type of traffic that is being filtered. You should also not confuse it with the *in* and *out* parameters of the *access-group* command. If you will recall, on the PIX/ASA you can only have one ACL applied to an interface in the case of the 6.*x* OS or one ACL in any given direction in the case of the 7.*x* OS. This is an important concept to grasp, particularly as it relates to a one-armed DMZ segment. In that scenario, the ACL that you will wind up building is likely going to be both an inbound and an outbound ACL since the traffic going from the DMZ to the inside network is considered "inbound," whereas the traffic going from the DMZ to the outside is considered "outbound." This ACL will then be applied to the DMZ interface using the *access-group* command with the *in* parameter (since you want to filter traffic coming from the DMZ).

Creating Turbo ACLs

The PIX OS version 6.2 adds a new feature called Turbo ACL, which decreases the time it takes to search long access lists. Turbo ACL does this by compiling the ACL so that searches are deterministic and take fewer CPU cycles. The problem with uncompiled ACLs is that as they get larger, it takes more time to find a match, because the ACL is searched in a linear, top-down, fashion. A PIX with large, complex ACLs can cause a performance lag as well as increase latency for packets that pass through it. The PIX can decrease search times for ACLs with 19 lines or more when the global *access-list compiled* command or the individual ACL *access-list acl_name compiled* command is used. Turbo ACLs should be applied only to ACLs that have 19 or more lines, because compiled ACLs with fewer than 19 lines do not provide a performance upgrade compared with uncompiled ACLs. To configure a turbo ACL, you need to configure the ACL as you normally would, then apply the global or individual ACL compile command. The global compile command compiles all configured ACLs that have 19 or more lines. The individual command allows you select a specific ACL to compile, but the ACL must have 19 or more lines. If a change is made to a compiled ACL, the PIX will automatically recompile the ACL, so the change is reflected in the compiled ACL table.

With PIX software version 7.*x*, there is no longer a need to compile access lists. The software now automatically optimizes access list processing. From an upgrade perspective, any existing *access-list* statements with a *compiled* keyword are ignored and no longer accepted.

> **NOTE**
>
> The PIX requires approximately 2.1MB of Flash to run Turbo ACL, which limits chassis that can support this feature. This feature might not work properly on the PIX 501 and the PIX 506E chassis because they come with only 8MB of Flash installed and cannot be upgraded.

Time–Based ACLs

The PIX/ASA 7.*x* OS introduces support for time-based ACLs, where individual access list entries can be configured to be active and enforced during a specified time period. This new capability has been implemented via a new command (*time-range*) and the extension of the existing *access-list* command with a new keyword (*time-range*). To implement time-based restrictions for an access list entry, perform the following steps:

1. Define a time range via the new *time-range* command.
2. Create or modify an access list entry to use that time range via the *time-range* keyword in the *access-list* command.

The format of the *time-range* command is:

```
time-range name
```

The *name* parameter assigns a name to the time range you are defining. Once you enter this command, you enter time range configuration mode. Within this mode, you use the *absolute*, *periodic*, and *default* commands to define the time range parameters. The *absolute* command defines an absolute time when a time range is in effect. Its format is:

```
absolute [end time date][start time date]
```

- The meaning of the *start* and *end* keywords is obvious.
- The format of the *time* parameters is *HH:MM* (e.g., 20:00 for 8 P.M.), and the format of the *date* parameters is *day month year* (e.g., 1 January 2006).

The *periodic* command defines a periodic time when the time range is in effect. Its format is:

```
periodic days-of-the-week time to [days-of-the-week] time
```

The parameters and keywords of the *periodic* command are identified and described here.

The first occurrence of the *days-of-the-week* parameter specifies the starting day or day of the week for the time range. The potential values for *days-of-the-week* are any single day or combinations of days, including Monday, Tuesday, Wednesday, Thursday, Friday, Saturday, and Sunday. In addition, the following values are valid:

- Daily
- Weekends
- Weekdays

The second occurrence specifies the ending day or day of the week for the time range. The second occurrence is optional and can be omitted if the ending days are the same as the starting days.

The first occurrence of the *time* parameter specifies the starting time; the second occurrence specifies the ending time and is *not* optional. The format of the *time* parameters is *HH:MM* (e.g., 20:00 for 8 P.M.). Multiple *periodic* commands are permitted per *time-range* command. In addition, if a *time-range* command has both *absolute* and *periodic* values specified, the *periodic* commands are evaluated only after the *absolute start* time is reached and are not further evaluated after the *absolute end* time is reached.

The *default* command restores the default configuration settings to the *time-range* command *absolute* and *periodic* keywords.

> **NOTE**
>
> Obviously, the time range feature relies on the accuracy of the PIX clock. Best practice would include the synchronization of the PIX clock with an NTP server.

Now that a time range has been defined using the *time-range* command, you must use it to specify an active time period for an access–list entry via the *access-list* command. The general format of this command with respect to time ranges is:

```
access-list id [line line-number] [extended] {deny | permit} {tcp | udp} {host
sip | sip mask | any} [operator port] {host dip | dip mask | any} [operator port]
time-range time_range_name
```

To make an access–list statement active for a particular time range, simply include the *time-range* keyword and the *time_range_name*, which is the name of a time range previously defined using the *time-range* command.

For example, suppose Secure Corporation has a business requirement to exchange data with a partner via FTP. The company has implemented an FTP server in its DMZ to provide a staging point for the exchange of files, as shown in Figure 6.28. The exchange of data via FTP occurs nightly at a specified time. Because Secure Corporation does not want the DMZ FTP server exposed unnecessarily when it is not being used, it has chosen to implement a time-based ACL to allow FTP traffic to/from the server only when necessary.

Figure 6.28 Time-Based ACL

```
PIX515(config)# static (DMZ,outside) 11.1.2.0 11.1.2.0 netmask 255.255.
    255.0 0 0
PIX515(config)# time-range PARTNER_FTP_TIME
PIX515(config-time-range)# periodic weekdays 20:00 to 22:00
PIX515(config-time-range)# exit
PIX515(config)# access-list INTERNET_TO_DMZ permit tcp any host11.1.2.4 eq ftp
    time-range PARTNER_FTP_TIME
PIX515(config)# access-list INTERNET_TO_DMZ permit tcp any host11.1.2.4 eq ftp-
    data time-range PARTNER_FTP_TIME
PIX515(config)# access-group INTERNET_TO_DMZ in Outside
PIX515(config)# exit
```

Monitoring ACLs

The PIX/ACL has a couple of commands that can display and monitor ACLs as well as check to which interface they are bound. The *show access-list* command shows the contents of an access list, the number of hits (matches) per entry, and whether the ACL is a Turbo

ACL or a standard uncompiled ACL. The *show access-group* command displays how the ACLs are bound to the PIX's interfaces. You can also use the *log* parameter in the *access-list* command to cause the firewall to log ACLs with matching entries for troubleshooting and diagnostic information.

Configuring & Implementing...

Tips on Inbound ACLs

Understanding how to properly create an ACL is very important to the integrity of your network. A mistake on an ACL can open holes that hackers can easily exploit. It is very important to be very specific when you're defining an access-list entry. The more specific the ACL, the fewer holes the hacker has to exploit.

The order of the ACE in the access list is also important. Many people make the mistake of making broad permit statements, then later in the ACL using a specific deny, or vice versa. Always remember that the PIX/ASA will stop processing the ACL when the first match is made, and any lines below the match will not take effect. We have put together some tips on how to configure an ACL for some common services and we present them here.

All access lists should start with an antispoofing ACL, which will prevent spoofing of the private address range (RFC 1918) from the Internet. A line for any public address space that your company has for internal use (not advertised to the Internet) should also be added here.

```
! To block spoofing of RFC 1918 Address ranges
Pix515(config)# access-list InboundACL deny ip 10.0.0.0
    255.0.0.0 any
Pix515(config)# access-list InboundACL deny ip 172.16.0.0
    255.240.0.0 any
Pix515(config)# access-list InboundACL deny ip 192.168.0.0
    255.255.0.0 any
```

This section of the ACL is quite simple. It allows users from the Internet to access the Web server via the standard Web port, TCP port 80, as well as SSL, TCP port 443.

```
! Allow WWW and SSL connections to the web server
Pix515(config)# access-list InboundACL permit tcp any host
    11.1.2.2 eq www
```

Continued

```
Pix515(config)# access-list InboundACL permit tcp any host
   11.1.2.2 eq 443
```

This section allows the use of Active or Passive FTPs to the FTP server. Because of the Application Inspection feature, you will not need to open any port besides TCP port 21. FTP usually requires ports 20, 21, and ports greater than 1023 to be open to support Active or Passive FTPs, but not the PIX/ASA. Application Inspection is discussed later in this chapter.

```
! Allow Active or Passive FTPs to the FTP server
Pix515(config)# access-list InboundACL permit tcp any host
   11.1.2.4 eq ftp
```

Since ICMP is connectionless, you need to explicitly allow ICMP echo replies to be allowed to re-enter the PIX/ASA and forwarded back to the client on the internal LAN to initiate the echo via the ping utility. If you notice that the destination address is not the internal LAN IP address range but is the address of the outside interface IP range, this occurs because, as an echo request from the internal LAN is sent through the PIX/ASA, it is translated to an address on the outside interface IP range (as configured in the previous NAT section of this chapter). The echo reply will be sent to the translated address; therefore, the ACL should specify the translated address as the destination and not the real internal address range.

```
! Allow ICMP echo reply from a ping initiate from an
   internal interface
      Pix515(config)# access-list InboundACL permit icmp any 11.1.1.0
      255.255.255.240
         echo-reply
```

Routing Through the PIX

The final step in the basic configuration of the PIX/ASA is to enable routing. By default, the PIX/ASA has no routes configured, so it does not know how to forward traffic. The PIX/ASA has three routing options: static routes, RIP, and OSPF. In this section we discuss how to configure static routing as well dynamic routing using the RIP and OSPF dynamic routing protocols.

Static Routing

Most PIX/ASA firewalls are configured using static routes because they are the simplest and most secure form of routing. Static routing hard-codes the next hop of a remote network so that the PIX/ASA knows in which direction to send traffic when a network is not directly connected. Usually a PIX/ASA has a default route pointing to the Internet and static route(s) pointing to networks or subnets on the internal LAN. The *route if_name ip_address netmask next_hop [metric]* command is used to define a static route. The *if_name* parameter identifies the route's outgoing interface. The *ip_address* and *netmask* parameters make up the remote network that you want the PIX/ASA to route to, and the *next_hop* parameter is the IP address to which the PIX/ASA will forward traffic that matches the specified remote network. The *metric* parameter sets a weight to a route in case there are multiple paths to the remote network. The route with the smallest metric to the same remote network will be selected unless it becomes unavailable; then the next hop with second smallest weight will be selected to reach a remote network.

To illustrate how static routes are configured, let's use our familiar network setup shown in Figure 6.29. In the diagram, three networks are directly connected to the PIX: the inside interface (192.168.0.0 /24), the DMZ interface (11.1.2.0 /24), and the outside interface (11.1.1.0 /28). These networks do not require any type of routing, either static or dynamic, because they are directly connected, and the PIX will simply ARP for hosts located on these interfaces. However, the internal LANs are not directly connected; therefore, they require static routes so that the PIX can forward traffic to the appropriate next hop. In this case, the next hop for both internal LANs (LAN A 192.168.1.0 /24 and LAN B 192.168.2.0 /24) is the Internal LAN router, or 192.168.0.2.

The first two configuration lines in Figure 6.30 show how to configure the static routing for both internal LANs. Now that we accounted for routing the internal LANs, we must turn our attention to configuring routing so that devices on the internal LAN and the DMZ can access the Internet. This could a daunting task if we had to configure static routes for every network on the Internet, but the PIX has an option that lets you define a default route for traffic for which the PIX does not have a specific route. In this case, the default route is the Internet router, or 11.1.1.14. The last configuration line in Figure 6.24 shows how to configure a default route to point the next hop, the Internet router. Notice that the syntax of the *route* command has been simplified by the use of double zeroes for the *ip_address* and *netmask* parameters. The expanded syntax of a default route is *route outside 0.0.0.0 0.0.0.0 11.1.1.14 1,* but the PIX allows you to abbreviate 0.0.0.0 for both the IP address and the mask to a simple double zero (0 0). The PIX/ASA will accept either the expanded or the abbreviated default route syntax. Assuming that the internal router is configured with a default route to point to the PIX as the next hop, the PIX is now capable of routing among the internal LAN, the DMZ, and the Internet. We discuss routing on the Internal and Internet routers in detail in Chapter 9.

Figure 6.29 Configuring Static Routes

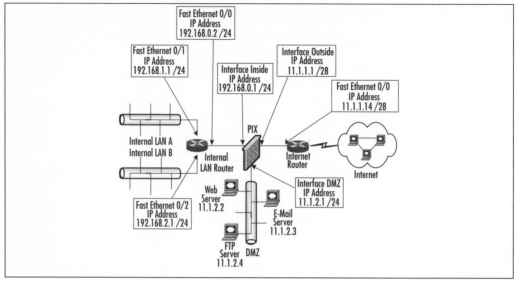

Figure 6.30 Static Route Configuration

```
Pix515(config)# route inside 192.168.1.0 255.255.255.0 192.168.0.2 1
Pix515(config)# route inside 192.168.1.0 255.255.255.0 192.168.0.2 1
Pix515(config)# route outside 0 0 11.1.1.14 1
```

Enabling RIP

In most PIX firewall implementations, the use of static routing meets the requirements for most DMZ designs. However, the PIX/ASA does offer dynamic routing capabilities that include support for Routing Information Protocol (RIP) versions 1 and 2 and OSPF. In this section, we discuss how to configure RIP, a distance-vector protocol that uses hop count to determine a route's metric. A device running RIP periodically updates its neighbors of the routes it knows about. Since the scope of this book is directed toward building a DMZ infrastructure, we assume that if you are going to configure RIP, you are well versed in its capabilities, so we will not go into RIP's details any further.

RIP was a common interior dynamic routing protocol before the more robust routing protocols such as OSPF and EIGRP came into play. Nevertheless, RIP can be found on many networks today, and the PIX can "talk" to devices, like routers, that run RIP to eliminate the administrative burden of adding a new static route to the PIX each time a new LAN is added to the internal network.

RIP is configured differently depending on whether you are running the 6.*x* or the 7.*x* OS.

Enabling RIP for PIX 6.x

The *rip* command is used to enable RIP on the PIX. Figure 6.31 shows how to configure RIP on the internal LAN or inside interface of the PIX. (Refer back to Figure 6.29 for the network setup.) In this case, the internal router is running RIP version 2 with MD5 authentication. The PIX needs to be able to communicate with the internal router so that the router can periodically update the PIX's RIP routing table. The PIX, in turn, needs to inform the internal router of the default route so that the internal router knows where to forward packets destined for the Internet. Once configured, if a new LAN is added to the Internal router, the router will send an update to the PIX notifying it of the new LAN without any extra configuration or static routes added to the PIX.

The first configuration line in Figure 6.31 enables RIP version 2 with MD5 authentication on the inside interface of the PIX. Note that MD5 authentication must also be set on the internal router, and the key (*mykey*) and key ID (*1*) must match for routing updates to take place between the router and the PIX. In this example, RIP is set to Passive mode, and the PIX will listen to only RIP version broadcast updates and update its RIP routing table accordingly. The second configuration line allows the PIX to advertise a default route back to the internal router so that it will know where to send traffic for which it does not have a specific route. The third line is the same as in the static route example, where the PIX will forward Internet-bound traffic to the Internet router.

Figure 6.31 PIX 6.x RIP Routing Configuration

```
Pix515(config)# rip outside passive version 2 authentication md5 mykey 1
Pix515(config)# rip inside default version 2 authentication md5 mykey 1
Pix515(config)# route outside 0 0 11.1.1.14 1
```

Enabling RIP for PIX/ASA 7.x

With the PIX/ASA 7.x command, Cisco changed the RIP configuration to work virtually identically to the configuration of RIP using the Cisco IOS. The *rip* command has been replaced by the *router rip* command, which places the firewall into the RIP router configuration mode. The RIP router configuration mode supports the following commands and is where the RIP routing configuration occurs:

- *auto-summary* Enable automatic network number summarization.
- *default-information* Control distribution of default route information.
- *distribute-list* Filter networks in routing updates.
- *network* Add/remove interfaces to/from routing process.
- *passive-interface* Suppress routing updates on an interface.

- *redistribute* Redistribute information from another routing process.

- *version* Set routing protocol version.

Configuring authentication for RIP is not performed in the RIP router configuration mode; rather, it is performed in the interface configuration mode of the interface that RIP will be running on. The command *rip authentication mode* is used to define the authentication method that will be used. The command *rip authentication key* is used to define the key and key ID that will be used for the authentication. So, working on the previous example, you would configure RIP for a PIX/ASA running the 7.*x* OS, as shown in Figure 6.32.

Figure 6.32 PIX/ASA 7.*x* RIP Routing Configuration

```
Pix515(config)# router rip
Pix515(config-router)# passive-interface outside
Pix515(config-router)# version 2
Pix515(config-router)# default-information originate
Pix515(config-router)# network 192.168.0.0
Pix515(config-router)# interface eth1
Pix515(config-if)# rip authentication mode md5
Pix515(config-if)# rip authentication key mypubkey key_id 1
```

OSPF

Starting with PIX OS version 6.3, the PIX/ASA supports the OSPF link-state routing protocol. Many large networks implement OSPF as the dynamic routing protocol and with this new feature allow the PIX/ASA to communicate with routers on the network running OSPF to dynamically update the routing tables on both the PIX/ASA and routers on the network. Since OSPF is fairly complex, we will not go into its configuration on the PIX/ASA, but be aware that the PIX/ASA can support it if necessary. For both the 6.*x* and 7.*x* OS, OSPF is configured by running the *router ospf* command to access the OSPF router configuration mode. The PIX/ASA's implementation of OSPF is robust and can support almost all the OSPF functions and features found in Cisco's router IOS. As with all routing protocols, if you decide to use this feature, be sure to use the OSPF authentication feature to ensure that you are sending and receiving routing information to trusted neighbors.

Configuring Advanced PIX/ASA Features

The PIX/ASA has many additional features that enable it to provide high availability, application layer security, and PIX/ASA management and support. The PIX/ASA supports features such as DHCP and VPNs that are out of the scope of this book. In this section, we cover topics such as failover, content filtering, cut-through proxy, application layer security, and securing some of PIX/ASA's management features.

PIX/ASA 7.x Security Contexts

One of the most interesting new features of the PIX/ASA 7.x OS is the introduction of virtual firewalls, or *security contexts*. Security contexts provide a means for allowing a single piece of hardware to function logically as multiple virtual firewalls. When you set up a security context, each context has its own security policies, interfaces, and supported features. This means that not all PIX firewall features are supported in security contexts. Some that are not supported when you have multiple security contexts include:

- Dynamic routing protocols
- VPN
- Multicast

When you start the PIX in single-context mode and convert to multiple-context mode, a new file called admin.cfg is created on the built-in Flash. This is the default administrator security context. You can store multiple security contexts on the same Flash, or you can have the PIX download them from the network using TFTP, FTP, or HTTP(s).

NOTE

When you convert from single security context mode to multiple security context mode, the original startup configuration is *not* saved, so always make a backup when you work with security contexts. The running configuration is used to make the two new security context files.

Use the *mode* command to place the Cisco PIX firewall in multiple security context mode. Our options for the *mode* command are:

```
PIX515(config)# mode ?

configure mode commands/options:
  multiple   Multiple mode; mode with security contexts
  noconfirm  Do not prompt for confirmation
  single     Single mode; mode without security contexts
PIX515(config)#
```

To go from single mode to multimode:

```
PIX515(config)# mode multiple
```

```
WARNING: This command will change the behavior of the device
WARNING: This command will initiate a Reboot
Proceed with change mode? [confirm]
Convert the system configuration? [confirm]
WARNING: This command will initiate a Reboot
Proceed with change mode? [confirm]
Convert the system configuration? [confirm]
!!
The old running configuration file will be written to flash

The admin context configuration will be written to flash

The new running configuration f



***
*** --- SHUTDOWN NOW ---
***
*** Message to all terminals:
***
***    change mode
file was written to flash
Security context mode: multiple




Rebooting...
```

When you confirm, the Cisco PIX will reboot itself to enable the new mode. We can confirm the mode by using the *show* command:

```
PIX515# show mode
Security context mode: multiple
PIX515#
```

To restore the Cisco PIX to single mode security context, we need to copy the original (you did make a backup, right?) to Flash:

```
PIX515(config)# copy flash:old_running.cfg startup-config
```

Then we will set the mode back to single:

```
PIX515(config)# mode single
WARNING: This command will change the behavior of the device
WARNING: This command will initiate a Reboot
Proceed with change mode? [confirm]
```

As you will see in the next section, one of the most valuable uses of security contexts is in configuring Active/Active failover.

The PIX/ASA Failover Services

When your DMZ design calls for a highly available firewall solution because downtime due to a problem with the firewall hardware will not be tolerated, consider using the PIX's failover feature. Historically, the PIX has supported failover in an Active/Standby mode of operation. What this means is that the failover feature allows you to set up a second PIX in Standby mode, and if the primary, or active, PIX should go offline, the secondary PIX will switch to Active mode and take over for the failed PIX. With the PIX/ASA 7.*x* OS software, Cisco introduced a new type of failover known as *Active/Active failover.* Active/Active failover is very similar to Active/Standby failover in terms of functionality, with one important difference—each firewall is configured to pass network traffic. This is done by running each firewall in multiple-context mode, with one context being active on the first firewall (and passive on the second firewall) while the other context is active on the second firewall (and passive on the first firewall). Each security context is then added to a failover group, which defines a group of security contexts. The failover group is then used to define the physical firewall that will be considered the primary firewall for the failover group and the firewall that will be considered the standby firewall for the failover group. Functionally, a failover group works similarly to the way the traditional Active/Standby failover functions. Consequently, unless otherwise noted, the failover concepts discussed in this section are applicable to both types of failover.

> **NOTE**
>
> When we talk about the primary and secondary firewall, we are referring to either the physical firewalls in an Active/Standby failover configuration or the physical firewalls for each failover group in an Active/Active failover configuration.

If the optional stateful failover feature is configured, the secondary PIX/ASA can maintain operating state for active TCP connections during failover, so users will not lose their sessions as the PIX/ASA fails over to its backup unit. To enable failover, the primary and secondary PIX/ASA firewalls need to be identical in terms of chassis, OS version, and hardware options. We cover the requirements for failover later in this section.

The PIX offers two options that provide connectivity for the primary and secondary PIX firewalls to exchange heartbeats and configuration information. The first option is a Cisco proprietary high-speed serial cable connected to a special serial failover port on the PIX. This option is not available to the ASA firewall. The second option is to use one of the

PIX/ASA LAN interfaces to carry heartbeat and configuration traffic. The advantage of using the Cisco proprietary high-speed serial cable to send heartbeat and configuration traffic is that it will not waste a LAN interface for a rather small amount of traffic. Instead, it uses a serial port specifically designed for failover. The disadvantage is that the high-speed serial cable is rather short (six feet long), and if the PIX firewalls are not physically located close together, you cannot use the cable-based solution, because the cable cannot be extended. If you have a situation in which the PIX/ASA firewalls are not physically located together, you can consider the second option, a LAN-based failover, which uses interfaces on each PIX/ASA to provide dedicated media for heartbeat and configuration traffic. The disadvantage of this option is that an interface on each PIX/ASA will be wasted just for heartbeat and configuration traffic. It is important to note that heartbeat and configuration traffic should not be confused with state traffic used for the stateful failover option, which the active PIX/ASA uses to send the standby PIX/ASA TCP state information. Although you can configure the PIX/ASA to carry heartbeat, configuration, and state traffic all on one interface on each PIX/ASA using the LAN-based failover option, doing so is not recommended.

When failover occurs, the standby PIX/ASA assumes all the IP addresses and MAC addresses on all interfaces of the failed PIX/ASA. Because there is no change to the IP address or MAC address information, other devices on the network will not be aware of a failure and that they are now communicating through a different device. Another feature of failover is that when a configuration change is made to the primary, it is automatically copied to the secondary PIX/ASA, and when a *write memory* command to save the configuration to Flash is issued on the primary, it also copies the configuration to the secondary's Flash.

What Causes Failover to Occur

To determine the health status of each PIX/ASA, the primary and secondary PIX/ASA poll each other. The poll interval is set using the *failover polltime* (*failover poll* for PIX 6.*x*) command; the default is 15 seconds. Polls, also called *heartbeats*, are sent over all interfaces, including the failover cable. If either PIX/ASA misses two consecutive heartbeats, each PIX/ASA will go through a series of tests to determine which PIX/ASA is in trouble. Each unit goes through four tests to determine its health: a Link Up/Down test, a Network Activity test, an ARP test, and a Broadcast Ping test. Each PIX/ASA firewall performs one test at a time. If one unit passes a test and the other unit does not, the PIX/ASA that passed will take over. If both PIX/ASA units fail, they move on to the next test. At the default poll interval (15 seconds), the PIX units can take up to 45 seconds to run through all the tests and determine whether failover should take place.

NOTE

When cable-based failover is implemented, the PIX will be able to immediately fail over to the secondary unit and skip the series of tests if the primary unit loses power due to a power failure or it is simply shut off. This is not possible with LAN-based failover, where a power failure of the primary unit must be detected via a series of tests.

Failover Requirements

To implement failover, you must make sure you have met all the following requirements before configuring failover:

- Both the primary and secondary PIX firewalls must be identical models. Only the PIX 515E, 525, and 535 support the failover feature.

- Both the primary and secondary ASA firewalls must be identical models. All ASA models support failover (the ASA 5510 must be running the Security Plus license).

- Run the same PIX or ASA OS version.

- Have the same amount of RAM and Flash.

- Have the same interface options.

- If encryption is required, the firewalls must run the same encryption type (DES or 3DES).

If you are configuring the stateful failover feature with the Cisco proprietary high-speed serial cable, the following items are required in addition to the standard requirements:

- Cisco proprietary high-speed serial to carry heartbeat and configuration traffic

- A dedicated interface on each PIX to carry TCP state traffic

- The interface used for stateful traffic must be, at minimum, set at 100Mb full duplex or at least as fast as the PIX's fastest interface

If you are configuring the stateful failover feature using the LAN-based failover option, the following items are required in addition to the standard requirements:

- A dedicated interface on each PIX/ASA to carry heartbeat and configuration traffic

- A separate dedicated interface on each PIX/ASA to carry TCP state traffic

- The interface used for stateful traffic must be, at minimum, set at 100Mb full duplex or at least as fast as the PIX/ASA's fastest interface

The last, but an important, requirement is to make sure you have the proper PIX/ASA license. At least one of the PIX/ASA's must have the Unrestricted license. The other unit can have the Unrestricted license, a Failover license, or a Failover Active/Active license.

Configuring Active/Passive Stateful Failover with a Failover Cable (PIX Only)

In this section, we cover how to configure stateful failover using the Cisco proprietary high-speed serial cable. In this setup, the serial cable is used to carry heartbeat and configuration traffic, and TCP state traffic is transferred to the secondary unit via a dedicated LAN interface. TCP state information needs to be passed from the active PIX to the standby PIX, so if a failure should occur, the secondary PIX can take over and the users will not lose their sessions.

As we mentioned earlier, cable-based failover uses a proprietary high-speed serial cable to carry heartbeat and configuration traffic between the primary and secondary PIX firewalls. The cable is labeled on each end with "Primary" and "Secondary" and should be connected to the each PIX's failover serial port. If you are using a combination of Unrestricted license and Failover license, you must plug the "Primary" end of the serial cable into the PIX with the Unrestricted license and the end labeled "Secondary" into the PIX with the Failover license. Figure 6.33 shows the rear of both the primary and secondary PIX units and where to plug in the serial cable. The diagram also shows the interfaces of the PIX. Notice that both PIX units have a total of four Fast Ethernet ports. Fast Ethernet interfaces 0, 1, and 2 are assigned to the outside, inside, and DMZ interfaces, respectively. The last remaining interface, Fast Ethernet interface 3, is dedicated to carrying state information from the primary unit to the secondary unit.

Figure 6.33 The Physical Layout of the Cable-Based Failover Setup

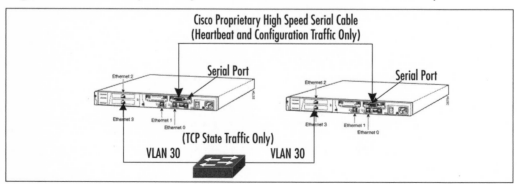

Before you start to configure cable-based stateful failover, you should first cable the units together, but make sure the secondary unit is shut down until the failover configuration has be entered into the primary PIX. The actual configuration differs depending on whether you are running the PIX 6.*x* or 7.*x* OS.

PIX 6.x OS Stateful Failover with a Failover Cable Configuration

First, start your failover configuration by configuring the interfaces. In Figure 6.34, we show the configuration for all the active interfaces on the PIX. The inside, outside, and DMZ interfaces you've seen before in our previous examples, but we added configuration statements for the interface that carries TCP state traffic called "stateful." Notice that the security level is set higher than the DMZ interface, the interface speed is set to 100Mb full duplex, and an IP address of 192.168.4.1 is assigned.

Figure 6.34 PIX OS 6.*x* Failover Preconfiguration

```
Pix515(config)# nameif ethernet0 outside security0
Pix515(config)# nameif ethernet1 inside security100
Pix515(config)# nameif ethernet2 DMZ security50
Pix515(config)# nameif ethernet3 stateful security90
Pix515(config)# interface ethernet0 100full
Pix515(config)# interface ethernet1 100full
Pix515(config)# interface ethernet2 100full
Pix515(config)# interface ethernet3 100full
Pix515(config)# ip address inside 192.168.0.1 255.255.255.0
Pix515(config)# ip address outside 11.1.1.1 255.255.255.240
Pix515(config)# ip address DMZ 11.1.2.1 255.255.255.0
Pix515(config)# ip address stateful 192.168.4.1 255.255.255.0
```

Once the interfaces have been configured, we move on to the failover section of the PIX configuration. Figure 6.35 shows the command necessary to configure cable-based failover. The *failover* command enables the failover feature. The *failover poll* command sets the poll interval in which the PIX units send heartbeats to determine the health of the units. In this case, the poll interval is set to 5 seconds, and if two consecutive heartbeats are missed, both PIX units will run a series of tests to determine whether you should be active. We reduced the poll interval from the 15-second default, so the time it takes to initiate failover tests and determine the active PIX is reduced. At the default settings, it could take up to 45 seconds to determine the healthy PIX, but at the new setting we reduced that number to about 25 seconds, and should a failure occur, it would be less noticeable.

The *failover ip address* command sets the IP address of the failover unit for each interface. When this configuration is copied to the secondary unit, it will use this address to communicate with the primary unit as well as allow you to Telnet or SSH into the secondary unit for management. The *failover link* command enables the optional stateful failover feature and tells the PIX on which interface to send the TCP state information. In this example we use the interface we named *stateful* to carry state information.

Figure 6.35 PIX OS 6.*x* Configuration of Stateful Failover with Failover Cable

```
Pix515(config)# failover
Pix515(config)# failover poll 5
Pix515(config)# failover ip address outside 11.1.1.13
Pix515(config)# failover ip address inside 192.168.0.3
Pix515(config)# failover ip address DMZ 11.1.2.5
Pix515(config)# failover ip address stateful 192.168.4.2
Pix515(config)# failover link stateful
```

At this point you are ready to power on the secondary unit. The PIX will automatically detect that the secondary unit is online, and the primary unit will then copy the configuration to the Flash on the secondary PIX. Once the pair is synchronized, the PIX units will function as an Active/Standby pair. We discuss how to manage and maintain failover status later in this section.

PIX 7.x OS Stateful Failover with a Failover Cable Configuration

Fundamentally you must perform the same failover tasks using the PIX 7.*x* OS as you do with the PIX 6.*x* OS, but the actual commands that you run have changed. The first step is to define the stateful failover interface and configure all the interfaces with the primary and secondary IP addresses that they should use. Instead of using the *failover ip address* command, the secondary IP address is assigned to the interface using the *standby* parameter of the *ip address* command. Figure 6.36 details the failover preconfiguration steps.

Figure 6.36 PIX 7.*x* Failover Preconfiguration

```
Pix515(config)# interface ethernet0
Pix515(config-if)# nameif outside
Pix515(config-if)# security-level 0
Pix515(config-if)# ip address 11.1.1.1 255.255.255.240 standby 11.1.1.2
Pix515(config)# interface ethernet1
Pix515(config-if)# nameif inside
Pix515(config-if)# security-level 100
Pix515(config-if)# ip address 192.168.0.1 255.255.255.0 standby 192.168.0.2
Pix515(config)# interface ethernet3
Pix515(config-if)# nameif dmz
Pix515(config-if)# security-level 50
Pix515(config-if)# ip address 11.1.2.1 255.255.255.0 standby 11.1.2.2
Pix515(config)# interface ethernet4
```

```
Pix515(config-if)# nameif stateful
Pix515(config-if)# security-level 90
Pix515(config-if)# ip address 192.168.4.1 255.255.255.0 standby 192.168.4.2
```

Once the failover preconfiguration settings have been configured, the next step is to configure the actual failover settings as shown in Figure 6.37.

Figure 6.37 PIX 7.*x* Configuration of Stateful Failover with Failover Cable

```
Pix515(config)# failover
Pix515(config)# failover polling 5
Pix515(config)# failover link stateful
```

At this point you are ready to power on the secondary unit. The PIX will automatically detect that the secondary unit is online, and the primary unit will then copy the configuration to the Flash on the secondary PIX. Once the pair is synchronized, the PIX units will function as an Active/Standby pair. We discuss how to manage and maintain failover status later in this section.

Configuring Active/Passive Stateful LAN-Based Failover

In this section, we cover how to configure stateful failover using the LAN-based solution. Instead of using the proprietary high-speed serial cable, which limits the physical distance the PIX firewalls can be set apart from each other as well as not being supported with the ASA, the LAN-based solution uses one of the PIX/ASA's interfaces for heartbeat and configuration traffic. You can connect the interfaces via a switch or a crossover cable, which enables the PIX/ASA units to be set further apart.

There are a few drawbacks to this method. The first is that an interface on each PIX/ASA will be used solely for the purpose of heartbeat and configuration traffic. The second is that a power failure in either unit will take longer to detect. Finally, the configuration requires configuring both units before failover will function.

Figure 6.38 shows how the LAN-based stateful failover is physically laid out. The diagram shows a pair of PIX firewalls with six Fast Ethernet interfaces. Fast Ethernet interfaces 0, 1, and 2 are assigned to the outside, inside, and DMZ interfaces, respectively. The fourth interface, Fast Ethernet interface 3, is a dedicated interface assigned to carry state information from the primary unit to the secondary unit. The fifth interface, Fast Ethernet interface 4, is a dedicated interface assigned to carry heartbeat and configuration traffic from the primary unit to the secondary unit. Cisco recommends that the heartbeat and configuration traffic (shown on VLAN 40) and TCP state traffic (shown on VLAN 30) be located on separate switches or connected via a crossover cable.

Figure 6.38 Physical Layout of LAN-Based Failover Setup

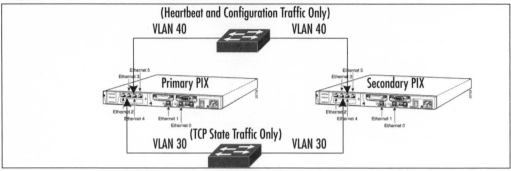

Unlike the cable-based solution, both PIX/ASA firewalls need to be configured before failover is fully operational. We begin with the primary unit, for which we need to define an interface for the heartbeat and configuration traffic, assign IP addresses to the failover unit, define the unit as a primary, and configure the stateful failover option. The configuration in Figure 6.39 should be combined with the configuration in Figure 6.34, which defines many of the interfaces, including the interface used for stateful failover.

In addition to the interfaces defined in Figure 6.34, we need to define another interface for heartbeat and configuration traffic. Figure 6.39 shows how to configure an interface named *heartbeat* with a security level of 95, an IP address of 192.168.5.1, and a speed defined as 100Mb full duplex. As with cable-based failover, we use the *failover* command to enable failover, set the poll interval to 5 seconds with the *failover poll* command, and set the IP addresses for all interfaces on the secondary unit using the *failover ip address* command.

The next group of commands is used to define the LAN-based failover. The *failover lan unit primary* command defines the PIX/ASA unit as the primary. The *failover lan interface* command tells the PIX/ASA on which interface to send and receive heartbeat and configuration traffic. In this example, we use the interface named *heartbeat*. For extra security, the PIX/ASA encrypts heartbeat and configuration traffic between the primary and secondary units by using shared keys. To specify the shared key, use the *failover lan key* command. We set the shared key in this example to *mykey*. The *failover lan enable* command lets the PIX know to disable cable-based failover and enable LAN-based failover. As with cable-based failover, the *failover link* command enables the optional stateful failover feature and tells the PIX/ASA on which interface to send the TCP state information. In this example, we use the interface we named *stateful* to carry state information.

Figure 6.39 Configuration of LAN-Based Failover (Primary)

```
Pix515(config)# nameif ethernet4 heartbeat security95
Pix515(config)# ip address stateful 192.168.5.1 255.255.255.0
Pix515(config)# interface ethernet4 100full
Pix515(config)# failover
```

```
Pix515(config)# failover poll 5
Pix515(config)# failover ip address outside 11.1.1.13
Pix515(config)# failover ip address inside 192.168.0.3
Pix515(config)# failover ip address DMZ 11.1.2.5
Pix515(config)# failover ip address stateful 192.168.4.2
Pix515(config)# failover ip address heartbeat 192.168.5.2
Pix515(config)# failover lan unit primary
Pix515(config)# failover lan interface heartbeat
Pix515(config)# failover lan key mykey
Pix515(config)# failover lan enable
Pix515(config)# failover link stateful
```

At this point, you need to configure the secondary PIX/ASA with the minimal number of statements shown in Figure 6.40 so it will be able to bring up the *heartbeat* interface. Once this process is completed, the primary PIX/ASA will be able to communicate to the secondary PIX/ASA via the LAN-based failover and copy its configuration to the secondary PIX's flash.

Figure 6.40 Configuration of LAN-Based Failover (Secondary)

```
Pix515(config)# nameif ethernet4 heartbeat security95
Pix515(config)# ip address stateful 192.168.5.1 255.255.255.0
Pix515(config)# interface ethernet4 100full
Pix515(config)# failover
Pix515(config)# failover poll 5
Pix515(config)# failover ip address heartbeat 192.168.5.2
Pix515(config)# failover lan unit secondary
Pix515(config)# failover lan interface heartbeat
Pix515(config)# failover lan key mykey
Pix515(config)# failover lan enable
```

Configuring Active/Active Stateful Failover with a Failover Cable (PIX Only)

Configuring Active/Active stateful failover with a failover cable is almost the exact same process as configuring Active/Standby stateful failover with a failover cable. As with Active/Standby failover, plug in the failover cable, being careful to connect the *primary* end to the primary firewall and the *secondary* end to the secondary firewall. Each interface on the primary firewall also needs to be connected to the corresponding interface on the secondary firewall through either a switch or a crossover cable. Leave the secondary firewall powered off, and turn on the primary firewall. Next we configure the clock on the primary firewall using the *clock* command.

> **NOTE**
>
> Do not power on the secondary firewall until the primary firewall is fully configured.

We must assign active and standby IP addresses to each interface on the primary firewall and enable the interfaces. In multiple-context mode, IP addresses must be configured from within each context, so use the *changeto* context command to switch between contexts. After configuring the active and standby IP addresses, the next step is to configure failover groups and designate if the firewall will be primary or secondary for each failover group. The command syntax is simple—for example, if the firewall will be primary for *failover group 1*, and secondary for *failover group 2:*

```
PIX515(config)# failover group 1
PIX515(config-fover-group)# primary
PIX515(config-fover-group)# exit
PIX515(config)# failover group 2
PIX515(config-fover-group)# secondary
PIX515(config-fover-group)# exit
```

All security contexts must be mapped to a failover group. The admin context and any unassigned contexts will automatically be mapped to *failover group 1*. The command syntax is:

```
PIX515(config)# context context_name
PIX515(config-context)# join-failover-group { 1 | 2 }
PIX515(config-context)# exit
```

At this point, simply enter the *failover* command on the primary unit. Boot up the secondary unit and enter the *failover* command. The configuration is complete! To enable stateful failover, follow the same steps as enabling stateful active/standby failover.

Configuring Active/Active Stateful LAN-Based Failover

To configure LAN-based Active/Active stateful failover, follow the same configurations as Active/Standby failover except for creating failover groups and preferences and assigning contexts to failover groups. So for example, you would assign different security contexts to different failover groups, allowing each failover group (and by extension security contexts) to operate independently in an active/active fashion. In essence, the actual implementation of active/active stateful LAN-based failover is no different from standby failover—it's just a manner of planning so that your security contexts are in different failover groups, thus allowing them to be assigned to different physical firewalls.

Testing and Monitoring Failover

The status of the failover feature can be viewed using the *show failover* command. This *show* command details whether failover is active, the status of each interface on both the primary and secondary units, and several other statistics. You might be confronted with a situation in which you need to force failover to occur for maintenance reasons or force the primary unit back into an active state after a fault has been fixed. Both these situations call for the use of the *failover active* command.

For example, to take the primary unit out of service for maintenance reasons, you can perform the *no failover active* command, which forces the primary unit to give up its active status and the standby or secondary unit to become active. When the maintenance on the primary unit is complete, you will use the *failover active* command to return the primary unit to active status. The *failover active* command is not limited to the primary unit; it can be used on either the primary or secondary, but if it's operational, all configurations changes should be performed on the primary unit.

NOTE

Should a fault occur and the PIX (configured for stateful failover) automatically fail over to the secondary unit, it will maintain state for TCP connections. However, once the fault on the primary unit is repaired and the primary PIX is forced to active status, all TCP will be disconnected because the secondary PIX does not send TCP state data to the primary unit. In other words, stateful failover occurs only from primary to secondary, not vice versa. You should consider returning the primary unit to active state after business hours or during times of low utilization, to minimize the loss of connections.

Blocking ActiveX and Java

Many security managers consider ActiveX and Java applets a security risk and require the firewall to block hosts on the internal LAN from downloading them from Web sites. ActiveX controls (also known as *OCX controls*) and Java can be downloaded by users who access Web sites that call for and download ActiveX controls and Java applets. ActiveX and Java can add functionality to a Web site in the form of interactive forms, calendars, and calculators. However, they can also be used for malicious activities, including taking control of the desktop, causing PCs to crash, collecting sensitive information, and initiating attacks on other machines. The PIX/ASA is able to block ActiveX and Java applets by commenting out the *<APPLET>, </APPLET>, <OBJECT>,* and *</OBJECT>* tags in the HTML code that so they cannot be executed. The PIX/ASA cannot discriminate between legitimate or malicious content, so the PIX/ASA will indiscriminately comment out this code. Therefore, all Web pages that rely on ActiveX and Java will not function properly.

Configuring the PIX/ASA to block ActiveX controls and Java applets is simple. Figure 6.41 shows the *filter* commands necessary to block them on TCP port 80 (the standard Web port). You can also narrow the scope of the ActiveX and Java filtering by specifying the source and/or destination addresses with the *filter* command.

Figure 6.41 Configuring ActiveX and Java Blocking

```
Pix515(config)# filter activex 80 0 0 0 0
Pix515(config)# filter java 80 0 0 0 0
```

NOTE

The PIX will inspect each packet containing the specified port and look for and comment out the *<APPLET>, </APPLET>, <OBJECT CLASSID>, <OBJECT>,* and *</OBJECT>* tags in the HTML code, but if the tag is spread across multiple packets, the PIX might not be able to block the ActiveX control or Java applet.

Content Filtering

The PIX/ASA does support content filtering, but it does so by utilizing a separate server running either the WebSense or N2H2 server. The WebSense or Secure Computing SmartFilter (formerly N2H2) server must be purchased separately from the PIX/ASA. All versions of PIX/ASA OS software support URL filtering (the filtering of HTTP requests). In addition, the PIX/ASA 7.*x* OS software supports filtering of HTTPS and FTP traffic through the external content filtering server.

The URL filtering feature is useful for limiting access to Web sites that could contain content that violates company policies, such as pornography and gambling. The PIX/ASA communicates with the WebSense or SmartFilter server to determine whether the Web content the user is requesting should be filtered or allowed.

Figure 6.42 shows how to configure the PIX to communicate with a WebSense server located on the PIX/ASA's inside interface with the IP address of 192.168.1.50 using the *url-server* command. The *filter url http* command specifies the range of source IP addresses that require HTTP filtering through the WebSense server. The *allow* keyword tells the PIX/ASA to allow all HTTP requests (even to filtered Web sites) to flow should connectivity be lost to the WebSense server. The *filter url except* command allows you the specify IP ranges that should be exempt from WebSense screening. In this case, users on the 192.168.2.0 /24 network are allowed to surf the Internet without URL filtering by the WebSense server.

Figure 6.42 Configuring URL Filtering

```
Pix515(config)# url-server (inside) vendor websense host 192.168.1.50
Pix515(config)# filter url http 0 0 0 0 allow
Pix515(config)# filter url except 192.168.2.0 255.255.255.0 0 0
```

For the PIX/ASA 7.*x* OS, configuring HTTPS and FTP filtering is also relatively straightforward once the URL server has been defined. This filtering is performed using the *filter https* and *filter ftp* commands, respectively, as shown in Figure 6.43.

Figure 6.43 Configuring HTTPS and FTP Filtering

```
Pix515(config)# filter https 443 0 0 0 0 allow
Pix515(config)# filter ftp 21 0 0 0 0 allow
```

Cut-Through Proxy   GALWAY COUNTY LIBRARIES

The cut-through proxy feature allows the PIX/ASA to authenticate users who access HTTP, FTP, and Telnet for inbound and outbound connections. Unlike standard proxy servers, the PIX/ASA authenticates users to an external RADIUS or TACACS+ database and, if allowed, the connection will be permitted directly between the client and the server. Access for HTTP, FTP, and Telnet services through the PIX/ASA can be applied on a per-user basis. When a user tries to access these services through the PIX/ASA, the PIX/ASA will prompt the user to enter a user ID and password. If the user has the required permission, the PIX/ASA will allow the requested connection to flow. If authorization is configured in conjunction with authentication, you can specifically restrict the Web, FTP, and Telnet hosts that a user can access.

The configuration in Figure 6.44 shows how to configure a cut-through proxy using the PIX 6.*x* OS. The configuration is similar to the AAA for management access to the PIX. We start by using the *aaa-server* command to configure the type of authentication server (RADIUS or TACACS+), IP address, interface, encryption key, and group tag. The next three commands enable the PIX to authenticate, authorize, and track all requests for HTTP access through the PIX initiated from the inside interface using the *aaa authentication*, *aaa authorization,* and *aaa accounting* commands. To complete the cut-through proxy implementation, the RADIUS or TACACS+ server also needs to be configured; refer to your RADIUS or TACACS+ documentation for information on how to do so.

Figure 6.44 Configuring User Authentication and Cut-Through Proxy for the PIX 6.*x* OS

```
Pix515(config)# aaa-server AuthOut protocol tacacs+
Pix515(config)# aaa-server AuthOut (inside) host 192.168.1.50 mykey
    timeout 5
Pix515(config)# aaa authentication include http inside 0.0.0.0 0.0.0.0
    0.0.0.0 0.0.0.0 AuthOut
Pix515(config)# aaa authorization include http inside 0.0.0.0 0.0.0.0
    0.0.0.0 0.0.0.0 AuthOut
Pix515(config)# aaa accounting include http inside 0.0.0.0 0.0.0.0 0.0
    0.0 0.0.0.0 AuthOut
```

As you would expect, configuring user authentication and cut-through proxy for the PIX/ASA 7.*x* OS is similar to the AAA for management access to the PIX. First you must configure the AAA server settings, and then you define the authentication, authorization, and accounting commands, as shown in Figure 6.44. The process of configuring user authentication and cut-through proxy for HTTP (you could just as easily substitute FTP or Telnet) is detailed in Figure 6.45.

Figure 6.45 Configuring User Authentication and Cut-Through Proxy for the PIX/ASA 7.*x* OS

```
Pix515(config)# aaa-server AuthOut protocol tacacs+
Pix515(config-aaa-server-group)# exit
Pix515(config)# aaa-server AuthOut (inside) host 10.21.120.46 mypubkey timeout 5
PIX515(config-aaa-server-host)# exit
Pix515(config)# aaa authentication include http inside 0.0.0.0 0.0.0.0
    0.0.0.0 0.0.0.0 AuthOut
Pix515(config)# aaa authorization include http inside 0.0.0.0 0.0.0.0
    0.0.0.0 0.0.0.0 AuthOut
Pix515(config)# aaa accounting include http inside 0.0.0.0 0.0.0.0 0.0
    0.0 0.0.0.0 AuthOut
```

NOTE

If you require a cut-through proxy with user authorization, consider using TACACS+, because the PIX does not support authorization with RADIUS. In addition, if you require extensive HTTP authorization, consider using the URL filtering feature.

Application Inspection

Translating network addresses can cause problems if an application embeds an address or port information into the payload of a packet. If this situation occurs, it could cause the application to reject the packet or session if the address or port in the header does not match the information in the payload.

To overcome this problem, Cisco has developed the Application Inspection feature. In the PIX 6.*x* software, this is also known as the *fixup*. In the PIX/ASA 7.*x* software, Cisco replaced the *fixup* command with the *inspect* command from the Cisco IOS. As packets are translated and pass through the PIX on known problematic application ports, the Application Inspection feature will check the payload of the packet for embedded addresses or ports, make the appropriate translations, and update the checksum. The packet is then forwarded to its destination, and the client or server on either end will be none the wiser that application inspection has taken place.

Application inspection also monitors applications that open secondary connections on separate ports to improve performance and allows dynamic ports to be opened for specific sessions. FTP is an application that requires application inspection because it starts a connection on the well-known TCP port 21 and then dynamically opens another port to transmit data. Application inspection is configured differently for the PIX 6.*x* OS than it is for the PIX 7.*x* OS.

Configuring PIX 6.*x* OS Application Inspection

The PIX 6.*x* application inspection functionality is configured through the *fixup* command. The configuration is relatively straightforward: Simply specify the protocol that the *fixup* will be applied to and specify any ports or additional information required by the given *fixup*. By default, application inspection is enabled for several well-known applications, including DNS, FTP, H323, HTTP, RSH, RTSP, SIP, SKINNY, SMTP, SQLNET, and TFTP, as of PIX OS 6.3(5). In addition to these defaults, you can also enable *fixup* for CTIQBE, ESP-IKE, ICMP, ILS, MGCP, PPTP and SNMP, as of PIX OS 6.3(5).

The configuration example in Figure 6.46 shows how to configure application inspection for HTTP on port 8080 using the *fixup protocol* command. Application inspection can also protect mail servers by only allowing certain SMTP commands to be executed on the mail server. This feature, also called MailGuard, allows only the following commands to be executed on the mail servers: *HELO, MAIL, RCPT, DATA, RSET, NOOP,* and *QUIT*.

Figure 6.46 Configuring Application Inspection

```
Pix515(config)# fixup protocol http 8080
Pix515(config)# fixup protocol smtp 25
```

Configuring PIX/ASA 7.x OS Application Inspection

The application inspection configuration commands were significantly changed in the PIX/ASA 7.x OS. The commands were largely changed to coincide with how application inspection is performed in the Cisco IOS, also known as *Modular Policy Framework* (MPF). This resulted in the *fixup* features being replaced by the MPF and protocol inspection features.

> **NOTE**
>
> You can still use the *fixup* command to configure application inspection in the PIX/ASA 7.x OS, but the command is automatically converted into the new protocol inspection commands. Consequently, it's a good idea to get into the habit of using the new commands.

Prior to MPF, most of these application inspection actions were an all-or-nothing proposition: Either all traffic transiting an interface was subject to the same policies, or none of the traffic was. With MPF, 7.x provides granularity to allow you to pick subsets of traffic from the whole and apply policies to it. MPF is new to PIX 7.x; there were no pre-7.x equivalents. Arguably, you could have some of this functionality in pre-7.x by cobbling together various parameters, but nothing as granular or flexible as MPF.

Depending on the protocol, inspection may or may not be enabled by default. All protocol inspection in PIX version 7.x is configured through the use of the MPF, which is a versatile and powerful way to apply protocol inspection to your firewall.

MPF has four main steps:

1. Defining a traffic class

2. Associating the traffic class with one or more actions

3. Customizing the parameters of the application inspection for the protocol in question

4. Applying the defined inspection to an interface

Defining a Traffic Class

Defining a traffic class is done through the use of the *class-map* command. The idea behind this command is that you want to identify a certain subset of the total traffic flowing through an interface. There are a number of possible methods of matching traffic, including:

- Using an access list

- Matching all traffic

- Using a list of predefined default IP protocols

- Matching traffic based on DSCP values

- Using a flow-based policy

- Matching specified TCP or UDP ports (without using an access list)

- Matching traffic based on IP precedence values

- Matching traffic based on RTP port numbers

- Matching a specified tunnel group

Prior to configuring any of these match conditions, the first step to configuring a traffic class is to define the traffic class and give it a name. To create a traffic class called *class1*, enter:

```
PIX515(config)# class-map class1
PIX515(config-cmap)#
```

You will notice that following this command, your prompt changes to *config-cmap*, indicating that you are now in class-map configuration mode and may enter commands relating to the specific class map (in this case, *class1*) that you have defined. At this prompt, you have the option of entering a description for this traffic class:

```
PIX515(config-cmap)# description sample traffic class
```

You also have the ability to rename the traffic class without removing and recreating it. In this case, we will rename the traffic class from *class1* to *class2*:

```
PIX515(config-cmap)# rename class2
```

The next step is to configure the traffic class to match certain traffic. To see all possible matching options:

```
PIX515(config-cmap)# match ?

mpf-class-map mode commands/options:
  access-list              Match an Access List
  any                      Match any packet
  default-inspection-traffic  Match default inspection traffic:
                           ctiqbe----tcp--2748      dns-------udp--53
                           ftp-------tcp--21        gtp----udp--2123,3386
                           h323-h225-tcp-1720       h323-ras-udp-1718-1719
                           http------tcp--80        icmp------icmp
                           ils-------tcp--389       mgcp---udp--2427,2727
                           netbios---udp--137-138   rpc-------udp--111
                           rsh-------tcp--514       rtsp------tcp--554
                           sip-------tcp--5060      sip-------udp--5060
                           skinny----tcp--2000      smtp------tcp--25
                           sqlnet----tcp--1521      tftp------udp--69
```

```
                          xdmcp-----udp--177
```

dscp	Match IP DSCP (DiffServ CodePoints)
flow	Flow based Policy
port	Match TCP/UDP port(s)
precedence	Match IP precedence
rtp	Match RTP port numbers
tunnel-group	Match a Tunnel Group

To match traffic by access list, you must configure an access list prior to configuring the traffic class. For example, to configure an access list called *acl1* that matches all traffic on TCP port 1111 and then apply it to the traffic class *class2*:

```
PIX515(config)# access-list acl1 permit tcp any any eq 1111
PIX515(config)# class-map class2
PIX515(config
-cmap)# match access-list acl1
```

To match any traffic, simply enter:

```
PIX515(config-cmap)# match any
```

The PIX default inspection traffic ports are shown in Table 6.3 (the table is courtesy of Cisco; see http://www.cisco.com/en/US/partner/products/sw/secursw/ps2120/products_configuration_guide_chapter09186a00804231c0.html, Table 21-2).

Table 6.3 PIX Default Inspection Ports

Protocol Name	Protocol	Port
ctiqbe	tcp	2748
dns	udp	53
ftp	tcp	21
gtp	udp	2123,3386
h323 h225	tcp	1720
h323 ras	udp	1718-1719
http	tcp	80
icmp	icmp	N/A
ils	tcp	389
mgcp	udp	2427,2727
netbios	udp	N/A
rpc/sunrpc	udp	111

Continued

Table 6.3 continued PIX Default Inspection Ports

Protocol Name	Protocol	Port
rsh	tcp	514
rtsp	tcp	554
sip	tcp, udp	5060
skinny	tcp	2000
smtp	tcp	25
sqlnet	tcp	1521
tftp	udp	69
xdmcp	udp	177

To match the PIX default inspection traffic ports, simply enter:

```
PIX515(config-cmap)# match default-inspection-traffic
```

To match traffic based on DSCP value, you may enter one or more of the following parameters, separated by a space:

```
PIX515(config-cmap)# match dscp ?
mpf-class-map mode commands/options:
  <0-63>   Differentiated services codepoint value
  af11     Match packets with AF11 dscp (001010)
  af12     Match packets with AF12 dscp (001100)
  af13     Match packets with AF13 dscp (001110)
  af21     Match packets with AF21 dscp (010010)
  af22     Match packets with AF22 dscp (010100)
  af23     Match packets with AF23 dscp (010110)
  af31     Match packets with AF31 dscp (011010)
  af32     Match packets with AF32 dscp (011100)
  af33     Match packets with AF33 dscp (011110)
  af41     Match packets with AF41 dscp (100010)
  af42     Match packets with AF42 dscp (100100)
  af43     Match packets with AF43 dscp (100110)
  cs1      Match packets with CS1(precedence 1) dscp (001000)
  cs2      Match packets with CS2(precedence 2) dscp (010000)
  cs3      Match packets with CS3(precedence 3) dscp (011000)
  cs4      Match packets with CS4(precedence 4) dscp (100000)
  cs5      Match packets with CS5(precedence 5) dscp (101000)
  cs6      Match packets with CS6(precedence 6) dscp (110000)
  cs7      Match packets with CS7(precedence 7) dscp (111000)
  default  Match packets with default dscp (000000)
  ef       Match packets with EF dscp (101110)
```

If you want to match traffic based on a TCP or UDP port without using an access list, you can use the *match port* command. For example, to match the same TCP port 1111 as in the preceding example:

```
PIX515(config-cmap)# match port tcp eq 1111
```

Note that the *match port* command allows you to specify ranges of ports. To do so, substitute *eq* with *range*, and then specify a lower and upper limit to the ports to match. For example, to match TCP ports 1111 through 1120:

```
PIX515(config-cmap)# match port tcp eq 1112
```

To match traffic based on its IP precedence, you may enter precedence values by name or number. For example, to match precedence values 2, 4, and 6:

```
PIX515(config-cmap)# match precedence 2 4 6
```

NOTE

The PIX supports multiple match commands only for the tunnel-group and default-inspection-traffic types. You may configure one of these commands in conjunction with any other *match* command. However, all other *match* commands cannot be configured at the same time; you must remove one before adding another.

Associating a Traffic Class with an Action

Once you have identified traffic of interest, the next step is to associate that traffic with a particular action, to actually perform the protocol inspection. To do so, the first step is to define a policy map. For example, to create a policy map named *pol1*:

```
PIX515(config)# policy-map pol1
PIX515(config-pmap)#
```

At this point, you will notice that the prompt is changed to *config-pmap*, indicating that all subsequent commands apply to the policy map. Just as with a class map, you have the option of adding a description to the policy map or renaming it. The next step is to specify one or more traffic classes to the policy map. For example, to specify the traffic class we created earlier (*class2*):

```
PIX515(config-pmap)# class class2
PIX515(config-pmap-c)#
```

Notice that now the prompt has changed to *config-pmap-c*, indicating that subsequent commands apply to the class map within the policy map. To enable protocol inspection, you may now use the *inspect* command. The following protocol inspection engines are available:

```
PIX515(config-pmap-c)# inspect ?

mpf-policy-map-class mode commands/options:
  ctiqbe
  dns
  esmtp
  ftp
  gtp
  h323
  http
  icmp
  ils
  mgcp
  netbios
  pptp
  rsh
  rtsp
  sip
  skinny
  snmp
  sqlnet
  sunrpc
  tftp
  xdmcp
```

For example, to enable FTP protocol inspection:

```
PIX515(config-pmap-c)# inspect ftp
```

Once you have completed the inspect configuration, you might want to return to the policy map configuration mode to define additional traffic classes. To do so:

```
PIX515(config-pmap-c)# exit
PIX515(config-pmap)#
```

Notice that the prompt has now returned to *config-pmap*. You may now enter additional configuration, or exit again to return to the main configuration mode.

Customizing Application Inspection Parameters

Although in general, protocol inspection will function without modifying the default parameters, at times you might want to tune the various options associated with a protocol inspection engine. To do so, you must use application maps. Application maps are available for a number of protocols, and we will go into detail on how to configure these, when available, in each application-specific section of this chapter. An application map called *httpmap1* is applied within the policy map configuration as follows:

```
PIX515(config-pmap-c)# inspect http httpmap1
```

Applying Inspection to an Interface

The final step to enabling protocol inspection is to apply the inspection you have configured to one interface, multiple interfaces, or all interfaces. To do so, use the *service-policy* command. For example, to apply the aforementioned policy map to the outside interface:

```
PIX515(config)# service-policy pol1 interface  outside
```

Similarly, if you want to apply this policy to all interfaces:

```
PIX515(config)# service-policy pol1 global
```

Intrusion Detection

The PIX/ASA's Intrusion Detection System (IDS) analyzes packets that enter a specified interface or interfaces on a PIX/ASA and compares them to 55 predefined attack signatures. The types of attack signature the PIX/ASA inspects for are related to the most common DoS attacks and information-gathering scans. Should the PIX/ASA detect a match, it can instantly drop or reset the session or send an alert. Figure 6.46 shows how to configure the PIX/ASA to inspect all packets coming in on the outside interface of the PIX/ASA. Should a match to an attack signature occur, all packets related to the malicious session will be dropped and the attack will be thwarted.

Figure 6.46 Configuring IDS

```
Pix515(config)# ip audit name DropAttacks attack action drop
Pix515(config)# ip audit interface outside DropAttacks
```

> **NOTE**
>
> This intrusion detection functionality should not be confused with the intrusion prevention functionality provided by the ASA with the AIP-SSM. Although the native PIX/ASA intrusion detection functionality provides some very basic and rudimentary intrusion detection and prevention capabilities, the AIP-SSM is a robust and full-featured intrusion prevention system that provides a tremen-

dous amount of functionality and flexibility. If you require IPS functionality with your firewall, you should use an ASA with the AIP-SSM instead of a PIX firewall. The AIP-SSM configuration is beyond the scope of this book.

FloodGuard and DNSGuard

The PIX/ASA has many features that protect it and resources it is protecting from DoS attacks. The FloodGuard feature protects the PIX/ASA from a form of DoS attack in which an attacker tries to overload the PIX with user authentication requests. To protect itself, the PIX/ASA actively closes certain half-open or idle connections to reclaim resources. This feature is enabled in PIX 6.x OS by the use of the *floodguard enable* command, a feature that is enabled by default. In the PIX/ASA 7.x OS, the *floodguard* command no longer exists, since *floodguard* is enabled by default and is always on.

DNSGuard identifies an outbound DNS query request and allows only a single DNS response back. A host may query several DNS servers for a response, and the PIX/ASA allows only the first answer to the query back in; additional responses from other servers are dropped. DNSGuard is enabled by default and cannot be configured or disabled.

Securing SNMP and NTP

Network management systems can manage the PIX's status via Simple Network Management Protocol (SNMP). For security reasons, the PIX/ASA allows only read-only SNMP access. To securely configure SNMP on the PIX/ASA, a shared key, or community string, is required to authenticate requests to and from the management system. The key must match on both the management system and the PIX/ASA firewall. As shown in Figure 6.47, the SNMP key is set to *mySNMPstring* using the *snmp-server community* command. The *snmp-server host* command specifies the management station that will communicate with the PIX/ASA and the interface in which the management station resides. In this example, the management station is 192.168.1.50, and it is located on the PIX/ASA's inside interface. Only devices specified with this command and the proper community string will be able to communicate with the PIX/ASA via SNMP. The *snmp-server host* command also allows you to specify whether the PIX/ASA will be polled by the management system (with the *poll* keyword) or whether the PIX/ASA will send traps to the management system (with the *trap* keyword).

Figure 6.47 Configuring SNMP

```
Pix515(config)# snmp-server community mySNMPstring
Pix515(config)# snmp-server host inside 192.168.1.50 poll
```

Network Time Protocol (NTP) allows the PIX/ASA to synchronize its clock with a time source. It is a good idea to have the clock set on all network devices, especially security devices, so that if an attack occurs, it will be easier to identify the sequence of events of an attack. Figure 6.48 shows how to configure NTP with authentication to ensure that the PIX/ASA is receiving its time from a trusted time source. In the example, the key is set to *myNTPkey,* and the NTP server is located on the PIX/ASA's inside interface and has the IP address of 192.168.1.50.

Figure 6.48 Configuring NTP

```
Pix515(config)# ntp authenticate
Pix515(config)# ntp trusted-key 1
Pix515(config)# ntp authentication-key 1 md5 myNTPkey
Pix515(config)# ntp server 192.168.1.50 key 1 source inside
```

PIX/ASA Firewall Design and Configuration Checklist

Use this checklist in designing and configuring your PIX firewall:

1. Gather DMZ requirements.

2. Design the DMZ environment to the specification of the requirements.

3. Select one of the five PIX or four ASA firewall chassis.

4. Select the optional components of the PIX/ASA firewall.

5. Select the correct PIX/ASA OS license (Restricted, Unrestricted, Failover, and Failover Active/Active).

6. Optionally, select an encryption license (DES and 3DES).

7. Configure the PIX/ASA's console and terminal interfaces.

8. Set security levels on the PIX/ASA interfaces.

9. Set IP addresses and speed/duplex settings on the active interfaces.

10. Configure outbound NAT statements.

11. Configure inbound NAT statements.

12. Configure outbound access rules controlling access from internal resources to specific resources on the Internet or other less secure interfaces.

13. Configure inbound access rules controlling access to resources on the DMZ. Remember to be as specific as possible.

14. Configure static or dynamic routing.

15. Should high availability be required, configure the failover or stateful failover feature.

16. If required, configure URL filtering, cut-through proxy, application inspection, and intrusion detection.

17. Lock down SNMP and NTP.

Summary

The PIX and ASA firewalls are powerful tools for protecting the enterprise's internal network and its DMZ. Built on a purpose-built operating system, the PIX and ASA firewall appliances can provide the security, performance, resiliency, and flexibility to meet all your DMZ infrastructure needs. Five PIX and four ASA firewall models can provide network architects with several different options to meet their needs—from a small DMZ environment to service provider-class environments. This chapter discussed several popular DMZ designs that will meet the needs of many DMZ planners. Use these designs to create the DMZ that best fits your requirements. Remember to choose your design based on your technical requirements and financial constraints. The PIX/ASA operating system is purpose-built and packed with features, which makes the PIX/ASA highly secure but at the same time provides many of the features found in firewalls based on general operating systems.

The PIX/ASA can be configured via a Web-based configuration and management tool called the Adaptive Security Device Manager (or, for the 6.*x* OS, the PIX Device Manager, or PDM) or via a command-line interface. In managing the PIX/ASA, always use a secure form of communication, such as SSH, which encrypts traffic between the client and the PIX/ASA, instead of Telnet, which communicates in clear text. This makes the PIX/ASA easy to configure and manage for both the novice and the advanced firewall administrator.

We covered how to configure many of the PIX/ASA's basic functions, including defining interfaces, NAT/PAT, access rules, and routing, which are essential to the PIX/ASA's secure operation. The PIX/ASA gives the DMZ planner the flexibility to individually set security levels to each DMZ interface, which can be used to control traffic and maintain the network's integrity. NAT and PAT can be used to hide network internal addresses or convert private IP addresses into publicly routable addresses. Access rules allow the DMZ planner to limit access to resources on the DMZ via predefined ACLs. The PIX/ASA can support a variety of routing protocols, including RIP and OSPF, but most DMZ infrastructures utilize static routing for its security, simplicity, and effectiveness. To provide additional functionality, we also covered how to configure failover for high availability, content filtering, and application layer security.

At this point, you have all the information you need to decide whether the PIX or ASA firewall is the right device for your DMZ infrastructure in terms or features, functions, and performance. Perhaps more important, this chapter gave you a good idea of how the PIX and ASA are configured and managed.

Solutions Fast Track

Basics of the PIX/ASA

- ☑ The PIX is a network security appliance with a purpose-built operating system, which reduces the risk of security flaws inherent in firewalls built on general-purpose operating systems.

- ☑ The ASA is a network security appliance based on the PIX operating system, which includes advanced IPS and Anti-X functionality into a single purpose-built device.

- ☑ There are five PIX models that can provide a high level of security and performance for networks of any size, from SOHO to a large enterprise or service provider.

- ☑ There are four ASA models that can provide a high level of security and performance for networks of any size, from SOHO to a large enterprise or service provider.

- ☑ The Adaptive Security Algorithm (ASA) allows the PIX to provide stateful inspection firewall services, track the state of all communications, and prevent unauthorized network access.

Cisco PIX/ASA Versions and Features

- ☑ The fact that the PIX/ASA has a purpose-built operating system does not mean it does not have the features of a firewall built on a general OS. In fact, the PIX/ASA has a strong security algorithm along with features that include but are not limited to URL filtering, content filtering, DHCP, and intrusion detection.

- ☑ In addition to securing the network, the PIX can support mobile user and site-to-site VPNs.

- ☑ The ASA devices can be configured in one of five editions: Firewall Edition, IPS Edition, Anti-X Edition, VPN Edition, and Business Edition.

- ☑ The PIX and ASA share a common OS. The latest main release of the PIX/ASA operating system is PIX OS version 7.2, which includes enhancements to VPN features, support for VLANs and virtual interfaces, support for virtual firewalls and security contexts, Layer 2 transparent firewalls, advanced Web filtering, tunneling application control, enhanced failover, and support for new, optional hardware.

☑ The ASA can be enhanced beyond traditional firewall functionality through the use of the AIP-SSM or CSC-SSM to provide integrated IPS functionality or threat protection and content control, respectively.

Securing Your Network Perimeters

☑ The PIX/ASA provides several design possibilities to secure your network and the DMZ, including the traditional "three-legged" firewall, multi-DMZ, and dual firewall internal/external firewall sandwich configurations.

☑ The PIX/ASA can support DMZs of all sizes and capabilities, including high-volume e-commerce sites.

☑ All the designs can also support high availability with the use of a second PIX/ASA as a hot standby firewall in the event of failure of the primary PIX/ASA. This can be configured in either an Active/Standby or an Active/Active failover configuration.

Making a DMZ and Controlling Traffic

☑ Apply security levels to active interfaces so that the PIX/ASA knows how to protect and restrict access networks and devices on each interface.

☑ NAT or PAT enables the PIX/ASA to hide addresses and translate private addressing to public addresses that are routable throughout the Internet. For the PIX to pass traffic between interfaces, either no nat-control or a NAT and/or PAT statement is required.

☑ Access control lists enable the PIX/ASA to restrict access to devices on all interfaces, including the DMZ.

☑ Routing allows the PIX/ASA to forward traffic out the correct interface and on to the receiving device or next hop. The PIX/ASA supports static and dynamic routing in the form of RIP and OSPF.

Advanced PIX/ASA Features

☑ Failover enables the PIX/ASA to provide high availability in case of a failure in either an Active/Standby or Active/Active fashion. In addition, the PIX/ASA supports stateful failover, so user connections through the PIX/ASA should remain active as failover occurs.

☑ URL, Java, and ActiveX filtering prevents access to restricted sites and protects users from downloading dangerous content and applications.

☑ IDS and application inspection delve into the packets to make sure there is no malicious activity flowing through the PIX/ASA.

PIX/ASA Firewall Design and Configuration Checklist

☑ Use the checklist at the end of the chapter when you are designing and configuring your PIX/ASA firewall.

Frequently Asked Questions

The following Frequently Asked Questions, answered by the authors of this book, are designed to both measure your understanding of the concepts presented in this chapter and to assist you with real-life implementation of these concepts. To have your questions about this chapter answered by the author, browse to **www.syngress.com/solutions** and click on the **"Ask the Author"** form.

Q: Does the PIX/ASA support other desktop protocols, such as AppleTalk and IPX?

A: The PIX/ASA supports only IP. If you need to pass AppleTalk or IPX protocols through the PIX/ASA, you must encapsulate them within an IP tunnel. Tunneling of protocols through the PIX can be dangerous and should only be done in a controlled environment.

Q: What routing protocols does the PIX/ASA support?

A: The PIX/ASA can support static routing, RIP (versions 1 and 2), and OSPF. The PIX/ASA does not support EIGRP and IGRP, Cisco's proprietary routing protocols.

Q: Can the PIX/ASA protect the internal LAN from viruses or worms?

A: By default, the PIX/ASA does provide some application-level protection for popular applications such as FTP and mail. In addition, the PIX does have IDS feature that can protect against 55 predefined attack signatures, providing protection against some popular DoS attacks. However, to protect against viruses and/or worms, you should consider an ASA with the AIP-SSM or CSC-SSM instead of PIX firewall to take advantage of the advanced filtering capabilities the AIP-SSM and CSC-SSM provide.

Q: Can a PIX 515 and PIX 515E used together for failover?

A: No. Both PIX/ASA units must be exactly the same model and must have the same amount of memory, Flash, and interface cards. Even though the PIX 515E is an enhanced version of the PIX 515, the models cannot be used together as a failover pair.

Q: Does the PIX/ASA have packet-capture capabilities, similar to a sniffer?

A: Yes. PIX/ASA version 6.2 supports packet-capture capabilities that allow the administrator to capture packets on specific interfaces and to filter captured packets via ACLs. The capture buffer can be viewed via the CLI or downloaded via a TFTP server.

Q: Does the PIX/ASA cut-through proxy work the same as a proxy server?

A: No. The PIX/ASA's cut-though proxy feature does not work like a standard proxy server, because the PIX/ASA will authenticate the user, and if permitted, the PIX/ASA will allow the client to communicate directly with the remote server. A standard proxy server will act as intermediate device where the client will request a connection to a remote device; it intercepts all requests to the real server to see if it can fulfill the requests itself. If it cannot, it forwards the request to the real server on behalf of the client, so the client never directly communicates to the remote server.

## Chapter 7

Firewall and DMZ Design: Check Point

Solutions in this chapter:

- **Basics of Check Point Firewalls**
- **Securing Your Network Perimeters**
- **Configuring the DMZ**
- **Configuring the Firewall**
- **Configuring the Security Rulebase**
- **Configuring the Address Translation Rulebase**
- **Configuring Network and Application Protections**
- **The Check Point NG Secure DMZ Checklist**

- ☑ **Summary**
- ☑ **Solutions Fast Track**
- ☑ **Frequently Asked Questions**

Introduction

A key component of any security policy is a well-designed DMZ. Because hosts in the DMZ are externally accessible over the Internet, your DMZ's design can make or break the overall security of your network. The DMZ can be the entry point through which malicious-minded individuals can enter your network.

There are two types of traffic to keep in mind when you're considering controlling traffic flowing to and from a DMZ: traffic originating from or destined for your internal network and traffic originating from or destined for the Internet. Although the connection point to the Internet is the most vital one, it is equally important to consider the access point to the internal network. Not only does this consideration provide a second layer of inspection for traffic traversing the DMZ to reach internal hosts, it also allows you to protect your network from malicious activity originating from within—an occurrence that's growing more and more common.

In this chapter, we review the basics of Check Point firewalls to give you a solid understanding of how firewalls operate and the feature they make available to you. We then go into detail about several features of Check Point's firewalls that are critical to developing a well-secured DMZ. These details include how to best configure Check Point's features to secure your network perimeters. Finally, we document the steps to set up the DMZ from scratch using Check Point firewalls, from the setup of the physical interface to rulebase configuration.

Basics of Check Point Firewalls

Check Point Software Technologies' firewalls are full-featured firewalls that run on a variety of platforms. These platforms include open systems and dedicated appliances manufactured by Nokia as well as a dozen other companies such as Crossbeam, Sun, IBM, and others. Additionally, Check Point firewalls run on top of a variety of operating systems (OSs), including SecurePlatform, Nokia's IPSO, Sun Solaris, Microsoft Windows 2000/2003, and Red Hat Linux.

Designing & Planning...

Operating System Selection

Choosing the operating system to use for your Check Point firewall is important to the overall effectiveness of the product in securing your network. In reality, Check Point installs as a driver at the network card level of the OS, and so the

Continued

security that Check Point provides under one operating system is, for the most part, the same as in any other. However, the features, performance, and maintenance options vary widely, depending on the underlying operating system.

In terms of features, Check Point usually implements additional features on SecurePlatform and Nokia IPSO that are not available in other OSs, such as ISP redundancy and route-based VPNs. In terms of performance, operating systems with large overheads, such as Microsoft Windows, will have a detrimental impact on the performance that a firewall can offer. In terms of maintenance, keeping the appropriate patches installed, ensuring full compatibility with all features, and having easy-to-use backup and restore functions are extremely important. Only SecurePlatform and Nokia IPSO provide the enterprise with patches that are easy to install with the appropriate firewall version and with integrated backup and restore functions that allow for complete disaster recovery in 30 minutes or less.

NOTE

Once you select your underlying operating system, the next decision is what platform to use. If you plan to use Solaris, AIX, or IPSO, you simply need to select the available appliances you will use (the Nokia appliances are discussed in greater detail in the next chapter). If you plan to use Microsoft Windows or Red Hat Linux, you can select an open system based on Intel or AMD processors from your preferred hardware vendor; see the Check Point Hardware Compatibility list at www.checkpoint.com/products/supported_platforms/secure-platform.html first. For SecurePlatform systems, you can also select an open system from your hardware vendor, or select from over a dozen different vendors, such as Crossbeam, Resilience, HP, Sun, Nortel, and others, that manufacture preinstalled SecurePlatform appliances.

Key features of Check Point firewalls are stateful inspection, network address translation, multiple types of authentication mechanisms, SmartDefense, Web intelligence, and content inspection; they provide malicious activity detection, antivirus, and other high-level application protections against activities such as port scanning, FTP bounce attacks, URL worms, spyware, and adware.

Check Point firewalls also have significant VPN capabilities for both site-to-site and remote access configurations. Check Point's site-to-site VPN is interoperable with products from all other major firewall vendors that implement the IKE and IPSec standards. For user VPN access, there are several VPN client alternatives: SecuRemote, a free VPN client from Check Point; SecureClient, a licensed VPN client that integrates a centrally managed personal firewall; and the SSL Network Extender, an SSL-based client that is ActiveX or Java based and downloads from a standard browser.

Choosing the Right Check Point Solution

Even for experienced Check Point professionals, keeping track of the various Check Point versions and commercial offerings is difficult. With a software-only solution, you can currently be running Check Point software purchased five or 10 years ago and have them updated to the latest available version.

Check Point Releases: From 1.0 to NGX R61

It's worthwhile to look at a quick timeline of Check Point releases. Check Point's original FireWall-1 solution ran on Solaris and was then ported to Windows NT. Constant version upgrades led to VPN-1/FireWall-1 version 4.1 and Check Point 2000, which became the most predominant version that Check Point had around 2000 and 2001.

In 2001, Check Point released NG (Next Generation), which could be considered version 5.0. Later Check Point released NG Feature Pack 1, Feature Pack 2, and Feature Pack 3 (versions 5.1, 5.2, and 5.3, respectively) and, in 2003, NG with Application Intelligence was released, with Release R54 (version 5.4). R54 included enhanced SmartDefense functionality. Subsequent releases included R55, which is still very widely used today, and R55W and R57, which included Web intelligence and content inspection functionality, although they are not widely deployed. In mid-2005, Check Point introduced NGX, a major upgrade from R55, with release R60. This release added Web intelligence to the regular product line. In April 2006, NGX R61 was released, adding content inspection (virus protection) for all product lines.

Keep in mind that you can have a license purchased in 2001 at version 4.1 and through the annually recurring Software Subscription be able to use that license to run NGX R61 software.

Check Point Solutions

The myriad of available Check Point versions can run on different platforms and with different packaged options. Until NG with Application Intelligence, there was an Enterprise product line, with FireWall-1 and VPN-1/FireWall-1 available for purchase, and the SmallOffice line for businesses of up to 100 protected IPs. There was also a short-lived VPN-1 Net product that was licensed based on VPN tunnels.

In 2003, Check Point changed its licensing scheme to the VPN-1 Pro and VPN-1 Express lines and discontinued VPN-1 Net and SmallOffice. All solutions included firewall and VPN functionality. The Pro line includes quality-of-service (QoS) capabilities and extended support for more VPN clients as well as unlimited gateway licensing. The Express line is limited to 500 users or fewer. In April 2006, Check Point once again changed its products to the VPN-1 UTM and VPN-1 Power lines. The UTM line includes firewall, VPN, IPS, and virus protection in one license, whereas the Power line includes firewall, VPN, IPS, QoS, and acceleration. There is also a UTM Power line, which includes firewall, VPN, IPS, QoS, acceleration, and virus protection.

The VPN-1 UTM Edge and Check Point Software Safe@Office round out the current product offerings. These are small, integrated appliances, as shown in Figure 7.1, with local Web-based administration; they include firewall, VPN, QoS, IPS, and antivirus for a small business of up to 100 users. The two products are nearly identical with the exception that the Edge products can be centrally managed from a SmartCenter, whereas Safe@Office can only be centrally managed through a dedicated product called a Security Management Portal. There are four hardware varieties: wired, wired with ADSL modem, wireless, and wireless with ADSL modem.

Figure 7.1 The VPN-1 UTM Edge Product Line

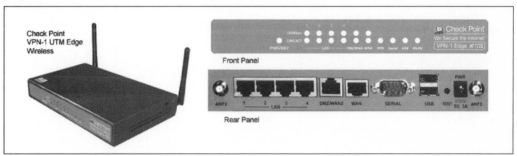

Management Architecture

Check Point's firewalls use a distributed architecture, where the management server, or SmartCenter, and the enforcement points, or gateways, can run on separate servers. As a result, it is possible to manage multiple gateways with a single SmartCenter or even have multiple SmartCenters with a high-availability configuration.

Check Point provides a comprehensive set of graphical user interfaces (GUIs), collectively called SmartConsole, to be used as a single configuration point for all firewall functionality. The SmartDashboard GUI provides separate views for the objects used in rulebases (computers, gateways, networks, services, and groups); the various rulebases; a VPN Manager; and a graphical view of your network. There are also the SmartView Monitor, SmartView Tracker, and other components, which run on either Windows or Solaris.

TIP

The SmartConsole for Solaris, also called the Motif GUI, requires the purchase of a separate license from Check Point and is less functional than the free Windows-based client. Unless you have a requirement for using a Solaris GUI, use the Windows version or run a virtual Windows machine in a *NIX system.

Because of the three-tiered architecture—SmartConsole, SmartCenter, and Security Gateway, as shown in Figure 7.2—there is a corresponding increase in management functionality compared with other models that use direct management access to the enforcement points. Moreover, all elements are independent of one another. If the SmartCenter is undergoing maintenance, the Security Gateway continues to work uninterrupted with the last policy installed.

Figure 7.2 Check Point's Three-Tiered Architecture

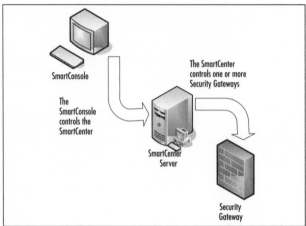

Stateful Inspection

The underlying technology behind Check Point firewalls is a proprietary inspection system known as *stateful inspection*. The premise behind stateful inspection is that it is ineffective for a firewall to determine whether to allow or deny each packet based solely on that packet's individual characteristics.

Check Point takes numerous other factors into account in examining packets, including data from all layers within the packet, data from previous related packets, and information received from related applications. Combine this with the capability to manipulate data within each packet as it flows through the firewall, and Check Point moves from the realm of simple packet filter to a much more robust solution capable of doing advanced Layer 7 protections. It's worthwhile to note that Check Point has a patent on stateful inspection and that other manufacturers' implementations of stateful inspection are not as complete.

Higher-Level Protections

Since the release of Check Point NG Feature Pack 2 and NG with Application Intelligence, SmartDefense was added to the firewall functionality. SmartDefense concentrates on network- and application-level protections, with an integrated intrusion prevention system (IPS) that is updated through the SmartDefense Subscription. The application-level protections are particularly useful for securing normally insecure services.

Later on, with R55W and now NGX, Web intelligence was added to the available features; it is a dedicated application-level firewall for Web traffic. Express CI and NGX R61 added content inspection, where you have the option of integrated antivirus protection from Computer Associates for Web, FTP, and e-mail traffic crossing the gateway. We will discuss SmartDefense, Web intelligence, and content inspection later in this chapter.

Securing Your Network Perimeters

Before configuring your DMZ, it is critical that you have a general security policy that addresses your network's overall security. It does no good to have a perfectly secure DMZ if other aspects of your firewall's security configuration are flawed and allow unintended access into your network.

The network perimeter is the interface or interfaces on your firewall that face a source that is not trusted. The most common example of this perimeter is an interface out to the Internet, but it is possible to have additional network perimeters—such as a connection to another organization's network or a second ISP—and the configuration for these would be the same.

Firewall Modes

Check Point firewalls can be used in any conceivable DMZ configuration, including the traditional "three-legged" design, a multi-DMZ setup, and the dual-firewall "sandwich" or "back-to-back" configuration, where separate firewalls protect the external and internal networks from each other.

Because Check Point's management architecture can involve separation of the SmartCenter from the gateways as well as separation of the SmartConsole from the SmartCenter, it is important to plan the location of each of these components when you're designing your network. Figure 7.3 illustrates a typical "three-legged" firewall design, with SmartConsole and SmartCenter separate from the gateway.

In this case, the SmartCenter is in the DMZ, whereas the SmartConsole GUI is on the internal LAN. Having the SmartCenter in the DMZ allows you to use that console to manage firewalls that are located on external networks, either on the Internet or on third-party networks, should you so desire. If the SmartCenter is to be used only to manage firewalls on the local network, it could be located on the internal LAN, which would provide additional security, since it would not be in a zone accessible from untrusted networks or from servers accessible from untrusted networks.

Figure 7.3 "Three-Legged" Firewall With Distributed Check Point Architecture

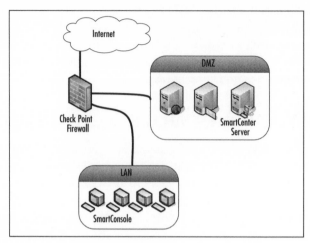

Note that the SmartCenter could be located on the internal LAN and still be able to manage external firewalls through NAT. However, this setup adds complexity to the management architecture.

Figure 7.4 illustrates a "back-to-back" configuration, where two firewall layers are used to separate internal resources from those that can be accessed from outside the perimeter.

Figure 7.4 "Sandwich" or "Back-to-Back" Firewalls With Distributed Check Point Architecture

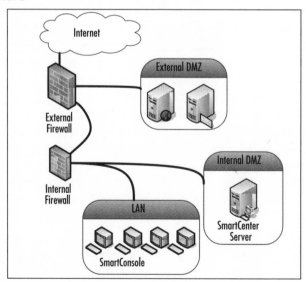

Routing Through Check Point

It is important to keep IP routing in mind when you are configuring the firewall. All routing functionality is handled by the operating system on which the firewall is installed; Check Point assumes that proper routing is in place to allow access to defined networks. Initial troubleshooting for any connectivity issue should be to determine whether appropriate routing has been configured on the operating system running the firewall.

Due to the fact that routing functionality is not part of the firewall's configuration, a discussion of that topic is out of scope here. Consult the documentation of your operating system or firewall appliance for information on how to configure static or dynamic routing in each environment. Both SecurePlatform Pro (an option for SecurePlatform) and Nokia's IPSO have built-in dynamic routing support for OSPF, RIP, and BGP.

Configuring Your DMZ

There is a wide variety of options that you might want to implement or have available on your DMZ, such as a redundant cluster, redundant connectivity, quality of service, and so on. Since a DMZ usually contains some of the most valuable IT resources in your enterprise, you want to ensure that it has the best possible connectivity.

ISP Redundancy

A feature that is very useful for highly available environments is the ability to have two ISPs connected to interfaces on the firewall, as shown in Figure 7.5. Check Point's ISP Redundancy option, available in SecurePlatform R55 and Nokia NGX, can be found in the Topology section of the gateway, in the SmartDashboard. You can have two different external interfaces, along with their default gateways, and choose whether a Primary/Backup configuration or a Load Sharing configuration will be used. You can even select specific nodes to monitor so that an upstream router can be checked.

NOTE

> Any ISP failover will result in the interruption of all connections, which will have to be reestablished through the second ISP. You also need to have a method for redirecting incoming connections through your second ISP, whether using your own IP addresses and BGP, Dynamic DNS, multiple DNS entries, or Check Point's ISP Redundancy DNS solution.

Figure 7.5 ISP Redundancy

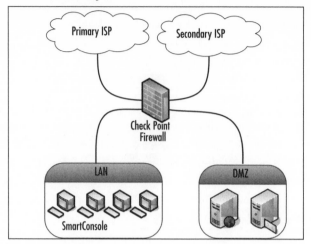

Clusters

All current Check Point products have a built-in high-availability option, whereby you purchase an additional gateway, usually at 80 percent of the original gateway price, and create an active/passive cluster that will act as a single entity for all purposes. An additional ClusterXL license can be purchased to create an active/active cluster for improved performance. This license is not required for Nokia IPSO clusters. Clusters behave like individual firewall objects.

SecureXL

SecureXL is an acceleration technology, originally developed by Nokia, which significantly enhances the throughput of a firewall by implementing pass/reject decisions at the network driver level. This license is now included in the VPN-1 Power line. Certain features such as fingerprint scrambling and QoS are incompatible with SecureXL and you will have to choose which feature is more important to you.

SecureXL is activated through the cpconfig program in the operating system running the firewall and selecting the option to **Enable SecureXL**. To verify it is working, use the **fwaccell stat** command from the command line.

Quality of Service

DMZ servers offer important services to both internal and external users. It is therefore preferable to guarantee a certain bandwidth, priority, or level of service to traffic accessing the DMZ. Check Point's QoS functions, previously called Floodgate, can offer both relative and absolute prioritization. For example, you could assign 1Mb to e-mail traffic, or assign it a higher priority than regular traffic. QoS is compatible with standards such as differentiated services (DiffServ) classes and low latency queuing (LLQ) systems, and it is configured in the QoS rulebase in the SmartDashboard. Configuring QoS is outside the scope of this discussion.

Configuring the Firewall

Once you decide on the kind of a DMZ you will have and the operating system, platform, and options you will implement, you need to configure the firewall object in the SmartDashboard, as shown in Figure 7.6. We assume that you have already installed the system, established Secure Internal Communication (SIC) if needed, and opened the Check Point SmartDashboard interface to the SmartCenter. Many of the steps to install a gateway are covered in the following chapter for both SecurePlatform and Nokia.

Figure 7.6 Configuring the Firewall Object in SmartDashboard

Configuring Interfaces

Setting up a DMZ requires at least two and usually three or more physical interfaces configured on the firewall. First you need to have the specific interfaces available on the server or appliance on which your firewall runs. Ensure that the interfaces are configured and recognized in the operating system. Both of these tasks are outside the scope of this discussion; consult your hardware and operating system documentation for more information.

Once the interfaces are available and ready to use, the next step is to update the list of interfaces of your firewall object. Edit the **Properties** of your firewall object, and choose **Topology**, and you will see the screen shown in Figure 7.7.

Figure 7.7 Configuring the Topology of a Gateway

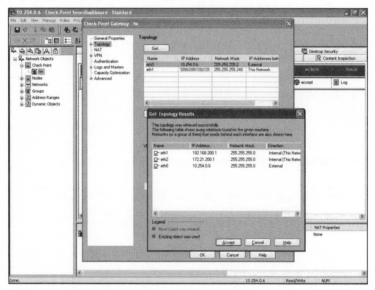

Click **Get…** and select **Interfaces and Topology**. If communication is established with the gateway, the SmartCenter will retrieve the list of interfaces and their topology. The topology is generated by pulling the static route list of the gateway. You might see the SmartCenter create new networks and groups so that each interface can be assigned a group containing the networks behind that interface. This process has been simplified. Previously each interface had to be entered manually by the administrator, who also had to ensure that the interface names were the same as in the operating system. That process is now automatically done by the Check Point software.

Configuring Interface Antispoofing

One popular method of breaching a network perimeter is via IP spoofing. A malicious user could attempt to use IP spoofing to manipulate his or her source IP address, appearing to originate from an address from within your network. The goal of this attack is to bypass deny rules you have in place, since the firewall may perceive the user's traffic as being part of your internal network.

To prevent IP spoofing, Check Point contains a comprehensive antispoofing feature. To configure antispoofing, first open the Check Point **SmartDashboard** and bring up the **Properties** of your firewall object. Choose the **Topology** tab, shown in Figure 7.8.

Figure 7.8 Configuring Interface Antispoofing Protection

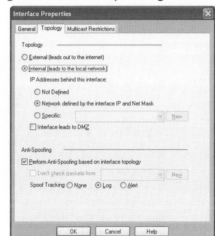

Each interface of the firewall is listed here. The field "IP Addresses behind interface" relates to the antispoofing configuration and specifies the type of host residing on that interface. The example shown in Figure 7.8 lists three interfaces: eth0, the internal network; eth1, the external, Internet-facing network; and eth2, the DMZ. If the field "IP Addresses behind interface" does not appear, this is because the addresses are defined as a host and not a gateway. Right-click the object and select **Convert to Gateway…**.

Highlight **eth2**, choose **Edit**, and then choose the **Topology** tab that appears, as in Figure 7.8.

Specify whether this interface is *external*, which means it faces untrusted networks, or *internal*, which applies to all other interfaces. Next, you need to specify the IP addresses hosted by this interface. Although there is a Not Defined setting, this choice is not recommended, because it removes the antispoofing capability for this interface.

Choose **Network defined by the interface IP and Net Mask** if the only network behind this interface matches the network defined in the General tab. Alternatively, choose

Specific and specify a previously defined network object, usually a group that contains networks, if there are additional networks hosted behind this interface.

By choosing either of the latter two options, you provide the firewall with the information it needs to perform antispoofing on this interface. More specifically, because the firewall is aware of the IP addresses behind each interface, it is able to check that traffic originating from each address is actually sourced at the matching interface.

To enable antispoofing, turn on **Perform Antispoofing based on interface topology.** You can also specify the tracking method the firewall should take when spoofing is detected. It is important to track spoofing so that you can take additional preventive action against the malicious user and his or her network.

Repeat this procedure for each interface on the firewall, and be sure to install the policy to have these changes take effect.

Configuring & Implementing...

Antispoofing Dropping Valid Packets

It is important to remember that when antispoofing is configured, you must ensure that all IP networks behind an interface are specified in the topology configuration. If a network is left out, the firewall will assume that traffic from that network is spoofed, and it will drop those packets. Therefore, when adding a new network to your firewall, it is important to remember the extra step of updating the topology information for the interface that will host that network. Also, if you inadvertently specify that the interface connected to the Internet is an internal interface, all connectivity to the outside world will be blocked until you correct the configuration.

In a critical failure, use the **fw unloadlocal** command from the gateway's operating system so that you restore control over the gateway and can send a fixed security policy.

Customizing Stateful Inspection

Another important aspect to securing the network perimeters is the ability to customize FireWall-1's stateful inspection mechanism. By adjusting these values as circumstances change around the network, you can ensure that you are taking full advantage of this powerful feature.

To access the stateful inspection properties, open the Check Point **SmartDashboard**, choose **Policy**, and then choose **Global Properties**, as shown in Figure 7.9. Next select **Stateful Inspection**.

Figure 7.9 Stateful Inspection

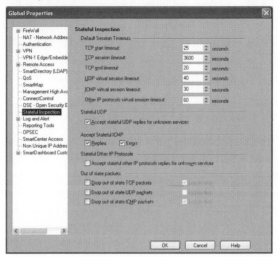

The first set of definable values is for session timeouts. All these values relate to the number of seconds that must elapse for various aspects of a TCP, UDP, and ICMP session. By shortening these values, you reduce the risk of DoS attacks penetrating your network perimeter. However, if the timeout values are too low, you could end up dropping valid connections to the network that are slow for other reasons, such as poor network or server performance. The default values are a good starting point and can be adjusted as required based on the performance of valid network traffic and the characteristics of malicious traffic.

Next are settings for stateful UDP. Selecting **Accept stateful UDP replies for unknown services** instructs the firewall to allow UDP connection replies, even if it is unaware of the service type. Enabling this option also allows you to select **Accept stateful UDP replies from any port for unknown services**, which allows UDP connection replies on any port, as opposed to only the port on which the connection originated.

Similarly, you can configure the way the firewall deals with ICMP requests in the next section: **Accept Stateful ICMP**. These settings relate to ICMP packets that are allowed based on stateful information about TCP or UDP connections. Selecting **Replies** allows ICMP reply packets, whereas selecting **Errors** permits ICMP error packets.

Selecting **Accept Stateful other IP protocols replies for unknown services** relates to packets that are not TCP, UDP, or ICMP. This choice instructs the firewall to accept these packets, provided they meet the usual state criteria.

Finally, the **Out of State Packets** section defines what the firewall should do with TCP, UDP, and ICMP packets that are determined to be out of state (those that the firewall's inspection mechanism doesn't know about or hasn't anticipated)—whether they should be dropped, logged, or both. For example, asymmetric routing (where an inbound path is different than the outbound path) will be a source of out-of-state packets. If you see a lot of these packets for seemingly valid connections, check the routing configuration in your operating system.

Configuring the Security Rulebase

Once the network perimeters have been configured, the next step is securing them. This section covers the setup and configuration of the Security Rulebase that will apply to the perimeters. This section covers adding network objects and configuring access rules to allow access to and from the DMZ.

Creating Objects and Servers

Once the DMZ interface is configured and ready for use, the next step is to install and connect the servers that are to reside in the DMZ to this interface. In general, you would connect the firewall DMZ interface to a switch and then connect the DMZ–residing servers to that switch. In this example, we have one Web server and one mail server sitting behind the DMZ, with IP addresses 192.168.200.2 and 192.168.200.3, respectively.

Define each server to sit in the DMZ as a network object by choosing **Manage** | **Network Objects** | **New** | **Nodes** | **Host** (see Figure 7.10).

Figure 7.10 Creating a New Host

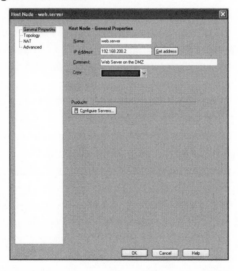

To configure the host, set the name, IP address, and an optional comment and color for it. By clicking the **Configure Servers...** button in the Host General Properties, you can specify the server role, as shown in Figure 7.11. There are three possible roles to select from. These roles classify the machine as a Web, mail, and/or DNS server, and classification will open up new protections to configure. For example, if you are creating a Web server, you can select its operating system (Windows, Solaris, Linux) and application engine (PHP, ASP, Perl, etc.), the port(s) it uses, and the firewall that protects it. You can also select which Web intelligence (WI) protections to activate for the server. For a mail server, you can select the

OS and the ports used for POP3, IMAP, and SMTP access. For a DNS server, you can select the domain authorized for that server, which means which external queries can be accepted to that server, or networks allowed for reverse DNS queries.

Figure 7.11 Configuring Hosts as Servers

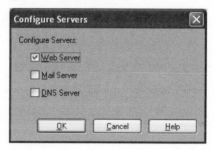

Define a network for administrator access by choosing **Manage | Network Objects | New | Nodes | Network** and entering a name, network address, netmask, and comment for it, as shown in Figure 7.12.

Figure 7.12 Creating a New Network

Creating Services

In some situations, a DMZ server may be utilizing a proprietary service. This service can use either a proprietary protocol or one that simply had its port number changed to hide the service from others. Check Point allows you to create any service that you want, with any port number, and to even specify that well-known services are running on different ports. Services can be categorized as TCP, Compound TCP, Citrix TCP, UDP, RPC, ICMP, DCE-RPC, and others.

To define a new service, choose **Manage | Services | New...** and select the type of service you want to create. For example, to create a new FTP service that answers to port 2121 instead of port 21, click the **Advanced** button of the **TCP Service Properties** dialog box. This will open a new dialog box where you will be able to select the protocol type, as shown in Figure 7.13. Select **FTP** for this example. This will allow FTP protections to be applied to the traffic as well as allow data connections in response to a request on port 2121.

Figure 7.13 Creating a New FTP Service

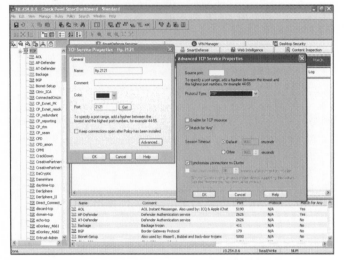

Creating Rules

Next we will define rules for HTTP and HTTPS access to the Web server and SMTP access to the mail server (see Figure 7.14).

The first rule permits any source IP address to access the HTTP (80) and HTTPS (443) TCP ports of the Web server; the second rule permits any source IP address to access the SMTP (25) port of the mail server.

Rule 3 allows only downloads from an FTP server on port 2121. To create such a rule, select **Manage | Resources | New | FTP...** and create a resource named **Download_Only**. In the **Match** section of the resource, select only **PUT**. Add the resource to rule 3 by selecting **Add with Resource** in the Service column, using FTP and the download resource you created.

Rule 4 allows access from the Administrators_Network to the DMZ using some management protocols such as SSH or Remote_Desktop (follow the previous procedure to create a Remote_Desktop TCP service with port 3389).

Rule 5 then blocks all other access to the DMZ.

Figure 7.14 Rulebase for DMZ Access

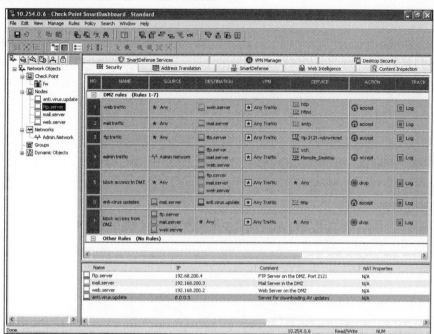

Two additional rules could be necessary. The first, Rule 6, allows HTTP and HTTPS access from the mail server to an antivirus update server, which can be a frequent request to keep the mail servers' software updated.

Finally, Rule 7 blocks all traffic originating from the DMZ. In the remote case that a DMZ server is compromised, it's important to prevent it from attacking the internal networks or other DMZs.

Combine a rulebase such as this with all the other perimeter security procedures mentioned in this chapter and you will have significantly increased the security of your DMZ hosts.

Configuring the Address Translation Rulebase

As is standard on most firewalls, Check Point supports Network Address Translation (NAT) with a variety of options. NAT is available in one of two modes: Hide and Static. In *Hide mode,* many hosts are hidden behind one routable IP address. In *Static mode,* there is a one-to-one mapping between internal and external IP addresses. Check Point also allows you to manipulate the service of translated packets.

You can use NAT in any number of scenarios when private IP addresses are used and need to access, or be accessed from, external networks. One of the most common instances where NAT is used is for access from workstations on the internal network to the Internet, for activities such as Web browsing or file transfers.

For a DMZ, you could use routable IP address on your servers or add another layer of security by using NAT to allow traffic to these servers. If you don't use NAT, your ISP will need to route the DMZ segment (which will probably be different from your external IP segment) to the external IP address of your firewall, which will then route connections to the DMZ. If you use NAT, you should use Check Point's automatic Address Translation rules so that the firewall publishes the ARP entries necessary for it to respond to the NAT IPs. Figure 7.15 shows an example of how to configure Automatic NAT rules for a DMZ Server statically to another IP.

Figure 7.15 Automatic Address Translation Configuration

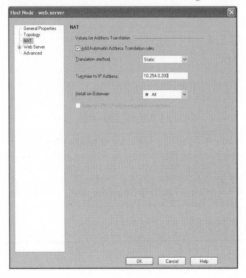

The Address Translation rulebase will be automatically updated with the appropriate rules. Moreover, it is usually unnecessary to NAT the connections from the internal networks to the DMZ networks. You can add a Manual NAT rule to the top of the rulebase, as shown in Figure 7.16.

Figure 7.16 The Address Translation Rulebase

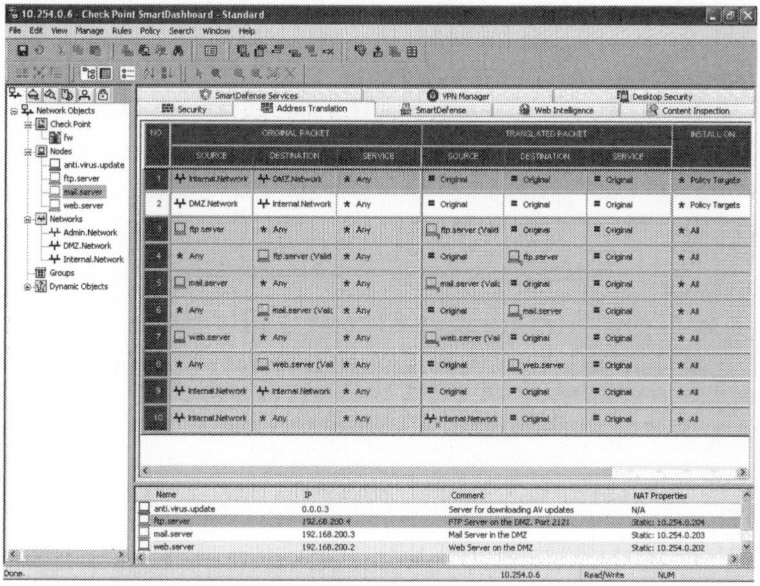

DMZ with Network Address Translation

Although using NAT for DMZ servers does provide an additional layer of security, it is also important to keep in mind the extra load it places on your firewall; translating large amounts of packets consumes its resources. Therefore, if you have a DMZ host that will have very high throughput levels, such as a busy Web server, it might not be practical to use private addressing.

Configuring Network and Application Protections

Check Point provides you with a number of tools to allow you to effectively secure your network perimeter. There are four distinct areas in which additional protections can be configured. These are protections that neither a packet filter nor even a stateful-inspection-only firewall can provide. These protections are network security in SmartDefense, which concentrates on things like scans and denial of service; application intelligence in SmartDefense, which concentrates on protection for high level services like SQL Server, peer-to-peer, and instant-messaging applications; Web intelligence, dedicated to protecting Web traffic only, and content inspection, dedicated to virus protection.

SmartDefense Network Security

SmartDefense is a very competent intrusion prevention system (IPS) that brings together various attack detection and notification systems present in previous Check Point versions. With all these options configurable from one location, the task of configuring your firewall to detect attacks is greatly simplified. Most of the features also have a monitor-only option. This makes it possible to monitor the traffic coming into the DMZ without responding to an attack. As with any IPS, it is important to get a sense of the traffic coming into and out of the DMZ and to try to identify and characterize legitimate traffic. When you turn on protection in Monitor-Only mode, you will see a small set of eyes in the check box, indicating that the firewall will only "look" at the connection.

To access the SmartDefense configuration dialog box, open the Check Point **SmartDashboard** and go to the **SmartDefense** configuration section, located next to the Security and Address Translation rulebases (shown in Figure 7.17).

Figure 7.17 SmartDefense General Settings

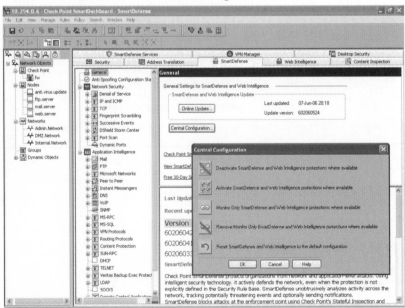

In the General section, you have the option to make an Online Update, where you will need to authenticate to the Check Point User Center. This option checks to see if any new versions of SmartDefense are available, and if there are, it allows you to install these updates.

There is also a link here to open the SmartView Tracker with a predefined SmartDefense filter. You can also use the Central Configuration button to globally activate, deactivate, set to monitor, or set to default settings for the SmartDefense configurations.

If you select **Anti Spoofing Configuration Status**, you can see if any gateways' anti-spoofing configurations need to be fixed.

Select **Denial of Service** and **Non-TCP Flooding** in the left side of the SmartDashboard window, as shown in Figure 7.18.

Figure 7.18 SmartDefense Non-TCP Connections

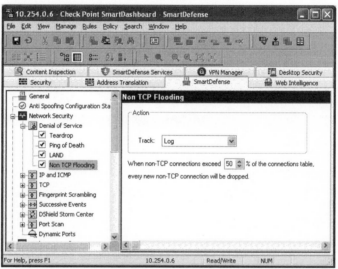

A denial of service (DoS) attack involves an attacker sending a large number of requests for particular services. Because the attack keeps your network so busy dealing with all the excessive requests, it is not able to respond to valid requests, or at least not at its usual pace.

SmartDefense provides protection against three types of DoS attack: teardrop attacks, which can crash servers by sending overlapping IP fragments; ping-of-death attacks, which can crash servers by sending ICMP packets exceeding the normal maximum packet size; and LAND attacks, which can affect network devices by sending packets with specific properties. New since R55 is the non-TCP flooding protection, which can limit the number of allowed non-TCP connections as a percentage of total connections.

To enable each of the three types of DoS attack protection, expand the drop-down list of attack types under the main **Denial of Service** option, and check each type of attack to enable. By default, all three are enabled, and it is probably wise to leave them enabled unless you have a specific reason to do otherwise. The single option available for each attack is the tracking setting, which specifies how the firewall should track detected attacks of that type.

Next is the IP and ICMP section. There are four types of verification in this category: packet sanity, max ping size, IP fragments, and network quota. The packet sanity verification looks at a number of aspects of each packet, such as headers and flags, searching for anything out of the ordinary. The max ping size setting allows you to specify how large ICMP request packets may be. The most useful configuration here for a DMZ is the network quota option, where you can create a block or alert when there are more than a specified number of connections per second from a specific source. This is very useful for blocking potential attackers before they can make a dent in your firewall performance. The Advanced section allows you to select network objects to which the protection will not apply as well as configure how long an attacker will be blocked. The software can then check to see if the attacker is still active, as shown in Figure 7.19.

Figure 7.19 Network Quota

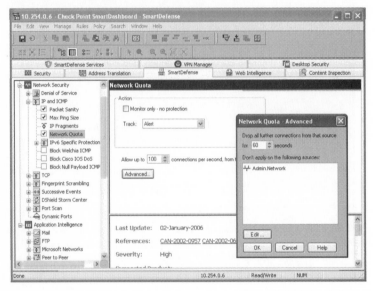

A SYN flood can slow down or stop a server by sending multiple incomplete handshake sequences. The acknowledgment step of the sequence is left out, so the server continually attempts to signal for this response, tying up its resources.

By choosing **Override modules' SYNDefender configuration**, you can enable SYN attack protection on enforcement modules, even if they have SYNDefender, a component of previous versions of Check Point FireWall-1/VPN-1, enabled. Disabling this option enables the **Early version SYNDefender configuration** option, which contains the traditional SYNDefender settings.

To enable SYN flood protection, choose **Activate SYN Attack protection** and then **Configure**, as shown in Figure 7.20.

Figure 7.20 SYN Attack Configuration

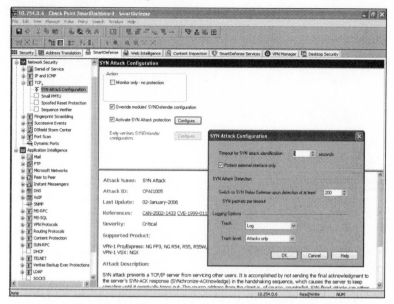

With the SYN Attack Configuration dialog box you can set the tracking option for SYN attacks detected and whether to track activity that is identified as part of a broad attack rather than individual occurrences. The timeout value specifies the number of seconds the firewall should wait for the acknowledgment part of the handshake before marking the session as possibly being part of an attack. The Attack Threshold sets the number of sessions without acknowledgments that must occur before the firewall concludes that a SYN attack is in progress. Finally, set **Protect external interface only** to ignore unusual SYN activity on all other interfaces other than external interfaces. This option is normally selected because SYN attacks originate on the Internet and usually from forged IP addresses.

The remaining two options in the TCP section are Small PMTU, Spoofed Reset Protection and Sequence Verifier. The Small PMTU section allows you to specify the smallest packet size allowed. This capability is useful because of the potential for an attack that involves sending a high number of very small packets, causing the network to slow down or stop because it is busy processing all these packets. The Spoofed Reset Protection can detect an abnormal number of RST packets in a specified time and block further RST packets from the source.

The Sequence Verifier function verifies that packets are being sent in the correct sequence. This prevents attacks that relate to packet sequence number manipulation. You have the option to track out-of-state packets that are anomalous or suspicious, or all out-of-state packets.

The Fingerprint Scrambling protection is useful for increasing the security of DMZ servers by making it harder to identify the operating systems running your DMZ server. You can activate ISN spoofing, TTL, and IP ID configurations, and they will change systems' normal responses to different queries. Be aware that these protections disable any kind of performance acceleration you have enabled, such as SecureXL, as described earlier in this chapter.

By selecting the **Retrieve and Block Malicious IPs** option in the **DShield Storm Center** section, you give the firewalls access to a list of active, malicious IP ranges detected by SANS's Dshield.org. This list is updated every three hours, and your firewalls would immediately block and report any connection originating from those IPs.

The final option in Network Security is the **Port Scan** detection. It can detect a host port scan, where a single machine receives a directed scan to list all its open ports, and a sweep port scan, where a specific service is scanned among different machines to determine, for example, which machines are running Web servers. There are options to exclude network objects or services from the scan. To block such scans, you will need to modify the **Global Properties | Log and Alert | Alert Commands** and create a user-defined script such as **sam_alert −I −src −t 600** to block the source of the attack for 10 minutes (you can look at *sam_alert* syntax from a command line: *sam_alert −h. sam_alert* is part of the default Check Point installation).

SmartDefense Application Intelligence

The Application Intelligence (AI) part of SmartDefense creates an application layer firewall and is continually updated to add new protections and protocols. By implementing AI, you can control and protect the use of many common and not-so-common protocols. It will even protect you from those ever-increasing critical vulnerabilities in an operating system or server application you are using. Although it is impossible to detail all the AI protections available (and Check Point is constantly adding new ones), let's examine some of the more useful current protections in NGX's Application Intelligence that relate to protecting DMZ servers.

Mail

In **Mail | POP3/IMAP Security**, you can apply protection to all mail traffic or to particular hosts defined as mail servers. You can block the use of identical usernames and passwords as well as set a maximum length for each. Additionally, you can block binary data or unknown commands in the mail traffic, as shown in Figure 7.21. Implementing this protection for a DMZ mail server is very useful, but you should closely monitor your logs when implementing any changes so that you can detect any inadvertent drops of valid e-mail.

Figure 7.21 Mail protection

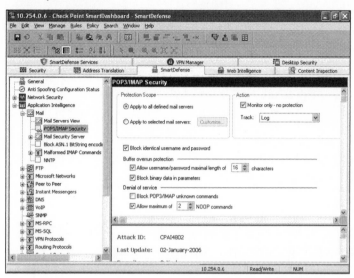

DNS

Next, click **DNS**. Here you have the option of implementing DNS protocol enforcement for UDP and TCP. You can also create a list of domains that will be blocked when querying the DNS servers. This is useful to block specific attacks such as worms. You should also activate the **DNS Cache Poisoning** protection, where you can implement scrambling, drop inbound requests, and block mismatched replies, as shown in Figure 7.22.

Figure 7.22 DNS Protection

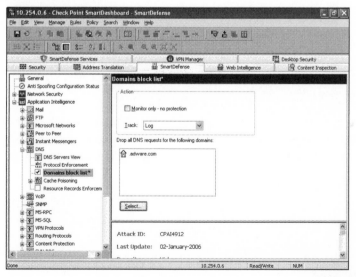

Peer-to-Peer and Instant Messengers

A great functionality of AI is being able to quickly and effectively block the use of peer-to-peer protocols such as Kazaa, Gnutella, eMule, BitTorrent, SoluSeek, DirectConnect, IRC, and Winny and instant messengers such as MSN Messenger, Skype, Yahoo! Messenger, ICQ, and Googletalk. Protection against these protocols is enabled by simply checking the boxes for those protocols, as shown in Figure 7.23. For each individual protocol, you can choose to block or to monitor only. In addition, you can block on the specific proprietary protocol or block the protocol when it tries to masquerade over the HTTP protocol. For MSN Messenger, you can even control which features you will block (file transfer, application sharing, white board, and remote assistant). You can also create a global list of exclusions for services or network objects that will be allowed to use these protocols.

Figure 7.23 P2P Protection

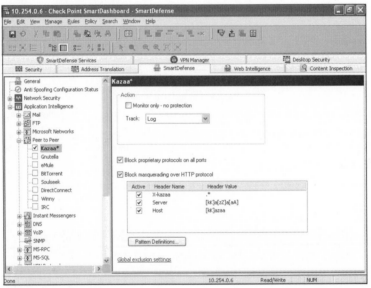

Microsoft Networks

One feature that's relatively unique to Check Point is that it can block propagation of worms within the Microsoft network protocols. In the **File and Print Sharing** section shown in Figure 7.24, you can block or monitor worms with a single click. Other protections include blocking null CIFS sessions and WINS attacks.

Figure 7.24 Microsoft Networks Protection

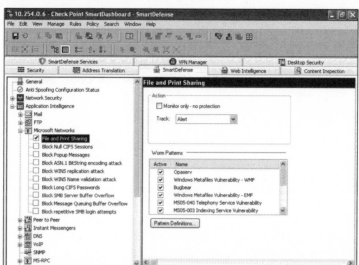

Microsoft SQL Server

Many database servers are located in DMZs, and the protections Check Point offers for Microsoft SQL Servers are especially powerful. You can block four types of attack on the SQL Monitor protocol: buffer overflow, version information, heap overflow, and network DoS attacks. Even more interesting is the protection for the SQL Server protocol, where you can select which port the SQL server uses, block attempts to log in with a blank password (a common default configuration mistake), block the execution of stored and extended stored procedures, enforce Windows Authentication (and block the less secure SQL authentication), and perform the protection on port 2433 as well, as shown in Figure 7.25.

VPN Protocols

The protections in this section relate to the VPN protocols that traverse the gateway. Two useful configurations in SSH enforcement are to **Block SSH v1**, which is a version known to have serious security flaws, and to **Block IKE Aggressive Exchange in IKE**, which has inherent authentication risks.

Routing Protocols

If you're using dynamic routing protocols in your network, you could activate Check Point's protections, which will block OSPF, BGP and RIP protocols that are not MD5 authenticated. However, you could be exposed to a DoS attack from external interfaces, so activate them mostly on internal networks.

Figure 7.25 SQL Server Protection

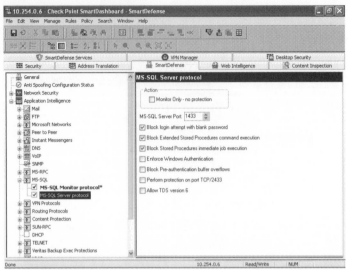

Keeping Your SmartDefense Up to Date

SmartDefense is continually updated, sometimes with four or more updates a week. These updates can be additional protections for existing protocols—for example, for new vulnerabilities discovered or new protocols being protected. You should read the full description of the available updates, both to learn what new protections are available and to prevent valid traffic from being blocked by a new update. You should subscribe to the SmartDefense Advisories and Updates mailing list by sending an e-mail to listserv@amadeus.us.checkpoint.com with the text "SUBSCRIBE SMARTDEFENSE-NEWS" in the e-mail body.

Web Intelligence

The Web Intelligence section provides deep protection for Web traffic, with advanced features that rival most dedicated Web security gateways. One caveat is that most of the Web intelligence protections, especially those that apply to hosts defined as Web servers, require the additional Web Intelligence license from Check Point. Most of the Web intelligence protections can have a protection scope that applies to all HTTP traffic or that applies only to selected Web servers (from among those hosts configured with the Web Server property). You can also select to monitor only the protections or to send an error page if blocked. The error page option can be a predefined HTML page that you configure or a redirection to another URL. Be aware that activating the error page has a performance impact on the firewall.

Malicious Code

Two important protections can be found in the Web Intelligence section: General HTTP Worm Catcher and Malicious Code Protection. With the **General HTTP Worm Catcher**, shown in Figure 7.26, you can activate protection against URL-based worms such as CodeRed and Nimda. You can also define or import additional worm patterns. As with many of the protections in Web intelligence, you have the **Monitor Only** option to set to monitor the protection and to send an error page if the attack is blocked.

Figure 7.26 General HTTP Worm Catcher

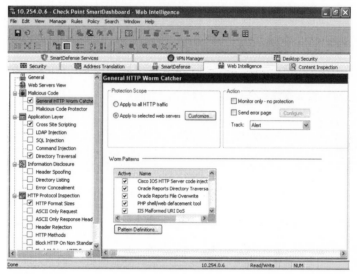

The other protection in this section is the Malicious Code Protector. This protection works like a virtual machine that disassembles machine code to detect attacks such as buffer overflows in URLs, HTTP requests, and bodies. It is very powerful, and you can customize it through two categories: memory consumption and speed and the search method, as shown in Figure 7.27.

Figure 7.27 Malicious Code Protector

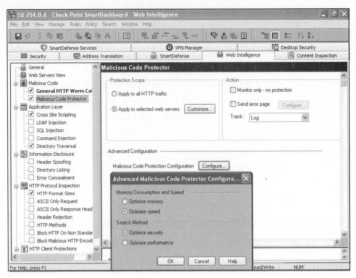

Application Layer

Application Layer Web protections refer to the use of commands within the HTTP stream that can be used to execute commands in misconfigured Web servers. You can activate protections against cross-site scripting, LDAP injection, SQL injection, command injection, and directory traversal attacks. The first three can be fine-tuned to accommodate commands that you would like to permit or specifically block.

Information Disclosure

With header spoofing, you can replace the responses that a Web server might send to identify its operating system, make, and version, to make it harder for attackers to specifically target vulnerabilities in a specific Web server or version. You can, for example, replace all headers containing the characters *IIS* in the value, to a simple *IIS*-only response. This hides the particular version in use. Other options you can activate prevent directory listings as well as error concealment. Error concealment will replace standard error message pages that a Web server sends and that usually identify the Web server or dangerous programming-related errors with a basic firewall-generated message or a customized error page. You can configure which error codes will be concealed and which application engines will be detected.

HTTP Protocol Inspection

With these protections enabled, as shown in Figure 7.28, you can specify the maximum size of URLs and HTTP headers and the maximum number of HTTP headers. In addition, you can configure which HTTP methods will be allowed as well as whether ASCII-only requests and response headers will be accepted. These protections can be applied to all HTTP traffic, to selected Web servers, or to connections related to URI resources. These protections prevent attacks that attempt to exploit poorly configured Web servers and unknown or zero-day Web vulnerabilities.

Figure 7.28 HTTP Format Sizes

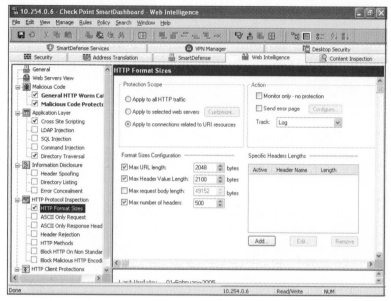

HTTP Protocol Inspection and Header Rejection

The header rejection protections are especially powerful because they allow all kinds of applications that use the Web protocol to be detected and blocked. SmartDefense updates these signatures that detect spyware, adware, and other applications, including MSN Messenger. You can also define your own signatures to detect specific applications. This function works by examining headers within the Web protocol and looking for particular header names and values that will identify specific applications (see Figure 7.29).

Content Inspection

With VPN-1 Express CI (in R57 and NGX 60A) and VPN-1 UTM (R61), Check Point has added content inspection to its product line. Right now content inspection means antivirus protection of SMTP, POP3, FTP, and HTTP through a partnership with Computer Associates.

Figure 7.29 HTTP Header Rejection

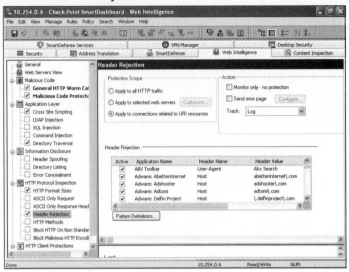

To enable virus protection, you need to edit the **Gateway** properties and select
AntiVirus within the Check Point products installed. That option will only be available if
the selected version is R57, R60A, or R61. Once the option is selected, you can edit the
interfaces in the **Topology** section of the **Interface Properties** dialog box and check the
box next to **Interface Leads to DMZ**, as shown in Figure 7.30.

Figure 7.30 Configuring an Interface That Leads to the DMZ

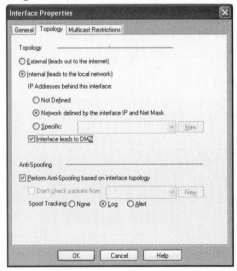

Within the Content Protection tabs, there are several settings to configure. **Signature Updates** allows you to see the latest signatures downloaded and select **Automatic Signature Updates**. Once you enter your **UserCenter Credentials**, signatures can be uploaded automatically to the gateways, either directly from Check Point or from the local SmartCenter.

For each of the four protected services, you can select whether the traffic scanned will be by file direction or by IPs. By file direction uses the interfaces defined as leading to the DMZ, as in Figure 7.31. The available options are:

- Scan incoming files arriving to the DMZ and internal networks, internal networks, or the DMZ
- Scan outgoing files leaving the DMZ and internal networks, internal networks, or the DMZ
- Scan internal files passing between the DMZ and internal networks or between all internal networks

Figure 7.31 Configuring Antivirus Protection for the DMZ

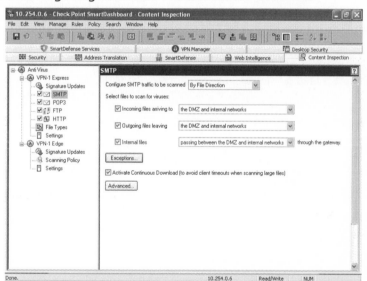

You can select network objects that will be exempt from the inspection. Checking **Activate Continuous Downloads** will prevent client timeouts when you're scanning large files. Also, you can select **Advanced Options** to configure the alerts that will be generated when a file is scanned, contains a virus, or is blocked. In addition, you can specify the notification messages, and for SMTP and POP3 traffic you can specify whether to block TLS traffic and scan MS Exchange specific data.

In the **File Types** section, you can select which file types to scan, pass, or block and whether they will have continuous downloads active.

Finally, in the **Settings** section, you can set the maximum file size to scan in Mbytes and whether large files will be blocked or passed without scanning. For archived files, you can configure the maximum nesting level and compression ratio, as well as the behaviors for when the antivirus engine is overloaded, if the scan fails, or if the engine fails to initialize.

Check Point NG Secure DMZ Checklist

Here is a checklist of the key elements to take into account when you're building a secure DMZ in a Check Point NG environment. Keep these in mind as you prepare and implement your DMZ, because they will greatly aid in both the ease of setup and the overall functionality and security of your Check Point NG DMZ:

- All firewall interfaces have IP addresses specified in their topology configuration.
- All firewall interfaces have antispoofing enabled.
- New network interfaces are added and configured in the operating system.
- Routable networks are assigned by the ISP and routed to the firewall.
- Define network objects for DMZ hosts.
- NAT is configured for outbound access from the internal network.
- Rules are added to the rulebase to allow access to DMZ hosts from the Internet.
- Rules are added to the rulebase to allow access to DMZ hosts from the internal network.
- Static or dynamic routing is configured in the operating system.
- SmartDefense is configured to detect, block, and log DoS and other attacks.
- Web intelligence is configured to protect against attacks on Web traffic.
- Content inspection is configured to detect and block viruses coming into or out of the DMZ.

Summary

Because the nature of a DMZ is to allow access from the Internet to hosts on your network, it is important to maintain a complete security policy surrounding access to these hosts. Building a secure DMZ with Check Point involves many aspects of the firewall's feature set. It is important to use these features to ensure that there are no weak links in your security policy.

Check Point's stateful inspection architecture provides a solid fundamental inspection layer for all traffic traversing the firewall to reach DMZ hosts. More effective than a simple packet filter, the ability to make filtering decisions based on packet state and context is a powerful mechanism from which your DMZ security will benefit.

Add to this the attack-prevention systems that are part of SmartDefense, such as application intelligence, Web intelligence, and content inspection, and the full picture of what it takes to build a secure DMZ comes into focus. Defining rules to allow specific access to hosts within the DMZ is a final step that must be done, keeping in mind only the access that is actually required to and from these hosts.

Solutions Fast Track

Basics of Check Point Firewalls

- ☑ Stateful inspection provides enhanced filtering based on state, context, and other information about each packet.

- ☑ NAT, configured manually or automatically, allows for translation of source, destination, and service for each packet.

- ☑ A distributed management architecture provides additional security by eliminating a direct connection between configuration client and enforcement point.

Securing Your Network Perimeters

- ☑ Enable antispoofing for all interfaces on the firewall to prevent spoof attacks.

- ☑ Use SmartDefense to protect your network from multiple types of attack, including DoS attacks.

- ☑ Customize stateful inspection to catch the maximum number of out-of-state packets.

Making a DMZ and Controlling Traffic

- ☑ Install DMZ hosts on a separate interface on the firewall.

- ☑ Add rules to the rulebase to allow access from the Internet to the DMZ and from the internal network to the DMZ.

- ☑ Configure static or dynamic routing in the operating system to allow access to and from the DMZ.

The Check Point NG Secure DMZ Checklist

- ☑ Follow the Check Point Secure DMZ Checklist when you're planning and running a Check Point DMZ.

Frequently Asked Questions

The following Frequently Asked Questions, answered by the authors of this book, are designed to both measure your understanding of the concepts presented in this chapter and to assist you with real-life implementation of these concepts. To have your questions about this chapter answered by the author, browse to **www.syngress.com/solutions** and click on the **"Ask the Author"** form.

Q: Do I need a separate physical interface on the firewall for the DMZ, or can I share another interface?

A: For the maximum level of security, you should have a separate interface for the DMZ. Using VLANs or other techniques, you could share another interface for the DMZ, but the firewall will not be able to protect the DMZ from traffic on the shared interface.

Q: The firewall is dropping legitimate packets because it reports they are out of state. How do I correct this?

A: One common cause of this problem is a configuration in which traffic is delivered to a node on one firewall interface and the node transmits the response on a different firewall interface. The stateful inspection engine will not recognize this traffic as legitimate. The solution is to ensure that all traffic moving to and from each node is using the same interface.

Q: Is it necessary to restrict traffic to or from the internal network to or from the DMZ? Can't I just open all access between them?

A: It is important to keep in mind that not all malicious activity comes from the Internet. You need to protect your DMZ from internal attacks as well, and so it is good security practice to only allow access that is actually required, even between the internal and DMZ segments.

Q: What is the best way to deal with alerts generated by SmartDefense?

A: In general, if SmartDefense has detected a security violation, it is a good idea to block all access from the offending host to your network, if possible. You can then notify the administrator of that network so that he or she can deal appropriately with the offending user.

Q: Is it necessary to have separate hosts for the enforcement point, SmartCenter, and GUI?

A: No. Your firewall will operate normally if two or all three of these components are installed on the same host. However, by dividing them into separate hosts, you gain the advantage of additional flexibility in terms of being able to manage multiple enforcement points. There is also an increased level of security if the SmartCenter is not on a host accessible to the Internet, such as the enforcement point.

## Chapter 8

Firewall and DMZ Design: SecurePlatform and Nokia Firewalls

Solutions in this chapter:

- **Basics of SecurePlatform Firewalls**

- **Basics of Nokia Firewalls**

- **Using cpconfig**

- **Nokia Firewall and DMZ Design Checklist**

☑ **Summary**

☑ **Solutions Fast Track**

☑ **Frequently Asked Questions**

Introduction

As we saw in the previous chapter, Check Point Software Technologies' firewalls can run on a variety of platforms. You can use open systems based on Intel or AMD processors or dedicated appliances manufactured by Nokia and a dozen other companies. However, two of the most popular and most powerful platforms continue to be Nokia's IPSO operating system and Check Point's SecurePlatform operating system. This chapter addresses these two platforms, including installation, initial configuration, and setting up Check Point for the first time.

SecurePlatform is a Linux-based operating system created by Check Point. It has been hardened and does not require an additional license for its use (except for the SecurePlatform Pro, required for dynamic routing). Since its introduction with NG Feature Pack 2, SecurePlatform has become one of the most widely deployed platforms, along with Nokia. Check Point has been doing all its research and development on SecurePlatform, with other operating systems being done later. SecurePlatform runs on almost any open system available: white-box systems with Intel Pentium IIs and 128Mb of RAM, up to dedicated server-class appliances running multiple CPUs and RAID configurations. In fact, SecurePlatform can run inside virtual machines from VMWare and Virtual PC, which is great for testing, troubleshooting, and more. The illustrations in this chapter were done while running on Microsoft's Virtual PC.

The Nokia IP Series is dedicated appliances that provide firewall services using Check Point firewalls. Nokia's underlying OS, IPSO, is based on the FreeBSD operating system. The IPSO OS has been hardened and does not require a license for its use. In addition, the IPSO OS is highly optimized for traffic forwarding. IPSO also provides a wide range of routing services and protocols. All Nokia IP Series appliances use IPSO, except for the IP40 appliances, a separate product line similar to the Check Point VPN-1 Edge appliances, which utilize different technology and are not discussed in this chapter.

Both SecurePlatform and IPSO have advantages over other operating systems for running your Check Point firewalls. Among these advantages are improved compatibility, more features, easier installation, easier upgrades and patches, and better maintenance and backup functionality.

This chapter refers to a Check Point NGX R61 installation in a distributed environment, which is the recommended way to plan your installation of NGX, and with a DMZ. A distributed installation consists of separating the SmartCenter Server from the security gateway. As we said in the previous chapter, the SmartCenter Server contains all the objects, security policies, user databases, time objects, logs, and so on that are required to push a security policy to a gateway. The security gateway will contain an inspect script that it received from your SmartCenter Server. The gateway will then determine whether or not to pass the traffic, according to the security policy it received.

Basics of SecurePlatform Firewalls

Check Point has been doing all its research and development on SecurePlatform, with other operating systems being done later. SPLAT (shorthand for *SecurePlatform*) has been taking over the market since its arrival with Check Point Next Generation Feature Pack 2. We will take a tour of SecurePlatform, looking at the various operating system capabilities and the Check Point-supported add-ons. Check Point has placed lot of emphasis on SPLAT, and many other operating systems have been replaced by an Intel-based system to run SPLAT as their underlying OS to run VPN-1 Pro. With the popularity of appliance devices in the market and the cost-effectiveness of utilizing Intel-based hardware instead of more expensive, proprietary hardware, Check Point is offering more flexible and cost-effective solutions by continuing to develop the SecurePlatform Operating System.

Even if you choose a dedicated appliance like Nokia for your firewalls, using a SecurePlatform system for your SmartCenter can save you a lot of money while giving you the performance and management you need.

Choosing the Right SecurePlatform Option

There are basically two hardware options if you decide to use a SecurePlatform system: dedicated appliances or open systems. Open systems are machines that you create, purchase, or customize yourself from any number of hardware vendors and then use the SPLAT CD to reformat the machines. It is usually less expensive to use an open system, and you would only get hardware support from your manufacturer. At the Check Point OPSEC Web site at www.opsec.com, you can find a list of recommended systems, performance ratings, and suggested prices from makers like IBM, Sun, Dell, and HP. It's very important to check the Hardware Compatibility list at www.checkpoint.com/products/supported_platforms/secure-platform.html before you make any purchases and then find out your system, NIC, or RAID card is incompatible.

Dedicated appliances come preinstalled with SPLAT, ready to be configured. They are also fine-tuned and pre-tested to avoid any incompatibilities. You can also benefit from your manufacturer's support team, which will be more familiar with Check Point-related problems than a generic vendor. You can find appliances from vendors such as Crossbeam, Corrent, i-Security, Resilience, SecureGuard, and Sun also listed at www.opsec.com.

Configuring SecurePlatform

The installation of SecurePlatform is designed to be a very easy process. In this section, we cover the installation process and the configuration of SecurePlatform as a SmartCenter Server. Although we will mostly use the command-line interface, there is a very complete Web graphical user interface (GUI) offered over HTTPS.

Installing SecurePlatform

To install SecurePlatform, use CD 1 of the Check Point Media Kit. (Up to R55, the media kit was a single CD; in NGX, it is two CDs, and in R61 you get a four-CD media kit.) Power on your machine with the SecurePlatform CD-ROM in the drive and a monitor and keyboard attached. The SecurePlatform installation program automatically starts and asks you to press **Enter** to continue, as shown in Figure 8.1. If your machine does not have a CD-ROM drive, you can use alternative methods for installation, such as a diskette or network boot. Refer to the user guide in the Check Point CD for further instructions.

Figure 8.1 SecurePlatform Installation Welcome Screen

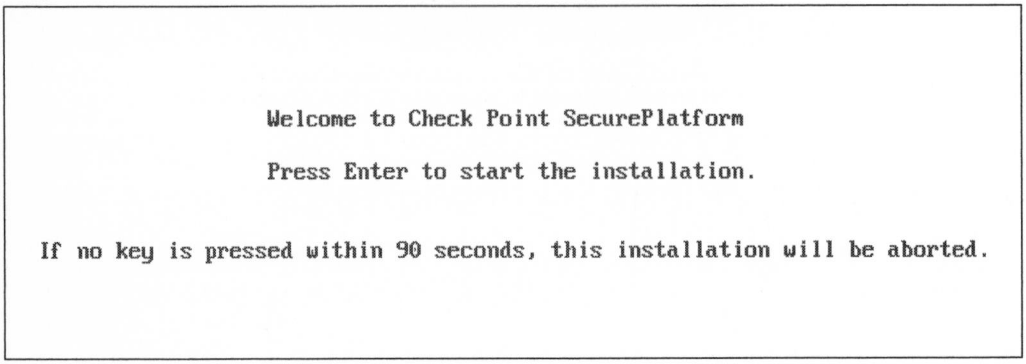

```
               Welcome to Check Point SecurePlatform

               Press Enter to start the installation.


   If no key is pressed within 90 seconds, this installation will be aborted.
```

When the welcome screen appears, press **Enter**. The installation program boots and loads the necessary drivers for the hardware it detects. After the SecurePlatform installation program is finished booting, you are presented with a screen summarizing the hardware probing results, as shown in Figure 8.2. This is a critical screen because if the machine doesn't find appropriate mass-storage devices (such as a hard drive), the installation will not continue, and if it doesn't detect your network cards you can also be looking at compatibility problems. In this screen you can add Linux or SPLAT drivers that you might have. If your system is suitable for SPLAT, press **OK**.

The next screen asks you which version you want to install. The options are SecurePlatform or SecurePlatform Pro. Unless your infrastructure requires advanced routing options such as OSPF or BGP, most users should choose SecurePlatform. Otherwise you need to purchase a SecurePlatform Pro license.

Figure 8.2 Welcome Screen After Hardware Scanning

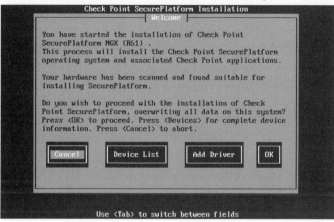

The next screen asks for some localization information. Choose the proper information to match your hardware. The next step asks which Ethernet device to configure. The default is the first NIC the system recognizes. In most cases, you will want to have the primary interface (and the IP address the hostname is tied to) be the external address—especially for VPNs. Once you select which NIC to configure, you can enter the IP address, network mask, and default gateway for the machine. Other NICs are configured once you reboot.

The next screen asks if you want to enable an HTTPS server for server configuration. If you plan to use the Visitor Mode feature of remote access VPNs, you should change the port to any other you like.

You are prompted to confirm the formatting of the hard drive, and then the installation program begins copying the SecurePlatform files. After this step is completed, you are prompted to reboot the machine, as shown in Figure 8.3.

Figure 8.3 SecurePlatform Complete Installation Screen

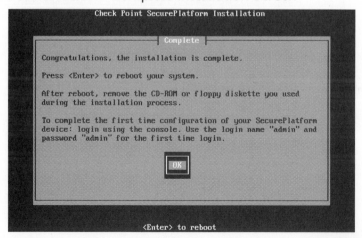

Initial Configuration

Once SecurePlatform is installed, you can access the command line via a monitor and keyboard, an *ssh* connection, or a serial connection. If you choose to use a serial connection, you should set your terminal program to 9600 baud, 8 data bits, no parity, and 1 stop bit and connect to COM1. This sequence is designed so that the SPLAT box can be set in a rack environment, without the need for a console or keyboard.

The default username and password are *admin* and *admin*. Once logged in, you must change your password to a strong password, and optionally change the username. After that, you will enter the Check Point restricted shell (CPShell), a Linux interface that provides you only a limited set of commands. To access the full Linux OS, use the *expert* command and enter the expert password, which initially is the same one as the admin user, but you are given the option of changing it. The expert password, in Linux terms, is the root user password.

> **! WARNING**
>
> For users who are familiar with the Linux operating system, it might seem easier or more efficient to configure the SecurePlatform manually via the file system. It is very important to utilize the tools Check Point supplies to configure the operating system, because the Check Point tools could alter more configuration files than is apparent.

The first thing you should do is use the *sysconfig*, which will show the Welcome Wizard the first time it is run. Type **n** for Next to advance among the wizard's screens. You will first see the Network Configuration screen, as shown in Figure 8.4. From here you should set the hostname (particularly important for a SmartCenter installation, so choose your hostname wisely), the domain name, the domain name servers, the network connections, and routing configuration. You should have no trouble configuring the first three sections.

Figure 8.4 The Welcome Wizard Network Configuration Screen

```
Welcome to Check Point SecurePlatform NGX (R61)

This wizard will guide you through the initial
configuration of your SecurePlatform device.

At any time you can choose Quit (q) to exit this Wizard.
Choose Next (n) to continue.

---------------------------------------------------------------
Press "q" for Quit, "n" for Next
---------------------------------------------------------------
Your choice: _
```

Let's look at the Network Connections Configuration screen, as shown in Figure 8.5. You have the option to configure a network connection, which you need to do for the interfaces to which you have not assigned an IP. In Linux, Ethernet interfaces have the prefix *eth*, and numbering starts at zero. Configure each interface with an IP address and network mask, and you can usually leave the broadcast address to the default. You can even set if as a dynamic interface, so that it receives its IP address via DHCP.

Figure 8.5 The Network Connections Configuration Screen

```
Choose a network connections configuration item ('e' to exit):
--------------------------------------------------------------------
1) Add new connection          4) Select management connection
2) Configure connection        5) Show connection configuration
3) Remove connection
--------------------------------------------------------------------
Your choice:
```

Two important options in the Network Connections Configuration screen are "Add new connection" and "Remove connection." SecurePlatform has built-in support for VLANs, and you can add up to 1024 VLAN interfaces to a single machine. Once you add a VLAN interface, you will be prompted for the VLAN tag (2–1024), and the new interface will then be named *ethX.Y,* where *X* is the physical interface and *Y* is the VLAN tag. You can also add secondary IPs to physical interfaces, even though from a security perspective it's not recommended. Other interfaces such as PPPoE, PPTP, and ISDN can be configured as well. When you're done, exit back to the Network Configuration screen.

The last option in the screen is the Routing option, which only allows you to set a default gateway if you didn't set it when initially configuring an interface. After the Network Configuration screen is the Time, Date, and Timezone screen. They are self-explanatory to configure.

You will then see a screen where you can Import a Check Point configuration file from a TFTP server. If you have made a backup on another system that you want to import into a new system, you can use this interface to import the backup and restore all configurations.

Initial Check Point Configuration

Once you step through these Welcome Wizard screens, you'll get to the Check Point installation wizard, as shown in Figure 8.6. Press **N** for Next, and in the next screen accept the license agreement and press **Y**. You will be prompted to select whether to install Check Point Enterprise/Pro or Express. Eventually those will be replaced by options for VPN-1 Power or UTM. In any case, select **Pro**. Even if you have an Express license, it will work with a Pro installation. In the next screen you also have the option of creating a new installation or importing a Check Point configuration from a previous installation.

Figure 8.6 Check Point Installation Wizard Welcome Screen

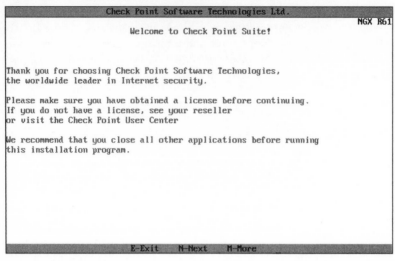

For a new configuration, you can now select the Check Point products to install, as shown in Figure 8.7. For a SmartCenter, you should choose **SmartCenter**, and optionally **UserAuthority** (a single sign-on product from Check Point), **Integrity** (available only on NGX R61 and higher), **Eventia Reporter**, and **SmartPortal** (a limited Web-based interface to the SmartCenter). For a security gateway, choose **VPN-1 Pro** and optionally the **Performance Pack**. If you selected a SmartCenter installation, you have to decide if it's Primary, Secondary, or Log only. You can have only a single Primary SmartCenter configured. Before installing the products selected, you need to confirm your selections.

Figure 8.7 Check Point Product Selection Screen

Once the products are installed, you'll see the prompts to finalize configuration of your Check Point installation: licenses, administrators, and GUI clients for SmartCenters, or activation key for security gateways. Then you will need to reboot your machine. You can then use the SmartConsole to log into a SmartCenter or use an existing SmartCenter to establish Secure Internal Communication (SIC) with the SmartCenter over a security gateway. Remember that if you have a security gateway, once you reboot it you won't be able to access it until a policy is installed into it.

SecurePlatform Configuration

After the initial SecurePlatform and Check Point configuration, you will eventually need to change or add some configurations. Use the *sysconfig* utility to see the screen shown in Figure 8.8.

Figure 8.8 The *sysconfig* Utility

```
Choose a configuration item ('e' to exit):
-----------------------------------------------------------------
1) Host name                      7) DHCP Server Configuration
2) Domain name                    8) DHCP Relay Configuration
3) Domain name servers            9) Export Setup
4) Time and Date                 10) Products Installation
5) Network Connections           11) Products Configuration
6) Routing
-----------------------------------------------------------------
(Note: configuration changes are automatically saved)
Your choice:
```

Some options that are available here include a full routing configuration for static routes and configuration of the built-in DHCP server in SPLAT. From the Products Installation option you can add products that you didn't install originally, such as Integrity or Eventia Reporter. The Products Configuration option opens the *cpconfig* utility to configure all Check Point options. With the Export Setup option, you send a configuration copy to a TFTP server.

SecurePlatform Maintenance

Some of the advantages of SecurePlatform as an operating system are all the built-in features for maintenance of the platform. You do not have to worry about patching the underlying OS, since Check Point patches and upgrades inclusive OS fixes as well. You can use the *Backup* and *Restore* commands for simple backups, *Snapshot* and *Revert* commands for complete disk copies, and the *Patch* command to install patches and upgrade your platform.

Backup, Scheduled Backup, and Restore

An extremely useful pair of utilities is *backup* and *restore*, for obvious reasons. *Backup* enables you to create a backup of the system configuration files and save them locally or send them to a TFTP or SCP server. All backups are stored in the /var/CPbackup/backups directory.

Use the *backup* command with no parameters to create a backup on the local system. Some available options are *–l*, to include logs in the backup (which could then increase to several gigabytes or more); *-t*, to send to a TFTP server; *—scp,* to send to an SCP server; and *–sched,* to schedule a recurring backup. For example, the command *backup —sched on 00:00 - w Sunday* would schedule a backup to run every Sunday at midnight.

Restore enables you to rebuild a system quickly after it is on the network. As with *backup*, you can restore a backup from a local file, a TFTP server, or an SCP server. Using *restore* without any command-line switches presents you with a menu that will walk you through the restore process, after you input the expert password. You will have the option to restore the system configuration and/or the Check Point configuration. If you find that the option to restore the Check Point configuration is not available, make sure that all the products installed on the backed-up server (i.e., Reporter, SmartPortal, etc) are installed on the server you're trying to restore.

Snapshot, Revert, and Snapshot Image Management

The *snapshot* utility enables you to create a full image of your SecurePlatform machine. After a snapshot is created, the Snapshot Image Management option is available at boot time.

To create a snapshot of your system, run the *snapshot* command and you will see an interactive menu where you can create a new local image or save it to TFTP or SCP and then proceed. It can take 20 minutes or more to create a snapshot.

An important difference between *backup* and *snapshot* is that in a backup, you only have the configuration files, whereas in a snapshot you have the entire contents of the disk. Also, to perform a backup you only need to exit the SmartConsole, but all Check Point services continue running. In a snapshot, all services stop (including the firewall and all traffic through it). You cannot schedule a snapshot.

The *revert* utility enables you to replace the current system state to a snapshot you created earlier. To revert to a snapshot, run the *revert* command and you'll see an interactive menu the reverse of the snapshot menu. You can also access the Snapshot Image Management option at the SecurePlatform bootup menu, as shown in Figure 8.9. You will be prompted for the expert password, and then you can revert from a TFTP or SCP server. It would be possible to format a new server, reboot, go into the Snapshot Image Management section, and reimage the machine in less than 20 minutes total.

Figure 8.9 Snapshot Image Management

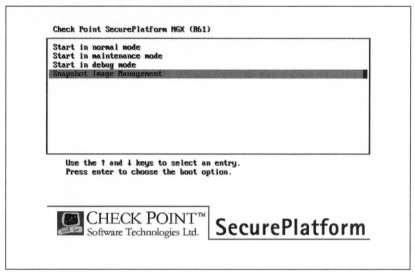

Patch Add

Periodically, you might need to add or update packages. You can add packages from either SmartUpdate or from the SecurePlatform command line. SmartUpdate is definitely the easiest way to upgrade, but if you have a management station running SecurePlatform or do not have a SmartUpdate license (which is included with a SmartCenter Pro license), you will be required to upgrade from the command line.

You should always read the release notes before upgrading. You can upgrade using a CD, a TFTP server, an SCP server, or files that you have copied over to the SecurePlatform machine. For example, to install a patch from a CD, use **patch add cd**, and the OS will read the CD and present a list of the available packages. To install a patch from a file on the local system, simply use **patch add** *<full_patch_path>*.

Basics of Nokia Firewalls

Nokia offers multiple platforms ranging from the IP40 series for the SOHO environment to the IP2200 series for carrier-class demands, as shown in Figure 8.10. One of the Nokia platform's key strengths is the use of a platform-independent OS and third-party applications, called IPSO. Current versions of IPSO can be used across most platforms, with the exception of the IP40/IP45, which is directly related to Check Point's VPN-1 Edge and therefore outside the scope of this chapter. Nokia uses Check Point firewalls to provide firewall services across all platforms, and they have the same behavior, the only difference being performance and hardware features. Another of Nokia's key strengths is the use of diskless platforms. Most of the current offerings can run directly from industrial-grade, solid-state

Flash memory storage, thereby eliminating the use of spinning media for their operation. This allows them to offer higher reliability and longer mean time before failure (MBTF). Nokia is the only hardware vendor that offers diskless platforms for running Check Point firewalls.

Figure 8.10 Nokia's Current Firewall Appliances

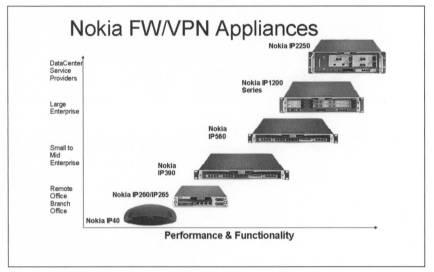

Choosing the Right Platform

Since the smallest Nokia IP appliance offers at least three 10/100 Ethernet interfaces, it is possible to design a DMZ solution with each appliance. In addition, Check Point FireWall-1/VPN-1 functionality is enabled by the features of the license, not by the software package. Since Check Point FireWall-1/VPN-1 is limited only by its license, it is important to choose the correct platform for the intended environment. In the next section, we discuss the current Nokia Platforms available and the environments in which they should be deployed.

Nokia IP260/265 Appliances

The IP260/265 appliances are rack-mountable, half-width 1RU platforms intended for the small to medium-sized enterprise environment. They contain four embedded 10/100 Ethernet interfaces, on-board hardware encryption acceleration, and full IPSO IP routing functionality. However, they are not expandable beyond the default configuration. The IP260 is a standard disk-based platform; the IP265 is diskless. With a 250Mb throughput, they are suitable for branch offices and small business.

Nokia IP390 Appliances

The IP390 appliance, released around March 2006, is an extremely capable platform for medium-sized to large companies. It ships with four embedded 10/100/1000 Ethernet interfaces, and there are two slots to add quad-port fast Ethernet cards or dual-port Gigabit Fiber cards. With a throughput of up to 3Gbps in a 1RU form factor, the IP390 can handle demanding environments at an affordable price. It is a diskless platform, although you can add a hard drive for local logging and additional storage.

Nokia IP560 Appliances

The IP560 appliance was released in late 2005, and it brings performance to new levels for the large enterprise. With a throughput of up to 6Gps, it can handle any job you throw at it with ease. It ships with four embedded 10/100/1000 Ethernet interfaces, and there are three slots to add quad-port Fast or Gigabit Ethernet cards or dual-port Gigabit Fiber cards. It is also a diskless platform, although you can add a hard drive for local logging and additional storage.

Nokia IP1220/1260 Appliances

The IP1220 and IP1260 are a carrier-class appliances, with a 2RU form factor and redundant features. They ship with four embedded 10/100 Ethernet interfaces, and there are four slots to add quad-port Fast or Gigabit Ethernet cards or dual-port Gigabit Ethernet or Fiber cards. It has the option of being a disk-based, diskless, or diskless with hard drive platform. The IP1260 includes redundant power supplies and mirrored disks; these features are options for the IP1220.

Nokia IP2250 Appliances

The IP2250 is the top-of-the-line, carrier-class appliance from Nokia. It has a 3RU form factor, redundant features, and hot-swappable options. It ships with four embedded 10/100 Ethernet interfaces and redundant power supplies. There are four slots to add quad-port Gigabit Ethernet or Fiber cards, eight-port Fast Ethernet cards, or even a single-port 10GBase-SR interface card. It is a diskless platform, with Accelerated Data Path technology, which incorporates traffic decisions in processors installed directly on the network cards.

Discontinued Appliances

Like many other hardware vendors, Nokia has an end-of-sale (EOS) policy for its appliances. Once an appliance is released, you can count on a minimum of a three-year sales life. However, once EOS is announced, Nokia has a generous three-year support time frame, during which the company supports and guarantees appliances under contract. After EOCS (end of contracted support), you're on your own. Many popular appliances are now EOS or EOCS. Some of them are:

- **IP110/IP120/IP130**   Small desktop-based appliances for running small offices, up to around 100 users. They have a maximum throughput of 100Mbps and 3 10/100 Ethernet interfaces. The main difference among the IP110, IP120, and IP130 is that they have 64Mb, 128Mb, and 256Mb of RAM, respectively.

- **IP330**   A Nokia workhorse some five years ago, this 1U appliance has a maximum throughput of 100Mb, 256Mb of RAM, up to five 10/100 Ethernet interfaces, and the option of a modem or WAN interface.

- **IP350/IP355/IP380/IP385**   Although not officially EOS in the Americas, Nokia will soon stop selling these great 1RU appliances. They have two slots for quad-port 10/100 cards or dual-port Fiber cards. The 3x5 models are Flash based.

- **IP440**   The most popular Nokia appliance five years ago. Very scalable, it could have up to 16 10/100 interfaces or a variety of WAN interfaces.

- **IP530**   A 2U appliance for the mid- to large enterprise. Had good performance, Fiber card support, and good expansion capabilities.

- **IP650**   An older 2RU appliance with features similar to those of the IP530, lower performance, but with optional redundant power supplies and disks.

- **IP710/IP740**   Carrier-class 3RU appliances, the first that had Gigabit firewall performance; it can have redundant power supplies and disks.

Nokia Appliance Comparisons

Table 8.1 lists all the platforms we've talked about and compares the most important features among them.

Table 8.2 lists some of the appliances that are EOS or EOCS.

Table 8.1 Currently Available Nokia Platform Specifications

	IP260/ IP265	IP350/ IP380	IP390	IP560	IP1220/ IP1260	IP2250
Form factor	1 RU	1 RU	1 RU	1 RU	3 RU	3 RU
Maximum FW throughput	248Mbps/ 227Mbps	350Mbps/ 1.5Gbps	3Gbps	6Gbps	2.4Gbps/ 4Gbps	7.5Gbps
Maximum 3DES VPN throughput	112Mbps	130Mbps/ 313Mbps	500Mpbs	1.7Gbps	1.19Gbps/ 1.49Gbps	1.9Gbps
Default memory configuration	512Mb	256Mb/ 1Gb	1Gb	1Gb	1Gb	2Gb
Maximum memory configuration	512Mb	512Mb/ 1Gb	2Gb	2Gb	2Gb	2Gb
Default # of 10/100 Ethernet ports	4	4/4	0	0	4	4
Max # of 10/100 Ethernet ports	4	12/12	8	16	20/20	36
Default # of 10/100/ 1000 Ethernet ports	0	0/2	4	4	0	0
Max # of 10/100/1000 Ethernet ports	0	4/4	8	16	8/8	8
Maximum connections per second	5.5k/4.8k	16k/19k	30k	58k	39k/62k	99k
Redundant power supply	N/A	N/A	N/A	N/A	Option/ integrated	Integrated
Flash-based (diskless)	IP265	IP355/385	Yes	Yes	Option	Yes
Mirrored disks	N/A	N/A	N/A	N/A	Option/ integrated	Integrated

www.syngress.com

Table 8.2 Nokia Appliances No Longer Available for Sale

	IP120/ IP130	IP330	IP440	IP530	IP650	IP710/ IP740
Form factor	Desktop	1 RU	4 RU	2 RU	2 RU	3 RU
Maximum FW throughput	117Mbps/ 100Mbps	130Mbps	236Mbps	460Mbps	317Mbps	1.3Gbps/ 2Gbps
Maximum 3DES VPN throughput (with accelerator, if available)	30Mbps/ 3Mbps	18Mbps	93Mbps	115Mbos	85Mbps	140Mbps
Default memory configuration	128Mb/ 256Mb	256Mb	128Mb	256Mb	256Mb	512Mb/1Gb
Maximum memory configuration	128Mb/ 256Mb	256Mb	512Mb	1Gb	768Mb	1Gb
Default # of 10/100 Ethernet ports	3	3	0	4	4	4
Max # of 10/100 Ethernet ports	3	5	16	16	20	20
Default # of 10/100/1000 Ethernet ports	0	0	0	0	0	0
Max # of 10/100/1000 Ethernet ports	0	0	0	4	8	8
Redundant power supply	N/A	N/A	N/A	N/A	Option	Option/ integrated
Mirrored disks	N/A	N/A	N/A	Option	Option	Option/ integrated

Nokia Support

Nokia's support is among the finest in the industry. The company has top-notch personnel who can assist in both Nokia and Check Point issues around the clock, with an excellent response time. Even better, appliance issues and Check Point software issues can both be handled by Nokia engineers. The company offers two support options, Essentials Support and Access Support. Both include access to the latest Nokia software versions, access to the company's help knowledgebase, and advanced hardware replacement for appliances. Access support allows customers to directly open cases with the Nokia TAC, whereas Essentials support is designed so that only authorized resellers can open cases on behalf of their customers. It is highly recommended that you always have a valid support contract. You can find more information at http://support.nokia.com.

Configuring the Nokia Appliance

The Nokia appliance arrives from the factory without configuration but with the most recent IPSO version and Check Point version installed. The initial configuration is usually done through the serial console port, and all Nokia appliances have a console port to connect to for configuration. They do not have display, keyboard, or mouse ports and so are designed for unattended rack installation.

Initial Appliance Configuration

The Nokia appliance arrives from the factory without configuration. All Nokia appliances have a console port to connect to for configuration. The console cable, a standard RS232 null modem cable, is provided with the Nokia appliance. Using a terminal emulator program, you can connect to the Nokia via a serial connection to begin the configuration. The terminal connection should be configured to use 9600 bits per second, 8 data bits, no parity, 1 stop bit, and no flow control. If you use the HyperTerminal program, be sure to use the latest, fully patched version; otherwise, it could activate the BIOS setup screen.

Once you have properly configured your terminal emulator and connected to the Nokia appliance, turn on the machine. You will see the initial startup screen and are prompted to enter a hostname for the appliance. You will also be prompted to choose and confirm a password for the user admin, as shown here:

```
Please choose the host name for this system.  This name will be used
in messages and usually corresponds with one of the network hostnames
for the system.  Note that only letters, numbers, dashes, and dots (.)
are permitted in a hostname.

Hostname? panama
Hostname set to "panama", OK? [y]

Please enter password for user admin:
```

```
Please re-enter password for confirmation:
```

Once you've chosen a password, you will be prompted to choose between using a remote Web browser Voyager or using the CLI to configure the Nokia appliance, as shown in the following example. Choose option **1** to use a remote Web browser. Choose option **2** if you do not have IP connectivity to configure the Nokia appliance. You may use either Lynx or CLISH, depending on the IPSO version you have. You will then be prompted to configure an interface for IP connectivity:

```
You can configure your system in two ways:

    1) configure an interface and use our Web-based Voyager via a remote
       browser
    2) configure an interface by using the CLI


Please enter a choice [ 1-2, q ]: 1

Select an interface from the following for configuration:

    1) eth1
    2) eth2
    3) eth3
    4) eth4
    5) quit this menu


Enter choice [1-5]: 1

Enter the IP address to be used for eth1: 10.1.0.1/16

Do you wish to set the default route [ y ] ?

Enter the default router to use with eth1: 10.10.200.200

This interface is configured as 10 mbs by default.
Do you wish to configure this interface for 100 mbs [ n ] ? y

This interface is configured as half duplex by default.
Do you wish to configure this interface as full duplex [ n ] ? y

You have entered the following parameters for the eth1 interface:

                  IP address: 10.1.0.1
                  masklength: 16
```

```
           Default route: 10.10.200.200
                  Speed: 100M
                 Duplex: full


Is this information correct [ y ] ?
```

After this process, you will get a few more prompts and eventually reach a login prompt. Then you can access the appliance via Voyager on a normal Web browser.

Nokia Voyager

The most common way of accessing and configuring Nokia appliances is the Nokia Voyager. Voyager is a complete Web-based interface that is installed with every IPSO installation, accessible via either HTTP or HTTPS. In IPSO versions up to 3.9, Voyager had a frameless Web interface and could also be accessed via a command-line utility called Lynx, essentially a command-line browser. However, with IPSO 4.0 and later, Voyager has received a complete overhaul and has become a frame-based interface incompatible with Lynx. In IPSO 4.0, the left-hand frame contains a menu tree that expands and collapses to show different settings. In IPSO 3.9, you would find those settings by scrolling down the Web page, as shown in Figure 8.11. Once you find the functions in either Voyager 3.9 or 4.0, they have very similar configuration options.

Figure 8.11 IPSO 3.9 and Earlier Voyager

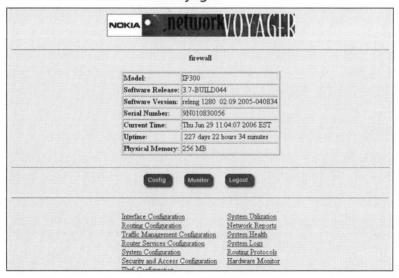

Voyager has two main sections, the configuration and the monitor sections, as Figure 8.12 shows for IPSO 4.0. In the Configuration section, you can change your passwords, manage the firewall and other packages installed in your appliance, get a configuration summary (useful to print and keep as a reference), and configure the following areas: interface, system, high availability, routing, traffic management, router services, IPv6, and asset information. In the Monitor section, you can monitor a cluster, transparent mode groups, the forwarding table, routes, and interfaces, and you can access sections for system utilization, reports, health, logs, routing, hardware monitoring, and IPv6 monitoring.

Figure 8.12 IPSO 4.0 Voyager Sections

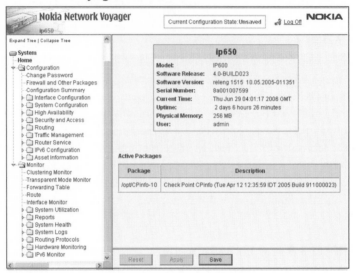

Designing & Planning...

Using Voyager

Voyager is a Web-based configuration tool used to configure the Nokia appliance. Voyager is intuitive and easy to use. We could go into each Voyager section to show you how to configure the Nokia appliance, but doing so would occupy too many pages for the purpose of this chapter. Instead, download the *Voyager Guide* from Nokia's support site at https://support.nokia.com for a full guide to Voyager configuration. For complex configurations, you can use CLISH to set up the Nokia appliance.

Using CLISH

Nokia introduced CLISH in IPSO 3.6 for IPSO configuration, and in IPSO 4.0 it has taken a predominant configuration role through the command line. Remember, Lynx has been eliminated from the regular distributions.

CLISH is a robust CLI that allows the administrator to define IPSO settings step by step or automatically through the use of a text file. CLISH is extremely useful when you have multiple appliances to configure. The syntax for the commands is the same whether they are input manually or through the use of a text file. To manually input the settings one by one, invoke CLISH by typing **clish**. To have CLISH read the input automatically from a text file, invoke the following command. In this case, the −*s* flag saves the configuration:

```
Nokia[admin]#clish -f <filename> -s.
```

Here are some other common commands and their uses. To configure the default gateway, use this command:

```
Nokia>set static-route default nexthop gateway address 205.226.27.2
    priority 1 on
```

To configure a static route, use the following command:

```
Nokia>set static-route 10.254.253.0/24 nexthop gateway address 10.254.254.2
    priority 1 on
```

To configure an interface's physical settings, use this command:

```
Nokia>set interface eth-s2p1 auto-advertise on duplex full speed 10M
    active on link-recog-delay 6
```

To configure an interface's logical settings, use these commands:

```
Nokia>add interface eth-s2p1c0 address 10.254.254.1/24
Nokia>set interface eth-s2p1c0 enable
```

To configure a proxy ARP entry, use the following command:

```
Nokia>add arpproxy address 10.254.254.152 interface eth-s2p1c0
```

Developing a standard template is very useful if you want to plan ahead and configure the Nokia appliances. A standard template is also very helpful if you configure Nokia appliances on a consistent basis. You will save configuration time by having the settings read into IPSO. You may use the pound sign (#) to insert comments. CLISH will not read the text preceding the # as configuration lines.

Here is a sample template file:

```
#Set Default gateway
set static-route default nexthop gateway address a.b.c.d priority X on
#Set Physical Interface
set interface eth-sXpX auto-advertise on duplex full speed XM active on link-
recog-delay X
#Set Logical interface
add interface eth-sXpXcX address a.b.c.d/x
set interface eth-sXpXcX enable
#Set Static route
set static-route a.b.c.d/x nexthop gateway address a.b.c.d priority X on
#Set Proxy ARP
add arpproxy address a.b.c.d interface eth-sXpXcX
```

For more information or additional command syntax, consult the *Command Line Reference Guide* for IPSO, available for download at https://support.nokia.com.

Time Constraints

Know how much time you have to implement the solution. You should have a pretty good idea of how much time is needed to implement your solution. Unfortunately, sometimes things do not go smoothly, and you will need to allocate time for troubleshooting. Estimate your time window to complete the project, and add some time for troubleshooting if something goes wrong.

You should also have an emergency backup plan in case the solution cannot be implemented in the time frame allocated. This is especially important when you're integrating a DMZ into an existing production environment. It is very easy to back out from changes in IPSO. Before you begin configuring an existing environment, you should back up the current configuration using Voyager. You can do so using the **Configuration | System Configuration | Backup and Restore** functions, and be sure to back up the **System** and **Check Point** settings. You may then restore to your original configuration at any time.

Operating System and Software Installation

The Nokia appliance comes preinstalled with IPSO and partner applications, including Check Point. However, it is not guaranteed that the latest software binaries are installed. The latest IPSO versions are available at http://support.nokia.com. All Check Point binaries must be obtained from Check Point's Web site. Keep in mind that you must have a separate valid logon and software subscription for each site.

Using Voyager

Choose **Config | System Configuration Section | Install New IPSO Image** in IPSO 3.9 or **Configuration | System Configuration | Images | Upgrade Image** in IPSO 4.0 to upgrade the IPSO operating system. Choose **Config | System Configuration Section | Manage Installed Packages | FTP and Install Packages** in IPSO 3.9 or **Configuration | System Configuration | Packages | Manage Packages** to upgrade or install third-party applications (i.e. Check Point). However, we recommend using the command-line interface for both, since they provide more feedback about the process and are not subject to timeouts that a browser could have.

Command-Line Installation of IPSO images

New IPSO images should be obtained from Nokia. These images are usually called *ipso.tgz*, but you should probably rename them to something like *ipsoX.XbYY*, to indicate the major IPSO version and the build version—for example, *ipso39b45*.tgz. Transfer the image to the appliance via SCP or FTP and then use the *newimage* command, as shown in Figure 8.13.

The $-l$ switch indicates that a locally stored image will be used, whereas the $-k$ switch prevents the image installation from deactivating the currently active packages. Once the image is installed, go to **Configuration | System Configuration | Images | Manage Images**, select the image to be used, and reboot. You can also Test Boot, which will reboot the machine, but if the new image is not confirmed within a set amount of time, the platform will reboot with the previous image.

The *newimage* command carries over the settings from the previous IPSO installation, unless it's an unsupported downgrade (check the release notes). To return a Nokia appliance to factory default settings, remove the /config/active link using the command *rm /config/active* at the command prompt and reboot the appliance. Use this command with caution because you will lose your settings on reboot.

Figure 8.13 IPSO *newimage* Command

```
ip650[admin]# newimage -l ipso41b13.tgz -k
Validating image...(no signature file found, continuing)...done.

Version tag stored in image:  .IPSO-4.1-BUILD013-03.27.2006-223017-1515

Setting up new image... done.
Checking if bootmgr upgrade is needed...
Upgrading bootmgr....
new bootmgr size is 1474560
old bootmgr size is 1474560
Saving old bootmgr.
Installing new bootmgr.
Verifying installation of bootmgr.

Will use /image/IPSO-4.0-BUILD023-10.05.2005-011351-1515 as root for next boot.
To install/upgrade your packages run /etc/newpkg after REBOOT

ip650[admin]#
```

Installing the Check Point Software

Use the *newpkg* command to install a third-party partner application. In this case you should have ready a Check Point package, usually called IPSO_wrapper_Rxx.tgz. Transfer the package to the appliance via SCP or FPT, and run *newpkg* as shown in Figure 8.14. The *−m LOCAL* switch indicates that the package is installed locally, and the *−n* switch indicates which package to install. Use the *−o* switch to indicate that an upgrade from a previous version should be made—for example, *−o $FWDIR*.

Figure 8.14 IPSO *newpkg* Command

```
ip650[admin]# newpkg -m LOCAL -n IPSO_wrapper_R60.tgz

Loading IPSO_wrapper_R60.tgz


Installing IPSO_wrapper_R60.tgz

    Running IPSO_wrapper_R60/INSTALL PRE /opt/IPSO_wrapper_R60 /opt/packages/./IPS
O_wrapper_R60.tgz IPSO_wrapper_R60/MANIFEST newpkg
    Running IPSO_wrapper_R60/INSTALL POST /opt/IPSO_wrapper_R60 /opt/packages/./IP
SO_wrapper_R60.tgz IPSO_wrapper_R60/MANIFEST newpkg
********************************************************************
It is required to configure Check Point products before activating them,
you can do so by re-login to the machine and running `cpconfig`
from the command line.

********************************************************************
Done installing IPSO_wrapper_R60

End of new package installation
cleaning up ..done
A reboot may be necessary to activate packages.
ip650[admin]#
```

Once you install the Check Point package, you have to log out and then log in so that you can configure the package initially with *cpconfig*. Since most Nokia appliances are used as security gateways, Figure 8.15 shows a sample initial *cpconfig* with the appropriate answers.

Figure 8.15 Initial *cpconfig* on Nokia Platforms

```
ip650[admin]# cpconfig

Welcome to Check Point Configuration Program
=====================================================
Please read the following license agreement.
Hit 'ENTER' to continue...

Please select one of the following options:
Check Point Enterprise/Pro - for headquarters and branch offices.
Check Point Express - for medium-sized businesses.
-----------------------------------------------------------------

(1) Check Point Enterprise/Pro.
(2) Check Point Express.
Enter your selection  (1-2/a-abort) [1]: 1

Select installation type:
-------------------------

(1) Stand Alone - install VPN-1 Pro Gateway and SmartCenter Enterprise.
(2) Distributed - install VPN-1 Pro Gateway, SmartCenter and/or Log Server.

Enter your selection  (1-2/a-abort) [1]: 2

Select installation type:
-------------------------

(1) VPN-1 Pro Gateway.
(2) Enterprise SmartCenter.
(3) Enterprise SmartCenter and VPN-1 Pro Gateway.
(4) Enterprise Log Server.
(5) VPN-1 Pro Gateway and Enterprise Log Server.

Enter your selection  (1-5/a-abort) [1]: 1
Is this a Dynamically Assigned IP Address gateway installation ? (y/n) [n] ? n
Would you like to install a Check Point clustering product (CPHA, CPLS or State S
ynchronization)? (y/n) [n] ? y
IP forwarding disabled
Hardening OS Security: Default Filter will be applied during boot.
This program will guide you through several steps where you
will define your Check Point products configuration.
At any later time, you can reconfigure these parameters by
running cpconfig
```

Using *cpconfig*

Once you have an installation of Check Point on your preferred operating system, you need to do some basic configuration to enable the graphical user interface (SmartConsole) to work. This is done through the *cpconfig* utility, which you will also use for adjustments after the initial configuration. The options available in *cpconfig* for SmartCenters and security gateways are different.

Common options that can be configured on *cpconfig* include these:

- **Licenses** Check https://usercenter.checkpoint.com/pub/usercenter/faq.html for licensing information in the Check Point UserCenter.

- **SNMP extensions** Use it to start the Check Point daemon so that SNMP tools can query the firewall.

- **Random pool** Used in various cryptographic operations.

Using *cpconfig* on SmartCenters

On SmartCenters, the *cpconfig* options are those shown in Figure 8.16. The options include:

- **Administrator** This will be a user who can connect to the SmartConsole and configure the firewall through the GUI. In NGX, you can define only one Administrator in *cpconfig;* the others are configured in SmartDashboard.

Figure 8.16 Using *cpconfig* on SmartCenters

```
[mgmt]# cpconfig
This program will let you re-configure
your VPN-1 configuration.


Configuration Options:
----------------------
(1)   Licenses
(2)   Administrator
(3)   GUI Clients
(4)   SNMP Extension
(5)   Random Pool
(6)   Certificate Authority
(7)   Certificate's Fingerprint

(8) Exit

Enter your choice (1-8) :
```

- **GUI Clients**   This is a list of IPs from which Administrators can connect to the SmartConsole. If you select specific IPs, implied rules will be created to allow access from those locations. If you select networks, hostnames, or Any, you will need to create rules that allow the CPMI service from those locations.

- **Certificate Authority**   Use this option to change the name used for the certificate authority. You normally shouldn't need to do this.

- **Certificate's Fingerprint**   Use this option to view or save the fingerprint of the certificate used by the management so that you can compare it to the one presented by the SmartConsole for authentication purposes.

Using *cpconfig* on Security Gateways

On security gateways, the *cpconfig* options are those shown in Figure 8.17.

Figure 8.17 Using *cpconfig* on Security Gateways

```
ip650[admin]# cpconfig
This program will let you re-configure
your Check Point products configuration.


Configuration Options:
----------------------
(1)   Licenses
(2)   SNMP Extension
(3)   Group Permissions
(4)   PKCS#11 Token
(5)   Random Pool
(6)   Secure Internal Communication
(7)   Disable cluster membership for this gateway
(8)   Enable Check Point SecureXL
(9)   Automatic start of Check Point Products

(10) Exit

Enter your choice (1-10) :
```

The options include:

- **Group Permissions** Used to select an OS group that can run the firewall services. You don't need to modify this option.

- **PKCS#11 Token** Used to select a PKCS#11 token that the gateway can use.

- **Secure Internal Communication** Used to change the SIC and reset the activation key the SmartCenter uses to take control of the gateway. If you change this setting, the security policy will be disabled and the gateway will wait for a SmartCenter to contact it and establish SIC.

- **Disable (or Enable) cluster membership for this gateway** Depending on whether or not the gateway will be part of the cluster, select or deselect this option.

- **Enable (or Disable) Check Point SecureXL** Enables (or disables) the software acceleration provided by SecureXL, which requires a separate license unless you're using the VPN-1 Power gateways that now include it.

- **Automatic start of Check Point products** Use this option to select the products that will start automatically with the gateway. Normally you don't need to change this setting.

Nokia Firewall and DMZ Design Checklist

Here is a sample checklist for planning your Nokia DMZ:

- Know what the DMZ will be used for.

- Read your corporate security policy dealing with DMZs.

- Have an accurate network diagram.

- Know how sensitive the internal network is.

- Select the proper DMZ to implement based on your corporate security policy.

- Develop a proper backup procedure.

- Set a reasonable time frame to implement the solution and include time to troubleshoot.

- Select the appropriate operating system or appliance for your needs.

- Decide on a standalone or distributed configuration.

- Always keep backups of current configurations with a maintenance schedule.

- The wizards guide you through the initial configuration.

- Use *cpconfig* to change options you need at a later time.

Summary

Check Point firewalls can be run on many platforms. SecurePlatform and Nokia firewalls are very secure and easy to use in implementing a DMZ solution. Check Point's SecurePlatform and Nokia's IPSO operating systems are highly secured OSs optimized to forward traffic and for firewall duties. In addition, their wide range of configuration tools makes them a very strong solution.

SecurePlatform is based on Linux and comes with the standard Check Point media kit. You can install SPLAT in an Intel- or AMD-based box in less than 20 minutes and configure it using all the provided wizards. Even if your security gateway runs on dedicated Nokia appliances, using SecurePlatform for a SmartCenter is a popular and intelligent choice. OS maintenance is handled through Check Point's hotfixes, and it has robust backup and restore functionality in case disaster recovery is needed.

IPSO is based on FreeBSD and is included on all Nokia IP appliances starting with the IP100 series. At the low end, the IP260 offers 250Mb of firewall throughput, whereas the IP2255 can offer 7.5Gb of throughput. These appliances are rock-solid and the only ones that can run Check Point in a diskless environment. Their support is among the best in the industry and highly recommended. Nokias also have robust backup and restore features for speedy disaster recovery.

Finally, it is important to remember that integrating DMZs and firewalls into your networks is only part of the whole security solution. Active log auditing, integrating intrusion detection devices, authentication, and security awareness training are some of the other integral components of corporate information management security.

Solutions Fast Track

Basics of SecurePlatform Firewalls

☑ SecurePlatform is a Linux-based operating system created by Check Point. It has been hardened and does not require an additional license for its use.

☑ Check Point has been doing all its research and development on SecurePlatform, with other operating systems being done later.

☑ There are basically two hardware options if you decide to use a SecurePlatform system: dedicated appliances or open systems.

☑ To install SecurePlatform, use CD 1 of the Check Point Media Kit and power on your machine.

☑ The default username and password are *admin* and *admin*. Once logged in, you must change your password to a strong password, and optionally change the username.

☑ The first thing you should do is use *sysconfig*, which will show the Welcome Wizard and help you configure the system.

☑ SecurePlatform has robust maintenance features, including *Backup/Restore* and *Snapshot/Revert*.

Basics of Nokia Firewalls

☑ The Nokia platform comes from the factory without configuration. The initial configuration must be done via local console access only.

☑ The Nokia platform can be managed via a console using a console cable provided by Nokia or by remote dial-in using an external modem or a PCMCIA modem.

☑ The Nokia platform can be remotely managed via SSH, Telnet, HTTP, or HTTPS. These settings are configured in Voyager. Refer to the *Voyager Reference Guide* for details on configuration.

☑ CLISH is the command-line interface shell for IPSO configuration.

☑ The *newimage −i* command is used to upgrade your IPSO operating system.

☑ The *newpkg* command upgrades or installs third-party applications.

☑ The Nokia appliance might not arrive with the latest software installed. Always check the Nokia and Check Point Web sites for the latest available software.

Using *cpconfig*

☑ Once you have an installation of Check Point, you need to use *cpconfig* to make basic configurations that enable the use of the graphical user interface (SmartConsole).

☑ The options available in *cpconfig* for SmartCenters and security gateways are different.

☑ Common options include licenses and SNMP extensions.

☑ On SmartCenters, options include administrator, GUI client, and certificate authority.

☑ On security gateways, options include secure internal communications, cluster membership, and SecureXL.

Frequently Asked Questions

The following Frequently Asked Questions, answered by the authors of this book, are designed to both measure your understanding of the concepts presented in this chapter and to assist you with real-life implementation of these concepts. To have your questions about this chapter answered by the author, browse to **www.syngress.com/solutions** and click on the **"Ask the Author"** form.

Q: What is an ideal setup for my Check Point DMZ system in terms of installation and gateways?

A: You should always try to have a distributed installation, where the SmartCenter is separate from the security gateway. This type of installation has performance, security, and disaster recovery benefits. For the SmartCenter, SecurePlatform is by far the best choice available. For security gateways, dedicated appliances like Nokia have significant advantages, especially regarding hardware replacement and support options.

Q: Does Nokia and/or SecurePlatform support the use of 802.1q VLANs?

A: Yes, both support 802.1q VLAN configurations. As a matter of fact, this configuration is recommended over multihoming an interface, since Check Point sees each logical interface as a separate interface. This creates a cleaner interaction with Check Point when you're dealing with antispoofing issues.

Q: I want to use one of Nokia's high-availability solutions, VRRP or IP clustering. Will I have to configure anything differently?

A: The basic principles and configuration still apply. If you are using high availability, you must create a gateway cluster in your Check Point-1 configuration. If you are using Check Point Sync to synchronize the state tables, you will lose one interface per Nokia as the dedicated sync interface. If you are using Nokia IP Clustering, you will lose another dedicated interface to IP Clustering Sync in addition to the Check Point sync interface. Plan ahead for your hardware requirements and choose the right platform.

Q: Does Check Point support port forwarding with its external IP address?

A: Check Point fully supports this functionality. This is another configuration of Static Port NAT where it takes advantage of the fact that the firewall is not listening on some ports, such as Port 80 for Web services. Since it is not used, some vendors allow the listening port to be used by an internal host on the DMZ.

Q: Does Check Point support other network protocols, such as IPX or AppleTalk?

A: No, Check Point supports only TCP/IP.

Q: What routing protocols does IPSO support?

A: IPSO supports static routing, RIP (versions 1 and 2), OSPF, IGRP, and BGP. You must configure Check Point security rules to accept this traffic.

Q: What routing protocols does SecurePlatform support?

A: SecurePlatform supports static routing only. With SecurePlatform Pro, it supports RIP (versions 1 and 2), OSPF, and BGP.

Q: How often do I need to interact with the operating system?

A: You will need to configure the operating system for changing interfaces and routes (and then get the topology in the GUI), rebooting the appliance, using *cpconfig*, reestablishing the SIC, and making backups. All other firewall configuration is done through the SmartConsole.

## Chapter 9

Firewall and DMZ Design: Juniper NetScreen

Solutions in this Chapter

- **NetScreen Basics**

- **Securely Managing Juniper NetScreen Firewalls**

- **NetScreen Configuration Basics**

☑ **Summary**

☑ **Solutions Fast Track**

☑ **Frequently Asked Questions**

Introduction

The Juniper NetScreen firewall helps implement solutions such as virtual systems, virtual routers, and zones that help you design, configure, and manage your enterprise DMZ. These solutions provide you with granular control over your network's security and help effectively identify DMZ boundaries. With this architecture, you can achieve optimal design, high security, and performance. This chapter introduces you to the solutions and the product range of Juniper's NetScreen and provides a brief summary of their technical specifications and features.

NetScreen Basics

Juniper Networks' premier security platform is the NetScreen firewall product line. The product line provides integrated firewall and IPSec virtual private network (VPN) solutions in a single appliance. The core of a NetScreen firewall is based on the stateful inspection technology, which provides a connection-oriented security model that verifies the validity of every connection while still providing high-performance architecture. The NetScreen firewalls are based on a custom-built architecture consisting of the Application-Specific Integrated Circuit (ASIC) technology. ASIC is designed to perform a specific task and to do that task at a higher performance level than a general-purpose processor. ASIC connects over a high-speed bus interface to the core processor of the firewall unit, a Reduced Instruction Set Computer (RISC) CPU.

The firewall platform also contains additional technologies to increase your network's security. NetScreen products support *deep inspection*, which allows you to inspect traffic at the application level to detect application-level attacks. This can help prevent the next attack on your Web servers, or deter someone trying to send illegal commands to your SMTP server. The deep inspection technology uses a frequently updated database and provides the ability to create your own regular expression-based signatures.

The Juniper NetScreen Security Solution

Juniper NetScreen Security solution includes firewalls, intrusion detection and prevention (IDP), the Secure Sockets Layer (SSL) VPN appliance, and security management software. In line with this discussion we will see how to implement the Juniper NetScreen-based DMZ for an enterprise network. We will discuss the products and features, the methods to manage NetScreen firewalls and configure interfaces, routing and policies, and NetScreen's advanced features, such as high availability, virtual systems, and content filtering.

Juniper NetScreen Versions and Features

The firewall product line has several tiers of appliances and systems. The newest range of Integrated Security Gateway (ISG) from Juniper offers firewall, VPN, and IDP. Juniper also offers a SSL VPN product under the product line known as Secure Access. The Secure

Access series offers a clientless remote access solution and a collaboration tool. The SSL VPN product line also includes the Secure Meeting application, enabling online collaborative meetings in which users can share their desktops and engage in instant messaging. Juniper's IDP prevents malicious traffic from residing on the network, compared to some products that only detect incoming traffic.

Juniper NetScreen Firewalls

The following is a quick review of all the products in the current NetScreen product line—from low-end appliances to high-end systems. Later in this section, we review the enterprise management options that Juniper Networks offers.

NetScreen 5XT and NetScreen 5GT

The NetScreen-5 series is designed for small offices, remote offices, and distributed enterprise networks. NetScreen-5GT ships in several versions: 5-GT 10-user and Plus, 5-GT ADSL 10-user and Plus, and 5-GT Wireless 10-user and Plus. NetScreen-5XT is available in 10-user and Elite versions. The Plus versions offer unrestricted IP addresses support. Table 9.1 summarizes the versions of NetScreen-5 series and their features.

Table 9.1 NetScreen-5 Series Feature Summary

Features	5-GT 10-User and Plus	5-GT ADSL 10-User and Plus	5-GT Wireless Plus	5-XT 10-User and Elite
Interfaces	5 x 10/100 Ethernet	5 x 10/100 Ethernet + 1 ADSL	5 x 10/100 Ethernet + 1 802.11 b/g Wireless Radio	5 x 10/100 Ethernet
Users	10 or unrestricted	10 or unrestricted	10 or unrestricted	10 or unrestricted
Firewall throughput	75Mbps	75Mbps	75Mbps	70Mbps
3DES VPN throughput	20Mbps	20Mbps	20Mbps	20Mbps
Concurrent sessions	2000	2000	2000	2000
VPN tunnels	10	10	10	10
Maximum policies	100	100	100	100

Continued

Table 9.1 continued NetScreen-5 Series Feature Summary

Features	5-GT 10-User and Plus	5-GT ADSL 10-User and Plus	5-GT Wireless Plus	5-XT 10-User and Elite
Security zones	2 (trusted and untrusted), support for 3 security zones when configured in Home/Work mode	2 (trusted and untrusted), support for 3 security zones when configured in Home/Work mode	4	2 (trusted and untrusted), support for 3 security zones when configured in Home/Work mode
Virtual routers	3	3	3	3

Additionally, the 5-GT products have embedded antivirus and antispam support, which the 5-XT products lack.

NetScreen-25 and NetScreen-50

The NetScreen-25 and NetScreen-50 series are designed for remote offices, small to medium-sized companies, and enterprise branch offices. Table 9.2 summarizes the features of NetScreen-25 and NetScreen-50.

Table 9.2 NetScreen-25 and NetsScreen-50 Feature Summary

Features	NetScreen-25	NetScreen-50
Interfaces	4 x 10/100 Ethernet interfaces	4 x 10/100 Ethernet interfaces
Users	Unrestricted number of IP addresses in Trusted interfaces	Unrestricted number of IP addresses in Trusted interfaces
Firewall throughput	100Mbps	170Mbps
3DES VPN throughput	20Mbps	45Mbps
Concurrent sessions	32,000	64,000
VPN tunnels	125	500
Maximum policies	500	1000
VLANs	16	16
Security zones	4	4
Virtual router	3	3

Continued

Table 9.2 continued NetScreen-25 and NetsScreen-50 Feature Summary

Features	NetScreen-25	NetScreen-50
Routing protocol	OSPF, BG, RIPv1/v2 routing protocols support	OSPF, BG, RIPv1/v2 routing protocols support
High availability (HA)	High availability through HA Lite	High availability mode: Active or Passive

Both NetScreen 25 and NetScreen 50 are available in basic versions that offer fewer sessions and VPN tunnels. These models also do not support VLANs and OSPF or BGP. Only HA Lite is supported for high availability. HA Lite relies on configuration synchronization only and does not provide tunnel and session synchronization.

NetScreen-204 and NetScreen-208

NetScreen-204 and NetScreen-208 are designed for medium-sized to large enterprises. Table 9.3 summarizes the features of NetScreen-200.

Table 9.3 The NetScreen-200 Series Feature Summary

Features	NetScreen-204	NetScreen-208
Interfaces	NetScreen-204: 4 x 10/100 Ethernet interfaces	NetScreen-204: 4 x 10/100 Ethernet interfaces
Users	Unrestricted number if IP addresses are in Trusted interfaces	Unrestricted number if IP addresses are in Trusted interfaces
Firewall throughput	375Mbps	375Mbps
3DES VPN throughput	175Mbps	175Mbps
Concurrent sessions	128,000	128,000
VPN tunnels	1000	1000
Maximum policies	4000	4000
VLANs	32 default VLANs (can scale up to 96)	32 default VLANs (can scale up to 96)
Security zones	4—can be up to 10	8—can be up to 10
Virtual router	3—can be up to 5	3—can be up to 5
Routing protocol	OSPF, BG, RIPv1/v2 routing protocols support	OSPF, BG, RIPv1/v2 routing protocols support
High Availability	Active/Passive, Active/Active	Active/Passive, Active/Active, Active/Active Full Mesh

Both NetScreen-204 and NetScreen-208 are available in basic versions. These versions have only 64,000 sessions and 500 VPN tunnels and support only RIPv1/v2 and Active/Passive high-availability options. These versions cost less than the advanced models. NetScreen Security Manager (NSM) can configure and manage all these appliances.

NetScreen-500

NetScreen-500 ships in two models: NetScreen-500 and NetScreen-500 General Packet Radio Services (GPRS). Refer to Table 9.4 for the feature summary of NetScreen-500. Please refer to the datasheet on the Juniper Web site for NetScreen-500 GPRS features.

Table 9.4 NetScreen-500 Feature Summary

Features	NetScreen-500
Slots	4
Interfaces	8 x 10/100 Ethernet interfaces, 8 Mini-GBIC or 4 GBIC
Users	Unrestricted number if IP addresses in Trusted interfaces
Firewall throughput	700Mbps
3DES VPN throughput	250Mbps
Concurrent sessions	250,000
VPN tunnels	5000 site-to-site VPN tunnels 10,000 remote-user (dial-up) VPN tunnels
Maximum policies	20,000
Virtual systems (VSYS)	Up to 25 virtual systems (by default you get 0 VSYS)
VLANs	100 default VLANs
Security zones	8 security zones (can go up to 50)
Virtual routers	2 virtual routers (can go up to 25)
Routing protocols	OSPF, BG, RIPv1/v2 routing protocols support
High Availability	High-availability modes: Active/Passive, Active/Active, Active/Active Full Mesh

The basic version of NetScreen-500 offers 128,000 sessions, 1000 VPN tunnels, RIP-only support, and Active/Passive high-availability mode.

NetScreen-5200 and NetScreen-5400

NetScreen-5200 and NetScreen 5400 are designed for large enterprises, Internet service providers (ISPs), and data centers. This is a high-end, high-performance offering from NetScreen. Table 9.5 summarizes the features of the NetScreen-5000 series.

Table 9.5 NetScreen 5000 Series Feature Summary

Features	NetScreen-5200	NetScreen-5400
Slots	2	4
Interfaces	2 x Fast Ethernet, 10GigE or 8 Mini-GBIC or 2 Mini-GBIC + 24 x 10/100 Ethernet interfaces	6 x Fast Ethernet, 10GigE or 24 Mini-GBIC or 6 Mini-GBIC + 72 x 10/100 Ethernet interfaces
Users	Unrestricted number of IP addresses in Trusted interfaces	Unrestricted number of IP addresses in Trusted interfaces
Firewall throughput	10Gbps	30Gbps
3DES VPN throughput	5Gbps	15Gbps
Concurrent sessions	1,000,000	1,000,000
VPN tunnels	25,000	25,000
Maximum policies	40,000	40,000
Security zones	Default 16 (up to 1000)	Default 16 (up to 1000)
Virtual routers	3 (up to 500)	3 (up to 500)
Routing protocols	OSPF, BG, RIPv1/v2 routing protocols support	OSPF, BG, RIPv1/v2 routing protocols support
High availability	High-availability mode: Active/Passive, Active/Active, Active/Active Full Mesh	High-availability mode: Active/Passive, Active/Active, Active/Active Full Mesh

The Juniper NetScreen ISG Series

The ISG series includes linear firewall and IPSec VPN performance and provides integrated firewall, VPN, and intrusion detection and prevention functionalities. Table 9.6 summarizes the NetScreen ISG features.

Table 9.6 NetScreen ISG Series Feature Summary

Features	NetScreen ISG 1000	NetScreen ISG 2000
Interfaces	4 x fixed 10/100/1000 plus up to 4 x Mini GBIC (SX or LX), or up to 8 x 10/100/1000, or up to 20 x 10/100	Up to 8 x Mini-GBIC (SX or LX), or up to 28 x 10/100
Users	Unrestricted number of IP addresses in Trusted interfaces	Unrestricted number of IP addresses in Trusted interfaces
Firewall throughput	1Gbps	4Gbps
3DES VPN throughput	1Gbps	2Gbps

Continued

Table 9.6 NetScreen ISG Series Feature Summary

Features	NetScreen ISG 1000	NetScreen ISG 2000
Concurrent sessions	250,000	512,000
VPN tunnels	2000	10,000
Maximum policies	10,000	30,000
Virtual systems	0 to 10	0 to 50
VLANs	250	500
Security zones	20 default (up to 40)	26 default (up to additional 100)
Virtual routers	3 (up to 10)	3 (up to additional 50)
Routing protocol	OSPF, BG, RIPv1/v2	OSPF, BG, RIPv1/v2
High Availability	High-availability mode: Active/Passive, Active/Active, Active/Active Full Mesh	High-availability mode: Active/Passive, Active/Active, Active/Active Full Mesh
IDP upgrade	Optional upgrade kit for Integrated IDP	Optional upgrade kit for Integrated IDP

In its basic edition, ISG–1000 offers 125,000 sessions, 1000 VPN tunnels, 50 VLANs, and RIP only and Active/Passive high-availability mode. ISG 2000 in its baseline edition provides 256,000 sessions, 1000 VPN tunnels, 100 VLANs, and RIP only and Active/Passive high-availability mode.

Juniper NetScreen Firewall Software

In the core of the Juniper NetScreen firewall is ScreenOS. In this section, we look at ScreenOS architecture, functions, and licensing options.

ScreenOS

ScreenOS, the operating system (OS) for NetScreen firewall, provides services such as dynamic routing, high availability, and management and virtualizes a single device into multiple virtual devices. This OS is designed as a *real-time operating system* (RTOS), which can respond to external world events in a time frame defined by the external world. On an RTOS CPU, performance is a concern because only one task can run at a time. Therefore, the idea is to minimize the time it takes to set up the CPU and begin executing a task. Another challenge for RTOS is memory allocation. Allocating this memory takes time and can slow down the OS while it's executing a task. As a result, ScreenOS preallocates memory to ensure that there is enough memory available to provide a sustained rate of service.

ScreenOS is more secure than open source operating systems because the general public cannot review the source code for vulnerabilities. ScreenOS also does not have the security exposure of Microsoft Windows. As a result, ScreenOS is exposed to fewer people, denying them a chance to learn about the OS or possible exploits for it.

Today's firewalls have to provide much more than just the regular Layer 3 and Layer 4 inspection. Filtering your ports, protocols, and IP addresses might not provide the security necessary for preventing sophisticated attacks. You need the ability to scan the packet for specific threats to the data. *Deep inspection* technology is the next step in the evolution of firewalls. Deep inspection allows you to inspect traffic at the application layer, relying on regular expressions (*regex*) to determine what content in a packet is malicious. For example, a virus spreading on the Internet attempts to exploit your Internet Information Server (IIS) vulnerabilities by sending a specific string of characters to your Web server. To identify this string, you can write a custom signature. You can then apply the custom signature to a policy to inspect the traffic in the policy for that specific string. Deep inspection implemented through ScreenOS is truly a jump in terms of evolution for the firewall.

Screen OS Licensing

ScreenOS licensing is a simple process. Every appliance comes with a serial number that you need to register at the Juniper licensing site. In addition, you need to enter into the support contract so that you get access to downloads, upgrades, and updates for your appliance. A valid support contract also ensures that you get telephone and e-mail support. Most important, your system's defense mechanisms are up to date.

You also need licenses for additional services such as content management (URL filtering or antivirus add-ons). You might have to buy additional virtual systems if they're required for your networks. We will learn about virtual systems and their benefits in a later section. You can upgrade entry-level appliances that come with 10-user support to unrestricted versions by buying additional upgrade licenses.

From the WebUI (introduced later in this chapter), go to **Configuration | Update | ScreenOS/Keys** to see the licensing information applicable on your appliance. The following is the licensing information of the NetScreen 208 used for the exercises in this chapter:

```
Model:               Baseline
Sessions:            64064 sessions
Capacity:            unlimited number of users
NSRP:                ActivePassive
VPN tunnels:         500 tunnels
Vsys:                None
Vrouters:            3 virtual routers
Zones:               15 zones
VLANs:               0 vlans
Drp:                 Disable
Deep Inspection:     Disable
Deep Inspection Database Expire Date: Disable
AV:                  Enable
Url Filtering:       Disable
```

Securely Managing Juniper NetScreen Firewalls

The first step to implementing NetScreen firewall security is learning how to manage it. Every NetScreen management utility centers around two types: the Web user interface (WebUI) and the command-line interface (CLI). There is a third type of management, an enterprise class of security, called the NetScreen Security Manager (NSM). WebUI and CLI are a requirement for managing the NetScreen firewall.

Each management utility has a few strengths and weaknesses, and you should not implement only one utility. Instead, you should take advantage of the range that NetScreen offers and use multiple configurations. For each type of utility, there is a different way to update ScreenOS, and some options may be more effective than other options.

Finally, it is critical that only authorized administrators have authentication rights and access to use these utilities to manage your firewall's configuration. NetScreen management utilities are console, Secure Shell (SSH), Web interface, and NetScreen Security Manager.

Console

The *serial console* is a nine-pin female serial connection. This option gives CLI access to the firewall. The console is used to initially connect to your device and to conduct *out-of-band management*. Out-of-band management is management that is not network-based, such as access via a modem. A serial console provides you with certain benefits that you do not get from using any other type of connection. The console provides a secure, physical, and dedicated access. Network connectivity issues cannot interrupt this connection, and no one can intercept your management traffic. It is completely secure because of its direct connection to the device.

When configuring the firewall over a serial port, you do not use network connectivity. As a result, using the serial console is an excellent option when you need to change Internet Protocol (IP) addressing on the firewall and guarantee connectivity. Only the serial console lets you view and interact with the booting process. This cannot be accomplished remotely because the OS has not started and it is unable to provide management services. Many devices, such as Unix-type servers and other embedded devices, use serial consoles to provide serial console management. On the NetScreen 5XP/5GT/5XP and NetScreen-500, use a DB9 female to DB9 male straight through serial cable to connect for console management. On the NetScreen 25/50/204/208/ISG 2000/5200/5400, use an RJ-45 serial cable with a DB9 female connector. Table 9.7 outlines the settings for connecting with a serial terminal or serial terminal emulator.

Table 9.7 The Serial Terminal Settings

Setting	Value
Speed	9600 bps
Character Size	8 bit
Parity	None
Stop Bit	1
Flow Control	None

SSH

Another form of command-line management is *Secure Shell*, or SSH. Like Telnet, SSH is a remote command-line utility, but without Telnet's security concerns. SSH provides an encrypted command-line session to the NetScreen firewall. It also provides protection from IP spoofing and Domain Name Service (DNS) spoofing attacks. SSH has two versions, v1 and v2. The versions are not backward-compatible. Version two is considered more popular because of its higher level of security. You require an SSH client that is compatible with the version of SSH you are using. Many UNIX-based operating systems include clients, but Windows-based operating systems do not. You can use a client named *putty* for Windows. It is free and easy to use. You can download it from www.chiark.greenend.org.uk/~sgtatham/putty/download.html.

WebUI

WebUI is the easiest management utility to use. Because of its simple point-and-click options, it gives the end user a jump-start into managing the NetScreen firewall. You can see in Figure 9.1 that the interface is simple. On the left side of the browser is the menu column that lets you choose from the various configuration options. This menu can be either Dynamic HyperText Markup Language (DHTML) based, the default, or Java based. The functionality of each type of menu is the same, but the look and feel is slightly different. By default the WebUI is configured to work over the Hyper Text Transfer Protocol (HTTP) only. It can, however, be configured to work over Hyper Text Transfer Protocol Secure (HTTPS), which provides a mechanism to secure your Web management traffic.

Figure 9.1 The WebUI Interface

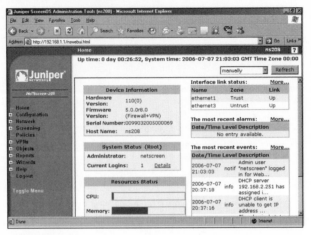

The NetScreen Security Manager

The NSM is a tool that can be used to manage multiple NetScreen devices. The NSM runs as an application on either a Solaris server or a Red Hat Linux server. It requires a separate license, and it is based on how many devices you want to manage. This product is most effective if you want to manage multiple devices at the same time. Figure 9.2 shows the NetScreen Security Manager interface.

Figure 9.2 The NetScreen Security Manager Interface

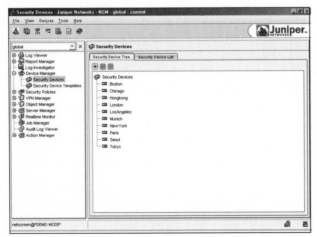

NetScreen Configuration Basics

While the NetScreen firewall platform was being designed, ideas were invited from the developers as to how a firewall should work by combining both conventional and original security concepts. These concepts are essential to effectively design your organization's network security and deploy, configure, and manage NetScreen firewalls. Let's look at these NetScreen core concepts before we start the configuration process.

Virtualization

Juniper NetScreen firewalls work on the concept of *virtualization*. Virtualization allows you to extract maximum performance from the firewall appliance (or system) and provides granular control over the security administration, users, network objects, VPN tunnels, and routing tables. This feature raises a doubt in the conventional method of thinking only two types of network exist: trusted and untrusted. How trusted are the trusted networks? This question leads to the concept of zones.

Security Zones

Zones are the core of the NetScreen architecture. A zone can be defined as a logical area. Several types of zones can exist on a NetScreen firewall. The first and the commonly used zone is the *security zone*. The two commonly used security zones are *trust* and *untrust*. The *trust zone* is assigned to the internal LAN, and the *untrust zone* is assigned to the Internet. Security zones are a key component of the policies and are used in policy configuration.

Different types of security zones are:

- **Layer 3 zones** Untrust, trust, DMZ, and global.
- **Layer 2 zones** V1-Untrust, V1-Trust, and V1-DMZ.
- **Function zones** Null, Self, Mgt, and HA are zones defined for specific purposes.
- **Tunnel zones** Untrust-Tun zone for VPN tunnels.

Virtual Systems

A virtual system (VSYS) is a unique security domain within a NetScreen firewall. Each virtual system contains its own address book, user lists, custom service definitions, VPNs, and policies. Virtual systems also have their own virtual system administrators. These administrators have access to a specific virtual system only. This limits VSYS administrators to their own virtual system, denying them access to other virtual systems and the root system.

Administering a virtual system is the same process as administering a regular appliance. The only difference is that you can have only one read/write administrator and one read-only administrator. A read/write administrator for a VSYS has the same privileges as a read/write administrator for an appliance. As the name goes, the read-only administrator can only view the configuration of the virtual system. The read-only administrator may review the firewall logs and configuration but is not allowed to make any configuration changes.

The root administrator of the entire firewall device is allowed to create and delete virtual systems. The root administrator is also required to give resources to the virtual systems.

For example, if you want to give a virtual system access to interfaces or virtual routers, you need to be connected to the system as the root administrator. A VSYS administrator cannot perform this type of task. Once the VSYS administrator has the interfaces or virtual routers (VRs) in the VSYS, it can do whatever it wants with them, but only after the root administrator gives the VSYS access to the resource.

Tools & Traps...

Sharing Nicely with Others

We have begun to discuss the idea of "shared" objects. A *shared object* is an object that can be used by multiple systems residing on the same physical firewall. On a virtual system, these consist of zones, interfaces, and virtual routers. Sharing the same objects across several virtual systems allows for the efficient distribution of resources.

In situations in which you are using a NetScreen-500 and it is configured with the maximum eight Ethernet interfaces, you want to ensure that in the long term you have enough resources available to you. This is where efficient sharing among all the available virtual systems and the root system is important. If you have long-term expansion goals, you will want your initial design to reflect these goals. You never want to be stuck in a situation where you need to redesign your network after several months of deployment because you failed to see the bigger picture in the beginning.

Virtual Routers

A firewall is nothing more than a glorified router. It essentially sends traffic from one location to another, determining the best path based on its routing table. A normal device that uses IP has a single routing table. The routing table contains all the known or learned routes. A NetScreen device uses the concept of the *virtual router*, or VR.

A VR is a logical construct within a NetScreen device. It provides you with multiple routing tables on the same device. The VR has many uses. VRs are bound to zones, and the zones are bound to interfaces. The NetScreen router will function much like a standard firewall device with one routing table. However, using two separate routing tables gives you the ability to separate your routing domains. For example, if you were to run Open Shortest Path First (OSPF) internally and Border Gateway Protocol (BGP) externally, you would have two separate routing domains. This allows you to securely separate your internally trusted routes with your externally untrusted routes.

Using a VR may seem like a complex process at first. However, it is just like using a traditional routing device. Think about multiple virtual routers in your firewall as having multiple real routers. The VRs will function the same way. Zones are bound to virtual routers. This determines which routers are used on your firewall. If your firewall supports it, you can create additional VRs. Figure 9.3 shows the WebUI VRs of a NetScreen appliance.

Figure 9.3 Virtual Routers

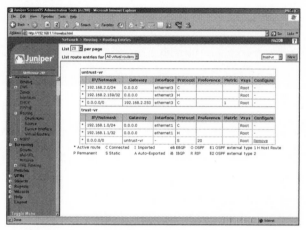

Interface Modes

A NetScreen firewall, by default, operates initially as a router. It allows each physical interface to use an IP address, allowing traffic to be forwarded between each interface. A NetScreen firewall, however, is not limited to this traditional type of firewall configuration.

The firewall allows its physical interfaces to run in a special mode called *transparent mode*. Transparent mode allows you to put the NetScreen firewall into Layer 2 mode, allowing the firewall to act as a bridge while still providing normal firewall filtering. Layer 2 mode is sometimes referred to as *drop-in mode*, where no IP reconfiguration of the network is required. The firewall is inserted between the router and the internal network. This setup is useful when you want to test the firewall's capabilities, with minimal or no reconfiguration of your network. The firewall offers full functionality, including VPN. You also have *route mode,* in which no address translation is performed, and *NAT mode,* in which address translations are performed. Interfaces that belong to trust zones are automatically configured to be in NAT mode, and untrust zone interfaces are in route mode.

Defining Interfaces

The following are the steps to define interfaces:

1 Assign zones to virtual routers.

2 Bind an interface to a zone.

3   Set up IP addressing.

4   Configure basic network routing.

After these steps are complete, you configure security policies. Security policies are discussed later in this chapter.

Assigning Zones to Virtual Routers

First, let's look at the zones we have configured on our device. This can be done from the command line as well as the WebUI. To view the zones using the WebUI, access **Network | Zones**. You can issue this command through a console connection. Figure 9.4 shows a Telnet connection established to a firewall.

Figure 9.4 Network Zones

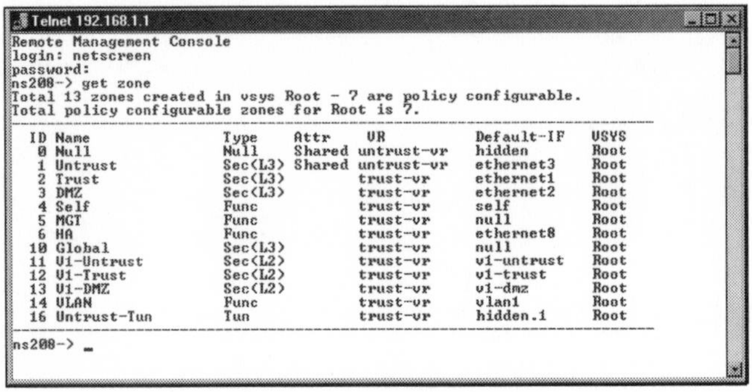

```
Telnet 192.168.1.1                                                      _ □ ×
Remote Management Console
login: netscreen
password:
ns208-> get zone
Total 13 zones created in vsys Root - 7 are policy configurable.
Total policy configurable zones for Root is 7.

ID Name          Type     Attr    VR            Default-IF   VSYS
 0 Null          Null     Shared  untrust-vr    hidden       Root
 1 Untrust       Sec(L3)  Shared  untrust-vr    ethernet3    Root
 2 Trust         Sec(L3)          trust-vr      ethernet1    Root
 3 DMZ           Sec(L3)          trust-vr      ethernet2    Root
 4 Self          Func             trust-vr      self         Root
 5 MGT           Func             trust-vr      null         Root
 6 HA            Func             trust-vr      ethernet8    Root
10 Global        Sec(L3)          trust-vr      null         Root
11 V1-Untrust    Sec(L2)          trust-vr      v1-untrust   Root
12 V1-Trust      Sec(L2)          trust-vr      v1-trust     Root
13 V1-DMZ        Sec(L2)          trust-vr      v1-dmz       Root
14 VLAN          Func             trust-vr      vlan1        Root
16 Untrust-Tun   Tun              trust-vr      hidden.1     Root

ns208-> _
```

It is a simple task to create a zone. However, before creating a zone, you should know the following:

- **Name** What you want to name your zone. It helps to be descriptive. If you have a DMZ for Web servers, naming it WebDMZ is more helpful than simply choosing DMZ02. This is really a personal preference. If you are creating a Layer 2 security zone, prefix the zone name with *L2-*.

- **Type of zone** You can create three types of zone: security Layer 3 zones, security Layer 2 zones, and tunnel zones.

To create a zoneusing WebUI:

1.   Access **Network | Zones** and click **New**.

2.   Provide a zone name.

3.   Choose the virtual router to which you want the zone to be assigned.

4.   Select the type of zone (Layer 3, Layer 2, or tunnel zones).

You may select other security options for the zone. Once a zone is created, you can modify any of its properties except its name. To change the name, you must delete the zone and recreate it using the desired name.

A NetScreen firewall can contain several types of interface. An interface allows traffic to enter a zone and leave a zone. If you want an interface to pass traffic, you need to bind it to a zone. Once you bind an interface to a zone, you can apply an IP address to the interface.

Binding an Interface to a Zone

First, let's bind an interface to a zone. We will bind the trust zone to the trust interface. This can be done in both the WebUI and the CLI. However, to change the zone you must first remove the IP address of the interface by setting it to **0.0.0.0/0**. Then you can select a new zone.

To bind an interface to a zone using the CLI, enter the command **set interface *interfacename* zone *zonename***, where *interfacename* is the name of the interface you want to bind and *zonename* is the name of the zone to which you want to bind the specified interface.

Setting Up IP Addressing

We will now assign the interface an IP address of 192.168.1.1 with a 24-bit subnet mask. This can be done in both the WebUI and the CLI. Modifying the IP address of an interface is the same as setting it up for the first time.

To assign an IP address to an interface using the CLI, enter the command **set interface *interfacename* ip *ipaddress netmask***, where *interfacename* is the name of the interface, *ipaddress* is the IP address you want to assign, and *netmask* is the netmask.

Tools & Traps…

Follow the Right Sequence

Consider an example: You have several soup bowls of increasing sizes. You place the smallest bowl upside down on the table and start placing the bigger bowls on top, one by one. Now try to pull out the innermost bowl! You can't.

Similarly, the sequence to define interfaces that we've just described needs to be followed. If you have already assigned an interface to a zone, you cannot assign it to a virtual router. To achieve this goal, you have to unbind the interface from the zone, disassociate the zone from the virtual router, and start afresh. Otherwise, you could receive the error message "**#untrust has interface bound. Remove them first.**"

Configuring Basic Network Routing

Our firewall is not yet fully functional. We need to follow these additional steps to completely set up the firewall:

1. Configure routing.

2. Create user, computer, and network objects.

3. Create service objects (if required).

4. Create policies.

When you want to connect to a remote network, you need to inform your firewall of the remote network's location. You would do this by adding network routes on your firewall. These routes tell the firewall where the remote network can be found. In this section, we look at adding a *static route* to access a remote network. We will also add a *default route*. A default route is also known as the route of last resort. So, if a packet on a device needs to get to a location and no other routes on the device are able to identify the next gateway for it to go to, it will use the default gateway. When a system is determining what route to use, it will always use the most specific route to the destination network first.

To add a static route using the CLI, enter the command **set route *ipaddress/netmask* interface *interfacename* gateway *gatewayip***, where *ipaddress* is the virtual router's IP address, *netmask* is the virtual router's netmask, *interfacename* is the next-hop gateway, and *gatewayip* is the IP address of the next-hop gateway.

To add a static route via the WebUI, access **Network | Routing | Destination** and click the **New** button on the top-right corner. Add the destination network and netmask. Choose the **Next Hop Virtual Router Name (untrust-vr)** or **Gateway (interface and Gateway IP address)**. Click **OK** to confirm.

Note that, in ScreenOS 5.3, you will find a Routing menu with four options: Destination, Source, Source Interface, and Virtual Routers. Previous versions have Routing Entries, Source Routing, and Virtual Routers options.

> **NOTE**
>
> Assume that we have *ethernet1* bound to a trust zone and in trust-vr. *Ethernet3* is in an untrust zone and in untrust-vr. All the packets that need to be routed to the Internet from trust-vr will have untrust-vr as the next hop. Untrust-vr will have a default route, 0.0.0.0/0, routed through *ethernet3*, which is connected to the Internet router. In essence, there is no direct connectivity to the Internet router from the trust-vr.

Configuring Security Policies

A *policy* or *access rule* permits, denies, or tunnels specified types of traffic between two points. You must first determine the source and destination zones for each policy. The *source zone* is where the source traffic is coming from. The *destination zone* is the location to which the destination traffic is going. Because zones are bound to interfaces, you are also inherently choosing which interface the traffic will use. This may help you when you're creating a policy, because the concept of zones is different from many other firewall products.

On a NetScreen firewall, there are three types of policy. Each policy contains the same five core components (Source Address, Destination Address, Service, Direction, Action). The only difference is the zones that each policy contains. A policy is classified by the source and destination zones that are used in the policy. There are three types of policy:

- **Intrazone policies** In an intrazone policy, the source and destination zones are the same.

- **Interzone policies** In an interzone policy, the source and destination zones are different.

- **Global policies** In a global policy, the source and destination zones are both in the global zone. The global zone is a special-purpose zone discussed later in this chapter.

NetScreen firewalls also have a default out-of-the-box policy that will drop any traffic that does not match any other policies. This default policy is a hidden global policy. Juniper offers it as a security feature to ensure that any traffic that you do not want to allow through is automatically dropped. This mitigates the risk of the firewall on the network by dropping any unmatched traffic. It is possible to change the behavior of this traffic from the CLI.

To override the default behavior (and therefore allow all traffic), enter the following command:

```
set policy default-permit-all
```

To change the firewall to deny all traffic by default, enter the following command:

```
unset policy default-permit-all
```

Components of a Security Policy

A policy is a single access control statement. When you create a policy, you must define five separate components:

- Source address (local area network or a specific computer)

- Destination address (remote network, remote server or a computer or domain)

- Service (HTTP, HTTPs, FTP, SMTP, and so on)

- Direction (inbound or outbound traffic)

- Action (permit, deny, or encrypt)

Address Book Entries

Source and destination IP addresses required to create a security policy are created and maintained in the address book. When using the command-line interface, you must create all your address book entries before you make your policies. However, when using the WebUI to create policies, you can create new address book entries as you create the policy. If you choose this latter method of creating address book entries while creating a policy in the WebUI, you can only specify the IP address and netmask for the entry. You will have to go back at a later time and edit the address book entry if you want to associate a name with the it. Figure 9.5 shows the WebUI address entry creation screen.

Figure 9.5 NetScreen WebUI Address Entry

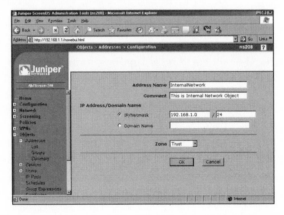

However, when you create a single network object, the netmask should be 32. Figure 9.6 shows a single computer object. The use of inappropriate netmask while creating the address book entries may produce varying results.

Figure 9.6 Creating An Address Book Entry for a Single Computer Object

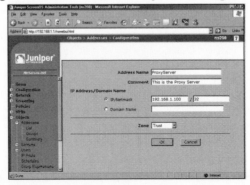

As you begin to amass many address objects, you will want a method to bring all of them together into logical containers. This is accomplished with the use of *address groups*. An address group is a logical container that groups together address objects. Address groups are very handy in creating policies.

Services

The next component in creating your policy is *services*. Services are the protocols that you use to access a system over the network. Services on a NetScreen firewall are represented by *service objects*. A service object is used to specify the applications that can be used in a policy. Every NetScreen firewall comes with a predefined set of services. The set of services that comes on your firewall varies by the version of ScreenOS you are running on your firewall.

Some protocols are also predefined because they function in a nonstandard way. One example is the FTP protocol. Because FTP sends special port redirects during its communication, Juniper has created a special mechanism to read inside the FTP connection to determine which ports to open up during the communication. Even though the predefined service allows only TCP port 21, the firewall is still able to dynamically allow ports based on the FTP communication.

It would be impractical for Juniper to create every service that exists. Juniper allows you to create your own custom service objects. These custom service objects can be used just like a predefined service object in your policy. To create a custom service object, you mention the protocol the custom service uses (TCP, UDP, or other), the source port, and the destination port.

Creating an Outbound Policy

Now that you are familiar with the components of creating policies, you can begin creating them. Polices are the main reason you are implementing your firewall in the first place—to control network traffic. You start by choosing the source zone and destination zone. In the policy creation screen, you choose the source network, destination network, service, and action. Optionally you may enable logging to monitor the traffic. Figure 9.7 shows an outbound policy.

Creating an Inbound Policy

Based on the network design, we might have to provide access to external users or networks to access services located in the internal network. Similar to the outbound policy, you have to choose the source and destination zones, source and destination networks, services that require access, and action (permit, deny, or tunnel). Dial-up VPN or remote offices may require access to your internal network. Careful planning is required when you're providing access to users outside your network. Additional security mechanisms such as virtual private network and authentication should be considered prior to allowing inbound access.

Figure 9.7 Configuring an Outbound Policy

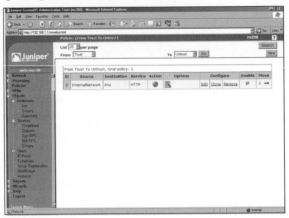

> **NOTE**
>
> Traffic returning as a response to a request from the internal network permitted by a security policy is not considered inbound traffic. Therefore, you may not require an explicit inbound policy to allow such traffic.

Configuring Network Address Translation

Juniper NetScreen has well-defined address translation architecture, functionality, and features. Probably no other firewall product has such clarity in defining Network Address Translation (NAT). Network professionals who are used to other firewalls may require a synchronization of terminologies from the other schools of thought to the NetScreen school of thought. Juniper NetScreen NAT features include:

- **Source NAT** Provides address translation on the source IP address. Source Port Address Translation (PAT) provides address translation on the source port. There are several methods of source NAT:

  - **Interface-based Source NAT** Provides the ability to NAT ingress traffic received in the defined interface, with NAT enabled with the last known egress interface. Source NAT is also performed by default.

  - **Managed IP (MIP)** Provides a static NAT functionality for one-to-one address translation. This feature can be used for either source or destination NAT capabilities.

- **Policy-based Source NAT** Similar in functionality to Interface-based Source NAT; the configuration is done on a firewall rule rather then a global interface setting.

- **Destination NAT** Provides address translation on the destination IP address. Destination PAT is another feature set that can be enabled at the same time, which provides address translation for the destination port. There are several methods of Destination NAT:

    - **Virtual IP (VIP)** Provides one-to-many address translation functionality. This feature can be used to translate the destination IP and the destination port at the same time.

    - **MIP** Can also be used in a destination one-to-one address translation and can be used for either Source or Destination NAT capabilities.

    - **Policy-based Destination NAT** Similar in functionality to Policy-based Source NAT except that it performs address translation on the destination IP or destination port on a per-firewall rule definition.

Source NAT

Source NAT is the most widely deployed method of address translation provided by vendors. It provides the ability to translate a source IP address to another IP address. By default (in NetScreen solutions), Source NAT is enabled on the interfaces by using the Trust security zone.

MIP

MIP provides the ability to perform a one-to-one mapping translation, which is referred to as *Static NAT*. This setting ensures that a host gets the same NAT every time traffic traverses the firewall, whether it's ingress or egress traffic. A MIP definition performs only NAT (not PAT); therefore, the IP address changes, but the protocol ports remain the same. Once a MIP is defined, a firewall rule is needed to allow access to the MIP.

All MIP definitions are placed within a global zone, no matter which security zone originally defined the MIP. Once a MIP has been defined, a firewall rule must be set up to allow for traffic destined for the MIP address. Within the firewall rule creation, the destination MIP selection can be from a global zone or the zone the MIP address was originally defined in.

The following example shows a typical MIP scenario. MIP is defined for you to access a Web server located on your private network from the Internet. Although this typically means an incoming translation, the Web server automatically gets the public IP for outbound translation, too.

To define the MIP on the Untrust interface (Ethernet3):

1. Go to **Network** | **Interface** | **Ethernet3** | **MIP** | **New** (see Figure 9.8).

Figure 9.8 Defining MIP

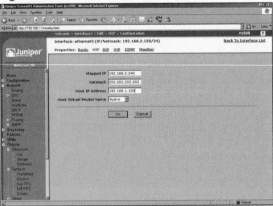

2.   Fill in the following:

Mapped IP: 192.168.2.240

Netmask: 255.255.255.255

Host IP Address: 192.168.1.100

Host Virtual Router Name: Trust-VR

3.   Define the firewall rule to permit traffic to the MIP. Go to **Policies | FROM | Untrust | TO | Trust | New** (see Figure 9.9).

4.   Fill in the following:

Source Address: Any

Destination Address: MIP (2.2.2.10)

Services: HTTP

Action: Permit

Note that in the lab scenario, the 192.168.2.0 range of addresses is used instead of public IP addresses. The 192.168.1.0 network is referred to as the *internal network*.

Policy-Based Source NAT

Policy-based source translations are accomplished by creating a firewall rule with Source NAT enabled. By default, the outbound interface's or egress interface's IP address in the destination zone is used as the newly translated source address. PAT is also enabled by default. The NetScreen policy is to use source NAT for traffic sourcing from the Trust side to the Untrust side. The Source NAT address will be the egress interface IP, in this case the Untrust Ethernet interface. Address objects must be defined before any firewall rule is created. Two address objects are created for this example, one for the Trust zone and one for the Untrust zone.

Figure 9.9 Configuring a Policy to Permit Traffic to the MIP

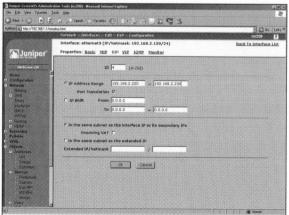

Dynamic IP

Several other methods can be used to translate the source address via the policy. These methods are primarily due to the functionality of dynamic IP pool (DIP pool) definitions. A DIP can be either a host range definition or a pool of address definitions. If it is a pool of address definitions, the pool must be in consecutive order. Therefore, it is important to note that no other IP(s) within that pool can be used anywhere else (e.g., a MIP definition).

DIP pool definition also offers the option to disable or enable PAT. Since the DIP pool is used only in Source NAT scenarios, PAT on the source ports can be utilized to increase the amount of usage for each address within the pool. Figure 9.10 illustrates the creation of DIP pool on the untrust (*ethernet3*) interface.

Figure 9.10 Creating a DIP Pool on the Untrust Interface

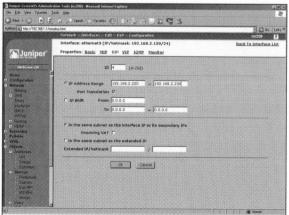

A DIP pool can also contain one IP range. For example, in defining the single IP address 2.2.2.2 within a DIP pool, the IP address range would be 2.2.2.2 ~ 2.2.2.2. This is an alternative way of using a different IP address than the one currently defined on the egress interface. It is recommended that you enable PAT within the DIP pool definition when you're creating for one IP range. Figure 9.11 shows the configuration of source translation by using DIP pool for the internal network. To access the Advanced Policy Settings screen, choose any policy and click the **Advanced** button at the bottom of the screen.

Figure 9.11 Configuring Source Translation Using the DIP Pool

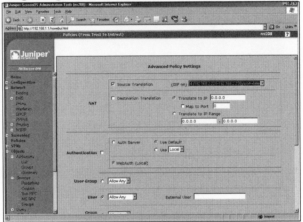

NOTE

When PAT is disabled in a DIP pool, the IP pool assignment remains the same for the host for all concurrent sessions. When PAT is enabled, the IP pool assignments rotate in a round-robin fashion for each new session.

Destination NAT

The following section illustrates how the NetScreen firewall solution handles destination address translations.

VIP

A VIP provides a one-to-many mapping scenario, whereas an MIP provides a one-to-one mapping. The one-to-many mappings a VIP performs are more related to a combination of destination Network Address Port Translations, or NAPTs.

VIP definitions are placed into the global zone, no matter which interface/security zone they were originally defined in. Once a VIP is defined, a firewall rule must be set up to allow for traffic destined for the MIP address. Within the firewall rule creation, the VIP can be selected from a global zone or the zone that the VIP address was originally defined in. Refer to the product documentation to find out the VIP capacity of various ScreenOS versions. Figure 9.12 shows single VIP 192.168.2.241 mapped to three different servers (192.168.1.10, 192.168.1.11, 192.168.1.12) offering HTTP, FTP, and SMPT services. As mentioned earlier, in real-life scenario 192.168.2.241 this example will be substituted with a public IP.

Figure 9.12 Configuring a Virtual IP

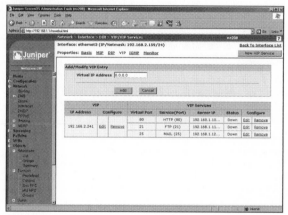

Policy-Based Destination NAT

Policy-based Destination NAT is also a subset setting within a firewall rule. Just like the Source-based NAT configuration, there is a separate definition in place to define a Destination NAT. Unlike Source NAT, there are no requirements to predefine settings on the interfaces. For example, you do not need to create a DIP pool before actually creating a destination NAT firewall rule. The address schemes for the newly translated destination are all defined within the firewall rule. Besides Destination NAT, a Destination PAT can also be defined. The options available to perform Destination NAT are as follows:

- Destination NAT to another IP
- Destination NAT to another IP with PAT to a different port
- Destination NAT to an IP range

NOTE

When you're using Destination NAT, it is important to know the NetScreen packet flow. Route lookup on the NetScreen device occurs *before* and *after* policy lookup. Policy lookup also entails Policy-based NAT functions. Therefore, there might be a need to create a route *before* or *after* a Policy-based NAT function takes place. Syngress Publishing has published a book, *Configuring NetScreen Firewall* (www.syngress.com/catalog/?pid=3120), that discusses these topics in detail.

Routing

NetScreen supports static routing and dynamic routing protocols such as RIP, OSPF, and BGP. Let's look briefly at configuring static and dynamic routing on NetScreen firewalls.

Static Routing

Static routing is often a simple way to set up a firewall and get it up and running within few minutes. A static route works well as long as the network is small and uncomplicated. However, when you have large networks, static routing might not be the right choice. You might have to implement routing protocols to perform automatic routing. However, static routes are always required. For example, when you want configure the default gateway on the untrust interface, you use static routing. You would require static routes when you configure the device to be in transparent mode.

To add a static route using the CLI, enter the command **set route** *ipaddress/netmask* **interface** *interfacename* **gateway** *gatewayip*, where *ipaddress* is the virtual router's IP address, *netmask* is the virtual router's netmask, *interfacename* is the next-hop gateway, and *gatewayip* is the IP address of the next-hop gateway.

Routing Information Protocol

The Routing Information Protocol (RIP) is one of the oldest routing protocols available today. It is highly inefficient, but this of course is made up for by its simple configuration. Almost all routing devices typically support the RIP protocol, even home user Cable/DSL routers. There are two versions of RIP: RIP version 1 and RIP version 2. NetScreen firewalls support RIP version 2. Even though the RIP protocol is old, it is mature and functions well in small networks.

RIP Concepts

The RIP protocol sends update messages to connected routers at regular intervals and when the network changes. This makes RIP a "chatty" routing protocol because it constantly sends information out to the network. RIP uses only one mechanism to determine the best route. It counts a hop or how many hops away a network is. It has a limitation of using up to 15 hops of distance. If a route's metric reaches 16 hops, the destination is considered unreachable.

Basic RIP Configuration

RIP is created on a per-virtual-router basis. To use RIP, you need to perform four simple steps on your firewall:

1   Configure a virtual router ID.

2   On the virtual router, create a RIP routing instance.

3   Activate the new RIP instance.

4   Configure the network interfaces to have RIP enabled.

Use the following steps to configure RIP via the WebUI:

1.   Access **Network | Routing | Virtual Router**.

2.   Click the **Edit** link of the virtual router you want to modify.

3.   Enable the **Virtual Router ID** option.

4.   Use the **Custom** field to enter an ID for the RIP.

5.   Click **Apply**.

6.   Click **Create RIP Instance**.

7   Enable the **Enable RIP** option (Figure 9.13).

8.   Click **OK**.

9.   Access **Network | Interface**.

10.   Click the **Edit** link of the interface on which you want to enable RIP.

11.   Click the **RIP** link at the top of the page.

12.   Enable the **Enable** option.

13.   Click **OK**.

Figure 9.13 Enabling RIP

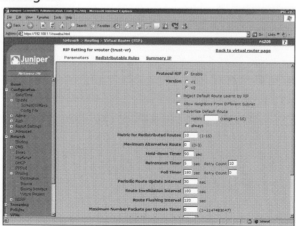

Use the following to configure RIP via the CLI:

```
ns208-> set vrouter trust-vr router-id 255
ns208-> set vrouter trust-vr protocol rip
ns208-> set vrouter trust-vr protocol rip enable
ns208-> set interface ethernet3 protocol rip enable
```

Use the following to verify RIP configuration via the CLI:

```
ns208-> get vrouter trust-vr
ns208-> get interface ethernet3
```

Open Shortest Path First

OSPF is a link-state protocol and is considered one of the best protocols to run for your internal network. The *Open* in OSPF represents that it is an open-standard protocol. OSPF sends out only periodic updates and is not considered a chatty protocol. It is extremely efficient and is supported by most modern routing equipment.

OSPF Concepts

Let's review a few OSPF concepts. These concepts are common throughout the configuration of OSPF as well as across various vendors' devices. Routers are grouped into *areas*. By default, all routers participating in OSPF are grouped into area 0, also known as area 0.0.0.0. On occasion you will want to divide your network into multiple areas. This is typically done in large networks.

Each router that participates in an OSPF network is classified as one of four types of router:

- **Internal router** A router with all interfaces belonging to the same area.
- **Backbone router** A router that has an interface in the backbone area. The backbone area is also known as area 0.
- **Area border router** A router that connects to multiple areas.
- **AS boundary router** A router that borders another autonomous system (AS).

Basic OSPF Configuration

Configuring OSPF is similar to configuring RIP because it is enabled on a per-virtual-router basis. Each virtual router is capable of supporting one instance of OSPF at a time. To use OSPF, you need to perform four simple steps on your firewall:

1   Configure a virtual router ID.
2   On the virtual router, create an OSPF instance.

3   Activate the new OSPF instance.

4   Configure the network interfaces to have OSPF enabled.

Use the following steps to configure OSPF via the WebUI:

1. Access **Network | Routing | Virtual Router**.

2. Click the **Edit** link of the virtual router for which you will configure OSPF.

3. Enable the **Virtual Router ID** option.

4. Enter an ID in the text box labeled **Custom**, next to the radio button you selected.

5. Click **Apply**.

6. Click **Create OSPF Instance**.

7. Enable the **OSPF Enabled** option.

8. Click **OK**.

9. Access **Network | Interface**.

10. Click the **Edit** link of the interface you want to enable OSPF on.

11. Click the link labeled **OSPF**.

12. Enable the **Enable Protocol OSPF** option.

13. Click OK.

Use the following to configure OSPF via the CLI:

```
ns208-> set vrouter trust-vr router-id 255
ns208-> set vrouter trust-vr protocol ospf
ns208-> set vrouter trust-vr protocol ospf enable
ns208-> set interface ethernet3 protocol ospf enable
```

Use the following to verify OSPF configuration via the CLI:

```
ns208-> get vrouter trust-vr
ns208-> get interface ethernet3
```

Border Gateway Protocol

BGP is the core routing protocol used on the Internet. BGP routing information is not broadcast like RIP or OSPF. Two BGP peers connect to each other form a Transmission Control Protocol (TCP) session. This session is then used to transmit all the routing data. BGP is a very complex protocol to implement and manage.

Use the following steps to configure BGP via the WebUI:

1. Access **Network | Routing | Virtual Router**.

2. Click the **Edit** link of the virtual router on which you will create a BGP instance.

3. Enable the **Virtual Router ID** option.

4. Enter an ID in the **Custom** field next to the radio button you selected.

5. Click **Apply**.

6. At the bottom of the page, click the **Create BGP Instance** link.

7. Enter the number of your autonomous system in the **AS Number** field.

8. Enable the **BGP Enabled** option.

9. Click **OK**.

10. Access **Network | Interface**.

11. Click the **Edit** link of the interface that you want to enable BGP on.

12. Click the **BGP** link.

13. Enable the **Enable Protocol BGP** option.

14. Click **OK**.

Use the following to configure BGP via the CLI:

```
ns208-> set vrouter trust-vr router-id 255
ns208-> set vrouter trust-vr protocol bgp 10245
ns208-> set vrouter trust-vr protocol bgp enable
ns208-> set interface ethernet3 protocol BGP enable
```

Use the following to verify BGP configuration via the CLI:

```
ns208-> get vrouter trust-vr
ns208-> get interface ethernet3
```

NetScreen Advanced Features

Because standard firewall features are not strong enough for more demanding environments, the mid- to high-range NetScreen firewalls provide support for the NetScreen Redundancy Protocol (NSRP). This protocol is the heart of all the high-availability (HA) options covered here. NSRP has been available for several years and was originally referred to as *HA*. HA setups are now commonly referred to as *NSRP setups* or just *running NSRP*. NetScreen firewalls can be implemented in Active/Passive, Active/Active, and Full-Mesh configurations. Figure 9.14 shows a Full-Mesh, highly available network design.

NetScreen Failover

NSRP is the protocol that redundant NetScreen devices use to talk to each other when they're running in various HA configurations. It is the language that allows them to exchange state information and make decisions. One of the main goals of HA is to have multiple redundant systems, wherein a second system can take over in case the first one fails. This is commonly achieved by duplicating the hardware. As with the NetScreen firewalls, any HA setup that is using NSRP implies that there are at least two firewalls of the same model working together. This group of firewalls is called an *NSRP cluster* or simply a *cluster*.

Figure 9.14 Full-Mesh Network Design

Virtualizing the Firewall

To minimize the amount of downtime caused when the first system in a cluster fails, it is important to ensure that the second system knows precisely what the first system is doing so that it can pick up without any interruption. In effect, what you want to do is shift the entire running firewall onto new hardware. When looked at this way, it makes sense to turn the actual firewall into a virtual firewall that has some hardware associated with it. This is precisely what is done in NetScreen firewalls. When NSRP is enabled, a virtual security device (VSD) is created, and the configuration for the physical interfaces change to apply to virtual interfaces called virtual security interfaces (VSI). The fact that these virtual interfaces are in turn associated with actual hardware is not important; all the configurations are done on the VSI. NSRP then takes care of associating the VSI to the correct physical interface.

By abstracting the firewall in this manner, it becomes relatively easy to move the firewall between different hardware units as necessary. It also becomes possible to have more than one VSD per physical firewall. A VSD is not a standalone entity; rather, it is always part of a *VSD group*, which spans both of the NetScreens in the cluster. There is one VSD per VSD group on each cluster member, and the VSD configuration is identical everywhere. VSD only acts as a container for the VSIs. Other configuration items, such as policies and routing, apply across all VSDs on a NetScreen.

Within a VSD group, one VSD is the designated *master VSD*. This VSD is the currently active VSD that is processing and forwarding traffic. The other VSD in the VSD group is the *backup*, which is located on the other NetScreen. The backup VSD is not processing traffic, which means that only one of the firewalls is active and processing traffic at any given time. This is known as an *Active/Passive setup*.

It is important to note that IP addresses assigned to a VSI follow the master VSD. This is slightly different from how Virtual Router Redundancy Protocol (VRRP) works. In VRRP, the backup unit has its own IP address and simply acquires the primary IP address upon failover. With NSRP, only one interface IP address floats between the NetScreens as necessary.

The *manage-ip* settings stay bound to the physical interface and do not follow the VSD. It would not be very useful if the IP addresses were also moved across to the active firewall, since that would render the backup firewall unreachable for management purposes. Thus, when the backup firewall becomes the master, it already has the manage IP address and then simply adds the VSI address.

Understanding NSRP States

As mentioned, the fundamental concept of NSRP is duplicating hardware—to be able to move the firewall functionality around as necessary using VSDs. As a consequence, at any given time each VSD is in one of six states, which determines the current role of the VSD. The possible states are:

- Master
- Primary backup
- Backup
- Initial
- Ineligible
- Inoperable

Understanding which state is used for what purpose is central to monitoring and controlling your NSRP cluster. Instead of simply explaining what each state is, let's look at the order in which the VSD transitions between the states.

When a VSD is first created, either due to a reboot or a configuration change, it is put in the *initial* state. While in this state, the VSD learns which other NetScreens are participating in the VSD group, synchronizes that state with the other VSDs if needed, and possibly partakes in the election process for the VSD that should become the master.

From the initial state, the VSD can move into either the *master* or *backup* state. If it wins the election process, this VSD takes on the task of processing traffic. If it does not win, it transitions into the backup state.

The election process used to determine the master VSD is reasonably straightforward. First, if there is no other VSD available, this VSD automatically wins the election. Second, if two VSDs are starting up at the same time, the winner is determined based on the configured priorities (**set nsrp vsd-group id X priority N**). The unit with the lowest priority value is the preferred VSD. If both VSDs have the same priority or if the priority is not configured, the VSD with the lowest Media Access Control (MAC) address wins.

Normally, an election is held only if there is no master VSD in the VSD group. However, if the starting VSD has preemption enabled (**set nsrp vsd-group X preempt**), it can force an election, which it would probably win due to having a better priority than the old master VSD.

A VSD in the backup state checks to see if there is already a primary backup VSD, and if there isn't, it makes itself the primary backup for the VSD group. As the primary backup, it is responsible for taking over the traffic processing should the master fail or step down. From the primary backup state, there are generally two directions the VSD can take: It either ends up promoted to master due to the old master VSD disappearing or it goes into the *inoperable* state.

A VSD puts itself into the inoperable state if it detects a failure that would prevent it from processing traffic. If this VSD were the master, any failure that resulted in a failover would result in this VSD becoming inoperable. In this state, the VSD does not participate in elections for the position of master VSD; however, it does continue to check for the failure condition. If that condition is remedied, as can be the case if the failure was caused by a monitored interface going down and subsequently brought back up, the VSD will progress from the inoperable state back into the initial state again.

The *ineligible* state is entered only by manual intervention. It is the *administratively down* state of the VSD. If for any reason you want to prevent the VSD from participating in the master election, thereby preventing it from processing traffic, you can put the VSD into the ineligible state using the *set nsrp vsd-group id X mode ineligible* command. The VSD group stays in that state until you use the corresponding *unset* command or NetScreen is rebooted without having saved the configuration. (The ineligible state can be kept across reboots if you save the configuration after entering the command.)

This explains the various NSRP states that a VSD can be in. If you are confident in this knowledge, you will have no problem understanding what the VSDs in your cluster are doing.

Building an NSRP Cluster

Before you can configure the NetScreens to be used in your NSRP cluster, you must do the cabling. For the traffic links, the three main choices are to connect the firewalls directly to the routers, connect the firewalls to the routers via switches or connect the firewalls in a full mesh. The HA links can either be directly connected between the NetScreens or connected via switches.

Adding a NetScreen to an NSRP Cluster

To add a NetScreen to an NSRP cluster, additional configuration is needed. The good news is that this is easy to do for a simple NSRP cluster. Once you have made it part of the cluster, you will probably want to add a few more configuration settings to make it fail over when appropriate. A NetScreen that has an NSRP cluster ID *greater* than zero is considered part of a cluster; valid cluster IDs range from 1 to 7.

Synchronizing the Configuration

Once you have cabled the NSRP cluster the way you want it, you must address the configuration side of things. Cluster members must have *near-identical* configurations to operate properly. The reason for near-identical and not *identical* is that some aspects must be unique to each NetScreen, including things such as the hostname and the management IP addresses.

Although it is possible to copy the cluster configuration from another cluster member using the *exec nsrp sync global-config* command, personal experience leads us to recommend configuring from scratch because it might not take a long time to configure an NSRP cluster.

The advantages of synchronizing the configuration using this method are that you know precisely what is going on at all times and there is no real risk of duplicate IP addresses conflicting with each other between the firewalls. This makes it possible to use this procedure safely when you're logged in remotely. Also, having the configuration files stored side by side makes it easy to compare them and see the differences using the *diff* command for UNIX and the *WinDiff* command for Windows.

Determining When to Failover–The NSRP Ways

Similar to the options provided on the low-end range of NetScreen firewalls, NSRP provides a number of methods that you can use to determine when a failover should be initiated. The options in some cases might seem identical to their low-end cousins, but do not confuse them—they are distinctly different, albeit subtly so.

Here is a list of reasons to fail over:

- Software crashes

- Hardware or power failure

- Link failure on monitored interfaces or zones

- Unavailability of one or more tracked IP addresses

The first two items, software and hardware failure, are detected automatically, without any need for explicit configuration. The last two items are available to provide flexibility in determining whether to fail over or not and must be explicitly enabled to be in effect. The NSRP IP tracking feature checks for the availability of a particular IP by regularly contacting it.

Looking into an NSRP Cluster

It would be impossible to provide listings of all the possible outputs from *get nsrp,* and we won't attempt to do so here. Also, there is a wealth of information available from the NSRP subcommand printouts; do a **get nsrp?** to see the options. Issue a **get nsrp** command on one of the cluster members and go through the output.

Taking Advantage of the Full NSRP

NSRP-Lite, a scaled-down version of NSRP, has a limitation. In the case of failover, any existing session and VPN information (among other things) is lost. Juniper NetScreen has an answer to this problem. It is called *Run-Time Object (RTO) mirroring*, and it is available only with the full NSRP. Enabling RTO means all the dynamic information is actively mirrored between the VSDs. In case of a failover, all this state information is already available on the new master VSD and can resume operation with a minimum of interference to the traffic flow. Examples are ARP cache entries, session table entries, IPSec Phase 2 security associations, certificates, and DHCP leases.

Another shortcoming of NSRP-Lite is that in an NSRP cluster, one firewall ends up sitting unutilized for most of the time. It can be hard to justify the purchase of an additional firewall when management counters with the argument, "It says here that it will not actually be used. Why do you expect me to spend money on something that will not be used?" Such setups are known as Active/Passive setups—one firewall is active and the other is passive. NSRP provides the ability to create Active/Active configurations, in which both firewalls actively handle traffic. Designing the network for Active/Active setups requires careful consideration, but once you have it set up and working, your network will run very nicely.

Failing Over

A chapter on HA and NSRP would not be complete without a more in-depth dissection of what happens when a failover occurs. We have already seen the reasons that a failover could occur. Additionally, the administrator can manually request a failover for maintenance purposes.

Once the primary backup VSD has determined that it must become the master VSD, a few things happen. First, the VSD promotes itself to master to prevent any other VSD from doing the same thing. Second, if the VSD has any links down, an attempt is made to bring them up. If a monitored link cannot be brought up, the VSD relinquishes its role as master and puts itself in the inoperable state.

Assuming that the VSD is the newly promoted master VSD with all relevant links up, it proceeds to send out gratuitous ARP requests. This is a very important aspect of the failover. These ARP requests tell the neighboring network nodes that the IP addresses configured on the VSIs are now reachable via a different path than before. This will cause switches to update their forwarding tables and routers to update their ARP tables. By default, four ARP packets are sent out on each interface.

As soon as the neighboring nodes have adjusted to this change, traffic is sent to this VSD instead of the old one. If RTO mirroring was enabled before the failover, this VSD already has a copy of the all run-time state and proceeds to handle traffic with no further disruption. Note that some packets might be lost during the time it takes for the neighboring nodes to reroute their traffic flows to the second NetScreen.

Configuring a Stateful Failover

Configuring failover includes creating NSRP clusters and defining VSD, VSI, and the interfaces to be monitored for a failover.

1. From the WebUI **Network | NSRP | Cluster**, provide the cluster ID and passwords for secure communication and authentication (Figure 9.15).

Figure 9.15 Creating NSRP Cluster

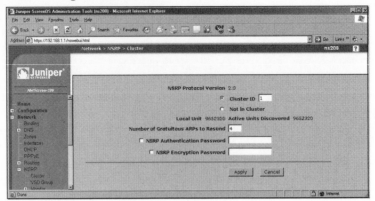

2. From the WebUI **Network | NSRP | VSD Group | Configuration**, set the group priority (Figure 9.16).

Figure 9.16 Setting VSD Group Priority

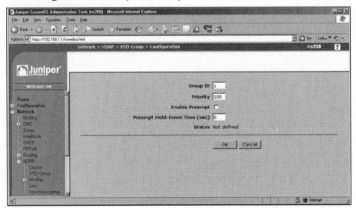

3. From the WebUI **Network | NSRP | Monitor | Interface | Edit**, choose the interfaces to be monitored and their priorities (weight) (Figure 9.17).

4. From the WebUI **Network | NSRP | Monitor | Zone | Edit**, you may choose the zones to be monitored and the weight (Figure 9.18).

5. From the WebUI **Network | NSRP | Synchronization**, choose the synchronization parameters (Figure 9.19).

Figure 9.17 Monitoring Interfaces

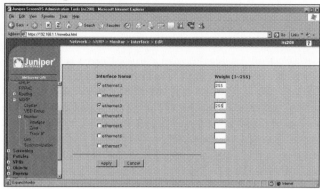

Figure 9.18 Monitoring Zones

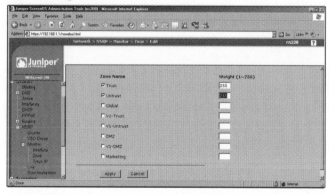

Figure 9.19 NSRP Synchronization Parameters

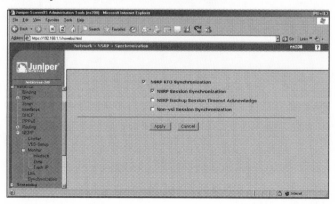

WARNING

For a successful failover for Active/Passive, Active/Active, and Full-Mesh configurations, apart from the NetScreen configurations, cabling the devices appropriately plays an important role. Physical wiring from the firewalls to internal switches and routers and between the firewalls requires careful planning.

Web Filtering

URL or Web filtering is the process of examining HTTP requests for content. Requests to inappropriate sites like those that host pornography, racism, or other offensive material can be blocked using this feature. This works by comparing the requested URL against a database of classified sites. URLs can be categorically permitted or denied with a variety of configuration settings, which depend on the filtering server/service used. These services charge a recurring fee for updates to the database because new sites are constantly created on the Internet. The URL filtering software provides Internet usage reports and also keeps track of repeat violators.

NetScreen firewalls now support the SurfControl Redirect protocol as well as the WebSense Redirect protocol, but not both at the same time. New integrated mode on the NS-HSC, NS-5GT, NS-25, and NS-50 provides URL filtering by loading a filter database directly on the device. Figure 9.20 shows the URL Redirect mode selection screen.

Figure 9.20 Choosing the URL Redirect Mode

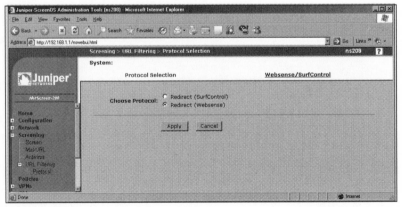

WebSense Redirect Mode

It is fairly straightforward to configure on the NetScreen device; the majority of work required is on the WebSense server side: configuring users, user groups, policies, and exceptions. To use WebSense with ScreenOS 5.3, select it as the protocol to use for URL filtering.

From the firewall side of things, setup is a snap. First, enable the **Enable URL Filtering** option. Next, type the IP address (or DNS domain name if configured for your WebSense server and your NetScreen has a DNS server configured) into the **Server Name** field. Enter the port number that the WebSense server is listening on for URL validation requests into the **Server Port** field (the default port is 15868). Now set a reasonable **Communication Timeout** value (10 is the default, but you might need more if the WebSense server is being accessed via a VPN). At this point, if the server is up and properly configured, a click on the yellow circle next to **Server Connection Status** should show that the server is running. Figure 9.21 shows the WebSense configuration screen.

There's also an option to set the behavior of the firewall in the event that the URL server cannot be contacted. Using this option to either block all HTTP or permit all HTTP is a policy decision you'll have to make on your own, depending on your business requirements and the stability of your WebSense setup.

Figure 9.21 URL Filtering Configuration with WebSense

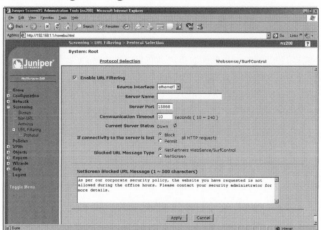

Once you configure WebSense and confirm its reachability, you might want to configure the policy to enable URL filtering. Edit the already created policy or create a new policy and enable the URL filtering check box to monitor the traffic and perform URL filtering. Figure 9.22 shows a policy with URL filtering enabled. Notice the WWW icon under the options.

SurfControl Redirect Mode

SurfControl Web Filter for Juniper Networks Security Devices is a competitor to WebSense, and with ScreenOS you now have a choice of URL filtering services to select from. Like WebSense, SurfControl will work with 512MB of RAM, but 1GB or more is preferred. SurfControl requires either an external MS-SQL database or an internal Microsoft Desktop Engine 2000 (MSDE2000) database. If an MSDE2000 database is not already installed, SurfControl will download and install it for you, similarly to the way WebSense handles a missing Web server, which is very handy. But unlike WebSense, SurfControl has an Integrated mode that uses public servers and does not require local installation.

Figure 9.22 A Policy With URL Filtering Enabled

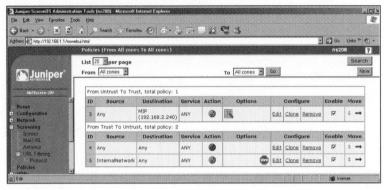

Since it's essentially the same concept, the configuration settings for SurfControl Redirect mode are the same as WebSense Redirect mode. To use SurfControl with ScreenOS 5.3, you'll first need to select it as the protocol to use for URL filtering. Then fill in the options as you would in WebSense, such as turning on **Enable URL Filtering**, setting a **Server Name**, **Server Port** (the default for the Surf Control Filter Protocol (SCFP) is 62252), and a **Communications Timeout** value. Now it's time to check the server availability.

SurfControl Integrated Mode

This mode is available on only the newer low- to midrange model NetScreen firewalls: the NS-HSC, NS-5GT, NS-25, and NS-50. SurfConrol Integrated mode also requires a feature key to activate. To use SurfControl with ScreenOS 5.3, you'll first need to select it as the protocol to use for URL filtering. The protocol used for this mode is the SurfControl Content Portal Authority (SC-CPA) protocol.

Once Integrated mode is selected, configuration options for this mode appear. Integrated mode URL filtering supports the concept of blacklists (always deny regardless of classification) and whitelists (always permit regardless of classification) right on the device. These lists, as well as custom URL lists, are created by accessing the **Screening | URL Filtering** option. In the custom list edit window, add a name to this category (Whitelist, Blacklist, Competitors, etc.), add your first URL, and click the **Apply** button. The category name will be saved and locked and the URL added to the list. Add more URLs (up to a maximum of 20) by entering them in the **URL** field and clicking the **Apply** button. When you are done adding URLs, click the **OK** button to save.

Antivirus

ScreenOS 5.0 introduced the new antivirus engine from Trend Micro. This feature is supported on middle- to low-end devices from NS-HSC through NS-208. A license key is required to activate the feature. Files sent via HTTP, FTP, POP3, IMAP, and SMTP are inspected for viruses right on the device. Access **Screening | Antivirus** to configure global antivirus parameters.

An antivirus is only as good as its virus database, so to stay protected, you need to stay updated. These settings are found by accessing **Screen | Antivirus | Scan Manager** in your WebUI. In this page, you will find important information such as AV license entitlement as well as how current your virus definitions are.

Activating AV couldn't be easier. Currently, there is only one AV object on the device (once the license is activated). Click **Objects**, and select **Antivirus**. Select the **scan-mgr** object from the **Available AV Object Names** column, and click the **<<** button to move it to the **Attached AV Object Names** column. Be sure to click the **OK** button to save the setting. Do this for each policy that needs antivirus scanning on any of the supported protocols.

Summary

Juniper NetScreen presents a variety of options, from low-end appliances for remote offices to high-end systems. Deep inspection (DI) technology, SecureOS, and features such as Web filtering and antivirus scanning extend the functionality of a firewall.

Solutions such as security zones, virtual routers, and virtual systems are a boon for enterprise security administrators to use to nail down the access and security levels using well-defined policies. Web-based interface and graphical NSM provides all the tools you'll need for remotely configuring and managing security devices.

The Juniper NetScreen product range provides comprehensive security for enterprises that are considering strengthening their DMZs. Enterprises can consider building a complete solution based on NetScreen firewall appliances, IDP, and SSL-VPN appliances.

Solutions Fast Track

NetScreen Basics

☑   The Juniper NetScreen firewall products have both the ICSA and Common Criteria certifications.

☑   Trend Micro antivirus is used for virus scanning on the firewall product line.

☑   Zones are used to separate logical areas inside of the firewall.

☑   Virtual routers allow for multiple routing tables in a single device.

☑   Deep inspection allows you to look inside of a packet for specific attacks.

☑   The Juniper NetScreen firewall design is based on ASICs, to increase its performance.

Securely Managing Juniper NetScreen Firewalls

☑ There are three methods for managing your firewall: the WebUI, the CLI, and the NSM.

☑ Physical interfaces can host multiple IP addresses on each interface.

☑ A policy is used to allow or deny traffic that passes through the firewall gateway.

NetScreen Configuration Basics

☑ There are three types of policy on a NetScreen firewall: intrazone, interzone, and global.

☑ The WebUI and the CLI can both be used for creating policies. However, it might be easier for people to use the WebUI because of its GUI nature.

☑ Each virtual router contains its own routing domain and routing table.

☑ Every NetScreen firewall supports at least two virtual routers.

☑ Virtual routers allow you to separate your routing design into separate routing domains on the same device.

☑ RIP is a distance vector protocol. Using RIP is the easiest of all the dynamic routing protocols supported by the NetScreen firewall.

☑ OSPF is an efficient link-state routing protocol. OSPF is more complicated to configure than RIP.

☑ BGP is used as the primary routing protocol on the Internet and requires careful planning to configure.

☑ Source NAT and Destination NAT options are available for address translation.

☑ A virtual system is a unique security domain inside a NetScreen firewall.

☑ Virtual systems can use components shared by the root system.

☑ You can define a virtual system so it will use its own virtual router.

☑ HA is all about risk mitigation; finding the right balance between availability and cost is not always easy.

☑ NSRP is the protocol used between firewalls configured in redundant clusters.

☑ VSDs are the logical containers used in configuring NSRP.

☑ VSIs are logical interfaces belonging to a VSD, which are configured with the IP addresses that should be possible to transfer between the firewalls when a failover occurs.

☑ When a failover occurs, the newly elected master VSD sends out gratuitous ARPs to announce the topology change to neighboring network nodes.

☑ SurfControl and WebSense are the two URL filtering options available with the Juniper NetScreen appliances.

☑ TrendMicro Antivirus is available on low-end appliances and can be integrated into policies for checking traffic viruses and malicious content.

Frequently Asked Questions

The following Frequently Asked Questions, answered by the authors of this book, are designed to both measure your understanding of the concepts presented in this chapter and to assist you with real-life implementation of these concepts. To have your questions about this chapter answered by the author, browse to **www.syngress.com/solutions** and click on the **"Ask the Author"** form.

Q: Security zones seem like a confusing concept. Other vendors get along with out them, so why use them?

A: Zones are excellent tools to provide logical separation between multiple areas of your network. As you will see in later chapters, in creating policies, zones simplify the process by identifying the two separate areas of your network you want to access each other. This can prevent you from accidentally creating access rules that will allow access to sections of your network that you did not intend to be accessible.

Q: Why would NetScreen limit the total number of policies that each device can have?

A: Each NetScreen device is designed to provide a specific rate of performance. Each NetScreen device could most likely support more policies, but that could degrade its performance. For each policy in the list, the NetScreen firewall checks it from a top-down perspective. Therefore, the longer the list of policies, the more time it takes to traverse the line.

Q: I have looked at the command-line interface and I do not feel that it is very effective to use. Why should I even use it when the WebUI is easier and quicker?

A: The WebUI is a very useful tool and it should be used in conjunction with the CLI. Each has its own pros and cons. Console access and CLI are useful when either the IP address of the management interface is not known or you want to set basic configuration parameters before accessing the WebUI.

Q: Is it possible to use IP address ranges as address objects?

A: When creating address book objects, you can only create objects based on subnetting. Even when you make a single host object, you are making it with a 32-bit mask only allowing for a single host. If you require a range of hosts, see if you can fit it into a subnet. If not, however, you will be required to create each host individually and then place them into a group.

Q: I am familiar with using other firewall software, and I am confused about why you would bind address objects to zones.

A: Having address objects inside of zones just furthers the zone concept. It is essentially binding that object into the logical location of a zone. Because most other firewall software programs do not use zones, they essentially have no need to organize address objects in any way other than by type.

Q: When would you need more than one virtual router?

A: Most people using NetScreen firewalls today are using only a single virtual router. This makes the NetScreen firewall function like a traditional routing firewall. However, when you want to use dynamic routing protocols on your device, using a virtual router is a great idea. This allows you to separate your two routing domains easily and effectively.

Q: What is the point of virtual routers?

A: Virtual routers are very effective when you're using dynamic routing protocols. This is typically when they are used.

Q: What are the purposes of using dynamic routing?

A: Dynamic routing allows you to dynamically update your network configuration. It is usually a requirement when you're using multiple locations with multiple subnets. Integrating it onto your firewall allows for seamless updates to your network and can ensure that resources can be accessed from almost anywhere in case of a link failure.

Q: Why doesn't the NetScreen firewall support IGRP or EIGRP?

A: Both IGRP and EIGRP are Cisco proprietary protocols.

Q: What are the advantages of using NAT?

A: NAT conserves IP addresses, provides a hidden identity for host(s), has the ability to use nonroutable addresses from the RFC 1918 space, addresses overlapping subnets, and maintains a cohesive network.

Q: What is the difference between a MIP and a VIP?

A: MIP provides a one-to-one Static NAT function, whereas VIP provides a one-to-many NAT function.

Q: What are the advantages of using Policy-based NAT over Interface-based NAT?

A: The number-one reason to choose Policy-based NAT over Interface-based NAT is the scalability. With Interface-based NAT, you are limited to performing address translation in only one flow direction; only the source address can be translated, you cannot turn off PAT, and it requires all ingress traffic to be translated. With Policy-based NAT, you can uniquely define address translation on a per-firewall rule definition, giving you the ability to control address translation flows, perform source and/or destination translation, and the turn PAT on and off.

Q: Can Interface-based NAT and Policy-based NAT configurations co-exist?

A: Yes. Interface-based NAT and Policy-based NAT can co-exist together. It is recommended that Interface-based NAT be disabled (set to Route mode) and that you use Policy-based NAT for your address translation needs.

Q: What is a DIP?

A: A DIP is used for Policy-based Source NAT functionality. A DIP can consist of one to many IP ranges.

Q: Virtual systems seem like a great idea, but are they practical for my environment?

A: Organizations very rarely use virtual systems. They are only practical to use when you require many separate firewalls. Only large organizations and ISPs have the type of environment that requires virtual systems. Even though the application of virtual systems may be beneficial to you, the cost may be prohibitive.

## Chapter 10

Firewall and DMZ Design: ISA Server 2005

Solutions in this chapter:

- Network Services Segment Configuration Options
- ISA Firewall Stateful Packet Inspection and Request/Response Paths
- Multiple Departmental Networks/Security Zones Connected to a Backbone Network
- Example Network and Perimeter Network Design
- Creating the ISA Firewall Network Representing the Corporate Network on the Network Services Perimeter
- Creating the Corpnet ISA Firewall Network
- Creating the Network Rule on the Network Services Perimeter ISA Firewall, Setting a Route Relationship between the Corporate Network and the Network Services Segment
- Creating an Intradomain Communications Access Rule on the Network Services Perimeter ISA Firewall and a DNS Server Publishing Rule
- Making Access Rules Running Outbound Access from the Network Services Segment on the Perimeter ISA Firewall
- Creating the Network Services Access Rules Giving Corpnet Clients Access to Network Services
- Configuring the Default Internal Network on the Edge ISA Firewall
- Creating a Routing Table Entry on the Edge ISA Firewall
- Joining the Edge ISA Firewall to the Domain
- Making Access Rules on the Edge ISA Firewall; Controlling Outbound Access from Corpnet Hosts; Hosts on the Network Services Segment
- Making Publishing Rules on the Edge ISA Firewall for Inbound Connections to Exchange Server Mail Services
- Creating a Routing Table Entry on Network Clients (Required Only If No LAN Routers Are Installed)

- Joining the Network Clients to the Domain
- Creating and Configuring DNS Entries in the Domain DNS
- Configuring the Firewall and Web Proxy Client Settings on the Edge ISA Firewall, and Enabling Autodiscovery
- Installing the Firewall Client Share on the Network Services Segment File Server
- Installing the Firewall Client on the Network Clients
- Connecting the Corporate Network Clients to the Network Services Segment

Introduction

The ISA firewall can act in a number of roles: as a front-end edge firewall that sits in front of the entire company, as a back-end firewall located behind another edge firewall that might be an ISA firewall or another type of firewall, or as a perimeter network firewall that walls off critical network servers and services from the rest of the network. We'll focus on the third configuration in this chapter.

In spite of eye-catching headlines about the death of the DMZ and the imminent demise of network security zones, the fact is that we who live in the trenches still need to live with the current reality, where network perimeters need to be defined to provide access controls on hosts connecting to other hosts belonging to different security zones. And although Network Access Protection (NAP; expected to be implemented in Longhorn/Vista) and IPSec-based domain isolation hold a lot of promise, there are and will be significant technological hurdles that have to be jumped before those methodologies will be applicable for widespread use.

Instead of proclaiming the death of the DMZ, security experts should be making the clarion call for increased *perimeterization*. You'll go a long way toward improving your network's security position by grouping hosts into different security zones, and putting firewalls and other network security devices between those zones that enable strong access controls on communications between those zones.

In this chapter, we'll examine the requirements and procedures involved with creating a network services segment separated from the rest of the corporate network by an ISA firewall. You can put an ISA firewall in front of the network services located on the services segment to help protect those critical network services from being adversely affected by outbreaks that take place on other network segments.

The key concept here is that only required communications are allowed to and from the network services segment; all other communications are blocked. In addition to limiting communications only to the hosts and protocols that are required for access, we will leverage the ISA firewall's advanced stateful packet and application layer inspection mechanisms to help secure the communications allowed to the network services segment.

Network Services Segment Configuration Options

As with all network security devices, and especially for network firewalls, there is no such thing as "one size fits all" when it comes to configuration. There is no replacement for understanding how your firewall works, and how to configure it to meet your organization's specific requirements.

We should look at two scenarios before proceeding with a step-by-step example for configuring a network services segment behind an ISA firewall. These scenarios are:

1. **Scenario 1** A local area network (LAN) router separates the edge ISA firewall from the rest of the corporate network.

2. **Scenario 2** No LAN router separates the edge ISA firewall from the rest of the corporate network.

Although there are variations on the second theme, our discussions of these two scenarios will hopefully make clear what your configuration options are when you do and don't have a LAN router on your network.

Scenario 1: A LAN Router between the ISA Firewall and Corporate Network

A high-level view of scenario 1 appears in Figure 10.1. In this scenario, there is a LAN router between the edge ISA firewall and the rest of the network. There also is a Route relationship between all internal networks located behind the edge ISA firewall. Network address translation (NAT) is used only for communications to the Internet.

In this scenario, hosts on the corporate network in front of the network services perimeter ISA firewall use a default gateway that is the local address of the LAN router. The LAN router is configured with a route of last resort (which allows it to access the Internet) that is the internal address on the edge ISA firewall. The LAN router is configured with a routing table entry that provides a route to the network ID located behind the network services perimeter network ISA firewall.

When a user makes a request to a server on the network services segment located behind the network services perimeter ISA firewall, the request is forwarded to the client's default gateway address, because the connection is to a nonlocal (remote) network. The packet is forwarded based on the routing table entry on the LAN router to the Internet Protocol (IP) address on the external interface of the network services perimeter ISA firewall, and then the network services perimeter ISA firewall routes the request to the server on the network services segment.

The black arrows in Figure 10.1 show the request path, and the red arrows show the response path. The server on the services segment sends the response to its default gateway, which is the IP address on the internal interface of the network services segment perimeter ISA firewall. The response is forwarded directly to the client making the request because the ISA firewall has knowledge of all network IDs to which it is directly connected. The response is *not* forwarded to the LAN router and then back to the client. Note that the request and response paths are not the same.

Figure 10.1 A LAN Router Separating the Edge ISA Firewall from the Rest of the Corporate Network

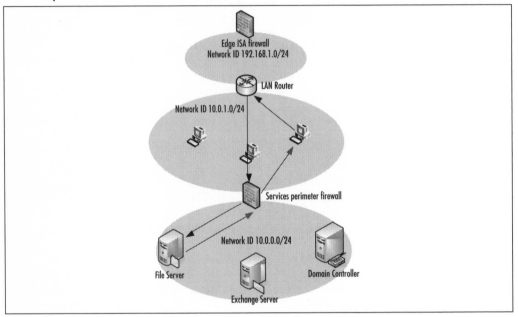

Figure 10.2 shows the request and response paths for connections made to the Internet. Notice in this case that the request and response paths are the same.

Scenario 2: No LAN Router between the ISA Firewall and Corporate Network

Now let's look at scenario 2, where there is no router between the ISA firewall and the rest of the network (see Figure 10.3). In this case, the clients on the corporate network use the internal interface of the edge ISA firewall as their default gateway address. The edge ISA firewall is configured with a routing table entry informing the edge ISA firewall of the correct route to network ID 10.0.0.0/24. The ISA firewall forwards the connection to the IP address on the external interface of the network services perimeter ISA firewall, which then routes the connection to the server on the network services segment.

Figure 10.2 Request and Response Paths for Connections Made to the Internet

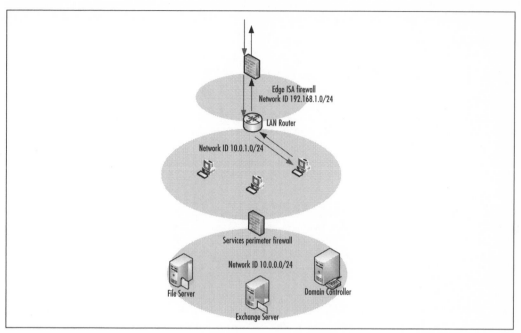

The response from the server on the network services segment is forwarded to the server's default gateway address, which is the IP address on the internal interface of the network services perimeter ISA firewall, which in turn forwards the response directly to the client machine that made the request. Notice that the request and response paths are not the same. This scenario works because the ISA firewall handling traffic has knowledge of and is not dealing with response traffic to connections it is not aware of. This will be made clear in the next figure.

ISA Firewall Stateful Packet Inspection and Request/Response Paths

Figure 10.4 shows a scenario where a system on the network services segment needs to *initiate* a connection to a host on the corporate network. A network management server on the network services segment makes a connection to a workstation on the corporate network in front of the network services perimeter ISA firewall.

Figure 10.3 No Router between the ISA Firewall and the Rest of the Network

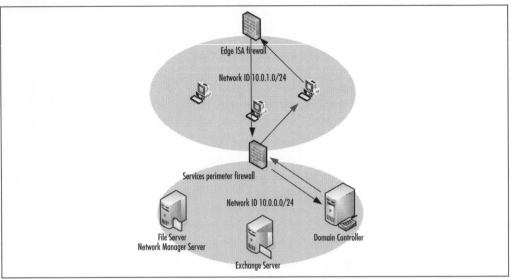

The connection is first sent to the network services perimeter ISA firewall's internal interface, as this is the default gateway of the network management server. The connection is then sent directly to the workstation, because the ISA firewall has knowledge of all networks to which is it directly connected. That is to say, the ISA firewall can do an Address Resolution Protocol (ARP) broadcast to get the Media Access Control (MAC) address of the workstation and send the request directly to that workstation.

A problem arises when the workstation tries to respond to the management server on the network services segment. Because the destination IP address of the management server is on a network *remote* from the workstation's network ID, the workstation sends the response to its default gateway, which is the internal interface of the edge ISA firewall. The response traffic is denied by the ISA firewall because the client is sending a SYN-ACK message back to the management server, but the ISA firewall never "saw" the SYN message from the management server to the workstation. Because the ISA firewall is a stateful packet inspection firewall, it drops the SYN-ACK because it isn't associated with a preceding SYN.

You can deal with this issue in several ways:

- Make sure that no servers on the network services segment behind the perimeter ISA firewall ever need to create new outbound Transmission Control Protocol (TCP) connections to hosts on the corporate network in front of the network services perimeter ISA firewall. This means that not only can you not place servers making outbound connections through the network services perimeter ISA firewall, but you also cannot use protocols where the clients make primary connections to the servers on the network services segment and require secondary connections from the servers on the network services segment.

Figure 10.4 A System on the Network Services Segment Initiating a Connection to a Host on the Corporate Network

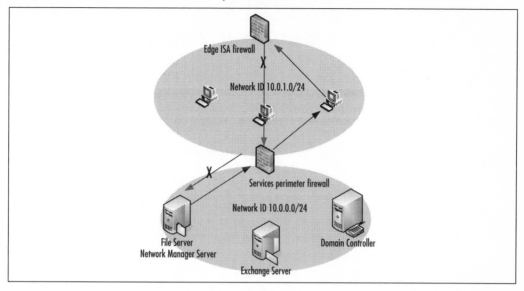

- Put a LAN router between the edge ISA firewall and the rest of the corporate network.

- Put a LAN router between the network services segment perimeter ISA firewall and the rest of the network.

- Create routing table entries on the hosts located on the corporate network in front of the network services perimeter ISA firewall so that they know the gateway address to reach the network services segment, which in this case would be the IP address on the external interface of the network services perimeter ISA firewall.

- Use multiple network interface cards (NICs) on the edge ISA firewall and place the network services segment on an ISA firewall network associated with one of the NICs. This avoids the routing and "network with a network" scenario.

Most enterprise networks will have LAN routers in place, so it's easy for these organizations to create the appropriate routing table entries to support this scenario. For small organizations that do not have LAN routers in place, you can get complete support for connections to and from the network services segment by automating routing table entries on the corporate network hosts located in front of the network services segment perimeter ISA firewall. You could use a logon script to enter these routing table entries on the clients using the *route add –p* command.

Multiple Departmental Networks/Security Zones Connected to a Backbone Network

Note that the issues mentioned earlier are specific for the "network within a network" scenario and when clients systems are "on a subnet" with an edge ISA firewall that must be reached from a host on a remote subnet that is part of the *same ISA firewall network*. This is not a problem when you have a backbone network configured and all the clients and servers are behind ISA firewalls.

For example, consider the network in Figure 10.5. In this scenario, we do not run into similar problems because there are no host systems on the backbone network, and therefore no host systems on a subnet of the edge ISA firewall's internal interface. All ISA firewalls contain routing table entries directing them to the external interface of the appropriate ISA firewall to reach the appropriate network ID(s) located behind any specific ISA firewall. Hosts behind each ISA firewall use the internal interface of their local ISA firewall as their default gateway, and the routing table entries on the ISA firewalls route the connection to the correct ISA firewall's external interface for the remote networks.

Note that we are assuming a Route relationship between all ISA firewall networks in this scenario. A mix of route and NAT relationships will work too, and can potentially simplify the routing table entries because segments that use a NAT relationship do not require routing table entries on the ISA firewall to reach the addresses behind the NAT. The responder only needs to reach the IP address on the external interface of the ISA firewall sending the connection, and in a backbone network scenario, all the external interfaces are likely on the same network ID. Whether you decide to use a route or NAT relationship depends on the type of access required.

Figure 10.5 A Network with No Host Systems on the Backbone Network

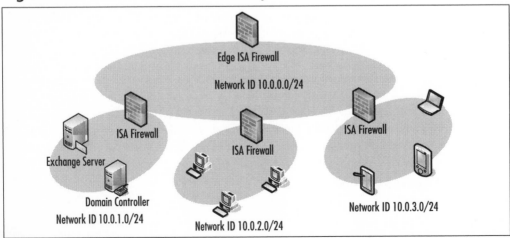

Note that for the route configuration to work most efficiently, each ISA firewall requires the appropriate routing table entries. You could get around this requirement if each ISA firewall used the edge ISA firewall as its default gateway, and the edge ISA firewall contained the appropriate routing table entries. This solution could potentially work, but performance would be abysmal because the edge ISA firewall would be routing connections between all network IDs on the corporate network.

Example Network and Perimeter Network Design

In this chapter, we will use the sample network shown in Figure 10.6 and outlined here:

- The default gateway for all servers on the network services segment will be the IP address on the internal interface of the network services perimeter ISA firewall.

- The default gateway for all hosts on the corporate network containing client systems is the IP address on the internal interface of the edge ISA firewall.

- Client systems are configured with a routing table entry that forwards connections to network ID 10.0.0.0/24 to the IP address on the external interface of the network services perimeter ISA firewall. This is required because we do not have a LAN router in this configuration.

Figure 10.6 Our Sample Network

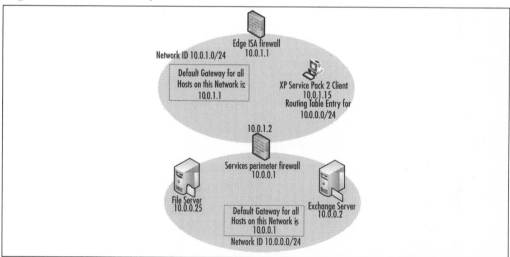

A Windows 2000 file server and an Exchange 2003 server are located on the network services segment. The Exchange server is also a domain controller, domain name system (DNS) server, Windows Internet Name Service (WINS) server, Dynamic Host Configuration

Protocol (DHCP) server, certificate server, and Remote Authentication Dial-in User Service (RADIUS) server. We will create Access Rules that enable connections to all the network services on the Exchange server and to file shares on the file server. The file server will host the Firewall client installation files so that we can avoid allowing file sharing protocols to any portion of the ISA firewall's local host network. The network services perimeter ISA firewall is already joined to the domain.

We will perform the following procedures:

- Create an ISA firewall network representing the corporate network on the network services perimeter ISA firewall.

- Create a network rule on the network services perimeter ISA firewall that sets a Route relationship between the corporate network and the network services network.

- Create an intradomain communications Access Rule on the network services perimeter ISA firewall that allows corporate network hosts access to the domain controller on the services segment for intradomain communications, and a DNS Server Publishing Rule that enables the DNS application layer inspection filter.

- Create Access Rules controlling outbound access from the network services segment on the perimeter ISA firewall.

- Create network services Access Rules on the network services perimeter ISA firewall enabling client access to network services, such as Outlook Web Access (OWA), Outlook Messaging Application Programming Interface (MAPI), Simple Mail Transfer Protocol (STMP), Postoffice Protocol version 3 (POP3), and Internet Message Access Protocol version 4 (IMAP4), and file shares.

- Create a routing table entry on the edge ISA firewall providing a path to the network services segment network ID.

- Join the front-end ISA firewall to the domain.

- Create a routing table entry on the network clients (required only if no LAN routers are installed) providing route information to reach the network services segment network ID.

- Join the network clients to the domain.

- Create a WPAD entry in DNS to enable autodiscovery for firewall and Web proxy clients.

- Configure the Firewall client settings on the edge ISA firewall (including Web proxy client configuration).

- Install the Firewall client share on the network services segment file server.

- Install the Firewall client on the network clients.

- Connect the corporate network clients to resources on the network services segment and the Internet.

Creating the ISA Representing the Corporate Network on the Network Services Perimeter

One of the most prevalent misconceptions regarding ISA firewall networks and how the ISA firewall sees the network world is how the ISA firewall deals with the default external network. Let's set the record straight: The default external network on the ISA firewall is defined as any IP address that *is not part of any other ISA firewall network defined on the ISA firewall.*

This means you can configure any collection of IP addresses that *aren't part of another ISA firewall network* to be part of a custom ISA firewall network. This includes the IP address(es) bound to the external interface of the ISA firewall (although the addresses on the external interface of the ISA firewall will always belong to the local host network).

This allows us to create a custom ISA firewall network that includes the IP addresses used on the corporate network between the edge ISA firewall and the network services perimeter ISA firewall. These addresses *do not* need to be part of the default external network, even though the corporate network is on the same network ID as the *external interface* of the ISA firewall. The term *external interface* only means that it's the interface with the default gateway configured on it, which typically is the closest to the Internet.

> **NOTE**
>
> Although the term *external interface* is used to denote the NIC that has the default gateway configured on it, the fact is that you can configure an ISA firewall that has no default gateway. This ISA firewall won't be able to access the Internet, and hosts serviced by that ISA firewall won't be able to access the Internet, but it illustrates that an ISA firewall does not require an external interface.

The value in making the corporate network located between the edge ISA firewall and the network services perimeter ISA firewall a separate ISA firewall network is that you can control the routing relationship between that network and any other network defined on the ISA firewall.

In the example network used in this chapter, configuring a custom corporate ISA firewall network on the network perimeter services segment ISA firewall will enable us to create a Route relationship between the default internal network behind the back-end ISA firewall and the corporate network located between the edge ISA firewall and the network services ISA perimeter ISA firewall. We can also create Access Rules controlling traffic moving to and from any ISA firewall network.

Creating the Corpnet ISA Firewall Network

Perform the following steps on the network services perimeter ISA firewall to create the Corpnet ISA firewall network:

1. In the ISA firewall console, expand the server name and then expand the **Configuration** node. Click the **Networks** node.

2. On the **Networks** node, click the **Networks** tab in the **Details** pane. Click the **Tasks** tab in the **Task** pane and then click the **Create a New Network** link.

3. On the **Welcome to the New Network Wizard** page, enter a name for the network in the **Network name** text box. In this example, we'll name the network **Corpnet**. Click **Next**.

4. On the **Network Type** page, select the **Perimeter Network** option and click **Next**.

5. On the **Network Address** page, click the **Add** button.

6. In the **IP Address Range Properties** dialog box, enter the **Starting address** and **Ending address** for the Corpnet ISA firewall network. In this example, we'll enter **10.0.1.0** for the **Starting address** and **10.0.1.255** for the **Ending address** (see Figure 10.7). Note that you don't have to include the entire network ID; you can include only the addresses that are actually in use on that network, or you can get even more granular and include only the addresses that you want to have a Route relationship with the default Internet network behind the network services perimeter ISA firewall so that you can later create another ISA firewall network representing other addresses on the corporate network that you want to create a NAT relationship with. Click **OK**, and then click **Next**. Figure 10.8 shows the results.

Figure 10.7 Entering IP Address Range Properties

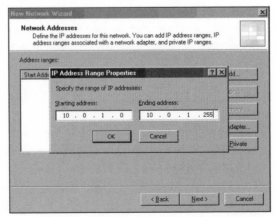

Figure 10.8 Network Address Ranges

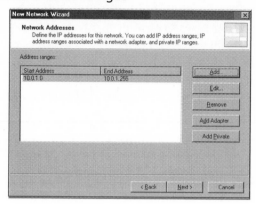

8. Click **Finish** on the **Completing the New Network Wizard** page. Figure 10.9 shows the results.

Figure 10.9 The Corpnet ISA Firewall Network

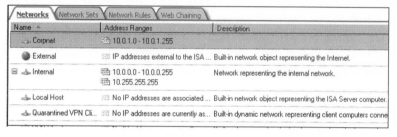

Creating the Rule on the Network Services Perimeter ISA, Setting a Route Relationship between the Corporate Network and Network Services Segment

In the scenario discussed in this chapter, the hosts on the corporate network are members of a domain that has its domain controllers located behind the network services perimeter ISA firewall.

An Access Rule must be created allowing hosts on the corporate network to communicate with the domain controller on the network services segment. Intradomain communications require that you have a Route relationship between the source and destination networks. For this reason, we will create a network rule that sets a Route relationship between the corporate network and the default internal network located behind the network services perimeter ISA firewall.

It's important to note that although there will be a Route relationship between the network services perimeter ISA firewall's default internal network and the Corpnet network, there will still be a NAT relationship between the network services perimeter ISA firewall's default internal network and the Internet. This is fully supported (and required), because private addresses are used on all networks behind the edge ISA firewall (in this scenario).

Creating the Network Rule Defining a Route Relationship between the Corpnet ISA Firewall Network and the Default Internal Network

Perform the following steps to create the network rule creating a Route relationship between the Corpnet network and the default internal network behind the network services perimeter ISA firewall:

1. In the ISA firewall console, expand the server name and then expand the **Configuration** node in the left pane of the console. Click the **Networks** node.

2. On the **Networks** node, click the **Network Rules** tab in the **Details** pane of the console, then click the **Create a New Network Rule** link in the **Tasks** tab of the **Task** pane.

3. On the **Welcome to the New Network Rule Wizard** page, enter a name for the rule in the **Network rule name** text box. In this example, we'll name the rule **Corpnet—Internal** (the default internal network behind the network services perimeter ISA firewall represents the network services segment). Click **Next**.

4. On the **Network Traffic Sources** page, click the **Add** button.

5. In the **Add Network Entities** dialog box, click the **Networks** folder and then double click the **Corpnet** network. Click **Close** (see Figure 10.10).

Figure 10.10 Adding Network Entities

6. Click **Next** on the **Network Traffic Sources** page.

7. Click **Add** on the **Network Traffic Destinations** page.

8. Click the **Networks** folder and then double click the **Internal** entry. Click **Close**.

9. On the **Network Relationship** page, select the **Route** option and click **Next** (see Figure 10.11).

Figure 10.11 Specifying That the ISA Server Should Send Traffic between the Source and Destination Network Entities

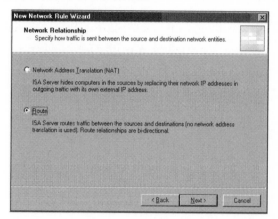

10. Click **Finish** on the **Completing the New Network Rule Wizard** page. Figure 10.12 shows the results.

Figure 10.12 The Completed Network Rule

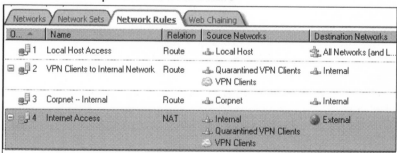

Creating an Intradomain Communications Access Rule on the Network Services Perimeter ISA Firewall and a DNS Server Publishing Rule

Multiple protocols are required to allow intradomain communications between hosts on the corporate network and domain controllers on the corporate network. Table 10.1 provides the details of this Access Rule. Table 10.2 provides details of the DNS Server Publishing Rule.

Table 10.1 Access Rule Allowing Intradomain Communications between the DMZ Host and the Domain Controller on the Default Internal Network behind the Back-End ISA Firewall

Name	Intradomain Corpnet—Internal
Action	Allow
Protocols	Microsoft CIFS (TCP)
	Microsoft CIFS (UDP)
	Kerberos-Adm (UDP)
	Kerberos-Sec (TCP)
	Kerberos-Sec (UDP)
	LDAP
	LDAP (UDP)
	LDAP GC (Global Catalog)
	RPC (all interfaces)
	NTP (UDP)
	Ping
From	Corpnet
To	Domain Controller
Users	All
Schedule	Always
Content Types	All Content Types

Table 10.2 DNS Server Publishing Rule

Name	Publish Domain DNS
Action	Allow
Protocols	DNS Server
Listener	Corpnet

Continued

Table 10.2 continued DNS Server Publishing Rule

To	10.0.0.2
Schedule	Always

Note that we are using an Access Rule rather than a Publishing Rule to allow access from the Corpnet ISA firewall network and the network services segment network. This is because we have a Route relationship between these two networks. As such, we have no need or ability to hide the addresses of the servers on the network services segment.

You might be concerned that you won't be able to leverage the ISA firewall's deep application layer inspection application filters when using Access Rules, but the fact is that you *can* benefit from the application layer filters for most protocols. If you check the protocol definitions associated with the application filters, you'll see that both inbound and outbound protocol definitions have the application layer inspection filters bound to them.

Unfortunately, the DNS filter is not one of the filters that you can use for both inbound and outbound access to stateful application layer inspection. Even though you can bind the DNS application layer inspection filter to the outbound DNS protocol definition in the user interface, the filter will have no effect.

You can test this yourself by binding the DNS application layer inspection filter to the outbound DNS protocol and then creating an Access Rule from the Corpnet network to the network services segment network using this DNS protocol definition. Now block DNS zone transfers in the **Enable Intrusion Detection and DNS Attack Detection** dialog box. After creating the Access Rule and configuring DNS intrusion detection, try to perform a DNS zone transfer using the *nslookup* utility and issuing the *ls −d <domain_name.>* command. You'll find that you can perform the zone transfers. In contrast, if you created a DNS Server Publishing Rule, the zone transfer would fail because the DNS application layer inspection filter would detect the intrusion.

For this reason, we will create two rules: a Server Publishing Rule for DNS communications and an Access Rule for all other intradomain communications. Although we could simplify the configuration by including the DNS protocol in the intradomain communications Access Rule, we would miss out on the added protection provided by the DNS filter.

Creating the Intradomain Communications Rule

Perform the following steps to create the intradomain communications Access Rule on the network services perimeter ISA firewall:

1. In the ISA firewall console, expand the server name and then click the **Firewall Policy** node in the left pane of the console.

2. On the **Firewall Policy** node, click the **Tasks** tab in the **Task** pane and click the **Create New Access Rule** link.

3. On the **Welcome to the New Access Rule Wizard** page, enter the name of the rule in the **Access Rule name** text box. In this example, we'll name the rule **Intradomain Corpnet—Internal**. Click **Next**.

4. Select the **Allow** option on the **Rule Action** page.

5. On the **Protocols** page, select the **Selected protocols** option from the **This rule applies to** list. Click **Add**.

6. Click the **Add Protocols** folder and then double click the following protocols:
    Microsoft CIFS (TCP)
    Microsoft CIFS (UDP)
    DNS
    Kerberos-Adm (UDP)
    Kerberos-Sec (TCP)
    Kerberos-Sec (UDP)
    LDAP
    LDAP (UDP)
    LDAP GC (Global Catalog)
    RPC (all interfaces)
    NTP (UDP)
    Ping

7. Click **Close** in the **Add Protocols** dialog box.

8. Click **Next** on the **Protocols** page (see Figure 10.13).

Figure 10.13 Selecting Protocols to Which to Apply Rules

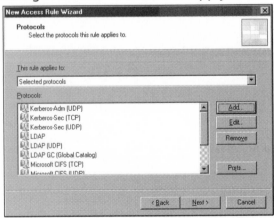

9. On the **Access Rule Sources** page, click the **Add** button.

10. In the **Add Network Entities** dialog box, double click the **Corpnet** entry and then click **Close**.

11. Click **Next** on the **Access Rule Sources** page.

12. Click **Add** on the **Access Rule Destinations** page.

13. In the **Add Network Entities** dialog box, click the **New** menu and then click **Computer**.

14. In the **New Computer Rule Element** dialog box, enter a name for the domain controller on the internal network (the network services segment). In this example, we'll name the computer **Object Domain Controller**. Enter the IP address of the domain controller in the **Computer IP Address** text box. Enter an optional **Description** if you like. Click **OK** (see Figure 10.14).

Figure 10.14 Naming the Domain Controller on the Internal Network

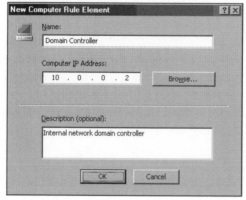

15. In the **Add Network Entities** dialog box, click the **Computers** folder and then double click on the **Domain Controller** entry. Click **Close**.

16. Click **Next** on the **Access Rule Destinations** page (see Figure 10.15).

Figure 10.15 Specifying Access Rule Destinations

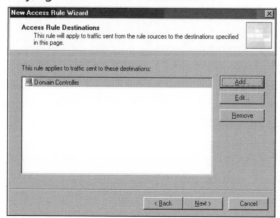

17. Accept the default setting, **All Users**, on the **User Sets** page and click **Next**.

18. Click **Finish** on the **Completing the New Access Rule Wizard** page.

Creating the DNS Server Publishing Rule

The next step is to create the DNS Server Publishing Rule. Perform the following steps on the network services perimeter ISA firewall to create the DNS Server Publishing Rule:

1. In the ISA firewall console, expand the server name and then click the **Firewall Policy** node.

2. On the **Firewall Policy** node, click the **Tasks** tab in the **Task** pane and then click the **Create a New Server Publishing Rule** link.

3. On the **Welcome to the New Server Publishing Rule Wizard** page, enter a name for the rule in the **Server Publishing Rule name** text box. In this example, we'll name the rule **Publish Domain DNS**. Click **Next**.

4. On the **Select Server** page, enter the IP address of the DNS server for the domain in the **Server IP address** text box. In this example, the domain's DNS server is located on the domain controller, which is at IP address **10.0.0.2**. We enter this IP address into the text box and click **Next** (see Figure 10.16).

Figure 10.16 Selecting a Server

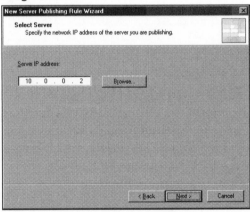

5. On the **Select Protocol** page, select the **DNS Server** option from the **Selected** protocol list. Click **Next** (Figure 10.17).

6. On the **IP Address** page, put a checkmark in the checkbox next to **Corpnet** and click **Next** (see Figure 10.18). There is an interesting vagary to this setting, which I'll talk more about at the end of this section.

Figure 10.17 Selecting the Protocol

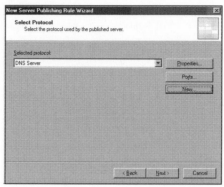

Figure 10.18 Choosing the Networks That Will Listen for Requests

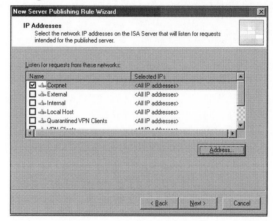

7.   Click **Finish** on the **Completing the New Server Publishing Rule Wizard** page.

I mentioned that there is an interesting twist to Server Publishing Rules when you have a Route relationship between the source and destination ISA firewall networks. To fully appreciate the situation, let's first examine what happens when there is a NAT relationship between the published server and the external client.

When there is a NAT relationship between the published server and the external client, the external client reaches the published server *using the IP address on the external interface of the ISA firewall configured to listen for incoming connections* for that specific Server Publishing Rule.

For example, if there were a NAT relationship between the published DNS server and the Corpnet network, we could choose the IP address 10.0.1.2 on the external interface of the network services perimeter ISA firewall as the listening address. Hosts that need to reach the published server would send DNS queries to the IP address used in the Server Publishing Rule listener, *not* the actual IP address of the published Web server.

In contrast, when there is a Route relationship between the source and destination ISA firewall networks, the external client reaches the published DNS server (or any other server *except* a Web server published using a Web Publishing Rule) using the *actual IP address* of the published server. So, even though we've created a DNS Server Publishing Rule that has a listener on the external interface of the network services perimeter ISA firewall, the external clients must use the actual IP address to reach the DNS server, which in this case is 10.0.0.2. The ISA firewall uses a method referred to as *port stealing* to make this possible.

Creating Access Rules Controlling Outbound Access from the Network Services Segment on the Perimeter ISA Firewall

You must create Access Rules allowing new outbound connections from hosts on the network services segment and any other network. In most cases, the only outbound connections you'll want to allow are those that enable access to the Windows update site or the Windows Server Update Service (WSUS) server on the corporate network. You would also likely want to enable outbound access to public DNS servers if your domain DNS servers are also providing Internet host name resolution.

Exactly what you want to allow as outbound from the servers on the network services segment is going to be very specific to your own implementation. In our current example, we're going to allow only outbound DNS traffic from the DNS server and outbound Hypertext Transfer Protocol (HTTP) and Hypertext Transfer Protocol Secure (HTTPS) traffic from all hosts on the network services segment to the Windows Update sites.

NOTE

You do not need to create outbound Access Rules from the network services segment to the Corpnet ISA firewall network to support the inbound Access Rules from the Corpnet ISA firewall network to the network services segment network. The ISA firewall is a stateful packet inspection firewall and will automatically allow responses to requests made from hosts on the Corpnet network.

Creating the Access Rule Allowing DNS Traffic from the DNS Server to the Internet

Perform the following steps to create the Access Rule:

1. At the back-end ISA firewall, in the ISA firewall console, expand the name of the server and then click the **Firewall Policy** node in the left pane of the console.

2. Click the **Create New Access Rule** link on the **Tasks** tab in the **Task** pane.

3. In the **Welcome to the New Access Rule** dialog box, enter a name for the rule in the **Access Rule name** text box. In this example, we'll name the rule **DNS to External**. Click **Next**.

4. On the **Rule Action** page, select the **Allow** option and click **Next**.

5. On the **Protocols** page, select the **Selected protocols** option from the **This rule applies to** list. Click **Add**.

6. Click the **Common Protocols** folder and then double click the **DNS** entry. Click **Close**.

7. Click **Next** on the **Protocols** page.

8. On the **Access Rule Sources** page, click the **Add** button.

9. In the **Add Network Entities** dialog box, click the **Computers** folder and double click the **Domain Controller** entry. Click **Close**.

10. Click **Next** on the **Access Rule Sources** page.

11. On the **Access Rule Destinations** page, click the **Add** button.

12. In the **Add Network Entities** dialog box, click the **Networks** folder. Double click the **External** network. Click **Close**.

13. Click **Next** on the **Access Rule Destinations** page.

14. On the **User Sets** page, accept the default entry, **All Users**, and click **Next**.

15. Click **Finish** on the **Completing the New Access Rule Wizard** page.

Creating the Access Rule Allowing Outbound Windows Update and Microsoft Reporting

Perform the following steps to create the HTTP/HTTPS Access Rule allowing access to the Windows Update and Reporting sites:

1. At the back-end ISA firewall, in the ISA firewall console, expand the name of the server and then click the **Firewall Policy** node in the left pane of the console.

2. Click the **Create New Access Rule** link on the **Tasks** tab in the **Task** pane.

3. In the **Welcome to the New Access Rule** dialog box, enter a name for the rule in the **Access Rule name** text box. In this example, we'll name the rule **Outbound to WU and MS Reporting**. Click **Next**.

4. On the **Rule Action** page, select the **Allow** option and click **Next**.

5. On the **Protocols** page, select the **Selected protocols** option from the **This rule applies to** list. Click **Add**.

6. Click the **Common Protocols** folder and then double click the **HTTP** and **HTTPS** entries. Click **Close**.

7. Click **Next** on the **Protocols** page.

8. On the **Access Rule Sources** page, click the **Add** button.

9. In the **Add Network Entities** dialog box, click the **Networks** folder and double click the **Internal** entry. Click **Close**.

10. Click **Next** on the **Access Rule Sources** page.

11. On the **Access Rule Destinations** page, click the **Add** button.

12. In the **Add Network Entities** dialog box, click the **Domain Name Sets** folder. Double click the **Microsoft Error Reporting sites** and **System Policy Allowed Sites** entries. Click **Close**.

13. Click **Next** on the **Access Rule Destinations** page.

14. On the **User Sets** page, accept the default entry, **All Users**, and click **Next**.

15. Click **Finish** on the **Completing the New Access Rule Wizard** page.

16. Click **Apply** to save the changes and update the firewall policy.

17. Click **OK** in the **Apply New Configuration** dialog box.

Your firewall policy should look like Figure 10.19.

Figure 10.19 The Completed Firewall Policy

Creating the Network Services Access Rules Enabling Corpnet Clients Access to Network Services

Now we're ready to create Publishing Rules and Access Rules that allow hosts on the Corpnet ISA firewall network and external clients on the Internet to access Exchange server and file server resources on the network services segment. Hosts on the Corpnet ISA firewall network will be able to connect to Exchange server and file server resources by going through the network services segment perimeter ISA firewall. Hosts on the Internet will need to traverse both the edge ISA firewall and the network services segment perimeter ISA firewall. Later we will create the rules on the edge ISA firewall to enable access to network services perimeter resources.

In this section, we will do the following:

- Create an OWA Web Publishing Rule on the network services perimeter ISA firewall.

- Create SMTP, POP3, and IMAP4 Server Publishing Rules.

- Create an Access Rule allowing access to file shares on the file server.

In our scenario on creating network services segments using ISA firewalls, I will assume that you have already deployed your certificate infrastructure and have already requested the appropriate Web site certificates to support Secure Sockets Layer/Transaction Layer Security (SSL/TLS) connections to the Exchange server's e-mail services.

If you haven't done this and are not sure how to start, I highly recommend the ISA Server 2004/Exchange Server deployment kit documents I created for Microsoft at http://download.microsoft.com/download/1/8/8/188ab94a-4ec5-4746-ac0f-a18177040fbf/isa2004se_exchangekit-rev%201%2005.doc (note that this is a very large document; if you need an individual Word file that applies to your network configuration from one of the chapters in the deployment kit doc, write to me at tshinder@isaserver.org and I'll send you the separate doc).

In the scenario used in this chapter, we've bound certificates to the OWA Web site, the SMTP site, the POP3 site, and the IMAP4 site on the Exchange server on the network services segment. Table 10.3 shows the common/subject names on the certificates bound to each site.

Table 10.3 Common/Subject Names Bound to Exchange Server Services

Exchange Server Service	Common/Subject Name on Web Site Certificate
OWA	owa.msfirewall.org
SMTP	mail.msfirewall.org

Continued

Table 10.3 continued Common/Subject Names Bound to Exchange Server Services

Exchange Server Service	Common/Subject Name on Web Site Certificate
POP3	pop3.msfirewall.org
IMAP4	imap4.msfirewall.org

In the following sections, we will create Access Rules, Web Publishing Rules, and Server Publishing Rules with the characteristics listed in Table 10.4.

Table 10.4 Resulting Firewall Policy on the Network Services Perimeter ISA Firewall

Order	Name	Action	Protocols	From/Listener	To	Condition
1	Exchange Server IMAPS Server	Allow	IMAPS Server	Corpnet	10.0.0.2	N/A
2	Exchange Server POP3S Server	Allow	POP3S Server	Corpnet	10.0.0.2	N/A
3	Exchange Server SMTP Server	Allow	SMTP Server	Corpnet	10.0.0.2	N/A
4	Exchange Server IMAP4 Server	Allow	IMAP4 Server	Corpnet	10.0.0.2	N/A
5	Exchange Server POP3 Server	Allow	POP3 Server	Corpnet	10.0.0.2	N/A
6	Exchange Server SMTPS Server	Allow	SMTPS Server	Corpnet	10.0.0.2	N/A
7	Publish OWA	Allow	HTTPS	OWA Listener	owa.ms firewall.org	All Authen-ticated Users
8	Publish DNS	Allow	DNS Server	Corpnet	10.0.0.2	
9	DNS to External	Allow	DNS	Domain Controller	External	All Users

Continued

Table 10.4 continued Resulting Firewall Policy on the Network Services Perimeter ISA Firewall

Order	Name	Action	Protocols	From/Listener	To	Condition
10	Outbound WU and MS Reporting	Allow	HTTP HTTPS	Internal	Microsoft Error Reporting Sites System Policy Allowed Sites	All Users
11	Intradomain Corpnet— Internal	Allow	Kerberos-Adm (UDP) Kerberos-Sec (TCP) Kerberos-Sec (UDP) LDAP LDAP (UDP) LDAP GC (Global Catalog) Microsoft CIFS (TCP) Microsoft CIFS (UDP) NTP (UDP) Ping RPC (all interfaces)	Corpnet	Domain Controller	All Users
12	File Server Access	Allow	Microsoft CIFS (TCP) Microsoft CIFS (UDP)	Corpnet	File Server 1	All Users

To simplify the configuration, we'll leverage the ISA firewall's Mail Server Publishing Wizard to create multiple Publishing Rules simultaneously.

Creating an OWA Publishing Rule on the Network Services Perimeter ISA Firewall

Perform the following steps on the network services perimeter ISA firewall to create the Web Publishing Rule that publishes the OWA Web site:

1. In the ISA firewall console, expand the server name and then click the **Firewall Policy** node.

2. On the **Firewall Policy** node, click the **Tasks** tab in the **Task** pane and then click the **Publish a Mail Server** link.

3. On the **Welcome to the New Mail Server Publishing Rule Wizard** page, enter a name for the rule in the **Mail Server Publishing Rule name** text box. In this example, we'll name the rule **Publish OWA**. Click **Next**.

4. On the **Select Access Type** page, select the **Web client access: Outlook Web Access (OWA), Outlook Mobile Access, Exchange Server ActiveSync** option and click **Next**.

5. On the **Select Services** page, select the **Outlook Web Access** checkbox and click **Next** (see Figure 10.20).

Figure 10.20 Selecting Services to Publish

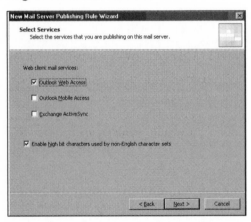

6. On the **Bridging Mode** page, select the **Secure connection to clients and mail server** option. This enables SSL-to-SSL bridging. Click **Next** (see Figure 10.21).

Figure 10.21 Enabling SSL-to-SSL Bridging

7. On the **Specify the Web Mail Server** page, enter the name on the Web site cer-
    tificate bound to the OWA Web site. In this example, the name is
    owa.msfirewall.org. Keep in mind that the ISA firewall will need to resolve this
    name to the actual IP address of the OWA site on the network services segment. You
    can do this with a HOSTS file entry on the ISA firewall, or set up a split DNS
    infrastructure.

      The split DNS infrastructure might be challenging in this scenario, because as
    you'll see later, we would need to create a triple split DNS to support name reso-
    lution for the ISA firewall itself, for hosts on the corporate network, and for hosts
    located on the Internet. Although putting together a well-designed split DNS
    infrastructure is fairly simple, some network admins have misconceptions that it's
    either insecure or difficult to manage. Both misconceptions are patently incorrect
    and you should not fall prey to them. We will create the HOSTS file entry on the
    network services perimeter ISA firewall after we've created all the Publishing and
    Access Rules. Click Next (see Figure 10.22).

Figure 10.22 Specifying the Web Mail Server

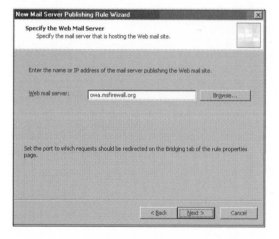

8. On the **Public Name Details** page, select the **This domain name (type
    below)** in the **Accept requests for** list. Enter the common/subject name on the
    Web site certificate that will be bound to the Web listener for this Web Publishing
    Rule. In this example, we have exported the Web site certificate bound to the
    OWA Web site and imported it into the machine certificate stored on the ISA
    firewall. Because this is the same certificate, it has the same common/subject name.
    Therefore, we enter **owa.msfirewall.org** in the **Public name** text box. Click
    Next (see Figure 10.23).

Figure 10.23 Specifying the Public Domain Name

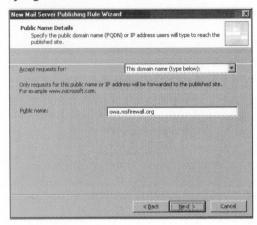

9.   On the **Select Web Listener** page, click the **New** button.

10. On the **Welcome to the New Web Listener Wizard** page, enter a name for the listener in the **Web listener name** text box. In this example, we'll name the Web listener **OWA Listener**. Click **Next**.

11. On the **IP Addresses** page, put a checkmark in the **Corpnet** checkbox and click **Next**.

12. On the **Port Specification** page, remove the checkmark from the **Enable HTTP** checkbox and put a checkmark in the **Enable SSL** checkbox. Click the **Select** button.

13. Select the OWA Web site certificate from the list in the **Select Certificate** dialog box and click **OK** (see Figure 10.24).

Figure 10.24 Selecting a Certificate

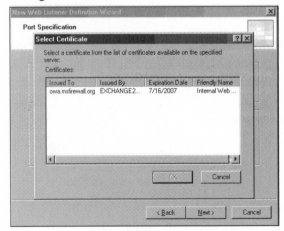

14. Click **Next** on the **Port Specification** page.

15. Click **Finish** on the **Completing the New Web Listener** page.

16. On the **Select Web Listener** page, click the **Edit** button.

17. On the **OWA Listener Properties** dialog box, click the **Preferences** tab.

18. On the **Preferences** tab, click the **Authentication** button.

19. In the **Authentication** dialog box, remove the checkmark from the **Integrated** checkbox. Click **OK** in the dialog box informing you that you don't have any authentication methods configured. Put a checkmark in the **OWA Forms-based** checkbox. Put a checkmark in the **Require all users to authenticate** checkbox. Click **OK** (see Figure 10.25).

Figure 10.25 Specifying Authentication Methods and Settings

20. Click **OK** in the **OWA Listener Properties** dialog box.

21. Click **Next** on the **Select Web Listener** page (see Figure 10.26).

22. On the **User Sets** page, click the **All Users** entry and click **Remove**. Click the **Add** button.

23. In the **Add Users** dialog box, double click the **All Authenticated Users** entry and click **Close**.

24. Click **Next** on the **User Sets** page.

25. Click **Finish** on the **Completing the New Mail Server Publishing Rule Wizard** page.

Figure 10.26 Selecting the Web Listener

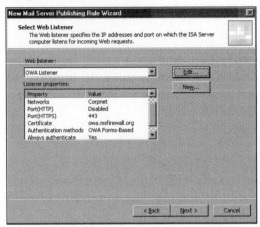

Your firewall policy should like that in Figure 10.27.

Figure 10.27 The Completed Firewall Policy

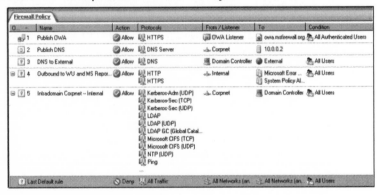

Creating SMTP, POP3, and IMAP4 Server Publishing Rules

The next step is to create the Server Publishing Rules that publish the rest of the Exchange server services. These include Server Publishing Rules for Secure Exchange RPC, SMTP, POP3, and IMAP4. We have the option to create these rules separately or all at once by using the Mail Server Publishing Wizard. We'll use the latter option to simplify things.

You might notice that we're not going to create a secure Exchange RPC Server Publishing Rule in this example, for the following reasons:

■   We're using a Route relationship between the Corpnet ISA firewall network and the network services segment.

■   The intradomain communications Access Rule is configured to allow inbound TCP 135 communications (the RPC [all interfaces] protocol definition).

Because we are using a Route relationship rather than a NAT relationship between the source and destination networks, we can't bind a specific IP address to the listener used in the Server Publishing Rule. When you use a Route relationship, the Server Publishing Rule listens on all addresses bound to the external interface using a feature known internally as *port stealing*. Because both the Secure Exchange RPC Server Publishing Rule and the RPC (all interfaces) component of the intradomain communications Access Rule are listening for similar communications, we end up with a conflict that prevents Outlook MAPI clients from connecting to Directory Services.

If there were a NAT relationship between the Corpnet network and the network services segment, we could bind multiple IP addresses to the external interface of the network services perimeter ISA firewall. Then we could create two rules—one for Secure Exchange RPC publishing and the other for RPC (all interfaces)—and use a different listening address for each rule. Machines on the Corpnet ISA firewall network would then connect to Secure Exchange RPC services or RPC (all interfaces) services using the IP address used for their respective rule's listener. This works because connections are made to the IP addresses on the ISA firewall's external interface when you have a NAT relationship between the network services segment and the Corpnet ISA firewall network.

It doesn't work when there is a Route relationship between the network services segment and the Corpnet ISA firewall network because hosts on the Corpnet ISA firewall network connect to the Exchange server *using the actual IP address of the Exchange server*. Because the hosts are connecting to the IP address of the Exchange server itself and not an IP address on the external interface of the ISA firewall, the ISA firewall's *port stealing* mechanism must listen and intercept RPC communications on *all IP addresses of the external interface*. This breaks the granularity required to allow both a Secure Exchange RPC Server Publishing Rule and an RPC (all interfaces) Access Rule on the same ISA firewall when there is a Route relationship between the source and destination ISA firewall networks.

You can confirm this by creating a secure Exchange RPC Server Publishing Rule in the scenario used in this chapter. Then attempt to make a connection to the Exchange server from the full Outlook MAPI client using RPC (don't use RPC/HTTP, because the inbound connection is HTTP, so the ISA firewall doesn't see the RPC communications tunneled in the HTTP header). You'll see that the connection seems to establish successfully, but if you open the **Connection Status** window in Outlook 2003, you'll find that the RPC connections are successful only to the Exchange server's Mail Services. No connection is established to Directory Services.

Creating Server Publishing Rules for POP3, IMAP4, and SMTP

Perform the following steps to create the Server Publishing Rules on the network services perimeter ISA firewall:

1. In the ISA firewall console, expand the server name and then click the **Firewall Policy** node.

2. On the **Firewall Policy** node, click the **Tasks** tab on the **Task** pane and click the **Publish a Mail Server** link.

3. On the **Welcome to the New Mail Server Publishing Rule Wizard** page, enter a name for the rule in the **Mail Server Publishing Rule name** text box. In this example, we'll name the rule **Exchange Server**. Click **Next**.

4. On the **Select Access Type** page, select the **Client access: RPC, IMAP, POP3, SMTP** option and click **Next** (see Figure 10.28).

Figure 10.28 Selecting the Access Type

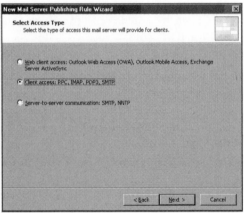

5. On the **Select Services** page, put a checkmark in each checkbox. This will allow us to connect to the Exchange server on the network services segment through the network services perimeter ISA firewall for all the services listed on this page (with the exception of the Exchange server's Network News Transfer Protocol [NNTP] service; we could create a separate rule for that if required). Note the comment on the page regarding the SMTP Message Screener. We will not deploy the message screener in this example, but you might want to consider it in your own deployment. You can install the SMTP Message Screener on the ISA firewall to filter both inbound and outbound mail. Even though the SMTP Message Screener won't be enabled, the SMTP filter is enabled and will protect SMTP communications moving through the network services perimeter ISA firewall. Click **Next** (see Figure 10.29).

Figure 10.29 Selecting the Services to Publish

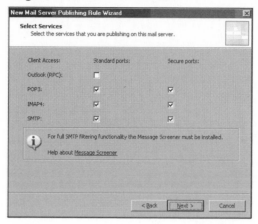

6. On the **Select Server** page, enter the IP address of the Exchange server in the **Server IP address** text box. In this example, the Exchange server's IP address is **10.0.0.2**, so we enter that value. Click **Next**.

7. On the **IP Addresses** page, put a checkmark in the **Corpnet** checkbox. Click **Next**.

8. Click **Finish** on the **Completing the New Mail Server Publishing Rule Wizard** page.

Your firewall policy should appear similar to that in Figure 10.30. Note that the Mail Server Publishing Rule Wizard added seven new Server Publishing Rules. Click **Apply** to save the changes and update the firewall policy. Click **OK** in the **Apply New Configuration** dialog box.

Figure 10.30 The Completed Firewall Policy

Creating an Access Rule Allowing Access to File Shares on the File Server

Now we can create the Access Rule allowing connections to file shares on the file server on the network services segment. We can enable either NetBIOS protocols or Direct Hosting (TCP 445). In this example, we'll enable only Direct Hosting, which is more efficient than NetBIOS protocols.

Perform the following steps to create the Direct Hosting Access Rule on the network services perimeter firewall:

1. In the ISA firewall console, expand the server name and then click the **Firewall Policy** node.

2. On the **Firewall Policy** node, click the **Tasks** tab in the **Task** pane and then click **Create New Access Rule**.

3. On the **Welcome to the New Access Rule Wizard** page, enter a name for the rule in the **Access Rule name** text box. In this example, we'll name the rule **Publish File Server**. Click **Next**.

4. Select the **Allow** option on the **Rule Action** page and click **Next**.

5. On the **Protocols** page, select the **Selected protocols** option from the **This rule applies to** list and then click **Add**.

6. In the **Add Protocols** dialog box, click the **All Protocols** folder and then double click the **Microsoft CIFS (TCP)** and **Microsoft CIFS (UDP)** protocols. Click **Close** (see Figure 10.31).

Figure 10.31 Adding Protocols

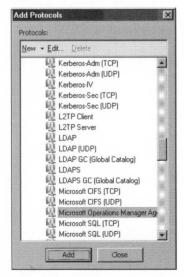

7. Click **Next** on the **Protocols** page.

8. Click **Add** on the **Access Rule Sources** page.

9. In the **Add Network Entities** dialog box, click the **Networks** folder and then double click the **Corpnet** entry. Click **Close** (see Figure 10.32).

Figure 10.32 Adding Network Entities

10. Click **Next** on the **Access Rule Sources** page.

11. Click **Add** on the **Access Rule Destinations** page.

12. In the **Add Network Entities** dialog box, click the **New** menu and then click **Computer**.

13. In the **New Computer Rule Element** dialog box, enter a name for the file server in the **Name** text box. In this example, we'll name it **File Server 1**. Enter the IP address of the file server located in the network services segment in the **Computer IP Address** text box. Enter an optional description if you like. Click **OK** (see Figure 10.33).

14. Click the **Computers** folder in the **Add Network Entities** dialog box, double click the **File Server 1** entry, and click **Close**.

15. Click **Next** on the **Access Rule Destinations** page.

16. Click **Next** on the **User Sets** page.

Figure 10.33 Specifying the New Computer Rule Element

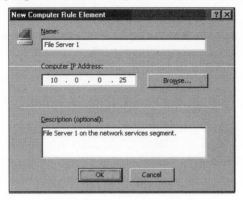

17.   Click **Finish** on the **Completing the New Access Rule Wizard** page.

Your firewall policy should look like that in Figure 10.34.

Figure 10.34 The Completed Firewall Policy

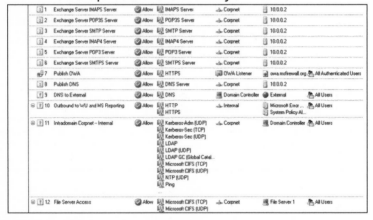

Configuring the Default Internal Network on the Edge ISA Firewall

When the edge ISA firewall was installed, it took its definition of the default internal network from the routing table on the edge ISA firewall device. The routing table entries indicated to the ISA firewall installer that the addresses 10.0.1.0 through 10.0.1.255 should be included in the definition of its default internal network. This is a correct configuration if the only network behind the edge ISA firewall was on network ID 10.0.1.0/24. However, in our scenario, this is an incorrect configuration and will cause problems with access controls on connections to and from the network services segment through the edge ISA firewall.

NOTE

If the ISA firewall device's routing table had been configured with a routing table entry for the network services segment located behind the network services segment perimeter firewall, the ISA firewall software's installer program would have seen this routing table entry and included that network ID as part of the edge ISA firewall's definition of its default internal network.

The reason for the problem with the initial settings for the default internal network on edge ISA firewall is that there is a Route relationship between the Corpnet ISA firewall network (which is the edge ISA firewall's default internal network) and the default internal network behind the network services segment ISA firewall. Because there is a Route relationship, connections from SecureNAT clients located behind the network services perimeter ISA firewall will reach the edge ISA firewall with their original client IP address included as the source address (note that this is not the case with proxied connections by Winsock [Firewall] and Web proxy clients). If we leave the edge ISA firewall's default internal network definition as it is now, connections from SecureNAT clients located behind the network services perimeter ISA firewall will be detected as spoofed packets.

ISA firewall networks are used to determine the validity of connections reaching the interface that is the "root" of a particular ISA firewall network. For the edge ISA firewall, the root of its default internal network is the internal interface which is on network ID 10.0.1.0/24. Any connections with a source IP address on that network ID are seen as valid. That is to say, they are seen as not being *spoofed*.

However, if a connection with a source IP address that is not part of the edge ISA firewall's default internal network's definition is made through the interface that is the root of the edge ISA firewall's default internal network (which is the internal interface of the edge ISA firewall), the connection is dropped as a spoof attempt. The ISA firewall assumes that it's not possible for an interface to accept a connection from a host on an ISA firewall network that isn't the same as that for which the interface is root.

NOTE

I'm using the term *root* to represent a point of exit and departure. The term *root* does not imply that the NIC's IP address or network ID defines what network IDs or subnets can be placed behind a NIC. You can put contiguous or discontinuous network IDs behind any NIC. The only requirements are that all IP addresses located behind any NIC on the ISA firewall must be included in the ISA firewall network for which that NIC is "root," and that no other ISA firewall network includes the same addresses. Another thing to keep in mind, which makes this concept easier to understand, is that addresses always lie behind an ISA firewall NIC. No addresses are ever in front of a NIC.

We can easily solve this problem by adding the IP addresses included in the network services perimeter ISA firewall's default internal network (which is the network services segment) to the definition of the edge ISA firewall's default internal network definition.

Adding IP Addresses of the Network Services Perimeter Segment to the Front-End ISA Firewall's Default Internal Network

Perform the following steps to add the IP addresses of the network services perimeter ISA firewall's default internal network to the definition of the front-end ISA firewall's default internal network:

1. In the ISA firewall console, expand the server name and then expand the **Configuration** node. Click on the **Networks** node.

2. On the **Networks** node, click the **Networks** tab in the **Details** pane, then double click the **Internal** network.

3. In the **Internal Properties** dialog box, click the **Addresses** tab.

4. On the **Addresses** tab, click the **Add** button.

5. In the **IP Address Range Properties** dialog box, enter the **Starting address** and the **Ending address** in the text boxes. In this example, we'll enter **10.0.0.0** and **10.0.0.255**, respectively. Click **OK** (see Figure 10.35).

Figure 10.35 Specifying IP Address Range Properties

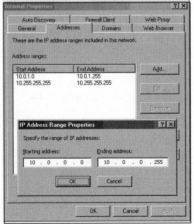

Click **OK** in the **Internal Properties** dialog box (see Figure 10.36).

Figure 10.36 The IP Address Ranges Included in the Network

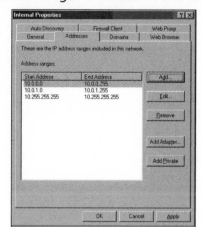

IP addressing information for hosts on the Corpnet network is determined by your requirements. The most secure configuration is to not provide users with a default gateway address that provides a route to the Internet. This forces all users to use the Firewall client and Web proxy configuration, which can be used to enforce strong user/group-based access controls, as well as block applications installed on users' computers from accessing the Internet. This also prevents users from using non-Winsock or Web proxy-compliant applications, such as Internet Control Message Protocol (ICMP) utilities such as PING and TRACERT.

Administrative users and servers can be configured with gateway addresses that route to the Internet. Administrators require the use of ICMP-based utilities, and servers do not have logged-on users, so both admins and servers require the facilities provided by the SecureNAT client configuration.

I should note that this can be problematic for networks that have LAN routers, as you must configure the clients to use the LAN routers as their default gateways. However, if you are using the ISA firewall as your edge firewall, this will not be a problem, as you can allow only administrative users access to non-Winsock protocols, such as ICMP and virtual private network (VPN) protocols.

Creating a Routing Table Entry on the Edge ISA Firewall

A routing table entry must be configured on the edge ISA firewall so that it knows the path to take to reach the network services segment. The ISA firewall should always be configured with routing table entries for all network IDs that can't be reached using the default gateway. In practice, this usually means that except for Internet addresses, there should be a routing table entry on the ISA firewall for all network IDs on your corporate network.

Note that if your ISA firewall is configured with a default gateway pointing to a LAN router, and all network IDs are reachable from that router, there's no reason to enter all network IDs in the ISA firewall's routing table, because the LAN router is performing the router duties.

At the edge ISA firewall, open a command prompt and enter the following:

```
route add -p 10.0.0.0 MASK 255.255.255.0 10.0.1.2
```

In the preceding code, *10.0.0.0* is the network ID for the network services segment behind the network services perimeter ISA firewall, *255.255.255.0* is the subnet mask for that network ID, and *10.0.1.2* is the IP address on the external interface of the back-end ISA firewall.

Figure 10.37 shows an example of configuring the routing table entry.

Figure 10.37 Configuring the Routing Table Entry

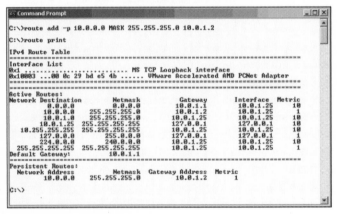

Joining the Edge ISA Firewall to the Domain

The edge ISA firewall should be a member of the domain so that you can fully leverage both the firewall and the Web proxy client configuration. Although you can use RADIUS authentication for Web proxy clients, there are significant limitations to RADIUS authentication in both the logging and the management realms. For this reason, I recommend that you avoid RADIUS authentication if at all possible. In addition, you must make the edge ISA firewall a domain member if you want to fully leverage the enhanced security and flexibility provided by the Firewall client.

The edge ISA firewall will be able to use the intradomain communications Access Rule created on the network services perimeter ISA firewall to access the domain controller. The edge ISA firewall is configured to use the DNS server on the network services segment, which is configured to support name resolution within the network and for Internet host names.

I should note that making the edge ISA firewall a domain member is specific for this scenario only, where the clients are located directly behind the edge ISA firewall. If you encounter resistance to joining the edge ISA firewall to the domain, you can easily place another ISA firewall in front of the edge ISA firewall in this scenario and then create rules that allow the required inbound and outbound connections, only not requiring any type of authentication. In this type of deployment, the ISA firewall would be acting in the same way as a typical "hardware" firewall.

Creating Access Rules on the Edge ISA Firewall, Controlling Outbound Access from Corpnet Hosts and Hosts on the Network Services Segment

Firewall policy on the edge ISA firewall will be highly customized based on your network's security requirements. You will need to decide together with your network security team who should have access to what Web sites and at what times of the day. Firewall policy is definitely something where one size does not fit all.

In the example provided by our sample network configuration, all hosts on the Corpnet ISA firewall network are configured as Firewall and Web proxy clients and are *not* configured as SecureNAT clients. The only exception is for administrator workstations, because network administrators will need access to non-Winsock protocols and utilities, such as PING and TRACERT.

We will create the following Access Rules:

- An Access Rule allowing the domain controller on the network services segment access to DNS outbound.

- An Access Rule allowing all authenticated users outbound access to all protocols. Note that in a production environment, you would create more granular access controls and create ISA firewall groups that allow users to access only the content they require to get their jobs done.

- An Access Rule allowing the servers on the network services segment access to the Windows reporting and Microsoft Update sites. We need this rule because the servers on the network services segment do not have logged-on users, so we will not be able to leverage the Firewall client to force authentication from server connections.

Table 10.5 shows the salient characteristics of these Access Rules.

Table 10.5 Access Rules on the Edge ISA Firewall

Order	Name	Action	Protocols	From/Listener	To	Condition
1	MU and Error Reporting–Servers	Allow	HTTP HTTPS	Network Services Segment	Microsoft Error Reporting Sites System Policy Allowed Sites	All Users
2	Outbound DNS for DNS Server	Allow	DNS	DNS Server*	External	All Users
3	All Open—Authenti-cated	Allow	All Out-bound Traffic	Internal	External	All Authenti-cated Users

* We will discuss the From configuration for this Access Rule shortly.

Creating the Outbound DNS for the DNS Server Access Rule

Perform the following steps to create the Access Rule allowing the domain controller on the network services segment outbound access to the DNS protocol:

1. On the edge ISA firewall, open the ISA firewall console and click the **Firewall Policy** node.

2. On the **Firewall Policy** node, click the **Tasks** tab on the **Task** pane and click **Create New Access Rule**.

3. On the **Welcome to the New Access Rule Wizard** page, enter a name for the rule in the **Access Rule name** text box. In this example, we'll name the rule **Outbound DNS for DNS Server**. Click **Next**.

4. Select the **Allow** option on the **Rule Action** page. Click **Next**.

5. On the **Protocols** page, select the **Selected protocols** option from the **This rule applies to** list and click **Add**.

6. In the **Add Protocols** dialog box, click the **Common Protocols** folder and double click on the **DNS** entry. Click **Close**.

7. Click **Next** on the **Protocols** page.

8. On the **Access Rule Sources** page, click the **Add** button.

9. In the **Add Network Entities** dialog box, click the **New** menu and click **Computer**.

10. In the **New Computer Rule Element** dialog box, enter a name for the computer in the **Name** text box. In this example, we'll name the computer **DNS Server**. Enter the IP address of the external interface of the network services segment perimeter ISA firewall. Note that we use the IP address of the external interface of the perimeter ISA firewall because there is a NAT relationship between the perimeter ISA firewall's default internal network and its default external network. Because the DNS queries the DNS server makes are to the Internet-based DNS server, the connection will be NATed. When the connection is NATed, the source IP address of the outbound connection is the primary IP address on the external interface of the perimeter ISA firewall. In this example, the IP address is **10.0.1.2**, so we'll enter that address. Enter an optional description if you like. Click **OK** (see Figure 10.38).

Figure 10.38 Adding a New Network Entity

In the **Add Network Entities** dialog box, click the **Computers** folder and double click the **DNS Server** entry. Click **Close** (see Figure 10.39).

Figure 10.39 Adding Network Entities

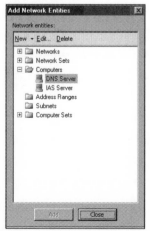

12. Click **Next** on the **Access Rule Sources** page.

13. Click **Add** on the **Access Rule Destinations** page.

14. In the **Add Network Entities** dialog box, click the **Networks** folder and then double click **External**. Click **Close**.

15. Click **Next** on the **Access Rule Destinations** page.

16. Click **Next** on the **User Sets** page.

17. Click **Finish** on the **Completing the New Access Rule Wizard** page.

Creating the All Open Rule for Authenticated Users

Perform the following steps to create the outbound Access Rule allowing all authenticated users outbound access to all protocols and sites:

1. On the edge ISA firewall, open the ISA firewall console and click the **Firewall Policy** node.

2. On the **Firewall Policy** node, click the **Tasks** tab on the **Task** pane and click **Create New Access Rule**.

3. On the **Welcome to the New Access Rule Wizard** page, enter a name for the rule in the **Access Rule name** text box. In this example, we'll name the rule **All Open—Authenticated**. Click **Next**.

4. Select the **Allow** option on the **Rule Action** page. Click **Next**.

5. On the **Protocols** page, select the **All outbound traffic** option from the **This rule applies to** list and click **Next**.

6. Click **Next** on the **Protocols** page.

7. On the **Access Rule Sources** page, click the **Add** button.

8. In the **Add Network Entities** dialog box, click the **Networks** folder and then double click **Internal**. Click **Close**.

9. Click **Next** on the **Access Rule Sources** page.

10. Click **Add** on the **Access Rule Destinations** page.

11. In the **Add Network Entities** dialog box, click the **Networks** folder and then double click **External**. Click **Close**.

12. Click **Next** on the **Access Rule Destinations** page.

13. On the **User Sets** page, click the **All Users** entry and click **Remove**. Click **Add**.

14. In the **Add Users** dialog box, double click on the **All Authenticated Users** entry and click **Close** (see Figure 10.40).

Figure 10.40 Adding Authenticated Users

15. Click **Next** on the **User Sets** page.

16. Click **Finish** on the **Completing the New Access Rule Wizard** page.

Creating the Microsoft Update and Error Reporting Sites Access Rule

Perform the following steps to create the Access Rule allowing servers on the network services segment access to the Windows Update sites and the Microsoft Error Reporting sites:

1. On the edge ISA firewall, open the ISA firewall console and click the **Firewall Policy** node.

2. On the **Firewall Policy** node, click the **Tasks** tab on the **Task** pane and click **Create New Access Rule**.

3. On the **Welcome to the New Access Rule Wizard** page, enter a name for the rule in the **Access Rule name** text box. In this example, we'll name the rule **MU and Error Reporting—Servers**. Click **Next**.

4. Select the **Allow** option on the **Rule Action** page. Click **Next**.

5. On the **Protocols** page, select the **Selected protocols** option from the **This rule applies to** list and click **Add**.

6. In the **Add Protocols** dialog box, click the **Common Protocols** folder and double click on the **HTTP** and **HTTPS** entries. Click **Close**.

7. Click **Next** on the **Protocols** page (see Figure 10.41).

Figure 10.41 Selecting the Protocols to Which the Rule Applies

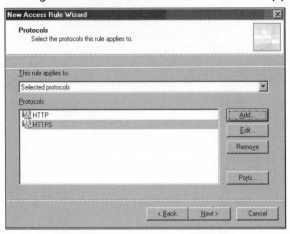

8. On the **Access Rule Sources** page, click the **Add** button.

9. In the **Add Network Entities** dialog box, click the **New** menu and click **Address Range**.

10. In the **New Address Range Rule Element** dialog box, enter a name for the address range in the **Name** text box. In this example, we'll name it **Network Services Segment**. Enter the start and end addresses in the **Start Address** and **End Address** text boxes. Enter an optional description and then click **OK** (see Figure 10.42).

Figure 10.42 Specifying the Range of IP Addresses

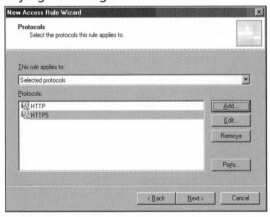

11. In the **Add Network Entities** dialog box, click the **Address Ranges** folder and double click the **Network Services Segment** entry. Click **Close** (see Figure 10.43).

Figure 10.43 Adding Network Entities

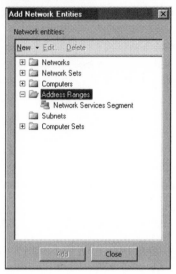

12.   Click **Next** on the **Access Rule Sources** page.

13.   Click **Add** on the **Access Rule Destinations** page.

14.   In the **Add Network Entities** dialog box, click the **Domain Name Sets** folder and double click **Microsoft Error Reporting sites** and **System Policy Allowed Sites**. Click **Close** (see Figure 10.44).

Figure 10.44 Selecting Domain Name Sets

15. Click **Next** on the **Access Rule Destinations** page.

16. Click **Next** on the **User Sets** page.

17. Click **Finish** on the **Completing the New Access Rule Wizard** page.

Before applying the configuration to the ISA firewall's firewall policy, make sure that you put the unauthenticated Access Rules before the authenticated rules. This is a good general approach to ordering firewall rules on your ISA firewall.

Click **Apply** to save the changes and update the firewall policy. Click **OK** in the **Apply New Configuration** dialog box. Your firewall policy should look like that in Figure 10.45.

Figure 10.45 The Completed Firewall Policy

O... ▲	Name	Action	Protocols	From / Listener	To	Condition
⊞ 📋 1	MU and Error Reporting – Servers	✅ Allow	🔒 HTTP 🔒 HTTPS	🖧 Network Services Segment	🗎 Microsoft Error Reporting sites 🔊 All Users 🗎 System Policy Allowed Sites	
📋 2	Outbound DNS for DNS Server	✅ Allow	🔒 DNS	🖥 DNS Server	⬤ External	🔊 All Users
📋 3	All Open – Authenticated	✅ Allow	🔒 All Outbound Traffic	🖧 Internal	⬤ External	🔊 All Authenticated Users
📋	Last Default rule	⊘ Deny	🔒 All Traffic	🖧 All Networks (and Local Host)	🖧 All Networks (and Local Host)	🔊 All Users

Creating Publishing Rules on the Edge ISA Firewall to Allow Inbound Connections to the Exchange Server Mail Services

Now we're ready to create Publishing Rules allowing access to Exchange server services for users on the Internet. We'll create Server Publishing Rules that allow access to the OWA, Secure Exchange RPC, SMTP, POP3, and IMAP4 services.

Creating an SSL Server Publishing Rule on the Network Services Perimeter ISA Firewall

We begin by creating an SSL Server Publishing Rule on the front-end ISA firewall. We must create a Server Publishing Rule rather than a Web Publishing Rule because the OWA form generated by the network services perimeter ISA firewall cannot be delivered through a Web proxy connection on the edge ISA firewall. The SSL Server Publishing Rule will enable a secure, end-to-end connection but will not allow the edge ISA firewall to perform stateful application layer inspection on the SSL connection moving through the edge ISA firewall. The edge ISA firewall will be limited, like a typical "hardware" firewall, to simple stateful packet inspection.

This is a limitation of our sample network design and should not be construed to imply that you can never use OWA FBA in a back-to-back ISA firewall configuration. For example, suppose you have a back-to-back ISA firewall configuration with a DMZ between the front-end and back-end ISA firewalls. You can use FBA on the front-end ISA firewall and configure its OWA Web Publishing Rule to forward basic credentials to the back-end ISA firewall's Web Publishing Rule. The back-end ISA firewall is configured to use basic authentication. In this case, we have single sign-on with FBA.

Creating the Network Services Perimeter Network OWA Web Publishing Rule

Perform the following steps on the edge ISA firewall to enable inbound access to the network services perimeter ISA firewall's OWA Web Publishing Rule:

1. In the ISA firewall console, expand the server name and click the **Firewall Policy** node.

2. On the **Firewall Policy** node, click the **Tasks** tab on the **Task** pane and then click the **Publish a Secure Web Server** link.

3. On the **Welcome to the SSL Web Publishing Rule Wizard** page, enter a name for the rule in the **SSL Web Publishing Rule name** text box. In this example, we'll name the rule **SSL tunnel to OWA**. Click **Next**.

4. On the **Publishing Mode** page, select the **SSL Tunneling** option and click **Next** (see Figure 10.46).

Figure 10.46 Specifying the Publishing Mode

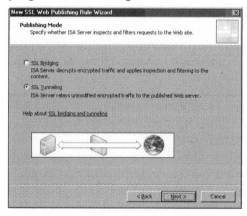

5. On the **Select Server** page, enter the IP address of the external interface of the network services perimeter ISA firewall. This is the address used by the listener on the OWA Web Publishing Rule on the network services perimeter ISA firewall. In this example, the IP address is **10.0.1.2**, so we'll enter that address and click **Next** (see Figure 10.47).

Figure 10.47 Entering the IP Address of the External Interface of the Network Services Perimeter ISA Firewall

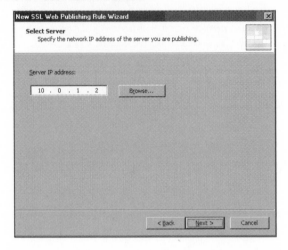

6. On the **IP Addresses** page, put a checkmark in the **External** checkbox and click **Next**.

7. Click **Finish** on the **Completing the New SSL Web Publishing Rule Wizard** page.

At this point, your firewall policy should look like that in Figure 10.48.

Figure 10.48 The Completed Firewall Policy

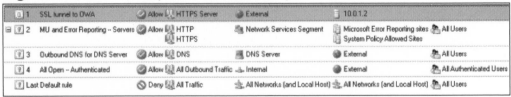

Creating Secure Exchange RPC, SMTP, POP3, and IMAP4 Server Publishing Rules

The next step is to create the Server Publishing Rules on the edge ISA firewall that provide access to the Server Publishing Rules configured on the network services perimeter ISA firewall. These Server Publishing Rules enable Internet-based hosts access to the Exchange server services on the network services segment.

Creating the Mail Server Publishing Rules

Perform the following steps to create the Server Publishing Rules on the edge ISA firewall:

1. In the ISA firewall console, expand the server name and then click the **Firewall Policy** node.

2. On the **Firewall Policy** node, click the **Tasks** tab on the **Task** pane and click the **Publish a Mail Server** link.

3. On the **Welcome to the New Mail Server Publishing Rule Wizard** page, enter a name for the rule in the **Mail Server Publishing Rule name** text box. In this example, we'll name the rule **Exchange Server**. Click **Next**.

4. On the **Select Access Type** page, select the **Client access: RPC, IMAP, POP3, SMTP** option and click **Next** (see Figure 10.49).

Figure 10.49 Selecting the Access Type

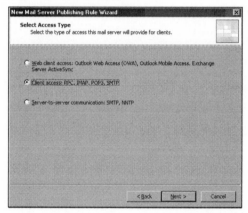

5. On the **Select Services** page, put a checkmark in each checkbox. This will allow us to connect to the Exchange server on the network services segment through the network services perimeter ISA firewall for all the services listed on this page. Note the comment on the page regarding the SMTP Message Screener. We will not deploy the message screener in this example, but you might want to consider it in your own deployment. You can install the SMTP Message Screener on the ISA firewall to filter both inbound and outbound mail. Even though the SMTP Message Screener won't be enabled, the SMTP filter is enabled and will protect SMTP communications. Click **Next** (see Figure 10.50).

Figure 10.50 Selecting the Services to Publish

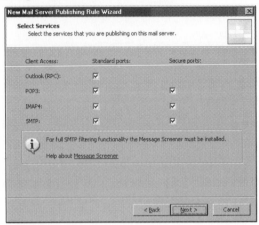

6. On the **Select Server** page, enter the IP address of the Exchange server on the network services segment in the **Server IP address** text box. In this example, the IP address is **10.0.0.2**, so we enter that value. Click **Next**.

7. On the **IP Addresses** page, put a checkmark in the **External** checkbox. Click **Next**.

8. Click **Finish** on the **Completing the New Mail Server Publishing Rule Wizard** page.

Your firewall policy should appear similar to that in Figure 10.51. Note that the Mail Server Publishing Rule Wizard added seven new Server Publishing Rules. Click **Apply** to save the changes and update the firewall policy. Click **OK** in the **Apply New Configuration** dialog box.

Figure 10.51 The Completed Firewall Policy

1	Exchange Server IMAPS Server	Allow IMAPS Server	External	10.0.0.2	
2	Exchange Server POP3S Server	Allow POP3S Server	External	10.0.0.2	
3	Exchange Server SMTP Server	Allow SMTP Server	External	10.0.0.2	
4	Exchange Server IMAP4 Server	Allow IMAP4 Server	External	10.0.0.2	
5	Exchange Server POP3 Server	Allow POP3 Server	External	10.0.0.2	
6	Exchange Server Exchange RPC Server	Allow Exchange RPC S...	External	10.0.0.2	
7	Exchange Server SMTPS Server	Allow SMTPS Server	External	10.0.0.2	
8	SSL tunnel to OWA	Allow HTTPS Server	External	10.0.1.2	
9	MU and Error Reporting -- Servers	Allow HTTP HTTPS	Network Services Segment	Microsoft Error Reporting sites System Policy Allowed Sites	All Users
10	Outbound DNS for DNS Server	Allow DNS	DNS Server	External	All Users
11	All Open -- Authenticated	Allow All Outbound Traffic Internal	External	All Authenticated Users	
Last Default rule	Deny All Traffic	All Networks (and Local Host)	All Networks (and Local Host)	All Users	

We need to do one more thing on the edge ISA firewall to make the Server Publishing Rules work correctly. Because there is a Route relationship between the Corpnet ISA firewall network and the network services segment, we will need to change the Server Publishing Rules on the edge ISA firewall so that the client requests appear to come from the edge ISA firewall. This allows us to use the Server Publishing Rules we created on the network services perimeter ISA firewall where the listener is listening on the Corpnet ISA firewall network.

Configuring the Server Publishing Rules to Use the ISA Firewall's Address as the Source IP Address

For each Server Publishing Rule created by the Mail Server Publishing Wizard, perform the following steps:

1. Double click on one of the **Server Publishing Rules** created by the **Server Publishing Rule Wizard**.

2. In the **Properties** dialog box for that rule, click the **To** tab.

3. On the **To** tab, select the **Requests appear to come from the ISA Server computer** option. Click **OK** (see Figure 10.52).

Figure 10.52 Specifying the Network Address of the Server to Publish

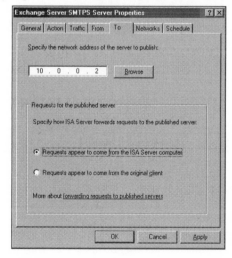

4. **Repeat** the procedure for all the Server Publishing Rules created by the Mail Server Publishing Rule Wizard.

5. Click **Apply** to save the changes and update the firewall policy.

6. Click **OK** in the **Apply New Configuration** dialog box.

Creating a Routing Table Entry on Network Clients (Required Only If No LAN Routers Are Installed)

Clients on the Corpnet ISA firewall network need to know the route to the network services segment. As discussed earlier in this chapter, you have two options: Use LAN routers that contain the appropriate routing table entries to reach the network services segment, or configure the clients with a routing table entry.

In this chapter, we'll create routing table entries on the clients. You can automate this process by using a logon script that contains the *Route add* command used to add the routing table entry. The command required is:

```
Route add -p 10.0.0.0 MASK 255.255.255.0 10.0.1.2
```

In the preceding command, *–p* makes the routing table entry permanent, *10.0.0.0* is the network ID of the network services segment, *255.255.255.0* is the subnet mask for the network services segment, and *10.0.1.2* is the gateway address used to reach that network.

Joining the Network Clients to the Domain

All the pieces are now in place to add the network clients to the domain. The network services perimeter ISA firewall has the appropriate Access Rules in place to join hosts on the Corpnet ISA firewall network to the domain. The procedure varies with the operating system you're joining to the domain. In this chapter, we're joining a Windows XP client to the domain.

Creating and Configuring DNS Entries in the Domain DNS, Including WPAD Entries

DNS infrastructure design is critical for all Windows environments. One of the most common reasons for connectivity and performance issues is a poorly designed DNS infrastructure. Proper DNS infrastructure is critically important in ISA firewall networking because the ISA firewall uses DNS name resolution for access control and security monitoring.

Clients on the Corpnet ISA firewall network will be configured as both Web proxy and Firewall clients. Web proxy and Firewall clients need to be able to locate the edge ISA firewall to access the Internet. Although you can manually configure each host with the proper information, it's much easier to automate the process using Web Proxy Auto Discovery (WPAD) entries in DNS and/or DHCP.

Web proxy and Firewall clients use WPAD entries in DNS and/or DHCP to find the address of the ISA firewall. After the clients find the address of the ISA firewall, the clients obtain configuration information from the ISA firewall. By default, the ISA firewall advertises configuration information on TCP port 80, which can be changed if required. However, if you use DNS-based WPAD entries, you *must* use TCP port 80. If you use DHCP for WPAD information, you can use any port you like to advertise autodiscovery information.

In this chapter, we will use DNS WPAD publishing. We will create a WPAD CNAME record based on the Host (A) record for the edge ISA firewall. The Host (A) record for the edge ISA firewall maps the name of the edge ISA firewall to the IP address on the internal interface of the edge ISA firewall.

Perform the following steps to create the WPAD entry on the domain DNS server on the network services segment:

1. At the DNS server, click **Start**, point to **Administrative Tools**, and click **DNS**.

2. In the **DNS** console, expand the server name and then expand the **Forward Lookup Zones** node. Click on the domain, which in this case is **msfirewall.org**.

3. Right click the domain name and click **New Alias (CNAME)**.

4. In the **New Resource Record** dialog box, enter **wpad** in the **Alias name (uses parent domain if left blank)** text box. Click the **Browse** button (see Figure 10.53).

Figure 10.53 Entering an Alias Name

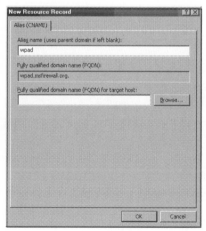

5. Double click the server name in the **Records** section, and then double click the **Forward Lookup Zone** entry. Double click the domain name and then double click the entry for the edge ISA firewall. In this example, the name of the edge ISA firewall is **remoteisa**, so double click that one (see Figure 10.54).

Figure 10.54 Selecting the Edge ISA Firewall

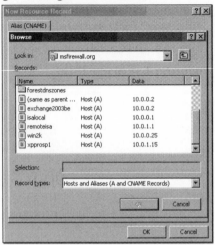

6.   Click **OK** in the **New Resource Record** dialog box (see Figure 10.55).

Figure 10.55 Applying Changes

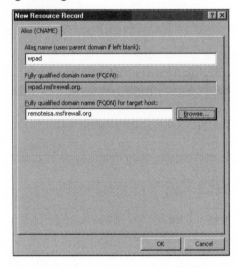

7.   The new CNAME record appears in the right pane of the console, as shown in Figure 10.56.

Note that the edge ISA firewall's IP address is included in the domain DNS because it was automatically added when the firewall joined the domain. If your domain DNS is not configured to enable automatic registration of DNS records, you'll need to create the Host (A) record yourself before you can create the CNAME record.

Figure 10.56 The New CNAME Record

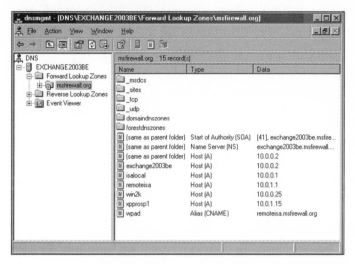

Configuring the Firewall and Web Proxy Client Settings on the Edge ISA Firewall, and Enabling Autodiscovery

In my experience, one of the least understood issues with ISA firewall configuration relates to the settings in the Firewall client configuration on the ISA firewall. For each ISA firewall network, you can configure Firewall client settings that are used by Firewall client systems located on that ISA firewall network. These settings allow you to set how the Firewall client software finds the ISA firewall, what destination addresses should be remoted to the ISA firewall, and which ones should not be serviced by the Firewall client software.

The best way to learn how these settings work is to get into the configuration interface. Perform the following steps on the edge ISA firewall to configure the Firewall client settings:

1. In the ISA firewall console, expand the server name and then expand the **Configuration** node. Click the **Networks** node.

2. On the **Networks** node, double click the default **Internal Network** entry.

3. In the **Internal Properties** dialog box, click the **Firewall Client** tab. On the **Firewall Client** tab, confirm that there is a checkmark in the **Enable Firewall client support for this network** checkbox. When this option is enabled, the Firewall client listener port, TCP 1745, is enabled and listens for connections from the Firewall clients on that ISA firewall network. In the **ISA Server name or IP address** text box, enter the fully qualified domain name of the ISA firewall. This is a critical setting. The default entry in this text box is the NetBIOS name of the

ISA firewall, which can create problems with name resolution. The name you enter into this text box is the name Firewall clients on the network will use to access the ISA firewall. If you leave just the NetBIOS name in this text box, there could be problems with name resolution related to fully qualifying the unqualified name. Although I am not saying that it won't work to leave just the NetBIOS name in this text box, I am saying that you will avoid difficult-to-troubleshoot issues with Firewall clients if you use a fully qualified domain name (FQDN) in this text box. Put a checkmark in the **Automatically detect settings** checkbox and do *not* enable the **Use automatic configuration script** and **Use a Web proxy server** checkboxes. You will get autoconfiguration information by using autodiscovery, and you don't need the **Use a Web proxy server** setting because the client will find the Web proxy filter component of the ISA firewall using the **wpad** settings (see Figure 10.57).

Figure 10.57 Enabling Firewall Client Settings

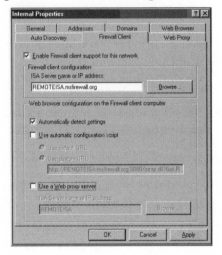

4. Click the **Domains** tab. On this tab, you enter your internal domain names so that the Firewall clients do not use the Firewall client software to handle connections to hosts on the internal domains. This is a tricky setting on multihomed ISA firewalls with multiple internal ISA firewall networks, but in this example, the edge ISA firewall has only a single internal network, so we won't run into those issues. In this example, we have a single internal domain, which is **msfirewall.org**. Click **Add** to enter the internal network domain (see Figure 10.58).

5. In the **Domain Properties** dialog box, enter the name of the internal domain in the **Enter a domain name to include** text box. Click **OK** (see Figure 10.59).

Figure 10.58 The Domains Tab

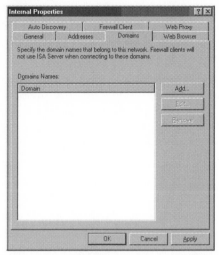

Figure 10.59 Entering a Domain Name

We can also configure the Web proxy client settings in the **Properties** dialog box of the ISA firewall network. Continue with the following steps to configure the Web proxy client configuration:

1. In the **Internal Properties** dialog box, click the **Web Browser** tab. On the **Web Browser** tab, confirm that there are checkmarks in the **Bypass proxy for Web server in this network** and **Direct access computers specified in the Domains tab**. The Bypass proxy for Web servers in this network setting allows the Web proxy client machines to bypass their Web proxy configuration when connecting to servers using a *single label name*. For example, http://server1 is a single label name. When the single label name is used, the Web browser ignores the Web proxy settings and connects directly to the Web server. This is known as *Direct Access*. When Direct Access is used, the client system must be able to resolve

the name itself, as the ISA firewall does not handle the connection and therefore does not perform name resolution on behalf of the client.

The **Directly access computers specified in the Domains tab** option enables the Web proxy client system to bypass the Web proxy configuration when connecting to hosts that belong to a domain included in the **Domains** tab. This is a useful option because the Web proxy client bypasses its Web proxy configuration and the ISA firewall when connecting to internal, trusted servers on the corporate network.

You can also add servers, domains, and addresses for Direct Access by clicking the **Add** button next to the **Directly access these servers or domains** list. You might want to put all the addresses in the ISA firewall network in the Direct Access list. For example, because we're in the **Internal Properties** dialog box, we could include all the addresses in the default **Internal** network. In a multihomed, multiple internal network design, this can be used for authenticated access control.

2. Confirm that there is a checkmark in the **If ISA Server is unavailable, use this backup route to connect to the Internet** checkbox and that the **Direct Access** option is selected (see Figure 10.60).

Figure 10.60 The Web Browser Tab

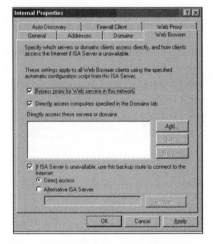

The last thing we need to do in the **Internal Properties** dialog box is enable **Autodiscovery** publishing. Perform the following steps to enable the ISA firewall to publish autodiscovery information:

1. Click the **Auto Discovery** tab in the **Internal Properties** dialog box.

2. On the **Auto Discovery** tab, put a checkmark in the **Publish automatic discovery information** checkbox. Leave the default port listed in the **Use this**

port for automatic discovery request text box as **80**. We must use TCP port 80 because we are using DNS for our WPAD entry (see Figure 10.61).

Figure 10.61 The Auto Discovery Tab

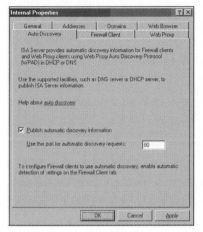

3. Click **OK** in the **Internal Properties** dialog box.

4. Click **Apply** to save the changes and update the firewall policy.

5. Click **OK** in the **Apply New Configuration** dialog box.

Installing the Firewall Client Share on the Network Services Segment File Server

The Firewall client software will be installed on all the client systems on the Corpnet ISA firewall network. Note that you should install the Firewall client software only on network client systems, and avoid installing it on servers. Although it is possible to install the Firewall client software on servers, there is little reason to do so, because servers typically do not have logged-on users (that is, interactive logons). You will avoid difficult-to-diagnose connectivity issues if you do not install the Firewall client software on network servers.

Although some ISA firewall administrators choose to install the Firewall client share on the ISA firewall itself, I highly recommend against this practice, as it requires Windows file sharing protocol connections to be made to the ISA firewall device itself. This creates an increase in the ISA firewall's attack surface that doesn't need to be there. Instead, install the Firewall client share on a file server on the network services segment. Remember, the ISA firewall is a network-level security device and connections to and from the ISA firewall device should be severely limited.

Perform the following steps on the file server computer on the network services segment:

1. At the file server on the network services segment, place the **ISA Server 2004 CD** into the CD-ROM drive. The **autorun menu** will appear. If the autorun menu does not appear, double click the **isaautorun.exe** file on the CD.

2. In the **ISA Server 2004 Setup** autorun menu, click the **Install ISA Server 2004** link.

3. Click **Next** on the **Welcome to the Installation Wizard for Microsoft ISA Server 2004** page.

4. Select the **I accept the terms in the license agreement** option on the **License Agreement** page and click **Next**.

5. Enter your user information and product serial number on the **Customer Information** page and click **Next**.

6. Select the **Custom** option on the **Setup Type** page.

7. On the **Custom Setup** page, click the **ISA Server Management** icon and click the **This feature will not be available** option. Click the **Firewall Client Installation Share** icon and click the **This feature, and all subfeatures, will be installed on local hard drive** option. Click **Next** (see Figure 10.62).

Figure 10.62 Selecting the Program Features to Install

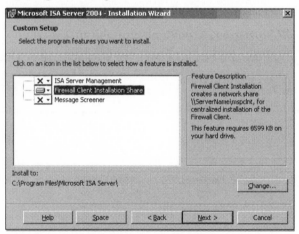

8. Click **Install** on the **Ready to Install the Program** page.

9. Click **Finish** on the **Installation Wizard Completed** page.

10. Close the **Internet Explorer** window that presents a page on how to **Protect the ISA Server Computer**.

11. Click the **Exit** link on the ISA autorun menu.

Installing the Firewall Client on the Network Clients

The Firewall client share is now installed on the file server and can be accessed using the \\server_name\mspclnt\setup.exe Universal Naming Convention (UNC) path. Any user logged on as a local administrator can install the Firewall client software. However, if some of your users do not run as local administrators, you'll need to find another way to install the Firewall client software.

Fortunately, the ideal solution to this problem is Active Directory Group Policy-based software installation. Because the client machines must be domain members to fully utilize the flexibility and increased security provided by the Firewall client, those domain members can have their Firewall client software installed automatically via Group Policy.

In the following procedure, we will create an Organizational Unit (OU) for machines that should have the Firewall client software automatically installed. We do this to prevent the Firewall client software from being installed on servers. There may be more elegant ways to approach this, such as using Group Policy filtering, but I'll leave that up to the Active Directory guys to figure out the most efficient way to assign the Firewall client software only to client systems and not to servers.

Note that in the following example, we'll create an OU that provides a Group Policy Object (GPO) linked to the OU that installs the Firewall client software. In a production environment, you will want to link other GPOs to the OU and order the GPO links appropriately.

Perform the following steps to create the OU, place a client system in the OU, and then use Software Installation to assign the Firewall client software to members of the OU:

1. On the domain controller on the network services segment, open the **Active Directory Users and Computers** console from the **Administrative Tools** menu.

2. Right click on the domain name, point to **New**, and click **Organizational Unit**.

3. In the **New Object—Organizational Unit** page, enter **Firewall Client Systems** in the **Name** text box. Click **OK**.

4. Click the **Computers** node and right click the client system name in the right pane of the console. Click **Move**.

5. In the **Move** dialog box, click the **Firewall Client Systems** node and click **OK**.

6. Right click the **Firewall Client Systems** OU and click **Properties**.

7. In the **Firewall Client Systems Properties** dialog box, click the **Group Policy** tab.

8. On the **Group Policy** tab, click the **New** button. Name the new GPO **Firewall Client Installation** and click **Edit**.

9. In the **Group Policy Object Editor** console, expand the **Computer Configuration** node and then expand the **Software Settings** node. Right click **Software installation**, point to **New**, and click **Package**.

10. In the **Open** dialog box, enter the UNC path to the Firewall client installation package file. In this example, the path is **Win2k\mspclnt\MS_FWC.msi**. Click **Open** (see Figure 10.63).

Figure 10.63 Entering the UNC Path to the Firewall Client Installation Package File

11. In the **Deploy Software** dialog box, select the **Assigned** option and click **OK** (see Figure 10.64).

Figure 10.64 Selecting the Deployment Method

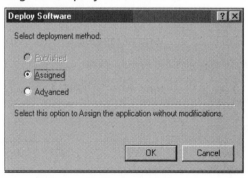

12. Close the **Group Policy Object Editor**.

13. Close the **Firewall Client Systems Properties** dialog box.

14.   Close **Active Directory Users and Computers**.

15.   Open a command prompt on the domain controller, enter **gpupdate**, and press **Enter**. When the client systems restart, the Firewall client software will install automatically.

Connecting the Corporate Network Clients to Resources on the Network Services Segment and the Internet

Now the clients on the Corpnet ISA firewall network are ready to connect to resources on the network services segment and the Internet.

Open the Web browser on the client and go to www.isaserver.org. You'll see log file entries on the edge ISA firewall that appear similar to those in Figure 10.65.

Figure 10.65 Log File Entries on the Edge ISA Firewall

10.0.1.5	69.20.55.133	80	http	Allowed... All Open -- Authentic...	MSFIREWALL\Adm...	http://www.isaserver.org/img/rec/msexchange.gif
10.0.1.5	69.20.55.133	80	http	Allowed... All Open -- Authentic...	MSFIREWALL\Adm...	http://www.isaserver.org/img/rec/windowsnetworking.gif
10.0.1.5	69.20.55.133	80	http	Allowed... All Open -- Authentic...	MSFIREWALL\Adm...	http://www.isaserver.org/img/rec/windowsecurity.gif
10.0.1.5	69.20.55.133	80	http	Allowed... All Open -- Authentic...	MSFIREWALL\Adm...	http://www.isaserver.org/img/rec/serverfiles.gif
10.0.1.5	69.20.55.133	80	http	Allowed... All Open -- Authentic...	MSFIREWALL\Adm...	http://www.isaserver.org/img/rec/ntfaxfaq.gif
10.0.1.5	69.20.55.133	80	http	Allowed... All Open -- Authentic...	MSFIREWALL\Adm...	http://www.isaserver.org/img/i_subtitle.gif
10.0.1.5	69.20.55.133	80	http	Allowed... All Open -- Authentic...	MSFIREWALL\Adm...	http://www.isaserver.org/img/rss.gif
10.0.1.5	69.20.55.133	80	http	Allowed... All Open -- Authentic...	MSFIREWALL\Adm...	http://www.isaserver.org/img/i_new.gif

Now open a share on the file server on the network services segment. You'll see entries like those in Figure 10.66.

Figure 10.66 Entries in a Share on the File Server on the Network Services Segment

3/9/2...	10.0.1.5	10.0.0.2	53	DNS Server	Initiated... Publish DNS
3/9/2...	10.0.1.5	10.0.0.25	0	Ping	Initiated... File Server Access
3/9/2...	10.0.0.1	10.0.0.2	123	NTP (UDP)	Closed ... Allow NTP from ISA Server to...
3/9/2...	10.0.1.5	10.0.0.25	445	Microsoft CIFS (T...	Initiated... File Server Access

Summary

We began this chapter with an in-depth discussion on network perimeters and how to design a functional network services segment via perimeterization. In subsequent sections, we provided detailed concepts and step-by-step instructions on how to configure the edge and network services perimeter ISA firewall to support secure connections from hosts located on the corporate network outside the perimeter to selected Exchange server services from Internet hosts.

## Chapter 11

DMZ Router and Switch Security

Solutions in this chapter:

- **Securing the Router**

- **Securing the Switch**

- **IOS Bugs and Security Advisories**

- **DMZ Router and Switch Security Best-Practice Checklists**

☑ **Summary**

☑ **Solutions Fast Track**

☑ **Frequently Asked Questions**

Introduction

When people think about securing their DMZs, they mostly think about firewalls, IDSs, VPNs, and hardening of servers within the DMZ. These are all parts of the process, but there is more to securing a DMZ than considering just these items. Some DMZ planners overlook hardening the routers or switches supporting the DMZ so that they cannot be exploited and used as tools to penetrate the network. Routers and switches provide the connectivity, both within the DMZ environment and to other areas of the network to which the DMZ is connected. This makes routers and switches prime targets for hackers to exploit and glean information about the network or simply use as springboards to other devices. Routers and switches on the DMZ, and anywhere else on the network, can also be used to protect resources that they connect via security features, including ACLs, port security, and private VLANs, to name a few. This chapter presents information on how to design and configure some important router and switch security features that enable them to run securely and protect the devices that they connect.

Securing the Router

This section covers how routers are implemented within a DMZ environment. We discuss topics such as the placement of routers in traditional DMZ environments, routing traffic into and out of the DMZ, applying access restrictions, and how to lock down the router's many features and services. In this chapter we use the Cisco router and IOS as the baseline for the examples. If you are using another vendor's router or switch, you might want to consult that vendor's appropriate documentation. Regardless of whose router or switch you use in your enterprise, the concepts introduced and discussed in this chapter are applicable across the board.

The configuration of the Cisco router Internetwork Operating System (IOS) is consistent across the entire Cisco router product line, especially as it relates to security. This makes it very easy to standardize security measures and policies across the network. This standardization allows the network administrator to create security templates that are applied to new router implementations.

The following sections provide valuable recommendations, techniques, and configuration information that will increase the integrity and security of your DMZ so that hackers will find it difficult, if not impossible, to hack into your network via the DMZ by exploiting your Internet-facing routers.

Router Placement in a DMZ Environment

In this section, we focus our attention on the routers involved in connecting the DMZ environment to the internal network and the Internet. Figure 11.1 illustrates an enterprise location with two internal LANs, a DMZ, and connectivity to the Internet. The diagram shows the use of three routers. One is a multilayer switch, which is a switch with routing capabilities (for simplicity, we'll call it a *router* from now on). A multilayer switch can increase routing performance when your network has a large number of users or VLANs, since the hardware that routes the traffic between VLANs is internal to the switch chassis and does not require any external connections. In Figure 11.1, the multilayer switch is directing traffic on the internal LAN.

The second device is an Internet router that provides connectivity to the Internet via a link to an ISP. Between these two routers is a firewall, which is just a router with the added ability to intelligently filter packets based on session state, among other things. The firewall is used to protect the internal LAN and provide secure connectivity to the DMZ's resources. In this example, we assume that static routes are configured correctly on the firewall, but if you need further details on how to configure the firewall to route traffic, refer back to the firewall configuration chapters earlier in this book. At this point we need to set up routing so that internal users can access resources on the Internet and so that a user on the Internet can access resources on the DMZ.

Figure 11.1 Router Placement in a Traditional DMZ Environment

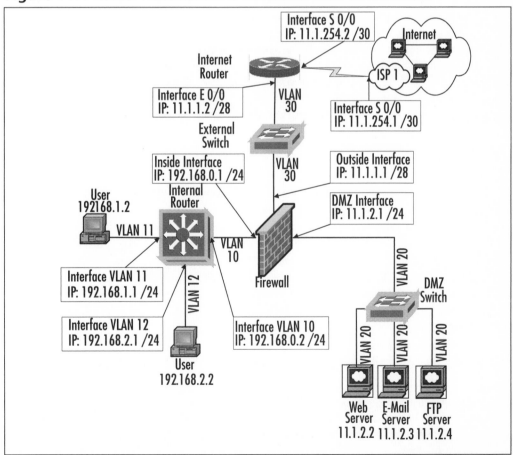

In Figure 11.1 you see a basic DMZ configuration. We placed a switch on the external leg of the firewall, connecting the router to the firewall. You could use a crossover cable to make this connection, but we placed it here because you could place a honeypot or IDS sensor outside the firewall. Either way, this setup is highly flexible based on your needs, but you should be aware of the reason we placed the routers and switches where they are in the graphic.

First, let's work on routing traffic from the internal LAN to the Internet. In this example, we assume that there isn't a proxy server and that users will access the Internet directly via a default route. All routers on the internal LAN need to know where to send traffic destined for a resource on the Internet. This can be accomplished by using a static route or a dynamic routing protocol such as OSPF or EIGRP. This could be a daunting task if you had to add static routes or dynamically route each network on the Internet (since there are currently over 150,000 Internet routes) on the internal routers—not to mention that it would take a lot of memory and CPU cycles.

NOTE

If you want to use a proxy server, make sure that the internal users can access the proxy server and in turn the proxy server can access the Internet. Proxy servers are usually located on the DMZ, which requires firewall configuration to allow users to access the proxy server as well as allow the proxy server to access the Internet. This approach prevents any direct communication between clients on the protected internal network and untrusted Internet resources; all communication must flow through the proxy server on the DMZ.

To reduce the amount of administration and computing power needed on internal routers, we will use a default route or gateway of last resort to route traffic to the Internet. This means that if a router does not have a specific route to a destination, it will forward the packet to its configured default route. In the example in Figure 11.1, the internal multilayer switch provides connectivity for the internal LAN segments. For users on the internal LAN who require access to the Internet, the internal router must have its default route or gateway of last resort set to the firewall's inside IP address. In this case, the router's default route would be 192.168.0.1. In turn, the firewall should check its routing table and forward the packet to the Internet router, 11.1.1.2.

Before the firewall forwards this packet, it needs to perform a NAT on the packet source address. The 192.168.0.0/16 network is a private network that could potentially be used in every IP network in the world; therefore, we need to translate the address to a public address that is assigned to our network, so we can be sure the return packets will make it back. In this case, we will use the external IP address of the firewall for the NAT, to conserve address space and simplify the configuration. We could have just as easily used an available address in the 11.1.1.0/28 network, if we were so inclined. The Internet router will then forward the packet to the ISP, where it will be routed to its destination, based on the ISP's dynamic protocols. The internal router requires two commands to implement a static route, as shown in Figure 11.2. The *ip route* command sets the default to 192.168.0.1 (the inside interface of the firewall), and the *ip classless* command lets the router route to unknown subnets.

Figure 11.2 Configuring a Default Route

```
InternalRouter(config)# ip route 0.0.0.0 0.0.0.0 192.168.0.1
InternalRouter(config)# ip classless
```

NOTE

If there are other routers in addition to the multilayer switch on the internal network and you are using a dynamic routing protocol, you should redistribute the default route into the routing protocol. This allows the default route to propagate dynamically to the other routers in the routing domain and saves you the effort of statically configuring the default route on every router. Also, if your topology contains redundant links, the dynamic protocol can automatically route around failed links. The redistribution procedure might differ, depending on the dynamic routing protocol in use. Refer to the following URL for more information on advertising a default route and selecting the routing protocol(s) used on your network: www.cisco.com/univercd/cc/td/doc/product/software/ios122/122cgcr/fipr_c/ipcprt2/index.htm.

At this point we have discussed how requests from the internal LAN are routed to the Internet. Now we must look at how the replies are routed back and how requests initiated from the Internet are routed to resources on the DMZ. The routing protocol of choice on the Internet is Border Gateway Protocol (BGP), which enables the dynamic routing of networks across the Internet. BGP is an Exterior Gateway Protocol (EGP) used to connect autonomous systems. In Figure 11.1, we showed the Internet router connecting to ISP 1 for connectivity to the Internet. In some cases, this router is provided and managed by the ISP, so the enterprise administrators do not have to worry about its configuration; they simply point their default route on the firewall to the Internet router's local Ethernet interface (11.1.1.2). The ISP will worry about advertising the enterprise's public addresses (11.1.1.0 /28 and 11.1.2.0 /24) across the Internet so that everyone will know how to reach these networks. However, if you (meaning the enterprise) manage the Internet router on your premises and the ISP manages the connection on its end, there usually will be two options. The first option is to point a default route to the ISP's border router on the serial connection, and the ISP will statically route your public address space (11.1.1.0 /28 and 11.1.2.0

/24) to your end as well as advertise it across the Internet. Figure 11.3 shows the routes needed to configure the Internet router for a default route to the Internet via the ISP as well as routes to reach the DMZ located on the DMZ leg of the firewall.

The second option is to use BGP to send and receive routing updates to and from the ISP. For networks with a single Internet link, there is generally no need to run BGP, since there is only one way in and out, but it can still be used if you prefer to employ some sort of dynamic routing protocol. Many enterprises aren't willing to suffer the downtime associated with an Internet link failure, though, so they will have multiple Internet links and routers. With multiple links, the enterprise can run BGP with each ISP and dynamically advertise their networks. The rest of the Internet will learn of the multiple paths to the enterprise's network, and the traffic can take the best path to the enterprise, depending on which paths are currently available. We will discuss BGP in more detail in the next section.

Figure 11.3 Configuring a Default Route

```
InternetRouter(config)# ip classless
InternetRouter(config)# ip route 0.0.0.0 0.0.0.0 11.1.254.1
InternetRouter(config)# ip route 11.1.2.0 255.255.255.0 11.1.1.1
```

Table 11.1 shows the routing tables for all enterprise-managed devices that are involved when static routes are used to configure the network shown in Figure 11.1. Notice how the Internet router has no knowledge of the internal LAN routes (192.168.0.0 /24, 192.168.1.0 /24, and 192.168.2.0 /24). This is because the private address space is not routable through the Internet; furthermore, the firewall translates the internal source addresses to public addresses on the 11.1.1.0/28 subnet.

Table 11.1 Routing Table

Device	Route	Next Hop
Internal Router	192.168.0.0 /24	Local—VLAN10
	192.168.1.0 /24	Local—VLAN11
	192.168.2.0 /24	Local—VLAN12
	Default	192.168.0.1
Firewall	192.168.0.0 /24	Local—inside interface
	11.1.2.0 /24	Local—DMZ interface
	11.1.1.0 /28	Local—outside interface
	192.168.1.0 /24	192.168.0.2
	192.168.2.0 /24	192.168.0.2
	Default	11.1.1.2

Continued

Table 11.1 Routing Table

Device	Route	Next Hop
Internet Router	11.1.1.0 /28	Local—interface E 0/0
	11.1.254.0 /30	Local—interface S 0/0
	11.1.2.0 /24	11.1.1.1
	Default	11.1.252.1

Border Gateway Protocol

As we mentioned in the previous section, BGP is the routing protocol used to dynamically route packets across the Internet. If you are using BGP in your environment, you will want to be sure that you sufficiently secure it so that hackers can't easily attack your BGP session. Let's first go through a quick review of how the BGP protocol works and then examine some options about how to secure it.

The design and configuration of BGP has been the topic of many books and articles, including the *BGP Case Studies* document located on Cisco's Web site at www.cisco.com/warp/public/459/bgp-toc.html. We assume that if you are considering administering a BGP connection to your ISP, you have extensive knowledge of the protocol and are comfortable supporting it.

BGP routes traffic between networks that are under different administrative controls. These networks are known as *autonomous systems (ASs)*. If you are running BGP, you will have an AS number assigned to your organization, just as each of your ISPs will have its own unique AS number assigned to it. BGP is able to scale to such large internetworks, such as the Internet, because it doesn't concern itself with what is inside the network of any particular AS. The details of the routing inside an AS are left to the Interior Gateway Protocols (IGPs) such as OSPF, RIP, and EIGRP. Instead of tracking every router hop that must be traversed to reach a destination, like IGP protocols, BGP tracks only the ASs that must be traversed to get there. This design allows for the AS to grow to a massive size, with hundreds or thousands of routers, and BGP won't need to treat it any differently than when the AS had only 10 routers. BGP allows government, education, and enterprise networks across the world to communicate with each other seamlessly. BGP is highly scalable, flexible, and very robust—and it needs to be, because there are well over 150,000 BGP routes on the Internet.

Some of the key features of BGP are:

- It is a path-vector protocol.
- It uses TCP port 179 to communicate, or peer, with neighbors.
- It supports classless interdomain routing (CIDR) to reduce the size of the Internet's routing tables by classless summarization.

- It is currently in version 4.

- BGP running between routers in two different autonomous systems is considered external BGP (eBGP), whereas BGP running between routers in the same AS is considered internal BGP (iBGP).

- It has an extensive number of BGP attributes that are used to decide the best path.

NOTE

AS numbers are assigned by the American Registry for Internet Numbers (ARIN). For the enterprise to receive its own AS, it must meet some requirements, including that the site must be multihomed, meaning that it has connectivity to more than one ISP. For more information on AS number registration, visit ARIN's Web site at www.arin.net/registration/asn/index.html.

BGP uses multiple attributes to describe every route entry in the BGP table and uses these attributes in the route decision process. These attributes can be classified into four categories:

- Well-known, mandatory

- Well-known, transitive

- Optional, transitive

- Optional, nontransitive

The well-known attributes are required to be recognized by all implementations of BGP, regardless of vendor. They are further divided into the *mandatory attributes*, which are required to describe every route, and the *discretionary attributes*, which are not. The *optional attributes* do not have to be supported by every BGP implementation and are divided into the *transitive attributes*, which can be propagated to other ASs, and the *nontransitive attributes* that cannot leave the originating AS. Some of the attributes that BGP uses are:

- **Next hop** A well-known, mandatory attribute that contains the address of the next-hop router that is used to reach the destination.

- **Origin** A well-known, mandatory attribute that defines how a network was originated. Values are *IGP* for routes originated in the same AS, *EGP* for routes learned outside the AS, and *incomplete* for routes injected into BGP through another protocol (redistribution).

- **AS-Path** The third well-known, mandatory attribute; records a list of the AS numbers that are between the local router and the route destination. When a router sends a route to a neighboring AS (via eBGP), it prepends its own AS number to the AS-Path. You will see later how this attribute is used in the decision process, but it is also used for loop prevention. If a router receives a route with its own AS number in the AS-Path, it can safely ignore the update so that loops are not created. Traffic should never pass through any particular AS more than once.

- **Weight** A Cisco proprietary parameter used to select the preferred path to a destination. This attribute is used only for decisions on the local router and is not propagated to any neighbor routers.

- **Local preference** A well-known, discretionary attribute that is also used to select a preferred path to a destination. This is a similar attribute to weight, except it is propagated throughout an AS so that all routers within an AS recognize and use the path with the highest local preference.

- **Multi-exit discriminator (MED)** An optional, nontransitive attribute that is used to suggest to an external AS the preferred route into an AS, when multiple paths exist. This attribute should not be propagated past the directly attached AS and does not have to be honored by the neighboring AS. The lower MED value is the preferred path.

- **Community** An optional, transitive attribute that provides a way of grouping destinations, to which routing decisions can be applied. You can think of this attribute as a tag that can be applied to a route or a group of routes. The BGP neighbor can decide to take certain actions with packets that match routes that are "tagged" with a certain community value. Just as with the MED value, a neighboring AS does not have to take any action just because a community has been assigned to a route.

On a Cisco router, BGP determines the best path for a route by applying the following 10 routing decisions, in order:

1. If the path specifies a next hop that is inaccessible, do not consider it.

2. Prefer the path with the largest administrative weight.

3. If the weights are the same, consider the path with the higher local preference.

4. If the local preferences are the same, prefer the path from which the local router originated.

5. If no route was originated, prefer the route with the shortest AS path.

6. If all routes have the same AS-path length, prefer the path with the best origin code. IGP is better than EGP, which is better than Incomplete.

7. If the origin codes are the same, prefer the path with the lowest MED metric.

8. If the paths have the same MED, prefer external paths over internal paths.

9. If the paths are still the same, prefer the path through the closest IGP neighbor.

10.   Lastly, prefer the path with the lowest IP address for the unique BGP router ID.

BGP is a very complex routing protocol. Trying to explain all its nuances in this brief section would not be possible. However, we do cover some basic features as well as how to secure BGP updates, because that is what you will be concerned about while securing your DMZ infrastructure.

> **NOTE**
>
> If you are taking in full BGP routes from your ISP, make sure that you have enough memory in the routers supporting BGP. Because the Internet has over 150,000 routes, you need a minimum of 128MB of RAM.

As we mentioned in the previous section, all ISPs offer a managed service that provides the customer with the equipment, configuration, and support needed for the links connecting the site to the Internet. This means that the ISP will take care of managing all aspects of running the Internet router pictured in Figure 11.4. All the customer has to do is connect the Internet router's Ethernet interface to the external switch (assuming the same topology as Figure 11.1) and configure a default on the firewall route to point to the Internet router. Easy, right? Well, if you've ever dealt with some ISPs, you know it can be difficult to get them to make changes, or even have them provide performance reports and statistics for the router and the Internet link. However, in many cases this is still the best option if you have limited technical resources and only one ISP.

Should you have multiple links to different ISPs and the technical resources required, it could be advantageous to control the Internet-facing router(s) yourself. This solution will allow you more control of the way Internet traffic enters and exits you network via the different ISPs. BGP has many "knobs and switches" (attributes) that allow you to shape the flow of traffic so that the best path is taken. Controlling the Internet-facing router(s) also gives you complete access into the router for detailed reports and statistics of router and Internet link performance as well as more visibility for applying and managing security and for troubleshooting problems.

In Figure 11.4, we show connectivity to the Internet via a link to ISP 1. For simplicity, we break ARIN's multihomed requirement for this example. The enterprise has a registered public address space (11.1.1.0 /28 and 11.1.2.0 /24) and an AS number (AS 200) that it wants advertised to the Internet so that internal users can access the Internet and users on the Internet can access resources on the DMZ. To accomplish this task, we need to configure BGP on the Internet router to advertise the enterprise's public addresses to its BGP neighbor at ISP 1 (which is fully managed by the ISP) as well as receive routing updates from ISP 1.

In global configuration mode, we enable BGP and set the AS number to 200 on the Internet router using the *router bgp* command, as shown in Figure 11.5. The *no synchronization* command disables BGP from checking its interior gateway protocol (IGP) for reachability before it advertises the route to its neighbor.

We use the *network* statement to tell BGP what local networks to advertise. In this case, we need to advertise the 11.1.1.0 /28 and 11.1.2.0 /24 subnets to the Internet. The *network* statement has the restriction that it will advertise the configured network only if it is in the local routing table of the router. The subnet 11.1.1.0 /28 is directly connected to the router, so it knows how to reach the subnet. However, subnet 11.1.2.0 /24 is not directly connected but is located on the firewall's DMZ interface. To advertise this route, we must add a static route for 11.1.2.0 /24 (the first line in the example), since we are not running an IGP in our DMZ. This allows the Internet router to advertise this route to its BGP neighbor, because it now exists in the routing table. Once we have established the AS and the networks we need to advertise, we can move on to establishing a neighbor to the ISP router.

Figure 11.4 A Single BGP Neighbor to an ISP

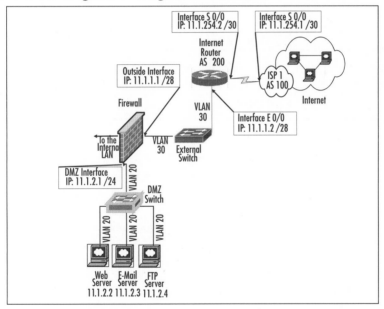

To configure a neighbor, we use the *neighbor remote-as* command to specify the neighbor IP address and AS number. In this example, the IP address of the neighbor is 11.1.254.1, and the AS for ISP 1 is 100. It is also a good idea to add a route map, distribution list, filter list, or prefix list to limit the routes being advertised or received by your AS. If you are in a multi-homed environment and you do not have filters in place to limit what is advertised to your ISPs, you can mistakenly become a transit AS by advertising all routes received from one provider to the other. If this happens, it can inundate your Internet link with unwanted traffic.

In the example, we use a *route-map* to allow the router to advertise only the enterprise's registered public address space (11.1.1.0 /28 and 11.1.2.0 /24) to the ISP using the *neighbor route-map* command and a route map that calls on access list 5. The *no auto-summary* command disables the autosummarization of advertised routes to their classful boundaries, such as 11.0.0.0/8. Assuming that the ISP has configured its end, at this point you should be able to establish a neighbor peering with the ISP and be able to share BGP routing information. To view the status of BGP neighbors, use the *show ip bgp neighbors* command or the *show ip bgp summary*; to view BGP routes, use the *show ip bgp* command.

Figure 11.5 BGP Example

```
InternetRouter(config)# ip route 11.1.2.0 255.255.255.0 11.1.1.1
InternetRouter(config)# route-map RoutesOut permit 10
InternetRouter(config-route-map)# match ip address 5
InternetRouter(config)# access-list 5 permit 11.1.1.0 0.0.0.15
InternetRouter(config)# access-list 5 permit 11.1.2.0 0.0.0.255
InternetRouter(config)# router bgp 200
InternetRouter(config-router)# no synchronization
InternetRouter(config-router)# network 11.1.1.0 mask 255.255.255.240
InternetRouter(config-router)# network 11.1.2.0 mask 255.255.255.0
InternetRouter(config-router)# neighbor 11.1.254.1 remote-as 100
InternetRouter(config-router)# neighbor 11.1.254.1 route-map RoutesOut out
InternetRouter(config-router)# no auto-summary
```

At this point, we have a pretty standard BGP configuration. We should be receiving any routes that we are configured to receive from our ISP (default-only, local customer, or full routing table, as examples) and we are advertising our networks, allowing our networks to be reachable across the Internet. Now we need to concern ourselves with how to secure our BGP session from tampering. To do this, we will enable the MD5 authentication feature, which can be used on a per-neighbor basis. This feature will generate an MD5 hash from the packet contents and then attach it to the update before it is sent to the neighboring device. The neighbor will then verify that the packet has not been tampered with by verifying the hash value before accepting the update. You will use the *neighbor password* command, which is shown in Figure 11.6, to enable this feature. Not all ISPs require this option to be set, but it is a good idea to implement it so that hackers spoofing the ISP can't inject bad routes into your Internet router. You will need to agree on a password and an implementation time, in advance, with your ISP because the BGP session will not stay connected unless both sides are configured with the same password.

Figure 11.6 Securing BGP with MD5 Authentication

```
InternetRouter(config)# router bgp 200
InternetRouter(config-router)# neighbor 11.1.254.1 password myBGPpassword
```

It is important to note that the password configured in Figure 11.6 is used as an example only. You need to make sure that you use a strong password for your BGP authentication, or else your network might not be as secure as you think. If you choose an easy password, it could be quickly cracked with a brute-force or dictionary attack, whereas strong passwords would take enough time as to make the process infeasible. If this password is compromised, the MD5 authentication will be of no use, since a hacker will be able to authenticate malicious traffic. Also keep in mind that enabling this feature, even with strong passwords, is no guarantee that your BGP session cannot be tampered with. For example, there is a theoretical DoS attack against the BGP authentication process in Cisco routers that could be used to disrupt your BGP session if you are not running a version of IOS that corrects for the vulnerability.

Another way to help prevent hackers from being able to inject faulty information or disrupting your BGP sessions is to implement the BGP TTL Security Hack (BTSH). An eBGP session, by default, can talk with only a BGP peer that is directly connected to the router. This is because the originating router will set the time-to-live (TTL) setting in the outgoing packet to 1, so if the BGP neighbor is not the directly connected device, the upstream device will decrement the TTL to 0 and drop the packet. However, in some situations you might need to establish an eBGP session between devices that are more than one hop away. The way around this problem is to use the eBGP multihop. When eBGP multihop is used, the TTL in the outgoing packet will be set to the number specified in the *multihop* command, allowing the packet to travel as many hops as required to reach the destination.

Although this might seem like some measure of security in itself, it really doesn't provide any security at all. One reason is that BGP doesn't require that inbound eBGP packets have a TTL of 1 when they arrive at the destination router. If you don't know how many hops away your eBGP neighbor is, you can set the eBGP multihop command to 255 hops and the session will still establish without issue, as shown in Figure 11.7. Even if this check was in place, it wouldn't stop a hacker from setting the TTL on the malformed BGP packets high enough so that the TTL is the correct value when it arrives at the target router. To remedy this situation, the BTSH was created. This feature alters the way the TTL is configured on the BGP peers. For this reason, BTSH and eBGP multihop cannot co-exist with each other; you must choose the one you want to use.

Figure 11.7 Configuring eBGP Multihop

```
InternetRouter(config)# router bgp 200
InternetRouter(config-router)# neighbor 11.1.254.1 ebgp-multihop 255
```

BTSH works by being configured with the number of hops between the eBGP peers and then setting the TTL for the configured session to the maximum number, 255. When the other peer receives the eBGP packet, it knows how many hops are between the two routers and expects the TTL to be set accordingly. If the two peers are two hops away from each other, they would expect a TTL of 253 when the packet arrives on the external interface. If the TTL is any lower, the packet will not be accepted. Since the TTL is already set to the maximum value, this approach prevents a hacker from being able to increase the value to compensate for the additional hops to send a malicious BGP packet to one of the peers. An example of this configuration is shown in Figure 11.8.

Figure 11.8 Configuring BTSH

```
InternetRouter(config)# router bgp 200
InternetRouter(config-router)# no neighbor 11.1.254.1 ebgp-multihop 255
InternetRouter(config-router)# neighbor 11.1.254.1 ttl-security hops 2
```

BTSH is a fairly new feature that was introduced in 12.0(27)S, which is part of the service provider train of code and was later added to 12.3(7)T and later.

Access Control Lists

Access control lists (ACLs) allow a router to filter traffic that passes through it based on a certain set of criteria. A router can filter a number of protocols, but since DMZs mainly use IP, we concentrate here on IP ACLs. ACLs can be applied inbound or outbound on any interface of the router and will filter based on a variety of fields in the IP header as well as the headers that belong to higher-layer protocols such as TCP, UDP, and ICMP. It is important to remember that ACLs are, for lack of a better term, dumb packet filters. They do not possess any of the intelligence that is included in stateful firewall products. They look individually at each packet, check the packet against the parameters of the access list, and make a decision for each packet. ACLs can be placed anywhere on your network, but in this section, we concentrate on creating and applying ACLs in key areas within your Internet/DMZ infrastructure. Depending on your design, you might need to place ACLs in other strategic areas to protect your network resources.

ACLs are processed top down, and when a match is found, the router executes the action (*permit* or *deny*) and stops checking for further matches. Therefore, the order of the lines that make up the ACLs is very important. Many people make the mistake of making broad *permit* statements, then later in the ACL configuring a specific *deny* statement, or vice versa. This might not provide the desired effect, so be careful when you're creating ACLs, because a simple ACL error can open holes in your network that hackers can exploit. All ACLs have an implicit *deny all* statement appended at the end, so if a packet is not explicitly permitted, it will be denied.

There two types of IP ACL: standard and extended. A *standard ACL* can only filter based on the source IP address and mask. The command to create a standard ACL is *access-list <access-list-number> <action> <source-IP> [source-wildcard] [log]* in global configuration mode. As you can see, the command has many parameters, which we have broken down here:

- **Access-list-number** Groups the ACL entries together. For standard ACLs, the number must be between 1 and 99 or between 1300 and 1999.

- **Action** Defines the action the router will take if the entry is matched. The values are *permit* or *deny*. The *permit* action allows the packet to continue; the *deny* action drops the packet.

- **Source IP** The source IP address of the packet. This can be any valid IP address or the keyword *any* to signify all IP addresses.

- **Source-wildcard** The wildcard mask or bits to applied to source IP to determine a range of addresses. If no wildcard mask is specified (it is optional), the router assumes you are specifying a single host.

- **Log** This statement at the end of a line will generate a log message upon a successful match of the specific entry. This message can be printed to the console, the internal log buffer or syslog, depending on how you have configured the logging facilities on the router.

The example in Figure 11.9 illustrates a standard ACL. The ACL number is 1 and only permits to a host with the IP address of 192.168.1.50 and any device within the subnet 10.10.0.0 /16. All other traffic is dropped and logged.

NOTE

ACLs can be used in many devices, not just routers. Today almost any device you purchase that offers some form of security is able to create an ACL.

Figure 11.9 Standard ACL Example

```
DMZRouter(config)# access-list 1 permit 192.168.1.50
DMZRouter(config)# access-list 1 permit 10.10.0.0 0.0.255.255
DMZRouter(config)# access-list 1 deny any log
```

An extended ACL can filter on the source and/or destination IP address as well as filter on source and/or destination port. Extended ACLs can also filter on other characteristics of each specific protocol—for instance, the flags in the TCP header and the many different functions of ICMP, to name a few. The command to create an extended ACL is *access-list <access-list-number> <action> <protocol> <source-IP> <source-wildcard> [operator [port]] <destination-IP> <destination-wildcard> [operator [port]] [log]]* in global configuration mode.

- **Access-list-number** Groups the access list entries together. For extended ACLs, the number must be between 100 and 199 or between 2000 and 2699.

- **Action**   Defines the action the router will take if the entry is matched. The values are *permit* or *deny*. The *permit* action allows the packet to continue; the *deny* action drops the packet.

- **Protocol**   The name or number of an Internet protocol. The most common values are TCP, UDP, IP, and ICMP. If IP is defined, it means anything that runs on top of IP, including but not limited to TCP, UDP, and ICMP.

- **Source-IP**   The source IP address of the packet. This can be any valid IP address or the keyword *any* to signify all source IP addresses.

- **Source-wildcard**   The wildcard mask or bits to apply to the source IP to determine a range of addresses. This field is not used when the keyword *any* is used in the previous field.

- **Destination-IP**   The destination IP address of the packet. This can be any valid IP address or the keyword *any* to signify all destination IP addresses.

- **Destination-wildcard**   The wildcard mask or bits to apply to the destination IP to determine a range of addresses. This field is not used when the keyword *any* is used in the previous field.

- **Operator**   This is optional; operands used to compare source or destination ports. Possible operands are *lt* (less than), *gt* (greater than), *eq* (equal), *neq* (not equal), and *range*.

- **Port**   The number or name of a TCP or UDP port (optional).

- **Log**   This statement at the end of a line will generate a log message upon a successful match of the specific entry. This message can be printed to the console, the internal log buffer, or syslog, depending on how you have configured the logging facilities on the router.

NOTE

We listed only some of the most common parameters used in an extended ACL. There are several other parameters for each specific Internet Protocol. Cisco routers also support named ACLs, where names can be given to the standard and extended ACLs instead of assigning a number. For further details on ACLs, refer to Cisco router IOS documentation or the following URL: www.cisco.com/univercd/cc/td/doc/product/software/ios122/122cgcr/fipr_c/ipcprt 1/1cfip.htm#1109098.

Figure 11.10 shows an example of an extended ACL. The ACL number is 102 and allows ICMP connectivity to and from any host, allows only SNMP access to devices on the

192.168.1.0 /24 subnet from all hosts, and lastly, permits UDP access from the 192.168.2.0 /24 subnet to the 192.168.1.0 /24 subnet. As with all ACLs, any access not explicitly permitted will be denied.

Figure 11.10 Extended ACL Example

```
DMZRouter(config)# access-list 102 permit icmp any any
DMZRouter(config)# access-list 102 permit tcp any 192.168.1.0 0.0.0.255
    eq snmp
DMZRouter(config)# access-list 102 permit udp 192.168.2.0 0.0.0.255
    192.168.1.0 0.0.0.255
```

To apply an ACL to an interface, use the *ip access-group <access-list-number> {in | out}* command in interface configuration mode. Access lists can be applied inbound or outbound on an interface. The example in Figure 11.11 applies ACL 102 inbound to Fast Ethernet interface 0/0.

Figure 11.11 Extended ACL Example

```
DMZRouter(config)# interface fastethernet 0/0
DMZRouter(config-if)# ip access-group 102 in
```

Configuring & Implementing…

Tips on Configuring ACLs for the Ingress Interface of Internet-Facing Routers

In the example in Figure 11.12, we show a typical enterprise branch office with an internal LAN, a DMZ, and connectivity to the Internet. The firewall will protect the internal LAN and the DMZ, but the LAN segment in front of the firewall is left unprotected, as is the Internet router. Assuming that you control the Internet router, meaning that it is not part of a service managed by your ISP, you can apply an ACL to provide some protection for devices connected to the outside LAN, including the Internet router, switches, and any other device that might be outside the firewall. ACLs can be applied to the ingress or egress interfaces on the router, to filter access. In this configuration template, we cover how to configure ACLs to protect against unauthorized access and prevent common hacking techniques. We then finish by discussing how to apply the ACL to the Internet-facing router's inbound interface, as shown in Figure 11.12.

Continued

All ingress Internet router ACLs should start with an antispoofing ACL, which will prevent spoofing of the special address ranges described in RFC 3330, *Special-Use IPv4 Addresses*. RFC 3330 is meant to be a collection of address assignments that have been made in other RFC documents and includes the private address ranges already assigned from RFC 1918, among others. These private address ranges, such as 10.0.0.0/8, 172.16.0.0/12, and 192.168.0.0/16, should be blocked at your Internet border because traffic sourced from these networks would never be valid. The exclamation point in the following cod was added for visual and explanation purposes only and is not needed, nor will it be shown in the configuration:

```
! To block spoofing of RFC 1918 Address ranges
IntRouter(config)# access-list 110 deny ip 10.0.0.0
    0.255.255.255 any
IntRouter(config)# access-list 110 deny ip 172.16.0.0
    0.15.255.255 any
IntRouter(config)# access-list 110 deny ip 192.168.0.0
    0.0.255.255 any
```

There are other address ranges listed in RFC 3330 that you will most likely want to drop in your ACL, such as the loopback range of 127.0.0.0/8, the Link Local range of 169.254.0.0/16, the Test-Net range of 192.0.2.0/24, and the multicast range of 224.0.0.0/4. Again, these are ranges that are assigned for special uses and should never be seen on the Internet. You need to understand your network and its traffic patterns well enough to decide if you also want to block all the other ranges listed in RFC 3330.

Some Web sites, such as www.cymru.com/Bogons/, also keep a list of network ranges from which you should never see Internet traffic sourced. They refer to these invalid address ranges as *bogons*, which include the addresses mentioned in RFC 3330, as well as IP blocks that haven't yet been assigned for allocation. Since these address ranges are not being assigned to users, there is no valid reason that you should see traffic on the Internet coming from these ranges. You could decide to manually filter these prefixes by creating an access list based on the list, or you can use one of the other available methods, such as a BGP peering session, to receive and filter these networks in a more automated fashion.

In addition to denying traffic sourced from the private and unallocated address ranges, we can also deny traffic that is sourced from the public address ranges that have been assigned to our enterprise. All valid traffic going into our network should have a destination of our public address ranges, but we should never receive traffic on our Internet connection that is sourced from our public address ranges. We can add a couple lines to our ACL to deny this traffic:

Continued

```
! Block spoofing of our public address ranges
IntRouter(config)# access-list 110 deny ip 11.1.1.0
    0.0.0.15 any
IntRouter(config)# access-list 110 deny ip 11.1.2.0
    0.0.0.255 any
```

Figure 11.12 Ingress Internet-Facing Router ACL

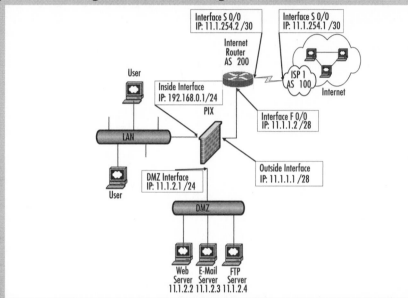

To allow only ICMP echo replies to enter the network from pings originated from the internal network, you must first permit the echo replies, then deny all other ICMP traffic so that pings initiated from the Internet will not be able to enter the network. This is an optional step but can be useful to prevent some DoS attacks:

```
! Allow ICMP echo reply from a ping initiated from the
    internal LAN
IntRouter(config)# access-list 110 permit icmp any any echo-
    reply
IntRouter(config)# access-list 110 deny icmp any any
```

Since the Internet router is the first line of defense against DoS attacks or worms, this ACL can be a point at which known attacks or worms can be thwarted or isolated. For example, to mitigate the exposure of the SQL Slammer worm, Cisco recommended the following ACL at ingress and egress points of the

Continued

network. This step is optional but can be an effective option in trying to prevent a fast-moving attack or worm from spreading any further:

```
! Stop the SQL Slammer worm from spreading
IntRouter(config)# access-list 110 deny udp any any eq 1434
```

After you have all the specific entries defined, you must add the *permit all* statement so that legitimate traffic can flow through the router:

```
! Permit all other access
IntRouter(config)# access-list 110 permit ip any any
```

The last step is to apply the ACL the Internet ingress points. In this case, we apply ACL 110 to Serial 0/0 on the Internet router:

```
IntRouter(config)# interface serial 0/0
IntRouter(config-if)# ip access-group 110 in
```

Security Banner

All network devices should present the legitimate end user, unauthorized user, or administrator logging into the system with a legal message prior to the login screen. The message should contain the following four statements, at a minimum:

- Unauthorized access is prohibited.
- Unauthorized access is unlawful, and violators may face civil and/or criminal prosecution.
- Access or attempted access to the system may be recorded and used as evidence in court.
- Any applicable federal, state, or local laws should be cited.

These notices help in the prosecution of any unauthorized person who attempts to enter and possibly succeeds in entering the system. Unfortunately, even criminals have rights, and to protect your network, these legal notices are necessary so that you can pursue conviction of intruders, should the need arise. The security banner should be a legal notice and not contain any information about the device such as its name, make, model, or function. This information could be useful to intruders trying to break into the system. You should always check with your legal and security departments prior to configuring the security banner on your devices to make sure it is worded correctly, meets corporate policies, and will hold up in court.

The Cisco router can display your legal message prior to the login screen with the use of the *banner login* command. Figure 11.13 shows an example of a security banner.

Figure 11.13 Configuring a Security Banner

```
DMZRouter(config)# banner login ^
          Warning!!!  You have accessed a private network.
             UNAUTHORIZED ACCESS IS PROHIBITED BY LAW
      Violators may be prosecuted to the fullest extent of the law.
  Your access to this network may be monitored and recorded for quality
     assurance, security, performance, and maintenance purposes.
  ^
```

NOTE

There are also different login levels for a Cisco device, and other banners can be constructed for these different levels. For example, let's say that you have Banner MOTD, which stands for *message of the day*. If you configure banners, make sure you test them to ensure that you have configured the proper one. If your device is compromised, you will not want to provide the attacker with any information whatsoever. Using tools such as a vulnerability scanner or analyzer, hackers can do entire scans (sweeps) of large IP address ranges, and the tools they use will provide them with the banner information. They can then go through the logs searching for any useful information. If you use banners, ensure that they provide *no* useful information at all.

Securely Administering the Router

This section describes how to configure the router so that management interfaces and services are protected and locked down. We secure all the entries into the CLI or via Web management. To secure this access, we need to secure all in-band and out-of-band connectivity options to include the console, auxiliary, Telnet, SSH, and HTML. This is done to prevent hackers from making changes to the router's configuration, gathering important network information, or using the compromised router as a launching point for other attacks. You will learn how to use TACACS+ or RADIUS servers to authenticate, authorize, and log access to the router. Lastly, we discuss using and securing management services such as SNMP, NTP, and syslog.

Console and Auxiliary Ports

Routers have console and auxiliary ports to allow direct serial access to the routers' CLI. By default, there is no security on these interfaces, so it is very important to secure these entry points into a router's CLI; if they are left unconfigured, a hacker with physical access to the router can literally connect a laptop to the router's console or auxiliary port and access the network with no interference. If you purchase a new router and basically configure it to pass traffic without locking it down using the methods described in this chapter, it is highly likely that you will suffer an attack. Access to the console and auxiliary port can be protected by a password or authenticated via a TACACS or RADIUS server. This type of access can be used for general maintenance and monitoring or when access via other methods, such as Telnet or SSH, is rendered useless due to configuration error or malfunction, whereas accessing the router via the console could be your last option to correct the problem before having to call Cisco's TAC for assistance.

NOTE

Cisco's TAC is responsible for providing Cisco customers with assistance for technical and configuration issues for all Cisco's hardware and software products, including the PIX firewall. Cisco's TAC can be contacted by phone or via the following URL: www.cisco.com/en/US/support/index.html.

By default, no password is set on the console and auxiliary ports. It is very important to apply a password via the *password* command to the console or auxiliary interface, to protect and discourage unauthorized personnel from attaching to the console or auxiliary ports and obtaining unabated access to exec mode. As always, the password should be a nondictionary word, difficult to guess, and it should contain a combination of letters, numbers, and special characters. A weak password will be easily cracked via a dictionary or brute-force attack (a topic that is covered in Chapter 15, "Hacking the DMZ."). Passwords can contain up to 80 characters, are case sensitive, and cannot begin with a number. When possible, use TACACS or RADIUS to authenticate access to the console port, because this allows for centralized control of the device and makes it easier to audit security violations. We discuss how to configure TACACS or RADIUS support later in this section. Always apply an *exec-timeout* timeout so that idle sessions will time out after a configured amount of time, such as 15 minutes, as configured in Figure 11.14. The example in Figure 11.14 illustrates how to use these commands to secure the console and auxiliary ports.

NOTE

If you want the most secure router (or switch) with virtually no way to penetrate it, consider using only out-of-band management via the console. If you lock your router in a closet or cabinet and use only console access, attackers can do very little in the way of penetration. This situation becomes a nightmare to administer, but then again, it is only an option for you to choose, depending on your need for high security or what your security policy dictates.

Figure 11.14 Configuring Console and Auxiliary Ports

```
DMZRouter(config)# line con 0
DMZRouter(config-line)# password H@rd2Cr@ck
DMZRouter(config-line)# exec-timeout 15 0
DMZRouter(config)# line aux 0
DMZRouter(config-line)# password H@rd2Cr@ck
DMZRouter(config-line)# exec-timeout 15 0
```

Telnet

The Cisco router provides the ability for you to Telnet to the CLI so you can manage and administer the device. The router usually allows for five simultaneous Telnet sessions from hosts or networks you specify via an ACL. As is the case with the console port, Telnet access can be protected by a password or authenticated via a TACACS or RADIUS server. Remember that Telnet traffic is sent in clear text, and if someone is sniffing your network, they can easily capture the router's Telnet password or the enable password, or if you are using AAA, they will be able to obtain a user ID and password and use them later for other malicious activity.

Figure 11.15 shows how to configure the five Telnet sessions (numbered 0 though 4) on the router under the *line vty 0 4* virtual terminal line configuration section. You can apply a password to the virtual interface via the *password* command. Remember to use a password that is hard to guess and is a combination of characters and numerals.

Follow the same rules of selecting a password as in the console section. For further protection, apply an access list that limits the hosts that are allowed to Telnet to the router. In this example, we used the *access-class* command to apply access list 10, which allows only the host with IP address of 192.168.1.50 to Telnet to the router. As with the console port, apply an *exec-timeout* timeout so the sessions will time out after an idle period, again set to 15 minutes in Figure 11.15. The *transport input* command specifies the type of protocol to allow on this line. In the example, we allow only Telnet sessions on this line.

Figure 11.15 Telnet Configuration Example

```
DMZRouter(config)# access-list 10 permit host 192.168.1.50
DMZRouter(config)# line vty 0 4
DMZRouter(config-line)# password H@rd2Cr@ck
DMZRouter(config-line)# access-class 10 in
DMZRouter(config-line)# exec-timeout 15 0
DMZRouter(config-line)# transport input telnet
```

SSH

One of the major weaknesses inherent to a Telnet session is that all data is sent in clear text. This can be a serious security vulnerability if someone is able to sniff your Telnet session to the router. This eavesdropping and snooping of your connection, either promiscuously or via a man-in-the-middle (MITM) attack, can provide just about any attacker with your full set of credentials because they will not be secured via encryption. The router can support SSH version 1.*x* and 2.0, depending on the IOS version, which gives the administrator secure access to the router's CLI. All traffic between the administrator's workstation and the router is encrypted, which will make it difficult for a hacker to capture IDs and passwords. Unlike Telnet, which is available by default on almost every operating system, an SSH client is required and usually needs to be installed on the workstation(s) that will be managing the router via SSH. As with the other access methods, the router can be protected by a password or authenticated via a TACACS+ or RADIUS server.

NOTE

To use SSH, you need SSH configured on the device you are going to connect to, and you must run an SSH client on your workstation. Most UNIX/Linux distributions provide SSH, or you can download SSH to use on other operating systems, such as Windows, from vendors that provide it. Two providers that are most common are located at www.ssh.com and www.openssh.org.

To configure SSH, an IOS loaded image must support DES or 3DES encryption to generate an RSA key. If the IOS meets this requirement, we can configure SSH as shown in Figure 11.16. The router must be assigned a hostname and a domain name prior to generating an RSA key. In this case, the hostname is *DMZRouter* and the domain name is *syngress.com*. To generate an RSA key, use the *crypto key generate rsa* command, which will prompt you to enter a modulus; at this prompt you need to enter 1024.

Depending on the router, this process could take some time to complete because the RSA key generation is processor intensive. Some of the lower-end router models can take several minutes to generate a key.

Once the prompt is returned to you, set the SSH timeout, which specifies how long the router should wait for the client to respond during the negotiation phase, using the *ip ssh time-out* command. In this example, it is set at 60 seconds, which is a good timeout, but you can set it however you see fit. You can also specify a limit for authentication retries, after which the connection is reset and the client will lose connectivity. In this case, the *ip ssh authentication-retries* command is used to set the authentication retry limit to 3.

When you're implementing SSH, it is necessary to create a local user database or authenticate users via a TACACS+ or RADIUS server because SSH requires a username and password.

In the example in Figure 11.16, we created a local user *dmzadmin* with the password *letmein* for simplicity. But again, in a production environment, we recommend using a TACACS+ or RADIUS server with strong passwords to authenticate SSH users. Like Telnet, SSH can support five SSH simultaneous sessions by default. Since the virtual terminal lines (line vty 0 4) default to using just the line password, we need to tell the router that we want to prompt for username and password, based on the locally configured user database. We can accomplish this by entering the *login local* command in the vty configuration.

As with the Telnet example, we used the *access-class* command to apply access list 10, which allows only the host with an IP address of 192.168.1.50 to SSH to the router, applied an *exec-timeout* timeout so sessions will time out after 15 minutes of idle time, and used the *transport input* command to only allow SSH sessions on this line. When we say *SSH to a router*, it's the same idea as though you were to Telnet to a router. For more information on SSH, visit this URL: www.cisco.com/warp/public/707/ssh.shtml.

Figure 11.16 SSH Configuration Example

```
DMZRouter(config)# ip domain-name syngress.com
DMZRouter(config)# crypto key generate rsa
The name for the keys will be: syngress.com
Choose the size of the key modulus in the range of 360 to 2048 for your
    General Purpose Keys. Choosing a key modulus greater than 512 may
        take a few minutes.
How many bits in the modulus[512]? 1024
Generating RSA keys.... [OK].
DMZRouter(config)# ip ssh time-out 60
DMZRouter(config)# ip ssh authentication-retries 3
DMZRouter(config)# username dmzadmin password letmein
DMZRouter(config)# access-list 10 permit host 192.168.1.50
DMZRouter(config)# access-list 10 deny any log
DMZRouter(config)# line vty 0 4
DMZRouter(config-line)# login local
DMZRouter(config-line)# transport input ssh
DMZRouter(config-line)# access-class 10 in
DMZRouter(config-line)# exec-timeout 15 0
```

HTTP and HTTPS

Some newer versions of the Cisco IOS support Web-based management and configuration of routers using HTML through a Web browser. This requires the router to run Web server code so that it can serve the HTML pages. Just like other Web server software, the IOS Web-based configuration tool has been found vulnerable to exploits. These exploits are corrected by performing an IOS upgrade on your router, which is a disruptive process that requires a reboot of the router. To make things worse, communication between the browser and the router happens in clear text, including usernames and passwords. Due to the lack of encryption and the possibility that more vulnerabilities will be found in the future, it is recommended that this feature be disabled. This feature is generally considered not very effective for the support and day-to-day maintenance of the router, so disabling it shouldn't cause much impact to your daily operations of the device. This feature is disabled by default, but if it's active, you might want to disable it using the *no ip http server* command.

If this feature is something that you need in your environment, you should instead use the secure HTTP server that was first available in version 12.2(15)T of the Cisco IOS. This will allow you to access the Web interface via an SSL encrypted connection. If security is your number-one concern, you might still want to leave this feature disabled, if for no other reason than to have as few processes running on the router as possible that could potentially be exploited.

> **WARNING**
>
> Sometimes you will not know that the HTTP server is running because it does not show up in the router configuration. Always try to disable the HTTP server, even if you do not see it in the configuration.

Enable Passwords

To keep an unauthorized user from making configuration changes, you should configure an enable password so that only authorized users can access the privileged mode. The enable password is separate from line passwords that allow a user access to exec mode. In exec mode, users can only show statistics and view interfaces, but once the user enters privileged exec (enable) mode, he or she can make any sort of configuration change.

There are two methods for applying an enable password. The first is via the *enable password* command, which should not be used because it is possible to reverse its encryption algorithm using several tools readily available on the Internet. The second method is via the *enable secret* command (as shown in Figure 11.17), which is the preferred method because it uses a nonreversible encryption method. Figure 11.17 shows the *enable secret* password being set, and then the partial output of a *show run* command, to show that the password has been encrypted in the configuration file.

Figure 11.17 Configuring Enable Password

```
DMZRouter(config)# enable secret H@rd2Cr@ck
DMZRouter(config)#^Z
DMZRouter#show run
```

```
Building configuration...
<lines removed>
!
hostname DMZRouter
!
logging queue-limit 100
enable secret 5 $1$FIyU$ibenevdkGwlNKnhtDhZIL/
!
<lines removed>
```

It is important to remember that even though the *enable secret* password uses a nonreversible algorithm, it can still be cracked with dictionary or brute-force attacks. For this reason, you should make sure that you use a strong password and change the password on a regular basis. If you do not use a strong password, the amount of time it could take for a hacker to break your enable password could be very short, whereas if you use a strong password it should take long enough to crack the password that a hacker won't be able to figure it out before you've changed it due to the regularly scheduled password changes.

To help reduce the risk of your router being compromised because you forgot to configure an enable password, all recent versions of the IOS code will not allow a user who is connected via a Telnet session to enter privileged exec mode (enable mode) if an enable password has not been configured. Figure 11.18 demonstrates how a router will respond when someone attempts to enter enable mode on a router lacking a password from a Telnet session.

Figure 11.18 Entering Enable Mode Via Telnet Without a Password

```
Trying 1.1.1.1 ... Open


User Access Verification

Password:
DMZRouter>en
% No password set
DMZRouter>
```

The *service password-encryption* command encrypts all clear-text passwords saved in the configuration of the router, such as the console, Telnet (vty), and user passwords, so they cannot be read directly out of the configuration when it is viewed. By default, this feature is disabled, but you should enable it on all routers. Although it is true that the algorithm used to encrypt the passwords is reversible and can be decrypted in a matter of seconds with software readily available on the Internet (if the hacker has access to the configuration file containing the encrypted passwords), it is still good practice to turn this feature on. If nothing else, it prevents people from seeing your passwords if they happen to be watching over your shoulder as you are working on a router. This command has no effect on the enable password that is set with the *enable secret* command, since that password is already encrypted with a different encryption algorithm that is nonreversible. This command does not encrypt SNMP community strings listed in the configuration. Figure 11.19 shows how to enable the password encryption service and then includes a partial output from a *show run* to show the encryption of the passwords.

Figure 11.19 Configuring Password Encryption Service

```
DMZRouter(config)#service password-encryption
DMZRouter(config)#^Z
DMZRouter#show run
Building configuration...
<lines removed>
!
username dmzadmin password 7 020A014F0603062F
!
<lines removed>
line vty 0 4
 access-class 10 in
 exec-timeout 15 0
 password 7 022E24490F542C336C4D02
 login
 transport input telnet
!
!
end
```

NOTE

If you take a closer look at the encrypted password and secret commands, you will notice a number between the command and the encrypted password. This number specifies the level of encryption that is being used on the password. The level 7 encryption is the reversible algorithm, which is best used to keep wandering eyes from seeing your passwords. The 5 means that the password was hashed with MD5 and is not reversible.

AAA

AAA stands for *authentication, authorization, and accounting,* which enable the router to verify, control, and track users who access the router for administrative purposes.

- **Authentication** The process of validating the claimed identity of an end user or a device, such as a host, server, switch, router, or firewall.

- **Authorization** Granting access rights to a user or groups of users.

- **Accounting** The methods to establish who performed a certain action, such as tracking user connections and logging system users.

The AAA feature can authenticate a user who logs into the router to an external RADIUS or TACACS+ server. RADIUS or TACACS+ servers contain the IDs, passwords, and privileges for each user defined to their databases. They can also log such information as the time a user logged to a system to the command a user entered. If the router receives a "Success" response from the RADIUS or TACACS+ server, the user will be allowed to gain access to the device. If a "Fail" message is received, the user will be denied access; it's as simple as that.

The AAA feature can also limit commands by authorizing each command an administrator enters. This feature is useful if you have many levels of administrator who have access to your routers. You might want some administrators to have only the ability to troubleshoot the router, which requires the use of *show, clear,* and *debug* commands, whereas you want to provide other senior or advanced administrators the ability to make configuration changes to interfaces, access lists, routing protocols, and so on. The accounting feature tracks and logs all the logins and changes an administrator makes. AAA is very useful for large organizations in which many administrators have access to the company's routers for management purposes and the security policy calls for each admin to have a unique ID and password, so changes to the router can be tracked and individual administrators can be held accountable. AAA can be applied to administrators accessing the router via the following access methods: console, Telnet, SSH, and HTTP.

AAA is a very useful feature that works very well for administrative access as well as for authenticating and authorizing users attempting to gain remote access via a network access server. A discussion of this topic is outside the scope of this book; if you need more in-depth information about AAA, check out the following site: www.cisco.com/univercd/cc/td/doc/product/software/ios122/122cgcr/fsecur_c/fsaaa/index.htm.

In Figure 11.20 you can see the commands necessary to enable AAA to authenticate users accessing the router for administrative purposes, authorization of commands an administrator can enter, and logging of administrative logins to a TACACS+ server. This example assumes that your TACACS server is already configured with usernames and authorization settings for all administrator accounts, since we are showing only the commands required to make the router communicate with the TACACS server. To enable AAA on a router, use the *aaa new-model* command in global configuration mode. To authenticate users who want to access the router to the TACACS+ server, use the *aaa authentication login* command. In this example, we use the keyword *default* to signify that it will be the default method for all sessions, including the console, Telnet, SSH, and HTTP.

With this option set as the default, from now on when you console, Telnet, SSH, or HTTP into the router, users will be prompted for a username and password instead of only a password. This prompt will ask the user to supply a full set of credentials that will not only be verified but logged as well. We also set a fallback option, should the router not be able to reach the TACACS+ server, to the enable password. If the TACACS server is down or if the router is off the network for any reason, you will still be able to log into the router using the enable password. The two *aaa authorization* command statements authorize all commands, whether in exec mode (level 0) or privileged mode (level 15), to the TACACS+ server, which verifies whether the administrator is authorized to execute a specific command. In the example, should the TACACS+ server be unreachable, the router will authorize all commands, since the backup method was set to no authorization (none). To log all the administrative sessions (logins and logouts) to the TACACS+ server, use the *aaa accounting exec* command. To specify the IP address of the TACACS+ server(s), use the *tacacs-server host* command. To specify the encryption key, which encrypts communication between the TACACS+ server and the router, use the *tacacs-server key* command. In the example, the TACACS+ server is 192.168.1.50 and the key is *MyTACACS-KEY*.

We have only brushed on some of the capabilities of AAA; again, refer to the URL mention earlier for more details on how to configure other aspects of the AAA feature.

Figure 11.20 Configuring AAA

```
DMZRouter(config)# aaa new-model
DMZRouter(config)# aaa authentication login default group tacacs+ enable
DMZRouter(config)# aaa authorization commands 0 default group tacacs+ none
DMZRouter(config)# aaa authorization commands 15 default group tacacs+ none
DMZRouter(config)# aaa accounting exec default start-stop group tacacs+
DMZRouter(config)# tacacs-server host 192.169.1.50
DMZRouter(config)# tacacs-server key MyTACACS-KEY
```

SNMP

Simple Network Management Protocol (SNMP) allows network management systems to monitor, collect statistics, and even make configuration changes to the Cisco router. SNMP version 1 is the most commonly used version of the protocol, but unfortunately it is the least secure because it uses a community string, which is like a password, that is passed over the network unencrypted, in clear text, just like Telnet. SNMP version 2 is considered more secure because it uses message digest authentication (MD5), so if your management system permits, use SNMP version 2 to manage your routers.

Cisco routers support SNMP versions 1, 2, and 3. If your management system does not yet support version 2 or greater, take a look at the example in Figure 11.21, which takes you through the steps to increase security for SNMP version 1. Since we know that the SNMP requests should come from only a management system, you should be able to create an access list that permits only the specific management system(s) to send SNMP messages to the router.

In the example, we created access list 10, which only permits the management system with the IP address 192.168.1.50, denies all other source addresses, and logs the failed attempts. The *snmp-server community* command is used to set the community string, define the rights (*RO* for read only or *RW* for read/write) and to apply an access list all in one line. In this case, we created two community strings—one for read-only access (*mySNMPReadKey*) and one for read/write access (*mySNMPWriteKey*). Both community strings have access list 10 applied to them, so only the specified management server can send the router SNMP messages. It is important to not use the well-known community strings *public* for read-only access or *private* for read/write access, because they are commonly used and easily guessed. Not only that, but most vulnerability scanners have a preset to scan all devices using common string names such as *public* and *private*. Try to use community strings that are a little more challenging (even the strings in the example are too simple), and try not to use the same community strings for all devices on the network. Furthermore, try to avoid SNMP on devices accessible by the Internet, if possible, because of its inherent weakness and vulnerabilities. If you need to run SNMP on devices accessible to the Internet, do not configure community strings enabling read/write, because if they are hacked, the intruder can possibly reconfigure the router, causing major problems.

WARNING

Using *public* and *private* (the default community string names) for any device on your network is not only unadvisable—it's a practice known to every hacker. Never use these strings, no matter what. Always change them or disable SNMP from the device.

Figure 11.21 Configuring SNMP

```
DMZRouter(config)# access-list 10 permit 192.168.1.50
DMZRouter(config)# access-list 10 deny any log
DMZRouter(config)# snmp-server community mySNMPReadKey RO 10
DMZRouter(config)# snmp-server community mySNMPWriteKey RW 10
```

Syslog

System logging (syslog) can record several events, from system status to security violations. These events can be sent directly to a console or terminal session, buffered in RAM, and/or sent to a syslog server. The information in the syslog can assist you in troubleshooting a system or network problem and recording matches or violations in an access list. This information can be time-stamped to determine the time and sequence of a problem or an attack. Syslog messages are tagged with one of seven severity levels: emergencies, alerts, critical errors, warnings, notifications, informational, and debugging. Each level has a numeric value, which can be seen in the help information for the logging commands, as shown in Figure 11.22. It is recommended to log syslog messages to both the internal buffer, which is stored in RAM, and a syslog server, because once the buffer in RAM is full, the oldest entry is overwritten, and when the router is reloaded, the entries in RAM are lost.

Figure 11.22 Syslog Severity Levels

```
DMZRouter(config)#logging trap ?
  <0-7>          Logging severity level
  alerts         Immediate action needed        (severity=1)
  critical       Critical conditions            (severity=2)
  debugging      Debugging messages             (severity=7)
  emergencies    System is unusable             (severity=0)
  errors         Error conditions               (severity=3)
  informational  Informational messages         (severity=6)
  notifications  Normal but significant conditions (severity=5)
  warnings       Warning conditions             (severity=4)
  <cr>
```

Figure 11.23 shows how to set up syslog to log events to the internal buffer and a syslog server. The *service timestamps log datetime msecs* command time-stamps log entries with the date and time (to the millisecond) for each recorded event. An alternate option is *uptime*, which shows when the event occurred in relation to when the router was last booted. The *logging trap level* command sets the severity level to be forwarded to the syslog server to *informational*, which means it will record all events from emergencies to informational events and send them to the syslog server. The *logging <syslog IP>* command sets the IP address of the syslog server to 192.168.1.50. The *logging buffered level* command sets the severity level for the internal buffer to debugging, which enables the router to log messages to RAM for all severity levels.

Figure 11.23 Configuring Syslog

```
DMZRouter(config)# service timestamps log datetime msecs
DMZRouter(config)# logging trap informational
```

```
DMZRouter(config)# logging 192.168.1.50
DMZRouter(config)# logging buffered debugging
```

All syslog messages that are generated by the router should contain the numeric severity level within the message. For example, every time someone exits global configuration mode, a message is generated noting that the configuration was possibly changed and the system will display which user was in configuration mode and the method of connectivity used. This message will look something like:

```
*Jun 29 00:28:00.797: %SYS-5-CONFIG_I: Configured from console by console
```

The number 5 in the *%SYS-5-CONFIG_I:* portion of the output shows that this message is severity level 5, or notifications, which is considered a "normal but significant condition," according to the output in Figure 11.22. In the case of this message, the configuration was done from the command line ("from console"), where no username was required, so the message states that the configuration was done "by console." If we connected via a Telnet session using a locally configured username, the output would look like:

```
*Jun 29 00:34:18.029: %SYS-5-CONFIG_I: Configured from console by dmzadmin on vty0
(1.1.1.1)
```

Notice that this message records the username, the vty the user connected on, and the IP address that the user was connecting from. The following are some examples of other messages that could be generated by your router and the severity levels of the message type:

```
*Jun 29 00:34:18.029: %HSRP-6-STATECHANGE: FastEthernet0/0 Grp 1 state Listen ->
Active
*Jun 29 00:40:31.473: %LINK-3-UPDOWN: Interface Serial1/0, changed state to down
```

The first message is generated by Hot Standby Router Protocol (HSRP) and is giving an informational message (severity 6) to record a state change in the protocol. The second message shows that the serial interface has lost signal and has been marked "down" by the router. This message is considered an error condition, which is severity level 3.

Configuring & Implementing...

The Importance of Logging Events

Logging events can be very useful for troubleshooting your network device, whether a router, switch, or server. However, log files are essential to determining how an attack compromised your network and what parts of the network were

Continued

attacked. Furthermore, log files are important to help prove in a court of law that an attack or an unauthorized event occurred.

On routers, logs can be saved to the router's memory buffer or sent to a syslog server. Log events sent to a buffer file in the router's memory are erased once the router is rebooted. This means that if the router is rebooted, it will lose all historical information, including very important data that could prove an attacker is guilty of penetrating the network. If you are not logging to a syslog server, an attacker can cover his trail by clearing syslog files of the devices he penetrated or by forcing the router to reboot. It is a good practice to send log information to a syslog file so that all log events are stored in a central place. Then if an attack occurs, the files can be quickly assembled and sent or shown to the proper authorities. It is also important for the logged events to have accurate timestamps (down to the second or even millisecond, if possible). To guarantee accurate timestamps, all devices on the network must have their clocks synchronized, which will make it easier to determine the sequence of events in an attack. You can synchronize the clocks on all devices on your network using Network Time Protocol (NTP), discussed in the next section.

Network Time Protocol

NTP synchronizes a router's clock with a time source, which helps keep time accurate on all network devices. When an attack occurs, it might be necessary to keep the time consistent on all network devices, to determine a sequence of events by checking the timestamps in the logs. Without this service enabled, it can be extremely difficult or even impossible to correlate events on different devices.

NTP time sources are ranked based on stratum, which is the number of "hops" a particular time source is away from an accurate time source, such as an atomic clock. The devices that receive their time directly from the accurate time source would be a stratum-1 time source. Time sources that synchronize from stratum-1 time sources would be considered stratum-2 time sources, and so on. There are many stratum-1 time sources available to the public on the Internet, hosted by universities and government agencies. A good place to start for information about NTP and a list of public time sources is the NTP Public Services Project, located at http://ntp.isc.org.

Many organizations will choose a group of devices to pull time from stratum-1 clocks so that they can then be used as internal time servers for the entire enterprise. This enables every device in your network to have synchronized time, allowing you to correlate logs between devices when an incident occurs. Enabling NTP requires only the *ntp server* command to specify the IP address of the time source. Multiple time sources can be configured, and a preferred time source can be selected. A router can also be configured as a time source for other devices to poll using the *ntp master* command. The only option for this command is the stratum level of the local clock, so if you are configured to pull time from stratum-1 time sources, you would configure your NTP master as a stratum-2 time source. Figure

11.24 shows how to further protect the NTP service by also configuring optional message digest algorithm 5 (MD5) NTP authentication. In the example, the router will synchronize its time with the NTP server (192.168.50.1) and authenticate using the key *NTPkey*.

Figure 11.24 Configuring NTP

```
DMZRouter(config)# ntp authenticate
DMZRouter(config)# ntp authentication-key 1 md5 NTPkey
DMZRouter(config)# ntp trusted-key 1
DMZRouter(config)# ntp server 192.168.1.50 key 1 prefer
DMZRouter(config)# ntp server 192.168.1.51 key 1
DMZRouter(config)# ntp master 2
```

Disabling Unneeded IOS features

As with many operating systems, some functions and features may be turned on by default to make configuration and management easier. Unfortunately, these functions and features can also give away vital information or expose the router to malicious attacks. In this section, we discuss some of the functions and features that can safely be disabled to mitigate the risk of an intruder obtaining network topology information or exploiting a weakness in the router's code. We strongly suggest that you read all this information very carefully because most routers are exploited due to unneeded, or more likely unknown, services that are running. This holds especially true for older routers with older versions of code. Newer routers come with current IOS that will normally not make available some of these exploits (such as directed broadcasts, for example, that could be used in a smurf attack). However, you can never be too sure, especially with your Internet-facing routers or routers within your DMZ. Remember, all it takes is a script kiddie with a tool like NMAP to check out what you have and possibly exploit it.

Before we begin, make certain that anything you consider disabling is not being used in your network, because by disabling services, you could break applications that might have been dependent on those services. One example is Cisco Discovery Protocol (CDP), which we discuss in the next section. Normally this service can be disabled without any ill effects, but the On-Demand Routing (ODR) feature uses CDP to propagate a default route to neighbors, and Cisco IP phones can use the protocol to negotiate power and QoS details with the upstream switch. You must be aware of the services that are in use within your networks before you start disabling these features.

Cisco Discovery Protocol

Cisco Discovery Protocol (CDP) is a Cisco proprietary network management protocol that operates on Layer 2. CDP allows a router to discover several characteristics of a directly connected neighbor, including the type of Cisco device, model, IOS, and IP addresses of the device. An attacker can use this feature to map out a network and determine other devices on the network and thus formulate an attack plan. This feature can be very useful for troubleshooting or managing a network, especially in very large environments, but it should never be used on an unsecured network such as the external or DMZ LANs. Network security is about managing risk, so you will have to weigh the trade-offs of using this feature on your internal LAN.

By default, CDP is enabled on all interfaces. To disable CDP on the entire router, use the *no cdp run* command in global configuration mode; to disable CDP on specific interfaces, use the *no cdp enable* command in interface configuration mode.

> ## NOTE
>
> As mentioned, make certain that none of your network management devices rely on CDP before you attempt to disable it. A general rule of thumb is, *never* use CDP on any device within the DMZ, because this protocol will be exploited to help map out what is located within your DMZ. If you have four Cisco devices using CDP in the DMZ, all it takes is one hacker to crack one of them to learn about the others.

Redirects

Cisco routers can tell a device whether there is a better router or other network device on the same subnet that can direct the packet to its destination in a more direct fashion. This prevents a packet from being received and sent out the same interface to another router on the same subnet. To accomplish this task, when the router receives a packet and the next hop is on the same subnet as the sending device, the router sends an ICMP redirect message to the sending device so that it will forward all future packets directly to the better next-hop router without involving the original router. This makes the path to the destination more efficient and direct; it also eliminates the unneeded processing of packets by other routers. Unfortunately, hackers can use ICMP redirects to shape and point traffic to other destinations and disrupt traffic flow. To disable ICMP redirects on a router, use the *no ip redirects* command in interface configuration mode. Please note that this is an interface configuration item, so it will need to be configured on every interface where you would want to disable redirects. ICMP redirects are enabled by default.

NOTE

As you can see, ICMP can easily be used to wreak havoc on a network. ICMP was meant to be used as an informational troubleshooting tool, but at times it can be manipulated to cause more bad than good. If you disable ICMP altogether, you will remove the option to use troubleshooting tools such as *ping* and *traceroute*. Make sure you enable and disable ICMP wisely to disrupt hackers looking to take advantage but so that you retain a way to troubleshoot your network. A word of advice: If possible, remove the ability for ICMP to be used for attacks (as you are learning about in this section) as well as to disable the ability to ping your Internet-facing router from the Internet.

Unreachables

When a router receives a packet and it has no route for the destination, it will reply with an ICMP unreachable packet to the original packet's sender. A hacker can use this information to figure out the subnets used on the network, which could be useful information to a hacker as he maps out the network and launches an attack. To stop a router from sending ICMP unreachable messages, use the *no ip unreachables* command in interface configuration mode. ICMP unreachable messages are enabled by default.

Directed Broadcasts

When a directed broadcast packet traverses a network, it behaves like a Unicast packet and is forwarded throughout the network as a Unicast packet would be. The difference is that when it reaches the router that is directly connected the destination subnet, the router will rewrite the directed broadcast packet as a link layer broadcast packet and flood the subnet. All replies are sent to the originator of the direct broadcast. Directed broadcasts are used in *smurf attacks*, in which a device continuously sends ICMP echo messages with a faked source address to a directed broadcast address so that all devices on the destination subnet will send echo reply messages to the false source address. The source address is usually spoofed to that of the target of the attack. The device with the real source address will be flooded with echo reply messages, which can severely degrade the device's performance. To prevent this type of DoS attack, use the *no ip directed-broadcast* command. This command stops the router from converting a direct broadcast packet to a link layer broadcast packet, thus saving lots of bandwidth on your Internet links if someone tries to use your site to launch one of these attacks. In most cases, directed broadcasts are enabled by default.

NOTE

Newer versions of IOS have this command already configured on the interface, but you should check anyway, just in case.

Proxy ARP

Proxy ARP enables hosts on the LAN that have no default gateway configured to determine how to get to other networks or subnets. A host sends an ARP request message to determine where to send traffic for a remote network or subnet to all devices on the subnet. If a router on the same subnet as the host has a route to the network or subnet in question, it will send a proxy ARP reply message to the host with its own MAC address, so the host can send to the router all traffic destined to the remote network or subnet. The router will then forward the packet to the destination. Even though proxy ARP has many legitimate uses, it can also be used by a hacker to determine which networks or subnets are connected to the network. Proxy ARP is enabled by default, but it can be disabled using the *no ip proxy-arp* command in interface configuration mode. With the use of DHCP servers or statically configured default gateways, it should not be necessary to enable the proxy ARP feature.

Small Servers

The term TCP and UDP "small servers" refers to a list of basic services that were designed as troubleshooting tools. Today, these services are rarely used, but if left turned on, they can be exploited to launch DoS attacks. Before we continue, let's quickly explain what a *service* is, as the term is used in this context. If you were to look at www.iana.org, you could easily find the port numbers for many known services such as Telnet (23), SMTP (25), and so on. Small services are the same, but they use very low port numbers and perform very basic functions. These services include *echo, chargen, discard,* and *daytime*. Each of these services is described below:

- **Echo** A TCP and UDP service designed to echo whatever is received back to the sender.

- **Chargen** Stands for character generator and is a TCP and UDP service that will generate a stream of ASCII characters. For UDP, a packet containing a string of characters will be sent in response to every UDP datagram received. For TCP, chargen will generate a constant stream of characters until the connection is closed.

- **Discard** A TCP and UDP service that will discard whatever is received.

- **Daytime** is a TCP service that will return the date and time configured on the router.

These services have legitimate functions, but they also leave the router vulnerable to certain types of attack. For example, character generation (*chargen*) can generate a string of ASCII data to a user who Telnets to TCP port 19 on the router, with the command shown here:

```
telnet 10.0.0.1 19
```

Although this is simple, an attacker can use the chargen service to tie up the CPU, which can severely degrade router performance. You can see the attack using the *show processes cpu* command while you have an open connection to the chargen service. You will see a rise in CPU usage, possibly up to 100 percent, depending on the CPU power of the router running chargen. If you capture the data stream with a sniffer you will see that this can generate thousands of packets in a matter of seconds. That's pretty bad for a service you will never use legitimately. One DoS attack involves the attacker causing the UDP chargen service on one device to send packets to the UDP echo service on another device. This will trigger a flood of traffic that will continue forever without some sort of intervention from the administrator. Since these services are so rarely needed (can you see a need to have a chargen enabled on your router?), it is recommended that you shut down these services by using both the *no service tcp-small-servers* and *no service udp-small-servers* commands in global configuration mode on all routers, including routers on the internal, external, and DMZ networks.

NOTE

Prior to IOS version 12.0, both TCP and UDP small services were enabled by default, but IOS 12.0 and greater TCP and UDP small services are disabled by default. Check the version of your routers and ensure that these two commands are not enabled, since there really is no need for them, especially on your Internet-facing routers.

Finger

The finger service is a carryover command from the UNIX world; it allows you to learn which users are logged into the router without you actually logging into it. This feature is not needed. If you need to know who is logged into your routers, consider using a TACACS+ or RADIUS server, which can produce reports on who is logged in. By default, this service is enabled. Use the *no ip finger* command in global configuration mode to disable the finger service on all routers on your network. Although this service is rarely used, it is recommended that you disable it, even if you don't see it disabled in your configuration. Finger is very informative, and many hackers boast about how much they can learn from devices that are running finger without administrators' knowledge. Many hackers find finger because it often won't show up as disabled in the configuration. Run the *no ip finger* command on your devices, or run a vulnerability scanner on your router externally to see if finger is in fact running.

Password Recovery

If your router is in an area that doesn't have adequate physical security, it is possible for someone to gain access to it using the password recovery procedure. This procedure, which requires a reboot, allows an attacker to access the router even though he does not know the passwords that were configured on the device. Since this procedure requires access through the console port of the router, it is generally safe to leave enabled, as long as you have good access controls into the areas where these routers physically sit. The problem occurs when someone who isn't authorized to access the router can gain physical access to the device.

If you are concerned about physical access to your device, you can disable the password recovery procedure with the *no service password-recovery* command. This command prevents someone connected on the console port of the router from breaking into ROMMON mode to bypass the password requirements. Since Cisco does not want to cause an administrator to never be able to access the device again if he or she forgets the password, the break sequence can still be used. The difference, though, is when password recovery is disabled and someone attempts to break into ROMMON; they are prompted to reset the router to factory defaults before they can gain access. This prevents someone with physical access to the router from gaining access with a working configuration on the device. To gain access to your network, they would have to reconfigure the router from scratch.

IP Source Routing

The Cisco router can support IP source routing where the information in the IP packet specifies the path the packet will take to the destination, instead of following the normal destination-based routing at each hop along the way. This capability can be dangerous because the packet sender can control the packet's path. If this feature is enabled, an intruder can manipulate the packet's path and possibly circumvent security points within the network. This feature should never be enabled, since source routing is rarely used. IP source routing is enabled by default and can be disabled with the *no ip source-route* command in global configuration mode.

NOTE

It should be noted here that packets could easily be created or forged. Most people think that it takes a college degree in programming to create a packet, but that only means that they haven't scoured enough of the Internet to find the tools they need. You can create falsified data using most protocol analyzers. When we talk about hackers causing most of these attacks against your routers (or any other devices), be aware that they are in fact creating or replaying data against you.

Bootp Server

If bootp services are not needed on the router to assign dynamic IP addressing to clients, it is recommended that this service be disabled. To disable this feature, use the *no ip bootp server* command in global configuration mode. Although vulnerabilities are not common, they can still be exploited by inundating the router with bootp requests, which can cause high CPU utilization and possibly cause the router to crash. The Bootp protocol is used by workstations and other devices to obtain IP addresses and other information about the network configuration. There should be no need to offer the service outside your internal LAN, which is usually provided by a separate server and not the router, and it could offer useful information to intruders.

Other Security Features

The security tips, services, and features discussed in the previous sections referred to standard features of the router IOS, which means that they are found in all IOS releases. However, Cisco does offer more security functionality through the many different feature sets the Cisco router offers, including an IOS firewall, IOS intrusion detection services (IDSs), and Security Device Manager (SDM) as well as VPN capabilities. In addition, many newer Cisco routers have a network module slot that can accept the IPS Network Module (IPS-NM). This module essentially provides a full-featured IDS/IPS device that fits into the network module slot and ties into the backplane of the router. These features allow the router to perform stateful packet inspection and detect attacks via signatures, just as their dedicated firewall or IDS appliance counterparts would, in addition to normal router functionality. This makes the router more than a device that directs traffic throughout the network; it becomes a legitimate security device.

Cisco has also started including its SDM product with many of the new routers and code versions. This tool can help you speed up deployments of new devices by walking you through configuration wizards. This tool can also be used to perform security audits on devices to help you gauge where the device may be vulnerable. Additional information about this feature can be found at www.cisco.com/go/sdm.

Since the focus of this book is to secure the DMZ, we won't cover every available security feature you can enable with Cisco-based devices, but if you need extra functionality, you can research it very easily on Cisco's Web site or with assistance of the Technical Assistance Center (TAC). It should be noted as well that this extra functionality does come at a cost, because these services require more memory and CPU power. Unlike dedicated firewall or IDS devices, where the hardware is optimized for these functions, the router relies on the software to provide firewall and IDS functionality. This means that the router might be bogged down performing all the extra services such as stateful packet inspection or intrusion detection, so latency could increase as traffic passes through it and routing updates are missed, which can cause serious network stability problems. A common rule of thumb is either scale up or scale out. In other words, don't be cheap when ordering a device to do it all, or simply use dedicated devices for dedicated services. In a large DMZ environment, use a dedicated firewall or IDS unit instead of the router IOS versions for these features. However, these features are useful for securing small to medium-sized locations requiring Internet access or for securing connections to business partners or third parties, so analyze your requirements and plan accordingly.

NOTE

In an enterprise DMZ environment, a router running the IOS firewall or IDS feature set should never replace a dedicated firewall device. Even though the router can perform many of the functions a dedicated firewall such as the PIX or an IDS unit, like the 4200 series sensor, can perform, it is not optimized for this purpose and is not recommended.

Securing the Switch

Switches have evolved over the last few years, from simple Layer 2 devices to very intelligent network devices that are able to cover all seven layers of the OSI model. Examples are the Cisco Content Services Switch (CSS) or the Content Switching Module (CSM) on the Catalyst 6500, which can load-balance up to the application level.

These innovations enable the switch to become a powerful tool for implementing a network infrastructure. Some of the functions and features added to the switch over its lifetime include VLANs, trunking, and Etherchannel as well as features to help secure the network, such as port security and private VLANs. The advances in switch hardware and software have also made the switch more than just a Layer 2 device and have bridged the gap between the switch and the router. Many of the new switches can now perform many of the upper-layer functions performed by the router, such as routing and ACLs; some switches can even perform application layer load balancing. As you can see, the switch is in a state of flux, with new enhancements evident in each release of switch software.

This part of the chapter mainly deals with securing the switch itself and some Layer 2 security-related features. Although there are many switches on the market, we recommend the Cisco Catalyst switch model line because these models are feature rich, highly secure, and have a CLI similar to the Cisco router line, which makes administration easier.

Cisco Switches

Unlike the Cisco router line, which uses a common operating system across all models, the Catalyst switch line uses two different operating systems. The first Catalyst switches were designed to run an operating system referred to as CatOS that ran on the supervisor cards that controlled the operation of these Layer 2 switches. As Layer 3 features were added to the switches to improve performance and scalability, IOS software started making its way into the Catalyst product line. This started with the Route Switch Modules (RSM) for the Catalyst 5000 series switches, which were routers built onto cards and installed into the Catalyst chassis. These cards ran their own version of the IOS operating system and ran completely separate from the CatOS software that controlled the Layer 2 features of the switch. For all intents and purposes, you had a router and a switch that were connected by the internal backplane of the chassis instead of Ethernet cables, and they had to be configured as separate devices. This design was also used on the first versions of the Multilayer Switch Feature Cards (MSFC) that were used in the Catalyst 6500 series switches. If you were running both operating systems within your Catalyst switch, you were running in "hybrid mode."

This design led to some interesting issues when you started adding redundancy within a chassis. Since these larger switches were designed as highly available data center class switches, they allow for redundant supervisor cards. The MSFC in the switch is actually a daughter card on the supervisor modules, so with two cards you can have redundant Layer 2 and Layer 3 features. The supervisors are designed to act in active/standby configuration; any sort of problem would trigger a failover, and the switch would operate from the second card. Since the MSFCs were designed as separate routers that attached at the backplane, that meant that the Layer 3 portion operated in an active/active configuration, just as though you had two routers attached to your switch. To make one MSFC take over for the other in the case of a failure, we must use all the features that allowed redundancy between two separate external routers, like HSRP, routing protocol metrics, and so on. In a redundant configuration with dual Supervisors with MSFC cards, you were required to configure one Layer 2 switch (active/standby) and two Layer 3 routers (active/active). Features such as Single Router Mode (SRM) were developed to reduce the Layer 3 configuration and complexity by making the MSFCs act in an active/standby configuration, but better overall integration of the devices in the switch was desired.

Cisco has been able to further integrate these components and started offering "native mode" software, which was a version of IOS that could control both the Layer 2 and Layer 3 functions of the switch. This allows the supervisor cards to work completely in an active/standby configuration and uses a common interface to control all Layer 2 and Layer 3 features of the switch. The 6500 series of switch was the slowest to reach this point, but all the other switches in the Catalyst product line have been migrated to running only IOS from the 2960s up to the 4500 series chassis-based switches. In some cases you still have the option to run in hybrid mode, but this will depend on which switch hardware you are using.

For this reason, the examples in this section pertain to only the IOS version of the Catalyst operating system. However, if you are running a CatOS version of the switch's operating system, the concepts and commands can be ported over to the CatOS. To complicate things further, the features of the Catalyst switch are not always consistent across the model line. To help clarify some features supported by each switch, we list some of the details of the most popular switches as they pertain to the DMZ.

NOTE

For more information on how to secure Catalyst switches running the CatOS version of the operating system, refer to www.cisco.com/warp/customer/473/103.html.

Catalyst Express 500

The Cisco Catalyst Express 500 is a line of low-cost switches that are intended for small businesses with limited network deployments. These are fixed-configuration switches that come with a limited feature set compared to the rest of the Catalyst line, so businesses do not have to pay for a large number of features that they would never plan to deploy. Most of the switches in this line have 24 nonblocking wire-speed Fast Ethernet Ports and two Gigabit Ethernet ports. There is also a model that contains only Gigabit Ethernet but is limited to a total of 12 ports. The various configurations have a varying number of ports capable of Power over Ethernet (PoE) for use with devices such as IP phones and wireless access points that receive both data and power over the Ethernet cable. All ports are capable of automatic medium dependent interface crossover (Auto-MDIX), which is a feature that automatically detects when a cross-over cable is required and can perform the cross in hardware so that the cable doesn't need to be replaced.

These switches are designed for ease of deployment and can be configured only through a Web-based interface that is accesses via HTTPS on a standard Web browser. The switch uses the Cisco Smartports feature, which is designed to automatically detect other Cisco Small-to-Medium Business (SMB) devices that are plugged into the switch and recommend QoS and security settings for the specific port. Since this switch was designed for end users in small environments and cannot be accessed via a command line, the security measures listed later in this chapter will not apply directly to this switch, but the Catalyst Express 500 line is included here so that you will have an understanding of the entire Catalyst product line.

To find more detailed information on this line of switches, visit www.cisco.com/go/catalystexpress500.

Catalyst 2960

The Cisco Catalyst 2960 series switch is designed to be an access layer switch that provides end stations access for small to midsized offices. The Catalyst 2960 has a fixed-chassis configuration that offers different combinations of 24 or 48 Fast Ethernet ports with 2 or 4 Gigabit Ethernet ports. The model numbers that contain a TT have either two or four fixed RJ-45 Gigabit Ethernet ports for use with copper cabling; the TC models use the dual-purpose Gigabit Ethernet ports. The dual-purpose ports have an RJ-45 port as well as a Small Form Pluggable (SFP) slot that are both considered the same interface in the software. You have the option of using either the RJ-45 port for a copper connection or inserting an SFP module for fiber optic connectivity. The switch's backplane performance is either 16 or 32 Gbps, depending on the model. This switch has the option of redundant power through the Cisco RPS 675, which is an external power supply that can provide secondary power to up to six switches.

The 2960 comes with a large number of Layer 2 features to give you all the flexibility you might need with this line of switch. They contain many security features, such as port security, DHCP snooping, IEEE 802.1x, and ACLs. In addition, this switch also contains all the latest QoS features to guarantee network bandwidth and delay for sensitive applications such as voice and video.

To see more detailed information about this line of switches, go to www.cisco.com/go/catalyst2960.

Catalyst 3560

The Cisco Catalyst 3560 series switch is designed as an enterprise-class access switch that offers multilayer capabilities. Like the Catalyst 2960, the 3560 has a fixed-chassis configuration that offers Fast Ethernet and Gigabit Ethernet connectivity. Cisco offers several different chassis options that can fulfill many of the Layer 2 needs of a medium-sized network as a standalone switch. This switch can also have Layer 3 functionality, including full IP routing, which allows it to be implemented in the core, distribution, or access layer, depending on the size of the enterprise network. This switch also supports redundant power with the Cisco RPS 675.

The 3560 has two available types of software image. The IP Base image (formerly known as the Standard Multilayer Image, or SMI) contains all the latest Layer 2 features and allows for some basic IP routing setups, although you are limited to RIP for routing updates. The IP Services image (formerly known as the Enhanced Multilayer Image, or EMI) allows you to use full Layer 3 capabilities for Unicast and multicast routing, including policy-based routing. This switch has the performance and functionality to interconnect the servers and firewalls in a small to medium-sized DMZ environment.

The 3560 is also the smallest product in the Catalyst line to support Cisco's network virtualization features. Network virtualization allows you to segment your network into multiple isolated areas while staying shared on the same physical equipment. In the same fashion that VLANs allow you to segment a switch into multiple virtual switches that cannot communicate with each other without passing through an external router (MSFC cards being considered "external"), Virtual Routing and Forwarding (VRF) allows you to create multiple virtual routers (which we will call VRFs) that are entirely isolated from one another. VRF was originally used to deploy MPLS VPNs in service provider networks, but this functionality can now be added as a feature to routers that do not support the MPLS protocol. On these routers, this feature is referred to as *VRF-lite*.

At a minimum, it is a great cost-saving feature when you can take, for example, a 3560 switch with 48 Fast Ethernet ports and turn it into 12 separate virtual routers with four Fast

Ethernet ports per VRF instance. When fully deployed throughout an enterprise, virtualization can enable you to quickly and easily add new isolated segments to your network without needing to ask for additional hardware resources. Network virtualization is not within the scope of this book, so we are offering only a brief overview of what virtualization can do for you. Virtualization is one of the components of Cisco's Service-Oriented Network Architecture (SONA); you can find more information about the SONA architecture, including network virtualization, at www.cisco.com/go/sona.

Designing and Planning…

Network Virtualization

Network virtualization is a concept that has recently started to get much more vendor support and customer attention. In the past, if you wanted to have completely isolated areas of the network, you were forced to purchase separate devices to build these areas. This can become very expensive as you end up running multiple, separate networks. With virtualization, you can create these separate devices, virtually, within the same physical device. This allows network administrators to quickly deploy new isolated segments of the networks with existing resources that might not be completely utilized. Although some vendors have implemented some half-measures that are referred to as virtualization, the VRF features available in some router and switch models allows for complete isolation between virtual devices. This means that there are separate routing tables, routing protocol instances, and interfaces for each VRF. When you start using these features, you will have to remember that you must specify to which VRF a command will apply. Even when you are just issuing a simple ping, you must specify which VRF to ping from; otherwise it will use the default VRF, which might not have any knowledge of the network you are trying to ping.

You have many options for connecting VRF instances on various devices, such as physical interfaces, logical interfaces, or tunnel interfaces. Physical interfaces are straightforward, since you will assign the physical interface to a VRF instance and connect the cable to the other device. Another option, which prevents you from quickly consuming all your physical ports, is to use logical interfaces such as dot1q. This lets you assign each dot1q VLAN to a different VRF so that you can connect multiple VRFs on different devices over a single cable. The third option is to use tunnel interfaces to connect devices that are multiple hops away. The general idea is to create a base or foundation infrastructure that interconnects all devices in the default VRF of each device. You can then use General Routing Encapsulation (GRE) tunnels or Multiprotocol Label Switching (MPLS) Label Switching Paths to interconnect additional VRFs without allowing them to access the default VRF. Even though the logical interface (such as the GRE tunnel

Continued

interface) is assigned to a particular VRF, the tunnel endpoints can be interfaces and addresses that belong to the default VRF. This allows a logical point-to-point connection to be established between two VRFs on devices that are multiple hops away from each other. An example of this kind of setup is shown in Figure 11.25.

Figure 11.25 Using VRF-lite and GRE to Virtualize the Network

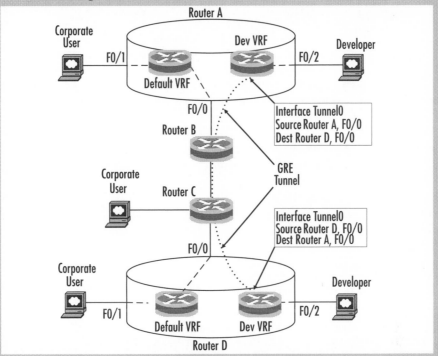

In this example, we see two routers that are implementing VRF-lite: Router A and Router D. Routers B and C are standard routers within the path between Router A and Router D. Each of these VRF-lite enabled routers have three Ethernet interfaces—F0/0, F0/1 and F0/2. In both routers we have moved the F0/2 interface into a VRF that is being used for the development department; the remaining interfaces (F0/0 and F0/1) have been left in the default VRF. For now, we want to forget about the Dev VRF and look at the base network infrastructure that has been created. We have a routed path between Routers A and D that flows through our standard routers B and C. This path allows the corporate user attached to Router A to reach the corporate user attached on Router D or Router C, but none of the corporate users will have access to reach the developers that are attached to the Dev VRF, since the Dev VRF is isolated from the rest of the network.

Continued

> Going back to the Dev VRF, if we look at the physical connectivity between Routers A and D, we do not have a path to let the developers communicate with each other, since the F0/0 interface of both routers is assigned to the default VRF and cannot also be assigned to the Dev VRF. Fortunately, we can connect these two Dev VRFs by using a GRE tunnel, because a GRE tunnel interface is allowed to transit the default VRF. The routers view the GRE tunnel as a direct point-to-point interface between the Dev VRF in Router A and the Dev VRF in Router D. Now the developers can communicate with each other, because their traffic will be encapsulated in a GRE header and tunneled through the base network, without giving the developers any kind of access to reach resources outside their VRF, such as the corporate users.
>
> This is just one small example of network virtualization deployed in a router. Cisco is starting to add virtualization into some of its other product lines so that you can have this same kind of functionality across all components in your routing paths. Keep in mind that although this feature can allow for great flexibility in your network designs, you still do not want to use this feature to allow a single device to house network segments from different security zones. You do not want to allow for the possibility of a hacker accessing your internal network by compromising a DMZ device that has been virtualized into different security zones.

Catalyst 3750

The Catalyst 3750 is Cisco's top-of-the-line series for fixed-configuration switches. The 3750 supports all the features of the Catalyst 3560 model that we just discussed but includes Cisco's StackWise technology for interconnecting multiple 3750 switches. These switches offer either 24 or 48 ports of Fast Ethernet and four Gigabit Ethernet SFP slots, as well as some models that also have PoE capabilities. If you need a larger number of Gigabit Ethernet ports, some models have either 12 SFP ports or 16 copper Gigabit Ethernet ports with a 10-Gig XENPAK uplink slot. The 10-Gigabit Ethernet is the newest standard of Ethernet to be standardized by the IEEE. This switch also allows for redundant power in the same manner as the 2960 and 3560, using the Cisco RPS 675.

The two main benefits of using a stacking architecture versus using Ethernet uplinks is that the stacking solution allows you to manage the entire stack as a single switch and you do not have to rely on spanning tree to prevent packet loops internal to the stack. The stack ring runs its own proprietary protocol that uses an internal header to direct packets passing across the stack ring. This protocol uses a token system, where the port that currently possesses the token can put a packet on the ring. As the packet traverses the ring, any port that needs to transmit the packet can make a copy for transmission before passing it to the next node in the ring. Once the packet reaches the originating port, it will remove the packet from the ring.

Each switch will have an "in" and "out" port on the back of the chassis for the stacking cables. The cables attach in a way that creates a ring topology that acts as the backplane between the switches that are a part of a stack. This ring is capable of running at 32Gbps, full duplex, and a break in the ring (meaning a switch or cable failure) can be corrected for in a matter of milliseconds by looping the disconnected ports, since traffic can flow in both directions on the ring. A single stack can support up to nine switches, and any model of switch in the 3750 line can be added to the stack, giving you the flexibility to add the ports and features you require into the stack. This allows the 3750 line to rival the port density of the 4500 and 6500 line of switches if the feature set in this line fits your needs better than the chassis-based switch solutions that will be discussed in the next sections.

The stack is designed to easily handle addition and deletion of switches from the stack. When a new switch is added to the stack, the master switch will copy the current software version and global configuration parameters to the new switch before it is included in the stack and allowed to pass traffic. The stack is also able to survive the loss of the master switch, because another switch will be selected as master, based on priority, in its place. To prevent disruptions when a switch with a higher master priority is added to the stack, the existing master will never relinquish its role unless it fails, thereby preventing unneeded master elections. Since the entire stack is managed as a single switch, this means that a single IP address is used to manage up to nine devices as though they were blades in a chassis-based solution, and the stack shows up as a single device to neighbors who are running CDP. This functionality allows for features to span across stack members, such as Etherchannel, which allows you to aggregate multiple Ethernet links into one logical link. With the 3750s, if you needed 3 Gigs of bandwidth for an uplink to your core, you could create an Etherchannel bundle that contains three Gigabit Ethernet links from three different switches within the stack. If you happened to lose one of the switches in your stack that was a part of that Etherchannel bundle, the uplink would continue to function as a 2 Gbps link instead of a 3 Gbps link until the failed switch was replaced.

Additional information on the Catalyst 3750 series switches, including a full list of benefits from the StackWise technology, can be found on the datasheets for the product at www.cisco.com/go/catalyst3750.

Catalyst 4500

The Cisco Catalyst 4500 series switch is Cisco's high-density, chassis-based switch solution, designed for edge deployments in medium-sized to large networks, and can support up to 10Gig Ethernet links. The brain of the Catalyst 4500 is the supervisor engine, which manages the configuration and controls all the other cards inserted into the chassis. Currently, there are three flavors of the 4500 supervisor engine: the Supervisor II-plus, the Supervisor IV, and the Supervisor V. All these supervisors run the IOS operating system and have varying levels of processing power and features. The Supervisor II-plus is mainly a Layer 2 card with some basic Layer 3 and 4 functionality. The Supervisor IV is a full multilayer supervisor card with increased processor power. The Supervisor V is a more powerful version of the Supervisor IV. The Supervisor V has increased performance from 64 to 96 Gbps and can perform certain switching functions in hardware, which further increases performance and reduces CPU load.

The 4500 offers four different chassis sizes, the 4503, 4506, 4507R and 4510R, which are 3, 6, 7, and 10 slots, respectively. The chassis that contain an *R* in the model number are capable of redundant supervisor modules; the other models are limited to a single supervisor. The remaining card slots can be populated with a variety of Fast and Gigabit Ethernet cards, depending on your organization's needs.

NOTE

The 4507R and 4510R chassis reserve Slots 1 and 2 for supervisor modules only. You cannot put standard line cards in either of these slots. For this reason, the 4507R does not offer any additional port density over the 4506. The benefit of the 4507R chassis is the ability to have the redundant supervisor module when more redundancy is required.

Like the other models, the Catalyst 4500 Cisco IOS software can support both Layer 2 and full Layer 3 features, including all the features of IP routing, QoS, security, and multicast routing. This switch can perform the Layer 2 switching functions within the wiring closet as well as in the distribution or core layer in a medium-sized network. This switch has the performance and functionality to perform well in a medium-sized DMZ environment. Additional information about the Catalyst 4500 line can be found at www.cisco.com/go/catalyst4500.

Catalyst 6500

The Cisco Catalyst 6500 series switch is a feature-rich, very flexible, and versatile switch that can provide high performance in all parts of the network, including your wiring closets, network core, server farm, and the DMZ. The 6500 is also designed as the switch with the highest levels of availability and performance throughout the entire Catalyst line. This level of performance is achieved by building as many features as possible into the hardware ASICs of the switch. That way, even in a feature-rich environment, very few packets will have to be punted to the processor for switching decisions, which can slow the flow of traffic through the switch. The Catalyst 6500 can operate between Layers 2 and 7, which allows it to provide simple Layer 2 connectivity to complex Layer 7 content load balancing. The Catalyst 6500 is a chassis-based switch with a variety of chassis types and line cards that can be inserted to accommodate any possible service requirement, from Fast Ethernet to 10 Gigabit Ethernet. The Catalyst 6500 can also accommodate WAN interfaces, ranging from T1 to OC-48, as well as a variety of service modules, making it a very powerful, modular, and versatile chassis.

For high availability, the chassis is designed for redundant power supplies and supervisor modules. Internal software features allow the standby supervisor modules to track the state of the switch so that in the event of a supervisor failure, downtime is limited to only a few seconds. Software upgrades between compatible versions can also happen with only a few seconds of downtime per switch, assuming redundant supervisors are being used. The latest versions of the Catalyst 6500 IOS software now support Cisco IOS Software Modularity, which is the latest enhancement to the IOS software architecture. In older versions of IOS, if a single process had a problem (for example, tried to write in the memory space of another process), the entire OS would crash and the device would reboot. With software modularity, these processes run independently of each other, and if a problem occurs, the problem process can be restarted automatically, without affecting the flow of traffic through the device. Since most of the switching is done in hardware, traffic can continue to pass through the switch while certain processes are restarting. This modularity also allows the administrator to apply patches to individual processes so that critical issues can be addressed in a timely manner and without disruption to the network. Previously, critical fixes were applied by upgrading to a newer version of IOS, which was difficult because you had to plan for scheduled downtime to apply the fix.

As with the Catalyst 4500, the brain of the Catalyst 6500 is located on the supervisor card, which provides multilayer switching capabilities. Two different types of supervisor engine are available, depending on how you plan to use your 6500 switch. The two models are:

- Supervisor 720 (Sup720)
- Supervisor 32 (Sup32)

The Sup720 is designed as a feature-rich Layer 3 card that contains many IP routing features built into hardware for increased performance and scalability. The Sup720 comes with a Multilayer Switch Feature Card, version 3 (MSFC3), which performs the Layer 3 functions and Policy Feature Card, version 3 (PFC3), which contains the ASICs that are used for implementing features such as routing, GRE, and QoS in hardware. The Sup720 also contains Switch Fabric Module (SFM) that increases the backplane speed of the 6500 to 720 Gbps. The Sup720 is offered in three different flavors: Sup720, Sup720-3B, and Sup720-3BXL, depending on the amount of processing power and advanced features you require. These different options describe the three versions of the PFC that can be installed onto the supervisor. The PFC3A is the standard PFC mentioned earlier; the PFC3B and PFC3BXL support some additional hardware features such as MPLS and an increasing number of VRF instances per device.

The Catalyst 6500 also has the ability to provide enterprise LAN access or edge services, such as WAN and Metro Ethernet, at a lower cost, for situations in which you do not require the same levels of performance as offered in the Sup720. The Sup32 comes with a PFC3B and supports a backplane capacity of 32 Gbps on a shared bus while supporting all classic and CEF256 modules available for the Catalyst 6500 line. This supervisor module enables the 6500 to complete with both the 4500 series and the 3750 series for edge connectivity. The decision becomes much more about which features and functionality work better for your environment and what sort of growth you expect in the future.

Other modules are also available to grow your investment in the 6500 to include the following optional components:

- Firewall Services Module (FWSM)

- Content Services Module (CSM)

- Intrusion Detection System Module (IDSM)

- Wireless LAN Services Module (WLSM)

- IPSec VPN Services Module (VPNSM)

- Network Analysis Module (NAM)

All these cards can provide this switch with the greatest features and functionality of any switch on the market. In other words, this switch can do it all and allows you to build the chassis that best fits your needs, from one with a very high Ethernet port density to one that is fully populated with services modules for advanced security and Layer 7 functionality. This switch can run on the Catalyst OS as well as the Cisco IOS, but new features and enhancements lag a few months on the CatOS version, so it would be in your best interest to ensure that you run IOS. The versatility, functionality, reliability, and performance this switch brings make it a favorite among DMZ architects. If you have a large DMZ infrastructure, consider using this switch; you will not be disappointed.

Securely Managing Switches

As with Cisco routers, Cisco switches offer many of the same management interface options to configure and support the switch, including the console, Telnet, SSH, and HTTP. In this section, we concentrate on the management interfaces of the Cisco Catalyst 2960, 3560, 3750, 4500, and 6500 series switches. Because they have similar CLIs, the same commands can be applied to all switches in these lines. Since all these switches have the ability to run Cisco IOS, we focus on the differences among the interface types as well as differences in configuration, in an effort to avoid duplicating the configuration described earlier, in the router section of this chapter.

One major difference you might notice is that switches do not have an auxiliary port the way the router does, so this topic is, of course, not covered here. We do cover how to configure the switch so that management interfaces and services (such as SSH, Telnet, console, and HTTP) are protected and locked down. We secure all the entries into the CLI to prevent hackers from making changes to the switch's configuration, gathering important network information, or using the compromised switch as a launching point for other attacks. You will learn how to use TACACS+ or RADIUS servers to authenticate, authorize, and log access to the switch. We also review using and securing managements services such as SNMP, NTP, and syslog.

NOTE

Technically, you would apply many of the same lockdown procedures you learned while reading about routers in the beginning of this chapter. It is important, however, that you read through this section to learn all the differences, especially with VLANs, as well as how to apply port-based security where needed. It's a sure thing that you will have a switch in your DMZ, so read on and learn where your network might be vulnerable and what to do about it.

Before we continue, we need to cover one very important point. Do not use a hub in your DMZ. For one thing, with today's technical advancements, using hub-based technology is simply ridiculous. If you invest the money in your infrastructure to build a DMZ in the first place, make certain that you at least "switch" this segment. As a result, you'll get more functionality out of the code running on the switch, as you will see in the following sections. You can also build virtual LANs, which are a very important security advancement, as you will learn shortly. Lastly, using a hub is dangerous if it is compromised. A compromised host could easily be made into a sniffer, and then the attacker will be able to eavesdrop promiscuously on every transmission that traverses that device.

Console

Out of the box, the switch acts like a dumb switch, with ports all set to auto-sense speed and duplex as well as all ports placed in VLAN 1. To initially configure the switch's features as well as other management interface options, you need to access the switch's console port, which provides direct serial access into the switch CLI. By default, there is no security on the console interfaces; therefore, it is very important to secure this entry point into the switch's CLI. If it is left unconfigured, a hacker with physical access to the switch can simply connect a laptop to the switch's console port and access the network without any interference. Access to the console port can be protected by a password or authenticated via a TACACS or RADIUS server. This type of access can be used for general maintenance or monitoring or when accessing the switch via other methods, such as Telnet or SSH, is rendered useless due to configuration error or malfunction. In this case, accessing the switch via the console could be your last option to correct the problem before you have to call Cisco's TAC for assistance.

By default, no password is set on the console port. It is very important to apply a password to this interface via the *password* command, to protect and discourage unauthorized personnel from attaching to the console port and obtaining unabated access to exec mode. As always, the password should be a nondictionary word, difficult to guess, and it should contain a combination of letters, numerals, and special characters. Line passwords can contain up to 25 characters, are case sensitive, and cannot begin with a number. When possible, use TACACS or RADIUS to authenticate access to the console port. We discuss how to configure TACACS or RADIUS support later in this section. Always apply an *exec-timeout* timeout so that sessions will time out after an idle period. The example in Figure 11.26 illustrates how to use these commands to secure the console ports.

Figure 11.26 Configuring a Console Password

```
DMZSwitch(config)# line con 0
DMZSwitch(config-line)# password H@rd2Cr@ck
DMZSwitch(config-line)# exec-timeout 15 0
```

Telnet

The Catalyst switch provides the ability to Telnet to the CLI. The switch allows up to 16 simultaneous Telnet sessions from hosts or networks you specify via an ACL. As was the case with the console port, Telnet access can be protected by a password or authenticated via a TACACS+ or RADIUS server. Remember that Telnet traffic is sent in clear text, so if someone is sniffing your network, they can easily capture the switch's Telnet password or enable password, or if you are using AAA, they will be able to obtain a user ID and password and use them later for other malicious activity.

To configure Telnet, you first need to configure the management VLAN, which is VLAN 1 by default, with an IP address, and if the switch will be accessed outside the local subnet, you need to configure a default gateway. Figure 11.27 shows how to configure the 16 Telnet sessions on the switch under the *line vty 0 15* virtual terminal line configuration section. Apply the password via the *password* command. Follow the same rules of selecting a password as in the console section. For further protection, apply an access list that limits the host(s) that can Telnet to the switch. In this example, we used the *access-class* command to apply access list 10, which allows only the host with IP address of 192.168.1.10 to Telnet to the switch. As with the console port, apply an *exec-timeout* timeout so that a session will time out after an idle period. In this case, it is 15 minutes.

Figure 11.27 Telnet Configuration Example

```
DMZSwitch(config)# interface Vlan10
DMZSwitch(config-vlan)# ip address 192.168.1.50 255.255.255.0
DMZSwitch(config-vlan)# no shutdown
DMZSwitch(config-vlan)# exit
DMZSwitch(config)# ip default-gateway 192.168.1.1
DMZSwitch(config)# access-list 10 permit host 192.168.1.10
DMZSwitch(config)# line vty 0 15
DMZSwitch(config-line)# password H@rd2Cr@ck
DMZSwitch(config-line)# access-class 10 in
DMZSwitch(config-line)# exec-timeout 15 0
```

NOTE

You should never use VLAN 1 as anything other than your management VLAN. As you might have noticed in the example in Figure 11.27, the management VLAN is set to 10 because all unassigned and inactive ports belong to VLAN 1 by default. If the management VLAN was set to 1, someone connecting to an unassigned port could attempt to access the management interface of this device. In addition, if you explicitly use VLAN 1 for your entire network, one compromised switch gives them all away—in other words, all management information is compromised. If VLAN 1 is limited to only containing the unassigned ports and doesn't have routed access to the rest of your network, you have reduced the risk of unauthorized access if someone manages to plug into an empty switch port.

SSH

One of the major weaknesses inherent in a Telnet session is that all data is sent in clear text. This can be a serious security risk if someone is able to sniff your Telnet session to the switch. Most recent versions of the Catalyst switch IOS can now support SSH version 1.*x*, which gives the administrator secure access to the switch's CLI. All traffic between the administrator's workstation and the switch is encrypted, making it difficult for a hacker to capture IDs and passwords. Unlike Telnet, which is available by default on almost every operating system, an SSH version 1.*x* client is required and usually needs to be installed on the workstation or workstations that need to manage the switch via SSH. As with the other access methods, the switch can be protected by a password or authenticated via a TACACS or RADIUS server. To run SSH on a switch, you need to obtain a special crypto version of the switch IOS software image, which enables you to switch to encrypt SSH sessions. To configure SSH, refer to the router section of this chapter, since the implementation of SSH on both the router and the switch are the same.

HTTP

Some newer versions of the Cisco IOS support Web-based management and configuration of switches using HTML through a Web browser. Unlike a router, some switches offer a more advanced HTTP interface that allows administrators to configure, manage, and support standalone switches as well as a cluster of switches. However, in a DMZ environment, it is recommended that this feature be disabled for security reasons because the communication between the switch and the Web browser is unencrypted. This feature is disabled by default, but if it is active, you can disable it using the *no ip http server* command. For best security results, do not activate this feature, especially in the DMZ.

Enable Passwords

To protect an unauthorized user from making configuration changes, you should configure an enable password so that only authorized users can access privileged mode. The enable password is separate from line passwords that allow a user access to exec mode, allowing a user to show statistics and view interfaces but not make configuration changes. As with the router, there are two methods to apply an enable password on a switch. The first is via the *enable password* command, which should not be used because it is possible to reverse it using several algorithms readily available on the Internet. The second method is the *enable secret* command, which is the preferred method because it uses a nonreversible encryption method. The *service password-encryption* command encrypts all passwords on the switch so that they are not shown in clear text when the configuration is displayed. As with the routers, the IOS software will not allow users connected via a Telnet session to enter enable mode if a password has not been set.

AAA

As with many features of the switch, AAA functionality and configuration are the same as the router's implementation of AAA. This makes configuring AAA consistent for all routers and switches across the network, improving the security integrity of the devices that support the network. With AAA you are able to validate the identity of an administrator, grant separate access rights to users or groups, and log changes made to the switch so that administrators are held accountable for their actions. Whenever possible, use AAA to secure the switches on the network.

Since the configuration of AAA is similar to the router's implementation, we only show you an example of how AAA is used to secure the DMZSwitch in Figure 11.28. In this example, we used AAA to authenticate administrative sessions, authorize all commands executed, and log all sessions on the switch to a TACACS+ server. Once AAA authentication is enabled, by default AAA will be used to authenticate, authorize, and log on all management interfaces, including the console, Telnet, and SSH. Therefore, all users accessing the switch will need to have a username and password to enter the switch.

Figure 11.28 Configuring AAA

```
DMZSwitch(config)# aaa new-model
DMZSwitch(config)# aaa authentication login default group tacacs+
    local-case
DMZSwitch(config)# aaa authorization commands 0 default group tacacs+ none
DMZSwitch(config)# aaa authorization commands 15 default group tacacs+
    none
DMZSwitch(config)# aaa accounting exec default start-stop group tacacs+
DMZSwitch(config)# tacacs-server host 192.168.1.50
DMZSwitch(config)# tacacs-server key MyTACACS-KEY
```

Syslogs, SNMP, and NTP

As we have seen, the advantage of having similar CLIs for both the switch and the router is that they share many of the same commands that make device configuration and support easier and consistent across devices. These similarities enable you to consistently configure and secure services such as syslog, SNMP, and NTP on routers and switches across the network. When you're configuring these services on the switch, be sure to follow all the same security precautions presented in the router portion of this chapter. Figure 11.29 shows a sample configuration for these services.

Figure 11.29 Configuring Syslog, SNMP, and NTP

```
DMZSwitch(config)# access-list 10 permit 192.168.1.50
DMZSwitch(config)# access-list 10 deny any log
DMZSwitch(config)# snmp-server community mySNMPReadKey RO 10
DMZSwitch(config)# snmp-server community mySNMPWriteKey RW 10
DMZSwitch(config)# service timestamps log datetime msecs
DMZSwitch(config)# logging trap informational
DMZSwitch(config)# logging 192.168.1.50
DMZSwitch(config)# logging buffered debugging
DMZSwitch(config)# ntp authenticate
DMZSwitch(config)# ntp authentication-key 1 md5 NTPkey
DMZSwitch(config)# ntp trusted-key 1
DMZSwitch(config)# ntp server 192.168.1.50 key 1
```

Security Banner

As we mentioned earlier in this chapter, security banners should be configured on all network devices on the network, including the switch. This banner is a legal statement that any unauthorized access to the device is prohibited; if it's violated, it could lead to criminal or civil prosecution. It is very important to configure this banner so that you'll be able to legally pursue a hacker who attempts and possibly succeeds at breaking into the network and disrupting business. As with many of the switch commands, the configuration of the login banner is the same as on the router, using the *banner login* command.

Disabling Unneeded IOS Features

Like the router, the switch has services, functions, and features that can be turned on by default on a switch's IOS to make configuration and management easier. Unfortunately, these functions and features can also give away vital information or expose the switch to malicious attacks. The switch might not have the extensive list of unneeded services that the router has, but it does have some of the potentially hazardous services enabled by default.

As with the router, TCP and UDP small servers and finger should *always* be disabled, since they provide no useful function, especially in your DMZ. It is also recommended that CDP be disabled to prevent hackers from obtaining important information about directly connected devices on the DMZ or outside the firewall. However, on the internal LAN, it might be necessary to run CDP because it is used for some plug-and-play functionality built into the Cisco IP telephony (AVVID) solution. As we mentioned earlier in the chapter, disabling unneeded services is a good idea; disabling needed services is not. Do an analysis of your network for the applications used and on what they depend, remembering that turning services off at times will paralyze an application you might depend on. The rule of thumb for DMZ-based services is less is better. Do not run what you do not need, analyze what you do need for vulnerabilities, and remove or replace as necessary. The configuration in Figure 11.30 shows how to disable some of the common unneeded services on the switch.

Figure 11.30 Disabling Unneeded Services

```
DMZSwitch(config)# no service tcp-small-servers
DMZSwitch(config)# no service udp-small-servers
DMZSwitch(config)# no ip finger
DMZSwitch(config)# no cdp run
```

VLAN Trunking Protocol

VLAN Trunking Protocol (VTP) is an automated method of distributing VLAN configuration information throughout a management domain. This process eases the pain of having to configure identical VLAN information on every single device you add to your network. VTP is a Layer 2 protocol that maintains VLAN configuration consistency by managing the addition, deletion, and renaming of VLANs within a VTP domain. VTP minimizes misconfigurations and configuration inconsistencies that can result in a number of problems, such as duplicate VLAN names and incorrect VLAN specifications. The switch has three VTP modes:

- **Server** In server mode, an administrator can create, modify, and delete VLANs and specify other configuration parameters for the entire VTP domain. VTP servers advertise their VLAN configurations to other network devices in the same VTP domain and synchronize their VLAN configurations with other network devices based on advertisements received over trunk links. VTP server is the default mode.

- **Client** In client mode, the switch will only receive VTP changes from servers. Switches configured as clients are not allowed to create, change, or delete VLANs.

- **Transparent** In transparent mode, the switch will not participate in VTP, which means it will not advertise its VLAN configuration and does not synchronize its VLAN configuration based on received advertisements. However, transparent network devices do forward VTP advertisements that they receive out their trunked ports, allowing VTP to function through the transparent device.

VTP is a very useful tool, especially in large networks, but if not secured properly it could be a point of vulnerability in your DMZ. As the network administrator, you will need to weight the benefits against the risks of having VTP in your DMZ infrastructure. If your environment is small enough that VTP doesn't offer much benefit, it is recommended that you do not use this feature, if only for the reason that you should keep the list of running services as small as possible. If your network is not properly protected, a hacker can inject faulty VLAN information, corrupting the VLAN databases on all switches in the VTP domain.

Since VTP cannot be disabled on a switch, you must set the device to transparent mode if you do not want it learning VLAN information from other devices. To change the switch from server mode, the default, to transparent mode, use the *vtp mode transparent* command in global configuration mode for all switches on the DMZ and outside the firewall. If VTP is something that would be beneficial to your DMZ environment, you should make sure you implement the MD5 authentication feature built into VTP. To enable this feature, use the *vtp password* command to specify the key that should be used for the MD5 hash.

VLANs

A VLAN is a feature that enables a switch or a group of switches to logically segment a network so that the network architect can group hosts across the LAN by department, application, or function instead of by the users' physical location. Each VLAN creates a separate broadcast domain, and broadcasts will not cross VLANs. VLANs operate in Layer 2, the data link layer. For communication of devices between VLANs to occur, Layer 3, network layer, routing needs to take place. Figure 11.31 illustrates a switch with three VLANs configured showing three different broadcast domains. Basically, the diagram shows how a switch can be configured to logically act like three different switches. VLANs are useful to cost-effectively partition your network into logical parts.

In recent versions of IOS code for Cisco switches, there are two ways to configure VLANs: VLAN database mode and config-vlan mode. In database mode, the switch allows you to configure VLANs in the normal range, which includes 1 to 1005, and save them to the VLAN database. In config-vlan mode, the switch allows you to configure in the normal as well as the extended range, which includes 1006 to 4094. In config-vlan mode, VLANs in the normal range are saved in the VLAN database, and VLANs in the extended range are stored in the switch's configuration file. To configure extended VLANs, the switch needs to be in transparent mode, since the extended range is not supported by VTP. Figure 11.32 shows how to set up a VLAN and select individual ports to the defined VLAN using config-vlan mode.

VLAN membership can be statically defined, as our example shows, or dynamically defined by a MAC address. In a DMZ environment, the ports used within the DMZ are usually statically defined to a specific VLAN. As shown in Figure 11.32, the configuration of VLAN 20 is started with the *vlan* command in global configuration mode. This command puts you in config-vlan mode, where the VLAN can be named and the maximum transmission unit (MTU) can be configured. In this example, VLAN 20 is given the name *DMZ2*, and the MTU is set to the default value of 1500 bytes. To statically define an interface to participate in VLAN 20, use the *switchport mode access* command to set the interface as a non-trunking single VLAN port, and use the *switchport access vlan* command to associate the port to a VLAN—VLAN 20, in this case. To show the status of the VLANs, use the *show vlan* command.

NOTE

Avoid using VLAN 1, the default VLAN for all ports on the switch. If trunking is necessary, use a dedicated VLAN other than VLAN 1, to avoid the possibility of VLAN hopping and double-tagged 802.1q attacks. Avoiding the use of VLAN 1 altogether will keep it from being used in access mode on any nontrunked ports. For additional security, you should disable any unassigned ports, but some switch administrators place them in an unused VLAN, which, in essence, has a similar effect.

Figure 11.31 A VLAN

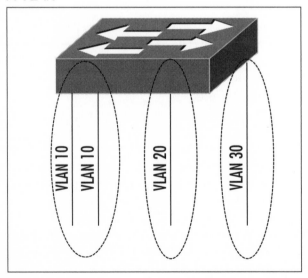

Figure 11.32 Configuring and Applying VLANs

```
DMZSwitch(config)# vlan 20
DMZSwitch(config-vlan)# name DMZ2
DMZSwitch(config-vlan)# mtu 1500
DMZSwitch(config)# interface fastethernet 0/1
DMZSwitch(config-if)# switchport mode access
DMZSwitch(config-if)# switchport access vlan 20
```

Designing & Planning...

Tips for Designing VLANs in a DMZ

VLANs are a cost-effective way to segment a network, because a single switch can be used to support many segmented LANs. This can be very useful on the internal network, where users are grouped by department, application, or function.

In a DMZ environment, incorrect use of VLANs can cause a security flaw or weakness in your network's defenses. Figure 11.33 shows *incorrect* use of VLANs. The diagram shows a small branch office or small enterprise office with an internal LAN, a DMZ, and connectivity to the Internet. A single switch is used to support the entire infrastructure and has three VLANs configured—VLANs 10, 20, and 30. VLAN 10 houses all the internal users, VLAN 20 supports the DMZ, and VLAN 30 connects the firewall to the ISP's Internet router at the site.

The problem with this implementation of VLANs is that a single switch logically partitions the various security zones on the network. The switch is not a security device and should not be counted on to securely partition the network, even with the use of VLANs. Each zone, the trusted internal LAN, the semitrusted DMZ, and connectivity to the untrusted Internet should have its own set of switches, and the switches should never have VLANs that cross zone boundaries. In the scenario pictured in Figure 11.33, the entire network could be in jeopardy should a hacker attack the switch, penetrate it, and exploit it. A simple configuration error could make the hacker's job that much easier to accomplish. Since the switch has ports outside the firewall, this makes it easy to attack. Should the switch be compromised, a hacker can bypass the firewall, because the switch has a presence on all parts of the network—a hacker's dream. At this point, the hacker can shut down ports, reconfigure VLANs, and so on to cause a major disruption and create security issue on the network. Furthermore, with a presence on the outside of the firewall, the switch is susceptible to DoS attacks and other forms of attack that focus on other features, such as trunking.

Continued

Figure 11.33 Improper VLAN Use

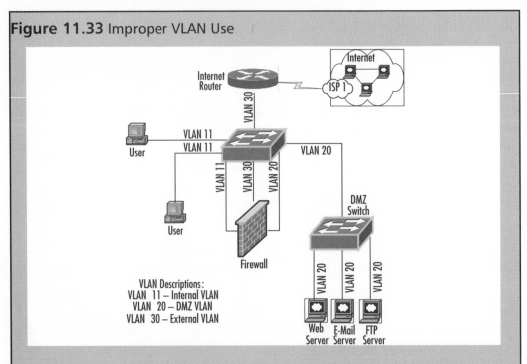

VLAN Descriptions:
VLAN 11 – Internal VLAN
VLAN 20 – DMZ VLAN
VLAN 30 – External VLAN

To mitigate these risks, use separate switches for each security zone. This solution prevents an attack on a switch from disrupting the entire network and compromising security. Figure 11.34 shows a proper VLAN implementation in which separate switches are used for each security zone, all separated by the firewall. The diagram shows an internal Layer 3 switch configured with VLAN 10 as the transit network between the internal switch and the firewall. VLAN 12 connects all the internal users to the internal switch, and VLAN 11 connects all the development users on their own subnet. Since the internal switch operates at Layer 3, it also acts as a router and allows routed access between the three VLANs configured on it. VLAN 30 only connects the outside or Internet-facing interface of the firewall to the ISP Internet router located at the site. Notice that there are two DMZ LANs supported by this firewall: one DMZ on VLAN 20 and the second on VLAN 25. These VLANs are located on the same switch, known as the *DMZ switch*. The connection between the DMZ switch and the firewall can either be an ISL or Dot1q trunk, so both VLAN 20 and VLAN 25 can pass across that link. The firewall will have two virtual interfaces that are assigned to the same physical interface: one for each VLAN. This allows the firewall to separate the two DMZ VLANs from each other. The use of VLANs to separate DMZs is a common and accepted practice in designing and building DMZs, because both DMZs reside in the same security zone, the semitrusted DMZ zone.

Continued

Figure 11.34 Proper VLAN Use

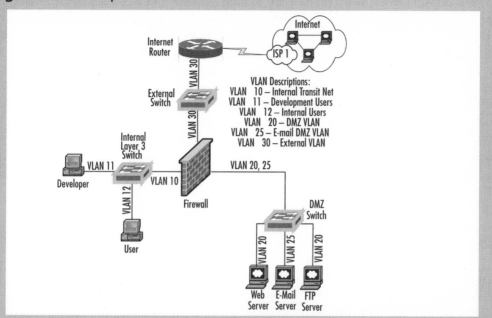

For further security, consider using a separate switch for VLAN 20 and VLAN 25. The use of multiple switches servicing each DMZ VLAN is usually complicated by the cost of the switches, additional physical firewall interfaces, and the common use of large, chassis-based switches that can accommodate a large number of servers, so some DMZ architects take the security risk in return for performance and manageability. In any event, an attack on a switch or switches on the DMZ will affect only the DMZ; the rest of the network will operate normally. This is because the switches in each zone are physically isolated, and connectivity between the zones is protected by the firewall. Therefore, if one switch is compromised, the attacker will need to penetrate the firewall's defenses before moving to or attacking another zone.

Private VLANS

Hackers often look to exploit a server or other end station that has not been hardened or patched to gain entrance to a network and launch further attacks from the compromised device. (You learned how to harden hosts on the DMZ in earlier chapters.) From the compromised device, the hackers have free access to any device on the local LAN segment because there are no firewalls or ACLs in the way to prevent them from attacking local devices. To reduce the risk of attackers using a compromised box to attack other devices on the same LAN segment, Cisco has introduced a feature called private VLANs (PVLANs).

DMZ segments are typically shared among many devices that have no interaction with each other, but they are on the same LAN segment, so they are free to talk to each other. For instance, a company's e-mail relay server might not need to communicate with the company's Web server, located on the same DMZ LAN, to operate normally. This can be a problem if a hacker compromises one of the boxes. Let's use the Web server as an example in which a hacker can exploit the server, then use the Web server to launch DoS or other attacks on the e-mail server or any other server on the DMZ.

To help solve this issue, Cisco has added the concept of a private VLAN to some lines of switches. A PVLAN allows you some control over intra-VLAN communication because you can isolate or group devices on a VLAN, keeping that group separate from the rest of the VLAN. With PVLANs, a port on a switch can be configured as an isolated, community, or promiscuous port. An *isolated port* on a switch can communicate only with the promiscuous port. A *community port* allows communication between other devices within the same community and the promiscuous port. The *promiscuous port* can communicate with all devices with the PVLAN, including the isolated and community ports. The promiscuous port designation is usually used for the default gateway device.

NOTE

Although you might think that this discussion is overkill on security for a DMZ, you would be surprised at how many engineers wish they knew how to add layers of security with PVLANs, as we are describing. If you need added security, this is one way to go. In your organization, you should assess the amount of security you need and apply it with tips and tricks such as the one described here.

Figure 11.35 shows how PVLANs are used to isolate and group servers so that devices can communicate only with other devices on the same LAN that provide normal communication and functionality. In this example, we isolated the e-mail relay server and grouped the Web and application servers. The switch's connection to the firewall is in promiscuous mode to allow communication to flow in and out of the DMZ LAN. The switch will only allow the e-mail server to communicate to the firewall to get to the internal LAN or the Internet. The Web and application servers are grouped into a community, meaning that they can communicate with any device within their community as well as the firewall so they can get to the internal LAN or the Internet. Assign IP addressing and masking as you would normally, through DHCP of static addressing. If you are using static addressing, be vigilant as to how you track your assignment, because when PVLANs are in use, it is possible for a ping to fail but the address you are pinging to be in use.

Figure 11.35 A Private VLAN

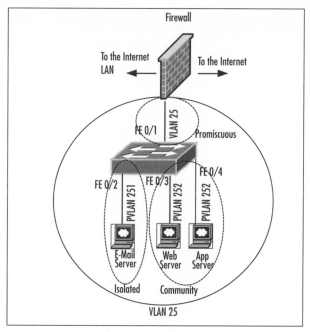

Not all Cisco Catalyst switches and Cisco IOS or Catalyst OS versions support PVLANs. As for the switches that do support PVLANs, not all support the community port functionality. If you are interested in using this feature, be sure to check the Catalyst switch documentation prior to implementation or purchase of hardware, or visit the following URL: www.cisco.com/warp/customer/473/63.html. This link requires a CCO login account for access.

To configure PVLANs, the switch must be set to transparent VTP mode. In this example, we configure PVLANs as per the diagram in Figure 11.35. Let's start with the configuration of primary and secondary PVLANs. PVLANs are configured similarly to a standard VLAN with the exception of establishing the role the PVLAN will play using the *private-vlan* command in config-vlan mode. The options include *primary*, which signifies the primary VLAN; *isolate*, which signifies that all devices on this PVLAN are set to *isolated*; and *community*, which groups devices that can communicate between one another. In Figure 11.36, we configured three PVLANs: the primary PVLAN (VLAN 25), isolated PVLANs (VLAN251), and a community PVLAN (VLAN 252). Once the roles of the PVLANs have been established, we need to associate the secondary PVLANs to the primary using the *private-vlan association* command in config-vlan mode of the primary PVLAN. In this case, we are associating secondary PVLANs, VLANs 251 and 252, to primary VLAN 25.

Figure 11.36 Configuring Private VLANs

```
DMZSwitch(config)# vlan 25
DMZSwitch(config-vlan)# private-vlan primary
DMZSwitch(config)# vlan 251
DMZSwitch(config-vlan)# private-vlan isolate
DMZSwitch(config)# vlan 252
DMZSwitch(config-vlan)# private-vlan community
DMZSwitch(config)# vlan 25
DMZSwitch(config-vlan)# private-vlan association 251,252
```

The next step is to configure the switch's interfaces (ports) and apply the PVLAN associations. We start with the promiscuous connection that supports connectivity to the firewall on Fast Ethernet interface 0/1, as shown in Figure 11.37. We use the *switchport mode private-vlan promiscuous* command to set the interface to promiscuous mode. Then we must map the primary and secondary PVLANs to this promiscuous interface using the *switchport private-vlan mapping* command. In this example, the port will be promiscuous for primary VLAN 25 and secondary VLANs 251 and 252. Next, the e-mail server on the Fast Ethernet interface 0/2 needs to be associated to the isolated PVLAN using the *switchport mode private-vlan host* command, to set the port to host mode, and the *switchport private-vlan host-association* command, to associate the port to isolated PVLAN 251. The same commands are used to set the Web and application servers, on Fast Ethernet interfaces 0/3 and 0/4, respectively, to community PVLAN 252. At this point the e-mail server will be able to communicate only through the firewall, and the Web and application servers can communicate between themselves and through to the firewall. To display PVLAN information, use the *show vlan private-vlan* command.

Figure 11.37 Applying Private VLANs to Ports

```
DMZSwitch(config)# interface fastethernet 0/1
DMZSwitch(config-if)# description Connection to the Firewall
DMZSwitch(config-if)# switchport mode private-vlan promiscuous
DMZSwitch(config-if)# switchport private-vlan mapping 25 251,252
DMZSwitch(config)# interface fastethernet 0/2
DMZSwitch(config-if)# description Connection to the E-mail Server
DMZSwitch(config-if)# switchport mode private-vlan host
DMZSwitch(config-if)# switchport private-vlan host-association 25 251
DMZSwitch(config)# interface fastethernet 0/3
DMZSwitch(config-if)# description Connection to the Web Server
DMZSwitch(config-if)# switchport mode private-vlan host
DMZSwitch(config-if)# switchport private-vlan host-association 25 252
DMZSwitch(config)# interface fastethernet 0/4
DMZSwitch(config-if)# description Connection to the App Server
```

```
DMZSwitch(config-if)# switchport mode private-vlan host
DMZSwitch(config-if)# switchport private-vlan host-association 25 252
```

Securing Switch Ports

The port security function is a Layer 2 security feature that allows the switch to block packets that enter a port that does not match a dynamically or statically configured source MAC address. This feature allows you to specify and limit the number of MAC addresses that the switch will accept from a particular switch port. This feature can prevent users from adding unauthorized devices to the network and discourage the unauthorized addition of hubs or other switches to the network. Another use of this feature is to prevent CAM over-flow attacks, which attempt to force the switch to flood all packets out all ports by flooding the switch with traffic from random MAC addresses. This flood of MAC addresses can fill up the CAM table, which tracks the switch ports a particular MAC address can be reached through, with invalid entries. If the CAM table is full of invalid entries, it won't have room to track valid hosts, and traffic to those valid hosts will be flooded out all ports, allowing an attacker to capture packets that wouldn't normally be sent to him.

There are three ways to define secure MAC addresses on most switches: static, dynamic, and sticky. *Static-secure* MAC addresses are manually configured on the switch port. *Dynamic-secure* MAC addresses are learned dynamically by the switch but need to be relearned when the switch is restarted. *Sticky-secure* MAC addresses can be dynamically learned or statically configured. When they're dynamically learned, the switch converts and enters them into the switch's configuration. Because sticky-secure MAC addresses can be written and saved to the switch's configuration file, there is no need to relearn any dynamic addresses after a reload. The switch will detect a port security violation when a MAC address that is not statically or dynamically defined tries to access a switch port, a MAC address that is statically or dynamically defined to a switch port attempts to access another switch port on the same VLAN, or the maximum number of allowed MAC addresses has been exceeded. The switch can be configured to react in protect, restrict, or shutdown mode when a violation occurs. In protect mode, the switch drops unknown source MAC addresses but will not log the violation. In restrict mode, the switch drops unknown source MAC addresses but records the violation. Shutdown mode is the switch's default setting; in this mode the switch will disable the port and record the violation.

The *switchport port-security* command is used to enable port security on an interface. This is the only mandatory command needed to configure port security. At this point, the switch will allow only one dynamically defined source MAC address to access the port, and if a violation occurs, the port will be disabled. At this point, you can add optional commands that define a static or sticky MAC address entry, change the number of MAC addresses that have access to the port, and change the switch's reaction to a violation. To specify a static MAC address, use the *switchport port-security mac-address* command. To specify multiple static entries, this command can be entered up to 128 times per interface on most switches. The *switchport*

port-security mac-address command enables sticky MAC addresses. To specify the maximum number of MAC addresses an interface can accept, use the *switchport port-security maximum* command. The maximum will vary from switch to switch; the default is one. Use the *switchport port-security violation* command to change the method by which the switch handles a violation. The valid values are *protect, restrict,* and *shutdown,* the default value. Use the *show port-security* command to verify your port security configuration. To clear dynamic or sticky MAC addresses, use the *clear port-security* command.

The example in Figure 11.38 shows port security enabled on two interfaces on the switch. On the first interface, the statically defined MAC address of *0001.0002.0003* will be the only address allowed to access the port. If a violation occurs, the switch will disable the port. On the second interface, the switch allows for 10 dynamically defined MAC addresses to access the port. The sticky command allows the switch to convert the dynamic MAC address and copy it to the switch's configuration so that when the switch is restarted, the MAC addresses will not have to be relearned. On this port, the switch drops packets from invalid MAC addresses and records violations.

Figure 11.38 Configuring Port Security

```
DMZSwitch(config)# interface fastethernet0/1
DMZSwitch(config-if)# switchport mode access vlan 20
DMZSwitch(config-if)# switchport port-security
DMZSwitch(config-if)# switchport port-security mac-address 0001.0002.0003
DMZSwitch(config-if)# switchport port-security maximum 1
DMZSwitch(config-if)# switchport port-security violation shutdown
DMZSwitch(config)# interface fastethernet0/2
DMZSwitch(config-if)# switchport mode access vlan 20
DMZSwitch(config-if)# switchport port-security
DMZSwitch(config-if)# switchport port-security maximum 10
DMZSwitch(config-if)# switchport port-security mac-address sticky
DMZSwitch(config-if)# switchport port-security violation restrict
```

IOS Bugs and Security Advisories

As you know, from time to time bugs or security vulnerabilities are found in software after it is released to the public. The software loaded in Cisco routers and switches is no different. Just as with Windows or UNIX operating system software, Cisco constantly releases new versions that contain new or enhanced functionality but also releases fixes for any bugs or vulnerabilities discovered in previous releases. It is very important to keep up to date on any potential security issues on your network, including making sure that the devices supporting your network infrastructure do not have any weaknesses. Cisco has set up a page on its Web site that announces security advisories and notices for its entire product line, including Cisco routers and switches. The page is constantly updated with new advisories and fixes to known problems related to Cisco hardware and software, as well as mitigation techniques for new attacks, to prevent them from spreading. This page also contains links on how to report an attack as well as how to report a vulnerability about one of its products to Cisco. You can find the Cisco Product Security Advisories and Notices page at the following URL using a valid CCO login ID: www.cisco.com/en/US/products/products_security_ advisories_listing.html.

> **NOTE**
>
> Cisco also provides several white papers called *SAFE Blueprints* that break down the parts of a network into separate modules and detail how to protect and secure each module. Many of the tips and items listed in this chapter can be found in these documents. Be sure to read these documents before designing and configuring your DMZ; they will provide you with sound network design and security strategies. The SAFE documents can be found at the following URL: www.cisco.com/go/safe.

DMZ Router and Switch Security Best-Practice Checklists

When you're designing and configuring routers and switches on your DMZ, make sure that you follow the checklists presented in this section to make sure that you have covered some of the important tasks that can increase your network's security and integrity. If you have already set up your DMZ, go through the list to determine whether you can improve security on the devices you already have in place.

Router Security Checklist

Here is a checklist to follow to ensure router security:

- Authenticate routing updates on dynamic routing protocols.
- Use ACLs to protect network resources and prevent address spoofing.
- Secure the management interfaces:
  1. Secure all management interfaces, including the console, auxiliary, and virtual terminal ports, using hard-to-guess passwords or a TACACS+ or RADIUS server.
  2. Use SSH instead of Telnet.

3. If possible, use AAA to authenticate, authorize, and log administrative access to the router using a TACACS+ or RADIUS server.

4. Disable the HTTP server, which disables configuration and management of the router through the Web browser.

- Lock down the router services:

    1. If possible, use SNMP version 2. Use ACLs to restrict access to SNMP.

    2. Disable CDP.

    3. Use authentication and ACLs to secure NTP.

- Disable interface-related services:

    1. Disable redirects.

    2. Disable ICMP unreachables.

    3. Disable directed broadcast.

    4. Disable proxy ARP.

- Disable unneeded services:

    1. Disable TCP and UDP small services.

    2. Disable CDP.

    3. Disable finger.

    4. Disable password security

    5. Disable IP source route.

    6. Disable the bootp server.

- Keep up to date on IOS bug fixes and vulnerabilities and upgrade (sometimes downgrade) if necessary.

Switch Security Checklist

Here is a checklist to follow to ensure switch security:

- Secure the management interfaces:

    1. Secure all management interfaces, including the console, and virtual terminal ports, using hard-to-guess passwords or use a TACACS+ or RADIUS server.

    2. Use SSH instead of Telnet.

    3. If possible, use AAA to authenticate, authorize, and log administrative access to the switch using a TACACS+ or RADIUS server.

4. Disable the HTTP server, which disables configuration and management of the switch through a Web browser.

- Lock down the router services:

  1. If possible, use SNMP version 2. Use ACLs to restrict access to SNMP.

  2. Use authentication and ACLs to secure NTP.

- Disable unneeded services:

  1. Disable TCP and UDP small services.

  2. Disable CDP.

  3. Disable finger.

- Use VLANs to logically segment a switch.

- Use PVLANs to isolate hosts on a VLAN.

- Use port security to secure the input to an interface by limiting and identifying MAC addresses of the hosts that are allowed to access the port.

- Do not use VTP on the DMZ switches. Configure DMZ switches for transport mode.

- Keep up to date on IOS bug fixes and vulnerabilities and upgrade (sometimes downgrade) if necessary.

Summary

As we have seen in this chapter, routers and switches do more than simply provide connectivity between hosts on a network. If implemented and configured correctly, they can also provide a higher level of security for the network. Routers direct traffic in and out of the enterprise network and are usually the first line of defense when the network is connecting to the Internet. Access control lists, or ACLs, on the ingress ports on the Internet-facing routers can provide the first point of defense on the network before traffic is forwarded to the firewall. Access lists can be used to prevent address spoofing, certain DoS attacks, and other known attacks from affecting the network. Since routers are key parts of an interconnecting network, they are prime targets of hackers. Hackers will try to infiltrate routers to glean information or use them as launching pads for further attacks. This is why it is important to lock down routers' management interfaces and services—to make them difficult for an intruder to hack.

As with routers, switches have an increasing role in network security. The switch provides many features, including port security. VLANs and PVLANs provide the tools to keep the devices on the DMZ secure. It is also important to lock down the switch's management interfaces and services so that hackers cannot break into the switch to change VLAN configurations, change port settings, or use the switch to connect to other parts of the network.

New attacks and new vulnerabilities are uncovered every day. It is very important to keep up to date on security notices and advisories posted on the various security Web sites as well as Cisco's site. When a flaw in the hardware or software of your network devices is exposed, it is very important to patch, upgrade, or find a workaround to the issue at the earliest possible time, to prevent an intruder from taking advantage of the vulnerability and break into or disrupt the enterprise network.

Solutions Fast Track

Securing the Router

- Router placement and routing in a DMZ environment are essential to connect the enterprise location to the Internet. Proper routing, whether statically or dynamically, is important to directing traffic to the Internet so that internal users are able to access the Internet and users on the Internet can access the DMZ.

- Often the Internet-facing router is the first line of defense in a DMZ infrastructure. Placing ACLs on the Internet-facing router's inbound interface can help protect the network from several types of DoS attack.

- Securing router management interfaces and services is important to prevent intruders from taking over the router and making configuration changes or using it as a launching pad for other attacks.

- It is also important to disable any unneeded services on the router to prevent security holes that could be exposed when these services are activated.

Securing the Switch

- Proper use of VLANs is essential to protecting the integrity of the network. Use physically separate switches and different VLANs in each security zone.

- Take advantage of the switch's security features, such as port security and private VLANs, to enhance security on the DMZ.

- Securing the switch's management interfaces and services is important to prevent intruders from taking over the switch and making configuration changes or using it as a launching pad for other attacks.

- It is also important to disable any unneeded services on the switch to prevent security holes that could be exposed when these services are activated.

IOS Bugs and Security Advisories

- Make sure that the router and switch software is free of any relevant bugs and any known vulnerabilities.

- Check any security notices and advisories on a regular basis for the latest attacks and mitigation techniques. Make changes or upgrades where appropriate.

- Take advantage of security white papers to identify security "best practices" and learn how to secure routers and switches on your network.

DMZ Router and Switch Security Best-Practice Checklists

- Follow the Security Best-Practice Checklists and make sure you have covered all the tasks that can help improve security for routers and switches on your DMZ.

Frequently Asked Questions

The following Frequently Asked Questions, answered by the authors of this book, are designed to both measure your understanding of the concepts presented in this chapter and to assist you with real-life implementation of these concepts. To have your questions about this chapter answered by the author, browse to **www.syngress.com/solutions** and click on the **"Ask the Author"** form.

Q: How much memory should my router have to receive the complete BGP routing table from my ISP?

A: We recommend a minimum of 128MB of RAM in the router to store a complete global BGP routing table from one BGP peer. If you store complete BGP routes from multiple peers, you must add more memory.

Q: How can I reset a BGP session?

A: When changes are made in the configuration of BGP, you usually have to reset the session to the neighbors for the changes to take effect using the *clear ip bgp* command. If you have enabled the "soft reconfiguration" option, you can resync routing updates without tearing down the TCP session.

Q: What is the difference between the *ip default-gateway, ip default-network*, and *ip route 0.0.0.0/0* commands?

A: The *ip default-network* and *ip route 0.0.0.0/0* commands are used to route any packets for which the router does not have an exact route match in its routing table. The *ip default-gateway* command is used only when IP routing is disabled on the router.

Q: Should I authenticate routing protocols? Which routing protocols support authentication?

A: Yes, you should always use authentication for routing updates so hackers can't tamper with routing tables. RIP v2, EIGRP, OSPF, and BGP all support authentication of routing updates.

Q: How do you route traffic between VLANs?

A: To route between VLANs, you need to have a switch with Layer 3 routing capabilities—for example, the 3560, 3750, 4500, and 6500 with MSFC—or connect the individual VLANs to a router.

Q: How many MAC addresses can you define using port security?

A: This number varies from switch to switch:

- 128 MAC addresses per interface on the Catalyst 2950/3550 series switches
- 1024 MAC addresses per interface on the Catalyst 4500/6500 series switches

## Chapter 12

DMZ-Based VPN Services

Solutions in this chapter:

- **VPN Services in the DMZ**

- **Designing an IPSec Solution**

- **Connecting B2B Sites**

☑ **Summary**

☑ **Solutions Fast Track**

☑ **Frequently Asked Questions**

Introduction

Virtual private networks (VPNs) are quickly supplanting leased lines as a cost-effective and practical way of providing WAN communication between a central network and various remote networks or extranet partner networks. However, implementing VPN services in the DMZ has its share of difficulties. For one, you must determine the placement of the VPN tunnel termination point. To identify the location for this device, you must conduct an evaluation as to the security of the device itself. Can it withstand an attack? Are there known vulnerabilities in the software?

Another factor that affects VPN device placement and VPN design is the function of the VPN. More and more companies are turning from dialup services to VPNs for remote access connectivity for telecommuters as well as mobile workers. The prime motivating factor in this move appears to be an overall lower total cost of ownership (TCO) of VPNs compared with dialup phone lines.

It is easy to get confused when we think about all the VPN technologies available, especially since many of them have different functions. To understand these technologies, it helps to step back and look at the basic definition of a VPN, which is just isolated network connectivity over a shared or public network. The word *virtual* refers to the fact that this connection must pass over a larger shared network as the transport mechanism, whereas the word *private* describes that this connection only offers connectivity between the endpoints, not the intermediate systems, keeping it isolated from the rest of the shared network. The term *VPN* is extremely generic and does not dictate a specific technology (such as IPSec or GRE), topology (point-to-point, full-mesh, remote access), the number of sites that can participate, or even what is being connected with this VPN (networks or single hosts). In most cases, this public network is the Internet due to its widespread use, but these concepts can just as easily apply to any kind of network that connects multiple separate entities.

As we just mentioned, when most people think of VPNs, they immediately picture an encrypted point-to-point connection that travels over the Internet between two sites. Although this might be the most common use of the term, there are other places where VPNs are used to enable services, such as MPLS-based WAN services. In these kinds of configurations, the service provider connects all users to the shared, high-bandwidth network with leased lines and then creates isolated, private routed networks between sites of the same company. This way, each customer has its own private WAN that offers direct site-to-site connectivity, and the bandwidth is limited only by the size of the circuits installed in each customer site.

Just like most people think of VPNs as traversing the Internet, they also mostly equate VPNs with IPSec. Other technologies, such as Layer 2 Tunneling Protocol (L2TP), Point-to-Point Tunneling Protocol (PPTP), Multi-Protocol Label Switching (MPLS), Generic Routing Encapsulation (GRE), and Secure Sockets Layer (SSL), VPNs have their uses as well as their drawbacks in constructing VPNs. Even so, certain VPN technologies are used in different ways. Still other proprietary solutions lie ahead, such as Cisco's Dynamic Multipoint

VPN (DMVPN) solution, which allows for the automatic creation of VPN tunnels between sites that have no direct knowledge of each other.

The preceding discussion was written to help you understand the depth and breadth of VPN services, but this chapter focuses specifically on the enterprise uses of VPN technology in the DMZ and mostly on connectivity over the Internet, since you have created your DMZ as a security measure to protect your systems from other users on this public network. The most common services used in these kinds of environments are IPSec and SSL VPNs, so most of our examples discuss these technologies.

VPN Services in the DMZ

VPN services in the DMZ are designed to provide connectivity to two primary groups of users:

- Business partners
- Remote users

Remote users can be further subdivided into three general categories:

- Branch offices
- Telecommuters
- Mobile workers

This section focuses on the various uses of VPN services as well as how these services can be leveraged to reduce the total cost of WAN connectivity for an enterprise.

A traditional corporate WAN is shown in Figure 12.1. Branch office networks are connected through either a circuit-switched data path such as ISDN, providing a low-end, broadband connection, or through packet-switched technologies such as Frame Relay or leased lines (T1, DS3, and so on). The cost of such a WAN topology increases significantly as the number of sites and the number of interconnections between the sites increase. For a fully meshed topology with four endpoints, six Frame Relay or serial connections are required. In general, a full meshed network with n nodes requires $(n(n-1)) / 2$ links. This system quickly becomes quite expensive as the number of nodes increases. VPNs provide dramatic flexibility in network design as well as a reduced total cost of ownership in the WAN.

There is a variety of ways to implement VPN services, including at the enterprise-edge router, the firewall, or a dedicated VPN appliance. Another possibility is the virtual private dialup network (VPDN). Primarily used for remote-access connection to an enterprise campus network, this type of VPN combines the traditional dialup network through the PSTN with either Layer 2 Forwarding (L2F) or L2TP. All these various technologies are available in today's marketplace, but the most popular VPN technology by far is the IPSec VPN. This type of VPN is the focus of this chapter.

Figure 12.1 Fully Meshed Enterprise WAN Connectivity

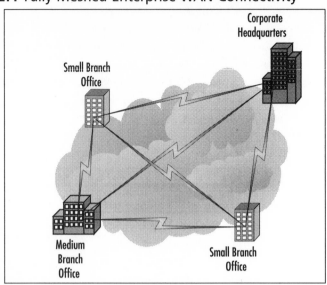

VPN Deployment Models

One of the first decisions to make when deploying a VPN is choosing a device to serve as the termination point for the VPN tunnel. This decision is primarily driven by the placement of the VPN tunnel endpoint but also the capabilities of the device that will serve as the tunnel endpoint. IPSec VPNs require devices capable of encrypting and decrypting all the traffic that traverses the VPN tunnel. Insufficient processing power will result in slow connection speeds over the VPN and poor performance overall. Many vendors address this problem by offering VPN accelerator modules (VAMs), which are onboard processors designed to offload the encryption and decryption operations from the central CPU to hardware designed specifically to handle these functions.

Deployment of VPNs in the enterprise DMZ is done primarily through the three models listed here and shown in Figures 12.2–12.4:

- VPN termination at the edge router
- VPN termination at the corporate firewall
- VPN termination at a dedicated appliance

Each of these deployment models presents its own difficulties that must be addressed in order for the VPN topology to be successful. One concern that must be addressed is the use of Network Address Translation (NAT). Due to its design, IPSec is not capable of traversing NAT devices. The problem comes when the NAT device changes information in the IP header of the IPSec packet. The changes will result in an incorrect IPSec checksum that is calculated over parts of the IP header. There are vendor workarounds for this problem, where the IPSec packet is encapsulated in a UDP or TCP packet and then transmitted to the other side. An IETF standard called NAT-Traversal, or NAT-T, has also been created to solve this issue and is defined in RFC 3947 and 3948. Having a detailed understanding of how your NAT mechanism works could be important for establishing a working VPN tunnel, especially if there are firewalls between the two VPN endpoints, so be sure to research the way your vendor is solving any NAT issues before you attempt to implement one of these features.

VPN Termination at the Edge Router

Termination of the VPN at the edge router has the benefit of ensuring that all VPN traffic must conform to external firewall policy, to reach the internal network. This topology (shown Figure 12.2) is best deployed for extranet connections where the business partners do not require access to the internal network but do require access to servers in the DMZ itself that might not necessarily be exposed to normal Internet traffic. Tunnel termination on the router eliminates the need to configure IPSec through NAT. As the number of business partners connecting through VPNs increases, the load on the routers due to the encryption and decryption of packets also increases. This situation requires the use of VAMs to offload the encryption/decryption process from the router CPU.

Figure 12.2 VPN Termination at Edge Routers

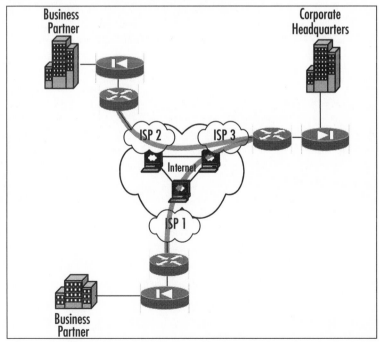

Designing & Planning…

The VPN Dilemma

When you're planning the type of network that you see in Figure 12.2, it is imperative that you understand what the cloud represents in the middle of all the sites, tunnels, and routers. This is the most confusing aspect of VPN design, and this explanation should help you understand why this chapter is included in this book and how it relates to a DMZ.

First, WAN links such as Frame Relay were traditionally used to get corporate data from one place to another over telecommunication circuits. A technology like Frame Relay was utilized in many deployments around the globe. Now, as more services are leaning toward IP (Layer 3 services such as voice and video), a faster and more flexible solution is needed. With the pervasiveness of the Internet, you can pretty much get an Internet connection anywhere, but this is not true with a technology like Frame Relay or ISDN.

Basically, with VPN technology, the ability to encrypt data over "any" connection has raised the bar. You can basically have a WAN connection with a user, business partner, or another site using a simple Internet connection instead of having to build a port and PVC, for example. The flexibility is great, and more important, the time to get a VPN up and running is much shorter, compared to ordering and provisioning circuits. The dilemma with the cloud in the figure is this: Basically, with VPNs, the cloud can be anything, but you will lean more toward the public Internet (and that is how the picture is labeled) when using VPNs because that's where your encryption investment will pay off. You need the encryption on the Internet. This is also why it is so important that you understand DMZ technology; now your WAN links will go out your traditional Internet connection, and most likely you will be hosting some form of services on the DMZ to utilize that public Internet connection.

As your network continues to grow, you could find that this model no longer fits your needs. Since routers are not normally designed as large-scale VPN endpoints, they tend to lack the features required to scale to a large number of tunnels or to perform VPN redundancy. When you have redundant Internet-facing routers, you will have to decide which router to use for VPN termination. This also means that if one of your Internet routers fails, you will lose all VPN tunnels that terminate on that device, even though Internet connectivity for the rest of the enterprise will continue working through the backup connection. VPN redundancy is much easier to implement on a device that has a failover partner that assumes all the same IP addresses as the master on failover.

VPN Termination at the Corporate Firewall

Termination of the VPN at the corporate firewall allows for direct access from branch networks to the internal corporate core network as well as any DMZ services that need to be accessible through that firewall. Remote users can then access all internal services without having to authenticate a second time. This particular topology (shown in Figure 12.3) is best reserved for LAN-to-LAN connections such as connecting a branch office to the corporate enterprise network or allowing access to and from a business partner's LAN. This topology also allows you to configure the tunnel and the access restrictions on the same device, which could ease administration of your VPN infrastructure.

Figure 12.3 VPN Termination at the DMZ Firewall

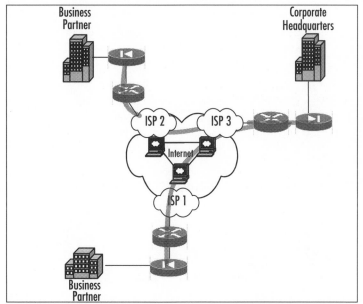

The drawback to this topology is that as more branch offices are connected to the corporate office, the load on the firewall increases due to the increased amount of encryption each VPN requires. When the load on the firewall reaches a point at which there is an overall impact on network connectivity, it is best to either add a VAM to the firewall or offload the VPN services to a dedicated device, which can be a VPN appliance or a firewall used for the sole purpose of terminating VPN connections. Your choice will depend on your needs, the device feature sets, and any vendor relationships you currently have.

VPN Termination at a Dedicated VPN Appliance

Dedicated VPN appliances are designed to provide VPN tunnel services in both LAN-to-LAN and remote access configurations. In larger deployments, you might want to have multiple VPN appliances to split up the load, if it is too much for a single device. If your company has thousands of users who will need remote connectivity to the office, you will be better served by a dedicated appliance (or a pair for redundancy) strictly for remote users while using another appliance or your corporate firewall for LAN-to-LAN VPNs.

Figure 12.4 demonstrates LAN-to-LAN tunnels built with a dedicated VPN appliance. In this particular topology, the VPN appliance is sitting parallel to the corporate firewall, with its own connections to the unprotected network and the internal LAN. Unencrypted traffic coming from the Internet would route through the corporate firewall to reach the internal network or DMZ network, just as in all the previous topologies. The VPN tunnels will be the only traffic that goes directly to the VPN appliance, and once it has been decrypted it will be sent to the inside networks. The "inside" network could be either the internal LAN or the DMZ segment, depending on where the "inside" interface of the appliance is attached. In this topology, there is an underlying assumption that the VPN appliance is secure and flexible enough to be deployed in this fashion. In the case where the VPN appliance doesn't have granular enough access controls or you are not comfortable with the level of security in the device, you might want to put a firewall or access list either inside or outside the VPN appliance (or both). This will depend largely on the recommended deployment strategy for each vendor's VPN device. You could also use another DMZ interface off the corporate firewall, but you will need to be careful of routing issues that could cause the reply traffic to bypass the VPN appliance, because this will break communications with the business partner.

Figure 12.4 VPN Termination at a Dedicated VPN Appliance

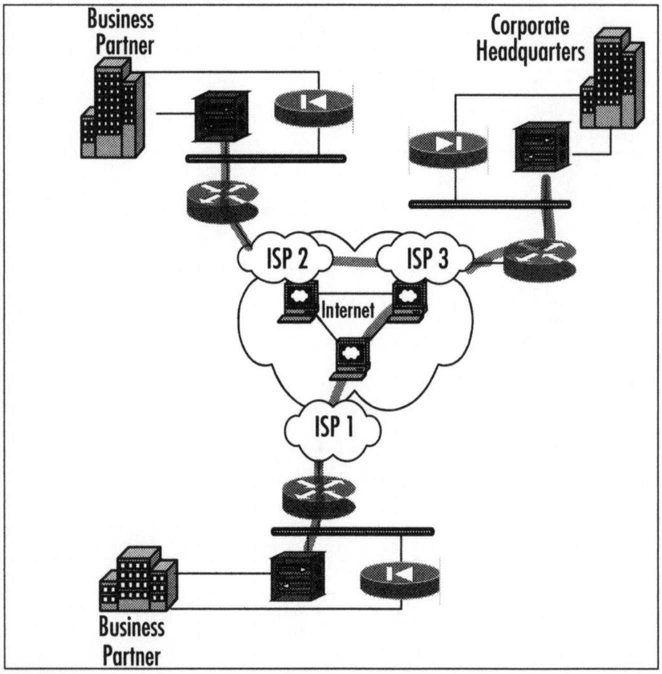

Although it's not shown in Figure 12.4, you also have the option of using the VPN appliance to offer LAN access to remote users who have Internet connectivity, but this will depend on the number of users that you will be supporting. With a large deployment of remote users, one option is to put another VPN appliance at the corporate office that sits parallel to the existing VPN appliance.

A further benefit to this deployment model is the ability to utilize the VPN appliances in conjunction with wireless networks. The original IEEE 802.11 wireless network specification had significant weaknesses that left wireless network open to easy attack and subsequently left the internal LAN open to attack as well. Isolating wireless networks "outside" the internal LAN in a DMZ and requiring users to utilize a VPN to access the corporate network helps address some of the weaknesses in wireless LANs (WLANs). You can read about WLAN VPN planning and deployment plans in Chapters 4 and 5.

Topology Models

The deployment models we've discussed represent how VPNs can be implemented to provide access to either the DMZ or the internal corporate network. This section focuses on the various topologies in which these models can be deployed. There are four general topologies to consider:

- Meshed (both fully and partially meshed)
- Star
- Hub and spoke
- Remote access

Each of these topologies is considered in greater detail in this section.

Meshed Topology

Like their traditional WAN counterparts, meshed VPN topologies can be implemented in a fully or partially meshed configuration. Fully meshed configurations have a large number of alternate paths to any given destination. In addition, fully meshed configurations have exceptional redundancy because every VPN device provides connections to every other VPN device. This topology was illustrated in Figure 12.1, although it was initially used to describe fully meshed WAN topologies. Even with the replacement of traditional WAN services such as Frame Relay or leased lines, fully meshed topologies can be expensive to implement due to the requirement to purchase a VPN device for every link in the mesh. A simpler compromise is the partial-mesh topology, in which all the links are connected to other links in a more limited fashion. A partial-mesh topology is shown in Figure 12.5.

Figure 12.5 Partial-Mesh VPN Topology

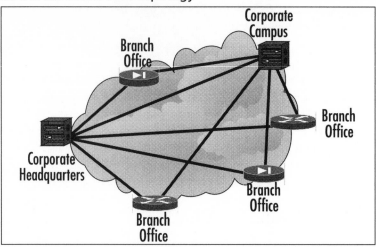

> **NOTE**
>
> Another issue you should be aware of with full versus partial-mesh topology is the number of tunnels you need to configure and manage. If you have 100 sites and add one router, think of all the connections you must make to rebuild a full mesh! You would be required to reconfigure every device in the mesh. In essence, the partial mesh is the way you want to go, but you might see an extra hop in the path from place to place because you will no longer have a single hop to any single destination. There is always give and take. Think about the method that suits your design needs, and implement that method accordingly. If a full mesh is required, this could be a great opportunity to look into Cisco's Dynamic Multipoint VPN (DMVPN) solution. This feature is briefly discussed with Cisco IOS VPNs in a later section.

Star Topology

In a star topology configuration, the remote branches can communicate securely with the corporate headquarters or central site. However, intercommunication between the branches is not permitted. Such a configuration could be deployed in a bank network so that compromise of one branch will not immediately lead to the compromise of a second branch without being detected. To gain access to a second branch, the attacker would have to first compromise the central network, which would hopefully be able to detect such an attack. A star topology configuration is shown in Figure 12.6.

Figure 12.6 Star VPN Deployment Topology

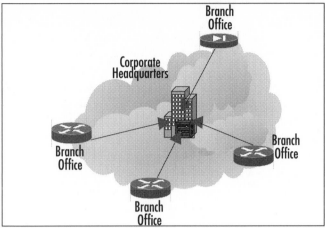

Hub-and-Spoke Topology

A hub-and-spoke topology by design looks very similar to the star topology. However, there is one significant difference: Unlike the star topology, all branch or stub networks in a hub-and-spoke topology are able to access other branch or stub networks. The central, corporate network works as a simple transit point for all traffic from one end of the network to another. As traffic transits through the central corporate network, the data is decrypted, inspected, and re-encrypted for transmission to the final destination. This topology has more risk inherent in the design than the star topology because an attacker who is able to compromise one branch network might then be able to attack another branch network through the VPN without being required to attack the central, corporate network. This topology is shown in Figure 12.7.

Figure 12.7 Hub-and-Spoke VPN Topology

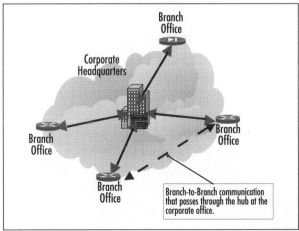

Remote Access Topology

A final topology to consider is the remote access topology. Built on either the star or the hub-and-spoke VPN topology (depending on the solution), this design focuses more on providing connectivity for remote users such as telecommuters, mobile workers, and other users who need access to corporate resources while working from outside the office. Most often these users have either dialup or broadband Internet connections with dynamic IP address assignment. Other users may travel the country, visiting potential customers and often need access back to company resources from customer locations. These users typically can load a remote access client onto laptop machines and create secure tunnels back to the corporate LAN from just about anywhere on the public Internet. Since these users' IP addresses are constantly changing, these users will authenticate with username and password combinations, although additional forms of authentication, such as digital certificates or tokens that generate single-use passwords for each VPN connection attempt are usually added. A remote access VPN topology is shown in Figure 12.8.

Figure 12.8 Remote Access VPN Topology

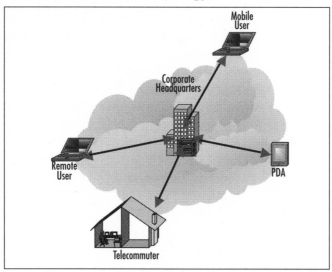

Since IPSec connections can sometimes be difficult to establish from remote networks that have strict firewall policies, companies have been forced to find solutions to make their resources more accessible to their remote employees. Some vendors have built in methods of tunneling the VPN traffic over more accessible ports, which can be chosen by the VPN administrator. Most people will try to use ports such as 80 or 443, since nearly everyone will allow certain areas of their network have access to the Web. SSL VPNs are also another solution for this issue. SSL VPNs allow users to gain access to company resources without loading any clients onto a machine. A user will only need to access a secure Web page with her Web browser for login to then be able to access resources through a Web-based portal page. Since not all applications can be supported through an SSL VPN portal page, some vendors offer IPSec-like connections by allowing the remote users to download a small Web applet to create a point-to-point tunnel over port 443 with the SSL VPN appliance.

The next topic we examine is deciding where to place the VPN endpoints within your network.

Placement of Devices

Now that we have looked at some of the more common designs of the VPN, we need to know where to place the VPN endpoint devices in our network. We'll make many of these decisions by reviewing areas of the networks that will need to be accessible through these VPNs as well as the features that are available in the VPN endpoint itself. All VPN endpoint devices need at least one interface with a public, unique IP address so that they will be accessible from anywhere on the Internet.

With NAT Traversal (NAT-T), it is possible to use a private address with NAT to make the device publicly accessible. Be aware that this approach may limit your functionality and complicate your VPN setup. If the device is sufficiently hardened, it can sit directly on the unprotected network, but if you are not comfortable with the device's security, you might want to put the external interface behind another DMZ interface of a firewall. If your VPN endpoint's external interface is behind a firewall, you will need to make sure you know all the ports that need to be allowed through the firewall.

For a basic IPSec tunnel, you will need UDP port 500 for Internet Key Exchange (IKE) and IP protocol 50 for ESP, which is the most common IPSec VPN method. You may also need IP protocol 51 if you are using AH for your tunnels. ESP and AH are described in the "Designing an IPSec Encryption Scheme" section later in this chapter. Other ports may be required if you are using a NAT traversal technique and depending on which one you are using. Some of these ports are defined by the protocol standards; others can be user defined, depending on the vendor implementation. This means that you will need to know the features you will use with your VPNs so that you can create a firewall policy accordingly.

Next, we will want to be very comfortable with how granular we can be with access controls on the VPN endpoint device. This will help us decide where we should connect the internal interface of the VPN endpoint device. If the device allows you to easily create policies for user groups, you might feel comfortable putting the inside interface of the VPN device directly into the internal or DMZ network. If you are using your firewall as a VPN endpoint, your device would already be configured in this fashion, and no additional links will be required. Otherwise, you might be more secure by placing the inside interface of the VPN endpoint in front of a firewall, which can restrict access. If the VPN endpoint's interface seems to be difficult to manage for larger deployments with many access restrictions, you might want to minimize the configuration on the endpoint by assigning IP addresses to users from address pools assigned per group. This way the firewall could be used to enforce access policies on the different user groups. Since each group has a range of IP addresses available for allocation, the firewall can still control policies for different user groups by referencing the address range assigned to a particular group.

The basic concept is to keep in mind what you are trying to accomplish and figure out how to best implement the solution in your particular environment. Most designs are governed by business needs, which could force your network to be configured in a way that is less than ideal from a pure networking perspective. This makes it impossible to create a cookie-cutter design for all VPN deployments.

Business Partner Connections

In addition to branch offices and other remote connections such as data centers, many enterprises have business partners that require secure communications to servers (such as database servers or servers running middleware applications) within the corporate DMZ. There are several ways to ensure such communication, including WAN connectivity, LAN-to-LAN VPNs, and remote access VPNs. WAN connectivity includes such technologies as MPLS, Frame Relay, leased lines, and dialup connectivity.

Although these services can have significant costs associated with them, they might be the way to go for connections that can't very well suffer downtime or performance issues. Although VPN connectivity over the Internet can be much less expensive, it is also much more difficult to troubleshoot when issues arise. For example, if your VPN tunnel has to pass though five different service providers and one of the providers in the middle starts having performance issues, you might have a very difficult time trying to contact someone to report the issue. If you can manage to find a contact number to call, it is still unlikely that anyone will talk to you if you aren't a direct customer of that service provider. This can lead to extended periods of poor performance that cannot be easily corrected, since you cannot control the full path traffic will take through the public Internet. When you are dealing with a single service provider for your WAN services, you will already have the contacts established to quickly respond to performance and downtime issues.

In many situations, though, the cost of WAN connectivity cannot be justified, and performance issues on the VPN tunnel are mostly an inconvenience, as opposed to a major business risk. In these situations, you might want to use a LAN-to-LAN VPN. Such VPNs have the benefit of being able to take advantage of your redundant Internet connectivity as well as being much less expensive than WAN connectivity, while offering the same sort of access to business partners. The downside of using LAN-to-LAN tunnels lies in the difficulty getting certain vendor solutions to interoperate. In recent years, many vendors have made their solutions more flexible, and most vendors can interoperate with each other, but in some cases the VPN administrators from both sides might have to spend a significant amount of time troubleshooting their configurations.

A remote access VPN solution can also be a good fit, depending on the nature of access required between your company and the business partner. When a limited number of people need access to your resources, it could be easiest to allow those users to connect through a mechanism such as an IPSec VPN client or SSL VPN solution, if a VPN client cannot be installed on the remote machines. Assuming that you already have a client VPN solution in place, it is a very simple process to add a few new users and create the appropriate access restrictions. This usually takes much less time than setting up a LAN-to-LAN VPN, especially when the VPN administrators from both sides are trying to set up a multivendor tunnel.

The downside of an IPSec client VPN lies with the support of the client software, such as application conflicts or connection problems due to firewalls or NAT configurations at the business partner's site. If your remote access solution allows you to configure SSL VPNs, you can bypass many of these client-related issues, since SSL VPNs are established through a Web browser and nothing needs to be installed on the client machine. A SSL VPN could be especially useful if the business partner needs access to only a small number of resources that can be set up in a portal page. If more open access is needed, or if your applications aren't supported by the SSL VPN Web portal, most SSL VPN solutions do allow for full "tunnel-like" access via a small client that is downloaded and executed through the browser if this sort of access is needed and the business partner won't allow you to install a software package on their machines. Although this type of access via an SSL VPN solution could be useful in certain situations, most SSL VPN vendors openly admit that, if possible, you are better off using a full IPSec client for this type of access.

The next section covers remote access solutions in more detail. Because there are many different solutions out there, we cannot cover all vendors that offer these types of solutions, so we discuss only the more popular solutions available.

Remote Access Services

Remote access services can benefit greatly from VPNs, and IPSec-based VPNs in particular. Companies can move away from central dialup servers and 1-800 numbers and toward a decentralized model. In this model, shown in Figure 12.9, companies contract with local service providers for dialup service to the Internet for remote users. These services usually consist of a small software package that presents the user with local dialup numbers for any city to which the user might have traveled. The user can then connect to the Internet using one of these local dialup lines, to avoid any long distance charges. To access the corporate network, users must dial into the local service provider (Step 1) and authenticate to the service provider's access server. Once service provider access is granted, the user must use a VPN to access the corporate network (Step 2).

To allow users to authenticate against corporate resources when they dial into the service provider's access server, a VPN can be used to connect the service provider's access server with an authentication server in the corporate DMZ. This enables the service provider to authenticate users in accordance with the corporate security policy. In this model, the easiest VPN technology to deploy is IPSec-based VPNs. The need to invest in access server hardware is eliminated, along with the extra phone lines and their cost, and is replaced with a new business expense: the cost of the dialup service from the provider.

Figure 12.9 Decentralized Access Using VPN

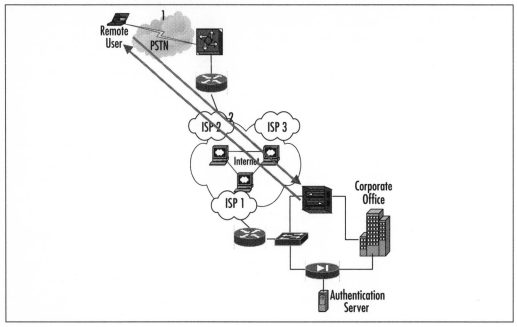

In addition to decreasing costs for dialup services, this solution also allows remote users to connect through the plethora of wireless and broadband Internet services that are scattered across the country. Hotels and convention centers usually offer some form of wired and wireless Internet access, Starbucks has teamed with T-Mobile to provide hotspots at every Starbucks coffee shop, and T-Mobile and WayPort compete to provide Internet access at many airports across the United States. Additionally, most home users subscribe to broadband services such as cable modem or DSL. These users would only need to start up their VPN client to connect into the corporate network and access their network resources.

As mentioned in the previous section, an SSL VPN solution is also ideal for this type of configuration because you rule out some of the troubleshooting involved when users are trying to gain remote access from behind a firewall and the required NAT traversal ports are not opened. The SSL VPN solution also boasts the ability to eliminate troubleshooting the VPN client itself, because the only software required is a Web browser with access to the Internet. Again, although this solution may sound excellent because of the lower support and troubleshooting overhead, you will need to evaluate the services your users require and decide whether an SSL-based VPN solution will fit your needs.

Nokia

Nokia VPN services are offered in a variety of platforms: dedicated VPN appliances and an integrated firewall/VPN appliance. The Nokia appliances are diskless-based, purpose-built platforms running a Nokia proprietary operating system. These appliances range from the small Nokia 5i VPN gateway for small offices to the 500i VPN gateway for corporate networks. In addition, Nokia produces larger gateways, the 50, 105, and 500 series appliances, in an "s" version that provides SSL VPN capabilities instead of IPSec VPNs. Nokia's firewall/VPN appliance integrates Check Point's VPN-1/FW-1 software on a hardened platform running Nokia's operating system IPSO. Nokia's VPN offerings provide a variety of features, some of which are listed here:

- **IP clustering** Nokia VPN appliances can be grouped together into a "virtual" appliance gateway.

- **Active session failover** This feature enables the use of active session failover for uninterrupted service. It allows the individual gateways to share security associations, to provide a seamless transition from one gateway to another in the event of failure.

- **Centralized management** As more VPN nodes are added to corporations that look to VPNs as a low-cost alternative to traditional WANs, a simplified, centralized management structure is critical.

- **Firewall integration** The firewall/VPN appliance provides for a tight coupling of a secure proprietary networking OS integrated with third-party applications designed for security solutions.

- **SSL VPNs** Providing SSL VPN connectivity to users without the need of a client software package provides access to corporate resources through the standard Web browser.

For greater ease of management and quick configuration of VPNs, the Check Point software includes Simplified Mode VPN setup, which condenses the normal multistep VPN setup and management processes into a more user-friendly process that allows the administrator to define VPN communities. These communities are just a collection of settings to which the administrator can add remote gateways objects. This way, all devices within a community receive the same VPN settings without having to manually configure each tunnel. This makes it quick and easy to deploy VPNs, whether they are remote access, intranet, or extranet VPNs.

It is important that you understand how to set up multiple VPN systems to see which one is cost effective and a good fit for your organization. You can learn more about Nokia's VPN and firewall solutions at www.nokiausa.com/business/security/.

Juniper NetScreen VPNs

NetScreen VPNs are integrated with the NetScreen firewall product. They allow for access control as well as authentication and network segmentation. NetScreen firewalls utilize a "security zone-based" model in which the network is separated into areas, or zones, that are distinct and separate from one another. The zones can be one or more physical or logical interfaces. This structure allows the device to cover VPN tunnel interfaces as well.

Each zone is governed by its own security policy, and the NetScreen firewall applies the policies between pairs of security zones, to control the type of traffic allowed between the zones. NetScreen products offer a variety of VPN features:

- **Redundancy** Although path redundancy at the physical layer is critical to recover from a connection failure, redundancy at the logical VPN layer is also important to minimize downtime. NetScreen VPNs support full redundancy in their VPNs by utilizing "standby" tunnels that mirror the VPN's security associations. In the event of failure in the live tunnel, the standby tunnel takes over in less than 1 second.

- **Dynamic VPNs** Dynamic VPNs help minimize the time required to manage VPNs. This is achieved through the use of dynamic routing through the VPN tunnels, to communicate network topology as well as link state information.

- **Security zones** As mentioned, security zones allow the network administrator to divide the physical network into a series of virtual sections with various levels of trust. Security zones can be implemented with their own individual security polices. The policies can offer firewall, VPN, and DoS mitigation capabilities. This structure provides several benefits, including an increased interface density, containment of unauthorized users and attacks, simplified management, and lower policy creation costs.

You can find additional information about Juniper's security products at www.juniper.net/products/.

Cisco VPNs

Cisco has integrated VPN technology into most of its networking products. These products include routers, PIX and ASA firewalls, and the VPN 3000 series concentrator. Most, if not all, of Cisco's IOS versions for its routers have an optional feature set that includes VPN and firewall service. Each of these devices provides approximately the same level of VPN services, as described in the sections that follow.

Cisco IOS VPN

IOS VPN services allow the network administrator to terminate the VPN tunnels at an external or internal interface of the router. This allows considerable flexibility in the design of the VPN. Some of the more important site-to-site VPN features available in Cisco IOS are:

- **Diverse networking environment support** IPSec is a Unicast, IP-only protocol, but Cisco's IOS VPN software features accommodate multicast and multi-protocol traffic. In addition, when combined with GRE, routing protocols are supported across the VPN. Scaled mesh VPN topologies are supported through Cisco's Dynamic Multipoint VPN (DMVPN) feature, which allows network administrators to better scale large and small IPSec-based VPNs by combining GRE tunnels, IPSec encryption, and Next-Hop Resolution Protocol (NHRP). DMVPN requires manual configuration of a hub-and-spoke VPN topology but then allows the spoke sites to learn about each other via the hub site. The spoke sites can then automatically create spoke-to-spoke VPN tunnels so that further traffic can bypass the hub site. This scheme allows for an easier deployment of meshed VPN topologies by automating the provisioning of connections between spoke sites as well as dynamically setting up connections based on network traffic. You can find additional information about the DMVPN solution at www.cisco.com/go/dmvpn.

- **Timely, reliable delivery of latency-sensitive traffic** Cisco's IOS VPN feature set enables traffic to be prioritized up to the application layer. This facilitates differentiated QoS policies by application type rather than just TCP port number. This system results in increased transmission reliability and better response time of business-critical applications traversing the VPNs.

- **V3PN solution** By combining advanced QoS, telephony, networking, and VPN features with purpose-built hardware platforms, Cisco's VPN offerings are able to deliver a VPN infrastructure capable of transporting converged data, voice, and video traffic across a secure IPSec network. This is known as Voice- and Video-Enabled VPN, or V3PN. More information about this solution is available at www.cisco.com/go/v3pn.

- **VPN scalability and feature sets** Cisco's IOS VPN supports a wide variety of features that are essential to VPNs. These features include data encryption, tunneling, broad certificate authority support for public key infrastructure (PKI), stateful VPN failover, certificate auto-enrollment, stateful firewall, intrusion detection, and service-level validation.

- **VPN management framework** Managing multiple VPN devices over multiple sites requires not only robust VPN configuration management and monitoring capabilities but also device inventory and software version management features. Cisco's CiscoWorks VPN/Security Management Solution (VMS) combines Web-based tools for configuring, monitoring, and troubleshooting enterprise VPNs as well as other devices such as firewalls and network- and host-based IDS.

PIX and ASA Firewall VPN

The PIX and ASA firewall product lines also provide VPN capabilities. These capabilities are designed to allow businesses to securely extend their networks across low-cost Internet connections to mobile users, business partners, and remote offices. The PIX and ASA firewall's VPN provides several key features:

- **Standards-based IPSec VPN** The Cisco solution provides for a standards-based, site-to-site VPN utilizing the Internet Key Exchange (IKE) and IPSec protocols.

- **Multiplatform, multiclient support** The Cisco PIX and ASA firewall's VPN supports a wide range of remote access VPN clients, including Cisco's own software VPN client on various platforms (Microsoft Windows, Linux, Solaris, and Mac OS X) and Cisco hardware-based VPN clients (PIX 501, 506E, VPN 3002 client, and the Cisco 800 and 1700 series routers). In addition to supporting IPSec-based VPNs, the PIX and ASA firewalls also support PPTP and L2TP clients that are found in Microsoft Windows operating systems.

- **Encryption** The PIX and ASA firewalls utilize one of three cryptographic algorithms for data confidentiality and integrity protection. These algorithms are the 56-bit Data Encryption Standard (DES), the 168-bit Triple DES (3DES), and the Advanced Encryption Standard (AES) algorithm. The AES implementation in the PIX and the ASA supports up to 256-bit encryption.

Additional information about PIX firewalls can be found at www.cisco.com/go/pix. You'll find additional information about ASA devices at www.cisco.com/go/asa.

3000 Series VPN Concentrator

The third major product in Cisco's VPN lineup is the 3000 series concentrator. The concentrator provides dedicated VPN services for remote access as well as LAN-to-LAN connectivity. The 3000 series provides for a wide range of models, from the 3005 for small enterprise networks to the 3080, designed for large enterprise networks. The 3000 series concentrator includes a software client that allows for easy configuration of IPSec tunnels by remote users. Additionally, a hardware version of the client, the 3002 concentrator, provides remote IPSec connectivity for telecommuters. Another benefit of the 3000 series VPN concentrator is the SSL VPN support that is built into the box, allowing you to deploy an SSL VPN solution without buying a dedicated box, although if your deployment becomes large enough, you will want it to run on dedicated hardware. Cisco has more information about the VPN 3000 platform at www.cisco.com/go/vpn3000.

Cisco EasyVPN

A recent software enhancement that simplifies VPN deployment in Cisco devices is Cisco Easy VPN. This feature centralizes VPN management and provides for the single deployment of consistent VPN policies and key management methods, thereby simplifying remote-site VPN management. The software consists of two components: the Easy VPN Remote and the Easy VPN Server.

The Cisco Easy VPN Remote feature allows Cisco IOS routers, Cisco PIX and ASA firewalls, and Cisco VPN 3002 hardware clients or software clients to act as remote VPN clients. These devices can receive security policies from a Cisco Easy VPN Server, thus minimizing VPN configuration requirements at the remote location. This cost-effective solution is ideal for remote offices with little IT support or large customer premises equipment (CPE) deployments in which it is impractical to individually configure multiple remote devices. This feature makes VPN configuration as easy as entering a password, increasing productivity and lowering costs as the need for local IT support is minimized.

The Cisco Easy VPN Server allows Cisco IOS routers, Cisco PIX and ASA firewalls, and Cisco VPN 3000 concentrators to act as VPN head-end devices in site-to-site or remote access VPNs, where the remote office devices are using the Cisco Easy VPN Remote feature. Using this feature, security policies defined at the head end are pushed to the remote VPN device, ensuring that those connections have up-to-date policies in place before the connection is established. In addition, a Cisco Easy VPN Server-enabled device can terminate VPN tunnels initiated by mobile remote workers running Cisco VPN client software on PCs. This flexibility makes it possible for mobile and remote workers, such as salespeople on the road or telecommuters, to access their headquarters intranet data and applications. Additional information on the EasyVPN solution is at www.cisco.com/go/easyvpn.

Windows VPN

Microsoft has integrated VPN solutions into its Windows 2000, Windows XP Home Edition, Windows XP Professional, and Windows 2003 products. Additionally, a downloadable application, the Microsoft L2TP/IPSec VPN client, is available; it allows users of older versions of Microsoft Windows (such as NT 4.0, ME, and 98) to create VPN connections. Additional information as well as a download link for this client is available from Microsoft at www.microsoft.com/technet/prodtechnol/windows2000serv/support/vpnclientag.mspx.

The implementation of VPNs in Windows is based on a combination of IPSec and L2TP, as described in RFC 3193. For every L2TP connection, the IPSec Encapsulating Security Payload (ESP) Transport Mode is negotiated utilizing 3DES as an encryption algorithm. L2TP encapsulates PPP frames to be sent over a variety of network protocols, including IP, X.25, Frame Relay, or asynchronous transfer mode (ATM) networks. L2TP is documented in RFC 2661.

L2TP over IP uses UDP to send the tunneled data. The packet payloads are L2TP-encapsulated PPP frames that can be encrypted and/or compressed. In this case, IPSec provides the encryption of the payload data. Figure 12.10 shows the structure of an IP packet containing an L2TP packet.

Figure 12.10 IP Packet Transporting an L2TP Frame

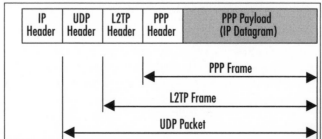

In addition to the L2TP/IPSec VPN solution from Microsoft, there is also support for PPTP as a VPN technology in the Windows operating system. PPTP functions are divided between a PPTP Access Controller (PAC) running on a dial-access platform and a PPTP Network Server (PNS) that operates on a general-purpose operating system. Windows allows for the PAC and the PNS to exist on a single platform by utilizing Windows Remote Access Service (RAS) for the PAC dialup capabilities as well as the VPN service for the PNS. PPTP uses an enhanced GRE mechanism to provide a flow- and congestion-controlled encapsulated datagram service for carrying PPP packets. Some service providers do not allow GRE packets to traverse their networks, so that could be an obstacle to deploying PPTP as a VPN solution.

Designing an IPSec Solution

This section focuses on the design of an IPSec solution for a given scenario. The focus here is on the identification of the various needs that drive the choices within an IPSec design.

Designing & Planning...

Tuning VPN Traffic

As noted earlier in the chapter, placing the VPN in the network depends on whether the tunnel endpoint should terminate at the edge router, on a dedicated VPN appliance, or on the firewall itself. However, we failed to cover one aspect of this question: the amount of VPN overhead and its effect on the firewall or edge router. Due to the nature of IPSec, which encapsulates the data it is carrying, the IPSec packet sizes are larger than can normally be handled by a router. Therefore, IPSec traffic tends to get fragmented by an edge device such as a router, resulting in poorer VPN performance. Another possible side effect occurs when packets are marked "Do Not Fragment" in the IP header. When these packets are encapsulated and become larger than a router can accept, the packet will be dropped, never reaching the destination.

To accommodate this situation, it is generally recommended that the Maximum Transmission Unit, or MTU (i.e., the maximum packet size), be reduced to accommodate the additional IPSec headers. It is best to reduce the packet size to approximately 1400 bytes (from the standard 1500 bytes in an Ethernet packet), although this number can change depending on the amount of overhead that is added. For example, additional overhead is added for DSL lines that use PPPoE for connectivity to the service provider, which could require you to reduce the MTU further.

Continued

If the MTU is set too large, you will likely see some erratic behavior, such as being able to ping a host but being unable to connect to it with something like Remote Desktop. The FTP protocol is great for demonstrating the effects of incorrect MTU settings. A user with the default MTU of 1500 is connecting over a DSL line, which requires PPPoE, and establishes an IPSec VPN back to the office. Everything connects successfully, so the user fires up an FTP client so that a fairly large file can be transferred to the office. The user connects to the FTP server, authenticates successfully, and then tries to upload the file. Nothing happens; the client just sits there attempting the transfer, which won't go through.

This is a common problem that is caused by an incorrectly set MTU size. Most of the packets that pass between client and server during the login phase are small packets that contain FTP control commands. Even browsing through directories can work fine, as long as the directory listing isn't too long, but once the file attempts to transfer, the user starts having problems. Since the file is multiple megabytes large, the user's operating system will start breaking down the file into chunks small enough that adding the TCP and IP headers will add up to 1500 bytes. Then, when the VPN client encapsulates the packet into IPSec (and adds another UDP and IP header, if UDP encapsulation is being used), the packet will be much larger than 1500 bytes, and we haven't even added the PPPoE header yet. This prevents only the data transfer from working, since that happens to be the only time full-size packets are being sent.

Designing an IPSec Encryption Scheme

Most vendors support one of three encryption schemes in their VPN solutions: the Digital Encryption Standard (DES), Triple-DES (3DES), and the Advanced Encryption Standard (AES). AES is the chosen replacement for the aging DES algorithm. DES provides for the use of a 56-bit encryption key that has been proven to be inadequate for long-term security needs. 3DES uses a 168-bit encryption key, is based on the DES algorithm used in a three-fold manner, and is considered a stop-gap measure until AES can be fully deployed. AES provides for key sizes ranging from 128 bits (the minimum required by NIST, according to the competition) to 256 bits and provides for the use of 192-bit keys.

The real choice of an encryption scheme comes down to the level of security needed in the VPN as well as the encryption speed desired. As noted earlier, DES has long been proven insecure against an attacker with sufficient computing means at his or her disposal. 3DES has yet to be compromised; however, it is significantly slower than DES and AES. AES has significant performance and security improvements over DES and 3DES, but it is still the proverbial "new kid on the block" as far as encryption algorithms go. Until now, no known attacks or weaknesses exist in AES that could result in the compromise of encrypted data. Given these factors, the choice comes down to 3DES or AES.

In addition to choosing an encryption algorithm, the administrator must decide to use either the IPSec Authentication Header (AH) or Encapsulating Security Payload (ESP) protocol. The AH protocol only affects the header of the packet and is used to verify integrity of the VPN packets; the payload that contains the data is left unencrypted. The ESP protocol, which is used in most VPN deployments, encrypts the payload of the packet while leaving the header untouched. Some vendors allow for both protocols to be used simultaneously, so that the header can have integrity services in addition to encryption.

There are also two different modes for IPSec tunnels: tunnel and transport. Tunnel mode is used between two VPN endpoints, such as VPN concentrators, PIX and ASA firewalls, or Cisco routers running IPSec capable versions of code. This tunnel can carry traffic for multiple hosts and/or subnets on each side. Transport mode is used between a VPN client and a VPN endpoint, such as the Cisco VPN Client connecting to a 3000 series concentrator. This means that your LAN-to-LAN VPN tunnels will be running tunnel mode while your remote access VPNs will be configured to use transport mode.

Designing an IPSec Management Strategy

Another thorn in the side of IPSec is management. For a VPN tunnel to be established between two peers, the peers must be able to negotiate a security association (SA). An IPSec SA is a one-way, cryptographically protected connection between a sender and a receiver that affords security services to traffic. The SA is defined for one direction only, and therefore a bidirectional connection (such as a VPN tunnel) requires two SAs—one for each direction. An SA is defined by three values:

- **Security Parameters Index (SPI)** This identifies the security association under which a received packet will be processed.

- **Destination Address** This is the address of the destination endpoint for the SA.

- **Security Protocol Identifier** This identifies whether the association is an AH-based or an ESP-based SA.

To establish an SA, the two VPN endpoint devices must have a way of authenticating each other. This can be accomplished through either a preshared key or digital certificates. Preshared keys require that the network administrator configure the secret key on all VPN devices that are going to establish tunnels with each other. This could require that the key be communicated to a party (such as an extranet partner) at the other tunnel endpoint through an out-of-band method. Additionally, since keys should be changed frequently, the administrator must coordinate changing keys at periodic intervals. Preshared keys are sufficient for a small deployment, but they quickly become unmanageable in a large, enterprise deployment of VPNs.

Another method of authentication between IPSec peers utilizes a PKI to provide the necessary information for a VPN endpoint device to authenticate to another. In this scheme, the signed X.509 certificates for both devices in the VPN are available from a certificate server at a certificate authority (CA). Each device retrieves the public key for the IPSec peer from the CA and uses it to encrypt its authentication challenge to the other side. If the peer is able to respond with the proper reply to the challenge, it is determined that authentication has succeeded. This method allows both sides to prove their identity before negotiating the SA. For small deployments, PKI requires more administrative overhead than preshared keys and is generally not recommended. For larger, enterprise-size deployments of VPNs, PKI provides significant benefits and is desired over preshared keys.

Designing Negotiation Policies

IPSec-based VPN tunnel parameters must be negotiated between the endpoint devices. This negotiation involves the announcements of encryption schemes the devices support (DES, 3DES, AES) as well as the message authentication code (MAC) hash algorithm that will be used to verify the integrity of the IPSec packets. Typical supported MAC hash algorithms include MD5 and SHA-1. These parameters are included as part of the tunnel SA and are negotiated using the Internet Key Exchange (IKE) protocol (formerly known as the Internet Security Association and Key Management Protocol, or ISAKMP).

The negotiation policy is where most issues occur when trying to establish a VPN tunnel between devices made by different vendors. All vendors must use the same options, since they are defined by the IPSec standard, but the default values for each vendor's implementations are usually different, which will prevent a quick-and-easy VPN setup between two different vendors' devices. By understanding which options make up the negotiation policy, you can quickly discover where a mismatch between two devices is occurring and make the appropriate changes to correct the problem.

VPN setup happens in two different phases, which can be reference by a few different names. The first phase is Phase 1 and is usually a Main mode negotiation. The alternate method is Aggressive mode, which is discussed in the next section. Some vendors sometimes refer to settings for Phase 1 as the *IKE* or *ISAKMP settings*, since this phase is handled by the IKE protocol. IKE negotiates an encrypted tunnel between the two VPN endpoints that is used to negotiate the IPSec SAs that define the traffic that can pass over the VPN. You can think of this as an encrypted connection that only the two endpoints use to discuss which IPSec tunnels need to be created or refreshed.

You need to be concerned with five options to make the Phase 1 negotiation successful:

- **Encryption algorithm** This is where you chose the encryption scheme that will be used to encrypt the Phase 1 traffic that flows between the VPN endpoints. The most common options available are DES, 3DES, and AES.

- **Hashing algorithm** This is where you chose the hashing algorithm you want to use to verify integrity and authenticity of the Phase 1 communications. The chosen algorithm is used to generate a keyed-hash message authenticate code (HMAC) that allows the other side to detect changes to the packet. The most common options are MD5 and SHA-1.

- **Phase 1 lifetime** This is the maximum amount of time that an IKE session can stay active before the connection must be torn down and recreated with new encryption keys. Some vendors implement this option in seconds; others use minutes. You need to be aware of which unit of measure each endpoint is using, so you can make sure these values match. The two most common default values are 24 hours (86400 seconds) and 8 hours (28800 seconds).

- **Diffie-Hellman group** – Diffie-Hellman is a protocol that is used to exchange private information (such as a shared secret) over an insecure transmission path. This allows the two sides to negotiate the shared secret for the tunnel, without letting someone who might be watching the conversation learn the password. The different group values relate to the key size used in the exchange. The larger the key size, the more secure the transmission will be. Some of the more common Diffie-Hellman groups are:

   Group 1 768 bits

   Group 2 1024 bits

   Group 5 1536 bits

   Group 14 2048 bits

- **Aggressive mode** A Main mode communicate requires six packets to be sent back and forth between the two endpoints. When Aggressive mode is enabled, this transaction can be shortened to three packets, which allows for quicker VPN setups. The problem with Aggressive mode is that it is less secure because some data is transferred before a secure tunnel is established. This mode is not required to be supported by all vendors.

Once the Phase 1 negotiation is complete, the two endpoints can start negotiating the IPSec tunnels that will carry the traffic between local and remote hosts. This is referred to as Phase 2 or Quick mode of the VPN negotiation process. Some vendors refer to these settings as the IPSec settings. It is possible for Phase 1 to be configured correctly but have mismatches in the Phase 2 configuration that will prevent traffic from flowing across the tunnel. It is even possible for only certain IPSec SAs to be configured incorrectly, causing some traffic to be unable to pass, while other traffic can traverse the VPN just fine.

NOTE

Remember that an SA only allows communication from a single host or subnet to a single remote host or subnet. This means that if you have three subnets on each side of the VPN tunnel, nine SAs will have to be created for all three local subnets to be able to send traffic to the three remote subnets. Another nine will have to be created to receive the inbound packets from the three remote subnets.

Phase 2 has more available options than Phase 1, so most of the VPN negotiation problems tend to be in the Quick mode configuration. These options are listed and explained here. This list covers the most common options, but since many VPN vendors might have implemented proprietary features, we cannot cover every possible option that a vendor may implement:

- **Encryption algorithm** This is where you chose the encryption scheme that will be used to encrypt the data that flows between the local and remote networks or hosts. The most common options available are DES, 3DES, and AES.

- **Hashing algorithm** This is where you chose the hashing algorithm you want to use for the IPSec SAs. The most common options are MD5 and SHA-1.

- **Phase 2 lifetime** This is the amount of time that the IPSec SA can pass traffic before it must be torn down and renegotiated with new encryption keys. This helps ensure that if someone does manage to crack the encryption for one of your SAs, they will only be able to decrypt a small amount of data. The default IPSec lifetime for most VPN devices is 1 hour (3600 seconds). Some devices can also implement a kilobyte lifetime for the IPSec SAs, so after a certain amount of data is transferred, a renegotiation occurs. "Responder Lifetime" error messages can be generated if one side is using both a seconds and kilobyte lifetime while the other is only looking at a seconds lifetime, although this situation usually doesn't prevent traffic from using the tunnel.

- **Perfect Forward Secrecy** The previous item describes how the keys used for the IPSec SA are renegotiated after an agreed-on amount of time has passed. The new keys to be used during the next time period can be derived from the other keys used in the exchange, which could allow a hacker to break multiple keys if the hacker manages to compromise a single one. Perfect Forward Secrecy (PFS) uses the Diffie-Hellman algorithm to derive the new keys, so there isn't a mathematical relationship between the new and old keys. This prevents a hacker from being able to derive other keys used in the exchange after a renegotiation occurs. As with Diffie-Hellman exchanges in IKE, you will have to configure the Diffie-Hellman group (key strength) you want to use in your implementation of PFS.

- **Local networks/hosts** This is where you define the list of networks and/or hosts on the local end of the VPN device that should be able to communicate over the VPN tunnel. This option can have many names, such as *interesting traffic* or the *local encryption domain*, depending on the vendor you are using. The local networks defined for VPN Endpoint A should be exactly the same as the Remote Networks defined on VPN Endpoint B.

- **Remote networks/hosts** This is a list of networks and/or host addresses that should be accessible on the remote side of the VPN tunnel. This option is sometimes referred to as *interesting traffic* or the *remote encryption domain*, depending on the vendor. The remote networks defined on VPN Endpoint A should be the exact same as the local networks defined on VPN Endpoint B.

Many of these options are global for all SAs associated with the VPN tunnel, but some of them are applied on a per-SA basis, such as the local and remote networks that will be traversing the tunnel. Some vendors allow you to specify both sides of the SA exactly how you want it; others will try to supernet the networks you input to the largest possible subnet to keep the SA count as low as possible. Some allow you to specify a network but create host-to-host SAs for each host within that subnet. When you start trying to establish tunnels between devices that are using these different options, you are very likely to end up with SA mismatches that will prevent the VPN from establishing correctly. You must be extremely aware of how your VPN device handles the SA definitions so that you can be sure to make your SAs match *exactly* what the other side expects to see. Sometimes this will require you to use any debugging modes available for your product that will tell you exactly what options are being sent and received, so that you can identify where the problem might exist.

Designing Security Policies

IPSec security policies are defined as a set of conditions that define an action. The conditions typically determine whether traffic passing through the device is to be encrypted and sent through the VPN tunnel or allowed to pass through unencrypted to a device outside the tunnel. For example, a simple policy would be:

If *<condition>* then *<action>*

Here, *<condition>* can be the source IP address, the destination IP address, the source or destination port, or the IP protocol being used. The *<action>* can be to deny the traffic, allow it, or pass it through the VPN tunnel. Figure 12.11 shows an example of a security policy being used to segregate IPSec traffic from non–IPSec traffic.

Figure 12.11 An IPSec VPN Security Policy

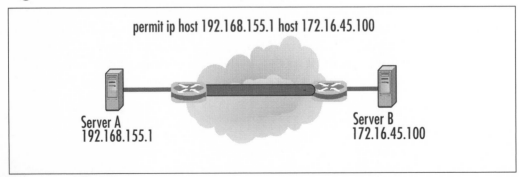

In this example, the security policy is shown at the very top. Any IP traffic with a source IP address of 192.168.155.1 whose destination is 172.16.45.100 is permitted into the tunnel. Once traffic has been identified as valid for the tunnel, the traffic is encrypted according to the tunnel encryption scheme. All traffic that does not match this security policy is allowed to pass through the router interfaces unencrypted and outside the VPN tunnel.

Designing IP Filters

IP filters can be used to restrict traffic coming from an external network through the VPN tunnel. These filters can limit access only to certain servers on port 80 or allow a broader level of access to the DMZ as a whole. VPN tunnel filters act like ACLs on firewalls and edge routers by giving administrators the ability to define traffic that is permissible. Unlike ACLs on routers and firewalls, IP filters tend not to be stateful and therefore may require more explicit rules to provide for proper two-way communication through the tunnel.

Defining Security Levels

Security levels are used to determine the security policies to implement and where. A network with a high security level might restrict traffic significantly, such that only encrypted traffic is allowed to access the network. Typically, networks with higher security levels contain more sensitive information and have a more restrictive access policy as well as a more restrictive security policy. Medium security levels allow a broader range of traffic in and out of the network but could still require strong authentication or encryption to protect the data in the communication. A low security network could allow plain-text communication protocols such as Telnet, FTP, or HTTP to access information on servers in the network. Furthermore, the amount of restriction on the traffic might be minimal.

This concept is also implemented in the PIX and ASA firewalls, where each interface is defined a security level. Traffic entering interfaces on higher security levels can automatically access networks of a lower security level without any explicit rules. To allow access from a lower security level into a network that is a higher security level, you will have to create explicit rules. For example, your trusted internal network could have full outbound access to the Internet automatically while traffic originating from the Internet cannot access your internal network without explicit rules.

Connecting B2B Sites

Business-to-business (B2B) connectivity has been made immensely easier with the emergence of the Internet and even easier still with the maturation and availability of VPN technologies. In the past, B2B connectivity utilized leased lines or dialup connections for the exchange of information and technology between two companies. VPNs have eliminated that need. However, trust is still of great concern. As with any business relationship, the trust between two companies can deteriorate at a rapid pace. Consider the relationship of Cisco

Systems Inc. and Dell Computer Corporation. In early 2003, the longtime business relationship between the two was terminated, with Cisco Systems citing Dell's entry into the switch marketplace as a factor.

Extranets

Extranets are B2B networks that are based on Internet network technology. An extranet can be viewed as part of a company's intranet that is made accessible to other companies or to the public or that comprises components that enable collaboration with other companies. Excellent examples of extranets include the Federal Express Tracking System (www.fedex.com/us/tracking/) and the UPS Tracking System (www.ups.com/WebTracking/track). These systems allow users to access both FedEx and UPS public sites, enter tracking numbers, and locate any package still in the system. Additionally, a user with either a FedEx or a UPS account can enter all the information needed to prepare a shipment form, obtain a tracking number, print the form, and schedule a pickup—all from the convenience of the user's computer and a Web browser. Other uses of extranets include:

- Private newsgroups between companies to share valuable experiences and ideas between business partners

- Sharing educational material or training programs

- Shared product catalogs accessible only to a select group within the industry

- Project management for intercorporate projects

As with any other connection, the main point to consider in terms of VPN extranet implementation is the termination point for the VPN tunnel. For extranets, there are two possibilities: at the edge router or at a dedicated VPN device in a DMZ leg of the firewall. It is not recommended that the VPN be terminated at the firewall, because of the need to ensure that the extranet business partner is controlled. Terminating the VPN at the inside interface of the firewall could provide the partner with significant access to corporate information as well as complete access to the corporate network. As we saw with Cisco and Dell, although the extranet partner might be trusted today, tomorrow that partner might well be a competitor.

VPN Security

VPN security is perhaps a more critical function of overall network security due to the fact that extranet VPNs rely on the security of business partners. Unlike remote office or branch networks that fall under the jurisdiction of the corporate security umbrella, extranet partners that connect into a corporate DMZ through a VPN might not follow the same methods or implement the same security policies. It is not unheard of for a secure network to be exploited by an attacker taking advantage of an extranet partner's VPN. This leads to the need to apply differing levels of trust to each VPN tunnel termination point. Many VPN appliances allow for the application of IP filters in the tunnel, much like a firewall. To ensure the highest level of security in the case of an extranet partner whose network security status is unknown, it is best to terminate the VPN tunnel at the edge router or at a VPN appliance in a designated DMZ off the firewall. These two cases are illustrated in this section.

In Figure 12.12, the termination point for the VPN tunnel allows the extranet partner's traffic to access the DMZ between the firewall and the edge router. This allows the tunnel to bypass the ACL on the edge router's external interface but still requires the traffic to comply with the firewall's security policy. In Figure 12.13, the tunnel is terminated at a VPN appliance in a second DMZ leg of the firewall. This tunnel also bypasses the ACL on the edge router as well as the security policy on the *external* interface of the firewall, but—for the traffic to access devices within the corporate headquarters network—the traffic must comply with a defined security policy on the firewall's DMZ interface. The traffic permitted by policy defined on this interface could be considerably different from the traffic permitted by the policy on the firewall's external interface. This provides the flexibility to provide a higher level of trust between the extranet partner's network and the corporate network. As an added level of security, you can deploy IDS at the extranet tunnel termination point to monitor traffic arriving from the external partner network.

Figure 12.12 Extranet VPN Termination on an Edge Router

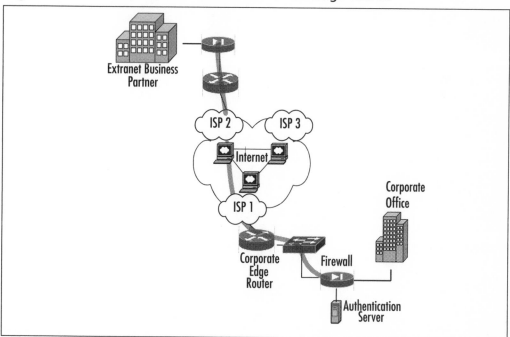

Configuring & Implementing...

Vendor IPSec Enhancements

One of the key issues that must be addressed when you're designing an IPSec VPN solution for extranets is the equipment to be used. IPSec itself is an IETF standard based on a whole range of RFCs, but there has been enough leeway and confusion in the development of IPSec that vendors have implemented proprietary enhancements to the protocols. At best, these enhancements can result in no impact in the configuration and implementation of the VPN. At worst, they can, in some cases, result in significant difficulties in getting a VPN tunnel to work, if at all. The IETF is working on resolving the issues with vendor enhancements to the IPSec protocol. The simple workaround is intended to ensure that either both parties are using the same vendor's VPN product or that the products being used are tested and certified as compatible with other vendor VPN equipment.

Figure 12.13 Extranet VPN Termination at a VPN Appliance

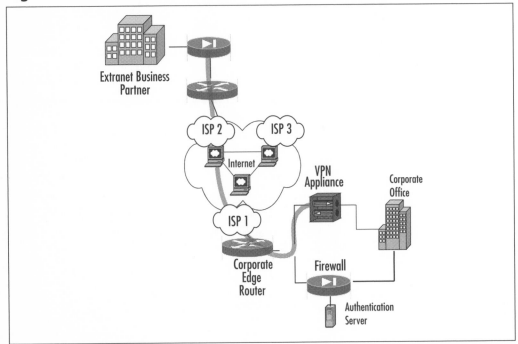

Active Directory Security

Perhaps a business partner requires more access to your corporate network than just data on a group of servers. Other methods, such as data mirroring or utilizing dual-homed servers, can accommodate such a case, the practical and more secure solution is to implement such a design using an IPSec VPN. Microsoft provides integrated software on the Windows server that allows for the deployment of a quick and easy VPN solution to address this scenario. This solution provides for greater ease on the part of the remote user as well as lower administrative overhead for the corporate administrator; it is achieved through the use of an IPSec policy that is maintained and managed using Group Policy objects stored in Active Directory.

Figure 12.14 shows an example VPN connection sequence using Windows Active Directory authentication. Here is the sequence of steps used in authenticating the user:

1. The remote user initiates a request to access the network via VPN connection. The user logs in using her username and password for the domain.

2. The VPN server requests authentication from the domain controller. If the VPN server is able to authenticate to the domain controller, the VPN server checks the authorization of the requesting user for VPN access.

3. If the domain controller authorizes the requesting user for VPN access, the VPN server and the remote client start an IKE exchange.

4. The domain controller authenticates the CA server and authorizes the CA server to issue a certificate to the remote user.

5. The remote user is issued a certificate from the CA. This certificate allows the encryption process to finish.

6. The IPSec VPN is now established and the remote user is able to access the corporate network with all the permissions she normally would have as if she were physically present at the corporate network and connected to it.

Figure 12.14 VPN Connection Using Active Directory Authentication

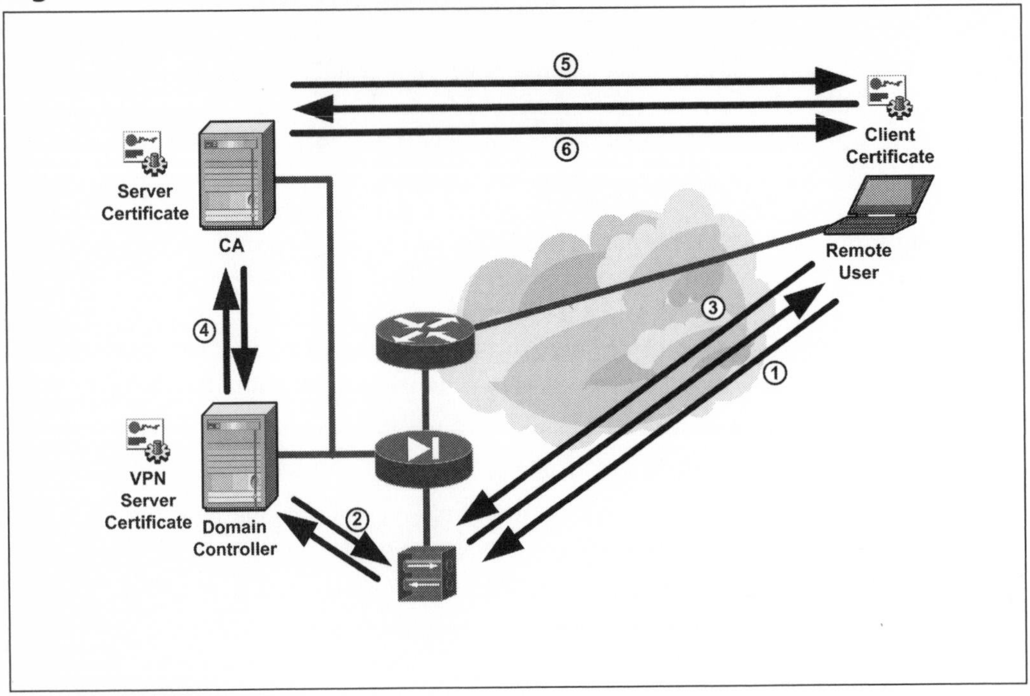

Summary

VPNs have quickly come to supplant traditional WAN technologies such as Frame Relay, leased lines, and dialup networks. They reduce the total cost of ownership of the WAN by eliminating recurring costs associated with those technologies and utilizing the underlying and nascent IP technology a company has deployed. The key to VPN utilization in a DMZ focuses on the deployment of the VPN in the DMZ itself.

There are three primary methods of terminating VPN tunnels in a DMZ: at the edge router, at the firewall, and at a dedicated appliance. Each method has its advantages and disadvantages. Terminating the VPN at the edge router allows traffic to reach servers outside the firewall and possibly inside the firewall, depending on the configured policy, but this solution can eat up resources on a device that is usually designed to pass packets as quickly as possible. Terminating a VPN tunnel at the firewall, however, allows direct access to the internal or DMZ network but could actually lower the security posture of the internal network if not configured well and can use up resources on the firewall, which could slow down processing of all traffic leaving your network. The last option is using a dedicated VPN appliance, which could require some extra attention to make sure it is implemented in a secure fashion; this is an additional expense when most companies already have edge routers and firewalls, but it allows for larger VPN infrastructures to be built without placing a burden on other devices in the network.

In addition to these deployment models, there are four deployment topologies to consider: mesh (both fully and partially), star, hub and spoke, and remote access. Each topology has advantages and disadvantages that should be carefully considered before implementation.

Once you've chosen the deployment method and topology for the VPN, the next step is to identify and design an IPSec security solution. This step includes identifying the encryption algorithm to use as well as the type of IPSec protocol and transport method. Tunnel negotiation characteristics must be decided as well, to ensure that both sides of the tunnel are configured properly. Determining the IPSec security policy will identify the traffic characteristics used to distinguish traffic destined for the IPSec VPN tunnel and traffic that will bypass the tunnel.

VPNs have advanced a long way since the days of leased lines and Frame Relay. The development of IPSec and other technologies has vastly changed the landscape with regard to WAN deployment, extranet partner connections, and B2B interaction and communication. As VPNs continue to mature, they will become the dominant force in these areas by helping drive down the total cost of ownership of the WAN.

Solutions Fast Track

VPN Services in the DMZ

- There are three general deployment models of VPN services in the DMZ: at the edge router, at the internal interface of the firewall, and at a dedicated VPN device in a DMZ leg of a firewall.

- The four topologies for VPNs are mesh (both fully and partially), star topology, hub-and-spoke topology, and remote access.

- The difference between a star topology and a hub-and-spoke topology lies in the fact that in a star topology, the branch or stub networks are not able to communicate with one another. They can only communicate with the central corporate network.

- IPSec is not capable of traversing NAT devices without some modification. The problem comes when the NAT device changes information in the IP header of the IPSec packet. The changes will result in an incorrect IPSec checksum that is calculated over parts of the IP header. There are workarounds for this problem, such as NAT-T.

■ When the number of VPNs connecting to the router, firewall, or VPN appliance becomes sufficiently large, it might be necessary to install a VPN accelerator module (VAM) into the device to offload many of the cryptographic functions used in the VPN.

Designing an IPSec Solution

■ There are three main choices for encryption schemes in IPSec: DES, 3DES, and AES. AES deployment is not as wide at present, so it might not be possible to use that encryption algorithm. DES has been proven insecure against an attack with sufficient resources. 3DES is the only current algorithm that is widely available and provably secure.

■ Message integrity is provided through the use of MD5 or SHA-1 with the HMAC hash algorithm.

■ Before an IPSec VPN tunnel can be established, the session parameters must be negotiated through the use of Internet Key Exchange.

■ There are five options to be concerned with during Phase 1, or Main mode, VPN deployments: encryption algorithm, hashing algorithm, lifetime, Diffie-Hellman Group, and Aggressive mode.

■ There are six main options to be concerned with during Phase 2, or Quick mode, negotiations: encryption algorithm, hashing algorithm, lifetime (seconds and/or kilobytes), Perfect Forward Secrecy, local networks, and remote networks.

■ IPSec security policies define the traffic permitted to enter the VPN tunnel.

Connecting B2B Sites

■ Extranets are B2B networks based on Internet network technology. An extranet can be viewed as part of a company's intranet that is made accessible to other companies or to the public or that comprises components that enable collaboration with other companies.

■ For partner extranets, there are two possible VPN deployment models: VPN tunnel termination at the edge router or VPN tunnel termination at a dedicated device on a DMZ leg of the firewall.

■ VPN security is a critical function of overall network security due to the fact that extranet VPNs rely on the security of the business partners.

Frequently Asked Questions

The following Frequently Asked Questions, answered by the authors of this book, are designed to both measure your understanding of the concepts presented in this chapter and to assist you with real-life implementation of these concepts. To have your questions about this chapter answered by the author, browse to **www.syngress.com/solutions** and click on the **"Ask the Author"** form.

Q: Why does IPSec have difficulty traversing a NAT firewall unmodified?

A: Incompatibilities between NAT and IPSec can be caused by myriad issues, two of which are described here:

- The AH protocol incorporates the IP source and destination addresses in the keyed message integrity check. NAT devices make changes to address fields and therefore invalidate the message integrity check.

- TCP and UDP checksums have a dependency on the IP source and destination addresses through inclusion of the "pseudo-header" in the calculation IPSec. ESP only passes unimpeded through a NAT device if TCP/UDP is not involved. This can be accomplished through the use of IPSec tunnel mode or IPSec/GRE. It is also possible for ESP to pass unimpeded through a NAT device if checksums are not calculated (as is done with IPv4 UDP).

    For a more complete overview of problems between NAT and IPSec, see the IETF Security Working Group's Internet draft, *IPSec-NAT Compatibility Requirements*, at www.ietf.org/internet-drafts/draft-ietf-IPSec-nat-reqts-04.txt.

Q: How does IKE work?

A: The Internet Key Exchange (IKE) protocol is designed to provide mutual authentication of systems as well as to establish a shared secret key to create in IPSec SA. IKE operates in two phases. Phase 1 provides mutual authentication of the systems as well as establishing session keys and is known as the ISAKMP SA. Phase 2 provides for setting up the IPSec SA.

Q: What is the significance of terminating a VPN tunnel on a firewall's internal interface?

A: Terminating a VPN tunnel on a firewall's internal interface allows all VPN traffic to access the internal directory in one hop. This might not be desirable, and if IP filters cannot be applied to VPN tunnel traffic, other methods, such as having the VPN tunnel terminate within an isolated VLAN, must be employed to restrict the traffic.

Q: What is the benefit of placing the VPN appliance in a DMZ leg of the firewall, as was shown in Figure 12.11?

A: Placing the VPN appliance in a DMZ leg of the firewall allows for the application of a unique firewall policy that is specific for the VPN traffic. The public interface of the VPN appliance sits outside the firewall while the private interface is in the DMZ leg of the firewall.

Q: What other types of VPNs are available besides IPSec?

A: Other VPN technologies do exist. They include Point-to-Point Transport Protocol (PPTP), which was originally developed by Microsoft, and Layer 2 Tunneling Protocol (L2TP), which was a merger of Microsoft's PPTP and Cisco Systems' Layer 2 Forwarding (L2F) protocol. PPTP is defined in RFC 2637, and L2TP is defined in RFC 2661.

## Chapter 13

Windows Bastion Hosts

Solutions in this chapter:

- **Configuring Bastion Hosts**

- **Testing Bastion Host Security**

- **Windows 2003 and Windows 2000**

- **Remote Administration**

- **Bastion Host Maintenance and Support**

- **Windows Bastion Host Checklist**

☑ Summary

☑ Solutions Fast Track

☑ Frequently Asked Questions

Introduction

Before we delve too deeply into the configuration of a bastion host, let's discuss just what is meant by the term *bastion host*. A bastion is generally defined as a stronghold or area that is exceptionally fortified against an attack. In network terms this could easily apply to most any security appliance. Typically, however, the term is used to describe a general-purpose networking device that has been intentionally hardened against attack because it will be providing some service to an untrusted network. In most cases, the untrusted network will be the Internet, but it could also be an extranet, wireless DMZ, or business-to-business (B2B) network. In short, much like the protective gates of an ancient castle, great effort is expended to secure a network device because you are *expecting* it to be attacked. The most common examples of a bastion host are an Internet-facing Web server or DNS server. These are servers that, by their nature, are exposed to the Internet and a nearly constant barrage of attacks.

At a high level, this hardening includes applying security patches, configuring logical access controls, and configuring operating system-specific settings to make the system more secure. Obviously, entire volumes could be and have been written to cover the hardening of specific operating systems. Therefore, this chapter provides a high-level overview of the steps that are needed to harden a Microsoft Windows 2000 or 2003 server, explaining the relevant concepts, pointing out any pitfalls or caveats in the process, and providing sources of additional information where applicable.

Configuring Bastion Hosts

When it comes to configuring a bastion host, try to take a minimalist approach. This host will be probed and attacked by people with a lot more free time to spend attacking the machine than you have to defend it. If the host has no services running on a given port, the proper response to traffic destined for that port is to ignore the packet. This means that compromising the system using traffic on a port the host isn't supposed to be listening to requires a pretty substantial security flaw in the host's TCP stack itself. Although these flaws do happen, as time goes on and the TCP stacks become more mature these types of exploits become less frequent. What this leaves as the most common exploit path is security flaws in the software that is listening on a given port. For this reason, you want as few processes listening on open ports as absolutely necessary.

Planning a bastion host takes time. If you decide to cut corners and put a machine into production with the intent of hardening the system "later," you could end up with a compromised system. Implementing a bastion host that can withstand the rigors of being visible on the Internet takes someone who is skilled and experienced with the operating system in question. There are a plethora of excellent books covering virtually every operating system currently on the market. Armed with an understanding of the role the host will play in the network and an understanding of the available options for a given operating system, you will be well prepared to successfully implement your bastion host.

Testing Bastion Host Security

Whether you are implementing a bastion host from scratch or securing one that you inherited, the first step will be to test the current security of the host. If you built, planned, and implemented the bastion host yourself, the next thing you will want to do is run a few tests to make sure it is as secure as you had planned. Similarly, if you are inheriting a pre-existing bastion host, the first thing is to determine the current state of the system. This step is vital so that you can know what work still needs to be done and so you can prioritize the remediation of any remaining vulnerabilities.

Vulnerability Scanning

If you are starting with a pre-existing bastion host that needs to be hardened, a vulnerability assessment is the first step. You need to begin by establishing a security baseline so you know what needs work and can prioritize your efforts. *Vulnerability scanning* is the process of performing automated checks for known security weaknesses. A wide variety of vulnerability scanners are available. Some are more invasive than others, meaning that their scanning is more likely to cause a service disruption. The closer the software comes to actually executing an attack, the more accurate is the estimate of your vulnerability to such an attack.

Unfortunately, the test is also more likely to cause some problems. Problems typically arising from a vulnerability scan are unresponsive services or software. In most cases these problems can be corrected by restarting the service or rebooting the machine, but in a production environment, such steps could be undesirable. In other cases, however, the testing can cause significant damage, such as data corruption when scanning a database. For this reason, any vulnerability scanning should be undertaken with great care. The tester also needs to ensure that he or she has explicit permission from upper management to perform the testing. This permission is for legal protection in case the testing causes any significant problems that result in financial loss.

Nmap

Truly a vulnerability scanner on its own, Nmap is typically the first tool an attacker will reach for, so you should be familiar with it as well. Nmap is the most widely used general-purpose, free port scanner; it's available from www.insecure.org/Nmap/. In addition to simple port scanning, Nmap can use a variety of techniques to attempt to see what ports are open on a host behind a firewall and attempt to scan without setting off any intrusion detection systems that might be listening. Nmap can also attempt to identify the OS through a technique known as *fingerprinting*. OS fingerprinting utilizes a variety of techniques such as inspecting the initial sequence number, supported TCP options, and initial window size. Nmap's primary role is to scan a machine and determine which ports on the machine are listening. Identifying the operating system and the types of software that are running will go a long way to help the hacker choose which exploits to attempt.

Although the number of options Nmap accepts can appear daunting, it comes with excellent instructions on its use. This is sample output of a basic scan with only the -O (OS detection) option enabled.

```
#nmap -O 192.168.1.99

Starting nmap 3.75 ( http://www.insecure.org/nmap/ ) at 2006-06-12 06:27 EDT
Interesting ports on 192.168.1.99:
(The 1660 ports scanned but not shown below are in state: closed)
PORT      STATE SERVICE
135/tcp open  msrpc
139/tcp open  netbios-ssn
445/tcp open  microsoft-ds
MAC Address: 00:11:D8:88:0F:B3 (Asustek Computer)
Device type: general purpose
Running: Microsoft Windows 2003/.NET|NT/2K/XP
OS details: Microsoft Windows 2003 Server or XP SP2

Nmap run completed -- 1 IP address (1 host up) scanned in 1.595 seconds
```

Nmap is natively a command-line tool, but you can download a GUI front end called Nmapfe that does a good job of turning the sometimes complicated command lines into a simple point-and-click screen. You can also find Windows ports of Nmap, though they don't run nearly as fast as the native Linux versions.

Nessus

Nessus is a true vulnerability scanner available from http://nessus.org/index.php. Although still free, the most current version (Nessus 3) is no longer open source. The Nessus system comprises two components: a server and a client. The server process does the actual scanning; the client is used to configure and run scans and view the results of a scan. Nessus is a very feature-rich application that can perform more than 10,000 types of checks via downloadable plug-ins. Nessus is available for Linux, FreeBSD, Solaris, Mac OS X, and Microsoft Windows. The licensing is relatively generous, but in some circumstance you must purchase a license. For full details on the licensing of Nessus, refer to the licensing FAQ located at http://nessus.org/plug-ins/index.php?view=faq.

You should periodically scan your hosts for vulnerabilities according to the requirements of your IT security policy. You should also perform a vulnerability scan any time significant changes are made to your bastion hosts. A significant change could include adding a new feature like enabling terminal services, performing an upgrade, or installing a new service pack.

The installation of Nessus is beyond the scope of this book. For an excellent reference on Nessus, see the Syngress Press book, *Nessus Network Auditing*. With Nessus successfully installed and running, you use the Nessus client to log into the server. In the example shown in Figure 13.1, the user *nessusroot* with a password of *password* is used to log into the server.

Figure 13.1 The Nessus Login Screen

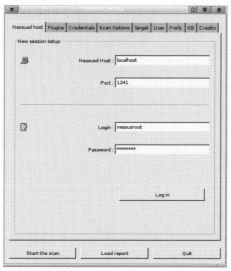

Once you are logged in, you have access to several tabs. Select the **Plug-ins** tab to choose the types of checks to perform by clicking in the check box and placing a check next to them. Use the **Target** tab to specify which machine to scan. Once you are satisfied with your choices, simply click **Start the scan**.

NOTE

Several types of check will not be fully tested by default. These are types of scan that run a higher-than-normal risk of causing an undesirable response from the target host, typically by causing a service to fail until it can be restarted or the host rebooted. Nessus's default behavior is to rely on the host's responses to guess whether it is vulnerable instead of actually attempting to exploit the vulnerability. This is a safer option, but the results are less reliable. To enable these plug-ins to perform a true test, you must remove the check next to **Safe Checks** on the **Scan Options** tab.

Once the scan is completed, a report window should open with the results. The interface allows you to go from pane to pane and drill down into your results. By selecting the **Subnet**, you are presented with a list of hosts in that subnet. When you select a **Host**, the Port pane populates and allows you to drill down into the results for a specific port. When you select a specific **Port**, you can then choose which results for that port you want to see. The specific nature of the vulnerability will be explained in the largest pane in the lower right, as shown in Figure 13.2.

Figure 13.2 Nessus Scan Results

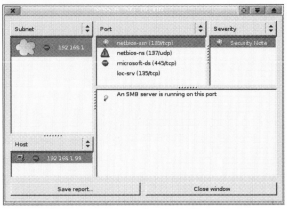

As you can see from the large number of available plug-ins, Nessus is a very powerful tool for determining vulnerabilities your systems might have. With the large number of supported operating systems and the ability to check for a wide range of vulnerabilities, Nessus fits nicely into many security toolkits.

Microsoft Baseline Security Analyzer

The Microsoft Baseline Security Analyzer (MBSA) is just that—a tool for checking the *baseline* security of supported Microsoft products. The primary page for MBSA is www.microsoft.com/technet/security/tools/mbsahome.mspx. There are different versions of MBSA, each supporting different platforms, so you will need to choose the version that is appropriate for you. The installation software is relatively short and lightweight, at less than 2MB. The MBSA interface, shown in Figure 13.3, is also very straightforward.

Figure 13.3 Microsoft Baseline Security Analyzer

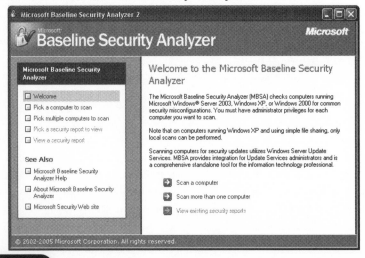

To scan a single computer, simply click **Scan a computer**, enter a computer name or IP address, and then click **Start Scan**. The results show an expected Microsoft bias. For example, in Figure 13.4, the MBSA tool has marked a red *X* because the system doesn't have all the disk partitions formatted as NTFS. Although it's true there is no file-level security with FAT32, there can be legitimate reasons for not using NTFS on all partitions.

Figure 13.4 Microsoft Baseline Security Scanner Results

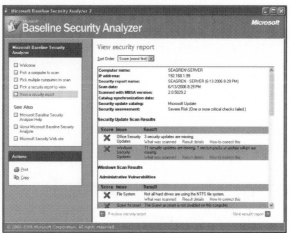

Using Vulnerability Scanning Results to Harden Bastion Hosts

Completing a variety of vulnerability scans against your bastion hosts is only the *first* step in testing their security. Running the scan only tells you where you are vulnerable. The vulnerability scanners do not finish the job for you. You still need to verify that the reported vulnerabilities are actually vulnerabilities and not *false positives*. It is not uncommon for vulnerability scanners to report something as a risk when in fact it is not. Verification can happen through a variety of means, both automated and manual. After identifying what is truly a risk, you may find yourself staring at a dauntingly long list of risks.

As is usually the case with a large project, the best approach here is to be methodical and tackle reasonable, bite-sized chunks at a time. A typical next step is to take the assembled report and sort the vulnerabilities according to priority. Start with the highest-risk items first. This is typically a subjective measure that factors in the vulnerabilities that can most easily be exploited, the criticality of the host in question, and the likelihood of the vulnerability being exploited. This revised and prioritized list will serve as your road map for the actual remediation.

Next you must begin the arduous task of securing the vulnerable machine. If you are lucky, some items on the list might be duplicate vulnerabilities, such that you may be able to automate the changes. For example, suppose your get a long list of directories that have the permissions set to give everyone full access. You could create a script to connect to the machine so that it iterates through the list of directories and corrects the permissions. Other times, each individual change that is needed might need to be made by hand. This process will likely be time consuming and require extensive communication with stakeholders. Many times, moving to a more secure configuration could result in some features being disabled. You should be cognizant of your organization's change control processes. Large-scale remediation efforts *will* bring unexpected problems, and a comprehensive change management process will help minimize the service disruptions that could result.

Ideally, vulnerability management should be a mature, cyclical process. As systems are updated, patched, and modified, the security posture of those systems will change. Vulnerability scanning should not be something that is done once and you're finished. The scanning should be repeated on a regularly scheduled basis that is in accordance with your organization's IT security policy. The schedule could be dictated simply by the calendar, or it could coincide with internal audit efforts. Vulnerability scanning and vulnerability remediation are ongoing processes that are never done.

Configuration Fundamentals

There was a time when Microsoft Windows servers were not even contenders to serve in the role of bastion host. Those times are gone; more and more Internet-facing servers have Windows as their underlying operating system. According to a netcraft.com survey of 88 *million* Web sites, Microsoft has gained nearly 15 percent in terms of market share in just the last three months (placing it at 30% share overall). The survey can be found here: http://news.netcraft.com/archives/web_server_survey.html. Apache is still the most widely used Web server, but Microsoft's Web browser IIS is definitely closing in. With proper planning and care, a Windows bastion host can be just as secure as any other operating system.

An important concept to keep in mind as you read this chapter is that the very nature of a bastion host impacts your strategy to protect it. For most systems connected to your network, you work under the assumption that the firewalls and routers on your perimeter will prevent unauthorized access to those systems. The average machine shouldn't really ever be reachable by an outside attacker. The bastion host, on the other hand, is exactly the opposite because it is designed to offer up some service to the outside world. You are working to secure the bastion host, *knowing* it will be exposed to hostile network traffic. This expectation will have a far-reaching impact on your planning and comes into play in virtually every design decision made concerning the bastion host.

This chapter's objective is to show you how to configure the bastion host in such as way as to minimize the chances of compromise and to minimize the damage that can be done if it *is* compromised. Of course, a well-implemented bastion host does not mean that due care shouldn't be taken when you're configuring the network infrastructure. A properly configured firewall and network architecture are vital components to keep the bastion host and the rest of the network as safe as possible from attackers.

Domain Members or Standalone Servers

Very early in the planning process, you will need to determine whether the bastion host will be configured as part of a Windows domain or as a standalone server. By allowing the server to be a member of a domain, you gain the ability to do some security work more easily. Things like pushing out policies to lock down the machine become much simpler when the bastion host is part of a domain. Security settings can be applied to parent containers and then propagated to the objects they hold. When considering this decision, remember the previous assumption: This machine will certainly be attacked. Realizing this, we want to minimize any damage that could occur if the host is compromised.

The same isolation that makes administration less convenient on a standalone server can also help insulate the network from harm if the server is compromised. If an attacker manages to gain control of the bastion host, he or she will only have the ability to compromise local accounts that have no access to the rest of the network. One of the attacker's first objectives will be to gain access to additional machines or accounts, so if the original compromised account is discovered and locked down, the attacker can maintain access. If the machine is not a member of a Windows domain, an attacker has a far greater challenge in gaining access to nonlocal accounts. For this reason, it is considered best practice for bastion hosts to be standalone servers.

The primary disadvantage of a standalone configuration stems from its limited administrative capabilities; however, steps can be taken to ease the administrative burden. In the following pages, we discuss several methods for enabling secure remote administration. If you determine that membership in a domain or active directory is absolutely necessary, there are some steps you can take to make things as secure as possible.

A final consideration is that by not making the system a standalone server, some additional work will be involved simply to permit domain communications. For example, if there is a firewall between the bastion host and the rest of the internal network, firewall rules will be needed to allow proper domain communication. This list of ports can get rather lengthy. The following are Microsoft's *recommendations* to allow a Windows 2000 server running Exchange 2000 domain connectivity:

- TCP53 (DNS)

- UDP53 (DNS)

- TCP80 (Web access)

- TCP88 (Kerberos to all domain controllers)

- UDP88 (Kerberos to all domain controllers)

- UDP123 (NTP to all domain controllers)

- TCP135 (EndPointMapper to all domain controllers)

- TCP389 (Lightweight Directory Access Protocol, or LDAP, to all domain controllers)

- UDP389 (LDAP to all domain controllers)

- TCP445 (Server message block to all domain controllers)

- TCP3268 (LDAP to global catalog servers)

- Plus one additional port that must be configured in the registry on all domain controllers the Exchange server will use

As you can see, allowing a bastion host to be a member of a domain through a firewall is not simple. If you are not careful, by the time you've configured the firewall to support a variety of bastion hosts sitting in the DMZ, each offering a variety of services, you could well end up having a complex firewall policy with a large number of exceptions for the necessary communications these servers require. At some point you might need to create additional DMZs, providing further isolation to keep the access control lists reasonable and limit damage if one of the systems is compromised. Of course, this comes with a price tag, in both real dollars for equipment as well as management and support overheard for the more complicated infrastructure.

Installation

As is so often the case, the first step of installing the operating system does not involve any software. The first step is careful planning. It is important to sit down and plan out what your needs are, taking into account items such as remote access and remote support, drive partitions, and memory. All of these factors should be laid out well before you sit down and actually load the operating system. Let's consider some of the implications of these choices.

Disk Partitions

When it comes to partitioning drives, people tend to fall into one of two camps: Either they have very strong opinions on how it "should" be done or they just don't care. At a high level, the options are to use one single partition per drive or use several partitions per drive. A majority of Windows systems tend to have the former. Windows can run just fine this way, but there are several advantages to segregating data onto different partitions and/or physical disks.

Performance is one advantage. By placing the data on different physical disks, you can allow greater bandwidth on the controller bus for data transfer. The most common example of this configuration is to place the Windows swap file on a different physical disk than the operating system. In truth, the real performance gains with this setup are very small, but when you are dealing with a production server having to process a high volume of data, it could make a difference. Another way to see performance gains is to consider that certain applications are prone to fragmenting their data. In some cases, this could happen because the application is inefficiently written; in others it could simply be the nature of the processing. In these instances, keeping the fragmented partition separate from the operating system partition could provide some noticeable gains.

There can also be security benefits to using multiple partitions. To be realized, many common exploits rely on well-known paths to files. This is true not only at the operating system level but for application vulnerabilities as well. In some cases you will have afforded yourself protection from an attack by simply having the vulnerable component on a partition other than the C: drive.

Once you have determined how you will partition your hard drives, you will need to decide how to format the partitions. There really isn't much of an option when it comes to formatting. The only real choice is NTFS. FAT32 offers no file-level security at all, so from a file system standpoint, everyone who accesses the system would have full control of all files. NTFS will allow you to configure access permissions on individual files or on entire directories; it is definitely the more secure choice.

Service Packs and Hotfixes

Now that your hard disks are partitioned and ready to receive the operating system, it's time to actually do the installation. It's worth noting that a clean install is always preferred over any type of in-place upgrade. This general rule is even more applicable when it comes to bastion hosts. Frequently the upgrade routine will enable certain features or disable other ones, with the intent of maintaining backward compatibility with settings or software on the original system. Often this can introduce a vulnerability that otherwise might not be there with a clean install. Most often, the upgrade process will not do a good job of removing unneeded software from the previous installation, resulting in leftover software or programs on the system that you don't need. Any of these programs could end up having a vulnerability an attacker could exploit. Whenever possible, it is most secure to perform a clean install on a freshly formatted system.

Once you have completed the new installation, you will need to bring the machine up to date on the latest patches and updates. You can go to Microsoft's Web site to have the machine automatically checked for updates. It can actually be difficult at times to locate the proper Web site to do a manual update, because most links will try to take you to the page to enable automatic updates. If you go to Microsoft's homepage and then navigate to **Microsoft Update**, you will be taken to the page to enable *automatic* updates. The URL to manually perform the scan and update is http://update.microsoft.com/windowsupdate/v6/default.aspx?In=en-us. Even from this Web page there is a button to "Enable automatic updates."

The update process on a clean installation will take some time. There will be dozens of updates, and several reboots will be required. Once this process is completed, you will have seen the "Enable automatic updates" button many times on the site, and you might be tempted to use it. Don't do it! Automatic updates are generally *not* recommended for mission-critical servers. If you configure automatic updates and allow the system to apply updates as they are released, if there is a new patch that breaks something on your server, you might not know it until it's already been applied. Automatic updates remove your ability to apply human judgment in choosing which updates to apply. If you do decide to enable automatic updates, you will be presented with a screen like the one shown in Figure 13.5.

Figure 13.5 Configuring Automatic Updates

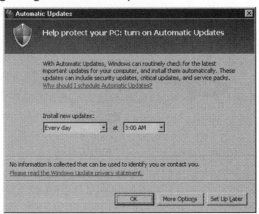

This screen allows you to choose when to apply the updates. A better option is to select the **More Options** button, after which you will see a screen with some additional choices. You should select **Notify me but don't automatically download or install them**, as shown in Figure 13.6.

Figure 13.6 Configuring Automatic Updates (Part Two)

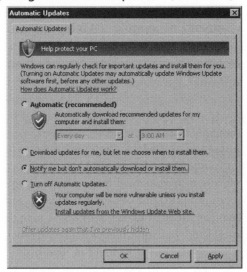

This is the best choice for a couple of reasons. As was previously discussed, applying the patches automatically could result in a system outage. Although Microsoft does test its patches extensively, it is impossible to test every conceivable combination of hardware and software, so sometimes problems do occur. Downloading the updates automatically and *applying* them manually might seem safe; however, the updates themselves could be very large. During this time the downloading of the update could adversely affect the network load or bandwidth to your bastion host. For this reason, the recommended option for a bastion host is either to only notify of updates or to simply disable automatic updates completely.

Another option is to use Windows Server Update Services (WSUS). WSUS allows you to download the updates to a single system on your network and then allow the client systems to use their automatic update functionality from your internal system. WSUS offers several advantages over automatic updates. WSUS allows you to centrally determine which updates to apply. WSUS also allows you to save on Internet bandwidth because you have to download the updates only once through the Internet. Client updates will then use your internal bandwidth. You can find more information on WSUS at www.microsoft.com/windowsserversystem/updateservices/default.mspx.

In either case, it is imperative that you don't completely forget about patching the devices. During the busy and sometimes hectic work week, it can be easy to neglect patches and updates. You should have a regularly scheduled change management process that includes a review of what updates are needed. The updates should then be applied during approved change windows and then reviewed to ensure that each update was applied properly and without adverse effect on the host. This managed process will ensure the bastion host's operating system is as current and secure as possible.

Removing Optional Components

Once the operating system is installed and updated, you can remove any unneeded components. These can include both hardware and software. Recall that the objective is to make the bastion host as secure as possible under the assumption that it will be attacked. You should remove any software on the system that is not needed for the bastion host to function properly. For example, although there might be no known exploits for the built-in Windows calculator (calc.exe), a vulnerability could be discovered in the future. Removing the software would remove that as a potential vulnerability in the future. Removing the Windows calculator might be considered extreme in some cases. You will need to carefully evaluate what components can be safely removed from your environment. Some components to *consider* removing or at least disabling could include the following:

- Unneeded network protocols such as NetBEUI, IPX, and possibly IPv6, if the environment is not a dual-stack network environment

- Unneeded software such as Active Desktop

- Unneeded hardware such as sound cards

Creating a New Local Administrator Account

The local administrator account should be renamed to something that cannot be guessed. Many exploits target the administrator account by its account name and have no provision for an administrator account that has been renamed.

After renaming the local administrator account, you should create an additional account with no privileges and name it *administrator*, then configure the account for maximum auditing (see the next section for auditing configuration). This lets you know if anyone is trying to access the system using the account named *administrator*. Barring a brief memory lapse, employees who are legitimately authorized to access the system will know that there is no usable account called *administrator*. This way, if someone does try to access through *administrator,* you will get a heads-up that someone is probably trying to compromise the system. Microsoft provides a complete prescriptive guide for securing both local and domain administrator accounts in the white paper *The Administrator Accounts Security Planning Guide*, which can be found at www.microsoft.com/technet/security/topics/serversecurity/administratoraccounts/default.mspx.

Security Configuration Using the Microsoft Management Console

The vast majority of security configuration is done via the Microsoft Management Console (MMC). Therefore, you should become familiar with this tool. You can access the console by navigating to **Start | Programs | Administrative Tools**. All the listed utilities such as Services are actually MMC snap-ins.

The MMC will show you a two-pane view. The left pane allows you to highlight a given snap-in, whereas the right pane shows you the details for the active snap-in. In the case of the Services snap-in, the left pane will contain only "Service (Local)."

To customize the MMC, go to **Start | Run**, type **mmc**, and click **OK**. This will open the full MMC. The first time you open it, the MMC will have no snap-ins loaded. For example, to load the Services snap-in, you would open the console and click **Console | Add/Remove Snap-in**; then, in the **Add/Remove Snap-in** window, click the **Add** button. In the **Add Standalone Snap-in** window, select the desired snap-in—in this case, **Services**—and click the **Add** button. Leave the default selection of **Local Computer** and click **Finish**. You can then close the **Add Standalone Snap-in** window by clicking **Close**.

Click **OK** in the **Add/Remove snap-in** window. This process can be repeated to add multiple snap-ins to your MMC console.

Figure 13.7 Add Standalone Snap-in Screen

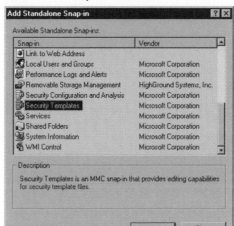

You will need to configure several security settings on your bastion host. These settings will control security options such as login restrictions, warning banners, and much more. You could configure all these settings by navigating and editing the registry directly, but a much simpler and safer method is to use the MMC. You can access and configure each setting individually by navigating through the MMC snap-ins separately, or you can configure and apply settings via one of the pregenerated security templates. The security templates simplify the hardening process by bringing configuration options from many different locations together using a single consistent interface (under a single snap-in).

You can open the Security Templates snap-in by adding it as you did the Services snap-in, choosing the **Security Templates** and the **Security Configuration and Analysis** snap-ins. The Security Templates snap-in will expand to show all the preconfigured templates. You can use this snap-in to edit these templates directly, or a better option is to right-click the template you want to start with, select **Save As**, and choose a name that is meaningful to you. This approach allows you to create security templates specific to your business needs and leaves the default templates intact.

Next you can import your template. Start by creating a new security configuration database by right-clicking the **Security Configuration and Analysis** snap-in and selecting **Open Database**. Choose a name ending in .sdb and click **Open**. Then select the **Security Configuration and Analysis** snap-in again, right-click and select **Import Template**, and choose one of the predefined templates or the one you previously saved. Hisecdc.inf, one of the more secure templates, is considered to be baseline security settings for a "high-security" domain controller. Once this is done, you need to right-click again, select **Analyze Computer Now**, and click **OK** for the log path, which reveals several expandable items under Security Configuration and Analysis. This places all the security-related settings in one location for easy access and management.

Account Lockout Policy

The Account Lockout Policy (Security Configuration and Analysis | Account Policies | Account Lockout Policy) allows you to configure the number of incorrect passwords that a user can enter before they're locked out of an account, how long the account stays locked out, and how long to reset the lockout counter. The following recommended settings will provide the most security an in average environment:

- **Account lockout duration** Represents how long the account will stay locked out. Setting this to zero means that the account will stay locked out until it's manually unlocked by an administrator. This is the most secure option, though even allowing the account to reset after as little as 10 minutes will slow down a hacker who is attempting to brute-force the password.

- **Account lockout threshold** Represents the number of invalid passwords that can be attempted before the user is locked out of the account. A setting of three invalid logon attempts is usually considered adequate. If the number is too low, a simple typo could result in an account being locked out. If the number is set to 0 (insecure), the account will never be locked out.

- **Reset account lockout counter after** Determines how much time will pass before the counter is reset. The default setting of 30 minutes is usually adequate. A longer setting is considered more secure.

The Account Lockout Policy setting and MMC console are depicted in Figure 13.8.

Figure 13.8 Account Lockout Policy

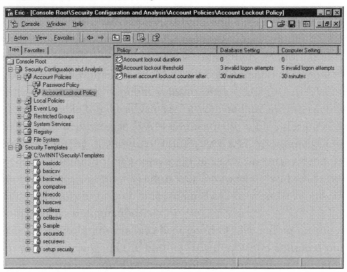

Audit Policy

The Audit Policy (Security Configuration and Analysis | Local Policies | Audit Policy) settings can be very important for a bastion host. Your audit logs can alert you to unauthorized activity before the system is compromised and after the fact can help you determine the series of events that might have led up to a successful compromise. You can review Microsoft's recommendations for securing Windows 2000/2003, including auditing settings, at www.microsoft.com/technet/security/prodtech/windows2000/secwin2k/default.mspx.

The most significant audit options are outlined here, along with some recommendations for the most secure settings. Auditing can have a significant impact on server performance. You must carefully weigh the benefits of having the audit trail versus the resources that will be consumed by enabling various audit options.

- **Audit account logon events** Set this to **No Auditing**. There is a subtle yet important difference between "audit *account* logon events" and "audit logon events." The account logon events occur only when a local account is used to log onto another computer. Because this is a standalone server acting as a bastion host, this event should never be triggered and is primarily useful for domain controllers.

- **Audit account management** Keep this set to **Success, Failure**, which tracks when passwords are changed, accounts are created and deleted, and group membership changes. The audit records generated by this setting should be closely monitored for signs of unauthorized activity that can indicate a system compromise.

- **Audit directory service access** Set to **No Auditing** since this is used to audit Active Directory (AD) activities. Because the most secure configuration for the bastion host is as a standalone server, the bastion host should never be exposed to any of these audit events.

- **Audit logon events** Set to **Success, Failure**. This is the single most important audit item. These audit events will let you know *who* and *when* someone is trying to log on, and perhaps even more important, whether they are succeeding. This setting will provide glaring evidence of brute-force logon attempts and hopefully give you a jump start on investigating the source and taking corrective action.

- **Audit object access** Keep at **Success, Failure**. This is another important audit setting. It will record access to objects such as printers, registry keys, folders, or individual files. Basically, it will audit anything with a system access control list (SACL) defined. This is explained in more detail later, in the "Registry and File System ACLs" section of this chapter.

- **Audit policy change** Keep at **Success, Failure**. This will trigger when someone modifies (or attempts to modify) your policies. An attacker who has successfully compromised a system may attempt to alter the system policy to give himself more freedom over the compromised system.

- **Audit privilege use** According to Microsoft, this setting will "Audit each instance of a user exercising a user right." This might sound handy at first, but in reality it often generates far too much data to be useful. If your environment justifies enabling auditing on these events, setting this option to only audit failures will usually suffice. Most often this option set to **No auditing** on production systems and only enabled for special troubleshooting activities.

- **Audit process tracking** Similar to "privilege use," this setting can generate a large amount of data and can have a significant impact on performance. In most cases, you should set it to **No auditing** unless you're diagnosing specific problems.

- **Audit system events** Keep at **Success, Failure**. This setting only triggers for events that affect the entire system, such as system start and shutdown, or for events that affect the system security or security log.

User Rights Assignment

The list of configurable events under User Rights Assignments is extensive. These settings (Security Configuration and Analysis | Local Policies | User Rights Assignment) allow you to configure what users (including the accounts that processes run as) can do. Rather than elaborate on all the specific settings in this category, we will examine only the most significant configurable events and make recommendations for the most secure settings for the majority of environments:

- **Access this computer from the network** You can safely set this option to **Authenticated Users** and remove all other access. You should make certain that "Anonymous Logon" is *not* in the allowed list. Users accessing this bastion host as a Web server will still have access as part of the IIS configuration.

- **Act as part of the operating system** *No accounts* should need this privilege. It allows a user to impersonate any other user on the system without authentication. This would pose a huge security risk and render your other auditing events meaningless. If an application needs this type of access to function properly, it should use the *LocalSystem* account, which includes this access by default.

- **Bypass traverse checking** This setting allows a user to navigate through directory trees, even if the user does not have access to a directory. It does *not* allow the user to list the contents of a directory to which he or she does not have the appropriate rights. This option should be set to **administrators** only.

- **Change the system time** Setting the time might not seem important at first glance, but it can be a huge security hole. If the time is set incorrectly, certain encryption systems such as IPSec will fail. Further, it becomes impossible to accurately correlate event logs, and critical transactions could fail, causing a denial of service for legitimate traffic. This setting should be set to **administrators** only.

- **Create token object** This setting allows an account to create a token that can then be used to gain access to any system resource. This right should not need to be set manually on any account. If it is needed, it should be assigned to the **localsystem** account.

- **Debug programs** This right will allow a user to attach a debugger to a process, which in turn will allow the user to access many sensitive internal resources. This right should be assigned with great care and usually shouldn't be needed on a production host.

- **Deny access to this computer from the network** This right should include the local administrator account. There is no legitimate need for the local account to access the system over the network.

- **Deny logon as batch job**, **Deny logon as service** Both of these rights should be set to the local **administrator**. By doing this, you ensure that if the local administrator account is compromised, the attacker will not be able to immediately install a service or batch job to further compromise system security.

Security Options

The Security Options group is also extensive (Security Configuration and Analysis | Local Policies | Security Options) and offers important security settings that impact the entire system instead of individual accounts. Many of these settings are discussed in the Microsoft security guide at www.microsoft.com/technet/security/prodtech/windows2000/w2kccscg/default.mspx. The following are the most important settings to configure:

- **Do not display last user name in logon screen** This option should be set to **enabled**. By displaying the last user to log on, you are giving any attacker who can get to that logon screen a first clue as to a viable account name to attack.

- **Message text for users attempting to log on** This message will be seen when someone attempts to log onto the console directly. This setting gives some legal protection against unauthorized access. Fill this in with a message stating that only authorized users should be accessing the system. Your legal department will likely already have the specific wording clearly defined; essentially, it serves to negate an attacker's claim that they didn't know they were doing anything wrong.

- **Message title for users attempting to log on** This is the title for the preceding message. Something suitably ominous such as **"Warning"** or **"Authorized Users Only"** should be adequate. Consult your legal department to be safe.

- **Number of previous logons to cache (in case domain controller is not available)** Because this is a standalone server, there should be no credentials to cache, so this option can be set to zero (which disables caching). Even if you are using domain authentication on your bastion host, the most secure setting is zero.

- **Rename administrator account** As mentioned earlier, the local administrator account is the most popular user account for attack. Changing this account name to something other than the default can help prevent the success of some automated attacks, such as an automated password-cracking attack against the local administrator account. You should avoid any obvious alternatives such as *Admin* or *root*.

- **Rename guest account** For the same reasons as the administrator account, this option should be selected as well. The guest account has few privileges, but it can still provide a local logon account and act as a first step toward elevating an attacker's privileges. Code Red, for example, adds *Guest* to the local Administrators group. Since this account name is mentioned specifically in Code Red's payload, merely renaming this account would prevent such a group membership modification from succeeding.

Event Log

Event log settings are designed to control how the event logs behave. Most of the settings are fairly self-explanatory and the ramifications of their configuration obvious. The only setting here that deserves special attention is the **Shut down the computer when the security audit log is full** option. You have to be very careful using this setting. If you set it to **enable**, when the security log reaches the size limit you specify, the system will shut down. Although this action prevents a user from getting away with activities that are not logged when the log is full, it can also be used to cause a DoS attack.

You should also configure some means of exporting the logs off the bastion host and into some central repository. This serves several purposes. For one, it keeps the logs safe, so if an attacker does manage to take control of the bastion host, he could delete the logs to cover his tracks, but he would not be able to delete the logs that have been exported and recorded remotely. Second, exporting the logs allows you to inspect the logs at a central location instead of trying to view all the event logs across your system. A centralized logging system is the only practical way to attempt any kind of event correlation, whereby events that might not be significant independently could indicate something significant when viewed in context.

The problem with this, of course, is that Windows servers lack any built-in method for exporting the logs. You can view the logs on a remote system using the Event Viewer, but this is not a practical way to inspect the logs of all your systems or even all your bastion hosts. The number of logs that will be generated will often be so great as to make manual inspection impractical or impossible. There are third-party products that will help you in this regard. Some will inspect and filter the logs on the host system, using an agent, and then send the ones that are deemed important to the central console. Others will export everything from the host to a central console and allow the console to determine what is noteworthy. You can find products to do this in both the native Windows logging format and, as is more common, Syslog format. Microsoft does provide some command-line tools that can allow some flexibility, but they cannot replace the features and ease of use of a dedicated product.

The following list highlights some of the Microsoft tools for manipulating event logs:

- **Logevent.exe (Windows 2000 Resource Kit)** Allows you to create an event you specify in the event log you specify.

- **Eventlog.pl (Windows 2000 Resource Kit, supplement 1)** Allows you to back up event logs, export event lists to text files, clear event logs, and query properties of event logs.

- **Eventquery.pl (Windows 2000 Resource Kit, supplement 1)** Allows you to display and filter event logs based on many fields such as time, date, source, category, and ID.

- **Eventcreate.exe (Windows 2003/XP)** Allows you to create an event you specify in the event log you specify.

- **Eventquery.vbs (Windows 2003/XP)** Allows you to filter and list events of a local or remote machine.

- **Eventtriggers.exe (Windows 2003/XP)** Allows you to configure a process to be executed when certain events are logged.

Restricted Groups

The Restricted Groups Policies allow you to specify who can be members of local groups. The obvious use of this feature is to restrict the accounts that could be members of the local administrators group. To edit the settings, simply select **Restricted Groups** in the left MMC pane and double-click the group you would like to edit in the right MMC pane (see Figure 13.9). Check **Define this group in the database** and then choose the desired user account to be permitted in the group you are editing. Click **Apply** and **OK** when you're finished. The local administrator account will always have administrative access, regardless of what you define here.

WARNING

If you apply this policy setting, both inclusion and exclusion are enforced. This means that if you apply this policy setting and an account you want to be in the administrators group is not listed, it will not be allowed. Basically, using this policy setting means that you are statically defining the members of the group in question.

Figure 13.9 Restricted Groups

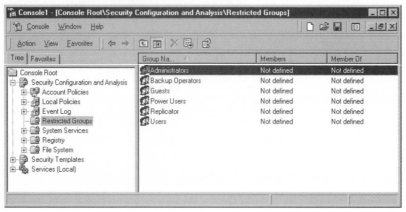

System Services

Most Windows systems installed with the default settings include a large number of services that are configured to run automatically. In addition, these services usually operate with elevated privileges such as *localsystem*. In an effort to minimize the number of services that can be attacked, you should disable any services that are not needed. Unfortunately, determining which ones are needed can often be difficult. You'll find a list of services and their purposes for Windows 2000 at www.microsoft.com/technet/prodtechnol/windows2000serv/deploy/prodspecs/win2ksvc.mspx. You'll find a similar listing for Windows 2003/XP at www.microsoft.com/technet/prodtechnol/windowsserver2003/technologies/management/svrxpser_7.mspx. These lists will hopefully provide a solid foundation from which to research the services that are essential to your particular environment.

When you select **System Services** in the left MMC pane, you will see a list of all the services on the machine in the right pane, as shown in Figure 13.10. For any given service, you can double-click the service name and edit the policy settings. The **Analyzed Security Policy Setting** window is shown in Figure 13.11. Once you choose to enable the policy for a specific service by checking **Define this policy in this database**, you can choose the state the service should be in (Automatic, Manual, or Disabled) by default. By clicking **Edit Security**, you can apply more granular controls over who can start or stop the service.

The **Database Security** window is shown in Figure 13.12. For services not needed on the bastion host, set the services to **Disabled** and ensure that only the local administrator account has full control. You can allow authenticated users to read, start, stop, and pause the services if you think it's needed. When you're finished, click **OK** twice.

Figure 13.10 Services Policy

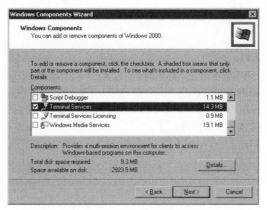

Figure 13.11 Service Security Policy Setting

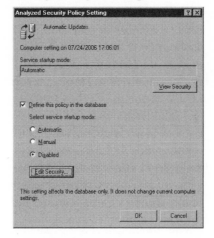

Figure 13.12 Services Security Policy

Microsoft has several guides that provide lists of suggested services that are needed depending on the role of the host system. For example, Table 4.11 of *The Microsoft Windows 2000 Security Hardening Guide* lists 46 services as the "minimum required." Of course, situations vary, but it provides a place to start your research and fine tuning. You can also find a variety of guides on the Web for disabling unneeded services. The key consideration for disabling unneeded services is to thoroughly test in a lab environment any applications that the bastion host will be running before you deploy the hardened policies to a production host.

Registry and File System ACLs

The Registry and File System settings allow you to configure specific access control lists (ACLs) on individual files, folders, or parts of the registry. These are the same permissions you could set by using the registry editor or the Security tab in the file properties. With some files, especially executables, you might find it advantageous to configure the ACL to deny the Everyone group access to those files. For other files, you might simply want to have a higher degree of auditing on their use.

To enable auditing on specific files, follow these steps;

1. In the left pane, navigate to the directory containing the file you want to audit. In this example we'll use **cmd.exe**, located in **C:\winNT\system32**.

2. Locate **cmd.exe** in the right pane and double-click the file.

3. Click **Edit Security**.

4. Configure the access settings for the file.

5. Click **Advanced**.

6. Select the **Auditing** tab at the top of the Access Control Settings for CMD.EXE window.

7. Click **Add**.

8. Select the group you want to audit access to CMD.EXE and click **OK**.

9. Place a check mark next to any events you want to audit—for example, **Traverse Folder/Execute File**.

10. Click **OK** four times to close all the windows.

Once you have configured all your policy settings to your satisfaction, you still need to apply those settings and save the template.

Applying the High-Security Policy

You can save your template by right-clicking **Security Configuration and Analysis** and selecting **Save**. This action does not *apply* the settings contained in the template; it only saves the template for future editing. To apply the settings, right-click **Security Configuration and Analysis** and select **Configure Computer Now**. You will be asked to verify the error log path. You may choose to provide a custom path and name or simply click **OK**. It is highly recommended that you choose a log filename that is meaningful to you, such as *New Password Policy.log*. Once the template has been applied to the system, you may begin testing the changes to make sure everything works properly. In the example, we configured auditing for execution of CMD.EXE. A screenshot of the generated log event is shown in Figure 13.13.

TIP

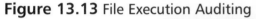

Many of the policy settings will take effect immediately, but some will take effect only after the system is rebooted. For this reason, is it recommended that you immediately reboot after making policy changes.

Figure 13.13 File Execution Auditing

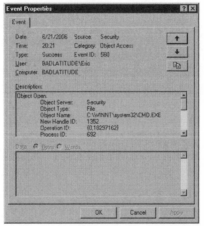

Configure Automatic Time Synchronization

Accurate system time is important to proper functioning of your bastion host. Without an accurate time setting, any logging will have unreliable time stamps. This will make any post mortem forensics difficult or impossible. Further, SSL and IPSec, two very common protocols found on bastion hosts, will fail if the system time is incorrect by a large enough margin. For this reason, you should have a way of securely maintaining an accurate system clock.

Plenty of third-party programs can use the Network Time Protocol (NTP) to keep the system time synchronized, but you can also do it with built-in tools. To use the Windows built-in time synchronization, you need to be running the Windows Time Service on the bastion host. When the Windows 2000 bastion host is a standalone server, this service is not configured to start automatically by default. You'll find an excellent article on Windows 2000

time settings at www.microsoft.com/technet/prodtechnol/Windows2000Pro/
maintain/w2kmngd/16_2kwts.mspx. The corresponding article for Windows 2003 can be
found at www.microsoft.com/technet/prodtechnol/windowsserver2003/technologies/secu-
rity/ws03mngd/26_s3wts.mspx. It's worth pointing out that synchronizing your time via
SNTP or NTP inside your DMZ is not advisable unless you also take steps to secure the
protocol. Different versions of NTP provide different levels of security, as follows:

- **NTPv1** No security features

- **NTPv2** Restrictions based on IP address, NTP traffic is unencrypted

- **NTPv3** Symmetric key encryption and authentication

- **NTPv4** Both symmetric encryption and PKI encryption

At the very least, you should configure the bastion host's time synchronization mechanism *not* to synchronize based on NTP broadcasts. This would allow an attacker to simply
broadcast false time updates to your bastion host. If your available time synchronization software does not provide the level of security you need, you can configure your NTP traffic to
use an encrypted IPSec tunnel to communicate with the time server.

Server and Domain Isolation

The recommended configuration for a bastion host is that it be a standalone server.
However, sometimes you can't configure things in the most secure way. Sometimes business
drivers and requirements require technical staff to make compromises on security. In the
event that you must implement your bastion host as a member of a domain, you can and
should take steps to provide as much isolation and protection as possible between the bastion
host and the domain controllers. One method to do this is through server and domain isolation. What follows is a *brief* overview of how server isolation and domain isolation work and
some of the pitfalls to be aware of when implementing them. For a detailed overview of
Microsoft's server and domain isolation methodology, see the TechNet website at
www.microsoft.com/sdisolation.

What Is Server and Domain Isolation?

In a nutshell, server and domain isolation are configurations whereby you can restrict
TCP/IP communications between trusted computers. You use Active Directory and Group
Policy to configure the permitted communications on the systems in question. This is
accomplished by establishing policy-enforced IPSec tunnels between isolated systems. They
are configured in such a way that the isolated systems can communicate with each other and
with other systems (even those not considered isolated), whereas systems that are not isolated
cannot initiate communications with the isolated systems. In this way you create a virtual
network that can act independently of the underlying topology. These methods are applicable
to Microsoft Windows XP, Microsoft Windows Server 2003, and Microsoft Windows 2000
Server (SP4 or later).

Domain isolation is accomplished by configuring domain member computers to accept only authenticated and secured communications from other domain member computers based on group policy settings. This configuration does not inhibit the domain computers from communicating to nondomain computers. As with many firewalls, by default the traffic is restricted inbound only; outbound communications are unhindered. *Server isolation* works the same way in that you configure the domain member server to accept only connections from other domain member computers, or if desired, only other domain member computers that are members of specific Active Directory security groups. The latter variation is called *group-specific server isolation*. Essentially, server isolation is IPSec policies defined via Group Policy Objects (GPOs). An excellent introductory paper can be downloaded from Microsoft here: www.microsoft.com/technet/itsolutions/network/sdiso/default.mspx.

How to Configure Server and Domain Isolation

The first step is to take an inventory of the network. You will need to evaluate several things, including what OS your systems are running, their logical communication requirements, and their positions in the Active Directory (AD) hierarchy. All these things will impact whether you can implement server and domain isolation as well as how it will be configured.

Performing a Host Assessment

Microsoft uses the terms *trustworthy* and *untrustworthy* to describe the functionality of the various operating systems within the scope of server and domain isolation (SDI). If the operating system is capable of natively supporting IPSec, belongs to an IPSec domain (AD), and can process the GPOs, it is considered trustworthy. Everything else is "untrustworthy" and will not be able to be included in an isolation group. These untrusted systems include OSs such as Windows 95, Windows 98, Windows ME, Windows NT, non-Microsoft OSs, or any machine regardless of its operating system that is not a member of a domain.

You will also need to verify domain membership for any hosts to include in an isolation group. As part of this verification, you should test that GPOs are being processed correctly by the host in question. The success or failure to process GPOs may be obvious during the day-to-day workload, but any systems that have issues will need to be corrected prior to implementing isolation. Otherwise, when you implement SDI, you could find that your systems cannot communicate properly.

Performing an Active Directory Assessment

The next step is to analyze your Active Directory structure. You will need to establish trusts between forests if you want hosts on different forests to be in the same isolation group. Domains will need to have trust relationships to properly manage IKE authentication. Your Organizational Unit (OU) structure will also impact implementation of isolation groups, since isolation groups are enforced via GPOs. This also impacts your planning, because GPOs are applied in order. The GPO defining the IPSec policy that is closest to the computer in the Active Directory domain structure will be used. Implementing SDI in a complex environment is not a trivial task.

Implementing Isolation Groups

Now that you know which hosts you are working with, you will need to determine group membership for these hosts. Communications between isolation groups can basically be broken down into the following categories;

- **Primary isolation domains** These are the bulk of the systems that will communicate securely with each other on a regular basis.

- **Untrusted systems** These are systems that are untrusted according to the previous guidelines.

- **Boundary isolation** These are systems that will be allowed to communicate with both trusted systems and untrusted systems. Conceptually, these systems are similar to systems found in a traditional network DMZ.

- **Exemption lists** These are untrusted systems that you want to allow trusted systems to communicate with, contrary to policy. Good examples here could be DNS servers or DHCP servers. With Windows 2000, these types of servers (infrastructure systems) must be on the exemption list; with Windows 2003, these servers can be included in the isolation domain.

You will need to define some groups that will be used to apply policy. Microsoft recommends separate groups for user accounts and computer accounts. By applying an isolation policy to a computer account that hosts an accounting application, you can ensure that isolation is enforced regardless of who logs into that machine. Similarly, by applying the isolation policies to a user account, you can require that users with administrative access use secured communications. Defining separate groups for user accounts and computer accounts allows you this level of flexibility in applying isolation policies. Although a given machine should not belong to more than one group, your users may well belong to multiple groups.

Creating the actual policies consists of three basic steps:

1. Create filter lists.
2. Create filter actions.
3. Create the IPSec policies.

Filter lists are basically access control lists that specify what traffic will need an action applied to it. You can define this traffic based on source or destination IP address, by protocol, or by TCP or UDP port numbers. *Filter actions* define how an IP packet is handled when it matches a filter list. Each filter action can have one of three security methods applied to it: Block, Permit, or Negotiate. The Block and Permit methods are self-explanatory. The Negotiate action will attempt to apply any of a series of security and cryptographic options in order of preference. You will also be able to set additional options on the policies to control the way a host responds to unencrypted traffic.

The IPSec policies also need to be defined via AD group policy. This is accomplished by defining the authentication methods used to establish trust between computers, the connection type, and whether or not the specific rule utilizes a tunnel configuration. The complete details for configuring these settings, as well as an in-depth explanation of the IPSec protocol, are beyond the scope of this book. You can find more information about Microsoft's IPSec support at www.microsoft.com/windowsserver2003/technologies/ networking/ipsec/default.mspx. Configure these settings via the IPSec Security Policy Management snap-in.

WARNING

Windows 2000 hosts support a limited number of IPSec policy types (three, to be exact). Windows 2003 or Windows XP systems support five additional policy types. If you need to apply policies to Windows 2000 hosts as part of your isolation groups, you should limit yourself to using only the three policy types that Windows 2000 supports (Local Policy, Active Directory Domain Policy, and Dynamic Policy).

The next step is the development of a deployment strategy. It is considered a best practice not to apply the policies to every system simultaneously. Create the appropriate GPOs for the IPSec policy, but remove the **Apply** right from the **Authenticated Users** group. Next configure the policies and assign them to GPOs. At this point, the new policies have not been distributed. Finally, place the computers to be included in the server and domain isolation design within the appropriate computer groups in the Group Policy. These systems will have read access to the GPOs. This approach provides control over when certain systems receive the new policy.

Despite the prospect of secured communications between hosts in isolation groups and the ability to enforce encryption at the host level, there are valid reasons to decide *not* to implement isolation groups. All the systems in the isolation groups will be doing additional authentication and possibly encryption, which will place additional strain on the processor, especially for high-throughput hosts. Although there are ways to mitigate the encryption overhead (such as NICs with integrated encryption chips), you should be aware of this potential issue. IPSec can also cause some protocols to fail. Notably the use of IKE via NAT can require the installation of patches on the OS. There are also some applications that simply don't work with IPSec due to the way they are written (such as including IP address in the data portion of the packet). IPSec is particularly problematic with hosts that are being load balanced. Finally, encrypted traffic between hosts will, by definition, prevent other devices from seeing the raw traffic. This will render ineffective many network inspection devices such as quality-of-service (QoS) devices, sniffers, and other troubleshooting tools.

As you can see, there are a host of potential hurdles to overcome in implementing isolation groups. Due to the SDI's complexity, extensive testing in a controlled lab should be a requirement before attempting changes on production systems. You need to develop a solid understanding of the underlying technologies and their implementation before applying that knowledge to your production network. Although isolation groups offer powerful functionality, it requires planning and caution to realize the benefits.

Remote Administration

The Remote Desktop Protocol (RDP) is the underlying protocol used to send screen images and other data across a Terminal Services session. It is worth noting that a Terminal Services session can be an entirely new session, meaning that you will not be able to interact with an existing, logged-on [user, or it can be a]session that can be shared with other users. The latter is far more common because it allows the support staff to see what the end user is seeing and more effectively diagnose the problem.

Using Terminal Services for Remote Administration (Windows 2000)

Terminal Services is the remote administration tool included in Windows 2000 Server, Windows XP, and Windows 2003. Because it allows you to act as though you were logged into the system directly, Terminal Services allows you to take full advantage of all the GUI applications for your administrative tasks. The Remote Desktop Protocol (RDP) is the underlying protocol used to send screen images and other data across a Terminal Services session. It is worth noting that a Terminal Services session can be an entirely new session, meaning that you will not be able to interact with an existing, logged-on user or a session that can be shared with other users. The latter is far more common because it allows the support staff to see what the end user is seeing and more effectively diagnose the problem.

Installing Terminal Services

On a Windows 2000 Server, follow these steps to install Terminal Services:

1. **Log on** as an administrator.
2. Go to the **Control Panel** and open the **Add /Remove Programs** tool.
3. Click **Add/Remove Windows Components**.
4. In the Windows Components dialog box, check **Terminal Services**.

5. If this machine is a standalone machine and you plan to publish applications from this terminal server, select the **Terminal Services Licensing** check box and click **Next**. If you will be using the Terminal Services functionality for remote administration only, you do *not* need to select this check box. This window is shown in Figure 13.14.

6. Choose the mode in which you want to run Terminal Services. There are two options, Remote Administration Mode or Application Server Mode. Then click **Next**, as shown in Figure 13.15.

Figure 13.14 Adding Terminal Services Components

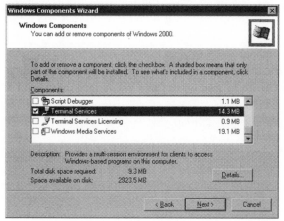

Figure 13.15 Terminal Services Modes

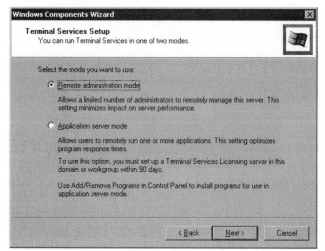

Once this process has been completed, you should discover that an additional service called Terminal Services is running. You will also have several new program shortcuts under Start | Programs | Administrative Tools. These are used for administrative tasks related to Terminal Services.

Securely Configuring Terminal Services

Administrative functions are often not given the attention they warrant when it comes to security. Although it is common knowledge that good passwords should be required for all systems on the network, administrative functions are sometimes performed via insecure methods. The assumption is that the host was in a relatively secure state before enabling Terminal Services, and therefore the next task will be to secure the Terminal Services functionality.

One obvious consideration is the level of encryption that will be used. The default behavior is to use 56-bit keys (Windows 2000) or 128-bit keys (Windows 2003), with the RC4 cipher to encrypt data flowing in both directions between the Terminal Services server and client. Although this approach *might* be adequate for trusted networks, for a bastion host you would want to increase the encryption strength. You should also change the default behavior for terminated sessions and some other settings, to be more secure. Follow these steps to secure Terminal Services settings:

1. Click **Start | Programs | Administrative Tools | Terminal Services Configuration**.

2. In the left pane of the snap-in window, select **Connections**.

3. In the right pane, double-click **RDP-Tcp** to open the Properties window (Figure 13.16).

Figure 13.16 Terminal Services Configuration

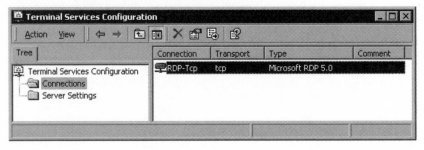

4. On the **General** tab of the RDP-Tcp Properties window, for **Encryption Level**, select **High** in the drop-down box (Figure 13.17). This choice will increase the size of the encryption key used, but it will not change the encryption algorithm.

Figure 13.17 RDP-Tcp Properties: General Tab

5. On the **Sessions** tab, check the box next to **Override user settings**, and set it to end a disconnected session after 1 minute.

6. Set the **Idle session limit** to something appropriate to your IT security policy, typically **10 minutes** or so.

7. Check the box next to **Override user settings** and set it to **End session** when session limit is reached or connection is broken (Figure 13.18).

Figure 13.18 RDP-Tcp Properties: Sessions Tab

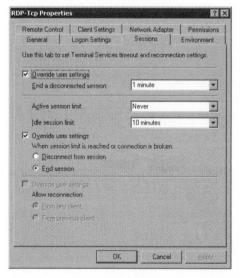

8. On the **Client Settings** tab in the Connection Section, uncheck **Use connection settings from user settings**, **Connect client printers at logon**, and **Default to main client printer**.

9. Under **Disable the following**, select all available check boxes (Figure 13.19).

Figure 13.19 RDP-Tcp Properties: Client Settings Tab

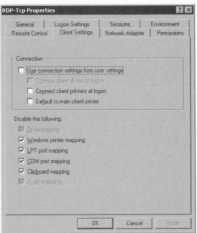

Remember, these settings represent the most secure configuration. You may have valid business justification to enable some of these. Just remember to take a minimalist approach and enable only what you need. In most cases, optional functionality such as remote printer redirection is not critical to performing the desired administrative tasks.

You also must evaluate weather the remote connection should be exposed to the Internet. Ideally, your administrative access can be granted only from internal IP ranges. If the administrator is not on the local LAN, he or she should be able to access the bastion host after being authenticated through some form of VPN and then connect to the bastion host. If you must expose Terminal Services to the Internet in general, it might be wise to change the TCP port that the terminal server is listening on for client connections. Generally speaking, hackers will recognize the default port of 3389 right away. Knowing this, they might spend a lot of effort trying to gain access to such a system. Changing the listening port doesn't make the service any more secure per se, but it might make it a little less of a target. If you set it to another well-known port, the attacker could assume that the listening service is the one commonly associated with that port and decide it's not worth attacking. This type of approach is usually referred to as *security through obscurity*. Some common examples are port 53 for DNS or port 22 for SSH.

Microsoft officially does not recommend changing the RDP port number, but it is relatively easy to do. To change the default port, you will need to follow a couple steps:

1. Go to **Start | Run** and enter **REGEDIT**.

2. Navigate to **HKEY_LOCAL_MACHINE\SYSTEM\CurrentControlSet\ Control\Terminal Server\WinStations\RDP-Tcp** in the left pane.

3. In the right pane, double click **PortNumber**.

4. Enter the new number you want to use (make sure you change it to decimal entry) and click **OK**.

You will then need to stop and start the Terminal Services service or reboot the machine for the changes to take effect. This process is covered in the Microsoft Knowledgebase article 187623. You will also need to change the port for the RDP *client*. Do this by exporting the connection information in the **Connection Manager** and editing the file with a plain text editor such as Notepad.exe. The entry for **ServerPort** should be changed to match the newly configured port; then reimport the file. If the client is Windows XP, you can simply specify the IP and port number at the Remote Desktop Connection window in the format *<IP>:<port>*.

NOTE

For further reading on RDP, you can find an in-depth article covering the most current version (RDP V5) on Microsoft's site: www.microsoft.com/windows2000/techinfo/howitworks/terminal/rdpfandp.asp.

Using RDP for Remote Administration (Windows 2003)

For Windows Server 2003, the task of remote administration is made simpler. RDP is installed by default, so all you need to do to enable remote administration is enable RDP and specify the users who are allowed to connect. The procedure to do this is outlined here:

1. Navigate to **Start | Control Panel | System**.

2. Select the **Remote** tab.

3. In the **Remote Desktop** section, check **Enable remote desktop on this computer**.

4. Click the **Select Remote Users** button and click **Add**.

5. Add any user accounts you desire to have remote desktop access.

6. Click **OK** three times to confirm your choices and finalize the changes.

Once RDP is enabled, the process for hardening the sessions is performed in the same manner as it is for Windows 2000, via **Start | Administrative Tools | Terminal Services Configuration**.

Bastion Host File Replication

As part of normal administrative tasks, it might be necessary to transfer files to and from the bastion host on occasion. The challenge in accomplishing this task is to do it in a secure manner with adequate authentication and encryption for the data being transferred. One method is to use the encryption for the Terminal Services session. If the Terminal Server is running Windows 2000 Server, it only supports client drive mappings via a Citrix ITA-based client, and those check boxes will be disabled automatically. You can get similar functionality through the RDPclip utility from Microsoft. It can be downloaded from ftp.microsoft.com/reskit/win2000/rdpclip.zip. Once you have downloaded it, simply decompress and run the included FXFRINST.bat on both the client and the Terminal Services server to install. This will allow you to share a common clipboard between the client and server.

Another alternative would be to enable FTP via an encrypted tunnel such as IPSec or SSL. Because *standard* FTP transfers all usernames, passwords, and data unencrypted, it should be avoided on the bastion hosts at all costs. This might be overkill for a functionality that will likely be infrequently used. The Secure Shell (SSH) often comes with a tool for secure file copy (SCP), which might be simpler to install and configure securely than an FTP server. SSH is discussed in more detail in the next section.

Command-Line Administration

If you can accomplish your administrative tasks on the command line without the benefit of a GUI, some additional options are available to you. Although Telnet is not encrypted, you can use IPSec to encrypt your Telnet session. This can be done via policies, in the same manner as configuring server isolation.

Another, more common method is via secure shell (SSH). SSH requires both an SSH client and an SSH server component. SSH is the industry standard for remote command-line access, and most systems come with it as part of the default install. Windows systems, however, are one among the few that do not. A variety of products, both commercial and free, is available to bring SSH functionality to Windows. One of the better-known commercial SSH clients is SecureCRT (www.vandyke.com). Most of the free versions are based on the OpenSSH (www.openssh.com) package, including a version for windows called PuTTY. Cygwin (www.cygwin.com) is a port of many UNIX tools for Windows, and it includes an SSH server. To add even more options, SSHWindows is a free package that installs only the minimum components of the Cygwin package to use SSH, SCP, and SFTP. Let's walk through setting up SSHWindows:

1. Download **SSHWindows** from sshwindows.sourceforge.net on the client and server.

2. Unzip the file, run the setup utility, and click **Finish**.

3. Under the directory where you installed OpenSSH for Windows, you must edit the **\etc\passwd** file.

4. If desired, create a separate group on the bastion host to hold users who will have access to SSH, and add the local user account of your admins.

5. Go to a command prompt, cd to the directory where you installed OpenSSH, and cd to the subdirectory **\bin**.

6. Enter the following command on the server to specify the groups that can connect via SSH: **mkgroup –l >> ..\etc\group**. This command will give *all* local groups permission to connect via SSH. You should open the group file and edit out any groups you do not want to have access.

7. Enter the following command on the server to specify a single account that is authorized to connect via SSH: **mkpasswd –l –u <accountname> >> ..\etc\passwd**. You must perform both these steps for SSH to work.

8. Edit the **Banner.txt** file located in \etc\ to match the banner specified by your IP security policy.

At this point you can connect to the remote system and access a command prompt over an encrypted session. Output from a successful connection is shown here:

```
I:\OpenSSH\bin>ssh sshuser@192.168.1.101
************ WARNING BANNER HERE ************
sshuser@192.168.1.101's password:
Last login: Sat Jun 24 20:05:22 2006 from 192.168.1.99
Could not chdir to home directory /home/SSH: No such file or directory
Microsoft Windows 2000 [Version 5.00.2195]
(C) Copyright 1985-2000 Microsoft Corp.

C:\OpenSSH>ipconfig

Windows 2000 IP Configuration

Ethernet adapter Local Area Connection:

        Connection-specific DNS Suffix  . : rr.com
        IP Address. . . . . . . . . . . . : 192.168.1.101
        Subnet Mask . . . . . . . . . . . : 255.255.255.0
        Default Gateway . . . . . . . . . : 192.168.1.1
```

This is the sample output from sending a file to the bastion host (192.168.1.101) via SCP:

```
I:\Internet\OpenSSH\bin>scp sample.txt sshuser@192.168.1.101:/
*********** WARNING BANNER HERE ************
sshuser@192.168.1.101's password:
Could not chdir to home directory /home/SSHUser: No such file or directory
sample.txt                              100% 1735     1.7KB/s   00:00
```

TIP

Although the SSH port in SSHWindows uses standard CMD.exe syntax, the *SCP* command and the *SFTP* command both use Unix-style paths. Also of note is the fact that unless it is configured differently, the SSH connection will assume that the directory you installed OpenSSH into is the starting root for client connections.

Bastion Host Configurations

At this point in the process of building your bastion host, you have a server that is at least minimally secure. Your bastion host is probably up to the task of being exposed on the Internet, but it is lacking one important feature. At this time the bastion host isn't really configured to *do* anything, it's just a base server build with remote administration enabled. Some of the most common functions for a bastion host are Web server, mail server, and DNS server as well as screening gateway. Here we discuss in detail the steps required to get your bastion host running as a secure Web server or mail server.

Configuring an IIS5 Server for Web Access

Microsoft's product for providing Web services is Internet Information Services (IIS). With the tight integration IIS offers with the underlying (Windows) operating system, many people find IIS a compelling choice to use as their Web server. IIS in its default configuration is not secure, however. The emphasis is on ease of use, not security. With proper planning and a little effort, IIS can serve as a secure public Web server.

Setting Up an Anonymous Public Web Site

IIS is an integral component of the Windows server platform if it is not installed during the initial system installation, simply navigate to **Start | Settings | Control Panel | Add/Remove Programs** and click **Add/Remove Windows Components**. Place a check mark next to **Internet Information Services (IIS)** or highlight it and select details. By checking all of IIS, you will likely install some components you might not need. At a minimum you need Common Files and World Wide Web Server, which will also automatically select the Internet Information Services Snap-in. When you're finished with your selections, click **OK** and click **Next**.

Once this is done, you will need to open the IIS snap-in in the MMC console. You can go to your saved MMC console and add it following the steps you used previously, or navigate to **Start | Programs | Administrative Tools | Internet Services Manager**. In the left pane of the MMC, double-click your server name, which will expand the view. Then highlight **Default Web Site**. You'll notice many of the paths use C:\inetpub, which is the default for IIS. Because this is the default and many automated hacking programs expect the default setting, we will want to change the default to something else. Follow these steps to create a new WWW instance in a nondefault location:

1. Right-click the **Default Web Site**, and select **Stop**.

2. Now remove it entirely by right-clicking again and selecting **Delete** and then **Yes** at the "Are you Sure?" prompt.

3. Create a new directory to serve as the WWW root, preferably not on the C: drive if possible.

4. In the left pane of the MMC, highlight the server name and select **New | Web Site**. This will begin the Web Site Creation Wizard.

5. Click **Next**, type a description for the Web site, and click **Next** again.

6. The next screen is **IP Address and Port Settings**. Typically, you can leave the settings on this screen at the defaults and click **Next**.

7. Enter the path to the home directory. In this example, create a new directory called C:\newWWW (or more preferably, D:\newWWW, or whatever drive letter you like if you have another physical disk in the system) and click **Next**. Leave **Allow Anonymous Access to this Site** checked if you need to allow anyone to access the site without logging in.

8. On the **Web site Access Permissions** page, you will need to leave the defaults (Read & Run Scripts) checked if you plan on using Active Server Pages (.asp). If not, you only need to check **Read**. When you're done with your selections, click **Next** and **Finish**.

Once this process is completed, the new site has been created. If you were to place an index file in the newWWW directory, you could connect to the server and view it via a Web browser. If you select the new site in the left pane of the MMC, you can see that many default WWW folders have been created for the new Web site. The next step is to lock down the configuration so that it cannot be exploited. To be safe, select the site again, and right-click and select **Stop** so that the new site is inaccessible. It is now secured.

Configuring an IIS6 Server for Web Access

The process for configuring IIS6 is very similar to the one used to configure IIS5. Navigate to **Start | Settings | Control Panel | Add/Remove Programs** and click **Add/Remove Windows Components**. Place a check mark next to **Application Server**. By default, all the minimum IIS components should be selected, but you can click details to verify the selected components. When you are satisfied, click **Next** and **Finish**. Next, add the **Internet Information Services (IIS) Manager snap-in** to your MMC console. To change the default Web root directory, follow these steps:

1. In the left pane of the MMC, expand the tree under IIS and the local machine name. Then expand **Web Sites**, and highlight the **Default Web Site**.

2. Right-click and select **Delete**.

3. Right-click the **Web Sites** folder and select **New | Web Site**, which will start the wizard.

4. Click **Next** and enter a description for the Web site, then click **Next**.

5. Enter the desired IP address to use, alter the TCP port to use (if desired), enter any host header information (if desired), and click **Next**.

6. On the next screen, click to browse to the path to the new Web root directory you have chosen, and click **Next**.

7. Select the desired permissions for the Web site. If you don't need any type of scripting support, you can leave it at **Read** and click **Next**.

8. Click **Finish**.

You should not be able to browse to your new Web site.

The IIS Lockdown Tool

The IIS Lockdown tool is a very useful tool Microsoft produces to help secure IIS via a scripted process. The first thing you need to do to take advantage of this tool is to download it from Microsoft at www.microsoft.com/technet/security/tools/locktool.mspx. It comes in the form of an executable; when it is executed, it starts the Internet Information Services Lockdown Wizard. To use the wizard, follow these steps:

1. Click **Next**.

2. Select **I Agree** at the End User License Agreement (EULA) screen, and then click **Next**.

3. The next screen is **Select Server Template**. If you choose any of the listed options, the Lockdown tool will preconfigure the settings for any known product requirements. These are high-level settings intended to be as generic as possible. It is very likely that you will need to fine-tune the settings when the wizard com-

pletes. If you need the Web server to serve in multiple listed roles, you should select **Other**. Leave **View template settings** checked and click **Next**. For our example, we will select **Dynamic Web Server (ASP enabled)**.

4. On the next screen, place a check next to any of the services you want to enable. Unchecked services will be disabled. If you check the **Remove unselected services at the bottom** option, unchecked services will be disabled *and* removed. The most secure approach is to check this option and remove any services you don't need, although at this point there shouldn't be any you didn't plan on using anyway. In this case we just left **Web service (HTTP)** checked and clicked **Next**.

5. The Script Maps window allows you to disable support for individual script types. The default should disable everything *except* Active Server Pages. Assuming these settings fit your needs, just click **Next**.

6. The **Additional Security** window has some very strong defaults. Unless you need something, leave these defaults and click **Next**.

7. URLScan is a great tool which does exactly that. It filters URLs as they are requested from the server and will block them according to a filter criteria you specify. Leave **Install URLScan filter on the server** checked and click **Next**.

8. Click **Next** to approve your selections and begin the lockdown process. Once it's finished, click **Next** again and **Finish**.

Finally, all that is needed is a few manual tweaks to the configurations. The next step is to fine-tune the URLScan tool.

NOTE

If you are using IIS 6.0, it includes built-in functionality that duplicates most of what the URLScan tool can do for you. Odds are good you won't need the URLScan tool at all with IIS 6.0, but if you choose to use it, only V2.5 is supported. You can read more about V2.5 and view a comparison with the built-in functionality of IIS 6.0 at www.microsoft.com/technet/security/tools/urlscan.mspx.

The URLScan Tool

The URLScan tool exists in a few different versions. There is one that comes with the IIS Lockdown tool (V2.0). You can also download a separate version that is V2.5. The added features in V2.5 are:

- **Change log file directory** Allows you to change the log directory instead of using the default.

- **Log long URLs** By default, the log lines are truncated to 1024 bytes.

- **Restrict the size of requests** Allows you to set limits on content length, URL length, and query string length.

If you need any of these functions, you will need to download and install the newest URLScan tool separately from the IIS Lockdown tool. By default, the URLScan log file and .ini file, which controls the way URLScan behaves, are located in %SystemRoot% \system32\inetsrv\urlscan.ini. The .ini file is heavily commented and fairly easy to understand. You should edit it to suit your specific needs and fine-tune the way URLScan works. The following are some of the more important security options within the .ini file:

- *UseAllowVerbs=* Setting this option to 1 or 0 basically determines whether the server is working off a white list or a black list approach. If you set it to 1, you must then specify all verbs that are allowed. Anything not explicitly specified in the .ini file will be denied (white list). If you set it to 0, you can specify a list of explicitly blocked verbs, and anything not explicitly blocked will be permitted (black list).

- *RemoveServerHeader=* Setting this option to 1 will cause the Web server to remove the server header from all responses. This is generally a more secure way to run, since telling attackers which Web server you're running only helps them narrow their selection of attacks to attempt. Another philosophy is to set it to 0, causing the server to send a server header, and then specify false information in the header by using the *AlternateServerName=* setting. You could, for example, claim in the header that you were running Apache instead of IIS. Again, this is *security through obscurity*.

Final Configuration Steps

The next step is to configure your Web site logging. If you choose to download the newest URLScan tool, you can specify the same logging directory for the URLScan tool as the Web site. Configure logging for the Web server by performing the following steps:

1. Open the **Internet Information Services** MMC plug-in. Highlight the server name in the left pane.

2. Right-click and select **Properties**.

3. On the **Internet Information Services** tab, in the **Master Properties** section, click **Edit**.

4. On the **Web Site** tab, make sure the check box next to **Enable Logging** is checked.

5. Click **Properties**.

6. In the **WWW Service Master Properties** window, at the bottom click **Browse** and set the logging directory to the one you have chosen, as shown in Figure 13.20.

7. Click **OK** three times to finalize the changes.

Figure 13.20 Specify Logging Directory

On the **Directory Security** tab, in the **Anonymous Access and Authentication Control** (**Authentication and Access Control** in IIS 6) section, click **Edit**. Make sure **Integrated Windows Authentication** is *unchecked* at the bottom. Because this server is for anonymous access, there is no need to allow the Web users to authenticate (or attempt to authenticate) with the Windows authentication system. This window is shown in Figure 13.21.

Figure 13.21 Disable Integrated Windows Authentication

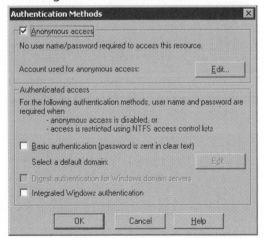

Next, on the **Home Directory** tab, click **Configuration** and then select the **App Debugging** tab. In the **Script Error Messages** section, select **Send Text error message to client**. If you leave the default, which is to send detailed messages to the client, you can provide an attacker with more detailed errors that he can use to refine his attacks. As is usually the case, the less information the attacker has, the better.

Setting Up a Secure Web Site

Often, if the contents of the Web pages need to be kept private in transit, you will want to enable some type of HTTP encryption. This is usually accomplished via Secure Sockets Layer (SSL). Those pages protected with SSL are denoted in the URL with *https://* instead of the normal *http://*. To enable SSL on the Web server, you will need a Server Certificate. Then you can make the necessary configuration changes on the server as follows:

1. Open the **Properties** for the Web site in the **IIS snap-in**.

2. Select the **Directory Security** tab and click **Server Certificate**.

3. This will start the **Web Server Certificate Wizard**. Click **Next**.

4. On the next screen you have the option to create your own certificate, assign an existing certificate, or import a certificate. If you need to present your site to third parties, you might need to get a certificate issued from a trusted third party, such as VeriSign.

   - If you select **Create a New certificate**, you will be given the option of preparing the request now to send later, or sending the request immediately over the Internet.

   - If you select **Assign an existing certificate**, you will be presented with a screen to select which certificate you want to use.

   - The **Import** option allows you to browse to and use a key in the form of a .key file. Once you have your certificate, you can go back and use the Import feature on the same wizard.

5. After the certificate has been imported, go to the same Properties screen again. On the **Directory Security** tab, select **Edit** in the **Secure Communications** section.

6. Check **Require secure channel (SSL)** and **Require 128-bit encryption**, and click **OK** twice to exit.

Configuring an IIS Server for SMTP

If needed, IIS can also server as a proxy for Internet e-mails. The IIS server can be configured to be the gateway for e-mail as it passes into or out of your protected network. This is a common configuration and offers increased security by not exposing your internal mail servers directly to the Internet. To enable SMTP on your IIS servers, follow these steps:

1. Navigate to **Control Panel | Add/Remove Programs | Add/Remove Windows Components**.

2. Highlight **Internet Information Services (IIS)** and click **Details**.

3. Check **SMTP Service** and click **OK**.

4. Click **Next** twice and then **Finish** after the files are installed.

5. Create directories and set permission on them to house a site root directory, a directory for mail with errors, and a logging directory.

6. In the MMC, the server name will have a new item under it called **Default SMTP Virtual Server**. Right-click it and select **Properties**.

7. On the **General** tab, make sure **Enable Logging** is checked.

8. Click **Properties** and then **Browse** to configure the directory to hold the SMTP logs.

9. Select the **Extended Properties** tab, and select as much information as your resources will allow. At a minimum you should log the **date, time, client IP address, user name, method, URI stem**, and **host agent**.

10. Click **OK**.

11. On the **Messages** tab, click **Browse** to configure the bad mail directory. IIS will place a copy of messages that could not be delivered or returned in this directory.

12. Click **OK**.

13. With the **Default SMTP Virtual Server** still highlighted in the left pane, right-click **Domains** in the right pane, and select **New | Domain**. This will start the new domain wizard.

14. Select **Remote** and click **Next**.

15. Enter the name of any domains that this SMTP server should process mail for. You can use asterisks for high-level domain names (i.e. *.microsoft.com). Click **Finish**.

16. Double-click and highlight **domains** in the left pane, then right-click the newly created domain in the right pane, and select **Properties**.

17. On the **General** tab, check **Allow incoming mail to be relayed to this domain**.

18. In the **Route domain** section, select the radio button to **forward all mail to smart host**. Enter the name of your exchange server and click **OK**.

19. Stop and restart the SMTP service for the changes to take effect.

Bastion Host Maintenance and Support

It cannot be stressed enough that completing these procedures does not mean your host is 100-percent secure. Even if you could theoretically take steps to protect your host from every exploit known today, there will be new ones discovered tomorrow. Security is an ongoing process. Your bastion hosts are a critical piece of your infrastructure and are one of the most visible targets in the organization for hackers to come after. You must have a schedule for security patches and updates as well as a schedule to review security logs and investigate anomalies. You should have a schedule for regular penetration tests and vulnerability scans, and the test results should be reviewed and researched. A bastion host is one of the most well protected parts of the network; it takes vigilance and effort to keep it safe on the Internet.

Windows Bastion Host Checklist

The following checklist provides a high-level summary of the steps needed to secure your Windows bastion host:

- Plan your hard disk partitioning layout.

- Perform a clean install of the OS.

- Update the system with the latest service packs and hotfixes.

- Remove unneeded system components.

- Configure local user accounts, renaming the defaults and creating new ones as appropriate.

- Customize and apply the high-security template.

- Configure time synchronization.

- Evaluate and configure IPSec policies if desired.

- Configure remote administration.

- Configure and lock down bastion host functional software.

- Perform routine maintenance and security testing.

Summary

Configuring a Windows server as a bastion host can be done, but it requires some planning and effort. With proper configuration, the Windows server can be just as secure in the role of bastion host as any other operating system. Further, the host of GUI tools and tight integration of tools can be a valuable asset in managing a complex configuration. The entire process of hardening a system to serve as a bastion host has to be done in the context of the role the host will serve and its place in the perimeter of your network.

Solutions Fast Track

Configuring Bastion Hosts

- ☑ Think minimalist, and be cognizant of the bastion host's role in all design decisions.
- ☑ Establish a security baseline. You have to know where you are to know how to get somewhere.

Configuration Fundamentals

- ☑ Do the up-front planning for things like server type (domain member or standalone), disk partitions, and other issues *before* you are sitting in front of a computer screen making choices.
- ☑ Perform a clean install and apply all operating system updates and patches.
- ☑ Configure accounts and security settings to suit your needs and limit exposures.
- ☑ Configure audit policy and log management settings so that you will know when something unusual or out of the ordinary occurs.

Remote Administration

- ☑ Determine whether you need a GUI for remote administration and if so, configure it as securely as possible. Use only encrypted protocols for all remote administrative tasks.
- ☑ Configure command-line remote access using encrypted protocols for all communications.
- ☑ Configure a means of transferring files for administrative purposes, and be sure to use encryption for all communications.

Sample Bastion Hosts Configurations

- ☑ Configure your bastion host as a Web server, hardening the default configuration into something that can last on the Internet.
- ☑ Configure your bastion host as an SMTP relay to securely act as your mail server's interface to the outside world without being compromised.

Ongoing Maintenance and Security Assessments

☑ Remember that all these processes should be repeated or at least verified regularly as part of an ongoing security program.

Frequently Asked Questions

The following Frequently Asked Questions, answered by the authors of this book, are designed to both measure your understanding of the concepts presented in this chapter and to assist you with real-life implementation of these concepts. To have your questions about this chapter answered by the author, browse to **www.syngress.com/solutions** and click on the **"Ask the Author"** form.

Q: Aren't there other, more secure operating systems besides Windows to use as a bastion host?

A: Microsoft often takes a bad rap in the media. Truthfully, at one time all Microsoft's efforts went toward making things easier to use, with security taking a back seat. Today, a Windows server *can* be just as secure as any other OS. The other OS might come with default settings that are more secure out of the box, but if you take advantage of the tools Microsoft provides, you can successfully harden your Windows server.

Q: What role does "out-of-band" management play for bastion hosts in a DMZ?

A: An out-of-band or management network can be useful for the bastion hosts. It allows you to move some of your management sessions completely out of the prying eyes of the DMZ. It's worth remembering that if a bastion host is compromised, the management network might have just became an extension of the external (untrusted) network. So all the appropriate security controls should be in place for the management network as though it were a DMZ itself. Otherwise, by adding a management network, you could be increasing your overall risk instead of reducing it.

Q: If IIS 6.0 has all the same features as the URLScan tool V2.5, why would I use the URLScan tool?

A: In most cases, you wouldn't. From a feature perspective, there probably isn't much reason to use the URLScan tool *if* you are running IIS6. About the only reason is if policies and/or procedures are such that the URLScan tool is entrenched and changing the configuration methods poses more trouble than it's worth.

Chapter 14

Linux Bastion Hosts

Solutions in this chapter:

- **System Installation**
- **Minimizing Services**
- **Additional Hardening Steps**
- **Controlling Access to Resources**
- **Auditing Access to Resources**
- **Sample Linux Host Configurations**

☑ **Summary**

☑ **Solutions Fast Track**

☑ **Frequently Asked Questions**

Introduction

The general concepts behind hardening a Linux bastion host are no different than they are for any other OS. You still need to minimize the installed software, update and patch the OS, and tighten the security settings. It is only the specific methods for accomplishing these tasks that vary with a Linux-based bastion host over a Windows-based one. The basic approach to hardening *any* bastion host (whether Linux, UNIX, Windows, or other) can be summarized in the following *high-level* steps:

1. Planning comes before doing.

2. Remember the bastion host's role during all stages.

3. Leave only the minimum components on the system to get the job done.

4. Take what's left and make it as secure as possible, avoiding default settings where practical.

In some ways, securing Linux to serve as a bastion host can be harder than if you were using a Microsoft product, because there are so many options. If you aren't thoroughly comfortable with the landscape, the task of sorting out what tool and configuration to use can seem daunting. On the flip side, this same weakness—Linux's extreme flexibility—is also its main strength. Those same bewildering number of options provide you with near-infinite flexibility in how you accomplish your objectives. In this chapter we walk through the steps for hardening a Linux computer and preparing it to serve in the role of bastion host. We cover the specific steps you need to take and contrast those with the same steps you would use on a Windows system. It is assumed that the reader has read or is at least familiar with the chapter on Windows bastion hosts and that the reader has at least moderate understanding of and experience using Linux.

System Installation

With various flavors of Linux becoming so popular, deciding to use Linux as the OS for your bastion host has never been easier than it is today. The Internet is overflowing with helpful articles and Web sites to help guide you through setting up a Linux system. Many vendors are offering brand-new systems with Linux already installed. Several distributions of Linux are specifically configured to be user friendly and help a novice learn the ins and outs of Linux. We will go through the steps of hardening your Linux system on the assumption that you are installing it from scratch. If it is preinstalled on your system, you will need to evaluate whether starting over with a clean install with settings you choose is worth the effort. If you inherited the system, starting over might not be an option, but many of these procedures can still serve as good guidelines for how you can lock down your newly inherited system.

Disk Partitions

Unlike Windows, Linux has some specific requirements for disk partitions. All the applications that could be running at any given time can require a considerable amount of RAM to run. Typically, more memory is required than the machine has physically installed. Fortunately, operating systems have a technique to make it appear that more memory is present using *swap space*. This swap space is presented to the application as though it were more RAM. In Windows, the swap space is in the form of a swap file, which by default is located on the same partition as the system partition. Linux, on the other hand, expects the swap space to be on a separate physical partition. This swap partition actually gets formatted specifically as a Linux swap partition, not as a standard file system. Some Linux distributions allow you to use a normal file for swap space, like Windows, but using a separate swap partition provides some significant performance increases and increased stability.

The amount of swap space that is needed will vary based on the programs that are loaded and the functionality you are using in them. When you use a swap file, this means the size of the file will need to change regularly, causing increased reads and writes to the disk, above and beyond what is needed to manage the program data, simply to manage the swap file itself. By contrast, if you have a separate swap partition, there is no disk activity to manage the swap file, only the activity required by the programs using the swap space. Stability can be enhanced using a separate swap partition as well. If the partition containing your swap file fills up with data, it can prevent the swap file from growing and providing the needed swap space for a newly loaded program. A dedicated partition for the swap space provides the desired isolation from user data and ensures that the swap space will be available.

Choosing a Linux Version

Because there are so many different versions of Linux available, you have a lot of choices here. The different versions may have some of the same core components, but each offers different sets of software packages, often with an emphasis on a particular type of functionality, such as security testing, general office productivity, or software development platforms. These variations are called *distributions,* or sometimes even *distros* for short. A good source of information on the various distributions is www.distrowatch.com. This site includes a brief summary of what the distribution is trying to accomplish and includes links to the home-pages and download locations. You can, of course, always do a Google search to find a distribution that does exactly what you are looking for. For a locally installed full installation, Fedora core (which we examine in the examples in this chapter) provides a lot of features and has extensive support documentation. If you just want to dabble, a live CD, such as SLAX, is a very user-friendly way to get your feet wet with Linux.

Choosing Distribution Media

One of the really nice features that Linux has over Windows is that it can be run from a variety of media. You can find distributions that are capable of running off a CD-ROM, full installs to the systems hard disk, and distributions that can run off a USB drive or even a floppy disk. Each media type offers some security pros and cons, and not every distribution is available on every media type. If you need the features of a specific distribution that doesn't come on the media you prefer, you might need to make a compromise. The decisions of media type and distribution selection will be made concurrently, unless you have some very specific requirements. You will need to research the media options and choose one that fits your environment; we review some of the pros and cons of each type in the following sections.

Full Installs

With the traditional install to the systems hard disk, much like Windows, you will boot up an installation CD and walk through a guided install process. Although it wasn't always the case, most of the distributions that are intended to be installed to the hard disk offer GUI install programs that are pretty easy to get through. There is no great advantage to using this type of distribution other than the size of the hard disk will allow you to install a lot of extra software. In a DMZ on a bastion host, this isn't necessarily desirable, and in many cases one of the smaller, more streamlined distributions would be more appropriate.

On the down side, this type of install will have all the same disadvantages of a Windows bastion host—namely, that the entire system is sitting on the hard drive, and if an attacker manages to compromise the root account, she will be able to install a virus or Trojan on the system that can survive future reboots, in addition to tampering with the contents of what is running in memory. Typically, if you discover that your bastion host has been compromised, unless you have some means of ensuring that the contents of the hard disk have not been tampered with, you must reinstall the entire system from scratch to guarantee the system's integrity. This type of install isn't really any better or worse than if you were using Windows for your bastion host operating system.

CD-ROMs

You can get Windows running off a bootable CD-ROM, but it takes a lot more work than it does with Linux. There are many versions of Linux designed specifically to run from a CD-ROM, allowing you to turn virtually any machine into a firewall, router, or general-purpose PC. There is an obvious security advantage to having all your configuration information on read-only media. Even if a hacker manages to compromise the system, all it takes is a reboot and your configuration can be restored to its previous condition. The system can still fall victim to a virus or Trojan but only until it is rebooted. Further, if there is a hardware failure, restoring the system is only as difficult as moving the CD to a new system and rebooting.

This same advantage also serves as a disadvantage. If you burn the entire OS and configuration settings to a CD, any time you need to make any adjustment you would need to burn and load a new CD-ROM disk. The cost of the CD media probably isn't an issue, because CD-ROMs are inexpensive, but such a configuration could hinder your ability to remotely administer the system. You would only be able to remotely make changes to the running configuration, whereas changes that will remain after a reboot will require someone local to burn and swap the CDs. If you needed to implement and test changes that required a reboot before they will take effect, this type of setup would make things a little more difficult. Finally, due to simple space limitations on a CD-ROM, you might not be able to fit all the needed software or functionality on a CD. All that being said, if the role of your bastion host allows the configuration and data to be relatively static, a live CD could be a very attractive option.

USB Drives

A Linux bastion host booting from a USB disk could offer the best compromise in security and flexibility. If you purchase a USB disk that includes a physical write-protect switch, you can make changes on the fly, as with a live system, and then write-protect the disk against modification when you are done. As the storage capacity of USB drives increases, you will be able to use a USB-based distribution that includes increasingly greater functionality. Whether you get the micro hard drive version or the solid-state USB disk, either will be more reliable than a diskette while offering the same benefit of allowing you to toggle the write-protect feature.

Diskettes

Although they probably won't be able to provide the functionality you are looking for in a Linux bastion host, many versions of Linux can fit on a 3.5-inch diskette. The primary advantage of these distributions is their very low resource requirements. Often these systems require only 8MB or 16MB of memory to function. The ability to toggle the write-protect switch on the diskette can also provide a high degree of configuration flexibility and security. Considering the unreliable nature of diskettes, they probably wouldn't be appropriate for any critical roles, though. Another disadvantage to diskettes is simply functionality. Whereas they can act as a simple router or firewall, they typically lack much in the way of features. Generally, these diskette-based distributions are single-purpose devices. Due to the space restrictions and small footprint, diskette-based distributions are almost always command line only, with no GUI for configuration or management.

Choosing a Specific Distribution

In conjunction with choosing the media to be used, you will need to choose the exact Linux distribution you want to employ. This decision can include a host of factors such as included features, personal preference, availability of documentation and support, and availability of technical support. Some distributions are known for being more beginner friendly or for supporting better security controls. One of the key differentiators for selecting a Linux distribution as a bastion host is technical support. Some distributions, such as Red Hat Enterprise Linux, are available with full technical support, which can be a major consideration for a corporate bastion host.

Once you have selected your preferred distribution, you should go through the installation process. If you are presented with any choices to install additional software, select **No**. We want to keep things to a minimum because our next steps will be removing any unnecessary software. The following steps assume you have the base Linux operating system installed and functional. I used the latest Fedora Core distribution for screenshots (V5) with the default GNOME window manager, but the procedures should be similar for most distributions.

Removing Optional Components

Windows has been the target of much scrutiny and ridicule for the size of its installation. Typically, Linux is seen as sleek and efficient. Well, this is partially true. The fact is that out of the box, if you don't take care to remove components, Linux can be pretty bloated. The default install of Fedora with none of the high-level optional software categories selected was just shy of 2GB, which isn't all that slim. The key difference between Linux and Windows is that with Linux you *can* remove or disable unneeded components (even including parts of the kernel itself) and strip the system down to a very lean and efficient machine. By contrast, tampering with the core OS files in Windows isn't really an option for most people.

Minimizing Services

Like a Windows system, your chosen Linux distribution will likely be installed with a large number of programs configured to run automatically, without human intervention. On Windows systems these programs are called *services;* on Linux they are called *daemons.* In an effort to minimize the amount of software that is running and thus reduce the number of software targets a hacker might try to exploit, you should disable any daemons that are not needed. Determining which daemons are needed will require some investigation and testing.

You'll find a list and brief description of daemons in Fedora Core 5 at www.mjmwired.net/resources/mjm-services-fc5.html.

To configure the daemons, navigate to **System | Administration | Services**. (Fedora actually uses the Windows terminology to refer to the daemons as *services*.) This will open the GUI interface shown in Figure 14.1.

Figure 14.1 Daemon Control Panel

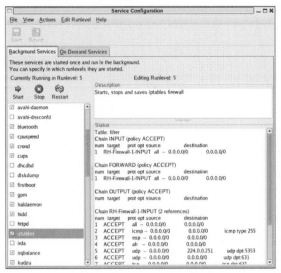

Highlighting a service in the leftmost pane will pull up a description and some additional details in the Description and Status panes, respectively. Disabling a service is as easy as removing the check mark next to the service in question, then clicking **Save** in the upper-right corner of the window and rebooting.

> **NOTE**
>
> Different services are handled differently with respect to the time at which your changes take effect. When changes are made to services managed through *xinetd*, *xinetd* is immediately restarted; thus your changes will take effect immediately. When the service is *not* managed by *xinetd*, the same is not true. In those cases you will need to either stop the service manually, go to a command prompt, type **telinit** *<runlevel>* and press **Enter** to reinitialize the run level, or simply reboot.

If you are administering the bastion host without access to a GUI front end, you will need to control daemons via the startup scripts. It's also a good idea to know how to control the daemons without the GUI because the GUI interface will vary from system to system. The methods for startup scripts can also vary from one distribution to another. The startup services in Fedora Core are managed by startup scripts located in /etc/rc.d/init.d. All you need to do is comment out the line that calls the specific script by inserting a # at the front of the line that calls it. You can also edit the individual scripts themselves for control of the way the services are initialized. The preferred way on Fedora Core is to use the *chkconfig* utility, which can be found in many distributions. You must be logged in as root to use this utility. Abbreviated output from *chkconfig --list* is shown in Figure 14.2.

Figure 14.2 Listing Services with *chkconfig*

```
[root@localhost ~]# chkconfig --list
NetworkManager  0:off   1:off   2:off   3:off   4:off   5:off   6:off
acpid           0:off   1:off   2:off   3:on    4:on    5:on    6:off
anacron         0:off   1:off   2:on    3:on    4:on    5:on    6:off
apmd            0:off   1:off   2:on    3:on    4:on    5:on    6:off
atd             0:off   1:off   2:off   3:on    4:on    5:on    6:off
autofs          0:off   1:off   2:off   3:on    4:on    5:on    6:off
avahi-daemon    0:off   1:off   2:off   3:on    4:on    5:on    6:off
avahi-dnsconfd  0:off   1:off   2:off   3:off   4:off   5:off   6:off
bluetooth       0:off   1:off   2:on    3:on    4:on    5:on    6:off
cpuspeed        0:off   1:on    2:on    3:on    4:on    5:on    6:off
crond           0:off   1:off   2:on    3:on    4:on    5:on    6:off
```

As you can see, *apmd* (which is used for monitoring and logging the battery status) is configured to start for run levels two through five. Since our bastion host has no battery to monitor, we can *disable apmd* for all run levels by entering:

```
chkconfig --level 123456 apmd off
```

If you want to *remove* the service entirely form the startup script, type:

```
chkconfig –del apmd
```

Removing Optional Software

As with Windows, you will also likely end up with some software you don't need. Removing the software is most easily accomplished with Pirut, the built-in GUI tool you can access by navigating to **Applications | Add/Remove Software**. Once it finishes checking what is currently installed on the system, you see the Package Manager window, which allows you to search for packages, install packages, or remove them. When you use the

Browse button, your interface is hierarchical and looks almost exactly like the one you used to install the operating system. The Package Manager window is shown in Figure 14.3.

Figure 14.3 Package Manager

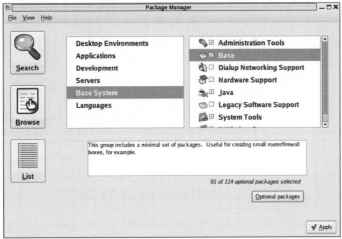

To remove the aforementioned *apmd* package, highlight the **Base System** category in the left pane, and then highlight the **Base** group in the right pane. Click **Optional packages** and a new window will open showing all packages in the **Base** group, as shown in Figure 14.4. Simply clear the check mark next to **apmd** and click **Close**. Back at the **Package Manager** window, click **Apply**. Click **Continue** on the next window to verify your changes, and finally, click **OK** when the update is completed.

Figure 14.4 Package Listing

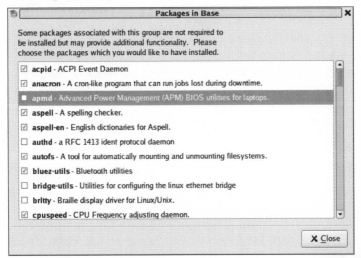

Packages can also be managed from the command line using the RPM Package Manager (RPM). You can view a list of all installed packages by entering:

```
rpm -q -a
```

For example, to install the *apmd* package, you would need to first obtain the package file itself (from www.redhat.com/download/mirror.html, for example) or use the RPMs that were included on the installation CDs. Then enter the following command to install *apmd*:

```
rpm -i apmd-3.2.2-3.2.i386.rpm
```

If the installation is successful, you should see output similar to the following;

```
Preparing...              ########################################### [100%]
   1:apmd-3.2.2-3.2        ########################################### [100%]
```

You can even install a package directly from the Internet by specifying the full FTP or HTTP path as the path to the RPM, as follows:

```
rpm -i ftp://somesite.com/5/i386/RPMS/apmd-3.2.2-3.2.i386.rpm
```

To uninstall the package, you must use the package name, which can differ from the name of the RPM file. To uninstall *apmd*, enter the following command, using the *−e* switch, for *erase*:

```
rpm -e apmd-3.2.2-3.2
```

TIP

There are various tools for package management. Here's a brief summary of the tools included in Fedora Core 5:

pup GUI tool for updating software, accessed at **Applications | System Tools | Software Updater**.

pirut GUI tool for managing software packages, accessed at **Applications | Add/Remove Software**.

rpm Command-line tool for managing software packages.

yum Yellowdog updater modified; command-line tool for managing software packages.

yum Extender A GUI interface for YUM (install with yum install yumex).

Pirut and yum will automatically ensure you have the most current version of a package. Both of these will also automatically check and install any dependencies for the software you install. Rpm does not include this functionality; you will need to check for dependencies manually when using rpm. YUM only works on RPM based systems, and not all systems will have YUM available/installed, therefore it is suggested that you understand how to manage packages with RPM even if you choose to use YUM for you day to day management.

There is no universal list to tell you which packages you should leave installed and which ones you should remove. You will need to evaluate each service based on your requirements. However, at a minimum the following services are ones you probably *do* need to have installed/running, unless you are very sure you don't need them:

- **haldaemon** Used for gathering and maintaining information concerning hardware devices

- **iptables** Manages IPTables firewalls

- **messagebus** Used for sending notification for certain system events

- **network** Manages the activation of network interface at boot-up

- **NTPd** Used to synchronize time via the NTP protocol

- **sshd** Runs OpenSSH server

- **syslogd** Used for system logging

- **xinetd** Manages the startup of services

Tools & Traps…

Services to Be Avoided at All Costs

There are some services that you would never want exposed to an untrusted network such as the Internet. In most cases this means they should not be running on a bastion host. These services include the following:

- **portmap** Used to manage RPC connections
- **Telnet** Used for unencrypted remote console access
- **rsh, rlogin, rexec** Used for unencrypted remote console access
- **nfs, lockd, mountd, statd** Used for Network File System (NFS) and related services
- **lpd** Printer service

All these services are inherently insecure. A variety of alternatives is available that take advantage of encryption and superior authentication methods. If you absolutely must use any of these services, you should protect them by tunneling them in IPSec or equivalent.

Choosing a Window Manager

While we're on the subject of cleaning out unneeded software, it seems like a good time to discuss window managers. Because Linux is natively a command-line based system, the graphical desktop environment is not an integral part of the operating system. Unlike with modern versions of Windows, you can simply remove the GUI altogether. This has several advantages, the most noticeable of which is that you will free up system resources. The simplest and most easily implemented remote access solutions are also command line only, which further lends itself to doing away with the GUI altogether. Finally, by not offering up an X Window session for remote use, that is one less listening port that needs to be opened on your bastion host, which means increased security.

If you decide a graphical interface is something you must have, you still must choose one carefully. They are not all created equally. Generally speaking, the more full-featured and visually appealing desktops are also the largest in terms of disk space and system resource requirements. Gnome and KDE are by far the most feature-rich, widely supported desktop environments. Gnome is not itself a window manager and comes standard with the Sawfish window manager. These two products also happen to be some of the largest and resource-intensive as well. If performance is a consideration, you will want to choose a lean and fast window manager such as IceWM (which is Gnome-aware) or Fluxbox. Some window managers can cause the loss of some features with different underlying desktops, so you will need to do a little research to make an informed choice.

Additional Steps

At this point, the basic system is in place. You have the desired software installed and should have the undesirable software removed. This covers only the most basic of hardening steps. The next steps will allow you to drill down into some of the more granular aspects of bastion host hardening. Now let's look at steps to synchronize time on the bastion host, keep the system patched, and more.

Configure Automatic Time Synchronization

Having an accurate system time is important to proper functioning of your bastion host. Accurate time on the bastion host is critical to having accurate audit logs, the ability to perform accurate forensics, and for maintaining secure (encrypted) communications. Fortunately, most distributions of Linux should support the newest versions of NTP by default. You will recall from the Windows chapter that different versions of NTP provide different levels of security:

- **NTPv1** No security features
- **NTPv2** Restrictions based on IP address, NTP traffic is unencrypted

- **NTPv3** Symmetric key encryption and authentication
- **NTPv4** Both symmetric encryption and PKI encryption

In the case of Linux, all you need to do is install the NTPD service, if it's not already installed, and then configure it to start automatically for the appropriate run levels. You can configure some of the NTP settings by navigating to **System | Administration | Date & Time**. You can then click the **Network Time Protocol** tab, as shown in Figure 14.5.

Figure 14.5 NTP GUI Configuration

Unfortunately, the GUI interface only lets your configure basic options, like adding time servers. You should make sure **Synchronize System clock before starting service** is the only option checked under **Show Advanced Options**. To configure the NTP security settings, you need to edit the file /etc/ntpd.conf and some additional files located in /etc/ntp/. For secure time synchronization with an NTP server, perform the following steps:

1. Edit **/etc/ntp.conf** and add the time servers you want to get time from; include the key to be used with each server, such as **server ourtimeserver.com key 12345**.

2. Ensure that **restrict default ignore** is in /etc/ntp.conf to set the default restrictions.

3. If needed, add a restrict line for any servers you want to *accept* NTP *requests* from.

4. Edit **/etc/ntp/keys** and configure a unique key to be used for each time server, using the desired algorithm; for example, **12345 A secretkey** would configure key #12345 as an ASCII string between one and eight characters long, with a value of *secretkey*. This key must be in the keys file of both the NTP server and the client for this to work.

5. Add the keys to the **/etc/ntp.conf** file. For example, to add key 12345 as a trusted key, enter **trustedkey 12345**.

6. Restrict the NTP configuration files to be owned and readable only by root.

You can view a detailed NTPD status by typing **ntpq −p**. If you enter **ntpq** and query associations, it will display the status of all associations, including an auth column indicating whether authentication is working properly, as shown in Figure 14.6. You'll find more information at www.ntp.org.

Figure 14.6 Viewing NTP Associations

```
# ntpq
ntpq> associations
ind assID status conf reach auth condition last_event cnt
============================================================
  1 38100  9414  yes   yes   ok    sys.peer  reachable 1
  2 38101  9614  yes   yes   none  sys.peer  reachable 1
```

Patching and Updates

Configuring your bastion host is a never-ending process. As new vulnerabilities are discovered and new features are added to software, you will need to upgrade your host to the most current version, especially if the updated version addresses a security flaw. Along the same lines, new versions of the core OS files will be released periodically. These updates, referred to as *kernel patches*, are similar in function to some Microsoft hotfixes that address core operating system functionality. Some kernel patches will be for features or options that don't apply to you, in which case you don't need the patch. Be aware that kernel patches can be applied incrementally, as they are released, or you can download and apply the latest kernel in its entirety.

Updating Software Packages

Keeping individual software packages up to date is pretty simple, and there are a couple of approaches you can take. The most straightforward method is to use the following RPM commands to *freshen* (-F switch) an installed package:

```
rpm −F apmd-3.2.2-3.2.i386.rpm
```

When you freshen a package, the newer version is installed, but only if an earlier version already exists. A good alternative is to use the *upgrade* option (by means of the -U switch), because this will install the new package, whether it is currently installed or not, and will remove any previous versions of the package that are present. Many experts advise simply using −*U* all the time instead of −*I* (for Install) to avoid any errors in case the package happens to already be installed on the system.

```
rpm -U apmd-3.2.2-3.2.i386.rpm
```

Updating the Kernel

There are two basic options for updating the kernel. You can download a newer kernel in its entirety and apply it, or you can download just a kernel patch and apply it. You can obtain the complete kernel or kernel patches from www.kernel.org. You should also check the Web site for your specific distribution to see if there are restrictions on which kernel will work with that distribution. In most cases you will have the choice of downloading a patch or patches or downloading the entire updated kernel. Patching the kernel generally requires a higher level of skill and a larger investment of time than installing a complete new kernel.

TIP

Kernel version numbers follow a specific pattern. There are several numbers separated by decimals, such as 2.6.17.4. In this example, the 2 represents the major version number, and the 6 represents the minor revision number. The third number represents the patch version, and the fourth is a minor revision of that patch. Essentially, the farther from the leftmost version number you get, the less significant the change. The high-level version numbers are pretty intuitive, but there is still more information hidden in a kernel version. If the minor revision number (the second number from the left) is even, that is considered a *stable* release; if it is odd, it is a *developmental* release. If the version number contains a dash, such as 2.6.17-3.4, it is a kernel that has been modified and produced by a specific distribution. The numbers to the right of the dash will follow a scheme specific to that distribution.

By entering the following command, you can determine the kernel you are currently running:

```
# uname -r
2.6.15-1.2054_FC5
```

The most current stable kernel on www.kernel.org is 2.16.17.4; however, on the Fedora site, we found the latest *Fedora Core* distribution release was 2.6.17-1.2145. Instructions on updating Fedora Core and a link to Fedora Core updates can be found at http://fedora.redhat.com/Download/updates.html. You can use Yum or RPM to update your kernel the same way you would with any other software package. One consideration is that using RPM will leave each kernel image sitting on the hard drive; over time this could account for a considerable amount of hard disk space. Yum will, by default, leave only the previous kernel in addition to the newest one and will delete all others.

Removing SUID Programs

Programs with the set user ID (SUID) bit set will be run with the permissions of the *owner*, not the user who is executing them. Obviously this could pose a big security risk. If an attacker were to locate a script with the SUID bit set and that was owned by root, and if the attacker could find a way to modify the script, he could do anything he wanted to the system, as though he were root. Although a script is the most likely target, an attacker could also gain root access if he could execute a buffer overflow against a binary program with the SUID bit set as well. The same considerations hold true for files with the set group ID (SGID) bit set. You can create a listing of all SUID and SGID files by entering the following command:

```
find / -perm -4000 -print
```

To list files with the SGID bit set, use the following command:

```
find / -perm -2000 -print
```

The list may be long, so redirecting the output to a file for review might be advisable. Unfortunately, some programs will not function properly without having the SUID or SGID bits set. Each instance will need to be researched and possibly tested in a lab environment to determine whether you can safely remove the bit. In all likelihood, either of those bits will be needed on some files, but reducing the number of files to a minimum will leave your bastion host more secure.

With all the obvious risks for using SUID and SGID programs, you might be wondering if using them is ever a good idea or simply an evil to be lived with. These bits can actually improve security in the right situation. For example, if a user needs to perform a routine maintenance action that requires root privileges, normally he needs to know the root password to temporarily gain root access and perform the task. By setting the file SUID and having it owned by root, you can give the user only permissions to execute the file but not modify it. Now he can perform the required task without ever knowing the root password.

SELinux Policy Development

SELinux, which stands for *security-enhanced Linux*, was developed in partnership with the National Security Agency (NSA). It provides a higher level of security by enforcing mandatory access control (MAC) through the kernel itself rather than by running additional processes in the user space. Because the enforcement is through the kernel, it can restrict the actions of any process, even a superuser (i.e., root) process. In fact, as far as the underlying components of SELinux are concerned, there is no concept of a root user, only security policies and security contexts. SELinux is available for many Linux distributions (see which ones at http://selinux.sourceforge.net/distros/redhat.php3) and comes included in some, such as Fedora Core. You can read the FAQ from the NSA at www.nsa.gov/selinux/info/faq.cfm for more information.

It is important to understand that SELinux is a work in progress. Currently, the setup and configuration can be rather complicated. You can enable SELinux on Fedora Core by navigating to **System | Administration | Security Level and Firewall**. On the **SELinux** tab, you must change the setting from Disabled to **Enforcing** *or* **Permissive** to enable SELinux, as shown in Figure 14.7.

Figure 14.7 Enabling SELinux

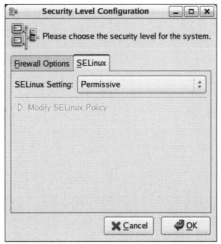

SELinux uses the *xattr* labels to generate persistent labels that describe the security context of a file or directory. These labels are not normally used; thus when you enable SELinux, you will get the warning dialog box shown in Figure 14.8. You must select **Yes** to enable SELinux, then **OK** on the **Security Level Configuration** window and reboot.

Figure 14.8 Relabel Warning Dialog Box

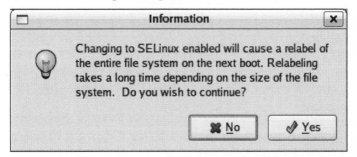

If you choose Permissive (which is recommended initially), the system will generate logs based on the SELinux policy but will not actually restrict any activities. This is useful for fine-tuning the rules until you get the system into a working state. Once you are satisfied with the SELinux rules, you can enable Enforcing mode, which will actually apply your configured policy. Policies can be defined as targeted or strict. The *strict* policy applies to all processes and files on the system; the *targeted* policy is applied only to specific files. Strict, while more secure, has been found to be very difficult to configure properly. Targeted is easier to configure and is the default policy type when SELinux is first enabled. You can check the status of SELinux by typing **sestatus**.

If you navigate back to the **Security Level Configuration** window and click the **SELinux** tab, then click to expand **Modify SELinux Policy**, you will be presented with a list of options to toggle various SELinux settings. These options are only a limited set of preconfigured choices to toggle settings in the SELinux policy files. For any serious configuration you will need to edit the files manually. You can also download a third-party SELinux policy editor from the SELinux Policy Editor Project (http://seedit.sourceforge.net/index.html). This package includes a simplified set of tools that is slightly less functional than the normal package. However, you can switch between using one or the other.

By reviewing the logs, you can see what actions the policy *would* have denied if it were enforced. If auditing has not been enabled, the *Access Vector Cache* (AVC) messages are found in /var/log/messages. If auditing has been enabled, they will be in /var/log/audit/audit.log. Further details on configuring SELinux are beyond the scope of this book. It is recommended that you read the documentation on the Web site of your chosen distribution as well as the official SELinux site (www.nsa.gov/selinux/).

TCP/IP Stack Hardening

Some means of attacking a computer system do not rely on weaknesses in the software that is providing a service but instead attack weaknesses in the underlying communications protocol. For Internet-connected systems, this means attacking weaknesses in the various protocols that make up the TCP/IP suite. Further, some of these weaknesses are intrinsic to the way the protocols work, and they cannot be removed. In those cases, you can still fine-tune the systems to make your hose more *resistant* to those attacks.

As with all security measures, they come with a cost. For example, a *SYN attack* occurs when an attacker initiates a high number of connections by sending a SYN packet, but the attacker never completes the TCP handshake. This causes the target machine to wait, with memory and CPU cycles being used on these half-open connections. The depletion of resources can cause performance degradation for all users of the system as well as reduce resources to the point where legitimate clients cannot make connections. One method of reducing your risk from such an attack is to reduce the length of time a connection can be in that half-open state before it is dropped, freeing up the resources. The downside to this approach is that legitimate clients traversing high-latency networks could have problems establishing a connection due to the short timeouts.

The way that you tune these settings, at least on some distributions, is through the *sysctl* utility. This utility allows you to configure various kernel parameters at run time. You can add settings to a script to be run at system startup, if desired. If you enter **sysctl –a | grep net.ipv4** you will see the list of available TCP/IP variables. In the previous example, to reduce the timeout of half-open connections, you would use the following command:

```
sysctl -w net.ipv4.tcp_synack_retries=3
```

The default value is 5, which means the half-open connection will not be dropped until three minutes have passed. Setting it to a value of 3 will result in only a 45-second timeout. Other values are possible, with a 1 equaling about nine seconds before timeout. As you can see, these changes will have a significant impact on the functionality of the host system, so they should be used with care. The following is a list of variables you might want to research and consider altering:

- **net.ipv4.tcp_synack_retries** Number of retransmissions in an attempt to complete the three-way handshake; a lower number is more resistant to attack.

- **net.ipv4.tcp_max_syn_backlog** Number of half-open connections that can be in the queue at any given time; a high number is more resistant to attack, at the cost of system memory.

- **net.ipv4.icmp_echo_ignore_broadcasts=1** Tells the system not to respond to a ping to a broadcast address. On systems this value is the default anyway.

- **net.ipv4.conf.all.accept_redirects=0 & net.ipv4.conf.all.send_redirects=0** Tells the system not to listen to ICMP redirects, which could be used to alter routing tables.

- **net.ipv4.conf.all.accept_source_route=0, net.ipv4.conf.all.forwarding=0 and net.ipv4.conf.all.mc_forwarding=0** Together these disable source routing, which is rarely used for anything other than attack attempts.

- **net.ipv4.conf.all.rp_filter=1** Tells the system to drop packets when the source and destination don't make sense based on the interface they came in on.

- **net.ipv4.conf.all.tcp_syncookies=1** Enables SYN cookies, allowing the connections to be made without using the backlog queue at all. If this setting is enabled, the *net.ipv4.tcp_max_syn_backlog* setting will have no effect. It is recommended to enable this setting.

Automated Hardening Scripts

Because there are so many settings to adjust and configure, it can be easy to miss a step. As a result, many people have developed semiautomated scripts to help harden a Linux system. The Cadillac of hardening scripts is Bastille-Linux. It has evolved from a crude basic script to a well-refined hardening system with a GUI interface. Bastille currently supports Red Hat

Enterprise Linux, Fedora Core, SuSE, Debian, Gentoo, Mandrake, and HP-UX, with a Mac OS X version in development. You can read about and download Bastille from www.bastille-linux.org.

You can pass only three options to Bastille, each of which tells it to run in a different mode. If you use *bastille –report*, the system will generate a Web based report of your host's current "hardness." The *–c* option will run the actual hardening script in a text-based mode, and *–x* will run it in a graphical mode, as shown in Figure 14.9.

Figure 14.9 Bastille Graphical Configuration

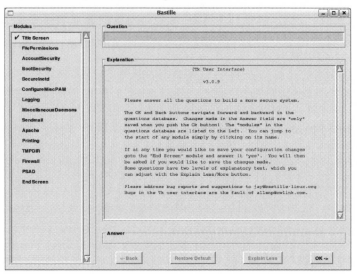

All you have to do to use Bastille is start it and it will present a series of questions you must respond to with a yes or no. Based on your choices, Bastille will configure various security settings automatically. These settings include removing SUID bits from some programs, disabling insecure services (such as rshell, for example), changing user account expiration and much more. The script will usually have the most secure choice as the default selection, except in cases where the more secure selection has a high risk of impacting normal functionality. When you are finished answering the questions, you will be prompted to choose whether or not to save the resulting Bastille configuration. You will then be prompted to choose whether you want to apply the configuration or not.

Controlling Access to Resources

The majority of the steps so far have been focused on controlling *how* a user can interact with the bastion host. Most of the steps so far were made under the assumption that the user already has connectivity to the bastion host, from which programs have the SUID bit set to the security context they use and the services that are available. Following a *defense-in-depth* philosophy, the next steps are to restrict *who* can interact with the bastion host. By restricting who may communicate with the bastion host, in addition to restricting what they do once they have established communication, we come closer to having a hacker-proof system.

Address-Based Access Control

From a networking perspective, the most common way to limit access is based on the IP address of the foreign system. A traditional firewall falls into this category. In this section we discuss some of the ways you can restrict access based on the IP address of the systems in question.

Configuring TCP Wrappers

TCP Wrappers functions similarly to a firewall, except where a firewall permits or denies traffic based on data contained in the IP header of the packet, TCP Wrappers filters access to services on the host it is running on. Services that are compiled against the *libwrap.a* library can make use of TCP Wrappers. When enabled, TCP Wrappers' attempts to access a given services will be compared against the /etc/hosts.allow file and then the /etc/hosts.deny file. Rules are checked sequentially, and processing of the rules files stops when a match is found. For example, if you wanted to allow only connections from Syngress.com to SSH on your bastion host while rejecting all other attempts, you would have the following lines in your hosts.allow and hosts.deny files:

```
/etc/hosts.allow
sshd : .syngress.com


/etc/hosts.deny
sshd : ALL
```

These two files accept several wildcards, such as *ALL, LOCAL, KNOWN, UNKNOWN,* and *PARANOID.* You can enable logging in the rule files as well, and configure the facility and severity of the log entry. With TCP Wrappers' limited functionality and syntax, you might wonder why you would ever use it over simply using the Linux firewall, IPTables. Because IPTables works at the packet level, if you want to deny access to a particular process, such as HTTP, you must do it based on port number. So if you use IPTables to explicitly block connection attempts to port 80, and the user starts the Web server and tells it to listen on port 8080, the connection will be allowed. With TCP Wrappers, you permit or deny access to a process. This distinction could prove invaluable if you have a service that uses a large number of listening ports or some type of service that is spawned as needed and the port number isn't always consistent, or if the packets are tunneled in another protocol, rendering identification via port numbers impossible.

Configuring IPTables

IPTables comes with virtually every distribution of Linux. It is a very functional firewall with an impressive array of features and options. To enable the IPTables firewall, simply navigate to **System | Administration | Security Level and Firewall**. On the **Firewall Options** tab, ensure that it is **Enabled**, as shown on Figure 14.10.

Figure 14.10 Enabling an IPTables Firewall

Depending on the distribution you choose, the default rules set for IPTables may vary. In the case of Fedora Core 5, the default rule set is to permit all outbound traffic and to permit all inbound traffic that is part of an established session. As you can see in the Figure 14.10, SSH was checked. Because the default configuration blocked all inbound connection attempts, checking that box will cause a rule to be created to allow an inbound connection for SSH (TCP 22). In addition to the preconfigured ports (services), you can add your own custom port in the **Other ports** section. This interface works well for simple packet filtering, but IPTables is capable of much more functionality than mere filtering. To get more advanced, you need to be comfortable with the command line. Next we will discuss what the rules look like and their meanings.

To use an example, this is the default output from the command *iptables −L,* which is to list all chains (we will see what a chain is shortly), shown in Figure 14.11. Your default rules probably won't look exactly like these.

Figure 14.11 An IPTables Chain Listing

```
[root@localhost ~]# iptables -L
Chain INPUT (policy ACCEPT)
```

```
target       prot opt source       destination
RH-Firewall-1-INPUT  all  --  anywhere            anywhere


Chain FORWARD (policy ACCEPT)
target       prot opt source       destination
RH-Firewall-1-INPUT  all  --  anywhere            anywhere


Chain OUTPUT (policy ACCEPT)
target       prot opt source       destination


Chain RH-Firewall-1-INPUT (2 references)
target       prot opt source       destination
ACCEPT       all  --  anywhere    anywhere
ACCEPT       icmp --  anywhere    anywhere      icmp any
ACCEPT       udp  --  anywhere    224.0.0.251   udp dpt:mdns
ACCEPT       udp  --  anywhere    anywhere      udp dpt:ipp
ACCEPT       tcp  --  anywhere    anywhere      tcp dpt:ipp
ACCEPT       all  --  anywhere    anywhere      state RELATED,ESTABLISHED
ACCEPT       tcp  --  anywhere    anywhere      state NEW tcp dpt:ssh
REJECT       all  --  anywhere    anywhere      reject-with icmp-host-prohibited
[root@localhost ~]#
```

To start with, let's review some basic IPTables vocabulary. *iptables* is the command-line utility for configuring the Netfilter firewall, which is integrated with the Linux kernel. Specifically, Netfilter is actually a set of hooks inside the Linux kernel that allows the various kernel modules to interact with the network stack. In short, this is what allows the firewall to do the actual work of packet manipulation.

- **Tables** *NAT* (used for NAT'ing), *filter* (used for packet filtering), and *mangle* (used for other types of specialized packet modification).

- **Chains** Basically, these are access control lists that tell the firewall what to do. There are built-in chains that are automatically processed by the tables (which start out empty), and you can create your own custom chains. Built-in chains are *FOR-WARD, INPUT, OUTPUT, PREROUTING,* and *POSTROUTING.*

- **Targets** These dictate what action should be taken when a rule is matched. The default targets are *ACCEPT, DROP, QUEUE,* and *RETURN.*

- **Commands** These are specific *uppercase* options on the command line used to manipulate the rules themselves; for example, *−A* to append a rule to a chain, *-D* to delete a rule from a chain, and so on.

- **Options** These are used to specify options for the rule-matching criteria, such as −*s* for source address and −*p* to specify the protocol to match.

Certain tables will process certain chains by default. The one we focus on for a bastion host is the filter table. If you do not specify what table to use when adding rules (with −*t* <*table*>) the default is to assume you are working with the filter table. The filter table processes the *FORWARD, INPUT*, and *OUTPUT* chains by default. Referring to the chain listing, you can see that the target for the built-in chains is to jump to the custom-created chain RH-Firewall-1-INPUT. This means all packets traversing the system will go through the same chain. You don't have to set it up this way. In fact jumping out to custom chains and then back to the built-in chains can be much more efficient. As an example, let's suppose that you have a long list of rules that only need to be checked against traffic to or from the accounting subnet. Now let's place this list on its own chain called *ACCOUNTING*. You can make a single rule that matches the accounting subnet and then jumps into the *ACCOUNTING* chain containing the lengthy list of rules. In this way the majority of your traffic is only checked against the single rule matching the accounting subnet instead of the entire list of rules found in the *ACCOUNTING* chain.

The man page for IPTables contains a wealth of knowledge, and the IPTables Web site has an excellent FAQ (www.netfilter.org/documentation/index.html#documentation-faq). The large number of features and flexibility can make management over the command line sometimes cumbersome. There are several GUI tools for creating and editing the Netfilter rules. Some of the most widely used GUIs are Firestarter, Firewall Builder (*fwbuilder*), and Guarddog. These allow you to more easily create the rule set without having to know all the command-line options for IPTables. To see what some of the GUIs look like, take a look at the main window for Firestarter shown in Figure 14.12.

Figure 14.12 Main Firestarter Console

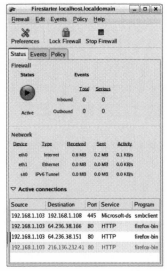

Auditing Access to Resources

Auditing serves an important role in network security. Not only does it allow you a means to know what is occurring on your systems in real time; it can also allow you to reconstruct a series of events after the fact, which can be especially important after a successful compromise has occurred. There are basically two types of auditing you can do. One is *kernel auditing*, which will log system calls, and the other is *syslog*, which can log most everything else.

Enabling the Audit Daemon

Enabling auditing is a very straightforward process. If you don't have *auditd* installed, go ahead and install it. It should be set to start automatically; if it's not, configure it to do so. The primary file for configuration of *auditd* is /etc/audit.conf. This file contains settings such as where to write the logs (defaults to /var/log/audit/audit.log), the log formatting, and what to do if the disk is full. Parameters of note are the *dispatcher, disk_full_action,* and *max_log_file_action*. Dispatcher is the program that the audit daemon will use to send all logs to *stdin*. This program will be run as root, so the program needs to be secure and used with caution. The *disk_full_action* is exactly what it sounds like: what should the daemon do when the disk that holds the log is full? *Max_log_file_action* tells the daemon what to do when the maximum log *file size* is reached.

> **TIP**
>
> If *auditd* is running, the logs for SELinux are written to the same location specified in the audit.conf file. If *auditd* is not running, the logs will instead be written to the *syslog* log (which is at /var/log/messages by default). You can view the logs directly or type **dmesg** in a terminal to view them.

The other relevant file for the audit daemon is /etc/audit.rules. This file tells the audit daemon what events to audit. By default, the file contains no rules. If you wanted to audit all calls for *mount*, for example, you would place the following line in your audit.rules file:

```
-a tools,always -S mount
-w /etc/fstab
```

This basically means to add a rule to the end of the *tools* list (-*a*), and *always* generate an audit event. The −*S* means the *syscall* to watch is *mount*. −*w* tells it to *watch* the /etc/fstab file for access attempts and log them. The usefulness of being able to keep such close tabs on the use of some of the more important system calls should be clear now. This is a very powerful tool for spotting intrusion attempts and other activities that could indicate someone is trying to do something they shouldn't be doing. The *watch* option does *not* accept wildcards, so −*w* /etc/*.conf will *not* work.

Enabling the Syslog Daemon

The daemon that supports *syslog* is *syslogd*. With current Linux distributions, you would be hard-pressed to find one that didn't come with *syslog* already enabled, but if you do manage to, you can install it like any other package. Once it's installed, you can control its behavior through /etc/syslog.conf. This rule file is relatively simple. Each line consists of a facility, a priority, and an action. Take the following example:

```
Mail.*          /var/log/maillog
```

This would tell the daemon to log all events from the mail subsystem, such as facility, regardless of their priority, to /var/log/maillog. Pretty straightforward. Examples of valid priorities are *debug, info, notice, crit, alert,* *, and *emerg,* which indicate the overall severity of the event. An asterisk (*) stands for all facilities *or* priorities, depending on where it is used. Unless a given facility isn't used or available on your bastion host, you should point the logs someplace for all of them. The action will typically point to a real file, but some other options are available. The most notable one from a security perspective is the *remote machine* action. This allows you to send the logs to a remote machine, which is a good idea. The syntax for the remote machine action is simply *@host*. If your bastion host were to be compromised by a hacker, any logs on that host would become suspect and of less value if legal action had to be taken. By sending the *syslog* events to a *syslog* daemon on another machine, you can ensure their integrity.

Viewing and Managing the Logs

Not that you have enabled all these logs, you will hopefully be generating a lot of useful auditing information. The issue then becomes what to do with all that data. You need a way to sort through it and pick out the most interesting pieces, then do something about it where necessary, preferably all in as automated a fashion as possible. The way to do this is through several handy log tools. One of the simplest of utilities is *dmesg*. It lacks any real features; it is merely a quick way to display the system message buffer.

A good Web site covering log analysis topics is www.loganalysis.org by Tina Bird. You can probably find a utility to do just about anything you want to do with log files, from sending e-mails for certain events to shutting down processes or just color-coding the events on the console. Two popular tools are *swatch* and *logwatch*. Of the two, *swatch* is the more lightweight, being easier to set up and having fewer options. *Swatch* is intended to parse the logs *in real time* and act on what it finds inside the logs according to the configuration you specify. *Logwatch* has a slightly different role: Its focus is on analyzing and reporting on log files, but not in real time.

Configuring Swatch

Since *swatch* (short for *simple watcher*) is relatively focused in its purpose, the setup and configuration are pretty simple. Some swatch behaviors can be set from the command line, but the rules to match must be in a configuration file. An example command line to invoke swatch would be *swatch -c /etc/swatch.conf –t /var/log/syslog,* which would tell *swatch* to use the configuration file (-*c*) at /etc/swatch.conf. If you don't specify which file to watch (-*t*), *swatch* will default to /var/log/messages or /var/log/syslog, in that order. If you don't specify a configuration file, it will echo everything to the console. You can use *–f <file>* to examine a file once instead of it running continuously with the –t options.

If you had the following lines in your configuration file, they would cause any line containing *denied* or *Denied* to echo to the console as yellow text and sound the bell once. Everything else would echo to the console as normal text.

```
watchfor         /[dD]enied/
echo yellow
bell 1


watchfor /.*/
echo
```

As you can see, configuring *swatch* is not difficult. Some of the key commands for security considerations and their use follow:

- **--script-dir=<*path to directory*>** Used on the command line. When *swatch* runs, it creates a temporary watcher script, which by default is written to the user's home directory. You should redirect the watcher script to a secured directory where it cannot be edited. A hacker with access to this temporary script could control what *swatch* reports and cover his tracks.

- **exec command** Used in the config file, this will cause matches to execute another command. This could be as simple as pager software, for example, or it could run a custom script to lock down the Netfilter firewall automatically.

- **Throttle hours:minutes:seconds,[use=message | regex | <reges>]** This is especially valuable because it controls how often duplicates of a given message will be acted on. This way a brute-force password cracker being run won't overload *swatch* with a nonstop scrolling message, possibly filling up your logging partition.

- **Threshold events:seconds,[repeat=no | yes]** This is another very important one. It allows you to ignore certain matches until they surpass a given threshold; in other words, threshold 4:60 will not perform any action unless the pattern matches four times within a 60-second window. This is very useful for things such as incorrect passwords. You don't want all sorts of alarms going off because the admin mistypes a password once, but many incorrect attempts in a short time frame may be a sign of a hacker at work.

Configuring Logwatch

Logwatch is intended to be more of a reporting tool than a live monitor. It has a host of command-line options. Logwatch will do some formatting of the output for you. For example, if you entered *logwatch —service sshd —print,* you'd get the output shown in Figure 14.13.

Figure 14.13 Output from Logwatch

```
[root@localhost ~]# logwatch --service sshd --print

################## LogWatch 7.1 (11/12/05) ##################
        Processing Initiated: Mon Jul 10 23:19:05 2006
        Date Range Processed: yesterday
                            ( 2006-Jul-09 )
                            Period is day.
     Detail Level of Output: 0
            Type of Output: unformatted
         Logfiles for Host: localhost.localdomain
 ##################################################################


-------------------- SSHD Begin ------------------------

SSHD Killed: 1 Time(s)

SSHD Started: 1 Time(s)

Illegal users from these:
    192.168.1.108: 4 times

Users logging in through sshd:
    root:
        192.168.1.108: 7 times

-------------------- SSHD End ------------------------


##################### LogWatch End #########################
```

As you can see, Logwatch can be invaluable in helping you sort through very large logs and extract the meaningful information in an easy-to-understand format. A command-line option of note is the *—archives —range all* option. This tells Logwatch to parse not only the log file specified but *all* archived files of that log family. For example, if used with the option —*logfile messages*, Logwatch would parse /var/log/messages in addition to /var/log/messages.* variations, such as /var/log/messages.1.

Remote Administration

It might be important to have remote administration capabilities for your bastion host. A key consideration with any administrative activities is to make sure unauthorized individuals aren't gathering information from those activities that can be used to compromise the security of the bastion host. This is true even if you are logging in directly to the console. The "guest" in the server room could be "shoulder surfing" to get your password. The same is even more true for remote administration because, by its very nature, your activities are having to traverse multiple devices and quiet probably hostile networks. Under these circumstances the key consideration is maintaining the confidentiality of the data (in this case, the administrative session) and restricting access to only authorized individuals. The challenge then becomes to provide your administrators with the needed functionality to do their jobs in a secure fashion. In this section we walk through the most common ways to accomplish this goal.

SSH

What secure shell (SSH) lacks in "flash" it makes up for in pure practicality. A secure, encrypted terminal session to the remote host is invaluable to an administrator, and with Linux's command-line-oriented design, very often no other remote access will be needed. Setting up SSH is pretty easy, too. Start off by installing the SSH daemon (*sshd*). Odds are very good it's already installed, because most distributions install it by default. Some command-line options should be configured to impact the security and operation of the daemon. This is not a complete list of options, only the most important ones from a security perspective:

- **–f <*configuration_file*>** Specifies the configuration file; *sshd* will not start without specifying a configuration file.

- **–h <host_key_file>** This option specifies the file containing the host key. You must use this option if *sshd* is *not* run as root. Because *sshd* will work without being run as root, you should configure it as a nonroot account and use this option.

The next step is to create a configuration file for *sshd*, which defaults to /etc/sshd_config if you don't specify an alternate file using the *–f* option. The following is a partial list of keywords containing only the most significant security settings. All the keywords and arguments *are* case sensitive:

- **AllowGroups** This specifies the groups allowed to log in based on group name. Wildcards are supported. The default is all groups. You should create a group specific to *sshd* users and populate it appropriately.

- **AllowUsers** This specifies the users allowed to log in based on username. The default is to allow all users. You can also specify *USER@HOST* to allow a particular user to log in only from a particular machine.

- **Banner** This is a typical banner message, which is usually a good idea to set to some ominous warning message approved by your legal department. This message is sent to the client *before* they log in and is only supported in *sshd* V2.

- **ClientAliveInterval** Specifies the time the session can be idle before *sshd* sends a message to the client requesting a response. The default is 0, which means the client will never see these requests and subsequently never be disconnected (see below). This setting will not actually disconnect the client.

- **ClientAliveCountMax** This setting specifies how many requests for a response can be sent to the client without receiving a response before the client is disconnected. The default value is 3, so if the ClientAliveInterval were set to 20, an unresponsive client would be disconnected after 60 seconds.

- **KeyRegenerationInterval** This specifies how often to regenerate the server key. The default is one hour. If resources allow, a lower setting would be more secure, depending on how paranoid you want to be.

- **LoginGraceTime** This specifies the time the daemon will wait for a client to authenticate themselves. The default is 600 seconds, which is far too long and just asking for a DoS attack. Set this to a lower number, such as 30 seconds or less.

- **PrintMotd** This will print /etc/motd *after* the user logs in. Same considerations apply to the *Banner* option described previously.

Once you have your configuration file and the *sshd* daemon started with all the appropriate options, you need to allow inbound connection on the *sshd* listening port (default is TCP22). Using a GUI-based tool such as the Security Level Configuration utility, this is simple. Navigate to **System | Administration | Security Level and Firewall**. On the **Firewall Options** tab, next to Trusted Services, place a check mark next to **SSH**. We covered this previously in Figure 14.9. Once this is done, click **OK**, and click **OK** again when the warning dialog box comes up. To make the same changes from the command line, you could enter:

```
iptables -A INPUT -p tcp -m state --state NEW --dport 22 -j ACCEPT
```

This would tell the firewall to append (*-A*) this rule to the *INPUT* chain. It would match the TCP protocol (*-p*) and look for the state to be a newly initiated connection (*-m state —state NEW*). When all this is true and the destination port (*—dport*) is 22, it will

ACCEPT the connection (*-j ACCEPT*). Remember, the *INPUT* chain is one of the built-in chains; yours might be different. In the case of Fedora Core 5, checking the box in the GUI would add the rule to the *RH-Firewall-1-INPUT* chain instead. You can also use *—source 1.2.3.4* to specify a source address, if known, but this might not be possible if your administrators will be accessing the bastion host from home.

Remote GUI

Even though you can get any administrative tasks done from an SSH session, maybe you're more comfortable using a GUI. The obvious question then is, How do I access a *secure* GUI session remotely? Typically it's done one of two ways: either using X Windows' built-in functionality or with third-party software such as VNC that's designed specifically to share desktops. In either case, you must encrypt the sessions somehow. The free version of VNC that's available for download, VNC Free Edition, uses an initial challenge response that hides the password, but after that the session is completely unencrypted. The current pay versions do support session encryption. Another commercial alternative is NoMachine NX server. Further information on this product can be found at www.nomachine.com. Because SSH and the X Server are a part of almost every Linux distribution and can provide the desired GUI session remotely, we will look at the settings needed to configure X Windows over SSH.

Tunneling X Windows over SSH isn't as complicated as it sounds, and if you're going to be doing the administration from a Windows machine, Cygwin/X is a free software package to provide the X Windows client and SSH client that will run on Windows. First, you need to open the appropriate ports on the Linux bastion host for inbound X Windows connections over SSH. The default SSH port is TCP port 22.

The X Server also includes its own rudimentary security mechanism. You must have a list of all user names or machine names that are allowed to connect to the X Server. This list is modified using the *xhost* utility. The process is very simple: Enter **xhost +bob** to add the *user* bob *or* the *machine* bob to the list of allowed X Server connections. Entering **xhost –bob** would remove that name from the allowed list. Finally, you need to ensure that the sshd_config must have ForwardX11 set to **Yes**. This allows the X Server to work over SSH, and in most cases it should default to **On**.

Bastion Host Configurations

Now that we have discussed the various ways to harden a Linux bastion host, it's time to do something with it. You probably don't want to have the bastion host exposed to the Internet without offering up some type of service. The most common Internet-exposed servers are FTP, Web (HTTP), mail relays (SMTP), and DNS servers. On Linux you don't need to buy any expensive software packages to have a secure, robust Web server or FTP server. Apache is the most widely used Web server on the Internet, and it's available for free. Here we examine the basic steps that are needed to provide these services securely over the Internet, and we focus on the steps that are needed *in addition* to the normal hardening procedures covered previously in this chapter.

Configuring a Web Server

Follow these steps to enable your Linux bastion host to serve as a Web server:

1. Install the Apache Web server software (*httpd*) and *openssl*. You can use any of the methods discussed previously to do so.

2. Configure the firewall to allow inbound connections to port 80 and 443 for HTTP and HTTPS, respectively. You can verify the ports are allowed by entering **iptables −L** to list the chains. There should be lines similar to the following;

    ```
    ACCEPT          tcp    --       anywhere          start NEW tcp dpt:https
    ACCEPT          tcp    --       anywhere          start NEW tcp dpt:http
    ```

3. If you are hosting a domain, you will want to add the domain and your server IP address to your /etc/hosts file.

4. Apache uses a configuration file to determine how it handles the Web site. You should read the documentation available at http://httpd.apache.org/docs/2.0/ for more information. The file is located at /etc/httpd/conf/http.conf by default. Edit this file if needed.

5. Assuming you want *httpd* to start automatically, go to **System | Administration | Services** and place a check next to **httpd** for the appropriate run levels.

6. Configure the appropriate monitoring for the log file (like *swatch*) if desired. The default location for the logfile is /etc/httpd/logs/.

7. At this point you should be able to connect to the Web server and see the Apache Test Page. The next step is to configure HTTPS. You can add your own content to /var/www/html and set the permissions to something appropriate for Web access, typically *read* only, or if scripts are used, *read* and *execute*; for example, **chown −R 755 /var/www/html**.

8. Install **mod_ssl**, which is the SSL/TLS module for Apache, and **openssl**.

9. Place your SSL certificate (obtained from a third-party CA) in a directory of your choice, and then edit the **/etc/httpd/conf/httpd.conf** file to include the following lines, which point to the certificate files. You should select a secured non-root partition to hold your certificate files.

    ```
    SSLCertificateFile          <path to certificate file>/server.crt
    SSLCertificateKeyFile <path to certificate file>/server.key
    ```

10. Edit the permissions to ensure that the server.key file is readable only by root.

Configuring an FTP Server

To configure your bastion host as an FTP server, follow these steps:

1. Select and install an FTP server daemon. Two good choices are *vsftpd* and *pure-ftpd,* but there are many others to choose from. If you are using a SELinux, *pure-ftpd* includes SELinux support, which must be downloaded separately. Some users have reported better performance from *vsftpd,* so that is the one we will use for this example; see the *vsftpd* Web site at http://vsftpd.beasts.org/ for more information.

2. After installing the daemon, ensure that the service is set to start automatically for the appropriate run levels.

3. Enable FTP inbound on the firewall, TCP port 21. At this point you should be able to connect to the FTP server from a remote host.

4. Edit the *vsftp* configuration file (must be owned by root) located at /etc/vsftpd/vsftpd.conf. What follows are some of the more security-oriented settings to be aware of. The default settings for *vsftpd* are pretty secure.

   - **anonymous_enable** The default is Yes, and if you comment out this line, the default will still be Yes. To disable anonymous, you must set this to No.

   - **ssl_enable** This should be set to Yes to support SSL-encrypted FTP transfers.

   - **dual_log_enable** Set this to **Yes**. It tells *vsftpd* to generate a *wu-ftpd* style log (/var/log/xferlog) in addition to *vsftpd's* own logging format (/var/log/vsftpd.log). The *wu-ftpd* style log will be understood by more log-parsing utilities.

   - **force_local_logins_ssl** Setting this to Enable will force all *nonanonymous* logins to use SSL.

   - **syslog_enable** Setting this to Yes will cause the logs to be written to the system log instead.

   - **tcp_wrappers** Setting this to Yes will enable *tcp_wrapper* support (*vsftpd* has to be compiled with *tcp_wrapper* support for this to work).

   - **userlist_deny** This option is used only if *userlist_enable* is set to Yes. Setting this option to No means that a user will be denied login *unless* he or she is explicitly listed in the userlist_file (/etc/vsftpd/user_list). It's also worth noting that the user will be denied *before* being asked for a password.

   - **userlist_enable** This is the reverse of *userlist_deny*. With *user_list enable*, the user_list file is checked, and *any names in the file* will be denied access before being prompted for a password.

- **anon_root** *<path>* This option sets the root directory for anonymous users only. This can simplify your security configuration by allowing different roots for authenticated users from anonymous users.

- **banner_file** *<path>* This is where you specify the security warning banner.

- **ftpd_banner** This setting sets a banner message from the configu file, instead of using a separate banner file. This setting will override the banner_file setting.

After setting these directives to the desired values and restarting *vsftpd*, you should be running a secure FTP server. Remember that file permissions are of particular importance when it comes to FTP servers. You must ensure that a hacker cannot edit any sensitive files, such as configuration files. Additional security can be achieved by running your FTP server from a *chroot* jail (explained in the following DNS example).

Configuring an SMTP Relay Server

Follow these steps to secure your SMTP relay bastion host:

1. Install Sendmail or another mail transfer agent (MTA) of your choosing. We use Sendmail in this example because it is the most widely used and is included by default with many distributions. If you check your configuration, you might find it's already installed and running.

2. Edit the **/etc/mail/local-host-names** file and add to it all domains for which you want to process mail. For the relay to work, either the sender or the receiver of the mail must be in this file or you will get an error.

3. Install **sendmail-cf**.

4. Edit the **/etc/mail/sendmail.mc** file and add/configure the following lines:

   - Edit the line **dnl define('SMART_HOST','smtp.your.provider')** with the name of your upstream mail server, and remove **dnl** from the beginning of the line.

   - Comment out the line that reads **DAEMON_OPTIONS ('Port=smtp,Addr=127.0.0.1, Name=MTA')dnl**. This line tells Sendmail to only accept mail from the local machine and is the default setting.

   - Add the following line to delete all the program and version information from the SMTP header: **define('confSMTP_LOGIN_MSG','')**.

   - Add the following line to remove version numbers in the HELP output; **define('HELP_FILE','')**.

   - Add the following line to enable privacy flags: **Define('confPRIVACY_FLAGS','authwarnings noexpn novrfy need-mailhelo noetrn')**.

5. Generate a new Sendmail.cf based on the new Sendmail.mc by entering **make –C /etc/mail** or **m4 /etc/mail/sendmail.mc > /etc/sendmail.cf**.

6. Add any domains you want to allow mail relay for in the **/etc/mail/access**. Use the format **somedomain.com   RELAY**. After configuring this file, generate a new db for Sendmail to use by entering **makemap hash /etc/mail/access < /etc/mail/access**.

7. Start and stop Sendmail for the new settings to take effect.

8. If there are any issues (or even if there are no issues), review the mail logs at /var/log/maillog.

Configuring a DNS Server

For this example we use BIND, the de facto standard DNS server. This section assumes that you have BIND working and are familiar with DNS. Due to the complexity of configuring a DNS server, we are only going to look at the security-related settings that should be used. Follow these steps in addition to the other hardening steps that were previously discussed to get your DNS bastion host up and running.

1. Edit /etc/named.conf as follows:

   - Remove the // for **query-source address * port 53;** by default, BIND will use an unprivileged port, but often only port 53 will be allowed through many firewalls.

   - Add the option **allow-transfer { 1.2.3.4; localhost; };** to the individual zone sections. This specifies that only the machine at 1.2.3.4 and the local host are allowed to perform a zone transfer. If you do not do this, hackers will use the zone information to locate target servers and help them construct a map of your internal network.

   - In the options section (which applies to all zones), remove the ability to answer queries for domains you don't own by adding the following: **allow-query { 192.168.1.0/24; localhost; };**. This says that only queries for 192.168.1.0 and the localhost are allowed.

   - In the individual zone sections, add **allow-query { any; };**. This says that anyone is allowed to query for those specific zones and is needed to provide DNS for the domains you own.

   - In the **Options** section, disable recursive queries except from internal sources. Add the following line: **allow-recursion { 192.168.196.0/24; localhost; };**.

2. Run **named** as a nonroot user in a *chroot* jail.

   - Create a **/chroot/named** directory.

- Create the user. In this example we will create the user **named**. Create a group called **named** as well. Set the shell for the user **to /bin/false** or something equally invalid, since this user should never need to log in directly. Set the home directory to **/chroot/named**.

- Create a subdirectory structure for the jail.

```
/chroot
  +-- named
      +-- dev
      +-- etc
      |    +-- other
      |          +-- slave
      +-- var
            +-- run
```

- Move named.conf to **/chroot/named/etc** and move any zone files to **/chroot/named/etc/other**.

- Give named access to **/chroot/named/etc/other/slave** (for any zones your name server acts as a slave) and **/chroot/named/var/run** to write statistical information.

- Create a device node for /dev/null and /dev/random:

```
# mknod /chroot/named/dev/null c 2 2
# mknod /chroot/named/dev/random c 2 3
# chmod 666 /chroot/named/dev/{null,random}
```

- Copy /etc/localtime to **/chroot/named/etc/**.

- Adjust the file location in **/chroot/named/named.conf** to point to the new jail.

3. Enable logging from inside the jail by editing the startup script for *syslog* by adding **-a /chroot/named/dev/log**.

4. Modify the startup script for **named** and add **–t /chroot/named –u named**.

5. Periodically you need to update the root.hints file. This can be downloaded from ftp://ftp.internic.org/domain.named.root. Reload **named** after updating the hints file.

Bastion Host Maintenance and Support

At this point you should be comfortable with the tools required to securely administer your Linux bastion host. Ongoing maintenance must be performed on a schedule. Changes should be handled in a systematic fashion. You should define maintenance windows and a change control policy whereby patches and upgrades are approved, implemented, and reviewed. Joining one of the many vulnerability mailing lists will help you stay informed about new vulnerabilities as quickly as possible. You can bet the serious hackers are all members of those mailing lists, so you probably should be too.

There should be a policy in place for log collection and review. Logs should be recorded, preferably on a read-only media for archival purposes. Logs should be regularly reviewed and suspicious activity investigated. This last point is key; all too often logs are generated but in many cases no one looks at them. Use of automated tools like *swatch* and Logwatch can help minimize the human labor involved in log analysis, but there will still be events that need to be looked at more closely. Remember that security is an ongoing process that requires continued education and effort to stay as hacker-proof as possible.

Linux Bastion Host Checklist

Use the following checklist when hardening your Linux bastion host. These steps are not specific to any particular role (such as a web server or SMTP relay). All these steps are critical; missing any single one could leave you vulnerable to hackers and result in a compromised system.

1. Research your needs for a Linux bastion host (support, media, functionality), and select a distribution accordingly.

2. Plan the partition layout, and give some forethought to providing space for the operating system, swap partition, system logs, and system data.

3. Install the OS, and remove and disable any optional software and services.

4. Apply patches and updates to the system kernel and software as needed.

5. Remove/minimize processes using the SUID or SGID bit.

6. If mandatory access control is desired, implement SELinux.

7. Harden the TCP/IP stack.

8. Configure TCP Wrappers.

9. Configure the Netfilter firewall via the GUI or IPTables tool.

10. Apply any needed encryption for sensitive data.

11. Enable and configure auditing as required.

12. Apply scheduled maintenance to keep the system secure.

Summary

As you can see, Linux has many free and powerful security tools at its disposal. With a little care and planning, a Linux bastion host can be *at least* as secure as a Windows bastion host, if not more so. Although they may take some getting used to, the package managers offer a powerful way to install and update packages. Windows users might find the interfaces a little odd, but the ability to download free software for firewalls, Web servers, and much more, all from a single interface, is something most Windows users don't easily have. Netfilter offers a powerful firewall with many advanced features built in, for free. There is no firewall with comparable functionality included with the Windows operating system. Armed with the knowledge in this chapter, you should be able to connect your Linux bastion host to the Internet and not get hacked, and if the system should be compromised, you will have logs to see it happening, or at worst, to reconstruct events so that it doesn't happen again.

Solutions Fast Track

System Installation

☑ Be cognizant of alternate OS media other than a traditional hard disk install.

☑ Research the strengths and weaknesses of a particular distribution and choose accordingly (not all are created equally).

☑ Prepare the hard disk (if needed) with forethought, especially with an eye for logging.

Removing Optional Components

☑ Think minimally. If you don't need the software in question, remove it.

☑ For services you need, control when they run. Some can be enabled as needed and don't need to be running at startup.

☑ Ensure that none of the "high-risk services" are running at all costs, and provide comparable functionality via more secure alternatives if needed.

Additional Hardening Steps

☑ Make sure your system's time is accurate. This is important for forensics and encryption.

☑ Make sure the kernel and software are patched and up to date, to avoid known vulnerabilities.

☑ Remove or minimize the use of SUID or SGID files.

☑ Consider applying SELinux for mandatory access controls. Research the implementation details fully before coming to a decision. SELinux can offer a lot of protection, but the configuration and management can be burdensome.

☑ Harden the TCP/IP stack to make it more resistant to inherent weaknesses.

☑ Run Bastille Linux in Report mode to see if there are things you missed, or use it to make actual changes to the system.

Controlling Access to Resource

☑ Implement TCP Wrappers to protect processes based on client IP addresses.

☑ Implement the NetFilter firewall. It's free and very powerful.

Auditing Access to Resource

☑ Enable *auditd* for auditing of system calls.

☑ Enable *syslogd* for normal *syslog* logging.

☑ Remember to log access to the logs themselves. Attackers will often attempt to delete or edit the logs to hide evidence of their activities.

☑ Configure automated log monitoring to make the volume of data manageable.

Frequently Asked Questions

The following Frequently Asked Questions, answered by the authors of this book, are designed to both measure your understanding of the concepts presented in this chapter and to assist you with real-life implementation of these concepts. To have your questions about this chapter answered by the author, browse to **www.syngress.com/solutions** and click on the **"Ask the Author"** form.

Q: If I were to run Linux from a CD-ROM on my bastion host, won't the performance be worse than if I used a hard drive?

A: Maybe. Many of the live CDs have the option of running entirely in RAM. If you have adequate hardware, this can result in an extremely fast system. If the host will need to manipulate a lot of data, using the hard disk might be unavoidable; however, you could still run from CD-ROM and customize the distribution to make use of the hard disk for data storage.

Q: Is IPTables the firewall or Netfilter? And what is this IPChains I hear about?

A: Netfilter is the actual firewall component, though it is very common for people to refer to the firewall as IPTables. Strictly speaking, IPTables is only the command-line interface for editing the rules that Netfilter uses. IPChains is the previous incarnation of IPTables and should no longer be used if possible.

Q: Is it any more secure to use the Netfilter firewall than TCP Wrappers?

A: They don't really do the same thing. The Netfilter firewall makes filtering decisions based on the contents of the headers of the IP packets alone. TCP Wrappers makes decisions based on only the source IP and the process name that is listening for inbound connections. The functions of the two overlap only slightly. They complement each other nicely, however, and using both of them provides *defense in depth*.

Q: Why *wouldn't* I want to run X Windows remotely? I like using a GUI instead of the command line.

A: For a bastion host, the objective is to minimize exposure to attack. And like any other software running on your bastion host, X Windows is simply one more listening service that an attacker can target. Using SSH only would always be the more secure option, though X Windows is used all over the Internet today without being compromised. In the end you will just need to research and weigh the pros and cons for your environment.

Index